The Great Irish Families

BLOOD ON THE HARP

Irish Rebel History In Ballad

(The Heritage)

BLOOD ON THE HARP

Irish Rebel History In Ballad

(The Heritage)

by

Turlough Faolain

The Whitston Publishing Company
Troy, New York
1983

Library of Congress Catalog Card Number 83-61046

ISBN 0-87875-275-7 (clothbound)
ISBN 0-87875-276-5 (paperbound)

Printed in the United States of America

Second Printing

To My Father,

An intellectual rebel
Who has spent his martial life
Fighting the rude Stranger
With gentle words. . . .

Acknowledgements

The author owes a substantial debt to many people who have helped him move this volume along its seemingly interminable journey from idle conversation to the printed page. A few words seem meager repayment for the gift of long hours and unselfish support without which this book would have remained trapped among the keys of my battered portable typewriter. If there remain errors of fact or fanciful interpretation of history, it is in spite of the yeoman efforts of those listed below.

To Caoimhím Ó Duhbhánaigh, for lending his Gaelic scholarship generally and for offering the added bonus of his splendid new translation of the *Lament for Art O'Leary;* to Mary Metraux Coyle, for grimly smiling when asked to redraw a map by someone who cannot draw a straight line; to Leslie Boyd, for the cheerful offer of her calligraphic hand; to Frank Sheridan, former Third Secretary of Ambasáid na hÉireann in Washington, for patiently pointing out little-travelled pathways; to the great Danny Doyle, for taking time from his busy schedule to run down information in Dublin; to Danny O'Flaherty of The Celtic Folk, for singing the Gaelic songs with a Connemara accent; to the gifted Paddy McGuigan, for taking the time to answer and for his *Irish Soldier Laddie;* to Barry Nelson of the Corrib Folk, for writing down lyrics long after the pub was closed; to the prolific and talented Pete St. John, for his haunting *Anne Devlin* and his wistful *The Frenchman;* to Brian Warfield of the Wolfetones, for his brilliant *The Protestant Men* (Skin Music); to the enthusiastic civil servants in the Main and Jefferson Reading Rooms of the United States Library of Congress, for falling all over themselves to help a stranger; to Joe Hickerson's staff in the Archive of Folk Song, for unaccountably pretending to be delighted by my being underfoot; to the anonymous librarian in the Rare Book Room, for waiving the requirements for references and going to get the books; to the harried librarians in the Music Reading Room, for suggesting every alternative except leaving; to the wizards of the Microform Room, for finding even those films whose numbers I wrote down incorrectly; to Frank and Sue Kelly, for allowing me to pore through their old broadside sheets; to countless musicians and barmen, for making my *real* research so much more pleasant; to Jackie Knoetgen, for believing and yet knowing how not to interrupt; to Patrick O'Flaherty, for the darts, beer, and friendship when I was feeling down; and, most of all, to my father, for the trenchant blue pencil and pithy margin notes that brought me crashing back to earth when I needed it most; to all of them and to so many more, my heartfelt and sincere thanks.

The nation . . . is the largest community which, when the chips are down, effectively commands men's loyalty, overriding the claims both of the lesser communities within it and those which cut across it or potentially enfold it. . . .

—*Carlton H. J. Hayes*

The *cláirseach* wild, whose trembling string
Had long the "song of sorrow" spoke,
Shall bid the wild *Rosg-Cata* sing
The curse and crime of Saxon yoke. . . .

—*Edward Walsh*

The Stranger shall hear thy lament on his plains;
The sigh of thy harp shall be sent o'er the deep,
Till thy masters themselves, as they rivet thy chains,
Shall pause at the song of their captive and weep!

—*Thomas Moore*

Whether nationalism as a process is a curse or a blessing, we have no stomach to declare. We have read enough history to make us timid, if not humble, about passing moral judgement . . . on great and long continued historic processes.

—*Carlton H. J. Hayes*

Preface

On an autumn Saturday night in 1981 a number of British sailors and marines were drinking in Ireland's Own, a pub in the Washington suburb of Alexandria, Virginia. The young men were ashore on liberty from *HMS Ariadne,* a Royal Navy frigate sent to America to participate in the bicentennial commemoration of George Washington's victory over Lord Cornwallis at Yorktown. Emboldened by copious amounts of Guinness, one of the marines passed a note up to The Celtic Folk, a popular folk band from Ireland who were entertaining the two hundred patrons.

The lead singer decided to read the missive aloud: "I've just come from a year's duty in Ulster . . . play me an Orange song!" Howls of outrage from the audience suggested the imminence of mayhem. The musicians, however, found a more effective way to handle the request. To the crowd's delight, The Celtic Folk began singing Irish rebel songs non-stop, enthusiastically accompanied by their English lead guitarist. Eighty minutes of unbroken medley later, the defeated young Britons quit the bar in disgust. The chorus of catcalls occasioned by their departure presumably still ringing in their ears, the embarrassed marines returned several nights later to rip down the Irish flag from above the pub entrance.

By stretching just a bit, we can extrapolate this event into the macrocosm of the Irish Rebel Tradition. All the necessary ingredients are there: the British in hostile country; the individual Englishman gone "more Irish than the Irish;" the natives ready to do illegal battle with the unwanted soldiery; the inhabitants turning instinctively to their bards; the balladeers intuitively wielding the uniquely Irish sword of rebel song; the British, disarmed in the battle of wits, impulsively striking back physically at the Irish. The Irish won the battle—and are happy to pass along the story—but the British did the most damage.

The tragedy, of course, is that the Irish National Tradition necessitates viewing such an episode in analogy. In any other situation, the young Englishmen would have been judged as just another group of frustrated young soldiers—not an uncommon sight in any bar. Eight centuries of experience with The Saxon, however, have made it almost impossible for the Irish to view any such incident so simply. Myopic? Probably. Paranoic? Possibly. Heart-felt? Indubitably. The Irish would reply with the nationalist equivalent of "just because we're paranoid doesn't mean that there's no one following us." And that, of course, is the problem: for eight hundred years someone has been. The Irish are not about to forget, or forgive, that history.

In 1169 Norman chivalry landed on the rocky promontory of Baginbun in County Wexford. The bewildering twists and turns of Anglo-Hibernian politics since that time have been crowded one upon the other in the history books, tending "to run together, as railway lines seem to meet in the distance," in the words of Oliver St. John Gogarty. Lost between those distant rails (and between the lines of the books) are the hopes and aspirations of the people who lived the events. They did, however, pass on at least one dimension of their lives that we "moderns" have only recently begun to appreciate. Alwyn and Brinley Rees describe this invaluable legacy:

> There is a growing awareness of the deep significance of realities that cannot be fully . . . explained by history and science. . . . [*Myth has*] proved an inexhaustible fount of inspiration for poets. . . . Only through blind arrogance can all this testimony be dismissed as of little or no significance.

It is those inspired poets who have given us the lyric—and myth—of Irish resistance since 1169. Their Gaelic verse was at once legend and rapier. The incident on the banks of the Potomac demonstrates that not the sanguinary saturation of Irish soil, not the shift to the language of the Stranger, not even the diaspora across the foam, have served to dull the keenest of Irish weapons: the rebel song.

If the lyric of the rebel song is "merely myth," it is a myth alive and kicking violently in modern Ulster. It is perhaps understandable that modern republicans often sing of 1798—when the concept of *poblacht* was imported from France—but it is a sign of something more than intellectual idealism that makes them sing of the Gaelic and Anglo-Irish rebel war-lords of 1534, 1570, 1598, 1641, and 1690. It is this emotional tie to the Irish past that is the basis of rebel song—and is at the root of the Irish Question itself. It is not enough to learn the "academic" history

of the island; it is the folk-history which the people believe . . .
and the folk-history is found in the songs. In the introduction
to her stunning anthology *1000 Years of Irish Poetry,* Kathleen
Hoagland outlines one reason that those not steeped in the tradition have difficulty learning it:

> There has been the problem of choosing poetry that would . . .
> be intelligible to an audience not familiar with Irish History, names
> and references. Therefore I have excluded some poems of a strict-
> ly historic or solely national content. . . . A complete explanation
> . . . would occupy more space than would the poem itself.

Hoagland is in fact correct; a familiarity with "Irish History,
names and references" *is* necessary to understand much of what
the poets sang. What they sang was resistance to the Stranger.
And they still do. The aim of this volume is to consciously
include the ballads "of a strictly historic or solely national content," to listen to that song of Irish rebel history from its largely
legendary birth up through the Emmet Rising of 1803, by which
time it had assumed its modern republican lyric.

    Some comments on format. First, because we are dealing
with folk-history, it is as important that we listen to the ballads
written long after the events themselves as it is to hear the lays of
the contemporary bards. Consequently, the reader will find such
as the boy-poet John Keegan Casey's famous *Rising of the Moon*
describing the emotions of the peasantry in 1798—even though
it was written a half-century afterwards. Second, since the
volume's task is to explain the songs within the tumultuous context of rebel history, the narrative is frequently intricate and
perhaps forbiddingly full of unfamiliar names. In explanation, I
can only suggest that it is meaningless to musically put one's
hope in "God and Our Lady, and Rory O'More" without men-
tioning the battle at Julianstown Bridge. Third, I unabashedly
admit dependence upon the careful research of those listed in
the **Bibliography**. My goal has been to play the role of middleman: to marry the efforts of the researcher, the academic historian, with that of the poet, the people's historian. Since the
reference-per-sentence style of many histories may intimidate
precisely those readers toward whom this book is targeted, I am
afraid the "pure" academician will have to be satisfied with a
chronological but unnumbered **Direct Quotations** section at the
end of the book.*

    A comment on the ballads themselves. The fact that folk-
song is a living tradition ensures that the lyrics undergo a con-

stant metamorphosis. The words to the rebel songs (and the Orange ballads) included herein are far from being chiselled in stone; the transferors of the Irish folk tradition have continually altered the way the story is told. There are few ways to discover the lyrics authored by the original balladeers, nor even when they were first written or sung. Even songs from the modern era are often changed by the singer who prefers his own words to the songwriter's. It is the way of folksong everywhere. The lyrics presented here, then, are not definitive; rather, they are the words that the author learned in boyhood, in the pubs, and even—occasionally—in the library.

A *caveat.* What was heard in English-speaking Wexford in 1798 was not heard in Gaelic Mayo. The enduring provincialism in Ireland makes it difficult to suggest that each ballad is truly representative of the era it describes. Irish resistance has always been against the Stranger—be he the Saxon from over the sea or the Irishman from over the hill (even today, for instance, the Catholic in Belfast has more in common with his urban Protestant neighbor than he does with his co-religionist in rural Connemara). To suggest that the "people of Ireland" felt a certain way at any juncture is a generalised conceit that cannot be justified without in-depth qualification beyond the scope of this book. It is a tightrope I walk in the hope that more skillful writers will clean up after me when I fall.

It is perhaps necessary that an explanation be offered to those who fail to find a favourite ballad. There are many thousands of songs that fit into the rebel *genre* in one way or another . . . in the English language alone. I have attempted to include songs that are historically "revealing" and, as often as possible, those that are still being sung (or narrated**). Unavoidably, some very popular ballads have been omitted for these and other reasons.

A word should also be said about those worthies who have blazed the trail which I follow. Much too little has been written about four modern writers who have already begun the task of putting the national music in perspective. Redfern Mason, an American participant of the early twentieth-century Gaelic Revival, made a grand start with his *Song Lore of Ireland.* The multitalented Patrick Galvin took the next giant step in 1955 with his *Songs of Irish Resistance.* In 1967 Georges-Denis Zimmerman published his monumental *Songs of Irish Rebellion;* covering the years 1780-1900, it is the definitive work on how the songs were sung "at the time." More recently, C. Desmond Greaves has covered another era with his *Easter Rising in Song and Ballad.* Each of these gentlemen is responsible for re-introducing some forgotten songs back into the mainstream of the rebel song tradition. To these four in particular, and to the millions who keep the songs alive in the traditional manner—by singing them—I offer a humble but hearty thanks.

If, as Galvin says, "Ireland's songs reflect Ireland's history with a fidelity probably unparalled in the world," there is a certain amount of background necessary to understand them. Even today, it is not unusual for the rebel songwriter to invoke the ghosts of the legendary Gaelic world of a millennium and more ago. To attempt comprehension of the rebel tradition is to begin in Irish prehistory and follow the march of the Gael from the time CúChulainn's successors met St. Patrick, and listen as the classic formalised poetry of the Druid evolved into the exhuberant defiant verse of the street balladeer. The manner in which the latter have sung about the former is what spurred this work.

The wild grim strength of Ireland comes alive in these ballads. A melding of energetic young ideas and wistful old memories, the rebel songs live on gloriously in our history, and tragically, in our present. I think it important that we remember that they were originally sung by a people who wanted to be left alone to live in peace. This work was begun on the assumption that those who refuse to learn from history will never learn to live with the future. Contemporary events sadly remind us that those who *dwell* in that history can lose touch with the present . . . thus never giving the future a chance.

Turlough Faolain
Lexington Park, Md.

*The plethora of footnotes, on the other hand, has little to do with scholarship, is apologised for in advance, and is due to the irrepressible verbosity of the author.

**Contrary to world opinion, not all Irishmen can carry a tune. Some poems—*The Man From God Knows Where* springs immediately to mind—are usually recited, and yet are very much in the Irish ballad tradition.

CONTENTS

Acknowledgements v

Preface viii

Table of Contents xiii

Table of Maps, Chronologies, and Calendars xviii

1 Introduction 2
    Our Heritage. 9

2 The Coming of the Stranger 13
    Unnamed Ballad 16
    Kincora 18
    Brian the Brave 20
    The Song of O'Rourke 24
    Avenging and Bright. 27

3 Assimilation of the *Sassenach*. 30
    The True Irish King 31
    The Battle of Callann 34
    The Dead at Clonmacnois .40
    When Shall the Day Break in Erin 46

4 The Twilight of the Gael 49
    The Siege of Maynooth. 54
    The Downfall of the Gael .58
    Shane O'Neill 63

5 The Desmond Wars. 67
    The Geraldines 68
    The O'Driscoll War Song. .76
    Follow Me Up to Carlow. .78

6 The Nine Years War 86
  O'Neill's War Song 92
  O'Donnell Aboo 97
  Cean-Salla 105
  Glenswilly 108

7 Plantation 112
  John O'Dwyer of the Glen 113
  The Hedge Schoolmasters 119

8 The Great Rebellion 128
  Rory O'More 128
  Brian Boy Magee 132
  Owen Roe's Address 136
  The Shady Woods of Truagh 139
  The Wexford Massacre 146
  The Death of Owen Roe 147

9 The War of the Two Kings 152
  The Rocks of Bawn 153
  Redmond O'Hanlon 156
  The Black-Backed Cow 161
  Lillibulero 163
  No Surrender 166
  The Maiden City 167
  The Boyne Water 171
  The Battle of the Boyne 172
  The Ballad of Galloping Hogan 176
  Galloping O'Hogan 178
  The Blacksmith of Limerick 180
  The Bridge of Athlone 183
  Ye Natives of This Nation 184
  After Aughrim's Disaster 185
  Lament for Patrick Sarsfield 188

10 Ascendancy and Wild Geese 193
   Ned of the Hill 194
   For the Green 198
   Shule Agra 199
   Clare's Dragoons 201
   The Flower of Finae 204
   The Blackbird 206

The Dirge of O'Sullivan Bear 208
Erin go Bragh 211
Carraigdhoun 212
The Cailín Dhoun 213
The Irish Brigade 215
Fontenoy 216
The Brigade at Fontenoy 218
The White Cockade 220
Bold Captain Freney 222
To the Battle, Men of Erin 223

11 Peasants and Patriots 227
Granuaile 228
The Lament for Art O'Leary 231
The Gaol of Clonmel 234
Honest Owen 237
Garryowen 239
The Bard of Armagh 241
Taxes 243
The Irish Volunteer 245
Unnamed Street Ballad 247
The Volunteers of '82 249
Kathleen ni Houlihan 251
Róisín Dubh 252
Brennan on the Moor 254
Lisnagade 256

12 The United Irishmen 260
Native Swords 263
The Boys of Mullaghbawn 265
Bold McDermott Roe 266
The Protestant Men 270
The Man From God Knows Where 273
Shan Van Vocht 278
Blaris Moor 281

13 The Eve of Rebellion 287
The Wake of William Orr 289
The Rising of the Moon 292
Lord Edward 298
The Brothers 301
Pat O'Donoghue 303

14 Explosion in Leinster 308
    The Wearing of the Green 311
    Prosperous 314
    Michael Boylan 316
    Captain Doorley and the Boyne 318

15 The Boys of Wexford 322
    Croppies Lie Down 323
    Dunlavin Green 325
    The Wind that Shakes the Barley 327
    Irish Soldier Laddie 329
    Boulavogue 331
    Kelly, the Boy from Killane 334
    The Banished Defender 336
    In Deepest Sorrow I Think of Home 338
    The Boys of Wexford 340
    The Battle of Vinegar Hill 342
    Sweet County Wexford 345
    Burke's Dream 347
    The Croppy Boy 349

16 Ulster Also Rises 354
    Henry Joy 358
    Henry Joy MacCracken 360
    General Munro 363
    The Wild Hazel Glen 364

17 Reprisal 368
    Rody McCorley 369
    Green Upon the Cape 371
    Michael Dwyer (I) 376
    The Vow of Tipperary 378
    The Patriot Mother 380
    Billy Byrne of Ballymanus 382
    The Suit of Green 383

18 The Year of the French 387
    The Men of the West 393
    The Frenchman 395
    Patrick Brady 397
    The Boys From the County Mayo 401
    Bodenstown Churchyard 404

Wolfe Tone 405

19 Bold Robert Emmet 411
   The Gallant Men of Ninety-Eight 413
   The Union 416
   No Rising Column 419
   Michael Dwyer (II) 421
   For God and Ireland 425
   Twenty Men From Dublin Town 426
   Anne Devlin 428
   Emmet's Farewell 429
   Bold Robert Emmet 430
   My Emmet's No More 432
   Nell Flaherty's Drake 433

20 Conclusion 437
   The Dead Who Died for Ireland 437
   Breathe Not His Name 438
   Forget Not the Field 439
   The Harp that Once Through Tara's Halls 440
   The Minstrel Boy 441
   By Memory Inspired 443
   The Three Flowers 444
   The Memory of the Dead 446

Irish Glossary 449

Bibliography 457

Direct Quotations 469

Index of Ballads 481

Index of Subjects 484

MAPS, CHRONOLOGIES, AND CALENDARS

Map, "Ireland" . . . (*Mary Metraux Coyle*) . . . Inside Front and Back Covers

Map, "The Great Irish Families". . . . (*M. M. Coyle*) . . . Inside Front Cover

Map, "Irish Battlefields, Massacres, and Confrontations,
1061-1691 . . . . (*M. M. Coyle*) . . . . Inside Back Cover

Map, "Ireland Before Brian Boru" . . . .(*M. M. Coyle*). . . . 15

Map, "Ireland on the Eve of the Norman Landing" . .(*M. M. Coyle*). . . . 22

Chronology, 1260-1460 32

Map, "Ireland at the Time of the Statutes of Kilkenny,
1366. . . . .(*M. M. Coyle*). . . . 42

Chronology, 1461-1567 51-52

Chronology, 1568-1585 69

Map, "Elizabethan Ireland". . . . .(*M. M. Coyle*). . . . 72

Chronology, 1586-1607 88

Chronology, 1605-1641 114

Map, "Plantations Under James Stuart". . . . .(*M. M. Coyle*). . . 117

Chronology, 1641-1653 130

Chronology, 1654-1691 154-155

Map, "The Cromwellian Settlement". . . . .(*M. M. Coyle*). . . 157

Chronology, 1692-1759 195-196

Chronology, 1760-1790 229

Chronology, 1791-1796 262

Calendar of Events, 1798 Rising. . . . .(*Leslie Boyd*) 296-297

Map, "The Rising in North Leinster, 1798" . . . .(*M. M. Coyle*). . . 310

Map, "The Wexford Rising, 1798" . . . .(*M. M. Coyle*). . . 324

Map, "The Ulster Rising, 1798". . . . .(*M. M. Coyle*). . . 356

Map, "The French Campaign, 1798". . . . .(*M. M. Coyle*). . . 389

Chronology, 1799-1803 413

BLOOD ON THE HARP

Irish Rebel History in Ballad

(The Heritage)

1

Introduction

"Give us a rebel song!"

The invariable request from the back of the room is easily and cheerfully answered in song by every Irish folk band south of Armagh. Curiously, the demand is as readily satisfied by the echoing *bodhrán*-beat of *Follow Me Up To Carlow,* celebrating an Elizabethan Irish rebel victory, as it is by the stinging lyric of *The Men Behind the Wire,* from the battle-streets of modern Belfast. In the long march of the Irish National Tradition, events four centuries apart are very much "on the one road." So long as the common threads of Saxon Perfidy and Defiant Resistance are present in the song, the audience considers its request fulfilled.

For the perplexed observer searching for the reasons behind the seemingly unending Irish hostility to the British Crown, one trip to an Irish pub is often more revealing than many to the library. As the lads on stage roar rousing elegies to martyrs long dead, attorneys and dustmen at the bar bellow out the refrains energetically, hoisting their pints to the Boys of the Old Brigade. Matrons in designer jeans and maids in Sunday frocks gleefully whoop, "Up the Rebels!", *their* drinks forgotten in the need to free both hands for clapping. An atavistic beast, eight centuries a-growing, has been loosed by the music. To understand the discouraging headlines of the Irish Today, it is essential to comprehend the Irish Yesterday in which that beast was spawned.

It has become a cliché to suggest that the Irish past may best be learned by listening to the ballads. As is true with many such commonplaces, this one holds more than a shred of truth; in the realm of the Irish National Tradition, at least, the cliché has a great deal of validity. The folk tradition suggests that the last eight centuries have been a constant struggle against the invader. Most modern historians would tend to disagree, citing a wealth of socio-economic data to emphasise that the view is simplistic. The cultural anthropologist, however, just might concur with the folk-historian, submitting that the reality perceived by a people—accurate or not—should not be underestimated. The problem, of course, is that the historian writes for other academics; the poet, on the other hand, sings for the people. If history is, as Carlyle counsels, a distillation of rumour, it makes little difference if the rumour is reported by a Macaulay or a wandering bard. And for all the hand-wringing it occasions in the groves of academe, the common folk are more likely to listen to the poet than the historian; they hear far more songs than they read books. The fact is simply that the folk history of Ireland *is* real to the common people, and *does* serve as their inspiration to the future. The Irish have a "tendency to live in their past," George Dangerfield remarks, "to cherish it and nurse it, because it is a past of indignities and oppressions, and has a more visceral and more poignant character to them than the English past has to their English neighbors." Eight hundred years of Anglo-Hibernian history—and perhaps fifteen centuries of Gaelic tradition before that—have been woven into the rich, evocative tapestry of Irish songs of resistance.

It is not merely the humble folk of Ireland who respond to the music. The modern scholar, perhaps comfortable himself with quiet pages of dry prose, is often surprised at the ease with which the rebel ballads arouse noisy emotions in the breasts of even waistcoated and bejewelled denizens of the middle and upper class. He may fail to understand that he is witnessing the musical equivalent of the classless, time-honoured Irish tradition of retiring to the pub to "talk a little treason." The use of balladeers for rabble-rousing has had a long history in Ireland. Emily Hahn refers to the practice among the ancient Gaelic chieftains . . . and the English response to it:

> Some lords used bards expressly to inspirit their fighting men. . . . In years to come the Normans detested this practice among the Irish, as did the English. Time after time the invaders passed laws against Irish harpists and bards, without effect.

To the sorrow and consternation of the Stranger, *no* sort of legislation seemed to have much effect on the Irish. For reasons inexplicable to the British—and perfectly obvious to the Gaels—the unruly Hibernians repeatedly ignored English law and custom, preferring instead to sing the story of a Brehon Law and Celtic folk tradition that had its origin in the dim mists of prehistory.

If the rebel song has become a distinct form in the folk music of the Irish, it has not always been. The birth of rebel balladry was not an event; rather, it was a process evolving from a Celtic culture that had always accorded an honoured place to the poet, the bard, and the storyteller. Relatively new to the folk-ways of the Gael—in the context of Irish history, the 1169 coming of the Normans is itself a recent event—the rebel song emerged first in Tudor Ireland in the form of *rosg catha,* bardic haranguing on the eve of battle. By the end of the eighteenth century, the song of resistance had settled into the Irish folk tradition with some permanence. To understand why the rebel ballad has become so important to the Irish, it must first be recognised that the folk-memories of the oldest continuous Western culture have never died. The Irish, quite simply, have never lost their primary identification as Irishmen.

When the Celts first arrived in Ireland sometime between 900-400 B.C., they discovered a bucolic society that had been thriving undisturbed by outside influence for thousands of years. Within the next millennium, the Celts and the "original Irish" had merged; by the time of Christ, there was a common poetry and language, a common Gaelic cultural identity. Unlike the shifting states of Europe whose borders were traditionally shaped by the most recent conqueror, Ireland was tucked out in the Atlantic with God-given boundaries that kept marauders away for sufficient centuries to allow a distinctive political and cultural entity to emerge. In the absence of foreign intervention—not even the Romans bothered to cross the Irish Sea—the isolated Gaels established a rude political system based on the *tuath,* or tribal clan. It was a sort of imperfect balance-of-power arrangement in which the various kings recognised each other's claim to tribal territory, even as they raided their neighbor's cattle. A pastoral people, the early Irish were generally more interested in adding to their herds than in establishing geographic hegemony over their rivals' lands. Although there was an *Ard Rí,* or High King, his position was largely that of "chairman of the board" when the most important chieftains met together on the royal Hill of Tara to settle their incessant squabbles. Of far more importance than the tribal political system was the culture that grew up within it.

Druidic poets gradually had become the custodians of the oral tradition—there was no written language.[1] These *ollúna,* or master poets, who also served as historians and genealogists, eventually became the dispensers of common justice. In many ways, the High Druids were more powerful than the kings; it would not be unreasonable, in fact, to call the cultural system a diarchy. Uisneach, the seat of these exalted magistrates in modern Westmeath, was probably of more importance to the prehistoric Irish than Tara, its more famous political equivalent almost forty miles to the east.

In those pre-Christian days, there was a definite pecking order among the pagan Druids. The *ollúna* were the final arbiters of the *Senchus Mór*, the sophisticated body of oral case-law—memorised by them in rhymed verse—that was to evolve into the famed Brehon Law. These mysterious hooded figures were the interpreters of a law to which even the kings were subject. A step below the High Druids were the *filí*, sort of local judge-poets who traditionally served individual tribal chieftains of the second-rank. The humble folk of Ireland rarely dealt with the lofty *ollúna* or *filí;* rather, the lowly clansmen heard their poems and stories from the bards and storytellers of the meanest order, the *seanchaithe*, who criss-crossed the island settling mundane disputes and "singing for their supper."[2]

These apprentice poets often told their tales through the long winter nights from *Samhaine* to *Bealtaine*—in modern parlance, All Saints' Day to May Day—when the cattle raiding had presumably died down for the season. It was not unusual for the people of an entire townland to crowd into the largest cabin to hear the bard spin out his sagas by the crackling hearth. The common Irish heard chronicles of legendary heroes and faery enchantments, of harrowing ghosts and romantic quests, of famous battles and spectacular duels. Nor were these extemporaneous performances: each *ollamh* was required to spend at least twenty years of apprenticeship as *seanchaí* and *file* in turn, learning by rote the entire oral lore of Ireland. In addition to the entire *Senchus Mór* and over 350 ritual sagas, the High Druids were required to commit the complete genealogy of all chieftains to memory word-for-word. The intellectual accomplishment of these illiterate early poets only comes clearly into focus when it is considered exactly what this meant:

> 1) The *Senchus Mór*—the great ancient law—codified first with the coming of the Christian scribes, was case law stretching back to the much older *Seanchus agus Félineachus na hÉireann*—the Ancient Laws and Decisions of the Féini, the "original Irish." The law was memorised in a distinct form of Gaelic verse, *Bearla Féini,*

a dead language that insured that the law was protected from re-interpretation "by idiom" (much as the use of Latin in the Catholic Mass insures the immutability of the ceremony). This ancient code, stretching back at least 2,500 years, reduced all offenses to civil wrongs, and was designed to compensate the victim rather than the society.

2) The sagas were also memorised precisely. *Táin Bó Cuailnge*, "the Cattle-Raid of Cooley," the story of CúChulainn, is the most famous of all Irish traditional tales. In the twelfth century Book of Leinster, a colophon is included with it: "A blessing on everyone who will memorize the *Táin* with fidelity in this form and will not put any other form on it." It was in fact part of the stylised ritual of the recitation for the storyteller to end his tale with the disclaimer, "That is my story! If there be a lie in it, be it so! It is not I who made or invented it."

3) The genealogies were the most difficult of all for the Druids. Irish tradition recognised four different gradations of "kingship." There was the chieftain of a single *tuath*, or *rí tuaithe;* the chief of several clans, also called *rí tuaithe;* the king of an entire province, *rí cóicid;* and the High King of the island, *Ard Rí.* The poets were responsible for memorising the complete genealogical structure of each of the chieftains on the island. When it is considered that there were about 150 *tuatha*, that the constant warfare must have caused frequent deaths and subsequent coronations, and that the kings were elected—changing the genealogy almost as often as the chiefs—the remarkable accomplishment of these guardians of the oral tradition is mind-boggling.

The tales of the *seanchaithe* were both history and news journal to the common folk of Ireland. It is not surprising that contemporary heroism and classical legend became confused . . . sometimes on purpose by *filí* intent on flattering their patrons. As the court poets composed verse praising their sponsoring chieftains, the wandering bards brought the heroic sagas to the rude homes of the countryside. The tradition endured far longer than might be supposed. Alwyn and Brinley Rees report that, as late as 1860 in one isolated locale, the "adventures of . . . Ossian were as true and real to the storytellers . . . and those who listened to them as were the latest exploits of the British Army to readers of newspapers."

When Christianity burst upon Ireland during the fifth

century, the influence of the pagan Druids was threatened. Two events, however, intervened to insure that the stylistic oral tradition would not disappear. First, St. Columcille (Columba of Iona) convinced the sixth century kings to retain their sponsorship of the *filí* as official court poets. Second, scribes in the new Christian monasteries began to record into Latin manuscript anything they could get their hands on—be it originally in Roman, Greek, or Gaelic. The position of the poets underwent a subtle metamorphosis; still held in awe by king and clansman, the *ollúna* and *filí* evolved into the Brehons, maintaining their bardic, historical, and magisterial duties while ceding religion to the Catholic monks. The kings, retaining their political preeminence, gradually became paramount in the society. Tara superseded Uisneach. The ritual and mythology of the pagan Celtic tradition had found a comfortable marriage with the new Christian influence. The result was a novel and uniquely Gaelic-Christian culture that retained its ties with the old ways. From that time, Christ and CúChulainn have marched together through Irish history.[3]

As administrators of a complicated but pervasive system of societal justice, the Brehons managed to maintain a state of relative order that enabled Ireland to become the "keeper of the flame of knowledge" during the European Dark Ages. The Irish chieftains continued to storm through each other's territory seeking cattle and slaves, but they dared not trouble the Brehon-protected monasteries. Meanwhile, the monks within laboriously copied the plays of Terence and Aristophanes, along with the legends of CúChulainn, for posterity (presumably wrinkling their collective noses at the content). While the centres of European learning slipped into shadow, St. Kieran was founding a great monastic university at Clonmacnois in 548. John F. Kennedy was not merely demonstrating pride of ancestry when he commented that "No larger nation did more to keep Christianity and Western culture alive in their darkest centuries." Famous monks such as Columbanus, Sedulius Scotus, Dicuil, and John Scotus Eriugena spread over Europe as educational and spiritual missionaries during the next several centuries. Ruth Dudley Edwards reports that by the ninth century Irish scholars:

> had a widespread European reputation. Charlemagne had appointed Irish masters to his palace schools, and during the ninth century Irish scholars . . . had an important role in the establishment of France as a centre of learning.

Soon after the founding of Clonmacnois, two other developments occurred which were to have a lasting impact on the
Gaelic tradition.   First, the monks began to chronicle Irish history.   Second, organised bardic schools began to appear.   No
longer would the history of the island be confined to a few *filí;*
now there was at once a written record of the Irish past, and
men who could both learn it and carry it to the people.   The
combination initiated an historical impulse that was in full
flower by the tenth century.   More important to the National
Tradition, researchers have found no trace of individual histories
of the 150 *tuatha* on the island.   The *Dictionary of Irish Literature* laconically notes that "from the beginning, the history
written was the history of Ireland."   It is perhaps not merely
coincidence that the full blooming of this historical impulse
among the Irish was to be chronologically congruous with history's only United Ireland.

One major reason for the spread of Irish educational missions to the continent was the onslaught of the Vikings in the
ninth century. Presumably, many monks were quickly convinced of the worthiness of missionary work abroad shortly after
the Danes found that the monasteries provided far better loot
than coastal fishing villages.   Although many of the Norsemen
were soon absorbed into Gaelic society, the power of those
living in the new Viking towns along the shore threatened to destroy the old order.   It provided the impetus needed for an ambitious Munster chieftain to unite the island politically for the
first time at the beginning of the eleventh century.   The fabled
Brian Boru was killed shortly thereafter as the Danes were ousted
"for good."   They were to return in the guise of their Norman
descendants in 1169.

The Irish had been able to largely absorb the Viking invasion for two major reasons.   First, the Northmen who came to
Ireland did not owe allegiance to a foreign nation-state; they
settled in Ireland precisely because they were on their own.
Second, the Vikings were merely after booty and had a vested
interest in seeing that the native Irish culture was not irreparably
damaged; so long as the native society survived, there was spoil
to be had.   The Normans turned out to be another matter altogether.   While the individual invaders were not averse to plunder,
they owed their nominal allegiance to a foreign state that wanted
to be cut in on the action.   When the Norman marcher lords of
Ireland began to side with the native Gaelic chieftains against

their supposed overlords in London, it was a direct threat to the modern nation making up on the Thames. The Crown of England was ambitious; it wanted political power in Ireland. When London finally realised that hegemony could not be exercised effectively in Ireland unless the native culture was supplanted, it just never occured to the Crown that the price would be so expensive.

Kings and ministers came and went in the early years of English "occupation" without appreciably affecting the lifestyle of the humble folk. When the Crown declared war on the Gaelic culture, however, it affected the Irish from king to kern . . . and poet. The people fought back with the weapons ready to hand. The *filí* fought back, too; in their acerb verse was born the rebel song.

Nationalism and rebellion in Ireland first truly became one during the Elizabethan era. The Irish began to invoke their folk heroes to help them jettison the English. The halcyon days of Brian Boru—and a United Ireland—were recalled fondly. The chauvinistic bards reminded the people that the Gaelic Ireland of Finn MacCool, Queen Maeve, and Cormac MacArt had developed an heroic culture while the Saxons were still ruffian serfs to dissipate Rome. The savage treatment meted out to the Irish was answered, as most things are in Ireland, by a question: "What else can be expected from barbarians?" The tragedy of Ireland for the last four centuries has been that, from their different perspective, the English have asked the same question.

The early seventeenth-century Flight of the Earls, with the resultant Ulster Plantation, was supposed to set the stage for the finale of the English play. It has been a long last act . . . its unending musical score is the subject of this work.

OUR HERITAGE

For much of the history of Ireland the literacy of the common man has been prevented by circumstances or prohibited by law. The Irishman has compensated for his lack of reading and writing skills with verse and music. C. Desmond Greaves affords an accurate appraisal of the importance of the folk balladry:

> Frequently sentimental, at times wildly romantic, of literary and musical quality as varied as the talents and circumstances of

those who wrote them, Irish songs gave a truer folk history than
the card-indexes of the colleges, because they recorded the emotions of the common people, emotions recalled often enough when
the events that occasioned them might be partly forgotten.
Given the conditions of his existence, it was perhaps inevitable
that the Irishman would sing songs of resistance. Given the continuity of his cultural tradition, it is not surprising that he would
look to the pantheon of ancient Irish heroes for his muse.

This ballad by Joseph Mary Plunkett echoes the ancient call
that sent men out to their fate on Easter Monday 1916 to declare
the Irish Republic. The martial poet was shot for his part in that
rising, since taking his own honoured place in the hagiology of
Irish martyrdom.

This heritage to the race of kings:
Their children and their children's seed
Have wrought their prophecies in deed
Of terrible and splendid things.

The hands that fought, the hearts that broke
In old immortal tragedies,
These have not failed beneath the skies,
Their children's heads refuse the yoke.

And still their hands shall guard the sod
That holds their fathers' funeral urn,
Still shall their hearts volcanic burn
With anger of the sons of God.

No alien sword shall earn as wage
The entail of their blood and tears,
No shameful price for peaceful years
Shall ever part this heritage.

The Irish rebel song exists for two primary reasons: (1) the
verse tradition of the Irish, and (2) the continuing insistence of
the Stranger that a military "solution" could be found to answer
the Irish Question. To get a feel for the poetic tradition, com-
pare this comment about ancient Ireland:

Verse was . . . the common literary medium. . . . There is one
essential fact about Irish poetry which must never be forgotten . . .

it is, and at all periods of its history has been associated with music.

—*Eleanor Knott*

with this one about recent times:

> The tradition of writing . . . and singing ballads at streetcorners or in the market place, has never died out in Ireland; it is still a *living* tradition to this very day. . . . Ireland's songs reflect Ireland's history with a fidelity probably unparalled in the world.

—*Patrick Galvin*

Over the centuries, the English have had no shortage of advisors "on the spot" in Ireland counselling against a military solution of the Irish Question. It is one of the tragedies of Anglo-Hibernian history that the British colonialist leadership in England has consistently disbelieved its professional soldiers in the field. Consider, for example, the following two dispatches, both of which were addressed to the authorities in London:

> Irishmen will never be conquered by war. They can suffer so much . . . ever at their advantage to flee or fight; so that a great army were but a charge in vain.

—*British State Papers*, 1541

> The Provisional IRA has the dedication and the sinews of war to raise violence . . . certainly for the forseeable future.

—*Captured British Army report*
published by the IRA, 1979

The folk culture of Ireland has drawn the heroes and villains of history in sharp detail, and recurringly returned to the weapons of an earlier day to fight the Stranger. Martyrdom, hunger-strike, and the power of the poet have been handed down through the generations from pre-Brehon Ireland. Over the long centuries, the larger-than-life figures of Gaelic legend have become one with the hapless creatures on the English gallows tree. In a very real way, Conn of the Hundred Battles is still alive on the streets of modern Belfast . . . with a *file* by his side.

CHAPTER NOTES (1)

1 — There was one exception. The *Ogham* system of cypher, a crude system found on totems and tombstones, did exist. The efficacy of *Ogham*—short lines "varying in number and position"—was limited. Tomás Ó Fiaich reports that "if a modern novel were to be written in it, it would require a surface over a mile in length."

2 — Nor did the nobles hear the sagas directly from the *ollúna* or *filí*. The poets of antiquity were not performers. A professional *reacaire* recited the poets' work, often accompanied by a harper. There is indeed much evidence that the poets were the only class allowed to travel freely about Ireland. Early Druidic law seems to have made some provision for keeping the common people loyal by denying them access to the blandishments of the neighboring septs (the problem, of course, is one not unfamiliar in our own time: one can almost hear the bards singing a few bars of "How do you keep them down on the farm after they've seen Clonmel?").

3 — Kathleen Hughes:

"One of the most exciting and historical facts . . . is that these two quite separate worlds, the Latin and the Irish, began to borrow ideas and techniques from each other . . . by this time some of the poets and lawyers had not only learned to read and write . . . they had also begun to apply their new knowledge to the Irish language and to their own traditional body of learning. The old method of learning by memory in the secular schools did not cease, but rather some poets and lawyers were coming into close contact with clergy of Latin education."

2

The Coming of the Stranger

The inviolability of the Celtic island was first breached late in the eighth century when the Vikings began to make sporadic forays along the shores of Ireland. At first, the raids were swift one-ship assaults on tiny coastal villages clearly unable to defend themselves. With increasing frequency, however, the shallow-draught longships appeared upriver searching for the monasteries, the most rewarding prizes.

Not able to muster defenders quickly enough to ward off these unpredictable attacks, the vulnerable monastic communities were forced to depend on the hereditary Irish ally, the sea. A quatrain, apparently written by a monk during the early ninth century, gives some idea of the Norsemen's impact:

> The wind is at war tonight,
> Whipping the waves of the white-winged sea;
> No fear to find the Irish Sea
> Crossed by savage Scandinavians.

At best, the sea was an inconstant ally.

In 837 the Vikings came to stay. The heretofore-isolated Irish must have looked on with awe as a fleet of over one hundred Norse vessels made their way boldly up the Rivers Boyne and Liffey, disgorging their axe-wielding, flaxon-haired warriors. The amazement would have turned quickly to horror when it became clear what the helmeted strangers were after. Within the century, the Danes had established permanent raiding bases all along the Irish coast. These "booty depots" were to evolve into the trading towns of Dublin, Waterford, Wexford, Youghal, Cork, Bantry, and Limerick. The squabbling Irish chieftains, unable to stand alone against the onslaught of the professional Norse commandos, began to turn to the savage tribes of Britain and Scotland for mercenary help. These *gallóglaigh,* or "foreign youth," were to become a staple of Irish fighting forces for the next eight centuries.

The Vikings were not interested in taking real estate for its own sake; certainly they had no desire to herd cattle or work the land. Rather, they were content to remain in garrison operating what has been called "a sort of primitive protection racket." They took to the countryside only on occasional plundering missions to chastise those tribes who would not come up with the required tribute. Since these were tactics not unfamiliar to the Gael, the Northmen soon came to be looked upon as just another group of strongmen by a society that admired strongmen. If these queer men of the North valued gold over cattle, it was no stranger than their butter-coloured hair to the bemused Irish. An almost inevitable merging of cultures began. The Danes, far from home, took Irish brides and learned the Irish language . . . unquestionably in that order. The Gaels, for their part, were pleased to learn the use of Norse weapons of War. Ensuing internecine wars took on the character of rows between contending coalitions of Norse-Irish with the battle-axe prominent on both sides.

Few Irish clans stood aloof from the intrigues. One that attempted to use the Norsemen for their own purposes was the declining Eóghanacht dynasty of the South. The Munster King Cellachán gathered an army of Vikings from Waterford and Limerick in 939 to resist the encroachments of the remarkable king of the Northern O'Neill, Murtough "of the Leathern Cloaks." Murtough had been little troubled by the martial ability of the Northmen, even defeating them at sea and plundering their settlements (the Viking towns were by now sufficiently established to be as vulnerable as had been the Irish monasteries a century earlier). In the ensuing campaign Cellachán was taken prisoner by the northerner and, when he returned to Munster after Murtough's death in 943, the Eóghanacht king found that the power vacuum created by his absence had been filled by the Vikings of Limerick. Though Cellachán managed to maintain his title until his death in 954, he could do little to prevent the Limerick Norse from moving further afield in their unending search for plunder. As they did, the DálCais, a minor Thomond clan, began to feel the sting of the Northern raiders for the first time. The Dálcassian King Mahon blamed the Eóghanachts for abdicating their "royal responsibility" and rose against them in 954. After ousting the old dynasty from the Munster throne at Cashel, Mahon turned on the local Vikings and drove them out of

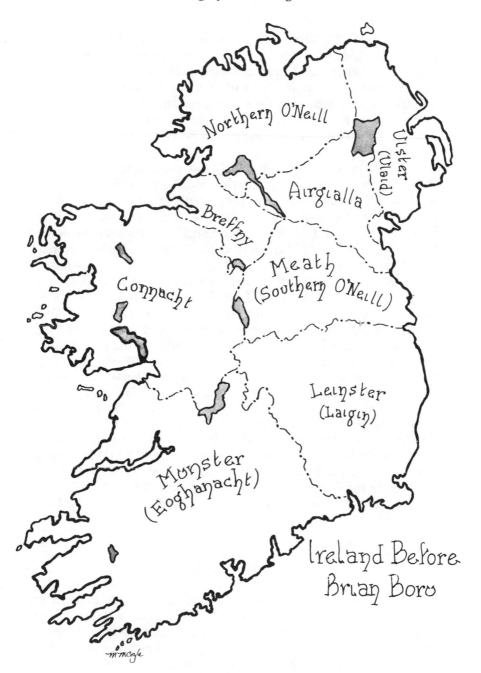

Northern O'Neill

Ulster
(Ulaid)

Airgialla

Breffny

Meath
(Southern O'Neill)

Connacht

Leinster
(Laigin)

Munster
(Eoghanacht)

Ireland Before
Brian Boru

mmcayle

Limerick in 967. The intrepid Danes soon returned and, with Eóghanacht aid, succeeded in killing the upstart Mahon in 976. The shaky Dálcassian claim to the suzerainty of Munster was swiftly assumed by Mahon's brother Brian MacKennedy, an ambitious war-lord who was now to storm out of the obscurity of Thomond with sword and battle-axe to emblazon his more familiar cant name on the pages of both Gaelic and Norse saga— Brian Boru.

As Brian launched his whirlwind campaign to "liberate" Munster, the young King of the Southern O'Neill, Malachy MacDonnell, recognised the Viking preoccupation with events in the South as his own opportunity. Malachy ousted the Danes from the North and forced the grudging submission of the Gaelic lords of Ulster and the Northern O'Neill. By 981 he had overrun the "Kingdom of the Ostmen" at Dublin, winning the appellation *Mór* ("the Great"), and had been proclaimed High King at Tara. Three years later, Brian's hold on the South was sufficiently secure to persuade malachy Mór to conclude a pact with the Munster lord: Brian was to hold sway in the South while the High King was acknowledged lord of the North.[1] When the Dublin Ostmen attempted a rising against Malachy in 998, the two kings defeated the penultimate Viking gasp at GlenMáma on the Kildare/Wicklow frontier. Brian took Dublin the next year.

In 1002 Brian—who had been strengthening his forces even in time of peace—made a triumphant "grand tour" of Ireland, flexing his military muscle and collecting cattle tribute from the clans. Malachy Mór got the message. In 1004 at Tara, Brian *Bóirhme*[2] became Emperor of the Irish. Until his death a decade later, Boru ruled as undisputed ruler of the island. For the first and—so far—last time, Ireland was a united land ruled by Irishmen.

Unnamed Ballad

The short decades of "autonomous unity" under Brian Boru and Malachy Mór have been romantically viewed by later generations of nationalists as the historical pinnacle of Irish political success. Hence the enduring war-cry: "*Re*unite Ireland!" Perhaps of more importance to the National Tradition is the *way* Brian unified Ireland. The sanguinary sword of Boru has stood example to countless Irishmen who have come to believe that only the martial tramp of the native will again free Innisfail from the Invader.

Lionel Johnson, author of the following verse, echoed that belief many centuries later "from his barstool in The Cheshire Cheese in London." Benedict Kiely submits that in "the company of the 'lost generation' of poets of whom he was one of the most notably lost," Johnson "could write about Ireland as nobly as he had written about the statue of King Charles at Charing Cross."

A terrible and splendid trust
Heartens the host of Innisfail:
Their dream is of the swift sword-thrust,
A lightning glory of the Gael.

Croagh Patrick is the place of prayers,
And Tara the assembling place;
But each sweet wind of Ireland bears
The tramp of battle on its race.

From Dursey Isle to Donegal,
From Howth to Achill, the glad noise
Rings: and the heirs of glory fall,
Or victory crowns their fighting joys.

A dream! A dream! An ancient dream!
Yet ere peace come to Innisfail
Some weapons on some field must gleam,
Some burning glory fire the Gael.

By 1013 Brian Boru's High Kingship was in trouble. King Svein of Denmark had conquered Britain, encouraging the Ostman King Sitric of Dublin and his ally MaelMórda of Leinster to rise against the *Ard Rí*. The rebellious sovereigns enlisted aid from Malachy's neighbors in Breffny and the Northern O'Neill, effectively neutralising the Meathman; Sitric and MaelMórda then simply outwaited a three-month siege by Brian on easily supplied Dublin. Boru finally lifted the "blockade" just before Christmas.

During the winter months, both sides prepared for the coming spring campaign. Sitric and MaelMórda managed to form an impressive coalition of Northmen from the Orkneys and Normandy, Danes from Scandanavia and Britain, Leinstermen, and Dublin Norse-Irish. The High King was not as persuasive among the Irish, demonstrating clearly that the "unity" of Ireland under Brian was more legend than fact. Outside of two minor clans, Connacht stood apart awaiting developments. Breffny and the Northern O'Neill remained hostile to Brian and Malachy, but sagely refused to commit openly for the "Foreigners of the West of Europe" until they could see which way the wind blew. Only the Southern O'Neill seemed willing to stand by the *Ard Rí*'s Munstermen.

On the eve of the 23 April 1014 Battle of Clontarf, the bitterest desertion of all befell the High King. For a reason not known to history, Malachy Mór led his Southern O'Neill army from the Irish camp near Dublin. Brian Boru, now seventy-three, was to fight the Good Friday battle with only two small renegade Connacht clans and a contingent of Scot gallowglass to add to his Munster forces.

KINCORA

What is known of the Battle of Clontarf suggests that the casualties exceeded ten thousand, a very great slaughter indeed for the times. Victims to the carnage were Brian Boru himself, his eldest son and heir Murrough, the High King's grandson Turlough, the Scot Prince Donald of Mar, and the flower of Munster's sub-royalty. The losses to the Dálcassians and their allied tribes of Munster ensured that the High Kingship would pass back to Malachy Mór, whose army, after all, was intact after Clontarf.

This James Clarence Mangan poem is ostensibly a translation of a Gaelic lament for Brian Boru by Giolla MacLiag, *file* to the slain *Ard Rí*. Brian's palace at Kincora was near by the southwestern shore of Lough Derg, just north of Killaloe. The castle referred to in the last quatrain is probably *BealBoru* ("Pass of the Tributes"), a lakeside outpost of the MacKennedy family supposedly once connected by a mile-long covered passage to Kincora. Its ruins are still visible overlooking the lough.

Oh where, Kincora! is Brian the Great?
And where is the beauty that once was thine?

Oh, where are the princes and nobles that sate
At the feast in thy halls, and drank the red wine?
Where oh, Kincora?

Oh where, Kincora! are thy valorous lords?
Oh whither, thou Hospitable! are they gone?
Oh where are the Dálcassians of the golden swords?
And where are the warriors Brian led on?
Where oh, Kincora?

They are gone, those heroes of royal birth
Who plundered no churches, and broke no trust,
Tis weary for me to be living on earth
When they, oh Kincora, lie low in the dust!
Low oh, Kincora!

Oh, never again will princess appear,
To rival the Dálcassians of the cleaving swords!
I can never dream of meeting afar or anear,
In the East or the West, such heroes and lords!
Never, Kincora?

Oh, dear are the images my memory calls up
Of Brian Boru!—how he never would miss
To give me at the banquet the first bright Cup!
Ah, why did he heap on me honour like this?
Why oh, Kincora?

I am MacLiag and my home is on the lake;
Thither often, to that palace whose beauty is fled
Came Brian to ask me, and I went for his sake;
Oh, my grief that I should live, and Brian be dead!
Dead oh, Kincora!

The Battle of Clontarf has often been trumpeted as a victory for Ireland. Certainly it was a disaster for the Danes—almost the entire coalition army was destroyed during the battle—but it is perhaps more accurate to describe the result as a political triumph for Malachy Mór.

The only Dálcassians of note to survive the 1014 campaign, Brian Boru's sons Donogh and Tadg, were soon quarrelling with each other over the Munster succession. In the power vacuum, Malachy had no real opposition when he re-assumed the High Kingship that he had ceded to Brian a dozen years earlier. When the Meathman himself died in 1022, however, it was the signal for a general free-for-all with the Crown of Ireland the elusive goal. No single provincial king had the military or political skill to do more than make a claim on the title for almost a century. The High Kingship was finally shakily assumed by Turlough O'Connor of Connacht in 1119. The chroniclers, though, name even O'Connor *Ard Rí* with the exclusion *co fresabra,* "with opposition."

BRIAN THE BRAVE

The political results of Clontarf left the Munstermen bitter. It had been the families of the South that had borne the brunt of the battle; it was the rest of Ireland that was fighting over the spoils. This old song well describes the feelings of the southerners during the century after the death of Boru.

As is common to Irish ballads, the use of metaphor makes the song equally valid in other eras: substitute "Norman" for "Dane" and the lyrics fit the Irish reaction to Strongbow in a later time; replace "Saxon" for "Dane" and the song can be sung about the Desmond Wars, still later.

Remember the glories of Brian the Brave,
Though the days of the Hero are over,
Though lost to Mononia and cold in the grave,
He returns to Kincora no more.
That star of the field which so often hath poured
Its beam on the battle is set;
But enough of its glory remains on each sword
To light us to victory yet.

Mononia! When nature embellished the tint
Of thy fields and thy mountains so fair,
Did she ever intend that a tyrant should print
The footsteps of slavery there?
No! Freedom, whose smile we shall never resign,
Go tell our invaders, the Danes,

That tis sweeter to bleed for an age at thy shrine
Than to sleep but a moment in chains.

Forget not our wounded companions who stood
In the day of distress by our side,
While the moss of the valley grew red with their blood,
They stirred not, but conquered and died.
That sun which now blesses our arms with his light,
Saw them fall upon Ossory's plain—
Oh, let him not blush when he leaves us tonight,
To find that they fell there in vain.

Turlough O'Connor's reign as *Ard Rí* from 1119-56 was marked by events that were to have great consequence for Ireland. Two provincial kings, Murtough MacLochlainn of TyrOwen and Dermott MacMurrough of Leinster, carried on with their own affairs as if the High King did not exist. In 1152 MacMurrough carried off Dervogilla, wife to Tiernan O'Rourke, overlord of Breffny and sometime ally of O'Connor whose avaricious gaze remained constantly upon the lands of Meath to his East—a "fiefdom" of MacLochlainn. The King of Breffny protested to the High King. O'Connor (or his Brehon) ruled that MacMurrough was to return the captive to O'Rourke along with a "fine" of one hundred ounces of gold. Dermott showed no reluctance in giving up Dervogilla—it is probable he had tired of the forty-five-year-old prisoner of love—but he was not about to give up anything of real value. The bitterness caused by this seemingly insignificant feud was to have an indirect impact far out of proportion to its contemporary moment: it was to provide the impetus for the Norman invasion of Ireland.

When the *Ard Rí* died in 1156, most of the Irish chieftains supported Rory O'Connor's claim to succeed his father. Certainly Tiernan O'Rourke did . . . if only because MacMurrough was supporting Murtough MacLochlainn's counterclaim. When the TyrOwen king died in 1166, Dermott MacMurrough found himself the only disputant to Rory O'Connor's right to the High Kingship. The vengeful O'Rourke—still looking for his hundred ounces of gold—was happy to lead the High King's forces against his old Leinster enemy. Dermott retreated to his clan stronghold in Wexford but found even Ferns Castle no sanctuary when his Leinster henchmen began to desert him,

Ireland on the Eve of the Norman Landing

presumably feeling ancient tribal ties of dubious value when faced with the prospect of battle against the combined forces of the Irish island. The deposed MacMurrough fled to Aquitaine to put his unhappy story before Henry II.

The ambitious King of England was off on one of his interminable continental adventures. The founder of the Plantagenet line, Henry was a thoroughly Norman descendant of the defeated Clontarf Norsemen with little understanding of, and little interest in, the Saxons he ruled as lord of England. If the King had little knowledge of Britain, it is certain that his knowledge of Ireland was even less comprehensive. The English monarch was nothing if not opportunistic, however, and it is entirely in character that he was not unreceptive to MacMurrough's plea for help. Although Henry was far too busy to get personally involved in squabbles among the tumultuous Irish, he was never averse to acquiring new domains at a bargain price. In the event he gave Dermott leave to recruit whom he would among the Norman barons of England and Wales, with the proviso that the potential volunteers would have to finance the venture themselves.

In truth, Henry II had another reason for wishing the adventure success. The Plantagenet had been feuding with his exiled Archbishop of Canterbury, Thomas à Becket, who was at the time under the defiant protection of Pope Alexander III. Ironically, the pontiff's predecessor Adrian IV (the only English pope) had in 1155 issued a papal bull, the *Laudabilitier,* which authorized Henry to:

> march into [*Ireland*] and carry out whatever tends to the honour of God and the welfare of that land, and . . . the people of that land shall receive you honourably and respect you as their Lord, as long as the rights of the churches are permanently preserved.

Busy elsewhere, Henry had not exercised his papal charge. The Norman King may now have found the prospect of seizing Ireland "in the name of the Pope" somewhat bemusing. Frustrated by the new pontiff's support of Becket, Henry must have felt a certain glee at this "heaven-sent" opportunity to tweak the papal nose.

Dermott MacMurrough went shopping for allies. The exiled King of Leinster was able to interest a number of restless Norman-Welsh nobles in the enterprise by making extravagant promises for landed sinecures. Chief among the Welsh knights was Richard FitzGilbert de Clare, Earl of Pembroke (better known to history by his *nom de guerre,* "Strongbow"), to whom was promised the hand of MacMurrough's daughter. Dermott, assured of aid as soon as his "heir-to-be" organised the Norman knights, returned to his Wexford home and meekly paid the hundred ounces of gold still owing to Tiernan O'Rourke.

On May Day 1169 the Irish near Bannow in Ballyteige Bay were presented with a sight that chilled the *Bealtaine* celebrations instantly: Robert FitzStephan, Myler FitzHenry, Robert de Barry, and thirty mounted, mail-clad Norman knights. The shining helmets of the sixty other horsemen disembarking with the Welsh barons probably impressed the astonished Irish more than the strange new weapon carried by the Flemish mercenary foot who also waded ashore. Their first impressions were to change as the Irish came under the destructive fire of the massed crossbows.[3] The next day, the Normans were joined by two hundred more under Maurice de Prendergast. The invasion of Ireland was on.

THE SONG OF O'ROURKE

(*The Valley Lay Smiling Before Me*)

Dermott MacMurrough's role in inducing the Normans to cross the Irish Sea has made the Leinster king the paramount villain in rebel history. The "false Dervogilla" also receives her share of the blame. Although the tale bears some resemblance to the Paris/Helen saga that precipitated the siege of Troy, Irish poets have been far less kind than Homer might have been to the pair whose dalliance brought the Stranger from over the sea to Ireland.

Seven-and-a-half centuries after the event, William Butler Yeats could still write passionately about their "blame":

> . . . . never, never
> Shall Diarmuid and Dervorgilla be forgiven.
>
> . . . .
> I had almost yielded and forgiven it all—
> Terrible the temptation and the place!

Though a defenceless plum such as Ireland would surely have been plucked by the avaricious Normans eventually, the treachery of MacMurrough foreshadowed what was later to be a recurring problem for Irish nationalists—the betrayal of Ireland by Irishmen. Such incidents have sadly spawned the proverb: "Put an Irishman on a spit and you'll find two to turn him.''

This Thomas Moore ballad demonstrates the lasting feeling of the Irish that still existed towards Diarmuid *na nGall* in the early nineteenth century, almost seven hundred years later. The scene of the poem may be seen from O'Rourke's Table, a fern and moss covered prominence near the village of Dromahair in County Leitrim, the ancient site of Breffny Castle.

The valley lay smiling before me,
Where lately I left her behind;
Yet I trembled and something hung o'er me
That saddened the joy of my mind.
I looked for the lamp which she told me
Should shine when her pilgrim returned;
But, though darkness began to enfold me,
No lamp from the battlements burned!

I flew to her chamber—twas lonely,
As if the loved one lay dead!
Ah, would it were death and death only;
But no—the young false one had fled.
And there hung the lute that could soften
My very worst pains into bliss,
While the hand that had waked it so often
Now throbbed to a proud rival's kiss.

There was a time, falsest of women!
When Breffni's good sword would have sought
That man, through a million of foemen,
Who dared but to wrong thee in thought!
While now—oh, degenerate daughter
Of Erin, now fallen is thy fame;
And through the ages of bondage and slaughter,
Our country shall bleed for thy shame.

Already the curse is upon her,
And strangers her valleys profane;
They came to divide—to dishonour,
And tyrants they long will remain.
But onward! The green banner rearing,
Go, flesh every sword to the hilt;
On our side is virtue and Erin,
On theirs is the Saxon and guilt.

Strongbow himself landed in Ireland during August 1170, over a year after the original Norman landing. Accompanied by a substantial body of troops, he overran Waterford and immediately claimed his prize, MacMurrough's daughter Eva. Under Norman law, Pembroke was now heir to the MacMurrough demesne of Leinster. Edmund Curtis correctly points out that Strongbow's claim "was sound enough in feudal law; but in Irish law it was unknown that a man should acquire a kingdom by right of a woman." Spurred to success by his lady or, more likely, his ambition, the new Prince of Leinster took Dublin in September.

After attacks by the native Irish were beaten back—most notably by a Norman surprise attack on Rory O'Connor at Castleknock, just northwest of modern Phoenix Park—there seemed little to thwart Strongbow's ambition to the High Kingship itself, particularly when Dermott MacMurrough died suddenly in the summer of 1171. That is, there was little until a suspicious Henry II landed in Ireland that autumn to check on *his* new possessions. The Plantagenet King allowed Strongbow to retain Leinster, but granted the lordship of Meath to Hugh de Lacy to counterbalance Pembroke's ambition. Further, with the unerring eye of the strategist, Henry made the towns of Wexford, Waterford, and Dublin part of his own immediate domain. The original spiritual commission to the Plantagenet to "enlarge the boundaries of the church" was beginning to look very much like temporal aggrandisement.

Rory O'Connor scrambled to maintain as much of his power as possible. In October 1175 the High King signed the Treaty of Windsor, giving Henry free reign over the lands that the Normans had in fact already conquered, while confirming O'Connor as *Ard Rí under the Crown* over the still-Gaelic marches.

Henry II shortly thereafter appointed John, Count of Mortain (later John of England), as Lord of Ireland. Prince John swiftly peopled Dublin with Saxons—primarily from Bristol—and made the area around the growing town as Norman-Saxon as possible. In this French-speaking Pale, the Irish language, dress, and customs were forbidden. It was the first attempt at "English" plantation in Ireland.

AVENGING AND BRIGHT

Many Irish septs saw no reason to abide by the terms of the Treaty of Windsor. Either Rory O'Connor was High King or he wasn't. If he was not—and under the treaty it looked as if he had signed away the claim—then he did not speak for them. Many of the sub-chiefs considered themselves released to make new alliances. The establishment of the Pale, of course, had done nothing to mollify their restlessness, no more had the actions of the Norman John de Courcy who, in direct contravention of the treaty, was carving himself out an independent domain in Ulster. There were few Irish who could speak Norman French or Saxon English, fewer still who had much use or understanding for the curious customs of the Stranger.

The clans surrounding the Pale treated the Saxon enclave as merely another source of profitable cattle raids. While these occasional Irish forays were not organised on other than a local scale, they became increasingly bothersome to the Crown. Giraldus Cambrensis, Gerald de Barry of Wales, who arrived in Ireland with Prince John in 1185, affords a contemporary Norman point of view of the authorities' problem, writing that the Irish raiders "used the woods as their strongholds and the marshes as their entrenchments." To the ritualised chivalry of the Normans, forced to erect castles and keeps as they spread out from the Pale, these were nettlesome and unfamiliar tactics.

As this ballad by Thomas Moore demonstrates, these guerrilla forays became an integral part of the tradition of Irish resistance. From a distance of centuries, the cattle raiders became heroic Gaelic warriors intent on avenging the Saxon rape of a glorious Celtic society.

Avenging and bright fall the swift swords of Erin
On him who have brave sons of Usna betrayed!
For every fond eye he hath wakened a tear in,
A drop from his heart-wounds shall weep o'er the blade.

By the red cloud that hung over Conor's dark dwelling,
When Ulad's three champions lay sleeping in gore—
By the billows of war which so often, high swelling,
Have wafted these heroes to victory's shore.

We swear to revenge them! No joy shall be tasted,

The harp shall be silent, the maiden unwed,
Our halls shall be mute, and our fields shall lie wasted,
Till vengeance is wreaked on the murderer's head.

Yes, monarch! Though sweet are our home recollections,
Though sweet are the tears that from tenderness fall,
Though sweet are our friendships, our hopes, our affections,
Revenge on a tyrant is sweetest of all!

Though in Ireland to stay by the end of the twelfth century, the Pale Normans were as much at a loss to understand the Irish culture as they were to comprehend that of Saladin's Saracens, who were battling the Crusaders of King Richard *Coeur de Lion* at the same time. Cambrensis, who tried, was reduced by the culture-shock to a sort of literary head-shaking:

> Although the Irish are fully endowed with natural gifts, their external characteristics of beard and dress, and internal cultivation of the mind, are so barbarous that they cannot be said to have any culture.

The reasons the Welshman advances for his conclusion are as revealing of Norman chivalry as they are of Irish "barbarism":

> They wear mantles instead of cloaks. . . . When riding they do not use saddles, leggings or spurs. . . . They regard weapons as a burden and they think it brave and honourable to fight unarmed. . . . They are a wild and inhospitable people . . . have not progressed at all from the primitive habits of pastoral living. . . . This people . . . has little use for the moneymaking of towns . . . and desires neither to abandon nor lose respect for the life which it has been accustomed to lead in the woods and countryside.

Cambrensis did find one saving grace among the Irish:

> It is only in the case of musical instruments that I find any commendable diligence in this people. They seem to me to be incomparably more skilled in these than any other people that I have ever seen.

When Gerald of Wales sums up by asserting that the Irish "are so removed in these distant parts from the ordinary world of men, as if they were in another world altogether," he is merely the first of many Britons who were to voice similar sentiments over subsequent centuries.

CHAPTER NOTES (2)

1 — In 982 Malachy had marched into Dál Cais itself and chopped down the sacred inaugural tree of the Dálcassian kings—presumably to demonstrate to Brian the latter's proper place in the scheme of things. In 988 Brian's unbridled ambition again caused Malachy to storm through Munster. In 994 the irrepressible Brian apparently decided to test Malachy's suzerainty yet again. It was still early times. The matter of who was High King was settled quite explicitly when Malachy Mór marched south into Tipperary from his Lough Ennell "Fort of the Shields," sacking Nenagh as a further lesson to the ambitious Brian.

2 — *Bóirmhe* (shortened to "Boru") was an appellation given to Brian after his 1002 tour of triumph around Ireland. In context, it means "of the [cattle] tributes."

3 — May 1169, a date deeply impressed upon the consciousness of every modern Irish schoolboy, was not seen by the contemporary Irish as particularly significant. Almost lost among the other entries that the Four Masters recorded from that year is the laconic entry: "The fleet of the Flemings came from England . . . they were seventy heroes, dressed in coats of mail."

Popular legends—and some historians who should know better—have suggested that the military superiority of the Normans was due simply to the appearance of the crossbow, the Irish supposedly having only battle-axe, sling, and pike. In reality the Celts had been using the bow before they arrived in Ireland some 2,000 years earlier (flint-tipped arrows and stone arm-bracers found by archeologists suggest that the Celts wielded the bow as early as 3,000 B.C.). Though not so large as the English longbow that was to afterwards dominate Crécy and Agincourt, the Irish bow, *properly used,* could be an effective weapon, even against the powerful crossbow. A similar Norman bow had, in fact, proved its worth against shielded Saxons a century earlier at Hastings. The real reason for the success of the Norman invasion was much more prosiac: the invaders were better led than the Irish.

3

Assimilation of the *Sassenach*

The first several centuries after the Norman landing in Ireland were to be characterised by the English Crown desperately trying, and failing, to prevent the Norman and Saxon settlers from merging into the Irish culture. One phrase became increasingly used by the English deputies in Dublin as they described the process to their superiors in London: the Britons were becoming *"Hiberniores hibernis ipsos"*—more Irish than the Irish.

The "Gaelicisation" of the Stranger had begun with the original invaders. Many of the Flemish mercenaries who had landed with Strongbow had remained in Ireland, learned Gaelic, taken Irish wives, and settled down on the land they had won as payment for their services. While the Saxon settlers in the towns managed to retain many of the customs of their former homeland, the continentals' easy acceptance of the lifestyle in the Irish countryside was to set an "ominous" precedent. Many of the transplanted Norman-Welsh nobles also found the Gaelic tribal life much to their liking. Taking to the role of Irish warlord with exuberant gusto, they quarrelled frequently and violently with each other and the native Irish chieftains. In Ireland to carve out personal domains in the first place, these new lords of the marches felt little empathy with the Pale English. The blandishments of life as an Irish tribal mandarin—not the least of which was the martial thrill of the traditional cattle-raid—seduced many a Norman lord. It was, in the words of Seán Ó Faoláin:

> an easy pastoral life . . . sealed in the minds of the people as the one true and lovely life, to be elaborated and adorned by every invention of the imagination, in law, poetry, saga, religion—for they peopled it with their gods and it was honoured by the druids, and the poets chanted it . . . it was an attractive existence [*that*] drowsed even the most disciplined invaders.

The Norman barons soon found that praise from the *filí* was heady wine indeed. Men who had landed in Ireland with imitative, chivalric dreams modelled on Roland and Lancelot soon found themselves emulating CúChulainn and Conn the Hundred-Fighter. On those occasions when the Crown itself took exception to the growing independence of these marcher lords, they showed as little reluctance in battling the forces of the increasingly remote English monarchy as they did in fighting their Gaelic neighbors . . . or each other. The gallowglass—now mostly from Scotland and the Hebrides—continued to find ready employment in Ireland.

THE TRUE IRISH KING

The incursions of the bellicose Norman barons were becoming a very real threat to the traditional domains of the Gaelic lords of the North and West. In 1258 the O'Connors of Connacht and the O'Briens of Thomond became sufficiently alarmed to recognise the claim of The O'Neill, Brian of TyrOwen, as *Ard Rí.* It was in reality little more than an alliance of convenience (the O'Donnells, unthreatened in their isolated TyrConnell, for instance, refused to participate[1]) but the acknowledgement precipitated a major TyrOwen raid against the Normans in Down. Brian's defeat and death at the Battle of Downpatrick in 1260 ended agitation for the return of the High Kingship to the O'Neills.

The most famous *file* of the era, Giolla Brighde MacNamee, memorialised the "rising" in a famous Gaelic lament for the fallen northern chieftain. The following Thomas Davis ballad commemorates the making of the High King two years earlier. The fourth verse, describing the coronation, is a reminder that from the time of Niall of the Nine Hostages in the fourth century to the Flight of the Earls in the seventeenth, there was no prouder title in Ireland than that of "The O'Neill."

The Caesar of Rome had a wider demesne
And the *Ard Rí* of France has more clans in his train,
The scepter of Spain is more heavy with gems,
And our crowns cannot vie with the Greek diadems;
But kinglier far before heaven and men
Are the emerald fields and the fiery-eyed clan,

CHRONOLOGY (Assimilation of the *Sassenach*)

1260 . . . . . .Battle of Downpatrick.

1261 . . . . . .Battle of Callann.

1270 . . . . . .Battle of Athankip.

1272 . . . . . .*Edward I.*

1292 . . . . . .Edward names Balliol King of Scots.

1297-98. . . . .Wallace Rebellion in Scotland.

1306-14. . . . .Robert the Bruce wages successful Scottish revolt, ousting English after Battle of Bannockburn.

1307 . . . . . .*Edward II.*

1315-18. . . . .Edward the Bruce invades Ireland, crowned king, crushed at Battle of Faughart.

1316 . . . . . .Battle of Athenry.

1318 . . . . . .Battle of Dysert O'Dea.

1327 . . . . . .*Edward III;* England invades France, Hundred Years War begins.

1348-49. . . . .Black Death reaches British Isles, reducing population of towns by one-half.

1356 . . . . . .Battle of Poitiers on continent.

1362 . . . . . .English language replaces French in courts of law.

1366 . . . . . .Statutes of Kilkenny.

1377 . . . . . .*Richard II.*

1381 . . . . . .Peasant revolt in England.

1390-94. . . . .Irish Gaelic/Middle Nation revolt; Richard II personally leads army to suppress rebels.

1396-99. . . . .MacMurrough revolt.

1399 . . . . . .*Henry IV* (Bolingbroke) seizes English Crown when Richard in Ireland running down MacMurrough.

1400 . . . . . .Glendower revolt in Wales.

1403 . . . . . .Hotspur rising in England put down at Battle of Shrewsbury.

1413 . . . . . .*Henry V.*

1415 . . . . . .Battle of Agincourt on continent.

1422 . . . . . .*Henry VI.*

1431 . . . . . .Joan of Arc turns English out of Orleans.

1449 . . . . . .Richard of York, Viceroy.

1453 . . . . . .Hundred Years War ends with French victory at Guienne; War of Roses begins with most Irish lords on side of York.

1460 . . . . . .Drogheda Parliament declares Irish independence; Richard of York killed at Battle of Wakefield.

The sceptor and state, and the poets who sing,
And the swords that encircle a True Irish King.

For he must have come from a conquering race—
The heir of their valour, their glory and grace;
His frame must be stately, his step must be fleet,
His hand must be trained to each warrior feat.
His face as the harvest moon, steadfast and clear,
A head to enlighten, a spirit to cheer,
While the foremost to rush where the battle-brands ring,
And the last to retreat, is a True Irish King.

Yet not from his courage, his strength or his name,
Can he from the clansmen their fealty claim;
The poorest and highest choose freely today
The chief that tonight they'll as truly obey.
For loyalty springs from a people's consent,
And the knee that is forced had been better unbent—
The *Sassenach* serfs no such homage can bring
As the Irishman's choice of a True Irish King.

Come look at the pomp when they make an O'Neill:
The muster of dynasts—O'Hagan, O'Shiel,
O'Cahan, O'Hanlon, O'Breslen, and all,
From mild Ardes and Orior to rude Donegal.
St. Patrick's *comharba,* with bishops thirteen,
And *ollum* and *brehons* and minstrels are seen
Round Tulacht-Óg Rath, like the bees in the spring,
All swarming to honour a True Irish King.

God aid him, God save him, and smile on his reign—
The terror of England, the ally of Spain—
May his sword be triumphant o'er *Sassenach* arts,
Be his throne ever girt by strong hands and true hearts.
May the course of his conquest run on till he see
The flag of Plantagenant sink in the sea!
May minstrels forever his victories sing,
And saints make the bed of the True Irish King.

THE BATTLE OF CALLANN

As TyrOwen rose against the Normans in the North, the MacCarthys of the Southwest were also ready to explode. A Crown grant of Décies and Desmond to John FitzThomas Fitzgerald[2] provided the spark. Fineen MacDonnell MacCarthy led his Kerry henchmen, the O'Driscolls and O'Sullivans, on a rampage through Munster. Despite reinforcement sent by the Dublin Viceroy, Robert d'Ufford, Fitzgerald was thoroughly routed by the Gaelic clans at the Battle of Callann, near Kenmare, in 1261. The MacCarthys maintained effective power throughout western Munster.

FitzThomas went forth to the slaughter all burning,
And the dame by Tralee waits the robber's returning;
With the deep-lowing creach, with the rich plunder laden,
The altar's best gold, the pearls of the maiden.

Winding down by the Ruachta his lances were gleaming,
Floating wild as a meteor, his banners were streaming,
He rode with the spells of all Desmond around him,
But the wrath of the Gael in its red vengeance, found him.

More swift than the eagle from Skellig's high eyrie,
Than whirlwinds of Corrin in hostings of faerie,
Dark as a storm o'er Dun Mór to the ocean-tired toiler,
Burst MacCarthy's fierce wrath on the part of the spoiler.

O'Sullivan Mór of the mountain and valley,
O'Connor, the chief of the tall-masted galley,
O'Driscoll, the scorge of the *Sassenach* sailor,
Left Cogan's proud daughter a desolate wailer.

For him who hath none from the gaunt wolf to save him,
To staunch the wide wound that the fierce clansmen gave him;
To weep the lost chief, with his battle-shield riven,
Cloven down by the war-axe, unhouselled, unshriven!

With the bold of the reivers that rode to the foray,
From Maing to Moyala, the girtles are gory,
The saffron-dyed shirts by the Cashin and Carrow,
Claim thy care at the fountain, fair maiden, tomorrow!

Chant the deeds of the warriors in chivalry vying,
The doom of the reivers, all prostrate or flying,
The false Saxon's fear: as rejoicing thou lavest
The blood-gouts that burst from the breasts of the bravest.

The need for constant vigilance against the Norman marcher lords was slowly making the Gaelic chieftains realise that the Stranger brought no quarter, individual resistance no reward, and the future no foreseeable relief.   The encroaching Normans finally forced the Gaels into alliances, some rather unusual. After Brian O'Neill's 1260 failure at Downpatrick, a number of frustrated northern chiefs, finally recognising the need for unity, petitioned King Haakon IV of Norway to accept the High Kingship of Ireland. Though Haakon's premature death scuttled the plan, the attempt itself was significant. The Irish had not yet forgotten the days when they elected their own kings.

As the MacCarthys had shown in the Southwest, even local alliances of Gaelic clans could withstand some overly ambitious Norman land-grabs.   Hugh MacFelim O'Connor of Connacht, instrumental in the conspiracies which had promoted Brian O'Neill and Haakon IV for the High Kingship, soon was forced to put together forces to defend his own lands in the West. Ralph d'Ufford and Walter de Burgo had taken Sligo and, by 1270 were cutting a swath through O'Connor lands in Roscommon with a large army.   By this time, however, O'Connor had found the answer: Scot mercenaries. At the ford of Athankip on the Shannon, Hugh O'Connor and his gallowglass butchered d'Ufford's army.   In the words of the annalists, "No greater defeat had been given to the English in Ireland up to that time." With the help of Donal of TyrConnell, The O'Donnell, O'Connor swept on to the east and had regained much of Meath within two years time.   Encouraged by the demonstration of Norman vulnerability, the O'Byrnes and O'Tooles of Wicklow also rebelled. By 1281 there was "great and general warfare between the foreigners and the Gael."

When Edward I sent John de Wogan to Dublin shortly thereafter to press the quarrelsome lords of Ireland for money to finance the Crown's war with France, it was a measure of how little London knew of the reality in Ireland. Wogan, though energetic in his attempt to fill the Crown's empty coffers, was unable to fulfill his royal commission. He found the island far from a British vassal-state; rather, Ireland had begun to assume the politically schizoid personality that was to characterise it through most of the Middle Ages.

Within the Pale, English law was administered in the manner of an English shire. Far from the towns were the wild western and northern lands, still governed by Gaelic chieftains under Brehon Law. In between was the Middle Nation—lands "administered" by the swashbuckling Norman-Irish descendants of the original Welsh freebooters, men becoming influenced more by their Gaelic peers and less by their nominal English overlords. The Norman-Irish lords of the Middle Nation were already becoming known as the "Old English" to differentiate them from the "New English," the settlers in the towns.

By this time, the bureaucrats in Dublin had divided Ireland into shires and liberties, the shires further broken up into baronies. Though these divisions had little immediate basis in political reality—only the Pale towns could be governed in the English manner—the imaginary boundaries of the smaller units would become important to the common Irishman in a mildly chauvinistic way. In Wexford, for example, where ten baronies were created, the difference in lifestyle was substantial between the Forthman of the benevolent coastal Southeast and the Bantryman who lived in the shadow of rugged Mount Leinster.

As Wogan tried unsuccessfully to get money out of the Irish, the Hibernians were watching with keen interest as the cramped passions of their kindred Scots burst into nationalism. The incident which triggered events north of the Tweed was the demise of King Alexander III in 1286. The accidental death of his only heir, the wee Margaret, Maid of Norway, precipitated a mad scramble for the Scottish Crown. By 1290 Edward I of England had successfully asserted his own right to name the new northern monarch. When he chose John Balliol of Galloway over Robert Bruce of Annandale in 1292, Edward managed to alienate half the proud Scottish lairds in one stroke. By becoming Edward's puppet, Balliol himself soon managed to irritate the rest, even his original supporters. Confronted with this unpopular authoritarian coalition, Scottish nationalism erupted with a vengeance. Led by William Wallace, an army of peasants and plebs stunned an English army at Stirling Bridge. Edward Plantagenet was astonished. He had moved to neutralise the major lairds but it had never occurred to the English king to worry about the common people. The Scot *schiltrons*,[3] squares of peasant pikemen, proved more than a match for English chivalry. Only when the famed Welsh longbowmen were hurried to the North was this remarkable "democratic" revolt put down at Falkirk in 1298.

As in Ireland, Edward I was to find that putting down Scottish rebellion and ruling the Scots were two very different things. As soon as one brush fire was extinguished, another seemed to break out. The big lairds themselves soon enthusiastically joined the *schiltrons'* Highland Game of defying the English king. By 1304 the Scottish nobles were looking to elect their own sovereign. Two years later they found him: Robert, Earl of Carrick. The grandson of the rejected claimant of 1290, he is better known to history as Robert the Bruce.

Fortuitously for the new King Robert I, Edward of England died in 1307. The political storm surrounding the succession of Edward II gave the Scot sovereign the respite he needed to consolidate his rule. Aided by the redoubtable Sir James Douglas, Robert reduced the English outposts in Scotland one-by-one, and by 1313 was making incursions into England itself. This was too much even for the pusillanimous Edward II. The full flower of feudal England ambled north to put down the upstart Scotsman. The Norman knights returned rather more hurriedly: on 24 June 1314 at Bannockburn, the English failed to use their Welsh archers once again. The Scots sent the southerners packing.

Across the Irish Sea, many of the Norman-Irish lords of Ulster—by now thoroughly assimilated into the Gaelic culture—cheered unabashedly at the Scot victory. Robert the Bruce was descended from the ancient Irish kings of Scotland and many of the Irish lords felt closer akin to the victors of Bannockburn than to the English of the Pale. In addition, most of the Gaelic clans of the North had long maintained ties with the Scots across the North Channel and, in truth, some had even fought in the Scottish campaigns against the English King. Consequently, when several of the Norman-Irish lords invited the Bruce to help them clear out the bothersome English from what they now considered *their* Celtic isle, Robert I, citing a "perpetual confederation of special friendship between us and you," was only too happy to oblige.

In May 1315 Robert's brother Edward landed at Larne with 6,000 men. The O'Neills, O'Hagans, O'Hanlons, O'Cahans, and other northern clans rose with several of the Norman-Irish lords

in support of the Scots. Having demonstrated in the Bannockburn operation that they were not averse to laying waste to their
own land, the invaders showed no hesitation at all in putting
Ireland to the sword when it suited their purpose. After thrashing the "plantation army" of Richard de Burgo, the Red Earl of
Ulster (and Edward II's champion in the North), at the Battle
of Connor in September, Edward de Bruce marched south.
The rampaging Scots-Irish army routed Sir Roger de Mortimer,
Lord of Meath, at Kells in December, and then defeated the
combined forces of the Butlers and Fitzgeralds at the motte of
Ardscull, near Athy, in January 1316. On *Bealtaine,* Edward
the Bruce had himself crowned King of Ireland.

Later that year, the King of Scots arrived in Ulster to see
personally how his brother was getting along. The two Bruces
marched south in February 1317, burning a swath of terror and
destruction through the heart of Ireland; their path reached as
far south as Callan in Kilkenny before swinging west to the
Shannon at Castleconnell, near Limerick. Two months after the
campaign had begun, the brothers Bruce were back in the North.
They had easily squashed what little opposition they had met
and laid waste through much of the island. The problem was
that they had neither gained popular support outside Ulster
nor found anyone really important who would come out and
fight.

Edward II was belatedly beginning to show some alarm.
Roger de Mortimer, now Lord Lieutenant, landed at Youghal
with Crown reinforcements just as the brothers Bruce were returning to the North. Quickly isolating the Scots in the wild
northern province, Mortimer settled down in the Pale to wait
them out. After Robert I returned to Scotland to mend some
fences on the English frontier, Edward de Bruce dawdled in
Ulster, frustrated by the lack of general Irish support for his
"crown" and not quite sure what to do next.

Faced with a foe who would not attack and with no real
prospect of a sympathetic general rising, de Bruce finally moved
south through the Moyry Pass in October 1318 resolved to find
and join battle with the Crown forces of John de Bermingham.
He did not live to regret the blunder. After the resulting Battle
of Faughart just outside Dundalk on 14 October, Bermingham
brought the head of Edward Bruce back to Mortimer in Dublin.
The Scottish adventure in Ireland was over.

The immediate result of the Bruce invasion was disaster

for everybody concerned. The *Annals of Clonmacnoise* judged Edward the "destroyer of all Ireland, in generall, both Saxon and Gael," suggesting that:

> there was not a better deed . . . done in Ireland than the killing of Edward Bruise, for there reigned scarcity of victuals . . . and the loss of men and women thro' out the whole Kingdom for the space of three years and a half that he bore sway, insomuch that men did commonly eat one another for want of sustenance during his time.

If the Scottish forays had not been popular with the Irish, they had been even more traumatic to the town English—by now they were convinced that all those living "Beyond the Pale" could not be trusted, that even the Old English were Irish at heart. Trevelyan seems to consider the Bruce incursion the genesis of the Pale English conception of the Irish as Enemy:

> The distinction set the tone for a policy that for centuries was fruitful of mischief. The colonists drew ever more rigidly the line between the two races, and proscribed native law, language, and custom, so far as their little power extended.

What the contemporary chroniclers could not foresee, as perhaps Trevelyan later did, was the legacy that the Bruces left to the folk-memory of the Gael: a royal champion had come from over the sea to deliver Ireland from the hated Saxon. To the British, the Scottish invasion became merely an historical anecdote, best forgotten; to the Irish, the reality would become poetic legend, never forgotten.

The major reason that Edward Bruce did not get general support from the Irish septs was that several in the West and Midlands had taken the opportunity presented by the Scottish adventure to rise against the Norman marcher lords in their own right.[4] One such rising in Connacht, led by Hugh O'Connell and Felim O'Connor, with the O'Briens and western O'Tooles as allies, had been crushed by the de Burgos at Athenry in August 1316, establishing the dominance of that Norman family in mid-Connacht. The O'Mores, O'Byrnes, and O'Tooles of mid-Leinster had meanwhile begun guerrilla agitation in support of Donal Kavanagh's claim to lordship of the province.

In Thomond during May 1318, the O'Briens had re-established their hold on the ancient kingdom by killing Richard de Clare at the Battle of Dysert O'Dea. By 1326 there was even a plot hatched to make Maurice FitzThomas Fitzgerald (soon-to-be first Earl of Desmond) King of Ireland. The annalists report that all the Gaels and Norman-Irish of Leinster and Munster were up in arms by 1336. The Gaelicisation of the Old English marcher lords was becoming complete. By 1340 even the proud de Burgos, who had put down the Connacht Irish only two decades earlier, had changed their family name to MacWilliam Burke.

The assimilation obviously was not going altogether unnoticed by the Pale English. Their complaints to London, however, were falling on uninterested ears. Edward III was embroiled in what would come to be called the Hundred Years War and had little time and less money for Ireland. The neglect by the English King was not the only factor favouring the lords beyond the Pale. When the Black Death visited the island in 1348-49, it hit the English towns far more severely than it did the Irish countryside.[5]

THE DEAD AT CLONMACNOIS

As the Old English adopted the Gaelic language and culture, they unavoidably listened to the native poetry and, in many cases, adopted the old Irish custom of taking a court *file*. In the case of one marcher lord, Gerald FitzMaurice Fitzgerald, who became third Earl of Desmond in 1359, no court poet was needed: Gerald the Rimer was accounted one of the finest Gaelic poets of the fourteenth century. It might fairly be said that the Gaelicisation process had ended. When the leading figure of the Norman nobility was acclaimed for his poetic skill in the ancient language it seems clear that the Old English were English in name only. The metamorphosis was complete.

Ballads such as this fourteenth century *caoine* for times past by Angus O'Gillan gave the lords of the Middle Nation an appreciation for Ireland's ancient glories. Though it was fast becoming the time of Men in medieval England, the formerly Norman marcher lords were happy to join the Irish preoccupation with long-dead Heroes. The translation is late-nineteenth-century by Thomas William Rolleston.

In a quiet watered land, a land of roses,
Stands Saint Kieran's city fair,
And the warriors of Erin in their famous generations
Slumber there.

There beneath the dewy hillside sleep the noblest
Of the clan of Conn,
Each below his stone with name in branching *Ogham*
And the sacred knot thereon.

There they laid to rest the seven Kings of Tara,
There the sons of Cairbe sleep—
Battle-banners of the Gael, that in Kieran's plain of crosses
Now their final hosting keep.

And in Clonmacnois they laid the men of Teffia,
And right many a lord of Breagh;
Deep the sod above ClannCreide and ClannConaill,
Kind in hall and fierce in fray.

Many and many a son of Conn, the Hundred-Fighter,
In the red earth lies at rest;
Many a blue eye of ClannColman the turf covers,
Many a swan-white breast.

In 1360 the Irish Viceroy complained to London that "many men of the English nation both in the marches of our land in Ireland and elsewhere there have recently assumed the condition of Irishmen." It was one thing for the isolated Old English of the countryside to adopt Irish ways, it was quite another that the folkways of the Gael were making inroads even into the Pale. Edward III took advantage of a tenuous peace with the French to send his son Lionel, Duke of Clarence and titular Earl of Ulster, to Ireland to repair the sagging fortunes of the Crown. Meeting some initial success in the area surrounding the Pale—even capturing the great rebel chief Art MacMurrough in 1362—Lionel soon despaired of bringing the distant degenerate Old English and defiant Gaelic chieftains to heel. The vast, wild land outside the Pale was patently beyond the practical ability of the English to govern.

Frustrated, Clarence called a 1366 parliament in Kilkenny to draft laws to rule where the Crown writ *did* run. The famous Statutes of Kilkenny drawn by this assembly were justified thusly:

> Many English . . . forsaking the English language, fashion, mode of riding, laws and usages, live and govern themselves accord-

Ireland at the Time of
the Statutes of Kilkenny, 1366

ing to the manners, fashions, and language of the Irish enemies, and have also made divers marriages and alliances between themselves and the Irish enemies aforesaid, whereby the said land and the liege people thereof, the English language, the allegiance due our Lord the king, and the English laws there, are put in subjection and decayed.

To halt the decay so ably described in the preamble, the Statues decreed that:

(1) Intermarriage was High Treason.

(2) Subscribing to or tolerating Brehon Law was High Treason.

(3) Englishmen adopting Irish names, titles, customs, speech, or dress incurred forfeiture of all their lands.

(4) Encouraging or harbouring Irish minstrels, rhymers, or storytellers was illegal.

(5) Traditional Gaelic *coyne* and *livery* were proscribed.

(6) Admitting Irish priests to monasteries or to benefices was prohibited.

There were many more.

In theory, the Statues of Kilkenny made the Irish second-class citizens in their own land. In practice the laws were ignored by the Irish, Old English, and Pale English alike. The prohibition against the "seditious" poets, for instance, not only left the *filí* unaffected, but actually supplied more grist for the rhymer's mill (it stretches credulity to imagine the great Earl of Desmond skulking about his castle surreptiously scratching his Gaelic verse). In any event, within the year the loyal English of the Pale were complaining again that rebels "rode in hostile array through every part of Ireland."

The real effect of the 1366 code was to acknowledge tacitly what the Duke of Clarence had already decided was clearly apparent: in two-thirds of Ireland, the King's writ did not rule at all. In truth, the Kilkenny Parliament had been called in the desperate attempt to save the ever-shrinking Pale from going the way of the rest of the island. It is a measure of the esteem in which the Statutes were held that many of the marcher lords were not even aware that the Crown had withdrawn their English titles. The Gaelic ways of the hinterland went on as before.

In 1375 the beleaguered citizens of Waterford complained of the "divers slaughters" of 130 of the king's men within a six-week period. In 1382 an Irish bishop reported that "the whole land of Munster, together with a great part of Leinster, is desolated and endangered" by "Irish enemies and our English rebels."

Two years later, Richard II tried to extricate the royal treasury from the whole Irish morass by granting sovereign rights in Ireland to Robert de Vere for life in return for a five-thousand-mark annual rent.   De Vere, also granted the grandiloquent title Marquis of Dublin, never set foot in Ireland . . . nor did the treasury gain a farthing from the deal.

In 1390 Art Oge MacMurrough, Gaelic lord of south Leinster, married an English heiress. When he discovered that his wife's lands would not accompany his *Sassenach* bride (because of the 1366 Statutes), he expressed his displeasure in a typically Gaelic manner: he went on a rampage. The marauding MacMurrough finally convinced London that the very existence of the Pale itself was in doubt. In 1394 the King of England landed in Ireland with more than ten thousand men.

The Middle Nation was brought quickly to heel in the face of this army, huge for its time. Richard forced the "Irish enemies and English rebels" alike to pay homage to his Crown. Even MacMurrough, whose guerrilla tactics had played havoc with the King's army, was induced to submit in exchange for an English knighthood and his wife's lands.   The wild Wicklow lord apparently tired of his new title and, soon after Richard's departure, once again drew his sword against the Crown. In a July 1398 skirmish at Kellistown, "Sir Art Oge" killed the King's favourite, Roger de Mortimer, Earl of March—heir to the throne of England—who Richard had left behind as Lord Lieutenant. The monarch was outraged. His loss of temper was to cost him his kingdom. When Richard II crossed the Irish Sea in May 1399 to chase the elusive MacMurrough about Ireland,[6] the Lancastrians seized the main chance in England. By the time Richard returned to Britain in August, he had neither the head of the Irish war-lord nor the Crown to place upon his own. Richard was swiftly imprisoned and Henry Bolingbroke enthroned in his place.

The Welsh rebellion of Owen Glendower in late 1400 convinced the new British king that he had more pressing concerns than Ireland. The morass of Irish politics was in fact to tempt neither Henry IV nor his immediate successors. The need to procure Welsh bowmen—the Lancastrian sovereigns kept their eyes fixedly on domestic security and continental adventure—made insubordinate Wales of more importance than ungovernable Ireland. In the meantime, of course, the customs of the Gael once again crept inexorably into the Pale. By 1435 the isolated

English in Ireland were wondering of Henry VI:

> How that his land of Ireland is well nigh destroyed and in-
> habited with his enemies and rebels, insomuch that there is not
> left in the nether parts of the counties of Dublin, Meath, Louth,
> and Kildare that join together, out of the subjection of the said
> enemies and rebels a scarce thirty miles in length and twenty in
> breadth, whereas a man may surely ride or go to the said counties
> to answer the king's writ and do his commandments.

Even this bare presence of England in Ireland, however, sufficed to prevent the Irish lords from joining together in other
than the traditional Gaelic tribal alliance. There was no push toward any sort of national unity; rather, the clan chiefs "rode in
the manner of war with banners displayed" intent on establishing
and maintaining their individual prerogatives, the English always
a bothersome factor in their calculations. The first half of the fifteenth century was dominated in the East and South by the Butlers of Ormonde and by the Fitzgeralds of Kildare and Desmond.
The Southeast was virtually an independent MacMurrough kingdom. The Southwest was the demesne of the MacCarthy More of
Kerry. The O'Neills, O'Donnells, O'Connors, MacWilliam Burkes,
and O'Briens controlled the North and West. A Gaelic poet of
the time described these great war-lords: "the principle of them
all is respect for the strong man . . . a man's inheritance will get
no recognition except he has strength to fight."

When Richard Plantagenet, Duke of York, arrived as
Viceroy in 1449, he found that his ready acceptance of the
status quo won him cheerful support from the unthreatened
marcher lords. Though he stayed in Dublin but a year, it was
time well spent. When the War of the Roses began in 1453,
Ireland—with the Butlers almost the sole exception—declared
for the Yorkists. In fact, just ten months before Richard was
slain at Wakefield in 1460, the great Irish lords had established a
parliament at Drogheda in which they freely elected the champion of the White Rose as "Lord of Ireland."

This parliament, the first ever called by the Irish themselves,
was to last for over three centuries. Besides declaring for
Richard, the participants—including Old English, New English,
and a surprising number of Gaelic Irish lords—proclaimed the independence of Ireland, albeit almost as an afterthought.[7] Sixty-
six years after an English king had first described the Irish as
"rebels," a rude Home Rule Movement had been born. Irish nationalism would never again disappear from the scene.

WHEN SHALL THE DAY BREAK IN ERIN

The Irish rebel tradition suggests that the Gaels have fought the English for over eight centuries. The corollary is that the fight has been for the cultural identity of the native Irish. While true to some extent, it is equally valid to point out that the cultural norm that many of the early Irish war-lords were trying to recapture was the freedom to battle each other without Crown interference.

The 1460 Drogheda Parliament provides a convenient touchstone from which to measure the growth of modern rebel Ireland. Curiously, although the independent Irish lords were threatening the very existence of English hegemony in Ireland, it took the personal popularity of the Duke of York to get the squabbling chieftains to work together for the first time. Even if it is probably not useful to suggest a specific date as the "beginning" of the rebel tradition—the growth of national consciousness was not an event but an evolving process that was to take its present form only after incorporating the alien egalitarian concepts of the French Revolution—one could still do worse than point to Drogheda, the nadir of English influence, as the time that the Irish began to realise that self-determination was at least possible.

This D. J. Downing song could almost have been written at any time from the late fifteenth century up to the modern era. It contains the two themes that were to become nearly universal in Irish rebel song: "Saxon Perfidy," and the intrinsic belief that the Future will someday regain the glory of the Past.

When shall day break in Erin?
When shall her day-star arise
Out of the East resplendent
To gladden watchful eyes?
When shall her wrongs become righted,
And her sad past forgotten be?
The day may be distant—what matter?
That will be her destiny!

Refrain:
Ireland is Ireland through joy and through tears,
Hope never fades through the long dreary years;
Each age hath seen countless brave hearts pass away
But their spirit lives on in the men of today.

Live yet the life of the brave, then:
Brothers go hand-in-hand,
Pause not in doubt or sorrow,
On for the dear old land.
What though the mighty be fallen,
Hope still triumphs o'er the grave,
Your hands may be winning the laurels,
Crowning the glories you crave.

Refrain

Ireland shall surely awaken
Out of her spell of despair,
Glowing her cheeks—Death's empire
Never was planted there!
Youth in her bright eyes is gleaming,
Liberty's ring in her voice,
That calls to her sons o'er the wide world
In nationhood's name to rejoice.

Refrain

As the marcher lords of Ireland chose sides in the English War of the Roses, they were unwittingly entering another, larger arena. No longer would the Gaelic and Old English mandarins be able to peer at the world from borders determined solely by the sword. Now, almost without realising it, they were entering the tortured universe of British power politics.

CHAPTER NOTES (3)

1 — The Donegal clan had little reason to join the general clamour against the Normans. Godfrey O'Donnell had some years earlier wrested control of the area from the O'Cannons and his brother Donal Oge had then guaranteed O'Donnell suzerainty at the Battle of Credran, halting the Geraldine expansion into the North.

2 — John FitzThomas Fitzgerald and his son Maurice FitzJohn were both slain at Callann. Maurice's grandson Maurice FitzThomas Fitzgerald was later to become the first Earl of Desmond. The Geraldines took their family name from John FitzThomas' uncle Gerald, first Baron of Offaly, who was also the ancestor to the earls of Kildare.

It was, by the way, from this bloody encounter at Callann which sprung the centuries-long feud between the Fitzgeralds of Desmond and the MacCarthys of Kerry.

3 — The *schiltron* was a hollow, circular "square" designed to make the most efficient use of the long Scottish pike. Even at close quarters, the peasants would merely retreat some few steps to be fighting back-to-back. The ritualised violence of Norman chivalry found this forerunner of the British square impenetrable without the longbowmen of Wales.

As with many such words, the description of the way these men fought soon became used to describe the peasant warriors themselves.

4 — Another reason was presumably Pope John XXII's blanket excommunication of anyone who supported the Scottish "King of Ireland."

5 — The return of the Plague in 1361, 1370, 1384, and 1398 was to further weaken the influence of the Crown in Ireland.

6 — An English observor who saw Art Oge MacMurrough gives us a hint of why he was so hard to catch. In so doing, the Briton also affords us a striking portrait of a late fourteenth century Gaelic lord:

> "I saw MacMurrough and a body of Irish more than I can remember descend
> the mountain. He rode a horse without saddle . . . it had cost him, they said,
> 400 cows. In coming down it galloped so hard that I for certain never saw hare,
> deer or sheep run with such speed. In his right hand he carried a great long
> lance, which he cast with much skill. He was a fine, large man, wonderfully
> active. To look at he seemed very stern and savage and an able man."

7 — The applicable statute read, in part:

> "That whereas the land of Ireland is, and at all times has been, corporate of
> itself by the ancient laws and customs used in the same, freed of the burden of
> any special law of the realm of England save only such laws as . . . had been in
> great council or parliament there held, admitted, accepted, affirmed and pro-
> claimed, according to sundry ancient statutes thereof made."

4

The Twilight of the Gael

Until the middle of the fifteenth century, the swaggering lords of Ireland had been more jealous of their domestic feuds than any political concerns of the remote English monarchy. It was in the time of the War of the Roses that the Irish chieftains began to involve themselves in the larger political rivalries surrounding the Crown. If the original reason was a personal "Gaelic-like loyalty" to Richard of York, the considerable Irish support of the White Rose was ultimately to cause a reciprocal British involvement in Irish affairs . . . particularly after the Red Rose of Lancaster adorned the Crown of England.

During the War of the Roses, the Yorkist faction in Ireland was led by the man the annalists termed "the most illustrious of his tribe in Ireland in his time," Thomas FitzJames Fitzgerald, the "Great Earl" of Desmond. After the Lancastrian defeat at Towton in 1461, Sir John Butler was almost the sole supporter of the Red Rose left among the major Hibernian lords. Nonetheless, Sir John—whose brother James Butler, Earl of Ormonde and Wiltshire, had been executed by the Yorkists—managed to rally a coalition army of British Lancastrians and his own Ormonde liegemen from Kilkenny and Tipperary to challenge Desmond. When the Great Earl and his Yorkist followers defeated Sir John of Ormonde at the Battle of Pilltown in 1462, the chroniclers reported "410 of the slain of his people interred, besides the number who were devoured by the dogs and birds of prey." A grateful Edward IV made the victorious Thomas Fitzgerald his Lord Lieutenant for Ireland the following year.

The Pale English were outraged. Desmond was the first marcher lord ever to be made viceroy; the Crown's apparent acceptance of the Great Earl's Gaelic ways must have seemed a direct threat to their ascendancy. Actually, the Desmond Geraldines were among the few Old English families that had remained relatively "pure-blood" Norman. Fitzgerald's real crime to the Dubliners was simply his popularity with the native Irish. Whatever the motive, however, the hue and cry raised by the New English of the Pale finally caused Edward IV to replace Desmond with John Tiptoft, Earl of Worcester, ostensibly to halt the imagined Fitzgerald-led drift toward Home Rule. The new Lord Lieutenant, commonly called "Tiptoft the Butcher" for his treatment of Lancastrians in Britain after Towton, proved an unfortunate choice. Worcester swiftly imprisoned and beheaded the seventh Earl of Desmond in 1468 for "trasons alliances and fosterages with Irish enemies." The annalists saw the execution of the Great Earl somewhat differently: ". . . he was killed in treachery by a Saxon Earl. . . ."

The Gaelic and Middle Nation leaders were shocked. Desmond had led them against the Yorkist King's enemies and his reward had been the block. After three centuries of English presence in Ireland, the marcher lords were beginning to suspect that it mattered little who was on the British throne, that it might be the Crown itself that was inimical to their interests. In the event Fitzgerald's execution would prove ultimately counterproductive. James FitzThomas, the eighth Earl of Desmond, married Margaret O'Brien, daughter to the Gaelic prince of Thomond—the first of many alliances that would hereafter bind the Desmond Geraldines and the native Irish. Young Desmond and his Munster liegelords refused to return to Parliament. Polarisation had begun in earnest.

Sixteen days after the October 1470 restoration of Henry VI, Tiptoft met the Lancaster axe on Tower Hill. The new Desmond-less Irish Parliament had not waited for Worcester's expected execution before electing Thomas, the seventh Earl of Kildare, as Tiptoft's successor. While the English were preoccupied with the events leading to the Lancastrian defeat at the Battle of Tewkesbury the next year, the head of the Kildare branch of the Fitzgeralds took the opportunity to establish himself firmly as the only great Anglo-Irish Yorkist lord left in Ireland. His family was to effectively rule the island for the next sixty years.

As the British continued their Lancastrain/Yorkist intrigues, Thomas Fitzgerald's son Garret FitzThomas succeeded to the Kildare earldom upon the father's death in 1477. Later to become known as Garret Mór, the new Kildare Geraldine promptly began solidifying his relationship with the leading families of Ireland. His sister and one of his daughters married O'Neills of

CHRONOLOGY (The Twilight of the Gael)

1461 . . . . . .*Edward IV.*
1462 . . . . . .Battle of Pilltown.
1463 . . . . . .7th Desmond, Viceroy.
1468 . . . . . .Tiptoft, new Viceroy, executes Desmond.
1470 . . . . . .7th Kildare, Viceroy; *Henry VI.*
1471 . . . . . .*Edward IV* restored by Battle of Tewkesbury.
1477 . . . . . .8th Kildare, Viceroy.
1483 . . . . . .*Edward V; Richard III.*
1485 . . . . . .Battle of Bosworth Field; *Henry VII;* Tudor era begins.
1487 . . . . . .Simnel's pretensions thwarted at Battle of Stoke.
1491 . . . . . .Pretender Warbeck arrives in Ireland.
1492 . . . . . .Columbus reaches America.
1495 . . . . . .Poynings Law.
1496 . . . . . .Kildare re-appointed Viceroy.
1498 . . . . . .Da Gama reaches India.
1504 . . . . . .Battle of Knockdoe.
1509 . . . . . .*Henry VIII.*
1512 . . . . . .Scots beaten at Battle of Flodden.
1513 . . . . . .9th Kildare, Viceroy; Machiavelli's *Prince* appears.
1517 . . . . . .Luther launches Reformation with 95 theses.
1519 . . . . . .Magellan sails; Cortes in Mexico.
1522 . . . . . .Zwingli begins Swiss Reformation.
1527 . . . . . .Charles V of France captures Pope Clement VII.
1532 . . . . . .Pizarro in Peru.
1534 . . . . . .Papal authority abolished in England; Silken Thomas revolt in Ireland.
1535 . . . . . .Fall of Maynooth.
1537 . . . . . .Silken Thomas and Kildare uncles executed.
1540 . . . . . .Jesuits founded.
1541-47. . . . .Henry VIII named King of Ireland, puts down O'More/O'Connor rising, institutes "divide-and-conquer" policy.
1542 . . . . . .Henry wars with Scots; Inquisition launched in Italy.
1543 . . . . . .Copernican Theory.
1547 . . . . . .*Edward VI;* Scots lose Battle of Pinkie.
1553 . . . . . .*Mary I.*
1554 . . . . . .Mary Tudor marries Philip of Spain.
1555 . . . . . .Mary repeals religious laws of Henry.
1556 . . . . . .Kings and Queens Counties created for plantation; Philip becomes King of Spain.
1558 . . . . . .*Elizabeth I.*

1559 . . . . . .Re-establishment of Church of England.
1560 . . . . . .John Knox in Scotland.
1561 . . . . . .Mary Stewart lands in Scotland, begins struggle with barons and
             Kirk.
1562 . . . . . .Shane O'Neill in London; French religious wars begin.
1565 . . . . . .14th Desmond imprisoned after skirmish at Affane; Battle of Glen-
             flesk.
1567 . . . . . .Battle of Farsetmore; Shane O'Neill slain; Scots revolt against Mary
             Stewart.

TyrOwen; another daughter married Pierce Butler of Ormonde; a third daughter married a MacWilliam Burke; a son took an O'Connor Offaly bride. Garret Mór Fitzgerald arrogantly made every match without the "required" prior approval of the King of England. Edward IV, perhaps recalling the furor caused by the Execution of Desmond, despaired of his new "Irish Problem" and formally, if reluctantly, recognised Garret Mór as viceroy in 1482.

Two years after the 1485 death of Richard III on Bosworth Field, ten-year-old Lambert Simnel arrived in Ireland in the care of Richard Simmons, an ambitious English priest who claimed the child was in reality the grandson of the popular Richard of York. The timing was propitious; a band of great Anglo-Irish lords were feeling sufficiently independent of the Lancastrian Henry VII to crown the boy Edward VI of England and Ireland. After the Dublin "coronation," a number of the Irish Yorkists joined the Earl of Lincoln when the latter landed in Britain with an army of German mercenaries to push the claim of the child. The pretender's sponsors were crushed by Henry VII at Stoke.

Though Kildare was almost certainly culpable in the Simnel Affair (Fitzgerald's brother Thomas Oge had ridden with Lincoln), Garret Mór's position was still too secure for the Crown to challenge directly. That was to change in 1491 when another pretender appeared at Cork. Claiming that he was Richard, the seventeen-year-old younger son of Edward IV who had disappeared from the Tower of London in 1483, Perkin Warbeck's outrageous claim was straight-facedly championed by most of the monarchs of Europe. Although Garret Mór was careful to hold himself aloof from this second pretender, Fitzgerald fence-straddling was no longer sufficient for the exasperated Henry VII. The continental support for Warbeck had decided the King of England: so long as the Geraldines and their ilk ran Ireland, the island would remain a strategic threat to Britain itself. Something had to be done to curb Kildare's power.

The something turned out to be an army of picked men under Sir Edward Poynings; it arrived in October 1494 charged with bringing the Irish to "whole and perfect obedience." Kildare, feeling himself guiltless in the Warbeck business, looked on self-righteously as the new Lord Lieutenant summoned a parliament at Drogheda. The first transaction of Poynings' carefully packed December assembly, however, was a bill calling for the arrest of Garret Mór. With the Geraldine safely ensconced in the Tower, the body proceeded to pass the legislation that is known to history as Poynings' Law: from that time forward, Irish parliaments could meet only by prior approval of the Crown, and could enact only that legislation which had been sanctioned by London. The Statutes of Kilkenny were reaffirmed, this time to be taken seriously. In the space of a few months, Poynings had effectively undone the drift toward Home Rule and, further, had made it illegal even to petition for redress.

After Poynings had gained the King the wanted legislation, Sir Edward found that its enforcement still depended on the sophisticated political ability of a strongman with a knowledge of the nuances of Ireland. Only one such man existed, and he was in the Tower of London. Henry VII relented, freeing a publicly repentant Garret Mór to stewardship of the island. Privately still hopeful of a Yorkist revival, the duplicitous eighth Earl of Kildare spent the rest of his life plotting against his Lancastrian enemies in the South and scheming with the Ulster lords to bring together a conspiracy with Scotland against the Crown. In the meantime, however, he brooked no interference with his *own* authority. In 1504 Kildare led his liegemen and a coalition of northern Gaelic clans against an increasingly threatening alliance of Connacht and western Munster septs led by Ulick Finn Burke of ClanRicarde and Turlough O'Brien of Thomond. The westerners were shattered in battle at the Hill of the Axes (Knockdoe) when Fitzgerald introduced a new factor to the Irish battlefield: firearms.[1]

When Garret Mór died in 1513, his son Garret Oge became the third generation Kildare Viceroy of Ireland. The Pale English (and the Butlers, from whom the young ninth Earl of Kildare had seized Clonmel in 1516) complained to a sympathetic ear at Henry VIII's court. Cardinal Wolsey's advice to the King was that there was danger in making the viceroyalty an inheritance of the Geraldines and that Ireland could be made to produce a profit under better, presumably Butler, leadership. It was but the first step in undermining Garret Oge's position. Interference with Fitzgerald's viceroyalty intensified over the next two decades. Finally, after Henry's marriage to Anne Boleyn—a Butler kinswoman—caused ominous Romanist rumblings in Ireland, Kildare was summoned to the Tower, leaving his son Thomas FitzGarret, Lord Offaly, as "acting Lord Lieutenant."[2] When Offaly heard an unfounded rumour that his father had been put to death in London during 1534, the brash young Kildare heir rode into Dublin at the head of a large band of gallowglass with swords unsheathed and silken fringes fluttering from their helmets (thereby affording Offaly the appellation "Silken Thomas"). Flinging down the sword of state and vowing vengeance for Garret Oge's "murder," the young hotspur declared himself an enemy of the Crown and rode riot through Dublin. Failing to take the Castle, Silken Thomas was left to work out his anger with bloody, madcap raids on the estates of the Butlers before finally retiring to the ancient Kildare Geraldine stronghold at Maynooth.

THE SIEGE OF MAYNOOTH

Silken Thomas made two major mistakes when he attacked Dublin. The obvious one, of course, was the failure to take Dublin Castle. The other blunder was to prove more costly in the long run: Archbishop John Alen, Thomas Cranmer's man in the Irish capital, was killed by Offaly's supporters. The Catholic prelate's death resulted in the excommunication of Silken Thomas and presented Henry VIII with the opening he needed to bring the entire Kildare Geraldine clan to heel.

No longer concerned about possible papal support on behalf of the still-Catholic rebel Irish, the English king dispatched Sir William Skeffington to Ireland with siege artillery, weaponry then almost unknown to the island. The cannon were predictably impressive to the Maynooth defenders; some were sufficiently awed to treat secretly with the new Lord Deputy. One, Parez, delivered Maynooth Castle to Skeffington on a March morning in 1535 for Saxon gold and the "Pardon of Maynooth."

As the ballad makes clear, Silken Thomas lasted longer on the run than the Irish "informer."

Crom, Crom Aboo! The Geraldine rebels from proud Maynooth,
And with him are leagued four hundred, the flower of Leinster's youth;
Take heart once more, oh Erin! The great God gives thee hope,
And through the mist of time and woe they true life portals ope!

Earl Thomas of the Silken Robes—here doubtless burns thy soul;
Thou beamest here a living sun, around which thy planets roll.
Then had our land, now scorned and burned, been saved a world of woe,
Oh, would that the Eternal Powers above that this were only so!

No more—no more—it maddeneth so! But rampart, keep and tower
At least are still—long may they be—a part of Ireland's power.
But who looks mid his warriors from the walls, as gleams a pearl
Mid meaner stones? This Parez, foster brother of the Earl.

Enough! We shall hear more of him; amid the hundred shafts
Which campward toward the Saxon host the wind upbears and wafts,
One strikes the earth at Talbot's feet with somewhat white—a scroll—
Impaled upon the barb—Oh! How exults the leader's soul!

He grasps it, reads: "Now, by St. George, the day at last is ours!
Before tomorrow's sun arise we hold yon haughty towers!
The craven traitor—but, tis well—he shall receive his hire,
And somewhat more to boot, God wot, than perchance he may desire!"

Alas, alas, tis all too true; a thousand marks of gold
In Parez' hands, and Leinster's bands are basely bought and sold.
Earl Thomas loses fair Maynooth and a hundred of his clan—
But worse, he loses half his hopes for he loses trust in man.

The morn is up, the gates lie wide, the foe pour in amain;
Oh, Parez, pride thee in thy plot and hug they golden chain.
There are cries of rage from battlements and melees neath in court,
But Leinster's brave, ere noon blaze high, shall mourn in donjon fort!

Twas but four days thereafter, of a stormy evening late,
When a horseman reared his charger in before the castle gate.
And gazing upwards, he descried by the light of the pale moon shed,
Imapled upon an iron stake, a well-known gory head.

"So, Parez, thou hast met thy meed! " he said and turned away,
"And was it a foe that thus avenged me on that fatal day?
Now, by my troth, albeit I hate the Saxon and his land,
I could, methinks, for one brief moment press the Talbot's hand!"

Skeffington finally ran down young Offaly in August 1535 and sent the rebel lord to the Tower to await the pleasure of Henry Tudor (his father, Garret Oge, was by now dead in fact). Silken Thomas was hanged along with five of his Fitzgerald uncles on a single gallows in 1537. The great house of Kildare, which had for three generations held a monopoly on the justiciarship of Ireland, was left with only a twelve-year-old claimant in exile on the continent.

The genocide of the Geraldines had been a policy of state taken after much deliberation. As a letter from Ireland had informed the King in 1536: "You highness must understand that the English blood . . . is in manner worn out of this land . . . is disminished and enfeebled; and contrariwise the Irish blood, ever more and more, without such decay encreaseth." Another missive had told Henry in 1537 that the Pale was "cramperned and crouched into an odd corner of the country." Not only was the Crown's authority limited geographically, but the King's men had not the faintest idea what was happening in the wild country just beyond those limits. An address to the King's Council admitted as much: "the country called Leinster and the situation thereof is unknown to the King and his Council." Only four years later, the London ministers were being told that "Irishmen will never be conquered by war." In short, Henry VIII ruled little of Ireland, knew less about the rest, and had no military way to deal with Irish resistance.

Characteristically, however, the Tudor king had swiftly grasped the crux of the problem: the Irish lords traditionally involved themselves in internecine strife; it had been only the reputation and power of the Kildare Fitzgeralds which had acted as a balancing force between the Old English and the Gaelic lords of the marches. The Geraldines' intermarriages and alliances had gained them a popularity and trust that no other family could match. Eliminate the Kildares and the wild Irish lords would return to their bickering ways. London would then *divide et impera* in Ireland by selective fanning of the feuds.

This the wily Henry proceeded to do. Four years after the

dark deed on Tower Hill, the Tudor declared himself King of Ireland and set out to Anglicise the island.[3]   Thomas Alfred Jackson describes the methods:

> The chief was first flattered with titles, honours, and a subsidy into becoming an agent of anglicisation. If he fell in with the plan he was made . . . the owner of all clan-territory. . . . If he accepted the title but did not introduce English-feudal tenures he was attainted as a traitor, his lands were confiscated and the English-feudal tenures were imposed on the clans by force. If the clans revolted either with the new lord-chief or against him, a punative expedition achieved the same result. . . . Every lord had to choose between (1) becoming a rent-hungry landlord on the English model, or (2) being attainted as a traitor, hanged as a "rebel," driven into exile, or disposed of by private assassination.

Henry Tudor had correctly surmised that duplicity would work where aggression did not.

By the time of Henry VIII's death in 1547, the Crown could claim effective control over perhaps half of Ireland.   Certain nobles such as Pierce Butler, first Earl of Ossory and ninth of Ormonde—whose family were old Lancastrian enemies of the Yorkist Geraldines, anyway—had been quite happy to submit to the "surrender and re-grant" policy of the King, meanwhile cheerfully joining the new Church of Ireland. Others such as the MacWilliam Burkes and the O'Briens, were more grudging but had finally given in, gaining the earldoms of ClanRicarde and Thomond.   Although the English had never effectively penetrated the wilds of mid-Ulster, even Conn the Lame, The O'Neill, had given up his honoured Gaelic title to become Earl of TirOwen (Tyrone) in 1542.   In all, over forty "English rebel" and "Irish enemy " lords had surrendered their traditional Irish titles for new ones in the English style.

Some few of the great lords, men such as Brian O'Connor of Offaly and Gillapatrick O'More of Laois, had fought back bitterly before finally succumbing to Lord Deputy Anthony St. Leger in 1546. The Crown made an example of their resistance: O'Connor was exiled, O'More imprisoned, and their lands were confiscated by the authorities.[4]   By 1550 the English Privy Council had decided to make these lands an extension of the Pale, the first major attempt at plantation since Prince John had brought the Bristol Saxons into Dublin. In 1556 Fort Protector (modern Port Laoise) became Maryborough in honour of Mary I; Daingean meanwhile became Philipstown after her

Spanish King.   Although angry at the new Queen's Catholic match, the English Parliament found no objection to passing the plantation legislation:

> The said King's and Queen's Majesties . . . shall have, hold and
> possess for ever, as in the right of the Crown of England and Ire-
> land, the said countries of Leix . . . and Offaly. . . .

The Irish were cleared off the plantation land from "king to kern" as the Crown attempted to resettle *Queens* and *Kings* Counties with loyal Englishmen. The plantation had hardly begun when Elizabeth I became Queen of England in 1558.

THE DOWNFALL OF THE GAEL

The major difficulty with the Surrender and Re-grant policy of the middle sixteenth century was that it did not take into account the "Gaelic heirs" to the ancient clan titles. It was all very well to make Conn *Bacagh* O'Neill the Earl of Tyrone, for example, but were his sons to succeed him under Celtic tradition or English law? In fact, under Gaelic law, not only was it possible that the chief might not be succeeded by his sons, but the lord did not even *own* his demesne; the lands were only his to rule during his lifetime. Upon his death, the clans would elect a new chieftain from among themselves. Understandably, the new leader would usually be the strongest among them—not always the son of the dead lord, and certainly not always the eldest son as called for by the feudal primogeniture of the English. The bitterness and confusion caused by this problem cannot be over-emphasised. The uncertainty in the succession of the Tyrone earldom in particular caused difficulty that was to be overcome only by three decades of savage warfare.

The most ferocious of the northern pretenders to the title O'Neill during the early days of Elizabeth's reign was Seán *an Diomais,* Shane the Proud. When his father Conn the Lame accepted the English title, surrendering the Irish one, Shane's right to the ancient Gaelic title was put in serious doubt. As the young Shane grew older, he would gradually go into rebellion against almost everyone but his own henchmen. Claiming personal allegiance from the MacMahons, Maguires, O'Hanlons, Magennisses, and O'Cahans, Shane was to become the scourge of the North. The wild chieftain's *file,* Farley O'Gnive, saw his O'Neill as a symbol of the permanence of traditional Gaelic values. In the following ballad, O'Gnive reaches back into his own poetic heritage to become a seer, singing achingly of the passing of an age. From the perspective of the twentieth century, Ó Faoláin comments tellingly:

> That old blind poet lying in the dark and telling his saga to his fellow-poets was part not merely of an old convention but of a convention that was already growing weary. It was growing too old to adapt itself to Change; like himself it had grown too blind to observe the realities. . . . That world of his and of O'Neill's . . . reached back too far, and was far too conscious of its own age and dignity, two things about which the intruding adventurers cared not a fig.

It had taken the Irish two centuries to master the battle-axe and repel the Viking. The new weapon brought by the English—the European concept of Nation—was not to be learned by the Irish until long after the Gael had passed from the scene.

This poem is one of the most famous in all of Gaelic literature. The translation given here, by Samuel Ferguson, has often been saluted as the one closest in spirit to the original.

My heart is in woe,
And my soul deep in trouble,
For the mighty are low,
And abased are the noble.

The Sons of the Gael
Are in exile or mourning,
Worn, weary, and pale,
As spent pilgrims returning.

Our course is fear,
Our nobility vileness,
Our hope is despair,
And our comeliness foulness.

There is mist on our heads,
And a cloud chill and hoary
Of black sorrow, sheds
An eclipse on our glory.

That the sons of the king—
Oh, the treason and malice! —

Shall no more ride the ring
In their own native valleys.

For the plain shall be broke
By the share of the Stranger,
And the stone-mason's stroke
Tell the woods of their danger.

The green hills and shore
Be with white keeps disfigured,
And the Mote of Rathmore
Be the Saxon churl's haggard!

The Gael cannot tell,
In the uprooted wildwood
And red ridgy dell,
The old nurse of his childhood:

The nurse of his youth
Is in doubt as she views him
If the wan wretch, in truth,
Be the child of her bosom.

We starve by the board,
And we thirst amid wassail—
For the guest is the lord,
And the host is the vassal!

Through the woods let us roam,
Through the wastes wild and barren;
We are strangers at home!
We are exiles in Erin!

And Erin's a bark
O'er the wide waters driven,
And the tempest howls dark,
And her side planks are riven!

And in billows of might
Swell the Saxon before her,—
Unite, oh, unite!
Or the billows burst o'er her!

Shane the Proud styled himself The O'Neill. The English more often, and accurately, called him the Grand Disturber. Actually, Shane's claim to the greatest of Irish clan titles was debatable even under Gaelic law.

When Conn *Bacagh* O'Neill had renounced the ancient title in 1542 to become first Earl of Tyrone (and Baron Dungannon), he had named wee Matthew O'Neill, son by his "wife" of the time (his third), as heir to his new English titles. Shane, eldest son by Conn the Lame's first wife, had more than a little reason to doubt Matthew's legitimacy as the boys grew up—Shane was slightly younger than Matthew. Shane was not particularly envious of the foreign appellations as the lads became young men, but he considered himself true heir to the now-open designation of The O'Neill, an ambition thwarted by the very presence of the young Baron Dungannon. By the time Conn the Lame died in 1559, Shane's problem had been solved: the O'Donnellys had murdered both the Dungannon heir and Matthew's eldest son Cormac. The dark deed had its desired effect. The aged and ailing Conn had accepted Shane as his tanist.

After Conn's death, his powerful nephew Turlough Luineach O'Neill of Strabane[5] supported Shane's claim, becoming in fact Shane's tanist while awaiting his own chance to claim the title of O'Neill. To further both their positions, Turlough murdered Matthew's third son Brian in 1562. Shane and Turlough were only sorry they could not get at Matthew's remaining sons, Hugh and Art. The wee Art was presumably in fosterage to a Gaelic family hostile to Shane; the teenaged Hugh, now Baron of Dungannon, had been rescued by the English and was being reared across the Irish Sea by the Queen's man, Sir Henry Sidney.[6] The annalists reckoned that Shane O'Neill "might have been called with propriety the provincial King of Ulster, were it not for the opposition of the English."

It was not yet an opposition dangerous to the wild Ulsterman. When Elizabeth ordered Thomas Ratcliffe, Earl of Sussex, to root Shane out of the Ulster wilderness, Sir Thomas had found himself chasing a will-o-the-wisp. Chasing northern warlords had long been like searching hayricks for needles, but when the arrogant Shane began treating with the Spanish as a result, London decided that things were getting out of hand. The Queen of England, attempting to delay *that* confrontation as long as possible, determined to drop the ineffectual stick and try the carrot. Perhaps recalling her father's divide-and-conquer

strategy, Elizabeth Tudor would now attempt to use the bellicose Shane to rid her of another nettlesome problem: the Redshanks of the Route, Scots gallowglass who had ousted the native
MacQuillans from the coastal glens of Antrim.   Led by James
MacDonnell, Lord of the Isles, these fierce Scottish warriors
made no pretence of allegiance to the Elizabethan Crown of
England; rather they offered fealty to Mary Stewart (the Queen
of Scots had just landed at Leith and was receiving the swaggering lairds at Holyrood).   Elizabeth invited the wild O'Neill chieftain to wait upon her in London.

        Shane the Proud arrived in England in late 1561 and spent
the winter astonishing the gaping court society.   Surrounded
by a pride of giant Ulstermen and gallowglass in full Gaelic re-
galia, this apparition from the Celtic past must have presented a
spectacle fully as divorced from the London of the time as
Buffalo Bill's Wild West Show was from that of Victoria three
centuries afterwards.   Elizabeth bestowed the curious title of
"the *Great* O'Neill" on Shane, perhaps in perplexed bemusement
at the strangely charming Irishman.   After laying waste to London society by his mere appearance, Shane agreed to attempt a
similar onslaught on the Antrim Scots with somewhat deadlier
weaponry.   O'Neill had nothing in particular against the MacDonnells—his Scottish neighbors would fight, after all, for the highest
bidder as long as it was not Elizabeth—but Shane needed little
encouragement to go to war with almost anyone.   First, however, O'Neill opted for a bit of territorial aggrandisement of his
own, securing his western flank with a crushing victory over his
bitter enemy Calvagh MacManus O'Donnell, titular head of
TyrConnell.   Shane finally turned to the Antrim Scots in 1565,
smashing them at Glenflesk, near Ballycastle.   O'Neill killed
James MacDonnell and his brother Angus "the Haughty," meanwhile taking Sorley Boye, another of the MacDonnell brothers,
as hostage.

        All the while the vulpine Shane was secretly plotting against
Elizabeth, even sending out overtures for the hand of Mary
Stewart (O'Neill's pride and ambition were legendary even in
his own time: one almost wonders if the Scots of Antrim were
finally attacked because of the fury of the rejected suitor—Glenflesk was contemporaneous with the Queen of Scots' marriage
to Darnley).   In any event, the sturdy Ulsterman's treachery was
not misplaced—the Queen of England had meanwhile been doing
her best to assassinate Shane.   After Sussex had failed in this

dark enterprise for the second time, O'Neill decided it was high time to change allies. O'Neill consequently freed Sorley Boye, though it turned out to be late in the game to try befriending the proud Scots of the Route.

The death of Calvagh O'Donnell at about this time convinced the ever-ambitious Shane that he now had the opportunity to regain the ancient power of The O'Neill in fact as well as name. The rebel's attack on TyrConnell in 1567 was shattered at the Battle of Farsetmore when Black Hugh, the new O'Donnell, treated Shane the Proud with somewhat less courtesy than had the lions of London society five years previously. With ClannConnell on his heels and the newly redcoated troops of the Crown blocking escape, O'Neill chose to throw himself on the mercy of his former prisoners, the MacDonnells, at Cushendun. It was a rash decision. His head was soon a hundred miles south, festooned upon the northwest gate of the capital city, grinning "scorn upon Dublin's Castle-tower." The thrifty Scots presumably found the thousand mark reward useful.

SHANE O'NEILL

Shane the Proud stood as the last real Gaelic warrior-chief in an Ireland fast succumbing to the blandishments of Tudor colonial society. He was a man representing a society, in the words of Ó Faoláin, that was:

> powerfully nostalgic, atavistically resurgent, long after the rest of Europe had begun to move forward to new ideas, new inventions, new codes, greater and finer elaborations in every branch of life.

In many ways he was a throwback to the days of CúChulainn and his own ancestor, Niall of the Nine Hostages. Yet, as Margaret MacCurtain observes:

> To write Shane O'Neill off as an archtypal example of Celtic savage is to do him an injustice. His grasp of diplomacy, his military skill, his authority which he exercised in Ulster, above all his realisation of the nature of the conflict he was involved in with Elizabeth's forces in Ireland, mark Shane O'Neill as an Irish Elizabethan surpassed indeed in moral and intellectual stature by the great Hugh O'Neill but claiming in his own right a certain greatness of achievement.

As the poet relates, the Ulster accent of Seán *an Diomais* "woke the ghost of Colm Cille" with "warrior words" and deeds which blocked the advance of English colonialism into the fastnesses of the North. London unsuccessfully attemped in turn to defeat him, cajole him, outwit him, and assasinate him. It is perhaps typically Celtic that this wild heroic war-lord finally brought himself down with Gaelic ambition.

The following late nineteenth century ballad is by Seumas MacManus, the famous nationalist poet and short story writer from Donegal. Best known today for his editing of *The Story of the Irish Race*, a history very decidedly from the Irish republican point of view, his poetry and ballads are often overlooked. Although occasionally wanting artistically, they accurately describe the importance of the old legends to the National Tradition.

On the wild and windy upland, Tornamona,
High above the tossing Moyle,
Lies in slumber, deep and dreamless now, a warrior
Weary-worn with battle-toil.
On his mighty breast the little canna blossoms,
And the scented bog-bines trail;
While the winds from Lurigaiden whisper hush-songs
Round the bed of Shane O'Neill.

Time was once, O haughty warrior, when you slept not
To the crooning of the wind;
There was once a Shane whom daisies could not smother,
And whom the bog-weeds could not bind—
Once a Shane with death-shafts from his fierce eyes flashing,
With dismay in fists of mail—
Shane, whose throbbing pulses sang with a singing lightning—
Shane, our Shane, proud Shane O'Neill!

Him the hungry Scot knew, and the thieving Saxon,
Traitorous *Éireannach* as well;
For their mailed throats often gurgled in his grasping,
As he hurled their souls to hell.
Sassenach, now, and flouting Scot, and Irish traitor,
Breathe his name and turn not pale,
Set their heel upon the warrior's breast, nor tremble—
God! The breast of Shane O'Neill!

Will you never, O our chieftain, snap the sleep-cords?

Never rise in thunderous wrath—
Though the knaves and slaves that bring a blight on Uladh,
Sweeping far a dread red swath?
O'er the surges shout, O you on Tornamona,
Hark, the soul-shout of the Gael!
"Rise O chief, and lead us from our bitter bondage—
Rise, in God's name, Shane O'Neill! —

The British swiftly installed Hugh O'Neill, the eldest surviving son of Matthew, in the family castle at Dungannon. Shane the Proud had been the last great Gaelic O'Neill of Ulster. The heir to Tyrone had been raised the proper English gentleman and was expected by London to keep the North quiet . . . for now the century-old spectre of the Geraldines was rising in the South.

CHAPTER NOTES (4)

1 — Putting down ClanRicarde did not, of course, solve the "native problem" in Connacht. The Gaelic Irish had become such an everyday threat to the major English trading centre of the West by 1518 that the city fathers passed an ordinance declaring that "neither O ne Mac shall strutte thro' the streets of Gallway."

2 — There is much evidence that Garret Oge had been treating secretly with the Earl of Desmond, who was in turn supposed to be dealing surreptitiously with Charles V, the Holy Roman Emperor (though the evidence of the latter is much more sketchy). The Butlers, Kildare's bitterest enemies, were kinsmen of Anne Boleyn, insuring that Henry VIII would hear much about the Fitzgeralds. How much true information the King received from this source is debatable. How much of it was favourable to the Kildares is not.

3 — English monarchs had traditionally based their claim to be "Lord of Ireland" on the *Laudibilitier* of the English pope Adrian IV. When Henry Tudor broke with Rome, the 1155 papal charter automatically became *passé*. Many of the Irish thought they were now subjects of Pope Paul III. Henry VIII had himself named King of Ireland to

nip that sort of sentiment in the bud.

4 — Although some of the suppressed clansmen of the middle counties became recon-
ciled to English dominion, others, such as the O'Mores, did not. Three subsequent
generations of O'More rebel chieftains—Rory, Rory Oge, and Eoiny MacRory—were to
fall to English arms. As late as 1641 still another Rory O'More would lead the Irish
attack at Julianstown Bridge.

The political rebels, by the way, were not the only ones considered a threat by
Dublin Castle. Among the prisoners taken by the Crown during the O'More-O'Connor
risings of 1546, in the words of the Four Masters, was "Teige O'Coffey, preceptor of
the schools of Ireland in poetry."

5 — Turlough's actual name was Turlough MacConallagh O'Neill. It is a sign of the
continuing importance of the Gaelic tradition of "fosterage" among the Ulster Irish
of the time that Turlough took the name of the clan who reared him, the O'Luinighs.
This cannot be explained away merely because Turlough Luineach was illegitimate—
Shane the Proud was often styled Shane Donnelly O'Neill (and sometimes simply
"Donnelly") after his foster family.

6 — Hugh's murdered older brother Cormac would seem to have been born about
1545, Matthew's third son Brian about 1553. Although there is yet much controversy
about the year of Hugh O'Neill's birth, there are various clues that suggest that the
future Arch Rebel was born within a year or so of 1548. If so, young Dungannon
would have been thirteen when he went to England, and twenty when he returned
to Ulster.

5

The Desmond Wars

It was in the time of Elizabeth Tudor that Irish resistance to the English Crown began to coalesce into what is now called the Rebel Tradition. Eschewing the *divide et impera* policy of her father, the Virgin Queen chose to subject Ireland with the sword. In his compelling *The Twilight Lords,* Richard Berleth sets the stage:

> During the reign of Queen Elizabeth I, England suceeded in conquering and colonizing large tracts of Irish land. In a series of squalid, destructive wars the face of Ircland was altered permanently, and the estrangement of the two countries, which had no exact beginning, hardened finally into a lasting emnity.
>
> Elizabeth's actions in Ireland are disastrous in retrospect, but at the time they seemed like good ideas. And they were carried out by a succession of the best of men. . . . Few emerged from the ordeal with credit or lasting gain. . . .
>
> The twilight lords themselves were the great feudal barons of Ireland: Gerald Fitzgerald, Earl of Desmond; James Fitzmaurice, Captain of Desmond; and the greatest rebel of them all, Hugh O'Neill, Earl of Tyrone. Caught between them and the invading English, the common people, the pawns at risk, were sacrificed by both sides without compunction.

While the Queen's ministers had been plotting against Shane O'Neill in the North, new trouble had been brewing in the South. By the 1560s, Thomas Butler, the Black Earl of Ormonde, and Gerald FitzJames Fitzgerald, the Pale Earl of Desmond, were renewing the family feud that had its roots in the War of the Roses. In May 1565 a seemingly insignificant boundary skirmish at Affane in Waterford led to the intervention of the Crown on the side of Ormonde, cousin to the Queen and head of the "most loyal Butlers." Gerald and his brother Sir John were summoned to England and confined at Southwark, leaving the administration of their vast Munster estates to their cousin James Fitz-Maurice, Captain of Desmond. Despite the Pale Earl's prostestations of allegiance, he was to be kept in England for seven years.

"For English contemporaries," Seán Ó Faoláin suggests, "the entry into sixteenth-century Ireland was an entry into a world as strange as the Indies were to Columbus." Elizabeth Tudor became convinced that the only way to make the Irish island comprehensible and halt the interminable feuding among Irish "princes as remote and unimaginable as the Great Khan," was to extend plantation from Kings and Queens Counties to the Desmond lands of the South. The conviction was to profoundly alter both Irish and English history.

By 1568 Sir Richard Grenville, Walter Raleigh, Humphrey Gilbert, and Sir Peter Carew were stealing huge tracts of Munster land with the blessing of the Crown. The freebooting ways of this new group of English adventurers accomplished one of the Queen's objectives in an entirely unforeseen manner: the ununitable southern Irish stopped their feuding, and united for the first time in history . . . against the British. The chroniclers tell of the breakout of the First Desmond War:

> James, the son of Maurice . . . was a warlike man of many troops this year; and the English and Irish of Munster; from the Barrow to Carn Uí Neid, entered into a unanimous and firm confederacy with him against the Queen's Parliament.

The authorities had blundered in imprisoning the essentially loyal fourteenth Earl of Desmond; James FitzMaurice, about whom the resistance rallied, was a violently papist Anglophobe.

THE GERALDINES

The Fitzgerald war-shout, "*Crom Aboo!*" rang out through the South and West of Ireland. The so-called Geraldine Confederacy came together for a common purpose: Barrys, Burkes, Roches, Kavanaghs, O'Faoláins, McSheehys, O'Connors, MacSwineys, and O'Dwyers found it more important to defend their lands than to steal each other's cattle. Even the MacCarthy More of the far Southwest and Black Tom Butler's sons Edmund and Edward joined the Fitzgeralds, remarkable occurrences considering the historic emnity those two families had shown the Desmonds. Whitehall looked on in horror. Plantation was supposed to have solved the Irish problem. Instead, it had touched off full-scale rebellion. It was not to be the last time in Irish history.

> ## CHRONOLOGY (The Desmond Wars)
>
> 1568 . . . . . .English adventurers carve up Munster; Mary Stewart flees to England.
>
> 1569 . . . . . .First Desmond War begins; Crown takes Kilmallock and Limerick; Hugh O'Neill established at Dungannon.
>
> 1570 . . . . . .Elizabeth excommunicated by Pope Pius V.
>
> 1572 . . . . . .Connacht rising put down; massacre of St. Bartholomew's Eve in Paris.
>
> 1573 . . . . . .Captain of Desmond flees to continent, 1st Desmond War ends; Pale Earl freed.
>
> 1575 . . . . . .Rathlin Island Massacre.
>
> 1577 . . . . . .Mullaghamast Massacre; Drake departs on round-the-world voyage.
>
> 1579 . . . . . .James FitzMaurice returns, sets off 2nd Desmond War; Battles of Springfield and Monaster.
>
> 1580 . . . . . .Earl of Desmond declares for rebels; general insurrection in Munster; Baltinglass leads papist revolt in Leinster; Battle of Glenmalure; massacre at Fort Del Oro.
>
> 1581 . . . . . .Baltinglass gives up revolt: Pale Earl cornered in Kerry.
>
> 1582 . . . . . .Sir John of Desmond slain; Pale Earl descends on Vale.
>
> 1583 . . . . . .Pale Earl killed; 2nd Desmond War ends; 2nd Munster Plantation begins.

This Thomas Davis song does more than celebrate the glory of the greatest of the Norman-Irish families. The "poet laureate of Irish Resistance" traces here the story of the Stranger becoming marcher lord, the marcher lord becoming native, and the native becoming rebel.

The Geraldines, the Geraldines, tis true in Strongbow's van,
By lawless force, as conquerors, their Irish reign began—
And, oh! through many a dark campaign they proved their prowess stern,
In Leinster's plains, and Munster's vales, on king, and chief, and kerne;
But noble was the cheer within the halls so rudely won,
And generous was the steel-gloved hand that had such slaughter done;
How gay their laugh, how proud their mein, you'd ask no herald's sing—
Among a thousand you had known the princely Geraldine.

These Geraldines, those Geraldines, not long our air they breathed—
Not long they fed on venison in Irish water seethed—
Not often had their children been by Irish mothers nursed,

When from their full and genial hearts an Irish feeling burst;
The English monarchs strove in vain, by law, and force, and bribe,
To win from Irish thoughts and ways this "more than Irish" tribe;
For still they clung to fosterage, to brehon, cloak, and bard—
What king dare say to Geraldine "your Irish wife discard?"

Ye Geraldines, ye Geraldines, how royally ye reigned
O'er Desmond broad, and rich Kildare, and English arts disdained:
Your sword made knights, your banner waved, free was your bugle call
By Glyn's green slopes, and Dingle's tide, from Barrow's banks to Youghal.
What gorgeous shrines, what brehon lore, what minstrel feasts there were
In and around Maynooth's keep, and palace-filled Adare,
But not for right or feast ye stayed, when friend or kin was pressed,
And foemen fled when *"Crom Abú"* bespoke your lance in rest.

Ye Geraldines, ye Geraldines, since Silken Thomas flung
King Henry's sword on council board, the English thanes among,
Ye never ceased to battle brave against the English sway,
Though axe and brand and treachery your proudest cut away;
Of Desmond's blood, through woman's veins passed on the exhausted tide;
His title lives—a Saxon churl usurps the lion's hide
And, though Kildare tower haughtily, there's ruin at the root,
Else why, since Edward fell to earth, had such a tree no fruit?

The Geraldines, these Geraldines, rain wears away the rock,
And time may wear away the tribe that stood the battle's shock,
But ever sure while one is left of all that honoured race,
In front of Ireland's chivalry is that Fitzgerald's place;
And, though the last were dead and gone, how many a field and town,
From Thomas Court to Abbeyfeale, would cherish their renown,
And men would say of valour's rise, or ancient power's decline,
"Twill never soar, it never shone, as did the Geraldine."

London already had its hands full in Scotland—Mary
Stewart had been in England only a short time and the northern
lairds had risen—but the Irish revolt of 1569 could not be ignored. The excommunication of Elizabeth was in the offing and
the Captain of Desmond was using the religious issue for all it
was worth. Playing wildly but effectively on the emotions of the
Catholic Irish, James FitzMaurices's denunciations of the Tudor
Queen and the plantation Church of Ireland were punctuated

with the perjorative terms "antichrist" and "heretic." Three years before the bloody counter-reformation terror of St. Bartholomew's Eve in France, the Irish were already trumpeting papist *jihad*. For the first time in Irish history, a native leader was discovering the unifying temporal uses of religion.

By autumn of 1569 four centuries of English influence in Ireland was in serious jeapordy. In Connacht, the Earls of ClanRicarde and Thomond had joined the rebels. Turlough O'Neill, disappointed in his claim to Tyrone, was raiding Crown herds in Fermanagh from the North, and in the far Northwest, the O'Donnells had risen. The only quiet realm was in mid-Ulster where Hugh O'Neill held sway. The plantation solution to the Irish question had precipitated another question altogether: the credibility of British dominion. England had put itself in the position of having to conquer an island that had been freely "surrendering" to Henry VIII scant years before.

Black Tom Butler, whose border fight with the Pale Earl had begun the conflagration, was ordered back from London to wean his kin from the rebellion and to "vanquish those cankered Desmonds." Meanwhile, Sir Henry Sidney, now the Lord Chancellor, sailed from Dublin for Cork, joining the newly created Lord President for Munster, Sir John Perrot, who had himself brought reinforcements from Britain. The Crown campaign started well.

Sidney marched north from Cork, splitting the Munster rebels by taking the Desmond stronghold of Kilmallock and continuing on to Limerick. Captain James FitzMaurice was forced back into the rugged mountain country around Killarney. Sidney, convinced that the Geraldine Confederacy was tottering, left the newly knighted Humphrey Gilbert in charge of the Kilmallock garrison while the Lord Chancellor himself marched north into Connacht, receiving the submission of John MacOliver MacWilliam Burke (who had raised the western Burkes and O'Flahertys) before returning to the Pale. At Kilmallock, Sir Humphrey's pacification program was brutal, but seemingly sufficiently effective to convince Gilbert that he had time to visit London. As soon as he did, the MacSwineys and McSheehys —the local Desmond henchmen—promptly rose up, overran Kilmallock, and ran the English garrison back to the southern coast. In one strike, the Geraldine rebellion was as strong as it had ever been. Sidney had been no more successful in running the Captain of Desmond to ground than had Sussex in chasing Shane the

Elizabethan Ireland

Proud a decade earlier. By the spring of 1570 the English were being bloodily reminded once again that it was one thing to take Irish land, another to hold it. Sir John Perrot thought he had the answer. Shrewdly, if unrealistically, the Lord President for Munster "outlawed bards and rhymers categorically . . . on grounds that . . . songs moved simple people to defiance and stirred kern and gallowglass to deeds of blood."

Presumably frustrated that he could not stop the music, Perrot spent the next two years slogging through the Irish countryside after the elusive James FitzMaurice. Berleth cites a contemporary account of the campaign faced by Sir John:

> The lurking rebels . . . lurk in ambush amongst the standing wood, playing upon all comers as if they intend to go headlong forward. On the bog they likewise presume with naked celerity to come as near our foot and horse as possible, and then fly off again, tripping after their pipes . . . knowing we cannot or indeed dare not follow them. And thus they serve us in the narrow entrances into their glens and quagmires of their mountains, where a few muskets well placed, will stagger a pretty army.

The years of coping with the dark bogwater and mournful mists of the wild southwestern wilderness began to have a cumulative effect on the Lord President. Perrot began to adopt the tactics, and then the customs, of the wraithlike James FitzMaurice in much the same way that American Indian fighters later found themselves wearing buckskin, living off the land, and adapting themselves to their environs. In almost Celtic desperation, Perrot was finally driven to challenge the Captain of Desmond to single combat in the Gaelic style.

London was furious. The vision of an English Lord President running about the bogs of Ireland behaving like a latter-day CúChulainn was more than British honour and dignity could countenance. Once again, an English leader was being absorbed by the bemused Irish. Encouraged, the *Mac anIarlas,* the sons of the "loyal" Earl of ClanRicarde, rose with Donnell "of the Wars" O'Flaherty of Connemara against the *Cailleach ghranna*[1] in 1572. Though the short-lived rising was put down fiercely at Aughnanure (through the efforts of the ambitious Murrough "of the Battle-axes" O'Flaherty), it did nothing to help Sir John Perrot's reputation. In virtual disgrace, he finally settled down to starve James FitzMaurice out. He eventually succeeded in the spring of 1573 when the intrepid Captain of Desmond escaped to the continent. The First Desmond War was over.

It had hardly been worth the price. The Munster plantation lands supposedly at stake had been ravaged; the English adventurers against whom the Geraldine Confederacy had risen had gone to look for greener pastures. Direct rule by the Crown was abandoned to the Pale Earl of Desmond who, along with his brother, was finally freed to return to his lands in 1574. Gerald was received as a conquering hero as he made his way across Munster to Askeaton, the Desmond Fitzgerald family castle by the Shannon. The Irish considered that they had won. They had good reason.

By 1576 Celtic Law again ruled the South of Ireland. The Geraldines ignored the English courts, swiftly reinstituting the Gaelic customs of tanistry and *éraic*. At a time when British savants were predicting that Elizabeth was destined to rule "an English empire of unbounded glory," the beleaguered city fathers of Galway were inscribing their new West Gate with the devout supplication, "From the Ferocious O'Flaherties, God Defend Us!" English common law had been displaced by that of the hooded Brehon in the very first colony of the British Empire. Worse, reports were reaching London that the rebel James Fitz-Maurice was successfully soliciting military aid from Pope Gregory XIII and Philip II of Spain.

The authorities neither had the resources to combat the resurgence of the Gaelic culture, nor could they do much about the continental intrigues of the Captain of Desmond, but they could, and did, demonstrate a certain amount of savage imagination in dealing with those still in outright rebellion. In 1575 the MacDonnells of the Route had evacuated their entire "civilian" population to Rathlin Island when hard-pressed by English troops. The British under Walter Devereux, first Earl of Essex, took the opportunity to land on the isolated North Channel island and massacre the Scots to the last woman and child. Two years later, the rebel O'Connors and O'Mores of the Kings and Queens County plantation lands were invited to a parley by the English governor, Sir Francis Cosby. Assured protection in the Queen's name, over 250 rebels arrived for a preliminary banquet at the Rath of Mullaghamast. None left alive.

In the summer of 1579 James FitzMaurice landed in Kerry with three hundred men. This time the Captain of Desmond was "officially" committed to a holy war against the "heretical Crown of England;" he had even brought along a papal legate, Father Nicholas Saunders, to serve as sort of staff theologian.

The Geraldines were probably not particularly impressed by the Roman rhetoric but, with the exception of the reluctant Earl of Desmond, they showed little hesitation in declaring for their old war-chief. The Second Desmond War was on.

The authorities swiftly put the Pale Earl in an impossible position. Sir William Drury, now Lord President for Munster, accused Gerald of treason, suggesting that Desmond could prove his loyalty by bringing James FitzMaurice to justice. The Pale Earl was well aware that Gaelic Law would free his henchmen from their liege-oaths if he attempted any such thing; besides, most of his clan chiefs had already joined the rebels. Desmond merely wanted to be left alone to run his desmesne. Barely a month after the Kerry landing, an event occured which was to make the Earl's naïve wishes moot.

In one of those accidents of history whose importance is sometimes underestimated, the martial Captain of Desmond was killed in a dispute over a horse. Upon the August death of James FitzMaurice Fitzgerald, the rebels had a disorganised enemy, a papal nuncio, three thousand men in the field, and a new leader: John FitzJames Fitzgerald (the same Sir John of Desmond who had been held in England with his brother Gerald during the First Desmond War). What the rebel army did not have was Gerald himself, nor the prestige that the Pale Earl could bring to the cause. That was soon to change.

At the September 1579 Battle of Springfield, Sir John's Irish destroyed an English force near Kilmallock, mortally wounding Sir William Drury in the process. Nicholas Maltby, named new commander of the Munster Crown forces by Drury's successor Sir William Pelham, soon tracked down the insurgent army near Croom and routed Sir John's force at the bloody Battle of Monaster in early October. As the fighting ranged closer to the Pale Earl's Shannonside retreat at Askeaton, Desmond remained within trying to remain aloof from the hubbub. The authorities, not satisfied with Desmond's officially neutral stance, ordered the Pale Earl to Dublin. He had spent enough time in English hands to know what *that* meant. He ignored the summons. On 3 November 1579 Gerald FitzJames Fitzgerald, fourteenth Earl of Desmond, was proclaimed a traitor for non-compliance. Maltby had succeeded in flushing a reluctant rebel into the open. The rebels—and the subsequent National Tradition—looked on the Pale Earl as without equal in "nobility, honour, and power." Such a view of Desmond "is fantastically untrue," according to Ó Faoláin, "and yet it is not in another sense untrue, and in its truth is the power and the poetry of Ireland, and in its untruth her indifference to all her children whom she sacrifices ruthlessly to her needs." Sacrificed to Irish Myth Desmond might ultimately be; for now, Gerald's emergence on the side of the rebels would insure that many a loyal Englishman would die with the sound of the Fitzgerald war-shout—"*Crom Aboo!*"—ringing in his ears.

THE O'DRISCOLL WAR SONG

When the honoured Earl of Desmond declared for the rebels, Ireland exploded. In southern Ulster, Turlough O'Neill used the occasion to recruit gallowglass for his recurring raids against the English cattle herds. The O'Connor Sligo and the O'Flahertys of western Connacht rose in sympathy, as did a relative of the latter, the redoubtable Grace O'Malley, pirate queen of Clare Island and Clew Bay.[2] The wild O'Byrnes and Kavanaghs came roaring down out of the Wicklows. Out of Kerry and south Cork, which had borne the brunt of the First Desmond War, came O'Sullivans, O'Driscolls, O'Mahonys, and O'Sheas to join the general clamour.

This Gerald Griffin song is evocative of that time. The O'Driscolls were the powerful rulers of Cape Clear Island and the area around Skibbereen. The song can be sung with equal effect to describe the O'Driscoll reaction to any attack by the Stranger —be the foreigner the Vikings, the English, or the Algerian pirates who sacked Baltimore in 1631. The author is most famous for his novel *The Collegians,* which inspired Boucicault's classic drama, *The Colleen Bawn.*

From the shieling that stands by the lone mountain river,
Hurry, hurry down with the axe and the quiver;
From the deep-seated Coom, from the storm-beaten highland,
Hurry, hurry down to the shores of your island.

Refrain:
Hurry down, hurry down!
Hurry, hurry down to the shores of your island.

Gallóglaigh and kern, hurry down to the sea,
There the hungry raven's beak is gaping for a prey;
Farrah, to the onset! Farrah, to the shore!
Feast him with the pirate's flesh, the bird of gloom and gore!

Refrain

Hurry, for the slaves of Bel are mustering to meet ye;
Hurry by the beaten cliff, the Nordman longs to greet ye.
Hurry from the mountain! Hurry, hurry from the plain!
Welcome him, and never let him leave our land again!

Refrain

On the land a sulky wolf, and in the sea a shark,
Hew the ruffian spoiler down and burn his gory bark!
Slayer of the unresisting, ravager profane!
Leave the white sea-tyrant's limbs to moulder on the plain.

Refrain

After a short guerrilla campaign which served to thoroughly
alarm the authorities—at Christmas 1579, for example, the rebels
overran the port city of Youghal—the Earl of Desmond withdrew
to the cover of the Slieve Mish, the Phantom Mountains, which
form a natural fortress ringing the Dingle Peninsula. The Crown's
response was a scorched-earth crusade by the Earl of Ormonde
and the Lord President of Munster that was to make Munster a
graveyard. According to the annalists, Thomas Butler and
William Pelham "shewed mercy neither to the strong nor weak
. . . killed blind and feeble men, women, boys, and girls, sick
persons, idiots and old people."
    In April 1580 Pelham reduced Askeaton, the ancient Fitz-
gerald stronghold. Sealing off the Pale Earl in Kerry, Pelham dispatched the faithful Maltby to the north to deal with the always
troublesome O'Flahertys and O'Rourkes, continuing on himself
to Castleisland and Castlemaine offering pardon to any rebel
who would bring in the head of another. That was all the incen-
tive needed by Cormac MacTeige MacCarthy More. Called by
Sidney the "rarest man ever born of the Irishy," Cormac
MacTeige still considered the Geraldines interlopers on tradi-

tional MacCarthy lands. Defeating a band of Desmond's men under James Oge Fitzgerald, son of the Pale Earl's youngest brother, Cormac dispatched James Oge's body to Cork where it was quartered and "pierced." Under pressure from both MacCarthy More and Pelham (who by this time had landed a force under Sir William Winter on Valencia Island in Dingle Bay) the Geraldine forces began to melt away. By summer 1580 the Earl of Desmond was a hunted man.

Just as it looked as if Gerald was trapped in the far Southwest, trouble broke out in the East. James FitzRoland Eustace, the ardently Catholic Viscount Baltinglass of Ballymore, fired himself by the zealous rhetoric of Father Saunders, stirred up a row among the Irish lords around the Pale. The displaced clan chiefs of Kings and Queens Counties were happy to join in; the disgruntled Turlough O'Neill, as usual, needed only the pretext to resume his cattle raids. In August, Fiach MacHugh O'Byrne led the O'Tooles and Kavanaghs against the Pale from the south, easily dispersing an isolated English expedition and killing its commander, Sir Peter Carew.

Pelham had been forced to hurry back from the Southwest to deal with the new threat, leaving Desmond unapprehended in Kerry. Dublin Castle meanwhile had been screaming to London for reinforcements. In mid-August 1580 Sir Arthur Grey, Baron de Wilton, arrived with another large army determined to solve the Irish Problem, in a phrase becoming all too common, "once and for all." After his early September investiture as Lord Lieutenant, Grey decided to march south to neutralise the malcontent O'Byrne. It turned out to be an unfortunate choice.

FOLLOW ME UP TO CARLOW

Lord Grey was trusting in the superiority of English numbers and discipline to defeat what he supposed were untrained Irish kern. What the new deputy had not considered was the geography. The untrammelled wilderness of the Wicklow Mountains favoured guerrilla tactics—tactics that the ferocious Fiach O'Byrne had mastered through long years of experience.[3] Grey marched out of Dublin in traditional English column.

The heavily laden Crown army moved southeastward from Naas, climbing all the time. By the time the long column snaked up through the valley of Glendalough, the English were beginning to appreciate the ruggedness of the terrain. The rebel O'Byrne waited patiently on his Ballinacor Mountain stronghold overlooking Glenmalure, the next valley to the south. When the British troops finally clawed over the mountains separating the two valleys, the Irish were ready.

As the leading elements of the Crown column descended into Glenmalure, the hills about erupted with the defiant sound of war-shout, *bodhrán,* and Irish pipe. Sir William Stanley, commanding the British rear, described the scene: the Irish "were laid all along the woods as we should pass, behind trees, rocks, crags, bogs, and in covert." The remnants of the British vanguard scrambled for the high ground, destroying all semblance of order in the main army itself. The Irish kern made short work of those who could not make the climb. "Were a man . . . slightly hurt," Stanley reported, "he was lost, because no man was able to help him up the hill. Some died, being so out of breath that they were able to go no further, being hurt not at all." Maltby, victorious the previous year at Monaster, was forced to watch the slaughter helplessly at Lord Grey's side: "The recruits wavered, the kern ran away to the enemy, and so the gentlemen were lost." The Lord Deputy left about five hundred men in the glen.

Kathleen Hughes, in describing the duties of Gaelic *filí* for a thousand years past, reminds that they "told their traditions before men went into battle, to inspire them with reminders of the heroic past, they praised the warriors' courage and prowess, they lamented those who were slain in war." In the same unbroken tradition of *rosg catha,* Doighre O'Daly, court poet to Fiach MacHugh O'Byrne, harangued the Wicklow men on the eve of the 1580 battle in Irish verse created for the occasion:

> Host of armour, red and bright,
> May we fight a valiant fight!
> For the green spot of the earth,
> For the land that gave your birth!

Three centuries later, Patrick Joseph McCall would set the following lyric to the martial tune of Irish pipe and *bodhrán* that had echoed through Glenmalure on that bloody September afternoon.

Lift MacCahir Oge, your face,
Brooding over the old disgrace,

That Black Fitzwilliam stormed your place
And drove you to the fern;
Grey said victory was sure,
Soon the firebrand he'd secure—
Until he met at Glenmalure
Fiach MacHugh O'Byrne.

Refrain:
Curse and swear, Lord Kildare,
Fiach will do what Fiach will dare;
Now FitzWilliam have a care,
Fallen is your star low;
Up with halberd, out with sword!
On we go, for by the Lord,
Fiach MacHugh has given his word,
"Follow me up to Carlow!"

See the swords of Glen Imayle
Flashing over the English Pale,
See all the children of the Gael
Beneath O'Byrne's banners;
Rooster of a fighting stock,
Would you let a Saxon cock
Crow out upon an Irish rock?
Fly up and teach him manners!

Refrain

From Tassagart to Clonmore
Flows a stream of Saxon gore,
Och, great is Rory O'More
At sending loons to Hades;
White is sick and Lane is fled,
Now for Black Fitzwilliam's head,
We'll send it over dripping red
To Liz and her ladies.

Refrain

Lord Deputy Grey had gambled and lost. Fiach O'Byrne pressed the confused Crown forces all the way back to the Pale.

In the spring of 1580, the Pale Earl of Desmond had been in hiding and the rebellion looked almost over; now, in early autumn, the English had suffered their worst military defeat in the four centuries they had been in Ireland. The Irish scented blood.

Turlough O'Neill, ever the opportunistic "Dragon of Tara," swept south from Ulster with five thousand men, driving Sir Hugh Magennis' loyalist forces before him. The O'Rourkes and O'Donnells resumed raiding in Leitrim. The O'Connors rose yet again in Connacht. James Eustace pressed Black Tom Butler severely in Kilkenny. Sir John of Desmond rallied the Geraldines of mid-Munster. Gerald of Desmond was again "in control" of the Southwest. With no central leadership, however, the Geraldine Confederacy was really more a description than a reality—the Irish seemed to be content to work separately to regain their ancient family lands. Nonetheless, the news arriving in Dublin was already all bad when suddenly it got much worse. Spanish aid, promised the late Captain of Desmond during his European travels, was finally arriving in Kerry.

It turned out that the expeditionary force that had landed on the far western end of the Dingle Peninsula was not the dreaded infantry of Spain; rather, the landing party was made up of mercenaries recruited specifically for the enterprise from the Italian principalities of Genoa, Florence, and Naples. The Bolognese in command, Colonel Sebastiano di San Joseppi, had only seven hundred men and no clear idea of his mission. After landing at Smerwick, he established a rude defensive position at nearby Fort Del Oro, and remained there awaiting contact by the rebels. James FitzMaurice, however, was long dead and the Earl of Desmond apparently had no idea that the Italians could make an admirable "papist rallying-point" about which to form a truly effective force in the European manner.

If Gerald did not understand the opportunity, Lord Grey understood the danger. Leaving Fiach O'Byrne and Baltinglass to their pillaging, and an ailing Turlough O'Neill to his plunder, the Lord Deputy marshalled the full weight of the Crown against the continental threat. Surmising that the eastern war-lords would be content with booty from the largely undefended Pale, he daringly denuded the English settlement of troops and had begun the investment of the Spanish by early November. This time Grey had guessed correctly. On 8 November 1580 the bewildered San Joseppi marched his men out of Del Oro under a white flag. After they had stacked their arms, the Italians were herded back into the fort. They were massacred to a man. To this day, "Grey's Promise" stands for an act of Saxon perfidy among the Irish.

Whatever the ethical considerations, the murder of the continental garrison at Smerwick had the desired military effect. Grey's Fort Del Oro victory marked an about-turn of the rebel fortunes in the Second Desmond War. O'Byrne and O'Neill drew back from the Pale. Maltby reasserted the power of the Crown in Connacht, putting down the rebellious Burkes and O'Rourkes, and driving the nettlesome O'Flahertys back into Connemara. James Eustace of Baltinglass gave up the cause, fleeing to the continent in the Spring of 1581. Captain John Elizabeth Zouche harried Sir John of Desmond's small force through the wastes of the South. Father Nicholas Saunders, the papal legate whose presence had given a bit of credence to the "holy war," died quite abandoned in April of an increasingly deadly enemy, starvation. Curiously, the Pale Earl of Desmond, originally so reluctant to join the rebellion, now refused to quit.

Sixteen years of almost constant warfare had made its mark on the land. The scorched-earth policy pursued by the English now began to pay its grisly dividend. Famine became deadlier to the Irish than the soldiers of the Crown. Holinshed reported that the people were "driven to eat horses, dogs, and dead carions, but also did devour the carcasses of dead men, whereof there be sundry examples."

As famine raged throughout Munster in the autumn of 1581, the indefatigable John Zouche plodded on after the Desmond rebels. The other English captains meanwhile began to quarrel over the blame for Crown reverses during the rebellion they considered all but over. Black Tom Butler was accused of not being sufficiently enthusiastic in his pursuit of James Eustace. Ormonde responded with telling remarks concerning Lord Grey's blundering march to Glenmalure. When Zouche rode down Sir John of Desmond in December 1581, the British leaders, feeling that the apprehension of the Pale Earl himself was only a matter of time, left Zouche to his own devices on the devastated land, meanwhile comfortably hurling imprecations at each other from the safety of the still relatively verdant Pale.

In June 1582 Gerald FitzJames Fitzgerald reappeared like a phoenix. Sweeping into the Golden Vale of Limerick with over a thousand men, he sent the unprepared Crown forces reeling. As usual, Fiach O'Byrne seized the opportunity to raid the southern

Pale; similarly, the O'Connor Offalys rose once more in Kings County. It was enough for London. Lord Grey and Captain Zouche were removed from their posts in August. Distinguished reputations had again fallen victim to Irish rebellion.

The Pale Earl's 1582 rebel campaign withered in the face of famine even worse than that of the previous year. Holinshed chronicles the conditions in Munster as:

> . . . so barren, both of man and beast, that whoever did travel from the one end of all Munster [*to the other*], which is about sixscore miles, he would not meet any man, woman, or child . . . nor see yet any beasts, but the very wolves, foxes, and other like ravening beasts, many of them laie dead, being famished, and the residue gone elsewhere.

Lecky views the "pictures of the condition of Ireland at this time" as "as terrible as anything in human history." By the spring of 1583 the remaining rebel Geraldines were once again holed up in Kerry. This time it was not the Crown that forced them into the West—even Black Tom Butler could not raise a band capable of feeding off the ravaged land. Desmond's army merely evaporated as his starving men wandered off in search of food.[4]

Gerald FitzJames Fitzgerald, the great Pale Earl of Desmond, spent the summer of 1583 hiding in the Kerry mountains near Tralee like a common outlaw. He was finally captured in the woods of Glenageenty during November by Owen O'Moriarty, a local tribal chief. Moriarty brought in the head of the rebel Earl for the thousand pounds of silver Dublin Castle had been offering as reward. The Desmond Wars, which had begun eighteen years earlier over an obscure border skirmish on the River Blackwater in Waterford, drew to a squalid close with a bounty hunt in the Slieve Mish of Kerry.

The two decades of warfare proved as ruinous to the old Gaelic culture as they had been to the land itself. The new administrators of what had been Desmond Ireland quickly divided Munster into counties on the English style (Connacht was also split into counties in 1585), carving up the land among a new group of adventurers for another, more lasting, attempt at plantation. A commission from Elizabeth addressed to "Robert Gardiner, Sir Henry Wallop, Sir Valentine Brown, Sir Robert Dillon, Sir Luke Dillon, and Joshua Smith" ordered "that the province should be repeopled and inhabited with good and loyal subjects" and, to that end, Her Royal Highness "had set down a plot." Thousands of homeless kern and gallowglass wandered unchecked about Ireland, foraging for food, and causing at least one English poet to urge the Irish bards to use their traditional influence to "Call back the stiff-nec'd rebels from exile/And mollify the slaught'ring gallowglass." Unfortunately, that influence was ebbing; the bards were themselves out of work. The poets had lost their noble patrons to the carnage and were also wandering the roads. As Hoagland comments, the great Gaelic verse had begun to disappear from the halls of the Irish aristocracy and find "a loving, though lowly, home among the people." The seeds of bitterness brought to the thatched cabins by these newly itinerant poets were to have much to do with the blossoming of the rebel tradition in Ireland.

The Desmond Wars had been an enormous drain on the Crown, too. London, viewing the unruly Irish island as a vast sinkhole that had swallowed men, treasure, and reputations, determined that Ireland would have to pay for the loss. As Lord Justice Henry Wallop scrambled with the Earl of Ormonde and the new group of freebooters for the spoils, the traditional power of the southern and western Gaelic lords disappeared forever.

CHAPTER NOTES (5)

1 — Literally, "the ugly hag," a cant name for Elizabeth Tudor that was, and is, popular in Connacht.

2 — The situation in the West was complicated. As early as March 1579 the Queen had directed her lieutenant in the area, Sir Nicholas Maltby, to conquer Connacht. Elizabeth R made certain that her soldier would not overlook the treason-abetting religious fraternities:

> "Divers houses, freight with friers, remain in some parts of that province . . . cause them to abandon those places, and compell them to change their cotes, and live according to our laws."

In the margin of the orders was an addition directing Maltby to be sure he included the rebel O'Connor Sligo in his "conquering." Two weeks later, Elizabeth granted the "Manor, Lordship, and Friary of Roscommon" to Maltby, presumably to spur him on to greater efforts against the O'Connors.

Connemara was handled differently. Murrough of the Battle-axes (called by the Irish "Morogh *ne doe* O'Flahertie") was pretender to The O'Flaherty title. Elizabeth made him a baron in the blatant attempt to suborn Murrough from his rebellious kinsmen.

Another western chieftain, Grace O'Malley of Burrishoole, was to become legendary in later centuries as *Granuaile*, a corruption of her Gaelic name that became another nationalist metaphor for Ireland. In her own time she was no less legendary. Lord Deputy Sidney called her the "most famous sea-captain . . . the most notorious woman in all the coast of Ireland." As one might expect of such a buccanneer, O'Malley was actually interested in nothing but maintaining her freedom from *any* encroachment, Irish or English. To secure her borders she married Donnell "of the Wars" O'Flaherty, outlived him, and married into another powerful western family, the MacWilliam Burkes (divorcing her new husband a year later after she had garrisoned his castles with her own men).

3 — A measure of the Queen's fury with the raids by the wild Wicklow lord is the grant she had given the year before to Sir Henry Harrington. In granting the Englishman "O'Birne's countrie," she had included definite instructions as to how he was to proceed. Harrington was to:

> "prosecute, invade, chase, withstand, punish, correct, in body, lands, and goods, by fire and sword, and all other ways and means, all rebels and malefactors of her Majesty's crown and realm. . . ."

After having secured Ballinacor, Harrington was to insure that:

> "no idle person, vagabond, or masterless man, bard, rhymer, or any other notorious or detected malefactor, doe haunte, remayne, or abide within . . . the bounds of your authoritie. . . ."

4 — That Desmond's force had melted away did not mean that the rebels had accepted English hegemony. A letter from the corporation of Waterford to Secretary "Cecill" complained that "good subjects in the county" were forced to become rebels or else starve. The March 1583 missive also observed that Donnell MacCarthy More—no friend to Desmond—refused his new title of earl "and is offended with any one that calleth him 'Earl of Clancair'."

6

The Nine Years War

The carnage of the Desmond Years had proved disastrous to both the English and the Irish, but the wars themselves had not been decisive to the future of Anglo-Hibernian affairs. After some four centuries of English presence on the Irish island, the Crown had achieved dominance in Leinster, and a reasonably secure foothold in Munster and Connacht. Without Ulster, however, the Norman invasion of Ireland could never be completed; the conquest of the northern province was the *sine qua non* in the conquest of Ireland. Ulster—with its trackless forests and its unremitting mountains, with its ancient Gaelic sagas and its curious papist piety, with its fierce Celtic chieftains and its wild Scottish rebels—had never really been penetrated successfully by the English. It was in the final ten years of Elizabeth Tudor's reign that the battle for the North was to be fought.

The previous decade (1584-93) was punctuated with sporadic risings by provincial clans not yet completely persuaded of English dominance, mostly in Connacht.[1] In addition, Sorley Boye MacDonnell, understandably bitter over the Rathlin Island massacre, kept Sir John Norris busy putting down the persistant Antrim Scot's raids in the North. Lord Deputy William Fitzwilliam had decided on another strategy to keep the Queen's peace on the other side of Ulster. In 1587 he shrewdly kidnapped young Red Hugh O'Donnell—son of Black Hugh of TyrConnell—to serve as hostage against possible trouble by that unruly and isolated Donegal clan. In May of the same year, an England battening down the hatches in the face of Spanish Catholic fury (Mary of Scots had been executed barely three months earlier and Philip II was already gathering the forces that would become the Spanish Armada the next year) recognised the Baron of Dunagannon as second Earl of Tyrone.

Sir Hugh O'Neill seemed the logical choice to hold Ulster

for the Queen. After spending his teenage years learning the ways of an English lord, the young Dungannon had returned to Ireland with Sidney, and had served loyally against the Munster rebels. O'Neill had also set about establishing his bona fides among the Gaelic lords of the North. He had mended the Tyrone/TyrConnell rift caused by Shane the Proud by marrying Joanna, daughter to Black Hugh. Dungannon had meanwhile carefully sworn "Gaelic allegiance" to Turlough Luineach O'Neill as titular head of the clan,[2] an action that had served to soften Turlough's reaction to Hugh's growing power, though the sullen Turlough was finally satisfied only by defeating Dungannon in battle and receiving meaningless titles from the English ("Captain of Tyrone" in 1569, "Earl of Clanconnell" in 1578) to compensate for Sir Hugh's. Dungannon had even been able to establish sporadic cordial relations with the wild MacDonnells of the Route, a feat that suggests more than a little diplomatic skill. From London, it looked as if the new Earl of Tyrone would hold Ulster peacefully for the Crown. All the while, Hugh plotted to rid himself of Shane's sons, clearing the way for his election to the title he really wanted—The O'Neill.

The Crown began slowly to get hints as to the extent of Tyrone's loyalty in 1588 when he "surreptitiously" aided some shipwrecked refugees from the Spanish Armada. When Hugh *Gaveloch* O'Neill, one of Shane the Proud's three remaining sons, reported to Dublin Castle in 1589 that Tyrone was treating disloyally with Philip II, Lord Deputy Fitzwilliam—presumably considering the source—refused to believe it. When in 1591 the same "Fettered Hugh" reported that Tyrone was now in bed with Angus Oge MacDonnell of the Route, Tyrone trumped up an excuse to execute Shane O'Neill's son as a traitor to the Crown. Lord Fitzwilliam understandably was beginning to wonder who the real traitor was.

There was reason for Tyrone's intrigues. In that latter year the Crown had forced the submission of the MacKennas and MacMahons of Monaghan and "Newry," gifting the loyal Nicholas Bagenal with the confiscated lands. It was becoming clear to Tyrone that Dublin Castle was not going to be content with the ravaged lands of Munster, Connacht, and the Midlands— the Crown had designs on Ulster itself. Under the covert guidance of Hugh O'Neill, the ostensibly loyal province of the North prepared to resist (the recently widowed Tyrone "began the campaign" by eloping with Bagenal's daughter, an action

CHRONOLOGY (The Nine Years War)

1587 . . . . . .Hugh O'Neill named 2nd Earl of Tyrone; Mary of Scots executed; Red Hugh O'Donnell kidnapped; Raleigh founds Virginia Colony.

1588 . . . . . .Spanish Armada dispersed; abortive rising in Connacht.

1591 . . . . . .Monaghan confiscated by Crown; Maguires begin border raids.

1592 . . . . . .Red Hugh escapes, named The O'Donnell.

1593 . . . . . .Tyrone proclaimed The O'Neill; Henry IV of France becomes Catholic.

1594 . . . . . .Nine Years War begins at Enniskillen; Ford of the Biscuits; general insurrection in south Ulster and north Connacht.

1595 . . . . . .Monaghan Fort cut off by rebels; Tyrone openly joins rebellion at Battle of Clontibret.

1596 . . . . . .Tyrone demands "Home Rule;" *Súgán* Earl of Desmond begins sympathetic revolt in Munster.

1597 . . . . . .Ineffectual Crown campaign in Ulster; heavy weather turns back Spanish fleet; Tyrone pardoned.

1598 . . . . . .Battle of the Yellow Ford; general rebellion in Ireland; Edict of Nantes ends French religious wars; Philip III becomes King of Spain.

1599 . . . . . .Essex lands in Ireland; Pass of the Plumes; Battle of Ballinafanad; parley at Bellaclynthe; Essex returns to London.

1600 . . . . . .Mountjoy lands, wages "scorched-earth" campaign; Docwra takes Derry; East India Company chartered.

1601 . . . . . .Spanish landing in Cork, Battle of Kinsale; Essex rebellion and execution in London; Dutch East India Company formed.

1603 . . . . . .Tyrone submits; *James I;* Tyrone pardoned, Rory O'Donnell named Earl of Tyrconnell.

1604 . . . . . .England makes peace with Spain; James pardons Irish rebels.

1605 . . . . . .Gunpowder Plot fails in England; Chichester Plantation begins in eastern Ulster.

1607 . . . . . .Flight of the Earls.

that won him the bitter emnity of the rest of her family). When Hugh MacCuconnacht Maguire, the young lord of Fermanagh, began border raids against his new Bagenal neighbors to the east and his old Bingham enemies to the south, the Earl of Tyrone publicly condemned Maguire's "outrages" while lending the youthful chieftain clandestine support.

In January 1592 occured an event which rocked Ireland. The eighteen-year-old Red Hugh O'Donnell was freed from his Dublin cell in a daring escape engineered by the O'Hagans, liegemen of Tyrone. Hugh O'Neill had divined the temper of the North accurately; the wily earl was accounted a hero for his *sub rosa* part in the release of the heir to the aging Black Hugh O'Donnell. The ambititious Tyrone had accomplished, moreover, another less-publicised goal in the escape. The O'Hagans had freed two other prisoners during the adventure, the surviving sons of Shane the Proud. While Red Hugh made it safely to the Ballinacor Mountain retreat of the old rebel Fiach O'Byrne, one of Shane's sons conveniently perished enroute to Glenmalure. The other ended up Tyrone's captive for the next nine years.

Despite his youthful years with the Sidneys in Kent, Tyrone was sensitive to the ancient tradition of Celtic Ireland. He had listened well to the bards, correctly judging the impact on the impressionable O'Donnells when his escape plan set the stage for the culmination of an old Donegal ballad:

When two Hughs, the Black and the Red,

Lawfully and lineally follow each other as O'Donnell,

The latter shall be *Ard Rí*

And banish the Stranger.

Events went precisely as Tyrone had anticipated. Red Hugh gave the Gaelic world of the North what the cold, calculating Hugh O'Neill never could. Ó Faoláin suggests that young O'Donnell "represented Gaelic resistance at its most obstinate and inspiring" and "fired the imagination of the clansman as soldier." If Tyrone was a manipulative seneschal in the English style who would never forget that the theatre of the world was much larger than the Irish stage, Red Hugh offered "the image of a popular hero as rooted in [*the Gaelic*] traditional life as some flashing hero out of the sagas." In May 1592 at the Rock of Doon near Kilmacrennan, an ailing Black Hugh proclaimed his son The O'Donnell, reviving the ancient Celtic custom of investing his successor before his own death.[3] Red Hugh promptly joined Maguire in the raids on the Binghams in north Connacht.

As the embers of northern rebellion began to smoulder anew, the heat was felt as far away as London. After the relative peace that had existed since the death of Gerald Fitzgerald, even the Queen seemed surprised:

We are informed that there remain within our realm of Ireland, divers perverse and obstinate persons who refuse to acknowledge, confess, and set forth our superioritie, prerogative, and prehemi-nence within our realm. . . .

The sheer inaccessibility of Ulster gave the northerners a certain

immunity that the Crown was not anxious to challenge in arms.
In the 1590s, the North was still a thickly forested land with
forbidding mountain refuges familiar only to the hardy clans who
peopled the area. Strategically, Ulster was a geo-military castle
with three easily defended gates, all already closely guarded by
hostile Gaels:

1)   *The Moyry Pass* — also known as the "Gap of the North," it was the
vital cut between Dundalk and Newry. Sir John Perrot described it as a
"broken causey besette on both sydes with bogges, where the Irish might
skip but the English could not goe; and at the two ends it was naturally
fenced with short and scrubbed wood." Irish tradition holds that the narrow pass could have, and had, been held single-handedly . . . by the great
CúChulainn.

2)   *The Gap of the Erne* — at Enniskillen, the traditional seat of the
Maguires, it bestrode the River Erne between the Upper and Lower Loughs
Erne.

3)   *Ballyshannon* — O'Donnell stronghold sitting athwart Lough Melvin,
and so providing a defender swift access to either Sligo or Enniskillen with
a flank protected by water.

      If the geography of the North was forbidding and the
O'Donnell/Maguire raids were nettlesome, a dark rumour that
reached Dublin in June 1593 was downright alarming. Fitzwilliam was told that Hugh of Dungannon, Earl of Tyrone by
grace of Her Royal Majesty Elizabeth I, had been elected The
O'Neill. The tale told to the Lord Deputy was true. The previous month at Tullaghoge—seat of the O'Hagans, justiciaries of
TyrOwen—Hugh had been proclaimed O'Neill according to the
ancient Gaelic ceremony. Though not yet himself in arms
against the Crown, Tyrone's hand would henceforth be felt behind every northern sword raised against the English.

      The Nine Years War began in earnest in February 1594
when the English took Maguire's castle at Enniskillen. In June,
Red Hugh O'Donnell and Hugh Maguire descended on the Gap
of the Erne with Scot gallowglass, O'Donnell neutralising the
pernicious British garrison while Maguire's horse streamed onto
the plains to the south. Brian Oge O'Rourke seized the opportunity to rampage through Sir George Bingham's holdings around
Ballymote in Sligo, attempting to oust the English from the
ancient O'Rourke lands taken from Brian Oge's father five years
earlier for aiding refugees from the Armada. Sir William Russell,
the new Lord Deputy in Dublin, responded by sending 2,500
men under Sir Henry Duke to the relief of Enniskillen. Maguire

met Duke on the River Erne at a point somewhat south of the castle. The English left behind only strewn bodies and supplies: sufficient of the former to cause the remnants of Duke's army to flee into Sligo, enough of the latter to gain the place for evermore the name "Ford of the Biscuits." Though Enniskillen itself did not fall to the rebels until the end of the year, the Maguires, MacMahons, MacCooleys, O'Donnells, and even the MacWilliam Burkes of Connacht roamed boldly about southern Ulster and northern Leinster through the remainder of 1594, threatening to isolate the Bagenal outpost at Monaghan.

"The Irish wars," in the words of Ó Faoláin, "were wars of the frontier and the forest. The frontier was wherever a fort or castle stood as a spearhead into the wilderness. Everywhere else was forest." Such a frontier was the beleaguered garrison of Monaghan when in May 1595 Sir Henry Bagenal, the Crown "Marshal of Newry," relieved the fort with long overdue supplies. When the relieving column set off on its return trip to Newry, it was set upon by an Irish force at Clontibret, thrown into disorder, and made its base only with great difficulty. The thrashing of the English troops, while not conclusive by any means, gave the Crown great reason for concern. Not only did Robert Cecil get a private communication from Ireland that "there were more hurt men . . . than was conveniant to declare" publicly, but the new English Secretary of State learned that the Irish leader at Clontibret had not been some easily dismissed Gaelic sub-chieftain; rather, the Ulstermen had been personally led by Hugh of Dungannon, Earl of Tyrone. Now as The O'Neill, the greatest of Irish rebels had openly and defiantly taken the field against the Queen of England. After 425 years of preliminary skirmishing, the true Battle for Ireland had begun.

To butcher an old cliché, you can take the Gael out of Ireland, but you can't take Ireland out of the Gael . . . so it was with Hugh O'Neill. The careful English indoctrination of the young lord of Dungannon had succeeded only in presenting the Crown with an opponent who understood both the British and the Gaelic mind. Almost as soon as he had been reinstated in TyrOwen in 1569, O'Neill had quietly begun to make alliances with the mandarins of the North. For over two decades he had moved constantly throughout Ulster establishing personal rapport with his family henchmen and those septs he would need to rely on later to claim the title of O'Neill. These sojourns, made under the cover of "hunts," also had given O'Neill the opportunity to train his liegemen in the use of modern firearms. In addition, Hugh had quietly began organising footloose refugees from the Desmond Wars into disciplined columns of *bonnacht,* the Irish equivalent of the mercenary Scot gallowglass. By the time O'Neill finally revealed his true hand, in the words of Berleth, he "was never to be in the position of leading kern . . . against trained infantry. He would come out of the north in his day with regiments of regular troops, led by seasoned officers, and he would wheel them through the South with a skill Grey might have envied."

Although the romantic nationalist legend of the Arch Rebel suggests that he was the last of the true Gaelic chieftains, such a stereotype does not really fit such a calculating political leader. After becoming Earl of Tyrone, O'Neill had proscribed Brehon Law, tying the northern Irish to himself in the manner of a European feudal lord. On the other hand, this war-lord who quoted Spenser and surrounded himself with English secretaries had a politician's appreciation of the benefit to be gained by encouraging those Gaelic customs that did not threaten his personal power base. This was a man who saw himself as a renaissance lord prepared to drag a tired culture into the seventeenth century by the scuff of its neck.

O'NEILL'S WAR SONG

By the time Hugh O'Neill was ready to challenge the Crown, he was prepared to wage war in the name of Irish nation that looked to him as its own natural leader. His alliances with the Ulster chiefs were a product of his own political acumen. His growing, if secret, connections with the displaced Gaels of the South were born of his opportunistic recognition of their bitterness at being thrown off the land. His treatings with the kings of Europe followed from his comprehension that if a strong Irish lord could not lead the Irish Celts into the modern world, the Queen of England would.

The following mid-nineteenth century lay by Michael Hogan catches the glowing spirit in the North on the eve of the Nine Years War. Hogan, called the "Bard of Thomond," was a Limerick wheelwright who was one of the very few Irish poets able to live on the earnings from his ballads.

Fierce is the flame of the vengeance of Erin
When roused by the blast of the battle to shine;
Fierce is the flash of her broad sword uprearing
To strike for her rights and her altars divine.
Haste, snatch the spear and shield,
Rush to the battlefield,
The Saxon is come from the towers of the Pale;
Sons of the vale and glen,
Children of mighty men,
Swell the dread war-note of conquering O'Neill!

Lightly the Red Hand of terror is streaming,
Like a fire-cloud of death on the hills of Tyrone,
Brightly the spears of ClanConnell are gleaming,
Like Swilly's blue waves in the beams of the sun.
Hark, the wild battle-cry,
Rings through the sounding sky,
Valley and mountain are blazing with steel;
Eagles and forest deer
Flee from the heights with fear,
Scared at the war-shout of conquering O'Neill!

O'Donnell descends from his father's dark mountains,
He comes, noble prince, to the strife of the Gael;
He comes like the rush of his own stormy fountains,
Sweeping impetuous over moorland and dale.
On to the Yellow Ford
Chiefs of the flashing sword,
Drive the proud *Sassenach* back to the Pale!
Fierce to the scene of blood,
Wild as a mountain flood,
Charge the stout warriors of conquering O'Neill.

Our war-shouts shall ring and our musket peals rattle,
Our swords shall not rest from the hot, weary toil;
Our plains shall be drenched with the red showers of battle,
Till the Godless invaders are swept from our soil.
Pikeman and musketeer,
Kern and bold cavalier!
The wolves and the ravens are scenting their meal;
Carve to them, red and fresh,
Plenty of Saxon flesh,
Follow your princely chief—conquering O'Neill!

Onward O'Neill, with thy Red Hand of glory,
Thy sword lighteth thousands to conquests and fame;
The annals of Eire are emblazed with thy story,
Her valleys are filled with the praise of thy name.
On with the Bloody Hand!
Shake the dread battle-brand!
Woe to the spoilers of green Inisfail;
Lo! Their red ranks appear—
Up! Every gun and spear—
Charge, charge, O'Donnell and conquering O'Neill!

Cut off from reinforcement after the Battle of Clontibret, Monaghan Fort was overrun by the rebels in June 1595. Hugh Maguire and Brian MacHugh MacMahon were soon in virtual control of Cavan while Red Hugh stormed into Connacht to aid the rising of the heretofore "loyal" Ulick and Richard Burke. That the Crown was totally unprepared for the onslaught was made painfully clear when Ulick killed George Bingham and delivered Sligo to The O'Donnell. In answer, Lord Deputy Russell gathered an army and gallantly, if rashly, plunged into the wilderness of Ulster looking for Tyrone himself. The O'Neill simply withdrew into the trackless forests and let the Deputy thrash about ineffectually until Russell finally got tired of the business and grumpily returned to Dublin. By fighting the Battle of Clontibret, Tyrone had cost the English almost half of Ireland. By refusing to fight Russell, he had proved to the English who was in real control of the land they had lost.

Dublin Castle was forced to consider seriously a startling missive that Tyrone presented in January 1596. As the Arch Rebel's fortunes soared over the next three years, he would continue to expand upon the remarkable document until it began to resemble the Home Rule demands made by Irishmen centuries afterwards. The O'Neill made nine major "requests" of London:

    1) Free liberty of "religious conscience."
    2) The return of confiscated Catholic property to the dispossessed churchmen.
    3) A Catholic university to be funded by Crown rents.
    4) A requirement that all political officials on the island would henceforth be Irishmen.
    5) The repeal of all laws that discriminated against Irishmen.
    6) Elimination of military conscription in Ireland.

7) The Earls of Tyrone and Desmond, and the O'Donnell, to be returned to their ancient lands, rights, and prerogatives.

8) Irishmen to have free right of trade and travel on a par with
Englishmen.

9) The Irish to have free right to build a navy.

If Irish nationalism had preceded Tyrone, it had done so without a coherent philosophy. Now, for the first time, a coalescing
group of Irish chieftains were beginning to look to a European-
style lord who was speaking for something more than a tribal Ireland. Here was an Irishman presenting the mighty Queen of
England a set of non-negotiable demands defining precisely what
they were fighting for. Here, in short, was a clear demand for a
modern Irish nation.

Elizabeth Tudor's reaction was to foreshadow that of a long
line of English monarchs after her: she was genuinely astonished
at the effrontery of Irish pretensions to self-determination. Even
the King of Spain misunderstood Tyrone, assuming that The
O'Neill was just another prideful Irish war-lord. The aging Philip
II, on the other hand, was still smarting from the defeat of the
Armada in 1588, and was happy to find another useful pawn in
his quarrel with the heretic British.

Tyrone could not have been unaware of the probable
English reaction to his demands. It is likely, in any event, that
they had been made primarily for domestic propoganda purposes. A case in point is perhaps the most subtle demand: the
call for the "restoration" of the Desmond lands of Munster to
James FitzThomas Fitzgerald, second cousin to Gerald, the slain
Pale Earl of Desmond. Called the *Súgán*, or "Hayrope," Earl of
Desmond (for Tyrone's creation of his claim as a "straw man"),
James FitzThomas had been elevated to a theoretical position
alongside O'Neill at the instigation of the far-seeing Tyrone in
the attempt to create a southern rallying-point for what was
threatening to become a unified Irish rebellion. The displaced
McSheehys and MacSwineys rallied at once to the Desmond
pretender. The irrepressible O'Byrnes of Wicklow, of course,
needed little prodding to join any rebel cause, no more did the
O'Connors of Kings County.

As the clans of Ireland began declaring for O'Neill, O'Donnell, and the *Súgán* Earl, the English leadership in Ireland once
again felt the reins of power slipping from their hands. Sir Henry
Wallop wrote to Cecil during February 1596, warning that:

The state of the realm was never so dangerous in the memory of man as it is at the present, in regard to the uniting of O'Donnell, and all the chieftains . . . with Tyrone . . . stretching itself unto all parts of this Kingdom . . . furnished with all the habilments of war. . . . They seem to be other enemies, and not those that in times past, were wont to attempt Her Majesty's forces in the plain field.

This, the Lord Treasurer seemed to be cautioning, was an opponent worth respecting—not only were the Irish uniting, but the forces they were marshalling looked to be ominously disciplined, perhaps capable of challenging the troops of the Queen in open battle in the European fashion. The next four years were to prove Sir Henry a savant.

In the spring of 1597, Dublin launched a huge offensive into Ulster. The major portion of the seven thousand men were commanded by Lord Burgh—still another Lord Deputy—as he struck through the Moyry Pass; the balance, under Sir Conyers Clifford, moved on the O'Donnells through Ballyshannon. The campaign was a disaster. Among the thousands of Crown casualties was Sir John Chichester, killed at the Old Mill Glen near Ballycarry by the MacDonnells, a clan now firmly on Tyrone's side. When Burgh's battered troops staggered back into the Pale, they had regained only one outpost: Portmore, two miles north of Armagh on the River Blackwater. For all the British dead, about all that was accomplished was to prevent Tyrone from moving through the Gap of the North to join the restless henchmen of the *Súgán* Earl of Desmond who were assembling in their thousands at the Glen of Aherlow. Even that slight attainment looked pointless: Maguire and O'Rourke had run Clifford out of Ballyshannon, and Red Hugh himself seemed poised to move south to aid a rising by Theobald MacWilliam Burke against Richard Bingham in Connacht. One Crown probe under Lord Trimleston made it only as far as the Meath/Westmeath border when it was destroyed by a band of Ulster rebels who had shadowed Burgh's retreat to the Pale (the site of the ambush would become known ever after as Tyrellspass in honour of the victorious rebel commander). Two Spanish fleets were making up for Ireland; one under Padilla had actually sailed, and was prevented from reaching the island only by a fierce autumn storm.

The situation was deteriorating so rapidly that the uneasy Queen of England was induced to sign a 14 September 1597 pardon of:

> Hugh, Earl of Tyrone, his children, brothers, known cousins, followers, tenants, and servants, residing within the county of Tyrone . . . and all other persons residing in the county of Tyrone.

The royal patent fooled no one. Both sides made the most of the truce to prepare for the inevitable resumption of hostilities. After Lord Burgh died in October—apparently of poison—a petulant Elizabeth immediately wrote her cousin Black Tom Butler, Earl of Ormonde and Ossory, complaining she had no one else in Ireland she could trust, and would he accept the commission of "Lieutenant-General and Captain of all our forces" in Ireland? As the Queen searched for an able commander, Tyrone settled in to starve out the isolated Crown garrison at Portmore, meanwhile doing his best to cool the blood of Maguire and O'Donnell as he negotiated with the dying Philip II for Spanish aid.

Ormonde, naturally more concerned with the *Súgán* Earl's threat to his own Butler lands in the South than he was with the exposed outpost on the Blackwater, put Sir Henry Bagenal in command of the column designated to relieve Portmore when the fighting resumed in 1598. Troops arrived all spring and summer from England, and when Henry "of the Battle-axes" was ready to march north in late July, he led 4,200 foot and 320 horse. The O'Neill had already sent out the call for a hosting of the clans.

O'DONNELL ABOO

(*The ClannConnell War Song*)

In response to Tyrone's call, the rallying-cry "*O'Donnell Aboo!*" rang throughout TyrConnell. From Ballyshannon to Malin Head, O'Cahans, MacSweeneys, and O'Doughertys dropped what they were doing to join the O'Donnells of Red Hugh. Similar war-shouts echoed throughout the North of Ireland. Martial MacMahons and O'Hanlons hoisted their banners in the name of Hugh Maguire. Antrim Scots who had helped throw back the English the previous year rallied again under Angus Oge MacDonnell. Bagenal's cautious approach into hostile Ulster gave even Brian Oge O'Rourke and Theobald MacWilliam Burke sufficient time to march to the hosting from Connacht. In an astonishingly short period, The O'Neill was able to boast of over five thousand men, six hundred of them cavalry. For the first time in over four centuries, the Crown forces were not to be faced by a maddenly entangled alliance of Gaelic tribes working at cross-purposes. This was a disciplined army of terrifying strength led by a single commander of extraordinary ability.

Tyrone chose the site of the coming battle. Leaving a skeleton force to maintain the pressure on Portmore, O'Neill positioned his army a couple miles south. He would intercept Bagenal's column as the redcoats crossed the little River Callan just north of Armagh. The English troops would have to cross the river at *Béal an Átha Buidhe,* so called from the colour of the banks and river bottom. It was to be known forever after as the Yellow Ford.

This rousing nineteenth century balled by Michael Joseph McCann gives us some idea of the excitement that ran through the northern clans on the eve of the battle. McCann taught at St. Jarleth's College at Tuam, County Mayo, before moving on to London to work as a journalist. The poetic similarity of this battle-march to *O'Neill's War Song* is striking.

Proudly the notes of the trumpet are sounding,
Loudly the war cries arise on the gale;
Fleetly the steed of Lough Swilly is bounding
To join the thick squadrons in Saimer's green vale;
On every mountaineer,
Strangers to flight and fear,
Rush to the standard of dauntless Red Hugh!
Bonnacht and gallowglass
Throng from each mountain pass,
On for old Erin, O'Donnell Aboo!

Princely O'Neill to our aid is advancing
With many a chieftain and warrior clan;
A thousand proud steeds in his vanguard are prancing
Neath borderers brave from the banks of the Bann;
Many a heart shall quail
Under its coat of mail,
Deeply the merciless foeman shall rue,
When on his ear shall ring,
Borne on the breeze's wing,
TyrConnell's dread war cry: O'Donnell Aboo!

Wildly o'er Desmond the war-wolf is howling,
Fearless the eagle sweeps over the plain;
The fox in the streets of the city is prowling,
All who would scare them are banished or slain.
Grasp, every stalwart hand,
Hackbut and battle-brand,
Pay them all back the deep debt so long due;
Norris and Clifford well
Can of TyrConnell tell,
Onward to glory, O'Donnell Aboo!

Sacred the cause that ClannConnell's defending:
The altars we kneel at, the homes of our sires.
Ruthless the ruin the foe is extending,
Midnight is red with the plunderer's fires.
On with O'Donnell then,
Fight the good fight again,
Sons of TryConnell, all valiant and true;
Make the false Saxon feel
Erin's avenging steel!
Strike for your country, O'Donnell Aboo!

The Battle of the Yellow Ford was joined on 14 August 1598. Tyrone caught Bagenal in line-of-march with perhaps half his column across the Callan. As O'Neill struck at the English van, Red Hugh O'Donnell fell on the rear. One analysis of the result—"the greatest victory ever won by Irish arms over English"—is scarcely Celtic hyperbole. The rebels suffered five hundred casualties; the English, three thousand, including their commander. It was the most complete rout of a British colonial army by native troops until the Zulu Wars of the late nineteenth century.

The news of the Irish victory in the North electrified the rest of the island, encouraging fence-straddlers to outright insurrection. The Irish nation had met the English in open battle in the continental fashion and won. The few Munster lords who had been standing by the Crown found their henchmen deserting *en masse* to The O'Neill's man in the South, the *Súgán* Earl of Desmond. For the first time since the era of Brian and Malachy, the Irish had a war-lord whose precedence was acknowledged by the other chieftains of Ireland. Perhaps most menacing of all to

English fortunes on the island was that Tyrone's victory at the Yellow Ford had excited the admiration and respect of the Catholic monarchs of Europe. The O'Neill's envoys were accorded the official courtesies due accredited ambassadors. Even James VI of Scots was said to be treating secretly with the new "Prince of Ireland." It was to cost London many men and much treasure to repair the damage done that August day.

In the South, the Earl of Ormonde found scant succour in the thought that it had been Bagenal instead of himself that had marched north to death; Black Tom was hard-pressed by the burgeoning forces of the *Súgán* Earl around Kilkenny. Lord President Thomas Norris of Munster, meanwhile, was barely hanging on at Mallow, sorely pressed by young Eoiny O'More— son of the rebel Rory Oge—who had swept south from Kings County. In Dublin, the English leaders quarreled over the blame, finally settling on Richard Bingham who was out in Connacht killing Burkes, and so unable to defend himself. Sir Conyers Clifford was named the new Crown Commissioner in the West. Tyrone, recognising that he had the squabbling English on the run, sent half his army south to aid the *Súgán* Earl. The northerners under Captain Tyrell joined Desmond, and the combined force swept westward through Munster, enabling the *Súgán* Earl to set up shop in the ancient Geraldine Castle at Askeaton. For all practical purposes, Ireland had been lost to the Irish . . . with the notable, and ultimately crucial, exception of the walled towns.

Elizabeth Tudor was perplexed, and not a little angry, at the turn of events across the Irish Sea. In March 1599 the Queen dispatched Robert Devereux, second Earl of Essex (son of the perpetrator of the Rathlin Island massacre) to Dublin as her new Lord Lieutenant. With him came the largest army ever to fly the red cross of St. George in Ireland, sixteen thousand men. The sovereign considered her intentions honourable:

> Our gracious intention hath not wrought in all men's minds a like effect, nor brought forth everywhere that fruit of obedience which we expected. [*Therefore*] we have been compelled to . . . reduce that kingdom to obedience by using an extraordinary power and force against them.

In more prosaic terms, since the quarrelsome Irish did not appreciate her "peaceful" attempts at plantation, Elizabeth of England was now prepared to nail the rebels to the wall. Unfortunately, she had chosen the wrong hammer.

Devereux was unwilling to march towards the sinews of Tyrone's strength in Ulster to "cut the root of the rebellion." Rather, he decided to first "shake and sway the branches" by challenging Eoiny MacRory O'More in recently liberated Queens County. Even young O'More turned out to be a match for Essex, however. The rebel chieftain's swaying branches swept so many plumed helmets from the heads of the English troops on one battlefield northeast of Abbeyleix, that the site became known after as the Pass of the Plumes. The 17 May fight was but one of many hit-and-run attacks on Devereux's flank and rearguard, none of which were decisive in itself but, put together, constituted a crushing strategic defeat for the British. Frustrated by O'More's guerrilla tactics, Essex retreated to Dublin. The discouraged English army had suffered frightful attrition and accomplished nothing. Now it began to desert. Within five months of his arrival in Ireland, Essex was to lose half his original force.[4]

The Queen was losing patience with her erstwhile favourite. The situation in Ireland was becoming embarrassing. Repeated orders issued from London, urging Essex in the strongest possible terms to march north and take on Tyrone directly. Devereux equivocated; having been treated himself to an unpleasant measure of Irish reality by O'More, the Lord Lieutenant received another jolt of it in mid-August via dispatch from the West. Sir Conyers Clifford's ill-advised campaign to halt Red Hugh O'Donnell's advance into Connacht had ended disastrously in the Curlew Hills of Sligo. The O'Donnell and Brian Oge O'Rourke had crushed Clifford's army so thoroughly at the 5 August Battle of Ballinafanad that the fleeing English had left the new Commissioner of Connacht's body behind on the field . . . along with hundreds of others. If O'More, O'Donnell, and O'Rourke were but lieutenants to The O'Neill, what, Essex must have been wondering, would it be like to face the great Earl of Tyrone himself?

Screwing up his courage, a feat presumably helped immeasurably by a stream of scathing missives from London, Devereux grudgingly inched toward Ulster in late August 1599. He did not get far. Essex found the dreaded O'Neill astride his path on the north bank of the River Glyde, near Ardee. The nervous Lord Lieutenant, uncomfortably aware that every previous attempt to storm into the North had ended in disaster, was not eager to try dislodging the well-positioned Tyrone. Even if the steadily dwindling Crown army *could* move the rebels, they would merely fall back on the deadly Gap of the North. In short, Essex was convinced that the Ulstermen were in perfect defensive array.

The two earls met in private parlay at the Glyde ford of Bellaclynthe (now known as the Ford of Aclint). It is not known what passed between the leaders, but it is at least certain that Tyrone did not speak from a position of weakness. The O'Neill well understood the words of Blind Teige O'Higgins, *file* to Brian O'Rourke: "To the warlike peace . . . none hath peace save men in armour." Whatever may have been discussed at Bellaclynthe, the result of the meeting was startling indeed to London. The Earl of Essex ordered the British camp struck and retired from the Glyde with his entire army. Predictably, the Pale English cried foul, accusing Devereux of plotting against the Crown. The charges flew fast and fanciful: Essex and Tyrone were linked with James Stuart, Pope Clement, the new Philip of Spain, and numerous others in an ill-defined conspiracy to deliver Ireland to the papists. Though Essex did plot against the Crown afterwards—he was beheaded in 1601—it is likely that, in this case, Tyrone had merely explained the tactical realities of the military situation at the Glyde to an already convinced audience. In the event yet another distinguished English reputation fell to Irish rebellion.

The discredited Devereux left for London after only six months in Ireland. Subsequent to his September departure, the war went on in a series of unco-ordinated and bloody skirmishes. The British held the coastal towns—by now overcrowded with refugees—the Irish the rest of the island. The O'Neill, always the consummate "Gaelic politician," made a winter Grand Tour of Ireland, accepting the 1600 political equivalent of the cattle tribute received by Brian Boru six centuries earlier. The shrewd Tyrone realised that the gesture would do more than fire the Gaelic folk-memories of the Irish; it would also demonstrate that he could boldly move about the island without fear of the redcoats. It was in fact extremely perilous for the Crown forces to move inland at all during the first half of 1600: Black Tom Butler was captured by the Geraldine rebels in Kerry, and Ormonde's chief lieutenant was taken by Eoiny O'More on Butler's own lands in Kilkenny. The only English success occurred in May when 3,500 men under Sir Henry Docwra landed in Tyrone's rear at Culmore and took an obscure monastic village on the River Foyle. Its name was Derry.

London was watching Tyrone's seemingly unending triumphs with more than a little trepidation. The Privy Council had been tossing the unpleasant reality of Ireland about so much that the facts themselves became transformed in the process. Demonstrating the collective fatuity for which it was deservedly famous, the Council somehow came to the conclusion that it could undermine the credibility of the *Súgán* Earl of Desmond by "officially" naming the imprisoned son of the Pale Earl as the "Fifteenth Earl." James FitzGerald Fitzgerald was consequently released from his English cell and sent to Ireland. The rebel Geraldines were not impressed. The Privy Council had forgotten once again that Gaelic law did not necessarily promote the first-born son. The ignored "pretender" was back in London by early 1601 and died the same year.

If her advisers were rope-dancers, Elizabeth Tudor was herself made of very stern material indeed. By the middle of 1600, she had finally found a Lord Deputy for Ireland to match her own mettle. Charles Blount, Lord Mountjoy, proved to be efficient, inflexible, and calculating—a worthy opponent for the hard-bitten O'Neill. Tyrone's biographer describes the Queen's new man in Dublin with admirable irony:

> Mountjoy was the one thing that the Irish nature dislikes intensely in an enemy and admires intensely in a leader—a calm patient man, slow to promise, firm in his word, not without evasion, relentless in his pursuit of any object, and most obstinate.

Blount, correctly surmising that O'Neill's men were living off the land while in arms, coldly burned the crops and slowly but inevitably forced the Ulstermen back into their northern wilderness—killing Eoiny O'More and Tyrone's nephew Brian MacArt O'Neill in the process. It was the policy of the Desmond Wars all over again. Lecky quotes a contemporary:

> Lord Mountjoy never received any to mercy but such as had drawn the blood of some of their fellow rebels. . . . McMahon and McArtmoyle offered to submit, but neither could be received without the word of the other's head.

In was a savagely effective policy. Shane O'Neill's son Arthur—held captive by Tyrone these nine years—escaped, rallying The O'Dougherty and Niall Garv O'Donnell against his former captor. Niall Garv was himself a prize recruit for the English. Chief rival to Red Hugh, he cared little for Tyrone's national vision of Ireland; the one passion of his life was becoming The O'Donnell. Niall Garv brought his henchmen to the Queen's cause, and delivered both Lifford and Donegal town to Docwra, thus solidifying the Crown bridgehead in Tyrone's rear. The ambitious O'Donnell pretender might have tempered his enthusiasm somewhat had he been privy to a letter that Mountjoy had sent to Cecil in July 1600:

> There be some few of these rebels of the most stirring sort that would make good rods to scourage these traitors and after be thrown into the fire themselves.

Nor were Mountjoy and Docwra the only ones launching attacks at the Earl of Tyrone. In eastern Ulster, Sir Arthur Chichester, Crown Governor of Carrickfergus, had taken advantage of O'Neill's other preoccupations to extend his own influence westward, going so far as to raid Tyrone's Dungannon lands via a "fleet" Chichester had built on Lough Neagh for the purpose. The O'Neill fought back desultorily as the net closed, patiently awaiting the long-overdue Spanish expedition to Ulster. Mountjoy, in no hurry himself, was meanwhile pouring troops into Munster, significantly relieving the pressure on the new Lord President of that province, Sir George Carew. The extra redcoats enabled Carew to turn the tide in the South, too. The *Súgán* Earl in time was forced literally to earth, hiding in the Mitcheltown Caves of north Cork with a price on his head.

The Spanish finally arrived in September 1601. Young Philip III's commitment turned out to be something less than Tyrone had been led to expect. The commander, Don Juan del Aguila, landed only 3,500 troops. Worse yet, the Spaniard had come ashore at the other end of Ireland from the Ulsterman, perhaps at the urging of the *Súgán* Earl who had his own envoys in the Spanish court. Kinsale, the landing site, was scant miles south of Carew's stronghold at Cork; it was 250 miles away from Tyrone's northern forces. Mountjoy and Carew promptly bottled up the invaders on the coast. O'Neill countered by making threatening moves towards Dublin; Mountjoy refused to rise to the bait. The warrior-chiefs of the North, seeing no help for it, gathered their troops and marched south. After years of unsuccessful attempts by the British to root them out of their trackless northern fortress, the lords of Ulster had been flushed from their stronghold by their own ally.

The march of the northern chiefs has itself become an important part of the Irish folk tradition. The Crown forces, of course, did everything possible to prevent the linkup. The trek to Kinsale was a remarkable saga of close escapes and extraordinary forced marches over impossible terrain—particularly the legendary journey over the frozen Slievefelim of Tipperary, called by Sir George Carew "the greatest march that had ever been heard of." Back home in Fermanagh, Eochy O'Hussey, *file* to the Maguires, wrote a classic Gaelic poem, imagining the hardships his young lord was undergoing on the march south through the early winter snows:

> Where is my Chief, my Master, this bleak night, *mavrone*!
> O, cold, cold, miserably cold is this bleak night for Hugh:
> It's showery, arrowry, speary sleet pierceth one through and
>   through,
> Pierceth one to the very bone!

The poet's fear for his chieftain "abroad in a strange land" was justified.[5]

The decisive fight in the three-month battle at Kinsale took place on Christmas Eve 1601. The Spaniards had fought gallantly while awaiting the Ulstermen, taking many more redcoat lives than Mountjoy and Carew could afford to lose. Now Tyrone had reached the killing ground. All of Ireland hung in the balance. Eighty leagues from their mountain fastnesses, the northerners no longer had the luxury of choosing the field, nor of fighting a defensive battle. Perhaps most vital of all, it was not a Henry Bagenal or a Conyers Clifford leading the English troops. Gaelic Ireland battered itself senseless that day against Lord Mountjoy's carefully considered counterattack.

CEAN-SALLA

The legend of Kinsale suggests that young O'Donnell counselled a reluctant O'Neill to attempt the frontal charge on the Crown at Kinsale. The story goes that the impetuous Red Hugh finally wore down Tyrone until the assault was ordered. In truth, Tyrone had no option but to attack. He was an island away from home in the dead of winter with an army that had just completed an astonishing forced march through some of the most rugged terrain in Ireland. His men faced the boreal blasts of Advent without shelter or supplies. Accustomed to living off the land when on the march, they found themselves stationary in an area already stripped clean by foragers from the three-month siege. Though the "Protestant Wind" stubbornly refused to blow, causing even the English besiegers severe shortages, the Spanish and Irish were near starvation.

   This ballad by James Clarence Mangan, sung from the point of view of a Red Hugh O'Donnell sailing to ask still more help from Philip III, perpetuates the myth that the Battle of Kinsale was a narrow thing turning on a few fleeing Irish "traitors" (actually Mountjoy and Carew destroyed the inept dawn assault piecemeal; the Irish rout was general). Considered by many to have had the greatest talent for translating Gaelic poetry into English verse without the loss of poetic imagery, Mangan has had a lasting impact on the National Tradition of Ireland. Curiously Kathleen Hoagland reveals that "while many of his lyrical versions . . . are true and exquisite," the nineteenth century poet actually "knew little Irish" and relied on the literal translations of John O'Donovan and Eugene O'Curry.

Weep not the brave dead!
Weep rather the living:
On them lies the curse
Of a doom unforgiving!
Each dark hour that rolls,
Shall the memories they nurse,
Like molten hot lead,
Burn into their souls
A remorse long and sore!
They have helped to enthral a
Great land evermore,
They who fled from Cean-Salla!

Alas for thee, slayer
Of the kings of the Norsemen!
Thou land of sharp swords
And strong kern and swift horsemen,
Land ringing with song!
Land whose abbots and lords,
Those heroic and fair,
Through centuries long,
Made each palace of thine
A new western Valhalla—
Thus to die without sign
On the field of Cean-Salla.

My ship cleaves the wave—
I depart for Iberia—
But oh, with what grief,
With how heavy and dreary a
Sensation of ill.
I could welcome a grave;
My career has been brief,
But I bow to God's will.
Not if now all forlorn,
In my green years I fall, a
Lone exile, I mourn—
But I mourn for Cean-Salla.

The plight of the Irish rebel leaders was desperate after the debacle at Kinsale. The *Súgán* Earl of Desmond had been unearthed in early 1601 and was in the Tower of London. Hugh Maguire had been slain in combat a year before. D'Aguila, after some haggling, now surrendered the Spanish expeditionary force. In the North, Docwra, Chichester, and Niall Garv O'Donnell had swept into the lands of the rebel chiefs in the absence of The O'Neill and The O'Donnell. The only hope left for the rebels was additional foreign intervention. Red Hugh, therefore, passed the title of O'Donnell on to his brother Rory, and took ship for Spain. He was followed by James Blake, an English agent with a case of deadly poisons. The Donegal chieftain died mysteriously at Salamanca in the summer of 1602.

Hugh O'Neill hacked his way back to the North to find the British holding Dungannon. Rory O'Donnell found his new Gaelic title meaningless—Niall Garv was also calling himself The O'Donnell . . . and held the Rock of Doon. The once great lords of Ulster were reduced to making guerrilla raids on their former holdings, staying barely ahead of pursuing Crown forces. The game was up. Finally convinced that no aid was coming from the continent, Sir Hugh of Dungannon, second Earl of Tyrone, The O'Neill of Ireland, resignedly marched to the River Boyne where he submitted to Lord Mountjoy on 30 March 1603. Unbeknownst to the rebel O'Neill, his bitterest enemy, Elizabeth of England, had died six days before he presented his sword to Mountjoy at Mellifont Abbey.[6]

GLENSWILLY

After the submission of Tyrone, the Gaelic lords of Ulster found themselves in an increasingly untenable position. Understandably distrusted for their martial past, they also found themselves the target of whispered accusations by land-hungry opportunists. Every instance of native opposition to Crown policy was laid at the feet of the once-powerful rebel chieftains. In fear of their lives, the Earl of Tyrone and Rory O'Donnell, now Earl of Tyrconnell, gave up the ghost. Along with O'Neill's three sons, his nephews Art Oge and Owen Roe, and ninety others, the harried Gaelic lords took ship from Rathmullen in Lough Swilly during 1607. The famous "Flight of the Earls" to the continent marked the effective end of Gaelic clan rule in Ireland.

The war-lords of Ulster had begun a diaspora of the Irish that was see many tearful farewells over the next three-and-a-half centuries. This ballad could have been written about any of them.

Attention pay, my countrymen,
And hear my native muse,
Although my song is sorrowful,
I hope you'll me excuse;
I left my native country
A foreign land to see,
I've bade farewell to Donegal,
Likewise to Glenswilly.

Brave stalwart men around me stood,
My comrades kind and true,
And as I grasped each well known hand
To bid a last *adieu*,
I said, "My gallant countryman,
I hope we'll yet be free
To see the 'Sunburst' proudly wave
O'er the hills of Glenswilly."

No more among the sycamore
I'll hear the blackbirds sing,
No more I'll hear the blithe cuckoo
Who welcomes back the spring,

No more I'll plough your fertile fields,
A chuisle geal mo chroidhe,
On a foreign soil I'm doomed to toil,
Far away from Glenswilly.

May peace and plenty reign supreme
Around Lough Swilly's shore,
May discord never enter those
Old homesteads any more;
And may the time soon come around
When I return to thee,
To live where my forefathers did
In dear old Glenswilly.

God bless you, dark old Donegal,
My own, my native land—
In dreams I'll see your heather glens
And towering mountains grand;
God bless the day, twill yet come round,
When I'll return to thee,
And live as my forefathers lived,
And die in Glenswilly.

The last rebel chieftain left in the North, Cahir O'Dougherty of Inishowen, burned the then-English garrison town of Derry in 1608. It was the last gasp of an ancient tradition. When O'Dougherty was killed two months later, Gaelic Ireland can be said to have died with him.

Most of the Elizabethan Gaels who had risen with the Fitzgeralds, O'Neills, and O'Donnells could not speak English; a century afterwards, perhaps only half of those who were to fight with James II and Patrick Sarsfield would speak Irish as their primary language; a hundred more years into the future, very few who would battle alongside Father John Murphy and Henry Joy MacCracken would be able to speak any Irish at all. As the Irish language disappeared, however, the folk-memories would not. Whether learned as *Aodh Uí Néill* or *Hugh O'Neill*, the name of the rebel Earl of Tyrone would achieve a stature in the Irish folk consciousness rivalled only by the already legendary CúChulainn.

CHAPTER NOTES (6)

1 — Galway, Clare, and Mayo became separate counties in 1585 after Sir Richard Bingham forced the most powerful of the rebel clan chiefs in Connacht to submit. Murrough O'Flaherty's surrender caused the O'Malleys, Burkes, and O'Dowds to follow suit.

Donnell Crone O'Flaherty, rightful heir to the O'Flaherty title, stubbornly refused to submit to the Crown for some years afterwards. When continual pressure by Bingham finally brought Donnell to his knees, the duplicitous *Sir* Murrogh "of the Battle-axes" proclaimed himself The O'Flaherty in 1589, rising against the Queen in his own right.

2 — Though the English government had abolished the title O'Neill when Conn the Lame had been named first Earl of Tyrone, Elizabeth had effectively restored its validity when Shane made his famous visit to London in the winter of 1561-62. When Shane's lands were attainted in 1569, the Crown not only "re-abolished" the old title, but made it a crime to use it in conversation.

3 — Under Brehon Law, a king was elected from among the inter-related "royal" families of a *tuath*. To prevent bloody squabbles upon the chieftain's death, a *tánaist*, or heir-apparent, was usually proclaimed while the king was still alive. To prevent a "palace coup" at the time of his death, an old or dying chieftain would occasionally step down in favour of the *tánaist* before his own demise—particularly if the heir was his own son.

The O'Donnell succession had been contested in arms for some years. If Shane O'Neill's passion in life was killing O'Donnells, an objective observer might well be tempted to suggest that Shane's passion seemed to be shared by the O'Donnells themselves. Red Hugh's accession at the Rock of Doon was bitterly resented by a powerful section of the clan led by Niall Garv O'Donnell. If the youthful Red Hugh's coronation had not been done in Black Hugh's lifetime, it is possible that it would not have been accomplished at all.

4 — Devereux was not the first English soldier to have this problem, nor would he be the last. Richard Berleth makes the point well:

> "The Crown had never sent a force to Ireland which was not eventually reduced 50 percent or more by desertion, defection, and an erosion of patriotism. So poorly fed and maintained were the Queen's soldiers in Ireland that they frequently sold their arms to the Irish for food and vanished into the local population for protection."

Until the time of Hugh O'Neill, the armies of the Irish had been little different from the English. Tyrone was the first Irish military officer able to command personal allegiance from other than members of his own clan.

5 — O'Hussey was writing here of Conn Oge Maguire. Brother to the dashing Hugh MacCoconnacht (who had begun the war nine years earlier), young Conn Oge had become Lord of Fermanagh when Hugh had been slain in an early 1600 skirmish.

6 — After word of Red Hugh's death in Spain had arrived in Ulster during October 1602, Rory O'Donnell had given up the fight. His submission had been accepted by the Queen. When Hugh O'Neill tried to submit in December, Lord Mountjoy refused the request, presumably under royal order.

Amidst the hundreds of rebel names listed as pardoned in the *Patent and Close Rolls of Chancery* is the following simple entry:

> "Pardon of Rory O'Donnell, of Tireconnell, in the province of Ulster; Caffara O'Donnell . . . Teige Oge O'Boy, alias O'Boile; Edward boy O'Boile, Brien O'Morrin, Connor O'Morrin, Gillechrist M'Morierty, and many others, followers of Rory O'Connell."

The date of the patent—26 February 1603—is less than four weeks before the death of Queen of England. It was one of the last documents dealing with Ireland that bore the "Elizabeth R" signature.

The rebel tradition is that Mountjoy kept the news of the Queen's death from Tyrone to induce the Arch Rebel's surrender. The truth is that it was only when the Lord Deputy was certain the sovereign was dying did he dare accept Hugh O'Neill's submission.

7

Plantation

When James Stuart was crowned James I of England in 1603, the Irish, remembering his romantic Catholic mother, hoped for more sympathetic treatment under the new sovereign than they had received under the Virgin Queen. They had mis-judged the Scot. He had been taken from Mary as a bairn and been raised a good Protestant. If he had any lingering sympathies with his papist heritage, they were well hidden from a cabal of English Catholic conspirators who were intriguing against the Crown in 1605. The virulent outbreak of British anti-Romanism that followed the discovery of the Gunpowder Plot did nothing to encourage James to pursue a policy of leniency toward the papists of either England *or* Ireland.

The Britain of Elizabeth I had been anti-Rome but had never been seriously troubled about dealing with Irish Catholic leaders if they could aid the Crown. Under the son of Mary of Scots, England became hysterically anti-Catholic. In the interim between the 1607 Flight of the Earls and the Great Rebellion of 1641, the Irish reacted by beginning to equate their papist pas-sion with an enthusiastic hatred of their new English masters. Trevelyan observes that:

> In such circumstances the Irish tribes finally became welded into the submerged Irish nation. The union of hatred against England, and the union of religious observance and enthusiasm be-came strong enough to break down at last the clan divisions of dateless antiquity, which the English also were busy destroying from outside. The abolition of the native upper class . . . left this peasant nation with no leaders but the priests and no sympathizers but the enemies of England.

There was substantial reason for this "union of hatred." The Stuart government was not content to discriminate spiritually against the papists; the authorities this time made the discrimination very much a temporal matter. The Irish were kicked off their land.

In May 1609 almost two million acres of northern land—confiscated from the estates of the rebel chiefs—was open to settlement. The Gaelic Irish were stunned. Under Celtic Law, the chieftains had not even owned the land, merely been lords over it, but the Gaels of the North were to find that the law of the English had finally come with a vengeance. Unlike the free-booting plantation attempts to the south where adventurers had attempted to make the land pay with native labour, the Ulster Plantation was designed from the outset to establish already-loyal subjects on Irish soil. This was to be invasion by leasehold. The greed of the individual landowner was to be subordinated to the equally rapacious needs of a new British imperialism.[1]

Ulster, virtually inaccessible to the Crown until the very end of the Nine Years War, was shired in the English fashion within a decade of Docwra's first landing on the Foyle. The City of London acquired the "Gaelic Countrie" around Derry and Coleraine, renaming it Londonderry, and dividing the new county among its guilds.[2] The other confiscated lands became the counties of Donegal, Fermanagh, Tyrone (also partially settled by the guildsmen of London), Cavan, and Armagh. By 1618 there were perhaps fifty thousand English settlers in the North of Ireland. In addition, there were about forty thousand Scots on land that had been the hereditary demesne of the Ulster septs since well before those wild tribes had conquered Scotland over 1,200 years earlier.

JOHN O'DWYER OF THE GLEN

When the Scot or English settler arrived in Ulster, he planted the best land. If the Gaelic natives were considered at all by the new arrival amidst the scramble for prime real estate, they were thought of as a lumberjack might think of wolves in a forest he is defoliating: his task is to defend himself against the wild canines, not to worry about their fate. As the settlers carved farm land from the virgin forests of the North, the Celtic Irish were forced to look on from the rocky highlands and the black-mirrored bogs. There was little the once-proud clansmen could do about it: by 1610 there were already fifty-six English garrisons established in Ulster.

CHRONOLOGY (Plantation)

1604 . . . . . .Act of Oblivion.

1605 . . . . . .Chichester Plantation in eastern Ulster; Barbados claimed as English colony.

1607 . . . . . . Flight of the Earls; Jamestown Colony in Virginia.

1608 . . . . . .O'Dougherty rising crushed in Ulster; Quebec founded by French.

1609 . . . . . .Ulster Plantation begins.

1610 . . . . . .Galileo's theories published.

1615 . . . . . .Villiers becomes favourite of James.

1618 . . . . . .Thirty Years War begins on continent.

1620 . . . . . .Pilgrims land in Massachusetts.

1621-29. . . . .Huguenots revolt in France.

1624 . . . . . .Richelieu chief minister to Louis XIII; England and Spain at war.

1625 . . . . . .*Charles I*, marries Henrietta Maria of France.

1626 . . . . . .Dutch establish New Amsterdam.

1627 . . . . . .Charles offers "Graces" to Irish Catholics; English war with France in aid of Huguenots.

1628 . . . . . .Villiers assassinated; Petition of Right by English Parliament.

1631 . . . . . .Algerian pirates sack Baltimore, County Cork.

1632-36. . . . .*Annals of the Four Masters* compiled.

1633 . . . . . .Wentworth, Viceroy; Laud, Archbishop of Canterbury; Charles I crowned King of Scots.

1634 . . . . . .English Catholic refugees found Maryland Colony.

1636 . . . . . .Laud imposes *Book of Canons* on Scotland

1638 . . . . . .Scot Presbyterians sign National Covenant against bishops, prepare for revolt against Crown.

1639 . . . . . .Covenanter Revolt in Scotland.

1640 . . . . . .Short Parliament; Scots invade England, Treaty of Ripon; Long Parliament.

1641 . . . . . .Wentworth executed; Ulster rebellion.

Thomas Furlong, Wexford poet and Gaelic translator, was a child at Ferns at the time of the 1798 Wexford rebellion. Later he would become a close friend to Dan O'Connell and an ardent repealer before his untimely death in 1827. Furlong translated this "Old Lament for the Slaughter of the Irish Nobility, the Confiscation of their Lands, and the Destruction of our once noble Woods by the ruthless Invader." It is, quite simply, a keen for the passing of an age.

Blithe the bright dawn found me,
Rest with strength had crowned me,
Sweet the birds sang round me,
Sport was all their toil.

The horn its clang was keeping,
Forth the fox was creeping,
Round each dame was weeping,
O'er the prowler's spoil.

Hark! The foe is calling,
Fast the woods are falling,
Scenes and sights appalling
Mark the wasted soil.

War and confiscation
Curse the fallen nation;
Gloom and desolation
Shade the lost land o'er.

Chill the winds are blowing,
Death aloft is going,
Peace or hope seems growing
For our race no more.

Hark! The foe is calling,
Fast the woods are falling,
Scenes and sights appalling
Throng the blood-stained shore.

Nobles, once high-hearted,
From their homes have parted,
Scattered, scared, and started
By a base-born band.

Sports that once were cheering,
Girls beloved, endearing,
Friends from whom I'm steering,
Take this parting tear.

Hark! The foe is calling,
Fast the woods are falling,

Scenes and sights appalling
Plague and haunt me here.

     As Lord Deputy Sir Arthur Chichester administered the
"official" Ulster Plantation, he meanwhile planted his own lands
around Belfast with Scots from the nearly Lowlands, as did his
Antrim and Down neighbors, Sirs James Hamilton and Hugh
Montgomery. The settlers in Ulster were of no better nor no
worse a class than pioneers are wont to be anywhere. In the
words of one of them who presumably considered himself a step
above the rest, "From Scotland . . . and from England . . . the
scum of both nations . . . came hither hoping to be without fear
of man's justice." The observation was perhaps unfair; it was the
very energy with which the planters reclaimed the primaeval
forest that transformed the North from the centre of Gaelic
culture to an English colonial farming community—and caused
the enmity of the native.
     There were some smaller English plantations in Longford,
Westmeath, Wicklow, and Wexford (the tortured justification for
the last was Art Oge MacMurrough's defiance of Richard II in the
1390s). Unlike the Ulster Plantation, however, these were administered by an emerging new Undertaker-Landlord class who
used the native Irish peasants as feudal tenants. The few Irish
lords reinstated after the Flight of the Earls were too shaky in
their own position to look after, indeed to care about, the
interests of the dispossessed Irish commons. Many of these
former chieftains threw off their Gaelic ways, embraced Protestantism, and sent their children to Britain to be raised proper
Englishmen—often as the price of their reinstatement. The landowning class, no longer to be freely elected by the Celtic septs,
was to become increasingly divorced from the humble Irish of
village and glen. The commoners had lost their leaders and been
thrown off the land. The very fabric of their everyday life,
tied intricately to their clan for millennia, had been rent by the
coming of the Stranger's laws. Forced to choose between the
unfamiliar English Protestant government that had caused them
so much grief and their last ties to the past, it is not surprising
that the common Irish chose their heritage.
     The Tudors had brought vast destruction to Ireland. Not
least among the institutions that almost disappeared from the
Irish landscape during the sixteenth century were the only real

Derry • Londonderry

Donegal

ULSTER
PLANTATION

Antrim
Carrickfergus

Down

Tyrone

Armagh

Sligo •

Fermanagh

Leitrim

Cavan

Dundalk •

Drogheda •

Dublin •

Galway •

• Athenry

Kings

Queens

Wicklow •

Arklow

Limerick •

New Ross • Wexford •
Carrick-on-Suir

• Kilmallock   Clonmel •   Waterford •

Dungarvin •

Dingle

Cork • Youghal •

Plantations Under
James Stuart

Baltimore •

D M°M Coyle

centres of education, the Catholic monasteries and the bardic
schools.   The seventeenth century British offered the Irish
nothing to replace what had been lost.   There were two educated
classes fast becoming itinerant on the island: the priests and the
poets.

The ancient *filí* were without noble patrons for the first
time in the folk-memory of the culture. As one of them,
Flaherty O'Malley Connor, wrote of his peers who had not yet
come to grips with the new order:

> Lughaidh, Tadhg and Torna,
> Famous poets of our land;
> Hounds they are with much learning
> Squabbling in an empty kennel.

The hounds, of course, finally found that they had to eat.   One
unhappy poet resented the new reality:

> My craft being withered with the change of law in Ireland,
> Alas, that I must henceforth take to brewing.

At least he had a "trade."   Most of his contemporaries had little
to offer other than their learning.   The once-great bards found
themselves roaming the byways of Ireland, passing along the oral
store of centuries in return for a meal and a roof over their heads.

The other group of newly itinerant Irishmen was the papist
clergy.   The Jesuits, for instance, had been present on the island
throughout the reign of Elizabeth and had been blamed, accurately in many cases, for a disproportionate amount of the
counter-reformation Irish resistance.   The defeat of the rebel
lords had also been a defeat for the Roman church; the land
whose missionaries had done so much to assure the continuity
of Western civilisation all across Europe had now become itself a
mission for continental Catholic apostles.

If Tyrone and Tyrconnell had conceded the battle for the
land, Rome was not willing to admit defeat in the fight for the
minds of the people.   As early as 1608 the Irish Privy Council
reported that:

> Priests land here secretly in every port in the realm . . . disperse
> themselves . . . in such sort that every town and country is full of
> them and most men's minds are infected with their doctrine and
> seditious persuasions. . . . Children and servants are wholly taught
> and catechised by them, esteeming the same a sound and safe
> foundation of their synagogue.

The first Capuchin Franciscans arrived in 1615; ten years later,
Discalced Carmelites spread over Ireland.   The Gaelic Irish clung

to the Catholic Church like survivours of a shipwreck cling to the only spars left afloat. The Mass, ejected from the once-familiar chapel, reappeared in *scáthlán* and *bothóg,* the mass-shelters of the countryside.

THE HEDGE SCHOOLMASTERS

The priests, like the bards, had found a new ministry, teaching their charges in the open air for the next two centuries. From these clandestine schools under the hedges of rural Ireland, the children learned the sanctity of the Mass and the old legends of the Gael. From these wandering men of the cloth and the harp, the Irish learned the curious, seemingly contradictory habit of praying to a Christian God and singing of pagan heroes. This late nineteenth century ballad by Seumas MacManus recalls the earnest men who kept learning alive on the island.

When the night shall lift from Erin's hills,
Twere shame if we forget
One band of unsung heroes
Whom Freedom owes a debt;
With brim high cups to brave ones then,
Their memory let us pledge,
Who gathered their ragged classes
Behind a friendly hedge.

By stealth they met their pupils
In the glen's deep-hidden nook,
And taught them many a lesson
Was never in English book;
There was more than wordy logic shown
To use in wise debate,
Nor *amo* was the only verb
They gave to conjugate.

When hunted on the heathery hill
And through the shadowy wood,
They climbed the cliff, they dared the marsh,
They stemmed the tumbling flood;
Their blanket was the clammy mist,
Their bed the windswept bent,

In fitful sleep they dreamt the bay
Of bloodhounds on their scent.

Their lore was not the brightest,
Nor their store, mayhap, the best,
But they fostered love undying
In each young Irish breast;
And through the dread, dread night and long,
That steeped our island then,
The lamps of Hope and fires of Faith
Were fed by those brave men.

The grass waves green above them,
Soft sleep is theirs for, aye,
The hunt is over and the cold,
The hunger passed away;
Oh, hold them high and holy,
And their memory proudly pledge,
Who gathered their ragged classes
Behind a friendly hedge.

In order to understand the conflicting passions that precipitated the cataclysmic events of the mid-seventeenth century,
it is vital to realise that open Irish resistance had been utterly
crushed. As Conor Cruise O'Brien has written:

> The natives were dispossessed, but not exterminated nor as-
> similated nor converted to Protestantism. Their Catholicism be-
> came the badge of their identity and their defiance.

The defiance was, however, an undergroud one of no pragmatic
use to the displaced Gael. On the other hand, there was one
institution that *was* able to use the gremlin of Rome to great
practical adavantage, the British House of Commons. The highly
respected J. H. Plumb has pointed out that even the popular
Elizabeth Tudor had managed the body but with difficulty; after
1601, "they were fundamentally out of hand—difficult to screw
money from and a hotbed of criticism." The activities of the
Commons were significant because Irish history between 1607-
41 had become essentially British history; Ireland was treated
as a sort of unruly ward of the English state. It was a time in
which the great landowners of Ireland considered themselves
English, whereas the Scots-Irish planters of Ulster became a

distinct community with close cultural and political ties to the dissenting Presbyterians of Lowland Scotland.

The policies of the Tudor monarchs had been generally representative of the wishes and spirit of the English people. The Stuarts were viewed by the Britons as a different kettle of fish altogether. James I, for example—a Scot whose myopic *Weltanschauung* was not in tune with that of the growing English colonial merchant class—was never to be forgiven by "the nation of shopkeepers" for his neglect of the Royal Navy and the consequent ascendancy of the Dutch as mistress of the seas. That many of the merchants most directly affected were Puritans with an increasing voice in the Commons was to prove crucial to the future of the British monarchy itself.

James Stuart's principal adviser was George Villiers, Earl of Buckingham (Duke in 1623). When the bloody carnival of the Thirty Years War broke out on the continent in 1618, Buckingham's appeasement of Catholic Spain and Austria caused anger within the growing Puritan faction and consternation even among the Anglican supporters of the Crown. The Dissenters would remember the Stuart flirtation with the European papists; in the meantime, Villier's influence in court remained undiminished, even after the death of James I in 1625. The minister's arrangement of the marriage of the new King Charles I to the Catholic Henrietta Maria of France, however, infuriated everybody but Charles and the eclipsed papists. Buckingham's attempt to mend his fences by aiding the French Huguenots against the rapacious policies of Cardinal Richelieu came too late to impress the now openly insolent Commons. Spoiling for a fight with the Stuarts anyhow, Parliament bitterly contested the increased taxes that would be necessary for Britian to have an impact on the sanguinary events in Europe. The increasingly independent assembly was flexing its muscles. In spite, Charles turned to Ireland, offering concessions to the remaining Catholic lords out of his royal "Grace and Bounty" in return for money.[3] Offering Irish papists The Graces served to envenom the Commons; likewise, the murder of Buckingham by a Puritan fanatic in 1628 only seemed to madden the legislators' passions further. The King was still faced with a desperate need for funds and a recalcitrant Parliament that held the pursestrings.

The lines for the coming civil war were coming clearly into focus. The Puritans and other Dissenters were, of course, firmly on the side of the Commons. The Church of England faction, led by Archbishop William Laud and his episcopacy, supported the sovereign. Trevelyan outlines the Puritans' dilemma . . . and solution:

> Laud and the bishops . . . were busy hunting [*the Puritans*] down. Puritans of all kinds,—and there were many different kinds,—must conform to the Anglican worship, or go to America,— or fight. At first they tried going to America. But after some years they found an opportunity to stay at home and make a bid for power,—the only way in those days to obtain toleration. The first of these movements founded the United States: the second founded English Parliamentary Government.

Many of those Englishmen who had not yet chosen a side found themselves edging away from the royalists; they saw the influence of the Catholic Queen in Charles' seeming reluctance to persecute papists. The King, with no help for it, looked again to Ireland for succour.

In 1633 Charles I sent Sir Thomas Wentworth to Dublin as Lord Deputy. Wentworth was an uncomplicated royalist interested only in making Ireland pay for his perpetually bankrupt lord. He was also a shrewd administrator. Demonstrating a rude intolerance for all opposition—be it Catholic, Puritan, Dissenter, or even Anglican—Wentworth proceeded to serve the King first, and govern Ireland second. The new Lord Deputy's analysis of his charges is described succintly by a biographer:

> It was to him self-evident that the wild Irish would be better men . . . if they gave up their savage ways . . . and turned as fast as possible into clean, industrious Protestants.

Indeed, had the wild Irish followed the advice it would have made scant difference; Wentworth treated the Protestants of Ireland no better than he did the Catholics, making a special point of harassing the Ulster Scots for their support of the anti-Crown faction in the Commons. Meanwhile, this loyal servant of the Anglican Crown began raising Irish Catholic regiments to serve Charles I.

There were some few indications that the British grip on Ireland was not as firm as it appeared. In 1631 a fleet of Algerian pirate vessels had swooped down on the coastal town of Baltimore in Cork, sacking the small village and taking off two hundred slaves. If the barbarous buccaneers of the Mediteranean could land with such impunity, why not the exiled papist Irishmen who were making reputations in arms on the continent? Two such soldiers, Thomas Preston, brother of Lord Gormanston, and Owen Roe O'Neill, nephew to the great rebel Earl of Tyrone, let it be known that they might be influenced to come back if armies could be raised against the English.

Nor had English domination completely killed the Gaelic intellectual spirit. During the years 1632-36 the *Annála Ríoghachta Éireann,* the "Annals of the Four Masters," had been compiled under the direction of Michael O'Cleary, a Franciscan lay brother of Donegal Abbey.[4] Colated from all the material then available on the history of Ireland, it is still the most informative source on the subject. Father Geoffrey Keating's *Foras Feasa ar Éireann,* "History of Ireland," had been written about the same time. The first popular history written for the Irish themselves, it is a model of eloquently simple Irish prose—with an equally uncomplicated nationalist fervour. The bards, meanwhile, became involved in the *Iomarbhaigh na bhFilí,* literally, the "Counterboasting of the Poets," which was essentially a poetic free-for-all that at least one nineteenth-century Gaelic scholar has suggested had as its object:

> to rouse and keep alive the national feeling and family pride of such of the native nobility and gentry as still continued to hold any station of rank or fortune in the country.

A somewhat less romantic twentieth-century observer sees the bardic contention in a somewhat different light, calling it a:

> colossal piece of pedantry . . . a mighty combat in words about the mythical theory of a mythical fifth century poet about the mythical origin of Ireland—this at a time when the conquistadors were in secure possession of the real Ireland from end to end.

As the Gaelic counterculture struggled to maintain its identity beneath the weight of the English political system, Sir Thomas Wentworth was very openly playing the role of an Irish Richelieu to Charles Stuart's Louis XIII . . . but not as ably.

The Lord Deputy's policies in Ireland were called tyranny by his many critics, "thorough" by Wentworth. A letter to his royalist ally Archbishop William Laud indicates the intensity of the Viceroy's devotion to the Crown:

> No such considerations shall fall in my counsels as my own preservation, till I see my master's power and greatness set out of wardship. . . . And thus you have my Thorough and Thorough.

One of Wentworth's proposed money-raising projects, the plantation of Connacht, was "thorough" enough to threaten the lands of the very Irish Catholics to whom the King had earlier turned with hat in hand to raise money (in return for the still-unfulfilled promises of The Graces) when the Parliament had earlier cut him off. It apparently never occurred to Wentworth that his enthusiastic efforts on behalf of his sovereign might be offset by the political liability of his heavy-handed actions.

As Wentworth continued to alienate every faction in Ireland and Charles I quarrelled with the Commons over prerogatives, Laud was making a blundering attempt to bring the Scottish Kirk to heel. The Primate of England had no temporal authority to meddle with the Scottish body—the Presbyterian Church was, after all, the state church north of the Tweed—so Archbishop Laud was attempting to change the liturgy of the Scot Church itself.[5] The angry Scots reacted by signing a national "Covenant with God" in 1638 that pointedly left both the British sovereign and the Church of England quite out of the equation. Trevelyan properly points out that "the country had not been so moved since the days of Wallace and Bruce." Even the great Earl of Argyle, chief of the Highland Campbells, was induced to sign the Lowland-inspired document (an action that in itself was ample reason for his Highland enemies to side with the Stuarts for the next century and more). The Glasgow church assembly not only ignored Charles' order to dissolve but went further, calling for Scotland's exiled sons to return from continental armies to serve in the burgeoning nationalist military forces of Alexander Leslie, Earl of Leven. The gauntlet had been flung at Charles Stuart's feet. The King called Sir Thomas Wentworth home from Ireland in 1639 to help him pick it up.

The Lord Deputy reacted in character. Before leaving for London, he stepped up recruitment of royalist Catholic legions. Further, he coerced the numerous Scots of Ulster—among whose devout Presbyterian population the Covenant had been circulating—to take the "Black Oath" of passive submission to the Crown. Rather than insuring obedience, the two actions succeeded only in pushing the bitter Ulstermen into the arms of the Puritans. If Scotland had heretofore been fighting the Commons' battle as well as her own, Wentworth's highhandedness no less played into the hands of the increasingly rebellious English parliamentarians.

Shortly after arriving in England, Wentworth was raised to Earl of Strafford for his zealous service to the Crown; he was by now the principal advisor to the King. Alarmed by the Scottish invasion of Northumberland and Durban, Strafford counselled Charles to summon Parliament for the money necessary to put down the Scot nation. The unruly Short Parliament which met on 13 April 1640 served only to acquaint the royalists with the true depth of disaffection with the Crown. In exasperation, Charles dissolved the assembly on 5 May.

Leslie meanwhile had not been waiting for events. Maneuvering the Scottish army like the professional soldier he was, the Earl of Leven had taken Newcastle by August, forcing Charles to negotiate a truce. The subsequent parley at Ripon resulted in the penniless Crown promising to pay the Scots army until Parliament was again called. After both the City of London and the East India Company had turned down the Crown's request for a loan, the King had no option: Charles reluctantly summoned Parliament in November 1640. This Long Parliament has often been named one of the major turning-points in the history of the English-speaking peoples. With the mailed fist of Scotland poised to strike, the legislators did not have to concern themselves with the normally present royal prerogative of dissolvement. The Commons, dragging a more reluctant Lords with it, eagerly abolished the Star Chamber, the High Commission, and other infamous perquisites of the Crown. Looking to a time when the leverage provided by Leslie's minions might not be present, the Parliament forced the King to acknowledge formally that it could not be again dissolved without its own acquiescence. Never again would it be possible to govern England without Parliament.

Perhaps the bitterest pill of all to Charles Stuart was his helplessness as the Parliament tried and attainted the hated Earl of Strafford. Wentworth's enemies were legion; his tunnel-vision in service to his monarch had seen to that. The Puritan parliamentarians discovered his prosecution to be an extremely popular proposition throughout England, Ireland, and Scotland: the Covenanters were pleased to be rid of the King's most loyal servant; the Gaelic Irish, Old English, Ulster Scots, and Dissenters of Ireland found they had at least an emnity of Strafford in common. Only the Church of English loyalists of Britain, their Cavalier contemporaries in Ireland, and the anti-Campbell Highlanders of Scotland stood by the King's favourite. The Lord Deputy of Ireland was beheaded on 12 May 1641 on Tower Hill.

Charles I, longingly viewing the nine-thousand-strong Gaelic Irish army still intact across the Irish Sea, now tried to win support among the Old English lords by finally confirming the Graces, delayed these fourteen years. The suspicious Irishmen were encouraged neither by the King's steadfastedness nor his ability to deliver, an attitude reinforced when the Puritan Lord Justices of Ireland intercepted the bill in Dublin before it could be confirmed by the Irish Parliament.

As the maddeningly entangled events in Britain and Scotland held centre stage, a small group of malcontent Gaelic Irish began preaching a gospel that was to become familiar in later centuries: "England's difficulty is Ireland's opportunity." A complicated military conspiracy was taking shape among not-quite-downtrodden Irishmen with names hauntingly familiar to aged veterans of the Elizabethan wars . . . O'More, Maguire, and O'Neill.

CHAPTER NOTES (7)

1 — Both Hugh O'Neill and Rory O'Donnell had visited James Stuart in London and had been officially pardoned by the King in May 1603, James I even going so far as to grant Rory the earldom of Tyrconnell (O'Donnell had actually been pardoned earlier by Elizabeth so that the King's treatment of the Donegal Gael was considered by those in the English court to show special favour). In 1604—before the Guy Fawkes affair—the pardon was extended to the other Gaelic rebels by the Act of Oblivion.

The confiscation of the six counties involved in the Ulster Plantation was actually in contravention of *Crown law.* It was not until 1615 that the lands of Tyrone and Tyrconnell were attainted, legally justifying the Plantation six years after it had gotten underway. Even under English law, only the Montgomery plantation of County Down was "legal;" Conn O'Neill had granted the Montgomerys the land around Newtownards much earlier.

Lord Mountjoy had been suggesting the new sort of plantation even while he was still battling the Ulster chieftains. He later described why settlers had been brought in to replace the Irish:

> "Because the Irish and Engish-Irish were obstinate in Popish superstition, great care was thought fit to be taken that these new colonies should consist of such men as were most unlike to fall to the barbarous customs of the Irish . . . no less cautions were to be observed for uniting them and keeping them from mixing with other than if these new colonies were to be led to inhabit among the barbarous Indians [*of the American colonies*]."

2 — Donal Ballagh O'Cahan of Dungiven was at first allowed to maintain Celtic dominion over his hereditary lands (his feud with O'Neill in 1606-07 was perhaps the final
straw that caused Hugh to flee the country). The Gaelic lord was, however, in the
way of the Plantation. He was imprisoned in 1609 and taken to the Tower, dying
there without trial while the Skinner's Company of London planted his former land.
A Captain Dodington built a new mansion on the shell of O'Cahan's castle in 1611.

One of the usual ways to differentiate a nationalist Ulsterman from his Unionist
neighbor is in his refusal to use "English" place-names. Draperstown, for example,
is still familiarly referred to as "The Cross" by the local Catholics. One of the most
curious of these place-name controversies is the Derry/Londonderry battle. County
Londonderry is commonly called "Derry" by Irish nationalists even though its name
was Coleraine before Plantation. The city of Londonderry, on the other hand, was
called Derry long before the Londoners completed its walls in 1613. For some reason,
its Protestant inhabitants have no problem in calling it "Derry" still, for all its smacks
of nationalism.

3 — The Graces, "the Irish analogue of the Petition of Rights" according to Lecky,
were in effect a bribe. The Catholic Irish lords agreed to raise £120,000 for
the Crown's coffers. In return, Charles was to guarantee that sixty years landed pro-
prietorship would relieve landowners of all Crown claims to the land; that Catholics
could practise law and fill government positions without taking the Oath of Supremacy; and that Connacht would not be subject to future Plantation. After Charles
had spent the money, he felt no need to fulfill his part of the bargain.

4 — O'Cleary, from the family that had traditionally provided the court *fili* to the
O'Donnells, worked with three assistants (Farfassa O'Mulcrony, Peregrine O'Cleary,
and Peregrine O'Duigenan) under the patronage of Ferghal O'Gara of Coolavin. The
Franciscan Abbey at Donegal had itself been destroyed during the Nine Years War
and, as early as June 1605, all seminary and monastic orders had been ordered out of
Ireland. It is likely the scholars worked in some protected ruin near the River Drowes
between Lough Melvin and Donegal Bay.

Wherever the work may have been completed, it is a treasure without which much
of what we know about Irish history would have been lost forever. The accuracy and
scholarship of the chronicles was attested to by the two most respected Gaelic intellectuals of the time—Conor MacBrody of Clare and Flann MacEgan of Tipperary.

5 — Laud's strategy was to impose the Church of England prayer book upon the
Scottish church. Had he succeeded, of course, the northern church would have been
Presbyterian in name only, a result that would have also affected the "Scotch-Irish"
of Ulster who looked across the North Channel for their liturgy.

8

The Great Rebellion

On 23 October 1641 Gaelic Ireland rose in rebellion. Out of the bogs and down from the rocky mountaintops of Ulster came Irishmen in their thousands determined to reclaim the glens of their grandfathers and pay off grim debts accumulated since the Flight of the Earls.

The Ulster rising had been planned to dovetail with the capture of Dublin Castle. Though the authorities fortuitously discovered the existence of the plot on the 22nd and so were able to protect the capitol, the sheer size of the explosion in the North suprised everyone—including Sir Felix O'Neill of Tyrone, titular leader of the rebels.[1] It was called the Great Rebellion in Ireland; to the Protestant English and Ulster Scots, it was the Great Massacre. The spontaneous nature of much of the rising ensured wanton bloodshed: it is probable that as many as four to twelve thousand Protestants were killed in the first months of rebellion—mostly Ulster planters.

Felix O'Neill and his brother Turlough marched south from their Tyrone headquarters at Caledon. The peasant army of the O'Neills moved toward Dublin, gaining lieutenants with famous Irish rebel names. In the vanguard as the insurgent army neared the River Boyne, for instance, rode Rory O'More of Kildare.

RORY O'MORE

The Great Rebellion was not due to any single cause, but to wrongs carefully remembered and imagined by the dispossessed Northern Gael. The British soldiery and magistracy had taken his patrimony, the heretic Church of England and supplanted his Catholic chapel, Scots planters were farming his land and swearing a covenant against popery. The Ulster Gael felt he had much to gain and little to lose by rebellion. When Rory O'More led the spearhead of the rebel army against an unusually disorganised Crown force at Julianstown Bridge in November 1641, the Irish peasants fought with a fanatical rage that caused the defenders to fall back on nearby Drogheda.

This stirring call to arms by Dr. William Drennan, painted as it is on the canvas of Irish folk-memory, captures the mood of 1641 vividly . . . and describes the reasons for the rising far more accurately than the sterile prose of many historians. Drennan, a celebrated Presbyterian minister-physician-pamphleteer of the 1790s, was one of the few nationalist leaders of that period who was to survive the United Irish uprising and yet remain free in Ireland.

On the green hills of Ulster the white cross waves high,
And the beacon of war throws its flames to the sky,
Now the taunt and threat let the coward endure,
Our hope is in God and in Rory O'More.

Do you ask why the beacon and the banner of war
On the mountains of Ulster are seen from afar?
Tis the signal our rights to regain and secure
Through God and Our Lady and Rory O'More.

For the merciless Scots, with their creed and their swords,
With war in their bosoms and peace in their words,
Have sworn the bright light of our faith to obscure,
But our hope is in God in Rory O'More.

Oh, lives there a traitor who'd shrink from the strife,
Who, to add to the length of a forfeited life,
His country, his kindred, his faith would abjure?
No! We'll strike for old Erin and Rory O'More!

The rebels soon found that atavistic enthusiasm would not be enough to overcome disciplined English soldiery. O'Neill failed to dislodge the garrison at Drogheda and, retiring to the north, suffered a rearguard defeat at Ardee. By that time, however, the Ulstermen were not alone; their spark—and a counterproductive December 1641 British Commons resolution outlawing Romanism—had lit a wildfire of rebellion across the island.

CHRONOLOGY (The Great Rebellion)

1641 (autumn). . . . .Ulster Rebellion begins; Battle of Julianstown Bridge; widespread local risings throughout island; Commons outlaws Catholicism in Ireland.

1642 (spring). . . . . .Adventurer's Act; Monroe lands in Ulster; Catholic Confederation formed in Kilkenny.

1642 (summer) . . . .Preston and Owen Roe O'Neill return to lead Confederate armies; English Parliament "declares war" on Charles I.

1643 (summer) . . . .Uneasy truce between Cavaliers and Confederates in Ireland; Solemn League and Covenant signed by British Commons; Louis XIV, King of France.

1644 (summer) . . . .Battle of Marston Moor.

1645 (summer) . . . .Battle of Naseby; Glamorgan negotiations in Ireland.

1645 (autumn). . . . .Rinuccini arrives with aid for Confederates.

1646 (spring). . . . .Ormonde Peace; Charles I surrenders to Scots; Battle of Benburb.

1646 (autumn). . . . .Ormonde Peace repudiated.

1647 (winter) . . . . .Scots deliver Charles to British Parliament.

1647 (summer) . . . .Siege of Trim; Ormonde surrenders Dublin to Jones; Battle of Dungan's Hill; New Model Army occupies London.

1647 (autumn). . . . .Charles escapes to Isle of Wight, signs "Engagement" with Scots.

1648 (spring). . . . .2nd Civil War begins; Old English/Cavalier truce in Ireland.

1648 (summer) . . . .Battle of Preston; Peace of Westphalia ends Thirty Years War on continent.

1648 (autumn). . . . .Cromwell marches into Edinburgh.

1648-49 (winter) . . .Rump Parliament; execution of Charles I; Prince of Wales assumes title of Charles II; 2nd Ormonde Peace in Ireland.

1649 (summer) . . . .Battle of Rathmines; sack of Drogheda.

1649 (autumn). . . . .Sack of Wexford; death of Owen Roe O'Neill.

1650 (spring). . . . .Ireton directs reduction of remaining royalist strongholds as Cromwell leaves Ireland.

1650 (summer) . . . .Charles II lands in Scotland; Battle of Dunbar.

1651 . . . . .Scots crown Charles II at Scone; Battle of Worcester; Battle of Scarrifholis.

1652 . . . . .Leaders of 1641 Irish rising executed; Anglo-Dutch War; Dutch found Capetown.

1653 . . . . .Last Irish resistance quelled, Cromwellian Settlement begins; Instrument of Government; First Protectorate.

All over Ireland, the remnants of the Old Gaelic septs seized the chance to recapture their heritage. The Fermanagh Maguires sacked the plantation lands of the Hamiltons, Coles, and Balfours. The O'Hanlons won back their ancient Armagh clan seat at Tanderagee. Luke O'Toole swept down from the Wicklows, taking Arklow Castle and investing the Black Castle at Wicklow town. In Cavan, Philip and Myles O'Reilly retook the old family castle at Cloughoughter. In the far Southwest, the Kerry poet-warrior Pierce Ferriter took Tralee, and then marched triumphantly through Cork into Limerick.[2] Gaelic Ireland was aflame.

If it was the native Irish who made temporal gains during the autumn and winter of 1641-42, it was to be the planters of the North who were ultimately to gain a spiritual tradition because of them. The "Popish Massacre of '41" was to become, in the words of John Mitchel, the "fifth gospel" of the Ascendancy. Upon this object lesson, the Irish landowners would ever after base their sermon to the lower-class Protestants on the dangers of political ecumenism. Whenever in the future the subject of Catholic rights would be advanced, there would be upper-class voices reminding the Ulster planters, as Mitchel suggests, that it was:

> the favourite enjoyment of Papists to rip up Protestant women with knives; to murder the mothers and then put the infants to their dead mothers' breast, and say: "*Suck, English bastard!*"—to delude men out of houses by offers of quarter, and then to cut their throats, and so on.

The Young Irelander goes on to claim with much justification that it would afterwards be equated with treason:

> if one presumed to deny or doubt the terrible drowning of Protestants at Portadown Bridge—or to question the fact of their ghosts appearing in the river at night . . . shrieking "*Revenge! Revenge!*"

Now two groups of Irishmen had innocent martyrs that could be invoked to justify future deeds.

The real Protestant casualty figures were bad enough but, in the way of the time, the reports reaching London spoke of massacres of twenty times the actual figure, perhaps exaggerated by cunning royalists pleased to have an excuse to petition the upstart Parliament for troops. The Commons hesitated, understandably reluctant to present the King with an army he might be tempted to use against the Parliament itself—particularly since Felix O'Neill was loudly proclaiming that Ulster had risen to protect Charles I from the Roundhead Commons. The King was in fact only *publicly* upset by the Irish uprising. Privately, he wrote cooly that he hoped "this ill news of Ireland may hinder some of these follies in England." The parliamentary skepticism seemed justified when the impatient Charles I ordered the arrest of John Pym, John Hampden, and three other foot-dragging parliamentary leaders in January 1642. Though the M.P.'s escaped, it did not help their colleagues' dilemma. The Irish rebellion had to be faced: not only were the Ulster Scots demanding revenge, but the Irish were showing ominous signs of unification under the dreaded banner of popery. Now, using the King's own Ripon Agreement as justification, the Commons gratefully looked to the rebel Scots. A Covenanter army under Major General Monroe landed in Ulster during April 1642. The Gaelic Irish were soon to discover they had no monopoly on massacre.

BRIAN BOY MAGEE

When Monroe landed in Antrim, he made Carrickfergus his base and sent out sorties to pacify the surrounding countryside. The General's idea of pacification was curious indeed. Receiving a friendly invitation to visit Dunlace Castle near Bushmills, Monroe took the opportunity to incarcerate his host, Randall MacDonnell, Earl of Antrim. Monroe's excuse for imprisoning the bewildered provincial lord was that his grandmother had been a daughter of Conn O'Neill and his grandfather the notorious Sorley Boye MacDonnell.

A more tragic event was Monroe's eradication of the entire Catholic population on the IslandMagee Peninsula, accomplished by cutting down the men and then throwing the women and children over the steep Gobbins cliffs. Slaughterford Bridge, named in honour of the episode, still stands landmark to the massacre. Perhaps a more poignant memorial is the lack of Catholics on the promontory 340 years after the murder.

This ballad by Ethna Carbery (Anna Johnston MacManus) was written in the late nineteenth century to commemorate the death of the IslandMagee Catholics.

I am Brian Boy Magee—my father was Owen Ban—
I was wakened from happy dreams by the shouts of my startled clan;
And I saw through the leaping glare that marked where the homestead stood,
My mother swung by her hair, and my brothers in their blood.

In the creeping cold of the night, the pitiless wolves came down—
Scotch troops from the Castle grim guarding Knockfergus Town;
And they hacked and lashed and hewed, with musket, rope and sword,
Till my murdered kin lay thick in pools by the Slaughterford.

I fought by my father's side, and when we were fighting sore,
We saw a line of British steel, with our shrieking women before;
The redcoats drove them to the verge of the Gobbins grey,
And prodded them—God, the sight!—as the sea it claimed its prey.

Oh, tall were the Gobbins Cliffs and sharp the rocks below,
And tender the limbs that met terrible death, my woe!
Mother and babe and maid, they clutched at the empty air,
With eyes opened wide in fright in that hour of despair.

The dawn that came was old and red, as red as the blood-soaked stream,
I slowly crept to the perilous brink—good God, it were a dream!
In all that island of black gloom, only I had life that day—
Death covered the green hillsides and tossed in the red-blue bay.

I shall go to Phelim O'Neill with my sorrowful tale and crave
A blue-bright blade of Spain in the ranks of his soldiers brave;
God grant me strength to flash and wield that shining weapon well
When the Gael shall sweep our foemen through the yawning gates of Hell.

I am Brian Boy Magee and my creed is one of hate,
Love and peace I've cast aside but for vengeance I will wait!
Till I pay back the four-fold debt for the horror I saw there,
When my brothers lay in their blood and my mother swung by her hair.

Events were moving swiftly in the three kingdoms. In late February 1642 the Dublin authorities of James Butler, thirteenth Earl of Ormonde, perhaps recalling the successful tactics of Lord Mountjoy four decades earlier, issued the following order to the commanders of the royalist Irish forces:

> To wound, kill, slay, and destroy by all the ways and means you may, all the rebels and adherents and relievers; and burn, spoil, waste, consume and demolish all places, towns and houses, where the said rebels are or have been relieved and harboured, and all hay and corn there, and kill and destroy all the men inhabiting, able to bear arms.

In London, meanwhile, Parliament had devised an imaginative *new* way to put down Irish rebellion. In March the Adventurer's Act was passed, placing 2,500,000 acres of Irish land on the block as reward for those who would help put down the papist insurrection. The response from land-hungry English burghers was encouraging. While Dublin Castle was reverting to the traditional scorched-earth policy, the English Commons had determined to put down the Irish by buccaneering; in effect, the parliamentary soldiery had been furnished a letter-of-marque . . . with Ireland both the prize and the prize money.

Alarmed by the sentiment in both London and Dublin, the Catholic Old English lords of Ireland saw no choice but to throw in their lot with the Gaelic rebels. In May 1642 at Kilkenny, the Anglo-Irish under Lord Gormanston and Bishop Rothe joined in confederation with Felix O'Neill's northern Gaels. Taking as their motto *"Pro Deo, pro rege, pro patria Hibernia unanimus"* (For God, for King, for a united Irish country), the Confederate Catholics of Ireland set up a provisional government. The Confederation announced its goals to be repeal of Poynings Law, liberty of conscience, and restitution of their ancient lands. The affirmation of support for the King, demanded by the Old English, was not a lightly declared avowal: Parliament declared war on Charles Stuart in August.

By the end of 1642 it would have been useful to have a playbill to identify the several armies fielding troops in Ireland. The Scottish troops of Monroe held much of Antrim and Down, the town of Londonderry, and the surrounding country. The Cavaliers—loyalist Anglicans led by Ormonde—held Dublin and the Pale. Murrough O'Brien, Lord Inchiquin, commanded an independent royalist army in Clare. Sir Frederick Hamilton had overrun most of Sligo for the Crown . . . and most of Fermanagh for himself. The Kilkenny Confederation had a half-dozen different "armies" in the field. Sir Charles Coote, alternately claiming allegiance to the Crown and Parliament, roamed about the island chasing them down. During 1642 the Catholic rebels had meanwhile gained desperately needed military leadership with the return of two professional soldiers from the continent: Thomas Preston of Desmond and Owen Roe O'Neill, gone these thirty-five years from Tyrone. Preston took command of the Anglo-Irish Catholics in the South; O'Neill became leader of the northern Gaelic rebels. The savage but bewildering campaigning continued in Ireland until September 1643 when a partially successful temporary truce was worked out. The contending forces settled uneasily down to watch the high drama unfolding across the Irish Sea.

The Scots had officially aligned themselves with the Commons that same September by the Solemn League and Covenant. Of perhaps more immediate importance than the pact with the Scots, however, had been the alliance between Parliament and the City of London. The Cavalier landowners were finding it difficult to convert their vast estates into specie to support the King's war effort; on the other hand, the merchants of the City, their port kept open by the now-parliamentary navy, were in a position to lend money to the Commons. Although the cash-poor royalists kept winning battles throughout 1643, the Parliament was winning the war. By late autumn, Charles I had lost the chance to exploit his early victories. To the north, twenty thousand Scots were finally marching to the aid of the Westminster army.

During the campaign of 1643 a young cavalry commander had been winning a military reputation among the heretofore faceless parliamentary officers. A Puritan M.P. for Cambridge, Oliver Cromwell was demonstrating a spectacular ability on the battlefield that was rivalled only by his talent on the floor of the English Commons. In early June 1644 a combined army of Covenanters under Cromwell and Alexander Leslie defeated Prince Rupert, Duke of Bavaria and nephew to Charles I, at the decisive Battle of Marston Moor. After the battle, the Roundhead leaders began to appreciate that military victory alone might not be enough. Cromwell's nominal commander posed the Puritans' dilemma succinctly: "If we beat the King ninety and nine times yet he is king still, and so will his posterity after him," observed the Earl of Manchester, "but if the King beat us once we shall all be hanged, and our posterity made slaves." After Marston Moor, rumblings of regicide began to be heard for the first time.

Parliament now raised the New Model Army under the command of Sir Thomas Fairfax. In June 1645 Fairfax defeated the last of the King's field forces at the Battle of Naseby. Charles, in desperate straits, sent Lord Glamorgan to treat secretly with the Catholic Confederation in Ireland, offering religious toleration in return for troops. The healthy skepticism of the papist leaders—who for almost four years had been defending themselves *against* royalist attacks while ostensibly fighting *for* the Crown—

proved to be well-founded when word of the meetings leaked and Charles immediately repudiated Glarmorgan. The only result of the clumsy intrigue was to push the artful Lord Inchiquin from the Irish loyalist side to that of the Parliament. On that bewildering stage of the 1640s, the players' exits and entrances began to take on an *As You Like It* air: many men played many parts . . . sometimes at the same time.

The Irish Catholics were not immune from this political and military merry-go-round. In October 1645 a fanatical papal nuncio, Giovanni Battista Rinuccini, arrived with £20,000 and arms for six thousand Confederates. The badly needed aid was not as helpful as the man was destructive. Father Rinuccini openly preached the establishment of an exclusively Catholic Ireland and, only somewhat more quietly, urged abandonment of the King, thereby undermining the basis for the Confederacy itself. The original rebellion may have been fanned by papist fire, but the Kilkenny pact had been born out of temporal necessity. Rinuccini's zealous politicking made the tenuous Catholic alliance ever more fragile.

As Coote's army plodded about Ireland after the Confederate rebels in the autumn and winter of 1645-46, Fairfax and Cromwell mopped up Cavalier resistance in Britain. By May 1646 Charles I was driven to the extremity of throwing himself on the mercy of the Scots. In the same month, General Monroe's Scot army in Ireland began a summer campaign that was to result in the famous Battle of Benburb.

OWEN ROE'S ADDRESS

In describing Owen Roe O'Neill's considerable political and military skill, Dr. Hayes-McCoy suggests that there was "something of Parnell in him, still more of Stonewall Jackson." One may debate the former assertion, but the events leading to Benburb lend credence to the latter: they bear an uncanny resemblance to those leading to Cross Keys-Port Republic in the Valley of Virginia.

Monroe's strategy was to gather three distinct Covenanter forces—from Antrim, Coleraine, and Derry—into one huge army along the Tyrone/Monaghan border, and then smash southward through the Midlands towards the heart of the Confederacy at Kilkenny. O'Neill, recognising the danger, marched up from his south Cavan camp to prevent the rendezvous. Owen Roe's plan was daring; his five thousand Gaelic Irish were outnumbered by each of the three armies toward which he was moving.

Arriving at Benburb on the River Blackwater just before Monroe's Antrim force of six thousand Scots, English, and Ulster planters appeared on the other bank, O'Neill dispatched his horse under Myles O'Reilly to Dungannon with the mission of screening off the Covenanter force moving down from Coleraine. The timing was critical. Owen Roe, well aware that Monroe had to move only six miles downriver to find the closest Blackwater ford, was cutting it close. In the event, it worked: the unexpected appearance of the Irish cavalry caused the overly cautious Coleraine column to take a defensive position, freeing O'Reilly's horse to gallop for the now-raging battle at Benburb. The horsemen arrived at a critical moment, flanking Monroe, thereby—Jacksonlike—confronting two enemy armies on the same day.[3]

This Phil O'Neill ballad imagines Owen Roe attempting to inspirit his troops on the eve of the battle. It may have happened; in an earlier day, the haranguing would have been done by his *file*.

Men of Ulster, marshalled round me
In your manhood and your might,
Once again prepared to battle
For your freedom and your right;
The hour for which we long have hungered
Now at last is close at hand,
When we strike again for vengeance
On the spoilers of our land!

For the worship of our fathers,
For the honour of our race,
For the glory of our Saviour,
Here today we take our place;
Glittering pike and trusty hackbutt
Speak the purpose of our souls,
As the rapid lightning flashes
Ere the sullen thunder rolls.

Gallant sons of old TyrConnell,
You whose fathers bled of yore,

In the sacred cause of Freedom
By the Bann and Bandon's shore;
Once again you join the combat
For your faith and fatherland,
Neath the standard of your country
Here today you take your stand.

Think of dauntless Hugh O'Donnell,
Done to death in foreign clime,
Yours' today upon those dastards
To wreak vengeance for that crime;
Tyrone's sons all, too, are ready
And impatient for the fray,
Where the fight is fast and fiercest,
Ever their's to lead the way.

Soldiers ever tried and trusted
In your hapless country's weal,
Once again you face the foemen
Neath the standard of O'Neill;
Think of haughty Shane of Ulster,
Murdered by a ruthless foe,
And pay back for treachery's action
By an overwhelming blow.

Think of Hugh, your gallant chieftain,
Mouldering in a foreign land;
From his friends and home and country,
By those Saxon robbers banned;
Think of every crime and outrage
Done your persecuted race;
Yours today by right our weapon,
Every insult to efface.

Think upon your hapless country
How in sorrow deep she pines:
Outraged maid and tortured matron,
Ruined hearths and rifled shrines,
Hunted priest and homeless peasant,
Pillaged land and burning towers;
God of Battle, steel our arms
In the task that now is ours!

Till each outrage is atoned for,
Till each stain is wiped away,
Till these brutal human fiends
For their hellish pastimes pay;
Till the Right is vindicated
And justice nobly done,
Till victory bless our arms
And the hard-fought fight is won.

THE SHADY WOODS OF TRUAGH

For the first years of the Catholic Confederation, Owen Roe O'Neill's Gaelic forces in the North had been the "poor sisters of rebellion." Sir Felix O'Neill's first blush of success had already faded when Owen Roe had arrived to take command of Ulster in the summer of 1642. Preston's Old English forces of the South, sorely pressed by Murrough O'Brien's royalists—and when Inchiquin changed sides, his parliamentarians—owned and used the lion's share of the Confederacy's limited resources. It is a measure of Owen Roe's leadership (or Monroe's lack of it) that the rebel general was able to keep the Scots bottled up in the North without substantial help from his Kilkenny allies.

When Rinuccini had landed with the resources needed to arm and train the Catholics, Innocent X's nuncio made certain that O'Neill's Gaels were supplied first. The action caused tension between Preston and O'Neill—ultimately disastrous to the alliance—but it did enable Owen Roe to train the forces that faced Monroe at Benburb, thus saving the Confederacy for one more year.

In addition to his trained forces, O'Neill benefited from the appearance of local leaders bringing reinforcements. One such was MacKenna, bethrothed to the daughter of Costelloe, The MacMahon of Monaghan.[4] Charles Gavan Duffy, co-founder of *The Nation* in the days of Young Ireland, wrote romantically of these volunteers:

> Down from the sacred hills whereon a Saint communed with God,
> Up from the vale where Bagnall's blood manured the reeking sod,
> Out from the stately woods of Truagh, M'Kenna's plundered home,
> Like Malin's waves, as fierce and fast, our faithful clansmen come.

Glaslough, MacKenna's family home, was only ten miles from the
Benburb battlefield.

From out the shady woods of Truagh
MacKenna rides at noon;
The sun shone brightly, not a cloud
Darkened the sky of June.
No eye had he for nature's charms,
They don't annoy his brain,
As through the vales he takes his way
And never draws a rein.

He has come to look on his Maureen,
For tomorrow he must go,
With his brave Truagh men to Benburb,
There to defend Owen Roe;
"I have come to look upon your brow
And hear your answer sweet,
For if in battle I should fall,
We ne'er again can meet."

"Go forth, my love, with my blessings, go
And smite the Saxon's forehead,
When you come back, I'll be your bride
Without another word."
With fond embrace they bid *adieu*
As the sun went sinking down
Behind the wooded western hills
That o'erlook Glaslough town.

MacKenna lightly mounts his steed
At the twilight of the eve;
It leads him over Dava Hills
And Truagh's woods so green;
Tonight he meets his faithful men
On the green hills of Tyrone,
To join the army of the North
At Benburb, on their own.

And well O'Neill was pleased to meet
These gallant mountaineers,
Who kept the Saxon wolf at bay

Round ancient Truagh for years;
Full well they fought on Benburb's plain
Where England's flag went down,
Few *Sassenach* escaped that night
Towards Carrickfergus Town.

Oh, autumn winds swirled through the woods,
The berries were ripe and red,
When MacKenna and his fair bride
In Glaslough church were wed;
And never in his father's hall
A fairer maid was seen
Than MacMahon's only daughter,
The gentle young Maureen.

The Battle of Benburb was an overwhelming tactical victory for the Catholic rebels; Monroe lost over 3,200 men to O'Neill's 300. Yet, it turned out to be only a defensive triumph, merely postponing the southerly march of the Covenanters. It is a military maxim—both tactical and strategic—that the culmination of a successful assault is a perilous instant. It is then that the gain must be exploited lest it be lost altogether to enterprising defenders. Monroe need not have worried; his enterprise was never tested by the Irish. Rather than turning his tactical victory to strategic advantage, Owen Roe marched south to Kilkenny intent on supporting the indefatigable Rinuccini, who was doing his fanatic best to spike an incipient peace treaty between Ormonde and the Old English. Though O'Neill managed to convince Thomas Preston to continue the "defense" against the Cavaliers for a time, it was questionable strategy at best. Not only had the chance been lost against the Scots, but the internecine squabbling within the unravelling Confederacy caused the Irish to lose sight of the real threat.

In January 1647 the British Parliament finally paid their Scot "allies" the money due under the Ripon agreement of 1640. In return, the Scots handed Charles Stuart over to the Parliament. The monarch was almost forgotten during the next six months, however, as the victors of the Civil War fell out among themselves. The New Model Army—by now thoroughly infiltrated by the populist Leveller movement[5]—called on the Commons to settle arrears of pay and establish toleration (of other

Protestantism than the Presbyterianism still espoused by Westminster). Fairfax, faced with possible mutiny within his own
army, ordered the military occupation of the City of London
and ousted the "offending" Presbyterians from the Commons.

To make the confusion complete, King Charles escaped to
the Isle of Wight in November. The sovereign immediately made
an "Engagement" with the Presbyterian Scots now unhappy with
the events unfolding in London. Charles promised the Scots that
he would establish Presbyterianism as the state religion if they
would restore his crown, an Engagement that understandably
stunned many of the King's Church of England Cavaliers. There
were now so many factions that anarchy and individual power
struggles threatened to determine the future of the three kingdoms: the British Parliament was controlled by the Puritans but
split by the champions of Presbyterianism; the New Model
Army was also controlled by the Puritans but had a strong Leveller element; the Scottish nation was divided by traditional feuds
within the Highlands, by ancient Highlander/Lowlander emnities,
and by the fresh quarrel between the old Anglican Cavaliers and
the newly royalist Presbyterians (the Engagers); the Catholic
Confederacy of Ireland was meanwhile riven by furious bitterness between the landless Gaels and the "English Irishry," a
split exacerbated by the "theological" dispute between the
Roman fanaticism of Bishop Rinuccini and the domestic prag-
matism of the Irish bishops; Ormonde's royalist New English
refused the King's new Engagement with the Scots; and so it
went.

In Ireland, the fighting dragged on. Thomas Preston had be-
sieged Trim in July 1647 with an army of Old English Irishmen
and Scottish papists. The following month, the parliamentary
forces of Lieutenant General Michael Jones had won a smashing
victory over Preston at Dungan's Hill. In the same month that
Charles escaped, Lord Theobald Taafe's Confederates were defeated by Inchiquin's now-parliamentary army. James Butler,
the King's beleaguered Lord Lieutenant, continued to offer the
"Ormonde Peace" to Bishop Rothe's Old English, promising to
confirm all land titles from 1628, repeal religious penalties, and
waive the supremacy oath in return for Catholic aid. It was, after
all, what the Anglo-Irish lords had been fighting for all along.
When Rinuccini torpedoed the deal again by reminding the
Gaelic Irish that it was not what *they* had risen for back in 1641,
Ormonde surrendered Dublin to Michael Jones and left for the

continent in exasperation.

Charles Stuart's Engagement with the Scots had meanwhile given new hope to the loyalists in Britain. Royalist risings broke out in Cornwall, south Wales, and Yorkshire in the spring of 1648, closely followed by full scale rebellion in Essex and Kent. An Engager Army of royalist Scots under the Duke of Hamilton was making up north of the Tweed. Even more ominous for the parliamentarians, a large portion of the "Royal" Navy mutinied in the name of Charles. The Second English Civil War had begun.

The New Model Army responded magnificently to the crisis. Fairfax and Cromwell swiftly suppressed the risings in the South, freeing the latter to meet the invading Engagers. In the August Battle of Preston, Lieutenant General Cromwell's Ironsides crushed the Scots and their Yorkshire Cavalier allies. Pressing on into Scotland, Cromwell came to agreement with the Presbyterian Kirk at Edinburgh, whose opposition to Hamilton had delayed the Engagers' march south just long enough for the Roundheads to be ready to meet them.

In Ireland, meanwhile, the early royalist successes in England had convinced Lord Inchiquin (who had overrun most of Munster in the name of the Commons, earning himself in the process the cant name "Murrough of the Burnings") to shift his allegiance for yet a third time: O'Brien negotiated a truce with Rothe's Old English Confederates in May. The chameleon-like Inchiquin and his new "English Irishry" allies now formally joined the Cavalier camp of Ormonde, the latter having returned to Ireland when Stuart fortunes seemed again on the rise. James Butler promptly gathered his new alliance into a large army and marched on Dublin, still held by the Roundheads of Michael Jones. The irrepressible Rinuccini hastily excommunicated everybody involved in this new Ormonde Peace, presumably including Bishop Rothe. Only Owen Roe O'Neill stubbornly refused to join the Cavaliers, going so far as to defeat Butler in pitched battle at Ballymore in Westmeath.

Things were just as confused across the Irish Sea. The English Parliament had fallen out yet again . . . this time over the fate of Charles I, who was once more in the hands of the Commons. The parliamentary division was ended in early December 1648 when Henry Ireton, son-in-law to the ascendant Cromwell, sent New Model soldiers to "purge" those Members who wished to negotiate with the King. The time for talking had long passed. The Rump Parliament brought the monarch to

trial.   Charles I of England was publicly beheaded at Whitehall
on 30 January 1649.   When the hooded executioner lifted the
sovereign's head to the crowd, the groans of horror and pity
from the audience were but the first signs of protest at this grisly
business of king-killing.

Europe was appalled.   In Scotland, the uneasy Covenanters
disowned responsibility for the regicide, even threatening to raise
new levies to avenge it.   Thomas Fairfax, who had been the most
formidable of Charles' military opponents, refused to take up
arms against the Scots, retiring from public life as his own protest at the execution.   Even the recalcitrant Owen Roe O'Neill
was caused to finally bring his Gaelic Irish into the Cavalier circle, provoking Rinuccini to depart for Rome in disgust.   On the
other hand, there was at least one Irish Cavalier who gauged the
full intensity of the Roundhead wind correctly: Roger Boyle,
Lord Broghill, shrewdly realised that the Regicides were quite un-
dismayed by the antagonistic public opinion.   The new leaders of
Britain swiftly abolished the House of Lords, established a Council of State, and had soon established the "Commonwealth and
Free State."   They meanwhile reinforced Michael Jones' be-
leagured Dublin army, a garrison also bolstered by the unexpected arrival of Broghill's formerly royalist troops.

At the Battle of Rathmines on 2 August 1649, Jones defeated the combined royalist armies of Ormonde and Inchiquin,
relieving the Dublin siege.   Murrough O'Brien, having changed
sides once too often, was still demonstrating his remarkable
instinct for self-preservation—he was not personally present with
James Butler on the battlefield.   Inchiquin's intuition was accurate; it was the beginning of the end for the anti-parliamentary
forces of Ireland.   Thirteen days after the fight at Rathmines,
another brilliant parliamentary soldier landed in Dublin to assume the post of governor.   Oliver Cromwell had come to Ireland.

Cromwell's first target was Ormonde's royalist garrison
under Sir Arthur Ashton at Drogheda.   Appearing before the
walls of the town on 2 September, it took the parliamentarian
artillerists a full week to set up their batteries.   The guns opened
up on the 9th and, Ashton refusing a demand to surrender, the
assault began on the afternoon of the next day.   The horror of
that evening is perhaps best described in Cromwell's own dispatch to the Council of State:

It has pleased God to bless our endeavours to Drogheda . . . the

> enemy were about three thousand strong in the town. They made
> a stout resistance. . . . We refused them quarter . . . I believe we
> put to the sword the whole number of defendants . . . the enemy
> upon this were filled with much terror . . . give the glory of this to
> God alone, to Whom indeed the praise of this mercy belongs.

A bloody but effective object lesson, the "mercy" at Drogheda
caused the Cavalier garrisons at Trim and Dundalk to flee without a fight, giving Cromwell the time to compose a rather length-
ier missive to the Speaker of the English Parliament describing
the fall of Drogheda:

> Upon Tuesday the 10th of [*September 1649*] . . . our men that
> stormed the breaches were forced to recoil . . . they made a second
> attempt . . . got ground of the enemy, and by the goodness of God,
> forced him to quit. . . . The enemy retreated, divers of them, into
> the Mill-Mount . . . our men getting up to them, were ordered by
> me to put them all to the sword. . . . I forbade them to spare any
> that were in arms in the town, and, I think, that night they put to
> the sword about 2,000 men . . . about one hundred of them pos-
> sessed St. Peter's churchsteeple. . . . I ordered the steeple to be
> fired. . . . The next day [*the West Gate tower and St. Sunday's
> tower*] were summoned. . . . When they submitted, their officers
> were knocked on the head, and every tenth man of the soldiers
> killed, and the rest shipped for the Barbadose. . . . I am persuaded
> that this is a righteous judgement of God upon these barbarous
> wretches, who have imbrued their hands in so much innocent
> blood . . . this work is wrought . . . not by power and might, but by
> the Spirit of God. . . . And therefore it is good that God alone
> have all the glory.

Cromwell seemed to be claiming that he was wreaking vengeance
only upon those who had "so much innocent blood" on their
hands; presumably he was referring to the Protestant blood
spilled by the Gaelic rising in 1641. If so, the Lord Lieutenant's
logic was tortured. He had taken his revenge against the very
garrison towards which those Irish rebels had marched in arms
eight years earlier. In reality, of course, Cromwell's course was
much more prosaic: he was simply consolidating the newly won
power of the Parliament as quickly as he was able. With this in
mind, Cromwell and his Ironsides moved south, rolling up the
coastal towns with ruthless efficiency. Only Wexford dared resist.

THE WEXFORD MASSACRE

Oliver Cromwell's men stormed the town of Wexford while negotiations were still going on. It was Drogheda all over again. The two massacres left a mark on the consciousness of the people of Ireland best expressed by a priest who witnessed (and barely escaped from) the carnage at Wexford. The cleric's judgement of Cromwell as the "pest of hell" has lived on among the Irish people for three-and-a-half centuries. Even that great champion of Empire, Sir Winston Churchill, lays the guilt for the subsequent Irish Problem squarely at the feet of the Roundhead general:

> Cromwell in Ireland, disposing of overwhelming strength, and using it with merciless wickedness, debased the standards of human conduct and sensibly darkened the journey of mankind. Cromwell's Irish massacres . . . by an uncomplicated process of terror, by an iniquitous land settlement, by the virtual proscription of the Catholic religion, by the bloody deeds already described, he cut new gulfs between the nations and the creeds. . . . Upon us all there still lies "the curse of Cromwell."

Over two thousand were killed at Wexford. This ballad by Michael Joseph Barry, one of the *Nation* poets, bitterly charges that some three hundred of the casualties—mostly women and children—occurred in the marketplace of the town after the battle was over.

They knelt around the cross divine,
The matron and the maid;
They bowed before Redemption's sign
And fervently they prayed.
Three hundred fair and helpless ones
Whose crime was this alone:
Their valiant husbunds, sires, and sons
Had battled for their own.

Had battled bravely but in vain—
The Saxon won the fight—
The Irish corpses strewed the plain
Where Valour slept with Right.
And now that man of demon guilt
To fated Wexford flew,
The red blood reeking on his hilt,
Of hearts to Erin true.

He found them there: the young, the old,
The maiden and the wife;
Their guardians brave in death were cold
Who dared for them the strife.
They prayed for mercy—God on high,
Before Thy cross they prayed;
And ruthless Cromwell bade them die
To glut the Saxon blade!

Three hundred fell—the stifled prayer
Was quenched in women's blood;
Nor youth nor age could move to spare
From slaughter's crimson flood.
But nations keep a stern account
Of deeds that tyrants do,
And guiltless blood to heaven will mount
And heaven avenge it, too!

While Cromwell was loose in the South, Owen Roe O'Neill was working a curious double game in the North. To protect his army's rear, Owen Roe formed a strange alliance with the parliamentary commander Sir Charles Coote to secure Londonderry against the Scot royalists. O'Neill apparently planned to march south in the name of the Crown against the parliamentary armies of Jones and Cromwell with another parliamentary army covering his base! It was late times in any event. O'Neill was taken ill in the autumn and died at Cloughoughter Castle in early November. Owen Roe was buried alongside Slasher O'Reilly at the Franciscan Friary in Cavan.

THE DEATH OF OWEN ROE

Perhaps inevitably, the story circulated that the last "Gaelic hope" of Ireland had been poisoned. This Thomas Davis song, based as it is on an old Gaelic ballad by the famous harpist-poet Pádraig MacLendon, propogates the fanciful legend that an English agent presented Owen Roe a pair of poisoned dancing pumps for a ball in Derry.

The scene is James Butler's County Waterford camp in November 1649. A courier from Cloughoughter has ridden non-stop to bring Ormonde the bad news.

Did they dare, did they dare to slay Eoghan Ruadh O'Neill?
"Yes, they slew with poison him they feared to meet with steel."
May God wither up their hearts, may their blood cease to flow!
"May they walk in living death, who poisoned Eoghan Ruadh!"

Though it breaks my heart to hear, say again the bitter words.
"From Derry, against Cromwell, he marched to measure swords;
But the weapon of the *Sassenach* met him on his way,
And he died at Cloch Uachtar upon St. Leonard's Day."

Sagest in the council was he, kindest in the hall;
Sure, we never won a battle—twas Eoghan won them all.
Had he lived, oh, had he lived, our country had been free;
But he's dead, but he's dead, and tis slaves we'll ever be.

O'Farrell and Clanrickarde, Preston and Black Hugh,
Audley and MacMahon, ye are valiant, wise and true;
But what, what are ye all to our darling who is gone?
The rudder of our ship was he, our castle's cornerstone.

Wail, wail him through the Island! Weep, weep for our pride!
Would that on the battlefield our gallant chief had died.
Weep the Victor of BeannBorb—weep him, young men and old;
Weep for him, ye women, your beautiful lies cold.

We thought you would not die, we were sure you would not go
And leave us in our utmost need to Cromwell's cruel blow:
Sheep without a shepherd when the snow shuts out the sky—
Oh! Why did you leave us, Eoghan? Why did you die?

Oliver Cromwell's exuberant rampage continued throughout
the rest of 1649. Waterford and Duncannon held out—they were
to fall to Ireton the next year—but most of the other southern
loyalist garrisons surrendered with alacrity. The stiffest opposition to Cromwell came at Clonmel in the spring of 1650. After a
furious battle, Black Hugh O'Neill, nephew to Owen Roe,
managed to spirit his entire force to freedom. The enraged Ironsides massacred the entire garrison at Gowran Castle, Kilkenny,
in reprisal. When Cromwell left in May to deal with the still

rebellious Scots,[6] he left Coote (presumably forgiven for his dealings with Owen Roe) in charge of the North, Lord Broghill (another Cavalier who had landed on his feet) to mop up Munster, and the steadfast Ireton in overall command.

Coote defeated Bishop Heber MacMahon's last Irish force in Ulster at Scarrifhollis on the River Swilly, and was pacifying Galway by the following year. Broghill meanwhile hanged another Irish Confederate prelate, Bishop Beotius MacEgan at Carraigadrohid, near Macroom, in 1650. In 1651 Broghill tracked down Pierce Ferriter in Kerry, ousted the Clare Confederate leader Conor O'Brien from the Pass of Inchicronan, and took Black Hugh O'Neill's surrender at Limerick. In 1652 Sir Felix O'Neill and fifty-one other Confederate leaders were executed. The next year Broghill hanged Ferriter near Killarney. The last Gaelic Confederate strongholds in Cavan and Galway also fell in 1653.

The "English" Civil Wars died a slow and savage death in Ireland. For all the blood, for all the fighting, for all the controversy, the Irish were left with one vivid, bitter memory—Oliver Cromwell. In the folk-history of Ireland, the sanguinary legacy of Cromwell was to come to represent the heavy hand of British rule in Ireland. In his excellent nineteenth century work on the Lord Protector, Samuel R. Gardiner suggests that:

> He stands forth as the typical Englishman of the modern world. . . . Even if Scotchmen forget the memories of Dunbar and Worcester, it is certain that Drogheda and Wexford will not pass out of the minds of Irishmen. It is in England that his fame has grown up . . . and it is as an Englishman that he must be judged.

One Kerry bard had put it slightly differently. Savagely poeticising Cromwell's legacy to the island, Egan O'Rahilly wrote that it was the parliamentary Lieutenant General and his Ironsides:

> Who gave plenty to the man of the flail,
> And left the heir of the land without "nothing."

CHAPTER NOTES (8)

1 — Most irredentist historians, perhaps trying to emphasise the "Gaelic nature" of the October 1641 rising, use O'Neill's Irish name, Phelim. In fact it was the Protestants of the time, stressing the barbarity of the Gaels, who refused to use "Felix," to which O'Neill had changed his name much earlier. Presumably the tale of massacre played better in England when the Irish culprits were led by "Phillom O Neal Cheife Trayter of all Ireland" than when led by "Sir Felix."

2 — Ferriter's bloody campaigns might lead us to suppose that he was a throwback, the sort of Gaelic poet who would have assumed a bellicose posture in support of his lord's latest cattle raid. In truth he was anything but. An unforgiving opponent in warfare, the Dingle gentleman-harper was a gentle pacifist in his verse. His most famous poem, *He Charges Her to Lay Aside Her Weapons,* is a thinly disguised love song urging Ireland to put down the habilments of war:

> I charge you, lady young and fair,
> Straightway to lay your arms aside.
> Lay by your armour, would you dare
> To spread the slaughter far and wide?
> ·
> Lady, we tremble far and near!
> Be with these conquests satisfied,
> And lest I perish, lady dear,
> Oh, lay those arms of yours aside.

3 — "Slasher" O'Reilly, commander of the Gaelic cavalry, became a legend in rebel history for this and a later, more tragic, action. Holding the bridge at Finae—between Loughs Shellin and Kinale—Colonel O'Reilly held a small force fast against repeated furious charges by the *Sassenach.* Heavily outnumbered, he kept fighting until his entire band was wiped out. Reinforcements from Granard arrived just in time to see the Slasher himself go down battling.

4 — Another MacMahon, Hugh Oge, had been one of the 1641 conspirators who had plotted to take Dublin Castle, along with Rory O'More and Lord Conor Maguire. When the plan was discovered by the authorities, The MacMahon was taken into government custody.

5 — The Levellers, headed by the radical John Lilburne, were calling for a full-scale political revolution. Before the Civil War, many Levellers had been unemployed, most had been landless. By autumn 1647 they had presented a manifesto to Fairfax calling for the abolition of both the monarchy and the Lords, the extension of the franchise to the landless, and complete revision of the law. In many ways the Leveller move-

ment anticipated the French revolutionaries of the late eighteenth century.

6 — Sixteen days after the execution of his father, the Prince of Wales was proclaimed Charles II by the Scots. Charles himself landed in Scotland in June 1650, promising to support Presbyterianism throughout the three kingdoms. Cromwell defeated the Scots at Dunbar that September and, after the Stuart heir entered England itself the next year to rally the remaining royalists, Cromwell crushed the rising at the Battle of Worcester in September. Charles spent the next nine years in exile.

9

The War of the Two Kings

By 1654 Oliver Cromwell had defeated all his foes, military and political—he was Lord Protector of the Commonwealth of England, Scotland, and Ireland. The Instrument of Government, the only written constitution in British history, governed the three nations. Though the Stuarts would be soon restored, never again would an English king rule autocratically. Henceforth, Parliament would skillfully wield the greatest of all weapons in a limited monarchy: the power of the public purse.

Ireland had been devastated by the Great Rebellion and the Civil Wars. One English officer noted that "A man might travel twenty miles and not see a living creature, either man or beast or bird." The land was so barren that hungry wolves roamed even into the towns looking for food. The physical destruction following the years of warfare was now to be joined by the political and social ravages of the Cromwellian Settlement.

The Commonwealth had enormous debts; sundry notes and promises accrued in the extremity of military necessity came quickly due. The Cromwellians were learning that winning a revolution is second only to losing one. The credibility of the Commonwealth itself was at issue. To take its place among nations, the Regicide government would have to honour its obligations. Fortunately for the Roundheads, there was a way to recompensate their creditors: Ireland could be made payment for the debts. All papist land in Ireland became forfeit to the government. Rebel landowners were executed and all others had their estates confiscated. Those Catholic lords not hanged for their part in the Irish risings were "re-granted" land in the western counties of Clare and Connacht. Even the "most innocent" among them received only two acres for every three they had forfeited elsewhere, and the scant yield of the poor western farmland made the settlement even more distasteful to the

Irish.   To the displaced landowner and his faithful *umhalach*, "To Hell or Connacht!" must have seemed debatable alternatives.

THE ROCKS OF BAWN

The Cromwellian Settlement was ostensibly applied to only the landowners.   What was of no concern to the debt-ridden Parliament was that, as Jackson points out:

> The Irish Catholic landlord in the majority of cases [*still*] stood to his tenants in the relation of a chief to his kinsmen. . . . In most cases where the landlord went, there his tenants followed, regardless of the fact they might have stayed.

Many labourers and ploughmen did in fact trudge westward with their unlucky lords; altogether over forty thousand Irishmen disappeared beyond the Shannon, most by the end of 1654.[1]

These new Connachtmen left behind their land to adventurers who had lent money to Parliament, to Puritan soldiers whose pay was in arrears, and most often, to speculators who bought up the largely unwanted land from parliamentary creditors who preferred cash.   As the speculators rounded up as much land as they could at bargain prices, the government was busy corralling orphan children and selling them at a profit as indentured servants to the Barbados and Virginia colonies.[2]

This old ballad suggests that the Irish left behind were not afforded particularly good farming land.   A "bawn" was originally a walled enclosure built by the Normans into which livestock could be driven to protect the herds from Irish raiders; later, the word became generic for "castle."   The singer, then, is bemoaning that he has been left to farm the quarries.   The song tends to confirm Lecky's suggestion that the Cromwellian Settlement was "the foundation of that deep and lasting division between the proprietary and the tenants which is the chief cause for the political and social evils of Ireland."   The ballad is still extremely popular today.

Come all you loyal heroes
Wherever you may be,
Don't hire with any master
Till you know what your work will be;
For you must rise up early
From the clear daylight till dawn,

CHRONOLOGY (The War of the Two Kings)

1658 . . . . .Death of Oliver Cromwell.

1660 . . . . .Stuart Restoration, *Charles II*; Boers settle South Africa.

1662 . . . . .Episcopacy restored; Ormonde returns as Viceroy.

1665 . . . . .London Plague kills 70,000.

1665-67. . . . . . . .Anglo-Dutch War.

1666 . . . . .Great London fire; Lowland Covenanter rising crushed at Pentland Hills; Calcutta "founded."

1667 . . . . .Irish Land Claims Court closes down.

1668 . . . . .Triple Alliance formed to counter French expansionism.

1670 . . . . .Duke of York openly avows Catholicism; Charles II deals secretly with Louis XIV; Hudson Bay Company formed.

1672-74. . . . . . . .Anglo-Dutch War; Willem of Orange-Nassau successfully defends Dutch against French and English by cutting dikes.

1677 . . . . .York's daughter Mary marries Willem.

1678 . . . . .Titus Oates "reveals" Popish Plot; Papist Disabling Act bars Catholics from Parliament.

1679 . . . .*Habeas Corpus* Act; Scot Presbyterian rising crushed at Bothwell Bridge.

1682 . . . . .Peter the Great, Tsar of Russia.

1683 . . . . .Monmouth exiled after Rye House Plot.

1685 . . . .*James II*; Argyle and Monmouth rebellions crushed, Bloody Assizes; Louis XIV begins campaign against Huguenots with withdrawal of Edict of Nantes; Clarendon, Viceroy.

1686 . . . . .Willem forms League of Augsburg against Louis XIV.

1687 . . . . .Tyrconnell, Viceroy; Declaration of Indulgence; Newton's *Principles* published.

1688 (spring). . . . .Catholic discrimination abolished; Prince of Wales born; Seven Bishops acquitted.

1688 (autumn). . . . .Willem and Mary land at Torbay with army; apprentice boys incident at Londonderry; James II flees to France.

1689 (winter) . . . . .*William III* and *Mary II* declared joint sovereigns with parliamentary supremacy; James lands at Kinsale.

1689 (spring). . . . .James rebuffed at Londonderry; Patriot Parliament.

1689 (summer) . . . .Battles of Killiecrankie and Dunkeld in Scotland; Schomberg lands in Ulster.

1690 (summer) . . . .William lands at Carrickfergus; Battle of the Boyne; James flees to France; Ballyneety Raid; Battle of Limerick; French fleet defeats Anglo-Dutch at Beachy Head.

1690 (autumn). . . . .Churchill takes Cork and Kinsale; William returns to England; French Jacobite troops return to France.

1691 (spring). . . . . .St. Ruth takes command of Irish Jacobites; Battle of Ath-
                lone.
1691 (summer) . . . .Battle of Aughrim; death of Tyrconnell.
1691 (autumn). . . . .Capitulation of Limerick; Flight of the Wild Geese.

I'm afraid you won't be able
For to plough the Rocks of Bawn.

My shoes they are well worn now
And my stockings they are thin,
My heart is always trembling,
Afeared I might give in;
My heart is nearly broken
From the clear daylight till dawn,
And I never will be able
To plough the Rocks of Bawn.

My curse attend you, Sweeny,
And give your horse some hay,
And give him a good feed of oats
Before you go away;
Don't feed him on soft turnips,
Put him out on your green lawn,
And then he might be able
To plough the Rocks of Bawn.

I wish the King of England
Would write to me in time,
And place me in some regiment
All in my youth and prime;
I'd fight for Ireland's glory
From the clear daylight of dawn,
And I never would return again
To plough the Rocks of Bawn.

    The Restoration of the Stuart monarchy in May 1660 was welcome news to the Catholic Irish. Not realising the tautness of Parliament's reins on Charles II, the Irish fully expected the King to set things right for the men who had fought so long and hard for his father. The re-establishment of the Church of Ireland within a few months of the Restoration gave the first hint that the new order was not going to provide a panacea for the ills of Ireland.[3] There *was* in fact some effort by the Crown to make restitution to the dispossessed. The problem, of course, was simply that there was not enough land to satisfy both the old and new landowners. James Butler, back in Dublin serving the Stuarts, wryly suggested the solution: "There must be new discoveries made of a new Ireland, for the old will not serve to satisfy these engagements." By 1667 about a third of the land taken by the Cromwellian Settlement had been returned to the original Irish owners. The claims court handling the rearrangment closed down that year, leaving nobody satisfied. The sullen Protestant landowners were bitter, believing that the bargain they had made with Parliament was being abrogated by the Stuart King. The papists were unhappy, too. Jonathan Swift would later describe why:

> The catholics of Ireland . . . lost their estates for fighting in defence of their king. Those who cut off the father's head, forced the son to fly for his life . . . obtained . . . those very estates the catholics lost . . . and thus gained by their rebellion what the catholics lost by their loyalty.

The Romanists of Ireland had ultimately lost two-thirds of the land they had owned before 1641; if that was to be the prize for defending the Stuarts, it should not be surprising that some of the papists lost all respect for the Crown and its law. The Catholics would never quite forget the Puritan lesson: there was profit in rebellion against the Crown.

REDMOND O'HANLON

Worst hit by the Cromwellian Settlement, and little succoured by the Stuart Restoration, were the Gaelic Irish of Ulster. It had been the men of the North that had risen that October night in 1641 to regain their ancient lands (though offering the public reason that they were defending the King from the Commons). A Gaelic fortress in 1601, Ulster had backed the losing side twice in a half-century and the Old Order had paid the tariff. By the time of the Restoration in 1660, the province had a five-to-two Protestant majority. Many classic Ulster names had found a new home in Connacht.

The O'Hanlons of Armagh were typical of many northern

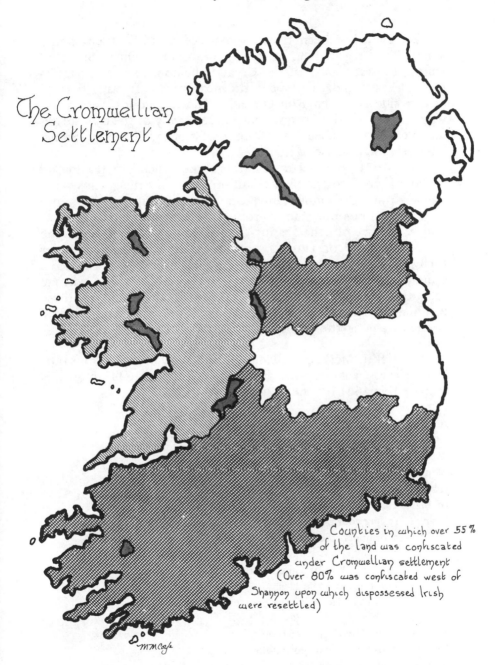

The Cromwellian Settlement

Counties in which over 55% of the land was confiscated under Cromwellian settlement (Over 80% was confiscated west of Shannon upon which dispossessed Irish were resettled)

MMCoyle

septs.   They had been first dispossessed in 1609, their family seat at Tanderagee going to the English Captain Oliver St. John. During the early days of the Great Rebellion, they had retaken the old castle and then spent the next decade fighting fiercely at the side of Owen Roe O'Neill.   The O'Hanlons were afterwards ousted by the Cromwellian forces, many of the clan suffering execution as rebels.   More went west of the Shannon.   Some, however, stayed close to home.

In 1671 one clan member, the legendary Redmond O'Hanlon, took to the Slieve Gullion of south Armagh, sweeping down from the mountains on unsuspecting English and Scot settlers in Monaghan, Tyrone, and Armagh.   O'Hanlon was representative of the rapparees—so called because of the short "rappers," or cudgels, that they often concealed under their cloaks—embittered outlaws who were to become a familiar sight in Ireland over the next two centuries. It is ironic that the Irish came to use an English nickname for these bandits; the Gaelic word for them, *toraidhe,* or pursuer, became common among the British to describe intense loyalists . . . as "tory."

Patrick J. McCall's ballad sings the story of the famous outlaw.   Never caught by the authorities, Redmond O'Hanlon was murdered in 1681 by one of his own band.

A shepherd that lives on Slieve Gullion
Came down to the County Tyrone,
And told us how Redmond O'Hanlon
Won't let the rich Saxons alone;
He rides over moorland and mountain
By night, till a stranger is found,
Saying, "Taking your own choice to be lodging
Right over, or under, the ground!"

If you whistle out "Whoo!" like a native,
He leaves you the way to go clear;
If you squeal out a "Hew!" like a Scotsman,
You will pay him a guinea a year;
But if you cry "Haw!" like a Saxon,
Och! Then tis your life or your gold!
By stages Count Redmond O'Hanlon
Gets back what they plundered of old!

Old Coote of Cootehill is heartbroken,
And Johnston beyond in the Fews
Has wasted eight barrels of powder
Upon him, but all to no use!
Although there's four hundred pounds sterling,
If Redmond you'd put out of sight;
Mind, if the heart's dark in your body,
Tis Redmond will let in the light.

The great Duke of Ormonde is frantic,
His soldiers got up with the lark,
To catch the bold Redmond by daylight,
But Redmond caught *them* in the dark;
Said he when he'd stripped them and bound them,
"Take back my best thanks to His Grace,
For all the fine pistols and powder
He has sent to this desolate place."

Then here's to you, Redmond O'Hanlon,
Long may Your Excellency reign,
High Ranger of woods and rivers,
Surveyor of mountains and plain;
Examiner-in-Chief of all traitors,
Protector of all that are true,
Henceforward, King Charley of England
May take what he gets, after you!

It was not rapparees in the wild Ulster mountains, however, that were the real danger to the Crown of England. The most important single threat to the stability of the Stuart was, as usual, the Crown's relationship with Westminster. By 1670 the King and Parliament were at daggers drawn. Charles II took great pains to remind the Members that Parliament had been a creation of the Plantagenet monarchy (leaving unsaid the implied caution that the assembly still existed only at the sufferance of the King). The parliamentarians just as heatedly reminded Charles II of his status during the Commonwealth (leaving unsaid the threat that the precedent of regicide had already been established). By now "there was a tradition," Professor Plumb suggests, "of conspiracy, riot, plot, and revolt among the ruling classes that stretched back to the Normans . . . violence in politics was an

Englishman's birthright." It was against this turbulent background that the players were to cast their shadows until the drama exploded into the Glorious Revolution . . . or, as it was to be called in Ireland, *Cogadh an Dó Rí,* the War of the Two Kings.

Charles II's arrogance towards Parliament had been demonstrated clearly as early as 1664 when the King went to war against the Dutch without consulting Westminster. The adventure had provided glory only for the sovereign's secretly Catholic brother James, Duke of York, who had seized New Amsterdam in his own name, incidentally providing Manhattan Island with the designation it has borne since. When the legislature had next met, it spitefully refused to pay for the "King's fiasco." Rather than accept the limits of royal prerogative, the King had sulked.

In 1678 occurred the singular affair of Titus Oates and the Popish Plot. A Baptist minster until the Restoration, and subsequently defrocked from both the Anglican and Roman churches, Oates was an unlikely candidate to have a dramatic impact on Britain, but the times and the mood were right and have an impact he did. This curious man produced a set of forged letters purporting to outline a Jesuit plot to massacre Protestants—including the King—and put the by-now openly papist Duke of York on the throne. Hatred of Rome and fear of a repetition of October 1641 were barely concealed spectres in the English public consciousness. Parliament was swift to feed the public hysteria. Embarking on wholesale trials and executions,[4] the Commons even went so far as to cheer when Oates stood before it accusing the Catholic Queen Catherine of complicity in the plot. That was too much even for Charles, whose safety all the agitation was supposed to be insuring. The King dissolved Parliament.

Parliament was ready for confrontation with the King when the assembly met again the next year. When a bill was introduced to exclude the Duke of York, heir to the childless Charles, from the royal succession, the King again was forced to resort to the by-now commonplace Stuart tactic of dismissing the Members. Titus Oates, whatever his original motive, had provided the Parliament with its Cause.

When Charles II died naturally in 1685, the dreaded event finally occurred, plot or no plot: an avowed Catholic was on the throne of England for the first time since Mary Tudor. In Ireland, hopes were high. When James II elevated the blatantly

Romanist Richard Talbot to Duke of Tyrconnell and then gave the new duke command of the Irish army, the Catholic Irish were understandably encouraged. Parliament, on the other hand, was appalled. A standing army of any sort stood as threat to Westminster, but an Irish Catholic standing army captained by a sworn papist looked a direct challenge to parliamentary power. When the new King made Tyrconnell Lord Lieutenant of Ireland in 1687 and then granted free worship to all subjects of the Crown, it was enough to chase many Irish Protestants back to Britain screaming "Popery!"[5]

THE BLACK-BACKED COW

(*Drimin Dubh*)

The Irish may not have been planning to join an Oates-like plot against the Crown, but it was no secret where their sentiments lay. Even before the death of Charles II, there had been high excitement of anticipation: not only was the Duke of York openly Catholic, but he was married to Mary of Modena—his second wife—who was also a papist. Large numbers of his adherents in Scotland and Ireland had already been calling themselves "Jacobites," from the Latin for James.

This old Gaelic song pre-dates the Glorious Revolution and demonstrates that whimsical metaphor was very much alive at the time . . . the *darling Black-Backed Cow* served to represent the Jacobite cause (the Irish idiom makes the proper translation the "dear black white-backed cow"). Though cattle rather than money had served as the symbol of value since pre-history in Ireland, perhaps only an Irishman could call his king bovine and mean it as a compliment. The translation is by Samuel Ferguson.

Ah, *Drimin dubh dílis,* ah pride of the flow,
Ah, where are your folks, are they living or no?
They're down in the ground, neath the sod lying low,
Expecting King James with the crown on his brow.

But if I could get sight of the crown on his brow,
By night and day travelling to London I'd go;
Over mountains of mist and soft mosses below,
Till I'd beat on the kettle-drums, *Drimin Dubh, O!*

Welcome home, welcome home, *Drimin Dubh, O*!
Good was your sweet milk for drinking, I trow;
With your face like a rose, and your dew-lap of snow,
I'll part from you never, ah, *Drimin Dubh, O*!

From the moment that James II came to the throne in 1685, his Crown had been in jeapordy. During the first year of his reign, he had been forced to suppress risings led by the Duke of Argyle in Scotland and by the Duke of Monmouth—the bastard son of Charles—in the West of England. The royal reprisals were savage, earning the name "Bloody Assizes" and, at least to the uneasy Protestants, bearing a suspicious similarity to the "Dragonnades" in France, by which the Sun King was crushing Calvinism at about the same time.

In 1687 James II unilaterally issued a Declaration of Indulgence that granted freedom of worship to *all* denominations. By affording toleration to the Dissenters, the King naively hoped to wean their support away from Westminster. Any bridges the King had built to the Dissenters by the indulgence were destroyed soon thereafter when the artless James appointed a Catholic priest to his Privy Council. The next year the King again went over the head of Parliament, asserting the royal prerogative of "dispensation" to remove all doubt as to his true hand: a second declaration was issued in April, specifically targeted to abolish discrimination against Catholics and ordering the writ to be read from the pulpits of the Church of England. When seven Anglican bishops had the temerity to submit a written protest, James arbitrarily arrested them for sedition. Even more distressing to the Parliament was a concurrent event; on 10 June 1688 Queen Mary presented the King with a Catholic heir. The Whigs[6] at Westminster found themselves faced with a monarch who was acting uncomfortably like the divine-right sovereigns of old and, with the birth of Prince James Edward, it was beginning to look as if the Catholic King was going to be able to force a papist future on an unwilling nation. James II, indeed the entire royal family, would have to go.

But who to replace James with? The unhappy experience of the Commonwealth was still fresh in the minds of the parliamentary leaders. They were not against the Crown *per se;* they were merely adamant that another Catholic should not sit on the throne of England. There was only one Protestant available who had the necessary "legal" qualifications: Mary, the eldest daughter of James by his first wife, Ann Hyde.[7] Not only did she fit Westminster's requirements, but her husband Willem, Prince of Orange-Nassau, was himself grandson to Charles I and was, therefore, third-in-line to the English Crown in his own right (behind Mary and her younger sister Anne). More important, Willem was game for the adventure. Even better, as Stadtholder of Holland and the United Netherlands, he had the troops to back up his wife's claim.

When the seven "seditious" bishops were acquitted amidst great popular approval on 30 June 1688, Parliament seized the opportunity to invite Mary and "William" to occupy the English throne. The Stadtholder, locked in struggle with Louis XIV, was not about to spurn an offer that could put the British fleet on his side against the Sun King. William landed on the Devonshire coast in November with fourteen thousand men. Led by John Churchill, Earl of Marlborough, the English army deserted to the Prince of Orange almost *en masse,* as did James II's other daughter Anne. The dispirited James threw the Great Seal of England into the Thames and flew to the court of France. The Jacobite's parting gesture was merely another sign of James' misreading of events—the growing power of the Parliament had long since superseded that of the Great Seal. On 13 February 1689 Mary II and William III were declared joint sovereigns of England with Anne named next in succession. The infant son of James II, Prince James Edward—history's Old Pretender—was specifically excluded. The War of the Two Kings was officially underway.

As the situation had deteriorated in England, Tyrconnell had not been idle across the Irish Sea. To Talbot, James was still King of Ireland, whatever the state of affairs in Britain. The Lord Lieutenant had rapidly seized the major strategic garrisons on the island, a process made easier by his having officered the Irish Army with large numbers of Catholics in the preceding years. By the time "Dutch William" had landed in Devonshire, Tyrconnell already held all of Ireland for James . . . with the significant exception of two isolated Williamite outposts at Enniskillen and Londonderry.

LILLIBULERO

Richard Talbot, Duke of Tyrconnell, was, to say the least,

not particularly popular among the Protestant planters of Ireland. His unswerving Romanism alone would have been enough
to earn him the emnity of the anti-Catholic lords; the obvious
anti-Protestantism of his viceroyalty also managed to gain him
the violent hatred of the lower-class settlers.

The oldest of Orange songs, *Lillibulero,* in the words of
MacCurtain, is the song "that whistled a king out of three kingdoms;" the doggeral verse attributed to Lord Wharton is still
often sung today in the North with updated, but no less bitter,
lyrics.[8] The disdain with which Tyrconnell was held by the
Ulster Scots is made obvious by the song. The spectre of the
bloody rising of October 1641 was still a living memory to the
uneasy Protestant farmers in 1688. The vision has unhappily
changed little in the past three centuries.

Ho, brother *Teague* dost hear the decree,
Lillibulero bullen a la;
That we shall have a new Deputy,
Lillibulero bullen a la.

Refrain:
Lero lero lero lero,
Lillibulero bullen a la;
Lillibulero lero lero,
Lillibulero bullen a la.

Ho, by my soul, he is a Talbot,
Lillibulero, etc.
And he will cut all the English throat,
Lillibulero, etc.
Though, by my soul, the English do prate,
Lilibulero, etc.
The Law's on their side and the divil knows that,
Lillibulero, etc.

Refrain

But if Dispence do come from the Pope,
Lillibulero, etc.
We'll hang Magna Carta and themselves on a rope,
Lillibulero, etc.
And the bold Talbot is now made a Lord,

Lillibulero, etc.
And with his brave lads, he's coming aboard,
Lillibulero, etc.

Refrain

Who in all France have taken a swear,
Lillibulero, etc.
That day will have no Protestant heir,
Lillibulero, etc.
Oh, but why does he stay behind,
Lillibulero, etc.
Oh, by my soul, tis a Protestant wind,
Lillibulero, etc.

Refrain

Now that Tyrconnell is come ashore,
Lillibulero, etc.
And we shall have commissions galore,
Lillibulero, etc.
And he who will not go to the Mass,
Lillibulero, etc.
Shall be turned out and look like an ass,
Lillibulero, etc.

Refrain

Now them old heretics all will go down,
Lillibulero, etc.
By Christ and St. Patrick the island's our own,
Lillibulero, etc.
There was an old prophecy out of the bog,
Lillibulero, etc.
That our land would be ruled by an ass and a dog,
Lillibulero, etc.

Refrain

So now the old prophecy's coming to pass,
Lillibulero, etc.
For James is the dog and Tyrconnell's the ass!
Lillibulero, etc.

Refrain

NO SURRENDER

In December 1688 Lord Antrim's Jacobite Redshanks appeared outside the walls of Londonderry. Inside, the huddled settlers and townsmen debated their options. The major argument among the Williamite refugees and their leader Robert Lundy was over how long the overcrowded town could hold on without aid. The decision was finally made to capitulate to the Jacobite Scots, presumably to avoid having to surrender to a Catholic force later on. As the "plumed and belted" Lord Antrim rode up to accept the official submission of the town, thirteen exasperated apprentice boys rushed up crying, "No Surrender!" and slammed the gates shut in the face of the Protestant Jacobite commander. So began the siege of Londonderry, the most glorious chapter in Orange-Irish tradition, a tradition as bitter and rich, if not so long, as the rebel.

Behold the crimson banners float
O'er yonder turrets hoary;
They tell of days of mighty note,
And Derry's deathless glory;
When her brave sons undaunted stood,
Embattled to defend her,
Indignant stemmed oppression's flood,
And sung out, "No surrender!"

Old Derry's walls were firm and strong,
Well fenced in every quarter.
Each frowning bastion grim along,
With culverin and mortar;
But Derry had a surer guard
Than all that art could lend her,
Her 'prentice boys the gate who barred,
And sung out, "No surrender!"

On came the foe in bigot ire,
And fierce the assault was given;
By shot and shell, mid streams of fire,
Her fated roofs were riven:
But baffled was the tyrant's wrath,
And vain his hopes to bend her,
For still mid famine, fire, and death,
She sung out, "No surrender!"

Again, when treason maddened round,
And rebel hordes were swarming,
Were Derry's sons the foremost found,
For king and country arming:
Forth, forth they rushed at honour's call,
From age to boyhood tender,
Again to man their virgin wall,
And sung out, "No surrender!"

Long may the crimson banner wave,
A meteor streaming airy,
Portentous of the free and brave
Who man the walls of Derry;
And Derry's sons alike defy
Pope, traitor, or pretender;
And peal to heaven their 'prentice cry,
Their patriot—"No surrender!"

With a month after William III's February 1689 coronation in England, James II had landed in Ireland. Summoning an Irish parliament for May, James rode north to put down the Enniskillen and Londonderry resistance. A Jacobite victory at Clady, just south of Lifford on the River Foyle, filled an already jammed Londonderry with more refugees, encouraging James to hurry to the city personally to accept Lundy's expected surrender. The overconfident King had not taken the mettle of the defenders into account.

THE MAIDEN CITY

In the long history of Orange/Green troubles in the North of Ireland, the Protestants have had but the two victories of Enniskillen and Londonderry to celebrate as actual triumphs-in-arms by "native" Protestants over Catholics. They have made the most of them; the victories, in truth, do form an heroic chapter in Irish history.

The Protestant Williamites of Fermanagh saved Enniskillen when they beat back the Jacobites at the Battle of Newtownbutler just east of Upper Lough Erne. The struggle for Londonderry was a closer thing.

Perhaps thirty thousand were crowded inside the walls of Londonderry when the Jacobites appeared on the heights of Creggan to the west. James Stuart soon found that the defenders were not at all disposed to surrender (they had put Lundy aside) and that, without proper siege guns, he had no way to make them submit without a protracted investment. Directing his troops to throw a boom across the River Foyle, cutting off the city's lifeline with the sea, the Jacobite King left for Dublin. The Williamites settled in for a slow descent into hell.

For 105 days the defiant defenders kept the besieging army at bay while suffering increasingly severe deprivation.[9] Only the animated efforts of the Williamite Major Henry Baker and George Walker, refugee rector of Donaghmore, kept up the spirit of the Derrymen as disease, exposure, and starvation took their toll. Finally, on 28 July 1689 the relief ships *Mountjoy* and *Phoenix* forced the boom at Culmore, and led a convoy of foodships through the breach. The Jacobites, with insufficient artillery to threaten the sealift, were forced to raise the seige.

This Orange ballad by Charlotte Elizabeth celebrates the gallant 1688-89 defense of what has become the Orange "holy city." Londonderry's resistance to James II is commemorated each year by Protestant Ulstermen by marches and parades on Apprentice Boys' Day.

Where Foyle his swelling waters roll northward to the main,
Here Queen of Erin's daughters, fair Derry, fixed her reign;
A holy temple crowned her, and commerce graced her streets;
A rampart wall was round her, the river at her feet;
And here she sate alone, boys, would be a maiden still,
Vowed the maiden from her throne, boys, would be a maiden still.

From Aughrim crossing over, in famous Eighty-Eight,
A plumed and belted lover came to the Ferry Gate;
She summoned to defend her our sires—a beardless race—
They shouted "No Surrender!" and slammed it in his face.
Then in a quiet tone, boys, they told him twas their will
That the maiden on her throne, boys, should be a maiden still.

Next, crushing all before him, a kingly wooer came
(The royal banner o'er him blushed crimson deep for shame);
He showed the Pope's commission nor dreamed to be refused,
She pitied his condition but begged to stand excused.

In short, the fact is known, boys, she chased him down the hill,
For the maiden on her throne, boys, would be a maiden still.

On our brave sires descending, twas then the tempest broke,
Their peaceful dwellings rending, mid blood and flame and smoke.
That hallowed grave-yard yonder swells with the slaughtered dead—
Oh, brothers, pause and ponder—it was US they bled!
And while their gift we own, boys—the fane that tops our hill—
Oh, the maiden on her throne, boys, shall be a maiden still.

Nor wily tongue shall move us, nor tyrant arm affright,
We'll look to one above us who ne'er forsook the Right;
Who will, may crouch and tender the birthright of the free.
But brothers, No surrender, no compromise for me;
We want no barrier stone, boys, no gates to guard the hill,
Yet the maiden on her throne, boys, shall be a maiden still.

William III sat uneasily upon his new throne. In Scotland, bands of Jacobite Highlanders were rising. In Ireland, virtually the entire island was behind James and his now-sitting Parliament. Worst of all to the Stadtholder—who had accepted the English Crown for what its fleet and resources could do for him in Europe—Louis of France was threatening his domains on the continent. With a superb grasp of the geopolitics involved, William decided that he had just enough time to suppress opposition in Scotland and Ireland before the procrastinating Sun King of France would be able to endanger the Dutch Williamite lands.

James was meanwhile happily basking in the applause of the Irish Parliament. The first truly "Irish" assembly in many centuries, the so-called Patriot Parliament which sat between May and July 1689 passed numerous laws, none of which were to have any staying power in the face of the storm about to explode over Ireland. Its importance as a symbol to later generations of Irish nationalists should not, however, be underestimated. Thomas Davis, for example, was to comment a century-and-a-half later that:

> it boldly announced our national independence in words which Molyneux shouted on to Swift, and Swift to Lucas, and Lucas to Flood, and Flood and Grattan redoubling the cry . . . Ireland was again a nation.

A French Jacobite general who had landed with James at Kinsale viewed the Patriot Parliament with less poetic, if somewhat more realistic, candour:

> All his other subjects have deserted him; this is the only body of men that he has now to appear for him; he is in their hands and must please them.

The interlude of the Patriot Parliament was soon over in any event; the war of the League of Augsburg against Louis of France was coming to Ireland.

In August 1689 a fleet of seventy Williamite vessels appeared at the entrance to Belfast Lough. Led by the octogenarian Marshal Schomberg—formerly a Protestant general in the service of the Sun King, the Marshall had left the service of France just four years earlier when Louis XIV revoked the Edict of Nantes—the Williamites landed ten thousand troops at Groomsport and immediately invested Lord Iveagh's Jacobite garrison across the lough at Carrickfergus. It took Schomberg only a week to take the port town. James II and Tyrconnell unaccountably allowed the Williamite general to secure the bridgehead unmolested. It was a grievous blunder. The elderly Marshal moved gingerly southward probing for the expected Jacobite resistance. He did not find it; instead, he found a smouldering Newry, torched by the Duke of Berwick—James Stuart's bastard son—when James II had ordered the Irish army to fall back first on Dundalk and, finally, to the River Glyde. The pleasantly astonished Schomberg found himself firmly ensconced athwart the strategic Moyry Pass by the autumn. Although plagued by disease, the Williamites had taken eastern Ulster with barely a skirmish. As the opposing armies wintered, the way into Ireland was open to the new King of England.

In June 1690 he came. Landing at Carrickfergus with a large army of Dutch, French Huguenots, and English, William III marched swiftly to join his lieutenant at Dundalk. James II, overruling Tyrconnell and de Rosen[10] who wanted to attack the Williamites at once, withdrew his army to the River Boyne, finally turning about on the southern bank to make his stand near the village of Donore.

The storied Battle of the Boyne began at dawn on 1 July 1690. King William having been slightly wounded in a night reconnaissance of the field, Schomberg assumed tactical command of the Williamite assault. The attackers crossed the river at several points but the major Dutch thrust, led personally by the Marshal, mustered in a concealing glen that sloped down from Tullyallen to the Boyne at the Oldbridge Ford. Old Schomberg himself was killed as the Williamites charged out from under cover to contest the ford, but his soldiers boldly continued the assault in the face of the concentrated Irish firepower. The battle raged unabated throughout the day until flanking raids by the superbly trained continental horse began to tell. The Jacobites fell back on Duleek in good order to protect their flanks from the repeated thrusts of the Williamite cavalry. As the evening wore into night the Irish finally broke, forming again on Dublin the following morning.

THE BOYNE WATER

The Battle of the Boyne is revered by the northern Protestants as their Independence Day . . . and so it was, though there was to be much carnage before the rest of the island was "liberated." The anniversary of the battle (12 July, new calendar) has become the focal point of the Orange celebrations. As modern Belfast echoes to the booming beat of the Lambeg drum, songs are offered up in praise of "King Billy." This ballad by Lieutenant Colonel William Blacker is still one of the most popular. It is also one of the best.

July the First in Ouldbridge Town there was a grievous battle
Where many a man lay on the ground by cannons that did rattle;
King James he pitched his tents between the lines for to retire,
But King William threw his bombballs in and set them all on fire.

Thereat they vowed revenge upon King William's forces
And oft did vehemently cry that they would stop their courses;
A bullet from the Irish came and grazed King William's arm,
They thought His Majesty was slain, yet it did him little harm.

Duke Schomberg then, in friendly care, his King would often caution
To shun the spot where bullets hot retained their rapid motion;
But William said, "He don't deserve the name of Faith's Defender,
Who would not venture life and limb to make a foe surrender."

When we the Boyne began to cross, the enemy descended,
But few of our brave men were lost, so stoutly we defended;
The Horse it was that first marched o'er, the Foot soon followed after,
But brave Duke Schomberg was no more by venturing o'er the water.

When valiant Schomberg he was slain, King William he accosted
His warlike men for to march on and he would be foremost;
"Brave boys," he cried,"be not dismayed for the loss of one commander,
For God shall be our king this day and I'll be general under."

Then stoutly we the Boyne did cross to give the enemies battle;
Our cannon, to our foes great cost, like thundering claps did rattle;
In majestic mien our Prince rode o'er, his men soon followed after,
With blow and shout put our foe to the rout, the day we crossed the water.

The Protestants of Drogheda have reason to be thankful
That they were not to bondage brought, they being but a handful;
First to the Thosel they were brought and tried at Millmount after,
But brave King William set them free by venturing o'er the water.

The cunning French near to Duleek had taken up their quarters,
And found themselves on every side still waiting for new orders;
But in the dead time of the night they set the fields on fire,
And long before the morning's light to Dublin did retire.

Then said King William to his men after the French departed,
"I'm glad," said he, "that none of ye seem to be faint-hearted;
So sheath your swords and rest awhile, in time we'll follow after,"
These words he uttered with a smile the day he crossed the water.

Come let us all with heart and voice applaud our lives' defender,
Who at the Boyne his valour showed and made his foe surrender.
To God above, the praise we'll give now and ever after,
And bless the glorious memory of King William that crossed the water.

THE BATTLE OF THE BOYNE

The unbent backbone of the modern Orangeman finds a
stiff brace in the folk-memory of the Boyne. The repeated
charges by the Williamites through the ford at Oldbridge and up
to the teeth of the Irish pikes and guns on the opposite bank
stand as a bold heritage proudly adopted by the northern Protestants. The legend of the anti-Rome English king crossing the
Irish Sea to protect the loyal citizens of Ulster has become a
firmly cherished constant in the folklore of the Protestant

society of the North.

As do the folk-memories of the nationalist Irish, however, the Orange "facts" sometimes get blurred in the resinging of the songs. King William, for example, had the full backing of the papacy in his attempt to wrest the Crown of England from James. His Irish campaign was neither for the rights of Ulster Protestants, nor against those of the papist Irish; rather, William was quite simply fighting an ally of his hated enemy, the Sun King of France. The Stadtholder "was a Calvinist, but he tolerated all religions," reports Robert Massie. "The Pope was his ally, so was the Catholic Emperor; there were Catholic officers in his army. Every other prejudice and antagonism was set aside; his sole vendetta was with Louis."

There are other honoured shibboleths of the Unionist folk-memory that are equally amnesic. The Jacobite forces, contrary to popular myth, did not wear green, nor did the Williamites sport orange. The men fighting for King James—and for the Jacobite pretenders after him—wore *white* cockades in honour of their Bourbon patrons. It is a bit of perhaps trivial irony that it was William's men who wore the cockades of green![11]

The fifth verse of the following song tells of the death of Marshal Schomberg and the Hero of Londonderry, George Walker, both casualties at the Boyne. Such Orange ballads are a reminder of an interesting musical phenomenon: while Irish rebels sing of martyrs and defeats, Orangemen sing of martyrs and victories.

A kingly host upon a stream, a monarch camped around,
Its southern upland far and wide their white pavilions crowned;
Not long ago that sky unclouded showed, nor beneath the ray,
That gentle stream in silver flowed to meet the new-born day.

Peals the loud gun—its thunders boom the echoing vales along,
While curtained in its sulphorous boom moves on the gallant throng,
And Foot and Horse in mingled mass, regardless all of life,
With furious ardor onward pass to join the deadly strife.

Nor strange that with such ardent flame each glowing heart beats high,
Their battle-word was William's name and "Death and Liberty!"
Then Ouldbridge, then they peaceful bowers with sounds unwonted rang,
And Tredagh, mid thy distant towers, was heard the mighty clang.

The silver stream is crimsoned wide and clogged with many a corse,
As floating down its gentle tide come mingled man and horse;
Now fiercer grows the battle's rage, the guarded stream is crossed,
And furious, hand-to-hand, engage each bold contending host.

He falls—the veteran hero falls, renowned along the Rhine—
And *he* whose name, while Derry's walls endure, shall brightly shine;
Oh! Would to heaven that churchman bold, his arms with triumph blest,
The soldier spirit had controlled that fired his pious breast.

And he, the chief of younder brave and persecuted band,
Who foremost rushed amid the wave and gained the hostile strand,
He bleeds, brave Caillemonte—he bleeds—tis closed, his bright career,
Yet still that band to glorious deeds his dying accents cheer.

And now that well-contested strand successive columns gain,
While backward James' yielding band are borne across the plain;
In vain the sword green Erin draws, and life away doth fling—
Oh! Worthy of a better cause and of a bolder king.

In vain thy bearing bold is shown upon that blood-stained ground;
Thy towering hopes are overthrown, thy choicest fall around;
Nor, shamed abandon thou the fray, nor blush though conquered there,
A power against thee fights today no mortal arm may dare.

Hurrah! Hurrah! For Liberty, for her sword we draw,
And dared the battle while on high our Orange banners flew.
Woe worth the hour—woe worth the state, when men shall cease to join
With grateful hearts to celebrate the glories of the Boyne!

James II left the Boyne battlefield as the Irish began to break, making his way posthaste to Dublin. Complaining upon his arrival to Lady Tyrconnell that his army had "run away," the King received a typically Churchillian rejoinder: "Yes, Your Grace, and *you* won the race!" In fact, James Stuart had not yet finished running; he was shortly in Waterford, and not long after, in France.

It is well at this point to remember that the Irish battlefield was centre stage in the European arena during 1690-91, perhaps for the only time in history. Without the continental perspective, however, the Irish locked in on the events of those years to such a degree that they *still* view the men and affairs of an importance far beyond that of "mere" heritage. Trevelyan makes the point with his usual insight:

> In the year 1690 Ireland was the pivot of the European crisis. The fate of Britain depended on William's campaign, and on the fate of Britain depended the success or failure of Europe's resistance to French hegemony. . . . But while Enniskillen, Londonderry, and the Boyne were but a stage in the forward march of British and world history, they became the central point of time in the imagination of the ruling race in Ireland.

The "subject race" was to find heroes for its songs of resistance later in the year.

The Boyne re-established English control of the North and East of Ireland. "Tyrconnell's Blackguards" withdrew to the line of the River Shannon to defend the still-Gaelic lands to which the native Irish had been forced by the Cromwellian Settlement. The Williamite army followed cautiously, probing for an opening. Major General Churchill established a secure Williamite left flank by investing Cork and Kinsale, but the right wing under Brigadier Douglas was turned back in late July by the Jacobites under Colonel Grace and, soon afterwards, by a horseman about to ride with glory unto the pages of Irish rebel legend, Brigadier Patrick Sarsfield, Earl of Lucan. Limerick, the centre of Jacobite resistance, was under the command of Tyrconnell and the French Duke of Lauzun. In early August 1690 the lumbering main column of the Williamite army wound through Tipperary *en route* to the Irish stronghold.

The Jacobite leaders were desperate. Limerick needed time . . . time not likely to be granted by a William anxious to be done with the Irish and get back to deal with the Scot Jacobites marauding through the Highlands. The city could withstand direct assault as long as the walls stood, but once the big Williamite siege guns were brought to bear, the defenders were doomed. Lauzun and Tyrconnell, sensing defeat, retreated to Galway, leaving the Duke of Berwick in military command. The Frenchman Boisseleaux was left behind as Governor of Limerick; his task was presumably to get the best terms possible when he surrendered the town. The French leaders, however, had no intention of capitulating without a fight. Seconded by Sarsfield and Dorrington, they furiously set about steeling the town's fortifications.

The Earl of Lucan now burst upon Irish history with a

blaze that has hardly dimmed over the centuries. Smuggled out of Ireland as a child, Sarsfield had been raised a soldier. As a young man, he had won plaudits from the Duke of Luxembourg, one of the ablest of Louis XIV's fine generals (and the man in whose service Sarsfield would afterwards die). Later joining Charles II's standing army in England, he had won further glory and a grant of land in Kildare helping put down the rebellion of the Duke of Monmouth—his brother-in-law—upon the succession of James II. Sarsfield's military reputation and stature as a great landowner made him the natural leader of the Irish at Limerick. Now he proceeded to buy the Duke of Berwick the time needed to fortify the town.

THE BALLAD OF GALLOPING HOGAN

At least five distinct bands of rapparees were swarming through the wild glens and mountains around Limerick by 1690. Faintly nationalist—and bitterly papist—the most notorious of these fierce outlaw gangs was led by the "White Sergeant," so-called for the White Cockade he sported to display his political/religious sentiments. Another famous rapparee was Michael Hogan whose band roamed the Tipperary mountains southwest of Nenagh. It was the latter who was to gain immortality in company with the Earl of Lucan.

Patrick Sarsfield reasoned simply: if Limerick could not withstand the shock of the Williamite batteries, then the artillery would have to be eliminated. The Prince of Orange had already invested the city and was awaiting the arrival of a 150-waggon supply train that was winding its way to the front from Thurles with the siege guns. Lord Lucan settled on a plan that brings to mind the later audacity of J. E. B. Stuart during the American Civil War: Sarsfield would take six hundred horsemen and ride entirely around the enemy army in the attempt to intercept the waggon train. Michael Hogan, "Galloping Hogan," was to be his guide.

The Irish horse rode north, crossing the Shannon quietly by night near BealBoru, the ancient Thomond ruin of Brian. Resting for the daylight hours in the Ballyhourigan Wood west of Keeper Mountain, they rode the next night with muffled hooves through the Slievefelim along the Tipperary/Limerick border. The Irish cavalry caught the Williamite siege column asleep and unsuspecting at Ballyneety in the small hours of the morning of 12 August 1690. The raiders spiked the artillery, galloping away to the report of a tremendous explosion. The Dutch were forced to send for more siege guns, giving the Limerick defenders the respite they desperately needed to shore up the defenses of the city.

Old Limerick is in danger
And Ireland is not free;
So Sarsfield sends a message
To a fearless Rapparee—
"Come ride across the Shannon
At the sounding of the drum,
And we'll blow the enemy siege train
To the land of Kingdom Come!"

Refrain:
Galloping Hogan, Galloping Hogan,
Galloping all along,
In his saddle is a sabre,
On his lips there is a song.
He's off across the Shannon
To destroy the enemy cannon,
And he goes galloping, he goes galloping,
Galloping, galloping on.

The Rapparee is bearded,
There's a twinkle in his eye;
As he rides into the city
The Limerick ladies cry:
"Captain Outlaw, my bold outlaw,
Will ye tarry here with me?"
"Och! I'm off to Ballyneety
To blow Dutch William's battery!"

Refrain

So tonight along the Shannon,
By the pale light of the moon,
There flows an eerie brightness
As of a faerie noon;
Then clippody-clop, resounding

Through the lattice of the shade,
The ghost of Galloping Hogan
Comes a-riding down the glade.

Refrain

GALLOPING O'HOGAN

As the Irish horse approached the siege-train camp at
Ballyneety, Hogan discovered the Williamite watchword from an
enemy camp-follower. By some spectacular stroke of irony, it
was "Sarsfield." Creeping upon the sentries, the Irish answered
the hail correctly. Leaping onto their horses, the Jacobites soon
amended their response in a somewhat louder tone of voice,
"Sarsfield is the word, and Sarsfield is the *man*!"
The successful raid was not without casualties; the Irish
horse had to battle their way back to Limerick around the
southern flank of the main Williamite army. This Percy French
ballad suggests that Hogan was one of those who fell "completing
the circle." Matthew Culligan-Hogan, on the other hand, has
made a convincing case for Galloping Hogan being one and the
same man as Major General Andre Miguel Hogan of the Portugese
army. The Iberian General Hogan commanded a cavalry raid
against the Spanish in 1712 remarkably similar to the Ballyneety
raid.

"They have sent for fresh artillery,
The guns are on the way,
God help our helpless Limerick
When dawns another day."
Thus speaks the gallant Sarsfield,
As sadly he recalls
The famine and despair that lurk
Behind those crumbling walls.

And yet one blow for freedom,
One daring midnight ride:
And Dutch William may be humbled yet,
For all his power and pride!
"Go! Bring to me The Galloper,

To Highway Hogan say,
'Tis Ireland hath need of him,
And him alone this day!' "

The General and the Highwayman
Are standing face-to-face,
The fearless front, the eagle eye,
In both of them we trace;
"Hogan, the night is dark and dread,
Say can'st thou lead the way
To the Keeper Mountain's black ravines
Ere dawns another day?"

"Lead on!" And well he led them,
Though the Shannon ford ran deep,
And though the white-tipped flood ran fierce
Around O'Brien's Keep.
The sentinel on Killaloe
Looked out but failed to see
Six hundred silent horsemen ride
Behind the Rapparee.

That night by Ballyneety's towers,
The English gunners lay;
King William's camp in safety lies
But twelve short miles away.
What need of further caution?
What Irish wolf would dare
To prowl around our camp tonight
So near the lion's lair?

An Irish wolf is near them now,
And Irish ears have heard
The chosen watchword for the night—
And "Sarsfield" was the word.
A tramp of horses: "Who's there? The Word?"
"Sarsfield!" the answer ran,
And then the sword smote downwards,
"Aye, and Sarsfield is the man!"

"To arms! The foe!" Too late, too late,
Though Villier's vengeful blade

Is wet with Hogan's life-blood,
As he leads the ambuscade.
Then foot-to-foot and hand-to-hand
They battle round the guns,
Till victory declares itself
For Erin's daring sons.

Oh! Sudden flash of blinding light!
Oh, hollow sounding roar!
Down history's page in Irish ears
It echoes evermore.
And Ballyneety's blackened tower
Still marks the famous place
Where Sarsfield staked his all to win
And won that midnight race.

The success of Sarsfield's Raid gave the defenders of Limerick an extra two weeks to strengthen the ramparts. It was a necessary respite. When William III finally ordered the first of three assaults on 27 August 1690, the battle was a close thing. Both sides were forced to commit their reserves; the Jacobites barely managed to oust the attackers from several breaches in the walls.

The Battle of Limerick was a tactical draw but strategically a definite victory for the Irish and French forces. The Irish Jacobites now had their own "Derry." William had run out of time. The defeat of the Dutch and English fleet by the French off Beachy Head had left Britain itself wide open to invasion. The Williamite King left Ireland, leaving the Dutch General Godert de Ginckel in command of his forces. With no help for it, de Ginckel lifted the siege of Limerick and retired to the East. Though Cork and Kinsale fell to Marlborough shortly afterwards, Connacht, at least, was securely Jacobite for the winter.

THE BLACKSMITH OF LIMERICK

As the Orangeman sings of the Boyne, the Irish rebel sings of Limerick. The gallant defense of the city thrust a new star onto the Irish rebel stage. As Trevelyan observes:

Sarsfield, the hero of Limerick . . . stood to the conquered as the representative man of the new Ireland, the faithful son of the *mater dolorosa*. The place occupied by Sarsfield in Irish history is significant. For he was no scion of an old tribal family. . . . The English had effectually destroyed the clan society and banished or slain the clan leaders. Sarsfield represented the new nation.

The Battle of Limerick was pulled out by the Jacobites when the townspeople joined the army defending the city. This song by Robert Dwyer Joyce suggests the loyalty that Lord Lucan commanded among the Irish of the time. The nineteenth century song is in itself testimony to Sarsfield's position in the rebel hagiology two centuries after the battle.

He grasped his ponderous hammer, he could not stand it more,
To hear the bombshells bursting and thundering battle's roar;
Said he: "The breach they're mounting, the Dutchman's murdering crew,
I'll try my hammer on their heads and see what that can do!"

"Now swarthy Ned and Moran, make up that iron well,
Tis Sarsfield's horse that wants the shoes so mind not shot nor shell."
"Sure now," cried both, "the horse can wait, for Sarsfield's on the wall,
And where you go we'll follow, with you to stand or fall."

The blacksmith raised his hammer and rushed into the street,
His prentice boys behind him, the ruthless foe to meet;
High on the breach of Limerick, with dauntless hearts they stood,
Where bombshells burst and shot fell thick and redly ran the blood.

"Now look, you brown-haired Moran, and mark, you swarthy Ned,
This day we'll try the thickness of many a Dutchman's head!
Hurrah! Upon their bloody path they're mounting gallantly;
And now, the first that tops the breach, leave him and this to me!"

The first that gained the rampart, he was a captain brave,
A captain of the grenadiers, with blood-stained dirk and glaive,
He pointed out and he parried but it was all in vain,
For right through skull and helmet, the hammer found his brain.

The next that topped the rampart, he was a colonel bold,
Bright through the murk of battle his helmet flashed with gold;
"Gold is no match for iron," the doughty blacksmith said,
As with that ponderous hammer he stretched his foeman dead.

"Hurrah for gallant Limerick!" black Ned and Moran cried,
As on the Dutchmen's leaden heads their hammers well they plied;
A bombshell burst between them—one fell with a groan,
One leaped into the lurid air and down the breach was thrown.

"Brave smith, brave smith!" cried Sarsfield, "beware the treacherous mine!
Brave smith, brave smith, fall backward or surely death is thine!"
The smith sprang up the rampart and leaped the blood-stained wall,
As high into the shuddering air went foeman, fort and all!

Up like a volcano they thundered wild and high:
Spear, gun, and shattered standard, and foemen, through the sky;
And dark and bloody was the shower that round the blacksmith fell,
He thought upon his prentice boys, they were avenged right well.

At that mighty roar, a deadly silent instant settled down;
Twas broken by a triumph-shout that shook the ancient town;
Again its heroes forward dashed and charged and fought and slew,
And taught Dutch William and his men what Irish hearts could do.

Down rushed the swarthy blacksmith unto the riverside,
He hammered on the foe's pontoon to sink it in the tide;
The timbers they were tough and strong, they took no crack or strain,
"*Mo bhron,* twont break," the blacksmith roared, "I'll try their heads again!"

The blacksmith sought his smithy and blew his bellows strong,
He shod the steed of Sarsfield but o'er it sang no song:
"*Ochon,* my boys are dead," he cried, "Their loss I'll long deplore,
But comfort in my heart, their graves red with foreign gore!"

    As the campaign of 1691 began, it was clear that the Williamites were not going to be content with the earlier "To Hell or Connacht" policy of the Roundheads; this time London was determined to take control of the latter, presumably leaving the Irish to the former. The French-Irish forces pinned down behind the Shannon were well aware that de Ginckel planned to flush them from their sanctuary.

    In May, Generals St. Ruth and d'Usson disembarked from France to take command of the Jacobites. The Williamite army started moving west a short time later. De Ginckel's strategy was simple: the main force under Hugh Mackay was to cross the

Shannon between Loughs Ree and Derg, at once threatening Galway and outflanking Limerick from the north. Mackay mustered his forces at Mullingar and marched on the Shannon just below Athlone in early June. An unsuccessful attempt to ford the river south of the town convinced Mackay that he would have to repair the partially destroyed bridge and cross at Athlone. The Irish under d'Usson, though ultimately unfortunate in the defense, gained new rebel martyrs in the battle for the crossing.

THE BRIDGE OF ATHLONE

Dutch carpenters had almost repaired the span at Athlone when an Irish sergeant of dragoons named Custume rushed the bridge with eleven volunteers. Tearing at the bridge repairs with axes, the Irishmen were cut down by a withering Williamite fire before completing their intended task. The Dutch, realising the danger, charged the bridge. They were beaten to the spot by eleven more Jacobites who accomplished the breach; the repairs came tumbling down under the weight of the bold Irish volunteers. Only two managed to make the safety of the Shannonside under heavy fire from the east bank of the river.

Does any man dream that a Gael can fear?
Of a thousand deeds let him learn but one:
The Shannon swept onward, broad and clear,
Between the beleaguers and broad Athlone.
"Break down the bridge!" Six warriors rushed
Through the storm of shot and the storm of shell;
With late but certain victory flushed,
The grim Dutch gunners eyed them well.

They wrenched at the planks mid a hail of fire,
They fell in death, their work half done;
The bridge stood fast; and nigh and nigher,
The foe swarmed darkly, densely on.
"Oh, who for Erin will strike a stroke?
Who hurl yon planks where the waters roar?
Six warriors forth from their comrades broke,
And flung them upon that bridge once more.

St. Ruth, in his stirrups stood up, and cried,
"I have seen no deed done like that in France!"

With a toss of his head, Sarsfield replied,
"They had luck, the dogs, twas a merry chance."
Oh, many a year on the Shannonside,
They sang upon moor and they sang upon heath,
Of the twain that breasted that raging tide,
And the ten that shook bloody hands with death.

YE NATIVES OF THIS NATION

General Mackay made a covered way to protect his carpenters as they attempted another repair on the Athlone bridge. The Irish burned it, leaving the Williamites apparently stranded on the eastern bank. D'Usson, confident that the siege of the town was over, withdrew the bulk of his forces to meet an anticipated crossing by de Ginckel further south, leaving only skirmishers under Colonel Grace to defend Athlone. The French general had misjudged the doggedness of his opposing number; the Dutchman attacked the crossing in full force. After ten days of brilliant defense, d'Usson's miscalculation allowed the Williamites across the Shannon in thirty minutes. It was to become a recurring theme of Irish rebel balladeers: the gallantry and sacrifice of the common soldier were to be all too often wasted by the decisions of his outclassed commanders.

The June 1691 loss of Athlone caused a rift in the Jacobite leadership. The Irish, repeatedly promised French military aid, had received only officers from Louis.[12] Now it looked as if even the French generals were no bargain. This old ballad by Barnaby O'Hanlon reflects the growing contemporary sentiment that it was Sarsfield, an Irishman, who had saved Limerick, whereas Athlone and the Boyne had been lost by the French.

Our ancestors formerly great valour they have shown,
Great exploits for Ireland's rights since Jamie's war was known;
Likewise the valiant Sarsfield, his losses did bemoan,
When he reproved St. Ruth for the losing of Athlone.

We rode with brave Lord Lucan before the break of day,
Until we came to Kinmagown where the artillery lay;
Then God He cleared the firmament, the moon and stars gave light,
And for the battle of the Boyne, we had revenge that night.

The Williamites were across the Shannon, threatening to drive a wedge into the heart of Connacht. St. Ruth was forced to offer open battle. He chose to make his stand at Kilcommedon Hill, a 350-foot ridge near the village of Aughrim in eastern Galway. Eighteen miles from Athlone athwart the Galway road, Kilcommedon was an admirable defensive position: flanked by bogs north and south, it could be approached only from the east via two "passes" through more marshland. The French general officer planned to induce a Williamite attack at Ballinasloe, fall back, and then counterattack the separated spearheads of de Ginckel's advance, cutting them off as they approached Kilcommedon Hill. Whatever the folk-musicians' view of St. Ruth, the Aughrim position suggests that the Captain-General was a polished and professional tactician.

The 12 July 1691 Williamite attack on this strong defensive position was as gallant as any in the annals of Irish warfare. It was successful for four reasons. First, Meloniere's Huguenots unexpectedly were able to beat off the counterattacks of Sarsfield's vaunted cavalry. Second, at a critical point in the Jacobite counterattack, the Irish foot discovered that their ammunition boxes contained balls incompatible with the bores of their weapons (causing the infantry to load their guns with pebbles and even buttons). Third, after the Williamite cavalry was repulsed on schedule, Henry Luttrell's Irish horsemen made no move to exploit the Dutch retreat; Mackay was enabled to re-form his shattered horse and attack again. Fourth, "a cursed [*cannon*] ball that carried such a measure of woe" killed St. Ruth just as the general was trying to turn his too-quickly advancing troops to meet the danger of the regrouping Williamite horse on their flank. Mackay seized the opportunity to enfilade the advancing Irish infantry. Bewildered by the unexpected assault when they had thought the battle won, the Irish foot fled. The Williamite horse rolled up the entire Irish line.

AFTER AUGHRIM'S DISASTER

Of the twenty thousand men in St. Ruth's army at Aughrim, fourteen thousand were Irish infantry. Almost half of them died in the battle and the subsequent rout. The rest of the army took to the safety of the wooded glens and mountains, scattering in all directions to flee Williamite wrath. The private soldier, as is normal in combat, suffered the terror and horror of the slaughter, in Swineburne's verse, "not with dreams but with blood and iron." For all the carnage, however, it was not among the common soldiery that Ireland suffered her biggest loss.

In the Irish custom, the Irish officers—mostly Gaelic and Anglo-Irish nobility—fought and fell alongside their men. Diarmuid Murtagh penetratingly observes that:

> Aughrim was more fatal to the old aristocracy of Ireland than Flodden had been to the knighthood of Scotland, or Agincourt to the chivalry of the French. After it the Catholic aristocracy disappeared from the Irish scene, and the political leadership of the Irish people passed into other hands.

The great blind poet Raftery, writing on the eve of the nineteenth century, put it more laconically: "It was at Aughrim on a Monday many a son of Ireland found sorrow, without speaking of all that died."

This traditional ballad tells of the flight of one small group of St. Ruth's beaten Irish Jacobites that managed to remain together for a short time after the battle. Sorely pressed by de Ginckel's troops, Sean O'Dwyer of the Glen and his band lived like rapparees until finally run to earth.

After Aughrim's great disaster,
When our foe in sooth was master,
It was you who first plunged in and swam
The Shannon's boiling flood.
And through Slieve Bloom's dark passes
You led our gallowglasses,
Although the hungry Saxon wolves
Were howling for our blood.

And as we crossed Tipperary,
We broke the Clan O'Leary
And drove a *creacht* before us
As our horsemen onward came;
With our swords and spears we gored them
And through flood and night we bore them,
Still, *Seán Uí Dhuir a ghleanna,*
We were bested in the game.

Long, long we held the hillside,
Our couch it was the rillside,

The sturdy oaken boughs,
Our curtain overhead.
The summer's blaze we laughed at,
The winter's snows we scoffed at,
And trusted in our long broad swords
To win our daily bread.

Then the Dutchman's troops they found us,
In fire and steel they bound us,
They blazed the woods and mountains
Till the very sky was flame.
Yet our sharpened swords cut through them,
Through their coats of mail we hewed them,
But *Seán Uí Dhuir a ghleanna*,
We were bested in the game.

Here's *sláinte* to your king and my king,
The sovereign of our liking,
And to Sarsfield, underneath whose flag
We'll cast once more a chance;
For the morning's dawn will bring us
Across the sea and sing us
To take a stand and wield a brand
Among the sons of France.

And though we part in sorrow,
Still, *Seán Uí Dhuir, a chara*,
Our prayer is—God Save Ireland
And pour blessings on her name;
May her sons be true when needed,
May they never feel as we did
For *Seán Uí Dhuir a ghleanna*,
We were bested in the game.

The Battle of Aughrim decided the Irish leaders. Tyrconnell
and Lucan had been aware all along that Ireland was a cat's-paw
is a far larger struggle. They had fought on after James II had
departed only because they believed that Louis of France was
going to send troops. With the Irish army shattered, Galway in
Williamite hands, and no French army on the visible horizon,
the Irish lords, from their remaining stronghold at Limerick,

asked de Ginckel for terms. When Tyrconnell died unexpectedly in August, Sarsfield was left to deal with the Williamites. The Earl of Lucan resignedly agreed to the Capitulation of Limerick on 3 October 1691.

De Ginckel, trying to wrap up the Irish campaign as swiftly as possible, had afforded the Irish generous terms. The very first article of the Treaty stipulated that "the Roman Catholics . . . shall enjoy such privileges in the exercise of their religion . . . as they did enjoy in the reign of Charles II." Signed by the Lords Justice of Ireland and ratified by William and Mary under the (new) Great Seal of England, the Treaty went on to promise "such further security as may preserve them from any disturbance upon the account of said religion." Officers and soldiers of the Irish army were to suffer no reprisals and were to be allowed to retain their possessions. The hastily drawn document was, however, full of loopholes. MacCurtain quotes a Galway Jacobite who was critical of the Treaty's formulations: "The articles were not so warily drawn but room was left for captious exceptions." In fact, a coach-and-four could have been driven through the Treaty's "exceptions." The loopholes were to leave sufficient flexibility for the Church of Ireland Protestants to subject the Catholic peasantry to a century and more of penal legislation.

Among the provisions of the Capitulation of Limerick was a stipulation allowing those Jacobites who wished to go to France the opportunity to do so at Williamite expense. In the event the English did not have to pay for the transportation of the Irishmen who chose to leave: two days after the agreement was duly signed and the remainder of the Irish army dispersed, a forty-four ship French fleet under Admiral Renault finally appeared in Dingle Bay. The Sun King's procrastination had lost Ireland, and with it any chance to use the British throne to extend French hegemony in Europe. The 3,200 troops aboard the French vessels, however, did find room to squeeze aboard the Earl of Lucan and fourteen thousand Irish Jacobite soldiers *en route* for the service of Louis XIV. The "Flight of the Wild Geese" had begun.

LAMENT FOR PATRICK SARSFIELD

Owen Roe O'Neill and Thomas Preston had returned after the Flight of the Earls to win glory on the battlefields of Ireland. The Irish soldiers who left in the Flight of the Wild Geese were destined to win their glory on the battlefields of the continent.

This poetic translation of a contemporary Gaelic Jacobite ballad is by Mangan. It captures what must have been the feeling in Celtic Ireland when Lord Lucan sailed for France.

Farewell, O Patrick Sarsfield, may luck be on your path,
Your camp is broken up—your work is marred for years—
But you go to kindle into flame the King of France's wrath,
Though you leave sick Ireland in tears.

May the white sun and moon rain glory on your head,
All hero as you are, and holy Man of God!
To you the Saxons owe many an hour of dread
In the land you have often trod.

I saw the royal Boyne, when its billows flashed with blood;
I fought at Grana Oge, where a thousand horsemen fell.
On the dark empurpled plain of Aughrim, too, I stood,
On the plain by Tubberdonny's Well.

To the heroes of Limerick, the City of the Fights,
Be my best blessing borne on the wings of the air!
We had card-playing there o'er our camp-fires at night,
And the Word of Life, too, and prayer.

But for you, Londonderry, may pague smite and slay
Your people! May ruin desolate you stone by stone!
Through you may a gallant youth lies coffinless today,
With the winds for mourners alone.

How many a noble soldier, how many a cavalier,
Careered along this road seven fleeting weeks ago,
With silver-hilted sword, with matchlock and with spear,
Who now, *mavrone,* lieth low.

All hail to thee Ben Hedir—but ah, on thy brow
I see a limping soldier, who battled and who bled
Last year in the cause of the Stuart, though now
The worthy is begging his bread!

On the Bridge of the Boyne was our first overthrow,
By Slaney the next for we battled without rest;

The third was at Aughrim. Oh, Eire they woe
Is a sword in my bleeding breast!

O! The roof above our heads it was barbarously fired,
While the black Orange guns blazed and bellowed around;
And as volley followed volley, Colonel Mitchell enquired
Whether Lucan still stood his ground.

But O'Kelly still remains, to defy and to toil;
He has memories that Hell won't permit him to forget,
And a sword that will make the blue blood flow like oil
Upon many an Aughrim yet!

And I never shall believe that my Fatherland can fall
With the Burkes, and the Decies, and the son of Royal James,
And Talbot the Captain, and Sarsfield above all,
The beloved of damsels and dames.

    The War of the Two Kings left the nationalist Irish with an irredentist heritage that has endured to modern times; no less important has been its legacy to the Unionist Irish. Dr. MacCurtain describes the war's endowment to both the rebel and Orange traditions:

> No Irish war has left such an indelible impression on the folk-memory of Ireland as the Williamite War. Gaelic poets, balladeers, set-dances and pipe music record the various peak-points of the war. "Lilibullero" . . . the poems of O'Brudair and Seamus Dall MacCuarta . . . (well-known set-dances) . . . the parades commemorative of the Boyne in Belfast and the Apprentice Boys' March in Derry are conscious invocations of a remembered past. It was the most exciting and colourful war of the plantation centuries, the last great stand when two sides were fairly evenly balanced, colonist and native Irish.

If the sides had not been clearly drawn before, they were now. The last papist lords were slain, in hiding, or gone to France. After the Treaty of Limerick, the ascendant Protestants of Ireland considered the Catholic Irish the enemy.

CHAPTER NOTES (9)

1 — Across the Shannon, along with the liegemen of many a displaced Gaelic lord, went the itinerant musician. The piper or harper who did not, found his condition changed considerably. An Irish musician was not a popular citizen in a Puritan-run society. Seán Ó Boyle describes one of the restrictions that these men faced:

> "In 1654, all harpers, pipers, and wandering musicians had to obtain letters from the magistrate . . . before being allowed to travel through the country. This passport contained full details of age, stature, beard, colour of hair and condition of life of the recipient. All musical instruments savouring of 'popery' were ruthlessly destroyed."

2 — Sir William Petty, Cromwell's Physician General, estimated that over 600,000 Irish died between 1641-53, out of a population of about 1,500,000. Orphan children, the unhappy product of all warfare, were a terrible problem after the savagery of the preceding decade. The sugar plantations of Barbados and tobacco plantations of the American continent could never get enough labour. J. H. Parry, in his excellent work on early European colonialism, reports that "transportation meant, for practical purposes, slavery. White labour from this source was less unwelcome than might be supposed." It is to be guessed that the Puritans, seeing no other solution ready to hand, sold the children across the Atlantic as a practical solution to a distasteful conundrum.

3 — Nor were the papists the only ones disappointed. Within a year of the Restoration, the Church of Ireland declared Quakers, Presbyterians, Anabaptists, and other Dissenters "enemies of the Church." Like the Catholics, the independent Protestant sects found life under the monarchy no less onerous than under the Commonwealth.

4 — Most of the Irish arrested in connection with this "purge" were of relatively low standing; in two cases, however, the aim was higher. Archbishop Oliver Plunkett was sent to London, tried, and martyred in July 1681. Archbishop Peter Talbot, brother to the future Duke of Tyrconnell, died in prison.

5 — When James II was crowned he had appointed the Protestant Edward Hyde, Earl of Clarendon, to the viceroyalty of Ireland (to replace the aging James Butler who had stood so loyally by the Stuarts during the Civil Wars). Clarendon was father to James II's first wife, Ann Hyde, and would be grandfather to two future queens of England, Mary II and Anne. That James would throw over such a staunch Protestant servant for an ambitious papist clearly made the appointment of Tyrconnell seem extremely ominous to the Parliament.

6 — The terms "Whig" and "Tory" came into popular use near the end of Charles II's reign. The Whigs were, in general, in favour of limiting royal prerogatives while their

opposite numbers usually supported the Kings "traditional" powers.

7 — Prince James had married Ann Hyde, daughter to Clarendon, during the year of his father's Restoration. Before her death as a converted Catholic in 1671, Ann had been delivered of two daughters who were raised as Protestants. Both Mary and Anne were to become queens of the realm.

8 — It is of some interest that this obviously anti-Gael song is macaronic. The Gaelic sections of verse would seem to have originally been sung in dialect Irish and since been corrupted (see **Irish Glossary**). Some sources have ascribed the song to the English Lord Wharton who was later to be instrumental in the passage of the Penal Laws. If so, it is significant that this great Williamite baron would have known sufficient Irish to be able to make fun of the language.

9 — A measure of the situation within the city walls can be found on a grocer's bill of fare. Near the end of the siege a mouse cost sixpence, a quart of horseblood, a shilling.

10 — When James II had landed at Kinsale on 19 March 1689, he brought arms but few men. The ones he did bring from France, however, were vital: officers. Without the professional leadership of the French, the Jacobite army in Ireland would have been little more than a badly led mob . . . with the exception, of course, of Tyrconnell's trained force.

11 — At this point in history, uniforms were still rare among the common infantrymen; rarer still were uniforms among volunteer forces; almost unheard of were standardised uniforms for an entire army. In the confusion of the hand-to-hand combat of the time, the means used to tell friend from foe were cockades, coloured ribbons or strips of cloth worn on the hats and arms of the troops.

The Stadtholder, on the other hand, rode into battle in the azure uniform of the Dutch Blue Guards. Over the light armour that covered his back and chest, William wore an orange scarf and sash, replicas of which adorn the Unionist marchers of modern Boyne celebrations.

12 — In March 1690 the French *had* landed seven thousand troops. The French troops, however, did not come gratis; an equal number of Tyrconnell's Irishmen were sent to the continent. After the 1690 fight at Limerick, the French troops left for France with Tyrconnell. When Tyrconnell returned with St. Ruth for the 1691 campaign, the French soldiery remained in France.

10

Ascendancy and Wild Geese

While the major Stuart/Orange confrontation came in Ireland, King William had also been faced with considerable opposition north of the River Tweed. The Highland clans in particular —out of bitterness for Argyle and the Campbells—gave the Scottish Williamites trouble. Led by John Graham of Claverhouse, "Bonnie Dundee," the kilted hordes had swept out of the North in 1689, defeating the Prince of Orange's Lowland allies under Hugh Mackay at Killiecrankie before being dispersed at Dunkeld. After the Irish had capitulated at Limerick, the Campbells felt sufficiently emboldened to take their revenge on the Jacobite MacDonalds in the horrible 1692 massacre at Glencoe. The fury of the victimised Highland clans was to find its ultimate expression in an almost mystical allegiance to the deposed Stuarts.

William III also had his hands full trying to maintain his continental possessions in the face of unceasing French pressure. To "Dutch William," Scot and Irish Jacobite agitation was now but a nuisance compared to his European concerns. He was not about to interfere with either the vengeance of the Campbells or the aspirations of the newly ascendant Protestants in Ireland, even when the latter repudiated the provisions of the Treaty of Limerick in an unabashed land-grab. In truth, William neither much liked his new subjects ("I am sure that this people has not been made for me, nor I for it."), nor cared particularly about the internal workings of his new demesne. Massie describes how William "ceded" formerly royal prerogatives to the parliamentary politicians of the three nations:

> He acquiesced in whatever Parliament asked, in order to keep its support for the struggle in Europe. He left domestic policy in the hands of others while striving to control foreign policy himself. . . . In essence a trade had been made: Parliament accepted William's war in order to protect the Protestant religion and assert its su-

premacy; William accepted Parliament's supremacy in order to keep England's support in fighting Louis.

Given this free hand, the Ascendancy landowners were quick to take the opportunity to add to their own holdings. As the now exclusively Anglican Irish Parliament began confiscating the estates of the officers who had fought with Patrick Sarsfield, many of the dispossessed took to the hills to fight back as rapparees.

NED OF THE HILL

(*Éamonn an Chnuic*)

Perhaps the most famous of the rapparees was Edmund O'Ryan of Knockmeill Castle. Best known as "Ned of the Hill" for his north Tipperary hideout on the mountain behind Cappaph White, O'Ryan was reputed to have earlier been a member of Galloping Hogan's band who had rallied to Sarsfield's call. What is certain is that he took to the hills sometime after the Capitulation of Limerick.

In 1702 a reward of £200 was offered for the head of "Edmund Knock Ryan" on the charge of murder. Constantly on the run, O'Ryan was forced to rely on sympathisers for shelter. At Foilclug, the rapparee took refuge in the house of one Dwyer, who promptly murdered his sleeping guest for the blood-price. In a beloved piece of Irish irony, Dwyer never got the reward. It seems that the man O'Ryan had slain had himself been a "common robber" who had accosted an English gentlewoman. Unbeknownst to Dwyer, the lady had set the authorities right and the reward had been withdrawn. Edmund O'Ryan was buried at Curraheen, near the village of Hollyford. Dwyer's grave is long forgotten.

Tradition asserts that O'Ryan was a talented Gaelic balladeer, author of the popular *Bean Dubh a Ghleanna* (Dark Lady of the Glen) as well as of the following autobiographical lay which stands symbol for the recurring tragedy of Irishmen "on the run" from the redcoats. A free translation from the Irish is given here.

"Who is that without
With passion in his voice
Who beats at my bolted door?"

CHRONOLOGY (Ascendancy and Wild Geese)

1692 . . . . . .Glencoe Massacre in Scotland; naval battle at Cap La Hogue ends French invasion threat.

1693 . . . . . .Sarsfield killed in Spanish Netherlands.

1694 . . . . . .Mary II dies; Bank of England founded.

1695 . . . . . .Irish Parliament rejects Treaty of Limerick, Penal Times begin.

1697 . . . . . .Treaty of Ryswick ends Franco-British war.

1698 . . . . . .Molyneux publishes case for Home Rule.

1699 . . . . . .Irish woollen exports restricted.

1701 . . . . . .War of Spanish Succession begins; James II dies, son James Edward hailed James III by Louis of France; British Act of Settlement provides for Protestant succession.

1702 . . . . . .*Anne;* Battle of Cremona in Italy.

1703 . . . . . .Anti-Popery Law in Ireland.

1704 . . . . . .Test and Registration Acts; Battle of Blenheim in Bavaria.

1705 . . . . . .Battle of Cassano d'Adda in Italy.

1706 . . . . . .Battle of Ramillies in Spanish Netherlands.

1707 . . . . . .Union of Scotland and England proclaimed; Hanovers named heir to British throne.

1708 . . . . . .Abortive Stuart landing at Firth of Forth.

1713 . . . . . .Treaty of Utrecht ends War of Spanish Succession.

1714 . . . . . .*George I;* Old Pretender recognised by France and Rome.

1715 . . . . . .Scottish Fifteen put down after Sherrifmuir; death of Louis XIV.

1719 . . . . . .Declaratory Act asserts power of Westminster over Irish Parliament.

1720-24. . . . .Swiftian pamphlets urge boycott of British goods, coinage.

1721 . . . . . .Walpole becomes "Prime" Minister; cabinet established.

1727 . . . . . .*George II.*

1733 . . . . . .Flying shuttle invented; Latin abolished in English courts.

1740 . . . . . .War of Austrian Succession begins.

1741 . . . . . .Famine in Ireland; cotton factories opened in Birmingham and Northampton.

1745 . . . . . .Battle of Fontenoy in Flanders; Bonnie Prince Charlie lands, Scottish Forty-Five begins with Battle of Prestonpans.

1746 . . . . . .Stuart pretensions crushed at Battle of Culloden Moor, pacification of Highlands begins.

1748 . . . . . .Treaty of Aix-la-Chapelle ends War of Austrian Succession; hereditary jurisdiction ends in Scotland.

1751 . . . . . .Clive seizes Arcot in India; revenue surplus quarrel in Irish Parliament.

1752 . . . . . .British adopt Gregorian calendar.

1754 . . . . . .1st iron-rolling mill in England.

1756 . . . . . .Seven Years War begins.

1757 . . . . . .Clive takes Calcutta; Pitt the Elder dominates British coalition government.

1759 . . . . . .Anti-Union riot in Dublin; Flood enters Irish Parliament, Patriot Party begins to form; Catholic Committee formed; Battle of Quebec in Canada.

"I am Edmund of the Hill,
Drenched and numb and wet
From walking long the mountains and the glens."
"My dearest, my treasure,
What should I do for you
But cover you with the skirt of my own dress?
For black gunpowder
Will densely be shot at us
And we should die together."

"Long on the run am I now,
In snow and in frost,
Daring not to near any man.
My fields are fallow,
My horses untethered
And wholly lost to me.
I have no friends
(I sorrow for that)
Who would harbour me early or late,
And so I must fly
Eastward over the sea
For it is there I have no kin."

The Protestant Ascendancy was not content with confiscation of the land. They now, in the words of Lecky, aimed to fortify their position by depriving the "conquered and hostile majority of every element of political and military strength." In the decades after Limerick, they succeeded admirably in their goal.

The means the Protestants used to solidify their privileged position in Irish society are known to history as the Penal Laws. This legislation, best personified by the title of a 1703 law—"An Act to prevent the further growth of Popery"—was unique in

Western history. Pogroms and persecutions against minorities had never been a rarity in Europe; this one, however, was directed against the undisputed *majority* of the people. There is perhaps no better way to demonstrate the pervasiveness and sweep of the Penal Laws than to list some of them.

1) Catholics could not teach, tutor, or go to school.
2) Catholics were excluded from the professions (with the eventual exception of medicine).
3) Catholics could not act as guardian to a child.
4) Catholics were excluded from all government positions (with the exception of rural magistrate when there were no Protestants available).
5) Catholics were required to pay double taxes for the militia.
6) Catholics were required to pay damages done by enemy privateers if England was at war with a Catholic nation.
7) Catholic tradesmen could have no more than two apprentices (except in the linen trade where dyed Irish linens were forbidden from all British colonies and subject to a thirty per cent duty even in Britain).
8) Catholics could not own a horse valued at more than £5.
9) Catholics could neither buy land nor inherit it from Protestants.
10) Catholics could not lease land for more than thirty-one years; neither could they lend money with land as security.
11) Catholics who died owning land were forced to divide it equally among all their sons.
12) Catholic children of any age who professed Protestantism could be taken immediately from their families; the authorities could then arbitrarily settle a portion of their fathers' estates upon them.
13) Catholic wives who converted to the Church of Ireland could likewise receive settlements of their husbands' property.
14) Catholic clergy above the station of simple parish priest were outlawed; all monastic orders were similarly banished.
15) Catholics were forbidden to attend public papist worship.
16) Catholics could not send their children abroad for education.
17) Catholics could not join the British Army or Royal Navy.

There were countless others.

Among the effects of the Penal Laws was to increasingly segregate the "poor" Catholic cottiers from the "rich" Church of Ireland landowners. The two groups grew entirely estranged, spawning separate cultures. The privileged class did not even, in the words of both Lord Chief Justice Robinson and Lord Chancellor Bowes, "presume any such person to exist as an Irish Roman Catholic."[1]

FOR THE GREEN

Under the circumstances of the Penal Times, it is not surprising that the Jacobite army of 1688-91 became fixed in the folk-memory of the defeated Irish. The legend of Patrick Sarsfield, impressive enough in life, soared after the bold exile was slain in the service of the King of France at the Battle of Neerwinden. Lord Lucan's 1693 death near the River Landen in Flanders was of the sort which Irish balladeers would certainly have invented were it not true. Sarsfield fell at the end of the battle when the British troops were in full flight. His last words, as he looked upon the retreating redcoats, were reputed to be, "Would it were for Ireland!"

This short lay by Dubliner Arthur Gerald Geohegan appeared in the *Irish Monthly* in the late nineteenth century. The irredentist poet has here transferred the nationalist Green of his own era to a time when the continental Irish "struck their blows" for the white lily of the French Sun King. "Kathleen" here stands metaphor for Ireland.

Do you remember long ago, Kathleen?
When your lover whispered low,
"Shall I stay or shall I go, Kathleen?"
And you proudly answered, "Go!
Join King James and strike a blow
For the Green."

Mavrone! Your hair is white as snow, Kathleen,
Your heart is sad and full of woe,
Do you repent you bade him go, Kathleen?
And she proudly answered, "No!
Far better die with Sarsfield so . . .
Than live a slave without a blow
For the Green."

Resentment of the Penal Laws was, of course, general in the Catholic community. The Irish quickly became consummate in avoiding the laws' most pernicious effects. The Mass, for one example, did not disappear; it merely moved once again from chapel to *bothóg*. The rapparees and highwaymen, for another, became folk-heroes; the humble folk were bitter and respect for the law itself became casualty. The authorities found it next to impossible to track down criminals, to get evidence against them, or even find juries willing to convict the ones they could catch. Bribery of the rural magistrates became endemic, not altogether startling when it is realised that Dublin Castle was obliged in many cases to use Catholics for the positions. Since the magistrates had to live among their fellow Catholics after the Crown judges left, they were not particularly energetic in the enforcement of Saxon Law.

The dark Irish night of the Penal Times was relieved by one flickering hope. If the baneful English laws could be avoided at home only by guile, bitter young Irishmen in their thousands found that the French were only too pleased to afford them an opportunity to strike back physically at the Saxon on the continent. The Flight of the *Géanna Fiáine* became a migration.

SHULE AGRA

The Wild Geese who had flown with Patrick Sarsfield formed only the nucleus for the burgeoning Irish Brigade of the French Army. "Recruiting Sergeants" covertly roamed Ireland looking for replacements for these legendary mercenary soldiers. In the Penal Times it was not hard to find recruits. One chaplain for the Brigade was to claim that close to 500,000 Irishmen *died* in the French service alone in the half-century following Limerick. If the figure is difficult to credit—it represents roughly seven per cent of the Irish male population for the period—the fact that such a number could be seriously proffered by a scholar itself demonstrates the pervasive effect of the Brigade's existence on the Irish of the time. The growing legend of the Brigade caught the imagination of the downtrodden Catholics at home; the reality caught more than imagination.

The departure of a young man to the carnage of the European battlefield was keenly felt; to many a plaintive lover left behind, it became a kind of inexorable tragedy. This simple but

haunting ballad is from the first half of the eighteenth century
when many young men left to join the Wild Geese.

The love song made the journey back-and-forth across the
Atlantic as folksongs will, and is often heard in America and
Ireland under the title *Shule Aroon.*

His hair was black, his eye was blue,
His arm was stout, his word was true,
I wish in my heart I was with you,
Go de thu, mavourneen slaun.

Refrain:
Shule, shule, shule agra,
Only death can ease my woe,
Since the lad from me did go,
Go de thu, mavourneen slaun.

I sold my rock, I sold my reel,
When flax was spun, I sold my wheel
To buy my love a sword of steel,
Go de thu, mavourneen slaun.

Refrain

I watched them sail from Brandon Hill,
Then I sat down and cried my fill,
That every tear would turn a mill,
Go de thu, mavourneen slaun.

Refrain

And so my love has gone to France
To try his fortune to advance,
If e'er he comes back tis but a chance,
Go de thu, mavourneen slaun.

Refrain

I wish brave Jamie would return to reign,
And bring my true love back again,
I wish and wish, but I wish in vain,
Go de thu, mavourneen slaun.

Refrain

I'll dye my petticoat, I'll dye it red,
And round the world I'll beg my bread
Till I find my love, alive or dead,
Go de thu, mavourneen slaun.

Refrain

To appreciate why the English government was content to let the Protestant Ascendancy run roughshod over the "Jacobite" majority in Ireland—and why the Catholic Irish considered joining the Irish Brigade a "patriotic" act—it is necessary to understand Britain's geopolitical stance in the first half of the eighteenth century. England had become a world power. This was the era in which the East India Company of London began to truly threaten its Dutch rival; when Gibralter and Minorca became British colonies; when Japanese magnolias were introduced into Britain by the growing English merchant fleet; when the American colonies began to pour their vast wealth into the burgeoning mercantile centre of Empire on the Thames. The focus of the financial world was shifting from Amsterdam to London. So long as Ireland was at "peace," the British were simply too involved in the growth of their colonial empire to be concerned with minor problems in their own backyard.

In the War of the Spanish Succession (1701-13), Britain was the dominant partner of the Grand Alliance—with Holland, Austria, Prussia, Savoy, Denmark, and Portugal—ranged against France and Bavaria. The Duke of Marlborough's famous victory at Blenheim in 1704 saved Austria and neutralised Bavaria. His triumph two years later at Ramillies established allied hegemony in the Spanish Netherlands. It was only French expansionism that was checked, however; even after the 1713 Treaty of Utrecht, France would present the British with a hereditary Catholic opponent that was openly sympathetic to the Jacobites of Scotland and Ireland.

CLARE'S DRAGOONS

On 23 May 1706 John Churchill won a signal victory over

the Elector of Bavaria and Marshal Villeroi of France at the village of Ramillies, thirty miles southeast of Brussels. While the brilliant English Captain-General suffered "only" four thousand casualties—inflicting fifteen thousand—the dispatches reveal that most of the allied dead were due to the Irish regiments in the French service. One Irish cavalry unit under Lord Clare took the only colours lost by the Grand Alliance during the battle. The captured battle-flags, those of the British Churchill Regiment and of a Scottish regiment fighting under the Dutch, were presented to a covent of Irish nuns at Ypres.

In Ireland, the tales of the Irish Brigade's exploits were becoming legend—the humble folk dreamed of the day when the Wild Geese would return like Owen Roe O'Neill to fight the British Crown on Irish soil. Except for a handful that were to sail with Wolfe Tone in 1798, they never came. This Thomas Davis song is perhaps more representative of the dreams of the downtrodden Irish peasant than of the hopes of the Irish private soldier in Europe.

When, on Ramillies' bloody field,
The baffled French were forced to yield,
The victor Saxon backward reeled
Before the charge of Clare's Dragoons.
The flags we conquered in that fray
Look lone in Ypres' choir, they say,
We'll win them company today,
Or bravely die like Clare's Dragoons.

First Refrain:
Viva la, for Ireland's wrongs!
Viva la, for Ireland's Right!
Viva la, in battle throng,
For a Spanish steed and sabre bright!

The brave old laird died near the fight
But, for each drop he lost that night,
A Saxon cavalier shall bite
The dust before Lord Clare's Dragoons.
For never when our spurs we've set,
And never when our sabres met,
Could we the Saxon soldiers get
To stand the shock of Clare's Dragoons.

Second Refrain:
Viva la, the new Brigade!
Viva la, the old one, too!
Viva la, the rose shall fade
And the shamrock shine forever new!

Another Clare is here to lead,
The worthy son of such a breed;
The French expect some famous deed
When Clare leads on his bold dragoons.
Our colonel comes from Brian's race,
His wounds are in his breast and face,
The *bearna baoghail* is still his place,
The foremost of his bold dragoons.

Second Refrain

There's not a man in squadron here
Was ever known to flinch or fear,
Though first in charge and last in rear
Have ever been Lord Clare's Dragoons.
But see, we'll soon have work to do:
To shame our boasts or prove them true,
For hither come the English crew
To sweep away Lord Clare's Dragoons.

First Refrain

Oh, comrades think how Ireland pines—
Her exiled lords, her rifled shrines;
Her dearest hope the ordered lines
And bursting charge of Clare's Dragoons.
Then fling your green flag to the sky,
Be "Limerick" your battle-cry,
And charge till blood floats fetlock-high
Around the track of Clare's Dragoons.

Second Refrain

THE FLOWER OF FINAE

This old ballad celebrates the glory of the Irish Brigade during the first decade of the eighteenth century. The song cites the 1702 defense of Cremona—in which six hundred Gaels of the Dillon and Burke regiments held the Italian city against Prince Eugene's nine thousand until Marshal Villeroi's French could relieve them; of the 1705 Battle of Cassano d'Adda near Milan—in which the Duke of Vendôme dispatched a body of Irishman to swim the Adda in the teeth of Eugene's guns and spike a battery that was playing havoc with the French defenses; and of the famous charge of Clare's Dragoons at Ramillies in 1706 which prevented Villeroi's defeat from becoming a rout. The Brigade's gallantry earned the exiles the appellation of *"Mes braves Irlandais"* from Louis XIV.

After her Fergus was slain alongside of Lord Clare, the heroine of this ballad presumably joined the sisterhood of the Irish dames of Ypres. By joining the cloister, the Westmeath lass could be near to the visible sign of her sweetheart's gallantry; the captured colours of Ramillies.

Bright red is the sun on the waves of Lough Sheelin,
A cool gentle breeze from the mountain is stealing,
While fair round its islets the small ripples play,
But fairer than all is the Flower of Finae.

Her hair is like night and her eyes like grey morning,
She trips on the heather as if its touch scorning,
Yet her heart and her lips are as mild as May Day,
Sweet Eily MacMahon, the Flower of Finae.

But who down the hillside than red deer runs fleeter?
And who on the lakeside is hastening to greet her?
Who but Fergus O'Farrell, the fiery and gay,
The darling and pride of the Flower of Finae.

One kiss and one clasp, and one wild look of gladness;
Ah! Why do they change on a sudden to sadness—?
He has told his hard fortune, no more can he stay,
He must leave his poor Eily to pine in Finae.

For Fergus O'Farrell was true to his sireland,
And the dark hand of tyranny drove him from Ireland;
He joins the Brigade in the war far away,
And he vows he'll come back to the Flower of Finae.

He fought at Cremona—she hears of his story;
He fought at Cassano—she's proud of his glory;
Yet sadly she sings *Shule Aroon* all the day,
"Oh, come, come my darling, come home to Finae."

Eight long years have passed, till she's nigh broken-hearted;
From her "reel" and her "rock" and her "flax" she has parted;
She sails with the Wild Geese to Flanders away,
And leaves her sad parents alone in Finae.

Lord Clare on the field of Ramillies is charging—
Before him, the *Sassenach* squadrons enlarging—
Behind him the Cravats their sections display,
Beside him rides Fergus and thinks of Finae.

On the slopes of La Judoigne the Frenchmen are flying;
Lord Clare and his squadron, the foe still defying,
Outnumbered and wounded, retreat in array;
And bleeding rides Fergus and thinks of Finae.

In the cloister of Yprcs a banner is swaying,
And by it a pale weeping maiden is praying;
That flag's the sole trophy of Ramillies fray,
This nun is poor Eily, the Flower of Finae.

The deposed James II had fled to France after the Battle of the Boyne with his tiny son James Edward, the Old Pretender. The Old Pretender's son—Prince Charles Edward Louis Philip Casimir—was later to become known in Britain as the "Young Pretender," in Scotland as "Bonnie Prince Charlie," and in Ireland as "The Blackbird." The Stuart pretenders, recognized as legitimate hiers to the English Crown by the Vatican and France,[2] were a source of constant worry to London. There was good reason. The succession of the House of Hanover to the British throne was the occasion for rising by the Jacobite Scots, the Old Pretender himself landing at Peterhead in 1715. Though the rebellion amounted to little more than a scare—the Duke of Argyle outbluffed the Jacobite Duke of Mar at Sherrifmuir, forcing James Edward's hasty departure—The Fifteen served to stoke the already burning "No Popery" blaze in England.

THE BLACKBIRD

As Scotland rose in 1715, Ireland watched quietly. Jacobite feeling was certainly pervasive among the Irish, but the natural leaders were "banish'd or slain" and the men who might fight were already in arms on the continent. Irish support for the Stuarts took the form of a sort of "Charley-over-the-Waterism," as one wag put it, a rude nationalist yearning for a Prince to lead the Irish Brigade home across the sea and free the Irish from the English yoke.

During the seventeenth century, and to a lesser degree in the eighteenth, traditional bards still roamed Ireland. A far cry from the *filí* of old, these vestiges of a vanished breed had primordial harps tucked under their arms and veritable libraries of balladry under their worn caps. Such a wandering poet was Claragh, so called from the hill where he was born. One lament he sang was in celebration of the Old Pretender, but could have easily been a keen for the passing of any Irish hero (or of the *file* who would no longer be there to sing of his prince):

> Mute are the minstrels that sang of him;
> The harp forgets its thrilling tone;
> The brightest eyes of the land are dim,
> For the pride of their aching sight is gone.

After the Capitulation of Limerick, street balladeers began to "replace" the traditional poets and musicians. Before the old harpists and pipers completely disappeared, young Edward Bunting was to save some of the ancient music by notating what he heard at the last Harper's Assembly in 1792.

This ballad from the Bunting collection may date to the early eighteenth century, and is generally considered the first Irish rebel lyric written in English. The "Blackbird" metaphor was used by the Jacobite Irish to represent both Stuart pretenders.

On a fair summer's morning of soft recreation,
I heard a fair lady a-making great moan;
With sobbing and sighing and sad lamentation,
A-saying, "My Blackbird most royal is flown.
My thoughts they deceive me,
Reflections do grieve me,
And I am overburdened with sad misery;
Yet if death it should blind me
As true love inclines me,
My Blackbird I'd seek out wherever he be."

"Once in fair England my Blackbird did flourish,
He was the chief flower that in it did spring;
Prime ladies of honour his person did nourish,
Because that he was the true son of a king.
But since this false fortune
Which still is uncertain
Has caused this parting between him and me,
His name I'll advance
In Spain and in France,
And I'll seek out my Blackbird wherever he be."

"The birds of the forest they all met together—
The turtle was chosen to dwell with the dove:
And I am resolved in foul or fair weather,
In winter or in spring, for to seek out my true love.
He is all my heart's treasure,
My joy and my pleasure,
And justly, my love, my heart shall follow thee;
He is constant and kind
And courageous of mind,
All bliss to my Blackbird wherever he be."

"In England my Blackbird and I were together,
Where he was still noble and generous of heart;
And woe to the time that he first went out hither,
Alas he was forced from thence to depart.
In Scotland he is deemed
And highly esteemed,
In England he seemed a stranger to be;
Yet his name shall remain
In France and in Spain,
All bliss to my Blackbird wherever he be."

It is not the ocean can fright me with danger,
For though like a pilgrim I wander forlorn,
I may still meet with friendship from one that's a stranger
Much more than from one that in England was born.
Oh, heaven so spacious,
To Britain be gracious,
Though some there be odious both to him and to me;
Yet joy and renown
And laurel shall crown
My Blackbird with honour wherever he be.

The almost inaccessible topography of the Irish Southwest made County Kerry "beyond the Pale" for much of the Penal

Times. Lecky describes the conditions:

> These districts—consisting almost exclusively of wild mountains and bogs, doomed by the nature of the soil to great poverty, traversed by few or no regular roads, far removed from all considerable centres of civilised life, and inhabited chiefly by a wild and wretched population of Cartholics—lay beyond the empire of the law.

A huge smuggling trade with the continent developed, a trade both necessary for survival and eminently "respectable" to the Kerry papists in their effort to circumvent the effects of the oppressive Penal Laws. Smuggling was, in truth, the only rural trade open to Catholics in which they could hope for more than subsistence living. The smugglers imported wine, tea, and tobacco, loading wool grown on Irish sheepwalks for the return trip. Also aboard was the most valuable contraband of all, listed as *Géanna Fiáine* on the boatsmen's bills of lading—recruits for the Irish Brigade.[3]

THE DIRGE OF O'SULLIVAN BEAR

Informing was a profitable, if dangerous, profession in eighteenth century Ireland. One Puxley, trying to take advantage of the "Saxon Bounty," informed on Murtogh Oge O'Sullivan, a smuggler working the Beara Peninsula in the far Southwest. After O'Sullivan had murdered Puxley for his trouble, the authorities duly dispatched a band of redcoats to run down the smuggler.

The fugitive's spirited defense resulted in the death of several British soldiers. O'Sullivan was in fact taken only after his frightened servant, Scully, wet his master's gunpowder. The furious Englishmen, under orders to bring their prisoners back to Cork for trial, followed only the letter of their instructions: the troopers brought O'Sullivan into harbour trailing from the back of their boat. Having saved the Crown the expense of the assizes, the soldiers festooned the Kerryman's head upon a spike at the South Gate Bridge.

Tradition has it that the original of this ballad was written by Murt O'Sullivan's aged nursemaid. Jeremiah Callanan, one of the few poets able to capture the nuance of Irish balladry in the English language, is responsible for this widely sung translation.

The sun on Ivera no longer shines brightly,
The voice of her music no longer is spritely,
No more to her maidens the light dance is dear,
Since the death of our darling O'Sullivan Bear.

Scully! Thou false one, you basely betrayed him,
In his strong hour of need when thy right hand should aid him;
He fed thee, he clad thee, you had all could delight thee,
You left him, you sold him, may heaven requite thee!

Had he died calmly, I would not deplore him,
Or if the wild strife of the sea-war closed o'er him;
But with ropes round his white limbs through ocean to trail him,
Like a fish after catching, tis therefore I wail him.

Long may the curse of O'Sullivan chase them:
Scully that sold him and the soldiers that slew him!
One glimpse of heaven's light may they see never,
May the hearthstone of hell be their best bed forever!

In the hole which the vile hands of soldiers had made thee,
Unhonoured, unshrouded, and headless they laid thee;
No sign to regret thee, no eye to tear o'er thee,
No dirge to lament thee, no friend to deplore thee.

Dear head of my darling, how gory and pale,
These aged eyes see the high-spiked on their gaol;
Your cheek in the summer sun ne'er shall grow warm,
Nor your eye again catch light, but the flash of the storm.

A curse, blessed ocean, is on thy green water,
From the haven of Cork to Ivera of slaughter;
Since thy billows were dyed with the red wounds of fear,
Of Muiertach Oge, our O'Sullivan Bear!

The disappearance of the last great Catholic lords after Limerick—and the consequent imposition of the Penal Laws—had insured that Irish "opposition" was to be led by Protestants for well over a century. Though political dissent with the Crown and championing Catholic rights were two very different things to most of the Ascendancy leaders, there were some few voices crying out in the wilderness. As early as 1698 William Molyneux had published *The case of Ireland's being bound by Acts of Parliament in England stated.* Precipitated by the English protectionist laws that were designed to destroy the Irish woollen competition with Britain, it is conceptually so kindred to the spirit of the American Declaration of Independence that it is possible it was consulted when that remarkable document was written seventy-eight years afterwards. Bishop George Berkeley, the noted philosopher, was driven to query "whether there be

upon earth any Christian or civilised people so beggarly wretched
and destitute as the common Irish?" Even the sympathetic
voices, however, dripped with colonial paternalism. Archbishop
Edward Synge scolded his fellow Anglicans:

> There are too many among us who had rather keep the Papists
> as they are, in an almost slavish subjection, than have them made
> Protestants, and thereby entitled to the same liberties and priv-
> ileges with the rest of their fellow subjects.

One iconoclastic voice, though, flashed forth from the groves of
academe with such withering effect that it has earned its owner
the appellation, "The Father of Irish Protestant Nationalism."
Jonathan Swift's pungent wit and incisive prose made him one of
the most respected minds of the century. A cousin of Dryden, at
grammar school with Congreve, educated at Trinity and Oxford,
Dean Swift had access to the most influential salons of London
and Dublin.

It would not be stretching an analogy unduly to suggest that
Swift's trenchant "pro-Irish" stance was a microcosm of what little national spirit there was in Protestant Ireland during his era.
The Dean of St. Patrick's would have been shocked by the suggestion of an independent Ireland in the modern sense; rather, his
skewering satire of the Crown (which, he suggested, "showed by
one satiric touch/No nation wanted it so much") was a Protestant Ascendancy view that London was too far removed from the
practical problems of Ireland to govern the island effectively. He
probably would have approved of the Home Rule arrangement
that Ireland would achieve under Grattan's Parliament in 1782.

Not having the forum of a parliamentary seat—Swift's
"Tory nationalism" did not endear him to the Whigs in Dublin
Castle—the Dean contented himself by firing off a steady stream
of scathingly satiric pamphlets on the folly of Walpole's government. His *Proposals for the Universal Use of Irish Manufacturers*
in 1720 urged the burning of everything British except coal. His
Drapier's Letters of 1722-24 counselled boycott[4] of the debased
halfpenny contracted in London for use in Ireland. Swift's most
famous pamphlet appeared in October 1729; entitled *A Modest
Proposal for Preventing the Children of Poor People from Being
a Burthen to Their Parents or Country*, it suggested that the children of the Irish poor could be fattened up to feed the rich instead of going to waste by starving to death or leaving "to fight
for the Pretender in Spain, or sell themselves to the Barbados."

Jonathan Swift provided the impetus to a feeling of "Irish-ness" to many of the Protestant Ascendancy. For the first time, an articulate spokesman of the Anglican landowning class was defining an estrangement from London that, deep down, many of his contemporaries were already beginning to feel. The banner of Irish nationalism had been discarded by the Catholic lords at Limerick. Now it seemed that there were some few Protestants willing to retrieve it . . . if not yet disposed to hoist it anew.

ERIN GO BRAGH

This eighteenth century street ballad expresses a philosophy probably quite close to that of Dean Swift. The references to England, Scotland, and Ireland joining hands together—if only Britain would recognize that Ireland wished to be her loyal, but equal, partner—is very much a Protestant Ascendancy "nationalist" sentiment. The reference to a land once "happy and free," however, is much more the memory of men in thatched country cabins recalling ancient Gaelic tradition. The two romances, married here within the same song, were to find a common frustration that would lead to rebellion by the end of the century.

Ye sons of Hibernia, however low in station,
Or wherever you be, come attend to my call:
Resist all attempts and unshackle your nation,
Old Ireland I mean, or alas, she must fall.
With burdens so great and her liberty sinking,
Its beauty nigh gone—on destruction its brinking;
Then on, my brave boys, don't let's stand by idly thinking.
While Ireland's our country, dear *Erin go bragh.*

Oh! Erin, my country, once happy and free
With pleasure I stood on thy once native shore,
But alas! Cruel fortune has turned foe to thee,
Oh! *Erin Mavourneen,* thy case I deplore.
Bound down by a shackle that's linked to a snare,
By foes base and keen who have filled thee with care;
Then on, my brave boys, we'll show we play fair,
For Ireland's our country, dear *Erin go bragh.*

Oh! England, your taunts and your censures give o'er,
And spite not that country that's equal to you,
But join hand-in-hand, each day and each hour,
With Scotland, our friends—all to each other true.
United in friendship, we'll join in a band,

Determined to fight for our kings, laws and land;
Then on, my brave boys, don't let us here stand,
While Ireland's our country, dear *Erin go bragh.*

As the years of the century wore on, the dichotomy between the "haves" and the "have-nots" became entrenched. One history has observed that the Protestants "developed the vices of slaveowners, becoming idle, dissipated, and neglectful of their duties." The Catholics, on the other hand:

> grew, as a serf-population always does grow, cringing, shifty, untruthful. They were lazy because they had nothing to work for, lawless because they knew the law only as an enemy to be defied or evaded wherever possible.

Previous and later generations of Irishmen rose against conditions far less oppressive than those existing under the Penal Laws. Unlike those other generations, however, the Irish of the eighteenth century lacked the strong young arms to wield the weapons—they were in France and Spain, in Austria and Portugal, bearing their pikes and guns under foreign banners. It was perhaps inevitable that the heart of many a *cailín* was over the sea with them.

CARRAIGDHOUN

With no future at home, "many a lad of twenty" determined to make his fortune on the continent before returning to wed his sweetheart. Not many came back. Those who did not fall in battle or succumb to disease were often reluctant to give up their fairly won status as respected veterans in exchange for serfdom in Ireland.

As this ballad by Cork-born poet Denny Lane indicates, young love was regularly thwarted by a combination of the reality of the Penal Laws and the blandishments of the continent. It was slowly sinking in that the thousands leaving to join the Irish Brigades of Europe might never return to fight for Ireland.

On Carraigdhoun the hearth is brown,
The clouds are dark o'er Ardnalee,
And many a stream comes rushing down
To swell the angry Ownabee;
The morning blast is sweeping fast
Through many a leafless tree,

And I'm alone for he is gone,
My hawk has flow, *ochone machree.*

The hearth is green on Carraigdhoun,
Bright shone the sun on Ardnalee,
The dark green trees bend tumbling down
To kiss the slumbering Ownabee.
That happy day twas but last May,
Tis like a dream to me,
When Donal swore, aye, o'er and o'er,
"We'll part no more, oh *stor machree.*

Soft April showers and bright May flowers
Will bring the summer back again,
But will they bring me back the hours
I spent with my Donal then?
Tis but a chance, for he's gone to France
To wear the *fleur de lis;*
But I'll follow you *ma* Donal *dhu,*
For still I'm true to you, *machree.*

THE CAILÍN DHOUN

Though the common folk did not openly oppose the Crown on an organised basis, the very separation of the Catholic cottier population from the centres of power insured the eventual growth of an Irish nationalist *jacquerie.* Not included in the day-to-day operation of the country—indeed, pronounced "enemies" by the British courts—the people not surprisingly turned to their Gaelic past. Jackson describes the process well:

> These people of the thatched cabins had once inestimably precious compensation. Around their turf fires they could hear retold again and again the legendary stories of the Gaels, and be solaced by poem, song, and music preserved from days which far outdated the oldest of their miseries—far-off days when the sun always shone and the blackbirds's whistle never failed in the glen.
>
> It was thus, and in these cabins, that the seed was kept alive which in due time would burst forth in the rich profusion of regenerated Irish Nationality.

This new note began to creep into the balladry. Even the plaintive love lament for the Irishman fighting the Saxon on the remote battlefields of Europe became less a keen and more a rebel song.

As I roved out one summer's morning,
I met a maiden of beauty rare—
The sweet wild roses the braes adorning,
Not half so sweet are, nor half so fair.
The brown thrush singing when the sun is sinking,
The blackbird piping when the sun is down,
And the little stars in the sky a-winking,
Sang not so sweetly as my *cailín dhoun.*

Oh, brown-tressed maiden of rarest beauty,
You've won my heart on this summer day,
To love you always will be my duty,
If you, fair one, won't say me "nay."
"Young man," she answered, "you are a stranger,
And I will never give my heart and hand
To any rover or to any ranger
Who will not fight for his native land."

"In the fields of France has my father battled,
My brothers too, neath the *fleur de lis,*
Where the sabres flashed and the cannon rattled,
Struck many a blow to set Ireland free.
And the English flag often sank before them,
But their graves are made by a foreign strand,
And sad and lonely do I deplore them
Who died away from their native land."

"Oh, bright-eyed maiden, the hours I'm counting,
Till the summons comes to the brave and true,
And the Green Flag flies over plain and mountain
And pikes are flashing, and muskets too.
And then, *astoreen,* when the battle's over,
I'll come and ask for your heart and hand;
And if I fall, forget not the rover
Who died for you and his native land."

Jonathan Swift died in 1745, a year of particular significance to the Irish Rebel Tradition. Two major events of that
year stoked nationalist fires in Ireland: the Battle of Fontenoy
and the Scottish Forty-Five.

Fontenoy, in what is now western Belgium, was the most
glorious single action of the many fought by the Irish Brigade.
On 11 May the French of Louis XV, in alliance with Frederick
the Great of Prussia, joined battle with the combined armies of
Austria, Holland, and England. The decision was a narrow thing.
The difference was the Irish Brigade.

THE IRISH BRIGADE

The Irish regiments in the French service were as noted for their unconventional discipline as they were for their reckless bravery under fire. Electing their officers in much the same way that Gaelic clans had elected their chiefs in antiquity, the Irish Brigade then fought for their leaders with a loyalty reminiscent of that shown to ancient Celtic war-lords.

This rousing Thomas Davis song recalls the Brigade on the eve of Fontenoy. The ballad brings to mind the perhaps apocryphal story of an irate Louis XV complaining to Charles O'Brien, Viscount Clare, that the ill-discipline of the Irishmen gave the monarch more headaches than all his other troops combined. The man who would shortly become Marshal Thomond of France is said to have replied whimsically, "Please, milord, your enemies make just the same complaint!"

The mess tents are full and the glasses are set,
And the gallant Count Thomond is president yet;
The veteran rose like an uplifted lance,
Crying, "Comrades, a health to the monarch of France!"
With bumpers and cheers they have done as he bade,
For King Louis is loved by the Irish Brigade.

"A health to King James!" and they bent as they quaffed;
"Here's to George the Elector!" and fiercely they laughed;
"Good luck to the girls we wooed long ago,
Where Shannon and Barrow and Blackwater flow;
God prosper old Ireland"—you'd think them afraid,
So pale grew the chiefs of the Irish Brigade.

But surely that light cannot come from our lamp,
And that noise: are they all getting drunk in the camp?
"Hurrah boys, the morning of battle has come,
And the generals' beating on many a drum."
So they rush from the revel to join the parade;
For the van is the right of the Irish Brigade.

They fought as they revelled—fast, fiery, and true—
And though victors, they left on the field not a few;
And they who survived fought and drank as of yore,
But the land of their heart's hopes they never saw more,

For in far foreign fields from Dunkirk to Belgrade
Lie the soldiers and chiefs of the Irish Brigade.

FONTENOY

It is not unusual for the victors of a battle to praise the ability and determination of the vanquished; it does, after all, serve to make the triumph seem all the greater. After Fontenoy, Irish balladeers and French troubadours did not need to exaggerate the steel of the British troops.

The French under Marshal Hermann de Saxe were dug in around the small hamlet of Fontenoy; their Prussian allies were entrenched somewhat further south around the village of Antoine. Lord Clare's five thousand Irishmen were on the left with the French, near the end of the line. The armies of the Alliance under the Duke of Cumberland were drawn up in battle array to the east with the Dutch opposite Antoine and the English and Hanoverians on the right opposite Fontenoy. Repeated frontal assaults by the Allies upon de Saxe's fortified redoubts had been beaten off when "Bloody Cumberland" ordered a final assault of sixteen thousand men led by his reserve under Lord Charles Hay. This column of infantry was launched out of the Bois de Barri, a wood just behind the allied lines, and was directed like an arrow straight at the heart of the French line. Cumberland's gamble almost paid off.

The bold British infantry marched in lockstep toward their goal, shrugging off appalling losses to the defenders' artillery. Hay's van broke through the left-centre of the French defenses. After de Saxe had foolishly hurled his cavalry reserve against this oncoming infantry, the French were faced with incipient rout. Louis XV, come to watch as spectator, hurried to fly with his courtiers. At that moment Clare's Irish burst suddenly onto Hay's right flank. The combination of British weariness, attrition, and lack of ammunition made the shock of the Irish assault irresistable. The English rallied bravely but the furious intensity of the Brigade's attack encouraged the wavering French to regroup, sealing the fate of Hay's troops. The French victory was complete.

In a fine example of the ballad as history, Thomas Davis here *sings* the story of the battle.

Thrice at the huts of Fontenoy the English column failed,
And twice the lines of St. Antoine, the Dutch in vain assailed;
For town and slope were filled with fort and flanking battery
And well they swept the English ranks and Dutch auxiliary.
As vainly through deBarry's wood the British soldiers burst,
The French artillery drove them back, diminished and dispersed;
The Bloody Duke of Cumberland beheld with anxious eye
And ordered up his last reserve, his latest chance to try.
On Fontenoy, on Fontenoy, how fast his generals ride!
And mustering, come his chosen troops like clouds at eventide.

Six thousand English veterans in stately column tread,
Their cannons blaze in front and flank, Lord Hay is at their head;
Steady they step a-down the slope, steady they climb the hill,
Steady they load, steady they fire, moving right onward still.
Betwixt the wood and Fontenoy, as through a furnace blast,
Through rempart, trench, and palisade, and bullets firing fast;
And on the open plain above they rose and kept their course
With ready fire and grim resolve that mocked at hostile force.
Past Fontenoy, past Fontenoy, while thinner grew their ranks,
They break, as broke the Zuider Zee through Holland's ocean banks.

More idly than the summer flies, French *tirilleurs* rush around,
As stubble to the lava tide, French squadrons strew the ground;
Bombshell and grape and roundshot tore, still on they marched and fired,
Fast from each volley, *grenadier* and *voltiguer* retired.
"Push on, my Household Cavalry!" King Louis madly cried:
To death they rush, but rude their shock—not unavenged they died.
On through the camp the column trod, King Louis turns his rein;
"Not yet, my liege," Saxe interposed, "the Irish troops remain!"
And Fontenoy, famed Fontenoy, had been a Waterloo
Were not those exiles ready then—fresh, vehement and true.

"Lord Clare," he says, "you have your wish—there are your Saxon foes."
The Marshal almost smiles to see, so furiously he goes!
How fierce the look these exiles wear, who're wont to be so gay,
The treasured wrongs of fifty years are in their hearts today:
The treaty broken ere the ink wherewith twas writ could dry,
Their plundered homes, their ruined shrines, their women's parting cry,
Their priesthood hunted down like wolves, their country overthrown!
Each looks as if revenge for all were staked on him alone.
On Fontenoy, on Fontenoy, nor ever yet elsewhere
Rushed on to fight a nobler band than these proud exiles were.

O'Brien's voice is hoarse with joy as, halting, he commands,
"Fix bayonets—charge!" Like mountain streams rush on these fiery bands;
Thin is the English column now and faint their volleys grow,
Yet, mustering all the strength they have, they make a gallant show.
They dress their ranks upon the hill to face that battle-wind,
Their bayonets the breaker's foam—like rocks, the men behind;
One volley crashes from their line when, through the surging smoke,
With empty guns clutched in their hands, the headlong Irish broke.
On Fontenoy, on Fontenoy, hark to that fierce huzzah,
"Revenge! Remember Limerick! Dash down the *Sassenach*!"

Like lions leaping at a fold when mad with hunger's pang,
Right up against the English line the Irish exiles sprang;
Bright was their steel—tis bloody now, their guns are filled with gore;
Through shattered ranks and severed files, the trampled flag they tore.
The English strove with desperate strength, paused, rallied, staggered, fled!
The green hillside is marted close with dying and with dead;
Across the plain and far away passed on that hideous wrack
While *cavalier* and *fantassin* dash in upon their track.
On Fontenoy, on Fontenoy, like eagles in the sun,
With bloody plumes the Irish stand—the field is fought and won!

THE BRIGADE AT FONTENOY

It was not only in the French service that the Wild Geese made their mark. In *Die Theresianische Militarakademie zu Neustadt,* the Austrian Military Academy, a third of the honoured paintings in the main hall are of Irishmen. There is good reason: there were forty-one Irish-born generals in the Austrian service during the eighteenth century. One of them, Field Marshal Thomas Brady of County Cavan, later became privy counciller and, finally, Governor of Dalmatia. Don Ricardo Wall became Prime Minister of Spain. Major General Count Peter Lacy led successful campaigns against the Swedes for Tsar Peter the Great of Russia. Miguel Hogan became a Portugese major general. Ambrose O'Higgins was the Spanish Captain-General of Chile, his son Bernardo became its Liberator. Macaulay comments tellingly about these Wild Geese:

> There were Irish Catholics of great ability . . . to be found every-
> where except in Ireland—at Versailles, at St. Ildefonso, in the

armies of Frederic, in the armies of Maria Theresa. . . . Scattered all over Europe were to be found brave Irish generals, dexterous Irish diplomatists, Irish counts, Irish barons, Irish knights of St. Louis and St. Leopold, of the White Eagle, and of the Golden Fleece, who if they remained in the house of bondage, could not have been ensigns of marching regiments or freemen of petty corporations.

The exiled Irish private soldier won no fewer accolades than his celebrated commanders. The echo of the Irish war-pipe reverberated throughout the battlefields of Europe as the Irish mercenary won an international reputation. Of the thousands of battles fought by Irishmen abroad, however, none surpassed Fontenoy in the folk-memory of their admirers at home.

By our campfires rose a murmur at the dawning of the day,
And the tread of many footsteps spoke the advent of a fray;
And as we took our places, few and stern were our words,
While some were tightening horse-girths and some were girding swords.

The trumpet blast has sounded our footmen to array—
The willing steed has bounded, impatient for the fray—
The Green Flag is unfolded while arose the cry of joy:
"Heaven speed dear Ireland's banner today at Fontenoy!"

We looked upon that banner and the memory arose
Of our hopes and perished kindred where the Lee and Shannon flows;
We looked upon that banner and we swore to God on high
To smite today the Saxon's might, to conquer or to die.

Loud swells the charging trumpet—tis a voice from our own land—
God of battles, God of vengeance, guide today the patriot band;
There are stains to wash away, there are memories to destroy,
In the best blood of the Briton today at Fontenoy.

With one shout for good King Louis and the fair land of the vine,
Like the wrathful Alpine tempest we swept along their line;
Then we rang along the battlefield, triumphant our hurrah,
And we smote them down still cheering, "*Erin, slanthagal go bragh!*"

See their shattered forces flying—a broken, routed line—
See, England, what brave laurels for your brow today we twine;
Thrice blessed the hour that witnessed the Briton turn to flee
From the chivalry of Erin and France's *fleur de lis.*

While the Wild Geese were winning glory on the continent, the Irish at home remained quiescent. The Scot Jacobites did not. Thirty years after the Old Pretender had been turned back by the Campbells in the Scottish Fifteen, another Stuart pretender arrived to try again. Bonnie Prince Charlie landed on Eriskay Island, set up court in Edinburgh, won a huge victory at Prestonpans, and took Carlisle. Swiftly gathering enthusiastic Highland supporters, the New Pretender rashly struck southward into England, reaching Derby before the unprepared English were able to respond. When they did, it was with a vengeance.

The Duke of Cumberland, fresh from defeat at Fontenoy, was in no mood to waste time on the Jacobites. Pushing the Highlanders back into Scotland, Cumberland used the newly established dominance of the Royal Navy to ferry troops into the North, outflanking the rebels. The Scot rebellion was finally crushed at the 1746 Battle of Culloden Moor. Prince Charles barely escaped with his life, making it back to the continent only through MacDonald guile. The last pitched battle on the soil of Britain, Culloden marked the end of realistic Stuart pretentions to the throne of the British Isles.

THE WHITE COCKADE
(*An Cnota Bán*)

The defeat of Bonnie Prince Charlie signalled the end of Celtic tribalism in Britain. The "Highland Question" was settled; henceforth, the Presbyterian Lowlands would be the dominant voice north of the Tweed. The Union of England and Scotland, proclaimed on paper in 1707, was now to become a reality.

In Ireland, the Protestant Ascendancy feared a sympathetic rising. They need not have worried. Irish sentiment for the Blackbird was a vague, leaderless, pro-Catholic nostalgia for the time of its grandfathers.

This old Gaelic song—translated here by Callanan—was a centerpiece of the "Stuart-nationalist" feeling of the eighteenth century. Irish war pipes had played it in battle for the last time at Fontenoy. Though it was Scottish pipes that retreated at Culloden Moor, the battle served as last hurrah for the Irish Jacobites as well. When next the Irish looked to France, the White Cockade of the Bourbons would be supplanted by the Tricolour of the Revolution.

King Charles he is King James' son
And from a royal line is sprung;
Then up with shout and out with blade,
And we'll raise once more the White Cockade.
Oh, my dear, my fair-haired youth,
Thou hast hearts of fire and of truth;
Then up with shout and out with blade,
We'll raise once more the White Cockade.

My young men's hearts are dark with woe,
On my virgin's cheeks the grief-drops flow,
The sun scarce lights the sorrowing day
Since our rightful prince went far away.
He's gone, the stranger holds his throne,
The royal bird far off has flown;
But up with shout and out with blade,
We'll stand or fall with the White Cockade.

No more the cuckoo hails the spring,
The woods no more with staunch-hounds ring;
The song from the glen, so sweet before,
Is hushed since Charles has left our shore.
The prince is gone; but he soon will come
With trumpet sound and beat of drum;
Then up with shout and out with blade,
Hurrah for the Right and the White Cockade!

By the middle of the eighteenth century, the rapparee tradition had become a fixture in the Irish folk culture. Though these highwaymen and brigands were by now a far cry from the bold rebels who had chosen to fight on for their land after the Capitulation of Limerick, the peasants were inclined to look on them fondly. Occasionally, a particularly daring rascal would be invested—through balladry—with the noble traits of a Robin Hood. The reality was far different, of course, but anyone who stood against Saxon law made a likely hero for the balladeers of the Penal Times.

BOLD CAPTAIN FRENEY

Captain Freney of the Cratloe Woods in south Clare was of the new breed of highwaymen. From humble origin, only his title was a rapparee remnant from the days when the men who took to the hills were Jacobite officers. Roaming Munster at will for over a decade, Freney was Ireland's answer to Ben Turpin. He later "retired" to New Ross a celebrity, accepted a job as a customs official, and wrote an autobiography (he even popped up in a Thackeray novel a century afterwards, appearing in Hollywood's version of *The Luck of Barry Lyndon* within the last few years). Freney claimed that the following ballad was based on a true incident.

One morning as, being free from care,
I rode abroad to take the air,
Twas my fortune for to spy
A jolly tailor riding by.

Refrain:
And it's, oh, bold Captain Freney!
Oh, bold Freney, oh!

As we rode on along the way,
We caught that tailor dressed most gay;
I boldly bid him for to stand,
Thinking he was some gentleman.

Refrain

Upon his pockets, I laid hold,
The first thing I got was a purse of gold;
The next thing I found, which did me surprise,
Was a needle and a thread, thimble likewise.

Refrain

You're a dirty trifle I disdain!
With that I returned him his gold again,
I'll rob no tailor; if I can,
I'd rather ten times rob a man.

Refrain

It's time for me to look about,
There's a proclamation just gone out:
To bring me in alive or dead,
With fifty pounds upon my head!

Refrain

The Scottish Forty-Five did have an impact in Ireland that was not immediately apparent. Lord Chesterfield, sent to Ireland as Viceroy at the time of the Jacobite landing in Scotland, relaxed the Penal Laws slightly to deflect attention from events across the Irish Sea. The narrow easing of restrictions on Catholics in trade was just enough for some papist merchants to achieve a modicum of commercial success. The growth in the population, with the parallel growth of the chief towns,[5] created for the first time an Irish middle class, consisting almost wholly of Dissenting Protestants and some prosperous papists. Catholic merchants and physicians (the only profession not proscribed) began to have direct dealings with peers who were not co-religionists.

As far removed from the wretched cottiers of the countryside as they were from the fox-hunting Protestant Nation, the burghers of the new middle class considered themselves quite unabashedly, and soon chauvinistically, Irish. These urban Dissenters and Romanists had no quarrel with the Georgian Crown, but had a Swiftian abhorence for the British Parliament.

TO THE BATTLE, MEN OF ERIN

Most of the attorneys, physicians, and tradesmen of the small but growing middle class were Dissenters: Methodists, Presbyterians, Baptists, and Quakers, who in strictly Anglican terms, were not considered "Protestant." Although the Penal Laws had been specifically targeted at the papists, much of the legislation had been drafted in such a way to make the Dissenters subject to the same restrictions as the Catholics. The Church of Ireland Ascendancy saw little reason to extend its own privileged position to the Dissenters. Though not "domestic enemies"—as

Lord Pembroke had named the papists—the Dissenters were very certainly not first-class citizens, either. The Ascendancy failure to amend the Penal Laws to exclude the Presbyterian defenders of Enniskillen and Londonderry brought, first, disillusionment and, finally, rebellion.

The first sign of the coming storm came in Dublin. In 1759 when rumours that a legislative union between Ireland and Britain was contemplated, the middle-class Dissenters of the capital erupted in the wildest riot in the city's history. The mob broke into the Irish Parliament, halted the carriages of Members, and killed the legislators' horses; a scaffold was even erected, presumably to threaten the politicans with a fate similar to that of their animals. Irish public opinion was making a raucous debut.

Most nationalist songs were written for the masses. There began to be exceptions to this general practice in the second half of the eighteenth century when poets of the middle class began to sing of grievances and solutions. By the time the teenaged Edward Bunting collected this song from its author in 1792, the Dissenters—and indeed even some of the Anglican Ascendancy—had long since begun to identify with the Wild Geese and the ancient Gaelic tradition.

To the battle, men of Erin,
To the heat of battle go,
Every breast the shamrock wearing,
Burns to meet his country's foe.
What through France thine eagle standard
Spreading terror far and nigh,
Over Europe's skies hath wandered
On the wings of victory.

Yet their vauntings we dismay not,
Tell us when ye, hand-to-hand,
Ever stood the charging bayonet
Of a right true Irish hand.
Erin, when the swords are glancing,
In the dark fight loves to see
Foremost still her plumage dancing
To the trumpet's jubilee.

For the first six decades of the eighteenth century, Ireland had been quiet. The Catholics, and to a lesser degree the Dissenters, had been forced to accept their lot. The rumblings of discontent among the humble Irish had remained below the surface, expressing themselves in secret smiles and quiet songs about the rapparees and the Irish Brigade. Even the Protestant Ascendancy had accepted their own status as second-class English gentry. The next forty years were to see the anti-English rumblings emerge into a groundswell of Irish nationalism that would finally burst into explosion at the end of the century.

CHAPTER NOTES (10)

1 – The perception of the Irish Ascendancy as a leisure-rich, parasitic, fox-hunting class has never really died among the commons of Ireland. The legacy of alienation between the landed gentry and the humble folk, dating from the Penal Times, makes Brendan Behan's definition of a landowner as "a Protestant on a horse" completely understandable—and only slightly funny—to the Irish.

2 – Although the Vatican had happily supported the claims of William and Mary during the War of the League of Augsburg against Louis XIV, the 1694 death of Mary, the British Act of Settlement in 1701, and the death of James II in that same year had changed Rome's policy. The Papacy supported Stuart pretensions to the British Crown until the death of Bonnie Prince Charlie in 1788.

The French, meanwhile, supported the Stuarts until two years after Culloden Moor when the War of Austrian Succession was ended by the 1748 Treaty of Aix-la-Chapelle.

3 – One family of smugglers from this area made profit enough during the eighteenth century to emerge as the local Catholic "gentry." The early nineteenth century scion of that clan was to emerge from Kerry and become "The Liberator," Daniel O'Connell.

4 – The word "boycott" did not actually come into use until the Land League times when a half-pay British officer of that name came into confrontation with the local peasants around Lough Mask in County Mayo. Dean Swift's idea, however, was identical to that of Captain Boycott's tenants a century-and-a-half afterwards.

5 — An admirable population study by John Carswell in 1973, using a number of different and often conflicting sources, places the Irish population at 1,000,000 at the time of Limerick. In 1780 it was 2,800,000.

11

Peasants and Patriots

The lot of the Irish peasant had changed very little during the long years of the eighteenth century. While some few Catholics had struggled into the new middle class of the towns, the cottiers of the countryside remained absolutely dependent for bare subsistence upon the whims of the landowners and the owner's agents. As the population had steadily increased making land more dear, a new spectre had appeared on the scene: the land speculator.

Under the Penal Laws, the peasant had no legal defense against this new curse. Subdivision and subletting had become a way of life, driving rents up still further. In some cases the "Big Lord" was five times removed from the peasant who actually worked the land. Often the landowner—safely insulated from the rural reality of Ireland amidst the social whirl of London and Dublin—had no idea how many tenants he had.[1] In truth, the ultimate limiting factor in sub-leasing had become starvation. If a peasant could keep alive and still pay the rent, the rate was considered "fair." On the other hand, if a peasant began to show signs of solvency, the rent was obviously too low and his immediate landlord would raise it (in turn, of course, *that* landlord's landlord would hike *his* rent . . . and so on through the middlemen up to the actual owner of the land). The practical result was that the rent was never lowered, even in bad years. The peasant paid increasingly higher rent until he had to choose between starvation or eviction. It was little matter to the land speculators; there was always someone who wanted the land. As late as 1844 the Devon Commission would report that "If you ask a man why he bid so much for his farm . . . more than he knew he could pay, his answer is, 'What can I do? Where could I go? I know I cannot pay the rent; but what could I do?' "

The Penal Laws provided much protection to the Ascendancy landowner, none to the Catholic cottier. The Irish peasant could be evicted arbitrarily even if he *did* pay his rent. Further, if he somehow managed to scrape together enough to improve the farm, the value of the land—and, consequently, its rent— would be raised. If the cottier did not punch a hole in the thatch for a rude fireplace, he would freeze; if he did, he was subject to a hearth tax. Finally, the peasant, though almost certainly Catholic or Dissenter, was required to submit an annual tithe for the support of the official Church of Ireland. Robert Fitzgerald, the Knight of Kerry, gives an enlightening view of the peasants' plight in his time:

> The lower orders are in a state of distress beyond anything known in the memory of man. The great rents of this country belong to persons resident out of Ireland, whose agents are severe in collecting them; the lower class . . . cannot dispose of their goods . . . the little money the country affords is carried off for absentees. . . . The miserable tenantry, when pressed by their landlords, bring them all their cattle . . . offer them at half-price . . . the common people are actually in a state of despair, ready for any enterprise that might relieve their present suffering.

The economic and political hopelessness of the Irish peasantry was conspicuous; it was not unique, however, in the Europe of the eighteenth century. What exacerbated the agony of the Irish to a degree unparalled by their continental counterparts were the tangible folk-memories of the Irish past. The Irish peasantry had no money nor were they in any case accustomed to using it; from antiquity, their normal means of exchange had been barter. Now, while the Ascendancy was a part of the London financial revolution, the landowners were pleased to maintain the peasantry in the old ways. The Gaelic oral tradition— still very much alive among the humble folk—reminded the Irish that those old ways did not even recognise private property in land. Their ancestors had elected their "landlords;" in return, those ancient chiefs had honoured the traditional system of common clan ownership. It is small wonder that the Irish looked back wistfully to those days.

GRANUAILE

This broadside ballad laments all that had been lost since the arrival of the hated Saxon six centuries earlier. Dating from

CHRONOLOGY (Peasants and Patriots)

1760 . . . . . .*George III*; French raid on Carrickfergus; Whiteboys appear in Tipperary.

1762 . . . . . .Whiteboyism made punishable by death.

1763 . . . . . .Peace of Paris ends Seven Years War.

1765 . . . . . .Stamp Act riots in Boston; Clive begins reforms in Bengal.

1766 . . . . . .British Parliament passes Declaratory Act for American colonies.

1767 . . . . . .Octennial Bill passed by Irish Parliament.

1770 . . . . . .North, Prime Minister; Boston Massacre; Cook discovers Botany Bay.

1773 . . . . . .Boston Tea Party; Jesuits dissolved by Pope Clement XIV.

1774 . . . . . .1st Continental Congress in America; Louis XVI becomes King of France.

1775 . . . . . .American rebellion begins at Lexington, British hire 29,000 Hessians to deal with rebels; Navigation Laws enforced in Ireland; Flood joins Government.

1776 . . . . . .Americans declare independence; *Common Sense* and *Wealth of Nations* appear.

1777 . . . . . .Burgoyne surrenders British army at Saratoga in New York.

1778 . . . . . .French join Americans; Irish Patriot politicians organise Irish Volunteers; 1st Catholic Relief Act; Non-Importation movement spreads rapidly.

1779 . . . . . .Spanish join French and Americans; British also battle Mahrattas in India; Irish Navigation Laws repealed.

1780 . . . . . .Lord Gordon anti-papist riots in London; Netherlands joins alliance against Britain.

1781 . . . . . .Cornwallis surrenders British army in Virginia.

1782 . . . . . .Rockingham forms Whig government; Dungannon Volunteer convention; 2nd Catholic Relief Act; Irish Parliament gains independence of English Privy Council; Mahratta War ends in India.

1783 . . . . . .Treaty of Versailles ends War of American Independence; Pitt the Younger forms ministry; Bank of Ireland founded.

1784 . . . . . .Foster's Corn Law.

1785 . . . . . .Peep o' Day Boys emerge in Ulster, Catholics respond with Defenders; steam engine installed in Nottinghamshire cotton-spinning factory.

1786-87. . . . .Botany Bay penal colony established in New South Wales.

1788 . . . . . .Britain forms Triple Alliance with Prussians and Dutch; Bonnie Prince Charlie dies; USA comes into being; George III goes mad, regency crisis in Britain; bread riots in France.

1789 . . . . . .French Revolution begins; George III recovers; Tammany founded in New York.

about 1765, the song uses the *aisling*—the traditional Irish vision-poem—to contrast the glory of that ancient Ireland with "poor *Granuaile*" under the British.

The use of this metaphor to denote Ireland seems to have been in common use since the War of the Two Kings. It is a corruption of the name of Gráinne Mhaol (Grace O'Malley), the fabled pirate queen in the time of Elizabeth Tudor who had been called by Richard Bingham "a noble traitress and nurse of all rebellions in the province [*of Connacht*] for forty years." The reference to Dan O'Connell indicates that the seventh verse was, in the normal genesis of folksong, either added or changed about seventy years after the ballad was first sung.

All through the North as I walked forth to view the shamrock plain,
I stood awhile where nature smiled amid the rocks and streams;
On a matron mild I fixed my eyes, beneath a fertile vale,
As she sang her song it was on the wrongs of poor old *Granuaile*.

Her head was bare and her grey hair over her eyes hung down,
Her waist and neck, her hands and feet, with iron chains were bound;
Her pensive strain and plaintive wail mingled with the evening gale,
And the song she sung with mournful tongue was poor old *Granuaile*.

The gown she wore was stained with gore all by a ruffian band,
Her lips so sweet that monarchs kissed are now gone pale and wan;
The tears of grief fell from her eyes, each tear as large as hail,
None could express the deep distress of poor old *Granuaile*.

On her harp she leaned and thus exclaimed, "My royal Brian is gone,
Who in his day did drive away the tyrants every one.
On Clontarf's plains against the Danes, his faction did prepare:
Brave Brian Boru cut their lines in two and freed old *Granuaile*."

"But now, alas, I must confess, avengers I have none;
There's no brave lord to wave his sword in my defense—not one.
My enemies just when they please, with blows they do assail,
The flesh they tore clean off the bones of poor old *Granuaile*."

"Six hundred years the briny tears have flown down from my eyes;
I curse the day that Henry made of me proud Albion's prize.
From that day down with chains I'm bound, no wonder I look pale!
The blood they drained from every vein of poor old *Granuaile*."

There was a lord come from the South, he wore a laurel crown,
Saying, "*Grania* dear, be of good cheer, no longer you'll be bound;
I am the man they call great Dan, who never yet did fail;
I have got the bill for to fulfill your wishes, *Granuaile.*"

With blood besmeared and bathed in tears, her harp she sweetly strung,
And, oh, the change, her mournful air from one last chord she wrung;
Her voice so clear fell on my ear, at length my strength did fail;
I went away and thus did say, "God help you, *Granuaile.*"

THE LAMENT FOR ART O'LEARY
(*Caoineadh Airt Uí Laoghaire*)

A commonplace event in 1773 poignantly demonstrates how pervasively the Penal Laws governed the life of the Irish. A Protestant named Morris spied a Catholic astride a horse worth more than five pounds—a violation of the law. Morris accosted the horseman and, as was a Protestant's right under the Penal Laws, offered the Catholic rider five pounds, claiming the steed as his own. The papist disdainfully struck Morris and galloped away. The County Cork authorities proceeded to track down the offending horseman, shooting him dead in Carraiganimma.

What made the incident more than business as usual was that the victim of the King's Justice was no mere Irish cottier— the rider was Arthur O'Leary, a colonel of the Austrian Imperial Army visiting Ireland on leave. The horse that O'Leary had been riding was his military steed.

The incident might have been forgotten except for the wife of the slain officer, Eileen, a poetess "of fire and power," as Donal Brennan accurately describes her. "The lament she wrote in Irish for him, full of sorrow and passionate love and burning anger, will survive as long as Irish survives." The *caoine* to her husband is generally considered the greatest lament ever written in the Irish language. Unfortunately, the Gaelic pathos of Eileen O'Leary's verse has successfully resisted "accurate" translation into English, though such worthies as O'Connor and Kinsalla have made the attempt.

The following is extracted from the effort of an astonishing young Gaelic scholar who is fighting the good fight for the Irish language in a most unlikely place—Washington, D.C. Caoimhín

Ó Duhbhánaigh's translation captures something of the proud
agony that subtly pervades the original.

My truest friend,
My mind still recalls
Yon fine day in springtime:
The hat looked so grand on you—
The gold band fixed round it—
The silver-hilted sword,
The stalwart right hand,
The menacing prance,
The trembling terror
Of treacherous enemies.
You mounted to ride
A trim snow-faced steed,
The Saxons they bowed
Down to the ground to you
(Not out of respect for you
But wholly out of fear),
Though at their hands you died,
My soul's beloved.

My friend truly
I never believed you would die
Till your horse returned to me
With her reins down to the ground,
With your heart's-blood upon her flanks
Back to your fine-tooled saddle
(Where you used to sit and stand);
I leapt up toward the threshold,
The second stride to the gate,
The third leap onto your mare.

I slapt her with open palm
And got her to gallop
As best as I was able,
Till I found you dead before me.
Nearby a lowly furze bush;
No pope, no bishop,
No cleric, no priest
To read over you the psalm,
But a wizened weathered old woman

Who spread over you her cloak-hem;
Your blood in streams flowed from you
But I did not stop to clean it
And, from cupped palms, I drank it.

My keen and painful sorrow
That I was not at your back
When the powder was fired,
So I would get it through the waist
Or the hem of my dress,
So I could let you fly away,
My grey-eyed rider,
For you were the best of them all.

May you know torture and want
You hideous villain, Morris,
Who took from me my man,
Father of my infant children—
The two of them at home
And the third in my womb
Who, no doubt, I'll never bear.

Why would anyone wonder
If O'Leary's land burst into flame
(And Ballingeary
And holy Gugan Barra)
For the sake of this skill-handed rider
Who used to harry the prey
While driving hard from Granach
When the trim hounds relented?
Rider with the roving eyes,
What happened to you last night?
For I thought to myself
The whole world could not kill you
When I bought your uniform.

And I will go across the waves
To discuss it with the King;
And if he pays me no heed,
I'll come back again
To the black-blooded brute
Who took from me my all.

Most Irish peasants seemed content to lament their misery. Some, however, were prepared to do somewhat more than sing sorrowful ballads. As early as the 1720s, secret agrarian societies had made violent, if sporadic, appearances in the countryside. By 1760 these bands had become something more than a nuisance; a widespread populist movement had emerged that was to plague the authorities for more than a century.

Familiarly known as Whiteboyism, this movement first gained prominence near Nenagh in County Tipperary and quickly spread through Cork, Limerick, and Waterford. Organised on a local level, their members bound by secret oath, the Whiteboys dealt out vigilante justice in defence of a Catholic peasantry unprotected by law. Their targets were landowners, agents, middlemen, tithe collecters, would-be tenants of land made available by eviction, and even peasants who continued humbly to pay extortionate rent in contravention of local Whiteboy policy. Also known as Rightboys and Levellers, the vigilantes used the only method available to them: outrage. These bands roamed by night, razing buildings and cattle-fences, branding and woolcarding flesh.[2] Perhaps the most effective of all their methods was the houghing and slaying of cattle—to a poor family, the ownership of a single cow was often all that held hopeless poverty at bay.

A parallel movement called Oakboyism surfaced at about the same time among the Presbyterian and Methodist farmers of Ulster. The Dissenters of the northern counties had many of the same complaints as the Catholics throughout the rest of the island and, consequently, reacted with much the same intensity.[3] Called Steelboys in the far North and Heart of Oak Boys in Monaghan and Armagh, the Dissenter societies of Ulster used terrorist methods comparable to those of the Whiteboys of Munster.

THE GAOL OF CLONMEL
(*Príosún Chluain Meala*)

By the seventh decade of the eighteenth century, perhaps seventy per cent of the rural Irish still spoke Gaelic in their daily communication. The Whiteboys were usually referred to as *Buachaillí Bána* because they wore white linen frocks over their clothes for disguise and indentification at night. The Oakboys of the North often wore sprigs of oak in their hats.

The singer of this ballad would seem to be a young Kerry-man awaiting execution for Whiteboy activities. Since the authorities started hanging the Whiteboys in 1762, the song probably was first heard shortly after that date.[4]

The years 1761-75 saw virtual war between the understaffed Munster authorities and the Whiteboys. It was not necessary to actually participate in agrarian depredation to be condemned; the mere taking of the Whiteboy oath became itself a capital offense. The hanging trees became so populated that Lord Chesterfield was driven to opine that if the military had shot half as many landlords as they had hanged Whiteboys, it would have been twice as good for the peace of the country.

As were many of the songs of the time, the *Gaol of Clonmel* was sung in Gaelic. As were few, the ballad was translated into an equally haunting English version. Included here are both the English-language version by Callanan and a literal translation from the Irish. The lyric is still heard in both languages.

The Gaol of Clonmel	*Príosún Chluain Meala*
No boy in the village	Tomorrow it will be a year
Was ever yet milder:	Since I left home
I played with a child	To go to Ardpatrick,
And my sport be no wilder;	Putting lace on my hat.
I'd dance without tiring	Whiteboys were there,
From morning to evening,	Scarpering at Dunhollow,
And the goal-ball I'd strike	As I lie sad and alone
To the lightning of heaven.	In the gaol of Clonmel.
At my bed-foot decaying,	My bridle and saddle
My hurley is lying;	Are lended this long time,
Through the boys of the village,	My hurling stick is warping
My goal-ball is flying;	Behind my bed;
My horse among neighbors	My ball is being struck
Neglected, may fallow;	By the lads of the valley,
While I pine in my chains	And would I hit a goal-shot
In the gaol at Clonmel.	As high as the men.
How hard is my fortune	Pray for me, Kerrymen,
And vain my repining;	I love your soft musical voices;
The strong rope of fate	I little ever thought

For this young neck is twining;
My strength is departed,
My cheeks sunk and sallow,
While I languish in chains
In the gaol at Clonmel.

That I should not return to you alive,
Or that our three heads
They would hoist upon three spikes
In the snow of the gloaming
And all other weather that may come!

Next Sunday the patron
At home will be keeping
And the young active hurlers
The field will be sweeping;
With the dance of fair maidens
The evening they'll hallow,
While this heart once so gay
Shall be cold in Clonmel.

If you are going to Iveragh,
Carry the news to my people
That I lay condemned in this place
And have only until Friday to live;
Gather the things for my wake
And a fine coffin for me;
That be the end of O'Donnell
And pray for him always.

If conditions were bad for the peasants of Munster and Ulster, they were incomparably worse for the cottiers of the western counties. The "Grazier Tribe," the landlords of Connacht, were largely absentee landowners who left the management of their vast estates to agents. The Big Lords commonly lived in Dublin or London and judged their agents' performance solely on the revenue produced by the land.[5]   The result was extreme poverty.   Arthur Young, an English agricultural expert who travelled Ireland in 1776-78 described the homes of the cottiers:

> The cottages of the Irish . . . called cabbins, are the most miserable looking hovels that can well be conceived. . . .   The furniture . . . in very many consisting only of a pot for boiling their potatoes, a bit of a table, and one or two broken stools . . . beds are not found . . . the family lying on straw.

Since the Connacht farmland was relatively unproductive, the task of the land-agent was not an easy one. Most, however, applied themselves to the challenge with great energy . . . to the misery of the tenantry. Enterprising and imaginative in wringing every shilling from the soil, the agents literally wielded the power of life or death over the peasants of the West on a season-to-season basis.[6]

HONEST OWEN
(*Eoghan Cóir*)

The condition of the peasants of Connacht was so wretched that they lived, in Young's words, as "slaves even in the bosom of written liberty." Far too busy struggling for survival itself to join any Whiteboy-like fights against injustice, the poor Irish of the West nonetheless bitterly resented the rapacious land-agents, the unseen landlords, and the Crown represented by them both.

Charles Bingham, Baron Lucan of Castlebar, was typical of the Big Lords of Connacht. Descended from the freebooting Richard Bingham who had been granted expansive acreages for his ferocity against the Irish during the Elizabethan era, Lucan was much too occupied in London society to ever visit his vast Mayo estates. The Baron employed several land-agents to wring the fiscal juices out of his unproductive Connacht lands. Owen Conway was one of the most efficient.

The land Conway managed was tucked away on the Mullet Peninsula in the far northwest corner of the county—a cultural backwater light years away from the salons of London. It is doubtful if any Bingham had ever seen the land personally. In a class of particularly cruel and venal taskmasters, Conway was apparently a standout. When he died in 1788 a local balladeer named Richard Barrett sang this paean in eulogy to the peninsula's most celebrated man.

The bitingly satiric elegy is as close to a rebel song as was sung in Connacht at the time. The following is a literal translation from the Irish.

Is this not a painful time in the countryside,
The sorrow and mental distress,
From where you leave Creagan
Until you arrive at Fallmore?
Such keening and mourning
You never heard before this
Although it is not surprising to us
Since, alas, Decent Owen has died.

He held everyone's love and affection—
The young man and the withered old man—
Rich and poor cared for him
Because of his great good heart.

With the elite and best in the land
He would spend gold pieces;
And with others, the poor, he wouldn't hesitate
In sharing a bottle of lager.

Tony Gavin is crying
And John Boyle has not long to live;
Since they lost their best friend in the country around,
Their hearts have been sorrowed
Amidst the village's grief; there never was buried,
I think, beneath gravestone or sod,
Any man who was dearer to those two
Than that lamented uncomplicated man, Honest Owen.

He was first-rate at rent-collection,
He did not fret about a month or two
Until the cow could be sold at the fair,
Or the bit of cloth from the loom.
Peader McGreavy's son Seamus said,
As he prayed to the King of Tears,
"As he treated the people,
May Christ treat him the same!"

One Thousand Seven Hundred
And Eighty-Eight
Was when he left the people
And never uttered another sound.
It is honestly written
That all living ends in the sod;
And as long as we *are* alive,
What harm for us to take a drop of drink?

As the agrarian societies resorted to popular justice in
Munster, there were those who used Whiteboyism as an excuse
for hooliganism. Bodies of *spailpín fánach,* spalpeens, travelled
from the poorer farming areas to the richer districts in search of
work. These young migrant cottiers rambled from hiring fair to
hiring fair leasing their strong backs. Having no stake in the land,
they were not above renting their fists as well . . . on either side
of the agrarian war.

GARRYOWEN

Some groups of youthful thugs used the cover of White-boyism to disguise wanton lawlessness. The "respectable" terrorists were often forced to issue proclamations disclaiming responsibility for "unauthorised" depredations—a practice all too familiar in our own day. These bands of young hoodlums were the forerunners of the faction-fighters of the next century.

This rousing song, made famous in the United States by Thomas Meagher's Irish Brigade in the American Civil War (and later by George Custer's Seventh Cavalry), was originally sung by the spalpeens of western Munster.[7] Johnny Connell and Darby O'Brien of the song were sons of Limerick brewers who aped the excesses of the local Ascendancy squireens during 1770-80. As the lyrics make clear, it was often difficult to differentiate between men committing outrage in defense of the peasantry and those doing it out of pure mischief.

Let Bacchus's sons be not dismayed,
But join with me, each joval blade;
Come booze and sing and lend your aid
To help me with the chorus:

Refrain:
Instead of spa we'll drink brown ale,
And pay the reckoning on the nail;
No man for debt shall go to jail;
From Garryowen in glory!

We are the boys who take delight in
Smashing the Limerick lamps, when lighting
Through the streets like sporters fighting,
And tearing all before us.

Refrain

We'll break windows, we'll break doors,
The Watch knock down by threes and fours;
Then let the doctors work their cures,
And tinker up our bruises.

Refrain

We'll beat the bailiffs out for fun,
We'll make the mayor and the sheriff run,
We are the boys no man dares dun,
If he regards a whole skin.

Refrain

Our hearts so stout have got us fame,
For soon tis known from whence we came;
Where'er we go they dread the name
Of Garryowen in glory.

Refrain

Johnny Connell's tall and straight
And in his limbs he is complete;
He'll pitch a bar of any weight,
From Garryowen to Thomond Gate.

Refrain

Garryowen is gone to wrack
Since Johnny Connell went to Cork
Though Darby O'Brien leaped o'er the dock
In spite of all the soldiers

Refrain

The Irish peasant had little to look forward to, no hope of escaping his losing struggle with the land and his landlord. The law itself forced him to look within himself for hope. His Roman Catholicism became even more deeply rooted; if he could not find relief in this life, he had at least something to dream of in the next.

While some few peasants slipped white smocks over their clothes and stalked into the Irish night, the vast majority nestled under the hedge with fugitive priests or huddled together in song around the hearth. While they looked to the afterlife for succour, the tenantry also looked to the past for inspiration.

THE BARD OF ARMAGH

The harper of this ballad remembers the joy of his long-lost youth. Much as the singer of *Granuaile* finds solace in the folk-memories of Gaelic antiquity, this bard contrasts his present lot with the "carefree" days under King James. Written by Thomas Campbell in 1801, the setting of the lay is the 1770s.

The title of the song may have been a metaphor for Patrick Donnelly, Catholic Archbishop of Armagh; the prelate is known to have disguised himself as an itinerant musician so that he could tend to his flock undisturbed by Priest Hunters.[8] Another notable trope is the ballad's reference to Phelim Brady's already dead "wife," Kathleen—a name fast becoming a synonym for Ireland.

Oh, list to the lay of a poor Irish harper,
And scorn not the strains from his poor withered hand,
But remember his fingers could move once more sharper,
To raise up the strains of his dear native land.

When I was a young lad, King Jamie did flourish,
And I followed the wars in my brogues bound with straw,
And all the fair *cailíns* from Wexford to Durrish,
Called me bold Phelim Brady, the Bard of Armagh.

How I love for to muse on the days of my childhood,
Though fourscore and three years have flitted since then;
Still it gives sweet reflection, as every young joy should,
For light-hearted boys make the best of old men.

At pattern or fair I could twist my shillelagh
Or trip though the jig with my brogues bound with straw,
Whilst all the pretty maidens around me assembled,
Loved bold Phelim Brady, the Bard of Armagh.

Although I have travelled this wide world all over,
Yet Erin's my home, and a parent to me;
Then oh, let the ground that my old bones shall cover
Be cut from the soil that is trod by the free.

And when Sergeant Death in his cold arms shall embrace me,
Oh, lull me to sleep with sweet *Erin go Bragh*—
By the side of my wife Kathleen, oh, please place me,
Then forget Phelim Brady, the Bard of Armagh.

If the seed of Irish nationalism had been kept alive in the rude cabins of the countryside, the cultivation was to be done in brick buildings beside the Liffey and Lagan. In addition to the societies of the night, two urban organisations that emerged during the 1760s were to have a major impact on the march of Irish nationalism. The Catholic Committee and the Protestant Patriot Party, though politically light-years divorced from the peasantry, shared the Whiteboys' resentment of the Crown's pervasive power in Ireland.

As has been seen, there had been an easing in some of the more onerous Penal Laws to forestall Irish support for the Jacobites during the Scottish scare of 1745. A small number of enterprising Catholic merchants had taken advantage of the "loopholes" to amass fortunes. This new *bourgeoisie,* under the leadership of Charles O'Connor, Thomas Wyse, and Dr. John Curry, founded the Catholic Association in 1759 to protect the new-found wealth of its members. Better known as the Catholic "Committee" (the most visible members were on the General Committee of the Association), its initial purpose was to convince London that it was possible for the Catholic commercial interest to be loyal to both King *and* Pope. The evolving Committee was later to become prominent in the parliamentary fight for reform of the Penal Laws themselves.

The Patriot Party, meanwhile, slowly emerged as the Loyal Opposition in the Irish Parliament. Forming in the Commons around Henry Flood, the Ascendancy son of a Chief Justice of the King's Bench, and in the Lords around Sir William Osbourne, a country squire, this political group was instrumental in the passage of the Octennial Bill of 1767, guaranteeing a parliamentary election every eight years. Ostensibly this new law would give the Opposition within the Protestant Ascendancy an opportunity to make inroads on the influence of the few powerful families who held a virtual stranglehold on the Irish Parliament. The real effect of the legislation, largely undiscerned at the time, was far different. Although it did in fact undermine the "authority" of the old power-brokers in the Parliament, it did not shift that power to the Opposition; rather, the control of patronage—and thereby real dominance of Irish affairs—transferred slowly into the hands of the Crown's official representatives in Dublin Castle.

As the English colonies in North America edged militantly towards revolution, the Patriot politicians in Ireland were listening intently to, in Flood's words, "the voice of America that shouted to liberty." As many of the younger Protestant squires, identifying with the defiance of the American landowners, flocked to Flood's side, London grew understandably nervous.

TAXES

Much of the British legislation that precipitated revolution in America was not unique to the colonies. American school-children still learn of the invidious tax laws passed in London "without representation." Over seven decades earlier in Ireland, William Molyneux had asserted that "to tax me without Consent, is little better, if at all, than down-right Robbing me." As the following old Irish street ballad demonstrates, resentment of the Crown's politico-economic stranglehold was not peculiar to the New World.

The burden of taxation in Ireland was borne largely by the farmers. In the fashion of the day, English land taxes were levied only upon acreage actually under cultivation. The Grazier Tribe, with vast tracts of real estate devoted to cattle, was often entirely exempt. On the other hand, the one-third acre set aside by the smallest farmer for the potatoes that would feed his family was taxed without exception. In addition, the tenantry were subject to the *cess*, a county tax which financed both road repairs and the assizes.

An attempt by the administration to raise additional revenue in 1773 by imposing a ten per cent surtax on absentee landlords was defeated in the Irish Parliament with the help of Flood's Patriots. The action well underlines that the Ascendancy Patriots, no friends of Westminster, were still less allies of the Irish peasantry.

Unfair treatment sparked revolution in the American colonies; in Ireland, such treatment had long been a way of life. The events of the next three decades were to demonstrate the Atlantic Ocean a far more effective moat than the Irish Sea.

All you young men and maidens come and listen to my song,
It is something short and comical, it won't detain you long.
Go where you will by day or night, the town or country through,
The people cry and wonder what with us they mean to do.

Refrain:
No wonder people grumble at the taxes more and more,
There never was such taxes in Ireland before.

They're going to tax the farmers and their horses, carts and ploughs,
They're going to tax the billygoats, the donkeys, pigs and cows;
They're going to tax the mutton and they're going to tax the beef,
And they're going to tax the women if they do not try to read.

They're going to tax the brandy, ale and whisky, rum and wine,
They'll tax the tea and sugar, the tobacco, snuff and pipes;
They're going to tax the fish that swim and all the birds that fly,
And they're going to tax the women who go drinking on the sly.

Refrain

They'll tax the ladies all that paint and those that walk with men,
They're going to tax the ducks and geese and turkeys, cocks and hens;
They're going to tax the farmers' boys that work along the ditches,
And they'll double tax old drunken wives that try to wear the britches.

They're going to tax the corn field, potato gardens too,
They're going to tax the cabbage plants, the jackdaws and the crows;
They'll double tax the hobble skirts and table up some laws,
But the devil says he'll tax *them* if he gets them in his claws.

Refrain

As resistance in America blossomed into full-scale rebellion, Dublin Castle moved to silence its chief opposition in Ireland by the simple strategem of seducing Henry Flood into accepting the post of Vice-Treasurer. The government, however, had miscalculated: it seemed there was no shortage of Patriots willing to retrieve Flood's discarded baton. The Earl of Charlemont, governor of Armagh, emerged as the new spokesman for the opposition in the Lords, along with young Henry Grattan, Charlemont's protégé, who spoke for the Patriot Party in the Commons. Inspired by the American example, the new leadership began to turn radical.

Charlemont and Grattan led the political fight for repeal of the onerous Navigation Laws (which Westminster had enacted to protect the British economy when American trade was cut off by the rebellion). Not content with the struggle to end the embargo on Irish trade, the new Patriot leaders soon also began to clamour for an independent Irish Parliament. Though the administration enjoyed a comfortable majority in Dublin during the early years of the American revolution, the increasingly precarious economic situation in Ireland—brought about by the combination of the Navigation Laws and American privateers prowling the coast—caused a steady erosion of Members to the Patriot side of the aisle.

After General John Burgoyne was stymied by Horatio Gates—or, more accurately, by Benedict Arnold—at the 1777 Battle of Saratoga in New York, the Patriot leadears in Ireland were presented their opportunity. The French, much encouraged by the surprising development in the New World, declared for the Americans the next year. Spain jumped on the American bandwagon not long after. The British Army, seriously under strength in the wake of the Seven Years War and now embroiled in the unexpectedly costly American adventure, did not have the personnel available to defend Ireland against potential Bourbon invasion. The Patriot leadership, seizing the moment, offered to "recruit" a volunteer force to defend the island. In fact, they had little recruiting to do. Beginning in Belfast in the summer of 1778, *ad hoc* volunteer bands had been appearing all over Ireland.

THE IRISH VOLUNTEER

The Volunteer movement spread quickly throughout Protestant Ireland. By the end of 1778 there were ten thousand men in arms, by summer of 1779, perhaps forty thousand. Lecky observes that:

> Never before in Ireland had public opinion shown itself so strong, so earnest, and so self-reliant. A sincere loyalty to the Crown, and a firm resolution to defend the country from invasion, were blended with a resolute determination to maintain a distinctively Irish policy.

Charlemont and Grattan were walking a political tightrope. While personally sympathetic to the American rebels, the Patriot leaders found it very much in the interest of their Volunteers to whip up public sentiment against the colonists' French allies. In the event it worked. When the French and Spanish fleets appeared in the English Channel during early summer 1779, the administration, with no viable alternative, grudgingly supplied the Irish Volunteers with sixteen thousand stands of arms. The Patriot leaders were now in command of a force that was a credible deterrent to the French. It would soon be "credible" to the British Crown itself.[9]

An anonymous Belfast street bard, presumably unaware of the Patriot politicians' dilemma, wrote this chauvinistic ballad blithely convinced the Americans were the enemy.

Ye daughters of Old Ireland, these lines to you I write,
Concerning your true lovers who have volunteered to fight
For their country's standard, to face their rebel peers,
It's pretty dame will see again our Irish Volunteer.

The worthy son of liberty who's got the heart to go
To sustain his country's dignity and face the rebel foe,
He's worthy of a lady's love, we'll all call him our dear,
He's strong and bold, and uncontrolled, our Irish Volunteer.

The cymbals are sounding, the trumpet shrill doth blow
For each platoon to form, we've got orders for to go;
Each pretty girl says to her love: "My darling, never fear,
You will always find us true and kind to the Irish Volunteer."

In the fearful hour of battle, when the cannons loud do roar,
We'll think upon our loves that we left to see no more;
And if grim death appears to us, its terrors and its fears
Can never scare in Freedom's war, our Irish Volunteers.

Come all ye worthy gentlemen who have the heart and means,
Be kind unto the soldier's wife, they hold your country's reins;
They will come back victorious, those gallant fusileers,
And bring again the flag unstained, our Irish Volunteers.

It did not take Charlemont and Grattan long to realise that an armed force the size of the Volunteers could be used to impress more than the French. Consequently, the Patriot Party leaders used the potential of this Irish "National" army to press London for a roll-back of the hated Navigation Laws. To demonstrate their influence, they used the Irish Volunteers quietly to fan the flames of a supposedly spontaneous "non-importation" movement. Hussey Burgh, perhaps the most eloquent of the Patriot politicians, concluded a speech on the floor of the Commons by reminding George III that temporary economic measures were not good enough, that it was "by free trade alone, that this nation is now to be saved from impending ruin." Grattan insured that the Dublin newspapers published the names of merchants that were selling English rather than Irish goods, lists that became shorter as the "non-importers" became more vocal. The Patriots were also careful to make public that the scarlet, green, blue, and orange uniforms of the Volunteers were all of *domestic* manufacture.

Unnamed Street Ballad

Almost every cottage in Ireland contained a spinning wheel and weaving loom. The burgeoning industrial revolution had not crossed the Irish sea. Cloth was not yet produced in factories, but by the peasants of Ireland working in their own homes. When the British declared the embargo as the American rebellion began, the jobbers no longer came to buy the peasants' cloth.

The lost income was all too often the difference between survival and starvation to the humble folk. When the "spontaneous" movement against the Navigation Laws began, it found instant popularity among the anxious masses. Since the Irish Volunteers were very much in evidence in the forefront of the national protest, they too found favour in the eyes of the lower class.

This broadside jingle was sung in 1778 by the Volunteers. Jonathan Swift would have approved.

Ye noblemen, in place or out,
Ye Volunteers, so brave and stout,
Ye dames that flaunt at ball or rout,
Wear Irish manufacture!

Thus shall poor weavers get some pence,
From hunger and from cold to fence
Their wives and infants four months hence,
By Irish manufacture!

Recognising the vast untapped political potential represented by the papist peasantry, Henry Grattan had also thrown in his lot with the Catholic Committee's ongoing attempts to chip away at the Penal Laws, holding that "the Irish Protestant could never be free till the Irish Catholic had ceased to be a slave." The sentiment had found favour with Edmund Burke and other Whig friends of the Committee in London who had managed to gather sufficient support to pass the First Catholic Relief Act in 1778. For the first time since the Flight of the Wild Geese, Catholics could buy land, albeit only after carefully swearing an oath of allegiance to the Crown.

In October of the following year, Grattan made an impassioned plea to the Irish Commons to petition London for "free trade." When a government spokesman rose to exclaim that the presence of uniformed Volunteers outside the hall smacked of blackmail, Hussey Burgh responded scathingly that the English had "sowed their laws like serpent's teeth, and they have sprung up in armed men." Indeed they had. That the Irish legislators did in fact agree overwhelmingly with the Patriot proposal *was* probably less due to Grattan's oratory than to artillery detachments of the Irish Volunteers, led by James Napper Tandy,[10] who were marching about outside with cannon bearing banners threatening, "Free trade or this!" In any case, the Irish Parliament recommended the legislation to Westminster, which repealed the onerous Navigation Laws in November 1779. Encouraged, Grattan tried to get the Irish Commons to accept a Declaration of Right in April 1780 as the first step towards Irish legislative independence. Henry Flood, by now working secretly with the Patriots again from his Dublin Castle office, prevailed upon Grattan to withdraw the foredoomed proposal until the party's position was stronger. Recalling Tandy's "persuasiveness," the Patriots now knew how to proceed.

In July, the Earl of Charlemont was elected Commander-in-Chief of the Irish Volunteers. He promptly began recruiting Catholics into the organisation. By the time Lord Cornwallis surrendered to the American rebels at Yorktown in October 1781, the Irish Volunteers numbered some ninety thousand men. The Whigs, brought to power in London in the wake of the debacle in Virginia, were well aware of the Volunteers' potential and were in no mood to challenge the Irish Patriot leaders. Without government opposition to the Irish cause, events began to move quickly.

Henry Flood, awakened to the drift toward independence and not wishing to be left out, resigned his Castle post, publicly rejoining the ebullient Patriots. The administration, now anxious to appease the Irish leaders, swiftly approved the demand for a *Habeas Corpus* Act for Ireland. The Patriots had the government on the run. When, back in 1780, a small Volunteer assembly in Monaghan had declared that:

> no Parliament had, has, or of right ought to have, any power or authority whatsoever, in this kingdom, except the Parliament of Ireland. . . .

it had been no more than wishful thinking. Now, however, things had changed. Now the Patriot-led Volunteers found they could move the governments of the two islands.

THE VOLUNTEERS OF '82

In February 1782 a convention of Charlemont's Ulster Volunteers—representing 25,000 armed men—met in assembly at Dungannon. After making the ominous point that "a citizen by learning the use of arms does not abandon any of his civil rights," the delegates unanimously resolved that:

> a claim of any body of men, other than the King, Lords, and Commons of Ireland, to make laws to bind this kingdom, is unconstitutional, illegal, and a grievance.

Then, by a vote of 141 to 2, the assembly held:

> the right of private judgement, in matters of religion, to be equally sacred in others as in ourselves. . . . That as men and as Irishmen, as Christians and as Protestants, we rejoice in the relaxation of the penal laws against our Roman Catholic fellow-subjects. . . .

Subsequent Volunteer conventions in Leinster, Connacht, and Munster ratified the Dungannon resolutions *in toto*. The Irish Patriot Party, via the rattling sabres of the Irish Volunteers, had offered a direct challenge to London.

The Whigs declined the contest. A direct result of the Dungannon convention was the Second Catholic Relief Act, giving Catholics equal property and leasehold rights with Protestants. Among the other provisions of the Act was one that eliminated registration of the priests. This Thomas Davis ballad recalls the part played by the Irish Volunteers in the political fight to wrest control of Irish affairs from London.

Hurrah! Tis done—our freedom's won—
Hurrah for the Volunteers!
No laws we own, but those alone
Of our Commons, King, and Peers.
The chain is broke—the Saxon yoke
From off our neck is taken;
Ireland awoke—Dungannon spoke—
With fear was England shaken.

When Grattan rose, none dared oppose
The claim he made for freedom;
They knew our swords, to back his words,
Were ready, did he need them.
Then let us raise to Grattan's praise,
A proud and joyous anthem;
And wealth and grace, and length of days,
May God in mercy grant him!

Bless Harry Flood, who nobly stood
By us through gloomy years;
Bless Charlemont, the brave and good,
The Chief of the Volunteers!
The North began, the North held on
The strife for native land,
Till Ireland rose, and cowed her foes—
God bless the Northern land!

And bless the men of patriot pen—
Swift, Molyneux, and Lucas;
Bless sword and gun which "Free Trade" won;
Bless God who ne'er forsook us!
And long may last the friendship fast
Which binds us all together;
While we agree, our foes shall flee
Like clouds in stormy weather.

Remember still, through good and ill,
How vain were prayers and tears—
How vain were words, till flashed the swords
Of the Irish Volunteers.
By arms we've got the rights we sought
Through long and wretched years:

Hurrah! Tis done—our freedom's won—
Hurrah for the Volunteers!

KATHLEEN NI HOULIHAN
(*Cáitilín ní Uallacháin*)

In the atmosphere created by the seeming British reluctance to face the guns of the Irish Volunteers, nationalist feelings soared. Public defiance of London was expressed unpunished for the first time in ninety years. It was heady wine indeed. The songwriters were as busy as the politicians. Rebel songs popped up like mushrooms; new lyrics were hastily set to old airs. Street balladeer and Gaelic poet alike sung of Irish glory and Saxon perfidy.[11] One such bard, unusual in that he wrote his verse in both English *and* Irish, was William Heffernon, a blind wandering poet from Tipperary.

The genesis of this song is particularly significant. Originally a Gaelic love ballad, the lay would now become a patriotic one in the English language. Using the original heroine's name as still another metaphor for Ireland,[12] the poet rewrote the lyrics to mirror the chauvinist sentiment at the time of the Irish Volunteers.

Our hopes run high, the time is nigh
To make the test of war;
Our plans are laid, our weapons made,
And soon our guns will roar.

Let others sleep! We watch will keep,
To hail a new day's dawn,
When the king's son shall be seen
With Kathleen ni Houlihan.

Our hated foes must not suppose
That we shall fear to die;
Though the clouds are dark, we still can mark
God's rainbow in the sky.

As the Red Sea sand became dry land
When Moses led Israel on,
May Jesus save thee,
Kathleen ni Houlihan.

The defiant alarum of the Irish Volunteers could now be heard in crescendo behind the major demand of the Irish Patriot Party. In late 1782 the Irish Parliament passed a "Declaration of Independence" by unanimous vote. The Whigs in London, still off-balance due to events in America, offered little resistance.

Flushed with success, Grattan, Flood, and Charlemont pressed for an Act of Renunciation by the Crown (of both Poyning's Law of 1495 and the Declaratory Act of 1719—the laws that gave Westminster the absolute right to legislate for Ireland). The British Parliament again acquiesced meekly. The new Dublin Parliament now had roughly the same relationship with the Crown as did Westminster. On paper, at least, the Irish were in charge of their own affairs for the first time in almost three hundred years.

Almost unnoticed in the euphoria of the Patriot triumph was the undisputed reality that the bureaucracy of Dublin Castle was still firmly in the hands of the Crown. While the Ascendancy could now pass legislation, it was still up to London to appoint the men who were supposed to enforce those laws. In the heady excitement of the moment, the Patriots failed to realise that the blatant power of the Crown had merely taken another form; hereafter London would wield power in Ireland through deft control of the Dublin Castle bureaucracy. Richard Brinsley Sheridan, in describing the manipulative behind-the-scene talents of one Castle official, would describe the system itself:

> Ireland, newly escaped from harsh trammels and severe discipline, was treated like a high-mettled horse, hard to catch; and the Irish Secretary was sent back to the field to soothe and coax him, with a sieve of provender in the one hand and a bridle in the other.

That the Crown's real dominance of the island had not been diminished was to become transparently obvious within two decades when the Castle was able to pressure the new Irish Parliament to vote itself out of existence.

RÓISÍN DUBH
(*The Little Black Rose*)

At about this time, the most popular of all Gaelic songs became yet another nationalist metaphor for Ireland. A seven-verse poem attributed to the sixteenth century bard Owen Roe MacWard, the ballad sings of love through the first six quatrains and becomes a "rebel paean" only in the last verse.

Included here are three translations of that last verse from the Irish. The first is literal; the second is by the 1916 rebel poet Pádraig Pearse; the third is the famous effort by James Clarence Mangan that turned this little love song into a sort of English-language "Gaelic National Anthem."

The sea will be turned to red tides and the sky to blood;
The world is in crimson battle on the edges of the heaths;
Every mountain glen in Ireland, every bog, shall rumble;
Ere the day shall die my Little Black Rose.

(from the Irish)

The Erne shall rise in rude torrents, hills shall be rent,
The sea shall roll in red waves, and blood be poured out,
Every mountain glen in Ireland, and the bogs, shall quake
Some day, ere shall perish my Little Dark Rose!

(Pádraig Pearse)

O! the Erne shall run red
    With redundance of blood,
The earth shall rock beneath our tread,
    And flames wrap hill and wood,
And gun-peal, and slogan-cry,
    Wake many a glen serene.
Ere you shall fade, ere you shall die,
    My Dark Rosaleen!
    My own Rosaleen!
The judgement Hour must first be nigh,
Ere you can fade, ere you can die,
    My Dark Rosaleen!

(James Clarence Mangan)

After the passage of the Act of Renunciation, Henry Flood was tempted to use the threat of the Volunteers one more time. Recognising that the makeup of the "independent" Irish Parliament represented British interests rather than Irish (the composition of the parliamentary districts, for example, was still that drawn up by Westminster), Flood wanted to use Tandy's marching columns to coerce the Dublin body into reforming itself. Lord Charlemont and Henry Grattan, although sympathising with the end, refused to countenance the use of force against *their* newly upgraded Parliament; Flood was forced to back down. Flood, on the other hand, maneuvered an alignment with Lord Charlemont to block Henry Grattan's attempt to interest the Irish Commons in repealing the extant Penal Laws.

While the Protestant politicians were jockeying, the peasants' life went on much as before. Although the Catholics could now legally buy land, there were few peasants with the wherewithal to take advantage of the opportunity. The Patriot Party's response to Grattan's attempt to enfranchise the Catholics had demonstrated clearly that the new Irish Parliament was going to represent only the twenty per cent of the island that was non-Catholic. For those peasants not willing to don the smock of the Whiteboys, however, there was still a vicarious way to tweak the Saxon nose . . . the country people could still root for the highwaymen.

BRENNAN ON THE MOOR

The rapparee tradition was still alive in the minds of the people at the end of the eighteenth century. Since the peasants felt no threat from the highwayman—they had little to steal—their sympathies were invariably with the outlaw as he earned his living by robbing the landowners and rich merchants.

By this time the rapparee was in no way a rebel; over the century since Limerick, he had sunk to common brigandage. The people remembered the tradition, however, and it was perhaps inevitable that the balladeers invested certain of the famous highwaymen with qualities that would have been envied by Galloping Hogan.

This song is the most famous of the genre. After a long career of "robbing on the King's Highway," William Brennan was finally caught and hanged at Clonmel in 1804. The original ballad had at least twelve verses; the seven most often sung today are included here.

Tis of a bold young highwayman, his story I will tell,
His name was Willie Brennan and in Ireland he did dwell;
Twas on the Kilworth Mountains he commenced his wild career,
And many a wealthy nobleman before him shook with fear.

Refrain:
And it's Brennan on the Moor, Brennan on the Moor,
Bold and undaunted stood young Brennan on the Moor.

A brace of loaded pistols he carried night and day,
He never robbed a poor man upon the King's Highway;
He robbed the rich, he helped the poor, like Turpin and Black Bess,
He always helped the widow and orphan in distress.

Refrain

One day upon the highway as Willie he rode down,
He met the mayor of Cashel a mile outside of town,
The mayor he knew his features, "I think, young man," said he,
"Your name is Willie Brennan, you must come along with me!"

Refrain

As Brennan's wife had gone to town, provisions for to buy,
And when she saw her Willie she began to weep and cry;
He said, "Give me that tenpenny," and as soon as Willie spoke,
She handed him a blunderbuss from underneath her cloak.

Refrain

Then Brennan being an outlaw upon the mountains high,
With cavalry and infantry to take him they did try;
He laughed at them in scorn until at length, it's said,
By a false-hearted woman he was cruelly betrayed.

Refrain

When Brennan heard his sentence, he made this bold reply:
"I own that I did rob the rich and the poor supply;
In all the deeds that I have done, I took no life away;
The Lord have mercy on my soul against the judgement day."

Refrain

"Farewell unto my wife and to my children three,
Likewise my aged father, he may shed tears for me;
And to my loving mother"—who tore her grey locks and cried,
Saying, "I wish, Willie Brennan, in your cradle you had died."

Refrain

The nature of the secret agrarian societies in Ulster began to change about 1785. The Oakboyism of the previous decades had been reasonably effective in keeping rents down in the northern counties. Now, due to the Catholic Relief Acts of 1778 and 1782, Catholics were permitted to lease land on an equal footing with the poor Presbyterian farmers. The inevitable increased demand had a predictable result: the landowners exploited the opportunity to raise prices. The northern secret societies blamed the Catholics rather than the landowners and shifted their dawn raids to meet the new threat.

Usually called the Peep o' Day Boys—sometimes The Wreckers or, simply, The Protestant Boys—these agressive new agrarian societies terrorised their new Catholic neighbors, sending many of them fleeing into the papist counties adjoining Ulster. The majority of the harassed peasants, however, stayed put. Forming countering bands called Defenders, the Catholics fought back.

LISNAGADE

On the 101st anniversary of the Battle of the Boyne, a band of Defenders attacked a procession of Down and Armagh Protestants that were commemorating the Orange victory. The Catholics apparently had been lying in ambush in the ruins of the ancient ring fort of Lisnagade just northeast of Scarva when the Presbyterian celebrants got word of their presence. When the Defenders sprung their "trap," it was no surprise; the Protestants put the attackers to rout.

It is of some interest that the symbol of the Defenders was a white flag (according to this anonymous ballad, it was embossed with *páidrín*, or rosary beads); even at this late date the Green of Irish nationalism had yet to make its appearance among the lower-class Catholics of Ulster. Also significant is that the Peep o' Day Boys were already calling themselves Orangemen although the Orange Order was not to make its formal debut for another four years.

Ye Protestants of Ulster, I pray you join with me,
Your voices raise in lofty praise and show your loyalty;
Extol the day we marched away with Orange flags so fine,
In Order to commemorate the conquest of the Boyne.

The first who fought upon that day, the Prince of Orange was,
He headed our forefathers in his most glorious cause:
Protestant rights for to maintain and popery to degrade,
And in memory of the same we fought at Lisnagade.

Twas early in the morning before the rise of sun,
An information we received, our foes each with a gun
In ambush lay near the highway, entrenched in a fort,
For to disgrace our Orange flag, but it chanced they broke their oath.

We had not marched a mile or so when the white flag we espied,
With a branch of podereens on which they much relied,
And this inscription underneath: "Hail Mary, onto thee!
Deliver us from these Orange dogs and then we will be free!"

At half an hour past two o'clock the firing did commence,
With clouds of smoke and showers of ball, the heavens were condensed;
They called unto their wooden gods to whom they used to pray,
But my Lady Mary fell asleep and so they ran away.

If "a voice from America had shouted to liberty," it had
been heard only by the Patriot Ascendancy of Ireland. The great
landowners had used the Irish Volunteer force to gain control of
their own affairs. The peasantry of the countryside and the middle class of the towns had been left completely out of the equation. Now the Catholics and Dissenters of Ireland were to hear
their own voice from over the sea . . . with the fall of the Bastille,
the citizenry of France would give liberty a new definition, a
populist one that was to shake the very foundations of British
hegemony in Ireland.

CHAPTER NOTES (11)

1 — This state of affairs continued on well into the nineteenth century. During the
Great Hunger, an army officer would relate the quandry of a typical Connacht land-

owner in 1846. The absentee Big Lord had let his acreage to a middleman who, in turn, re-leased the land to various other middlemen. By the time the landowner applied to the Quaker relief agency for food to feed his estimated sixty starving tenants, he was horrified to find that there were more than ten times that number living on his lands.

2 — Wool-carding was a particularly grisly business. It consisted of using a sharp-toothed metal comb—designed for use on sheep—upon human flesh.

3 — The peasants of Ulster did have marginally better conditions than their country-men in Munster, though I doubt if the fact afforded them much succour. The *Ulster Custom,* for one, protected the northern peasant from eviction if his rent was paid, a safeguard not offered to the leaseholders in the rest of Ireland. Productivity, however, was poor, and the "better conditions" under which the northern peasant laboured did not prevent the great "Scotch-Irish" emigration to the New World.

The disaffection with the Crown of these *émigrés* was to survive the Atlantic cross-ing. When the American colonies rose in the 1770s, it is not surprising that they found great support among the Ulstermen: many had relatives among the rebels.

4 — Another Whiteboy execution at Clonmel was somewhat more dramatic. In 1763 Father Nicholas Sheehy of Tipperary was arrested for "inciting to riot and rebellion." He was kept in custody for the next three years while he was tried and acquitted in three separate jurisdictions. Finally tried for murder (one that had occurred while he was in prison), the unhappy priest was hanged and quartered in the face of popular outrage. The pantheon of Irish martyrs got its first addition in some seventy years. The gap between slain heroes would never again be as long.

5 — Before Foster's Corn Law of 1784 provided landowners with large bounties for the export of grain, many Big Lords preferred the money realised from cattle grazing to that of cottier lease. This was particularly true in the West where the poor land made cattle a better investment than Irishmen.

Absentee ownership was chronic. In 1802 James MacParlan published a statistical study of eight of the nine Mayo baronies indicating that fifty-two of 115 landlords were absentee. Even those owners who were "resident," however, spent a great deal of time in Dublin attending to fiscal and social affairs.

6 — Lord Chesterfield reported that the peasantry "were used worse than negroes by their lords and masters." Arthur Young charged "the landlord of an Irish estate in-habited by Roman Catholics is a sort of despot, who yields obedience . . . to no law but that of his will." A 1795 prize-winning essay for the Dublin Society suggested that the peasants were subjected to "a degree of domestic tyranny difficult to imagine." Perhaps only slaves and the peasants of Russia lived under more onerous conditions than the humble folk of the Irish West.

7 — Garryowen is a community of the old town of Limerick. In English, it means "Owen's Gardens."

8 — By banning the bishops from Ireland, the Ascendancy apparently hoped that the priests would disappear (without bishops there could be no ordination of new priests). When the policy did not work, as Lecky tells us:

"A reward of £20, offered for the detection of each friar or unregistered priest, called a regular race of priest-hunters into existence."

9 — At this point, London still had good reason to trust the Patriot leadership. In 1760 the daring French naval commander Thurot had landed three frigates at Carrickfergus, taken the town, and tried to precipitate a Jacobite rising. Instead of support, the Frenchman was soon faced with a large volunteer force from Belfast which caused him to quit the town. The British fleet caught the French flotilla off the Isle of Man, where Thurot was killed in battle. The leader of the Belfast volunteers had been the self-same Lord Charlemont who was now offering to raise troops to defend the island against the French.

10 — This remarkably constant Irish rebel was, in 1779, a thirty-nine year old member of the Dublin Corporation. His consistent championing of the disenfranchised Catholics of the capital had already won him the sobriquet, "Tribune of the Plebs." Later the first Secretary of the Dublin Society of United Irishmen, he spent much of the 1790s in France clamouring for aid to overthrow the British in Ireland. In 1798 as a Brigadier in the French Army, he led an abortive one-ship invasion of the island which led to his imprisonment. Upon his release in 1803, Tandy immediately returned to France, intent on trying again at age sixty-three. Though he died soon afterward, his unvarying opposition to the British stands out even among the rebels of his time.

11 — As a young man, Yeats would write beautifully, if not precisely, about these eighteenth century poets:

"The political poetry of these men was no light matter in its day. Because of it they were hated and pursued by the powerful and the rich, and loved by the poor. They disguised their meaning in metaphor and symbol. The poet goes out . . . and meets a beautiful spirit weeping and lamenting. . . . On her he lavishes all his power of description, and then calls her Ireland. Or else he evades the law by hiding his sedition under the guise of a love-song. Then Ireland becomes his Kathleen, Ny-Houlahan, or else his Roisin Dubh, or some other name of Gaelic endearment."

12 — With confusing irony, the rebirth of this *Gaelic* ballad in the *English* language would give William Butler Yeats the title for his famous *English* language play celebrating the ancient *Gaelic* culture of Ireland.

_____

12

The United Irishmen

In 1789 the shock waves from the French Revolution re-verberated through the Western World. In Ireland, the reactions were largely predictable. The Protestant Ascendancy was horrified by the threat to monarchy and the privileged class. The downtrodden Catholic peasantry, not understanding the anti-clerical nature of the revolution, found a certain voyeuristic delight in the plight of the French aristocracy. The real excitement, however, was to be found among the middle-class Irish professionals and businessmen who saw their French equivalents thrust into prominence almost overnight. These men, primarily Belfast and Dublin Dissenters who had been active in the Volunteer movement, had no difficulty with the new French government's position on the Catholic Church.[1] To these middle-class intellectuals, Grattan's Parliament had been but the first step on the road to future Irish progress, dignity, and freedom. They thought they saw the second step being taken on the streets of Paris.

By the last decade of the eighteenth century, the shadow leadership of the remaining Belfast Volunteers had fallen to thirty-year-old Samuel Neilson. Originally from Ballyroney in County Down, Neilson had taken advantage of the boom years following the repeal of the Navigation Laws to become a prosperous industrialist. This young owner of the Irish Woollen Warehouse in Belfast was to spawn a movement that was to mature as the greatest menace to English dominion in Ireland between the Battle of the Boyne and the Easter Rebellion.

In 1790 Neilson recruited Thomas Russell, a twenty-three year old idealistic former librarian who had been posted to Belfast by the Army.[2] The alliance proved momentous. Captain Russell's closest friend was Theobald Wolfe Tone, a Protestant attorney and member of the Dublin Whig Club of Grattan and

Charlemont.[3]   Russell explained to Neilson that Tone, like themselves—and unlike their Patriot predecessors—espoused a radical
view of politics heavily stimulated by the intoxicating French
concepts of Liberty, Equality, and Fraternity.

The next year, Thomas Paine's *Rights of Man* found a ready
audience among the Dissenters.   It became fashionable for
liberal members of the middle class to address each other as
"*Citizen*" in the manner of the French revolutionaries. Republican broadsides began to appear on the streets of the cities.   One
of June 1791, apparently authored by Dr. William Drennan, an
Edinburgh-educated Belfastman, called for an end to sectarian
strife and proposed an "Irish Brotherhood" of Catholics and
Protestants to "answer questions" as to the "independence" of
Ireland.   Perhaps inspired by such broadsides, Wolfe Tone fired
off a salvo of his own: *An Argument on Behalf of the Catholics
of Ireland by a Northern Whig,* ostensibly addressed to the Presbyterians of Ireland, urged all parties to "forget all former
feuds" and work together for the good of the island.

Tone's pamphlet caused a sensation among the intellectuals.
John Keogh, Richard MacCormack, Edward Byrne, Dr. William
MacNeven, and John Sweetman of the newly radicalised Catholic
Committee immediately invited Tone to join them.   In Belfast,
Russell wrote to Tone at Neilson's inducement, inviting his friend
to help the northerners create a permanent organisation to repre-
sent their like views.   Tone accepted both offers.

The Society of United Irishmen held its first public meeting
in Belfast on 18 October 1791.   In addition to Neilson, Russell,
and Tone, the original membership included an American named
Digges, the brothers MacCracken,[4]   William and Robert Simms,
Thomas MacCabe, Samuel MacTier, and William Sinclair—good
Protestants all.   When Wolfe Tone returned from the North, he
helped form a Dublin chapter of the Society under the King's
Counsel Simon Butler, ably seconded by the broadsiding Dr.
Drennan and the iconoclastic Napper Tandy.   Two of Butler's
early recruits were Thomas Collins, a linen merchant who was
later to become a spy for the authorities, and Beauchamp Bagenal Harvey, a Wexford squire who was to become the slightly
bewildered commander of the 1798 rising in his home county.

Neilson had been busy in Belfast meanwhile, recruiting
among others Henry and John Sheares, Cork-born attorneys who
were to play their own part in the high councils of the Unitedmen on the eve of the rebellion seven years later.   In early 1792

CHRONOLOGY (The United Irishmen)

1791 . . . . . .Paine's *Rights of Man* and Tone's *Argument on Behalf of Catholics* appear; United Irish Society founded; Britain declares neutrality in French Revolution.

1792 . . . . . .*Northern Star* founded; Defenders appear in large numbers; Wollsontecraft's *Vindication* published; Corresponding Societies in London; Girondists form ministry in France, French Republic proclaimed, royal family imprisoned; French gain Austrian Netherlands; Danton's Jacobin's seize power in France.

1793 . . . . . .Louis XVI executed, Reign of Terror begins; Anglo-French war; Dublin Volunteer leaders jailed; Irish militia formed; French spy Jackson captured with document incriminating Tone.

1794 . . . . . .Unitedmen suppressed, go underground in Belfast; Fitzwilliam, Viceroy; British driven out of Netherlands; Jacobins ousted in France; *Habeas Corpus* Act suspended in Britain.

1795 . . . . . .Camden replaces Fitzwilliam; Cave Hill meeting, United Irish convention in Belfast; Defenders turn "nationalist;" committeemen recruiting in Ireland; Battle of Diamond, founding of Orange Order; Batavian Republic set up and Belgium absorbed by French; bread riots in Paris, French Directory established.

1796 . . . . . .Tone in France; Insurrection Act in Ireland, yeomanry created; Fitzgerald and O'Connor to France; Internment of northern United leaders; Dragooning of Ulster;United National Directory established; Napoleon conquers Italy; Spain declares war on Britain; French fleet appears in Bantry Bay.

Neilson and the brothers Simms founded the *Northern Star.* The radical mouthpiece of the Belfast Society, it gave a ready forum to the republican essays of Thomas Paine and to both Mary Wollstonecraft's *Vindication of the Rights of Women* and her *Answer to Burke's Reflections on the French Revolution* (Burke, ever the insightful political commentator, had foreseen the horrors to come in France). In addition, the journal aired the proceedings of the Paris Jacobin Society and found room for the work of such native "patriot poets" as James Orr of Ballycarry.[5]

As the United Irishmen continued to organise as legal middle-class "debating clubs," Wolfe Tone flung himself fulltime into the work of the now-Dissenter-controlled Catholic Committee. Accepting the post of Assistant Secretary, he was prominent in John Keogh's successful campaign for the Third

Catholic Relief Act that was passed, albeit grudgingly, by Parliament in April 1793. The landmark legislation gave the franchise to papists but, conspicuously, the right to hold public office was withheld. Curiously, the Great Catholic Unwashed were now at a point of ostensible political equality with their Protestant equivalents, but the Catholic middle class was not. As Lecky observes, "Nearly every post of ambition was still reserved for Protestants, and the restrictions weighed most heavily on the Catholics who were most educated and most able." The idealistic Protestant leaders of the Catholic Committee had found just how far the English were willing to go politically.[6] Events were passing the Committee by, in any case, and its influence waned after this time.

Since the fall of the Bastille, the head of the King of France had maintained a precarious existence upon the royal shoulders. The official birth of the French Republic on 22 September 1792 insured Louis XVI's date with the scaffold on 21 January 1793. It also insured war a month after the execution when the Regicides attacked the Netherlands. As in the American war, London became concerned immediately with the exposed position of Ireland. This time, however, the publicly expressed Jacobin sentiments of the United Irishmen convinced the Crown that the Irish Volunteers could not be trusted to defend the island.

The authorities were determined to suppress the Society. The Chairman and Secretary of the Dublin Unitedmen, Simon Butler and Oliver Bond, were jailed by fiat of the House of Lords. Their successors in the posts, Drs. William Drennan and Hamilton Rowan, were soon after arrested for sedition (their offense was printing an address to the Volunteers with the Gallic-sounding salutation, "Citizen Soldiers:"). The government rushed through legislation to prevent all private assemblies of delegates—thereby preventing a repetition of such as the 1782 Dungannon Volunteer convention—and made illegal the importation or manufacture of munitions.

NATIVE SWORDS

There was some reason for Dublin Castle's concern: Napper Tandy, Dr. Hamilton Rowan, and two new United Irish leaders, Oliver Bond and Henry Jackson, had collected the disorganised Volunteer remnants in Dublin into a new National Guard.

Formed in the manner of the revolutionary French National Guards, the new military group was parading publicly in uniform, brandishing an ominous emblem: the Irish harp with a Cap of Liberty substituted for the English Crown. This Thomas Davis song gives a feeling for that time in Dublin.

We've bent too long to braggart wrong,
While force our prayers derided;
We've fought too long ourselves among,
By knaves and priests divided;
United now, no more we'll bow;
Foul faction, we discard it;
And now, thank God, our native sod
Has Native Swords to guard it.

Like rivers which, o'er valleys rich,
Bring ruin in their water,
On native land a native hand
Flung foreign fraud and slaughter.
From Dermott's crime to Tudor's time
Our clans were our perdition;
Religion's name, since then, became
Our pretext for division.

But worse than all! with Limerick's fall
Our valour seemed to perish;
Or, o'er the main, in France and Spain,
For bootless vengeance flourish.
The peasant here grew pale for fear
He'd suffer for our glory,
While France sang for joy for Fontenoy,
And Europe hymned our story.

But now no clan nor factious plan
The East and West can sunder—
Why Ulster e'er should Munster fear
Can only wake our wonder.
Religion's crost when Union's lost,
And "royal gifts" retard it,
And now, thank God, our native sod
Has Native Swords to guard it.

After the crackdown in Dublin, there followed raids on Volunteer meetings and the *Northern Star* offices in Belfast. To replace the suppressed now-United-led Volunteers, the British imposed a lottery to draft a militia of fifteen thousand men. This new English-officered force, in the view of London, could be trusted to both defend the island against the revolutionary armies of the French and, incidentally, keep the bothersome United Irishmen in their place.[7] It apparently never occurred to the authorities to consider the reaction of the cottiers who were to be conscripted.

By this time, the activities of the peasant Defenders were becoming an increasing irritation to the Crown. No longer merely "defending" papists from the ravages of the Peep o' Day Boys, the Defenders had begun taking on the characteristics of Whiteboyism with primitive but menacing nationalist overtones. Appearing in large organised bands for the first time in the summer of 1792, the movement spread rapidly across the rest of the island from the counties adjacent to Ulster. In April 1793 alone —the month the militia lottery was made law—145 men were convicted of membership in Defender organisations. The authorities took the threat sufficiently seriously to sentence sixty-eight of them to death during March and April of that year. When conscription for the new militia began, Defender membership and activity grew dramatically in opposition. In July, for instance, a militia detachment fought a mob of two thousand Defenders near Wexford, killing eighty of the insurgents.

THE BOYS OF MULLAGHBAWN

Defender/Peep o' Day Boy violence had been sporadic until late 1791 when it broke out on a large scale in the North. The Ulster magistrates were far from evenhanded in their attempts to keep order. Influenced by the landowners—who were happy to have the Oakboys' heirs attacking someone else—the King's Justice came down far heavier on Catholic than Presbyterian perpetrators. In early 1793, for instance, twenty-one Defenders were sentenced to death in County Louth; there is no record of any Peep o' Day Boys being brought before the assizes.

Polarisation took place even within districts in which Catholics and Presbyterians had lived peacefully together for years. The 1787 death of kindly Richard Jackson of Forkhill, for example, proved a bane to the Catholics on his south Armagh estate. The men of Mullaghbawn, a parish on the Forkhill land just west of the Moyry Pass, banded together to resist the raids of The Protestant Boys that had begun on the death of the Squire. When conscription was enacted, this small Defender squad resisted; for their efforts, several were given transportation to the new prison colony at Botany Bay in Australia.

On a Monday morning early as my wandering steps did lead me,
Down by a farmer's station of meadow and green lawn,
I heard great lamentation that the wee birds they were making,
Saying, "We'll have no more engagements with the Boys of Mullaghbawn."

Squire Jackson was unequalled for honour or for reason,
He never turned a traitor or betrayed the *Rights of Man;*
But now we are endangered by a vile deceiving stranger
Who has ordered transportation for the boys of Mullaghbawn.

As those heroes crossed the ocean, I'm told, the ship in motion
Did stand in wild commotion as if the seas ran dry;
The trout and salmon gaping as the cuckoo left her station,
Saying, "Farewell to lovely Erin and the hills of Mullaghbawn."

To end my lamentation, we are all in consternation,
For the want of education, I here must end my song;
None cares for recreation since without consideration
We are sent for transportation from the hills of Mullaghbawn.

BOLD McDERMOTT ROE

The aims of the Defenders may have differed slightly from those of the Whiteboys who preceeded them (a contemporary account reports that they not only were swearing "the lower Roman Catholics to secrecy," but also *to the French when they land"*), still the methods of the newest agrarian societies were all too familiar. As Lecky tells us:

> Everywhere the Defenders were administering unlawful oaths and seizing arms. They were accustomed to burn the turf and root up the potatoes of those who refused to be sworn, cut down plantations for pike handles, dig up meadows, level banks, hough cattle,

rob or set fire to houses, ravish or murder. In eight months there were 147 acts of murder, robbery, or rape,[8] in the single county of Longford.

In some areas the threat of Defender retaliation made normal law enforcement problematical. The local authorities could be intimidated. As can be seen in this old broadside ballad, the fear of reprisal convinced the Roscommon constabulary at least that the execution of the local Defender "captain" would be most safely accomplished in Dublin.

Come all you wild young gentlemen so reckless and bold,
My hardships and my miseries I'm going to unfold;
McDermott Roe it is my name, a man of birth well known,
And by my wicked follies to destruction I was prone.

I headed the Defenders as their captain, tis the truth;
In the county of Roscommon I was called the undaunted youth.
One thousand men at my command, no rent I'd let be paid,
To face the army I did go and I was not afraid.

Part of my band being taken, swore to rescue them with speed,
Like Hector bold I ventured but, alas, did not succeed.
I fought as brave as any till my ear got shot away,
Nor did I turn a traitor or from my brave boys run away.

So McDermott Roe was taken and laid in Roscommon gaol,
Although my friends were rich and great, for me they'd take no bail.
Twice I was at assizes tried and each time guilty found,
But yet they dared not hang me there for fear of the country round.

There are many in the country would shed salt tears for me,
And venture life and limb to save me from the gallows tree;
Farewell dear honoured father, you've thousands lost by me,
Your troubled heart it grieves me more than the Saxon gallows tree.

To Dublin I was brought, the scaffold there for me,
Tis little thought I at the time of my nativity.
My father was a gentleman, my mother a lady gay,
One thousand was her fortune upon her wedding day.

There are estated gentlemen that do belong to me,
And did I live the quiet life, it's hanged I ne'er would be;
To back the poor against the rich with them did not agree,
And so McDermott Roe must die in shame and misery.

The Defenders of the countryside were as much an enigma to the United Irishmen as they were to the Crown. During May 1793 Napper Tandy attempted to infiltrate one such organisation in County Louth, a particular hotbed of Defender activity. Pursued by both the government (which wanted to hang him for taking an illegal oath) and the Defenders themselves (to whom he had given a false name), Tandy fled to America. The indefatigable old rebel would subsequently turn up in France urging support for the United Irish cause.

British fears of Jacobin involvement in Ireland were not unfounded. In 1793 the French Committee of Public Safety dispatched William Jackson, a Church of Ireland cleric sympathetic to the Revolution, to sound out the dissident elements on the island. The clergyman's mission was no secret to the British spies in Paris. The Crown discreetly managed to provide the French operative with a traveling companion, John Cockayne, an English attorney who reported Reverend Jackson's every move to Dublin Castle. The French spy's first visit was to Hamilton Rowan, still languishing in a prison cell on his sedition charge. Through one of Dr. Rowan's attorneys, Leonard McNally, Jackson was introduced to Wolfe Tone. When the French operative asked Tone to draft an estimate of the "state of Irish resistance," the Unitedman supplied him with an analysis which concluded:

> The Government of Ireland is only to be looked upon as a government of force; the moment a superior force appears it would tumble at once as founded neither in the interests nor the affections of the people.

When the incriminating document was posted to France—through Cockayne—the authorities arrested Jackson.

The capture of the document gave Dublin Castle the excuse it was seeking to suppress the Society of United Irishmen officially. In January 1794 Dr. Rowan was finally brought to trial for the "Citizen Soldiers" address, the use of the Gallic *citizen* now presumably proof of treasonous tendencies. He was defended magnificiently by John Philpot Curran, the greatest Irish advocate of the era. Rowan nonetheless ended up with a two-year sentence—due perhaps to the pressure put on Curran's colleague McNally, a Unitedman covertly providing privileged information to the Castle to stave off his own prosecution for espionage.[9] A deal had been struck in the meantime between the authorities and Wolfe Tone which allowed the prominent dissident to exile himself to avoid arraignment. Reverend Jackson was brought to trial later in 1794 but, in the face of overwhelming evidence, committed suicide before sentence could be pronounced.

In the summer of the same year, domestic English politics forced Pitt to appoint William Wentworth, Earl of Fitzwilliam, to the viceroyalty of Ireland as a sop to the Whigs. Although Wentworth did not arrive in Dublin until January 1795, when the new Lord Lieutenant did appear in the Irish capital, he came like a political thunderbolt. Taking his task at Dublin Castle much more seriously than the Prime Minister had anticipated, the idealistic Lord Fitzwilliam started right in on a series of reforms. When Wentworth sacked John Beresford, Commissioner of the Revenue—and the primary dispenser of Tory patronage—only four days after the new Whig Viceroy's arrival, the Dublin establishment was stunned. When Fitzwilliam dismissed Under Secretary for Military Affairs Edward Cooke a week afterwards, the Ascendancy was infuriated. The alarmed Anglican politicans made a strong argument to their friends in London: with an Irish Parliament in place and a reformer now at the head of the bureaucracy, the British were in serious danger of losing control of both the day-to-day administration and the manipulation of Irish patronage. Ireland, in short, was in danger of falling into Irish hands. Pitt speedily succumbed to the Tory outcry, recalling his new Lord Lieutenant in March 1795 and replacing him with the safely Tory John Pratt, Earl of Camden. It has been argued that the recall of Wentworth made rebellion inevitable. Certainly Lecky, writing almost a century later, thought the main chance to preserve peace had been lost:

> But from the day when Pitt recalled Lord Fitzwilliam, the course of [*Irish*] history was changed. Intense and growing hatred of England, revived religious and class animosities, a savage rebellion savagely repressed, a legislative union prematurely and corruptly carried, mark the closing years of the eighteenth century, and after ninety years of direct British government, the condition of Ireland is universally recognised as the chief scandal and the chief weakness of the Empire.

If Lecky overstates the case, it is not by much. The annulment of Fitzwilliam's viceroyalty did much to convince Sam Neilson and Wolfe Tone that constitutional agitation was not going to be enough. The dissidents were becoming rebels.

When Tone visited Belfast in May 1795 prior to finally leaving for exile in America, he found that the northern United-

men had gone underground. The irrepressible Neilson was holding meetings of the "Muddler's Club" at the Doctor Franklin
Tavern in Sugarhouse Entry, just down the street from his
woollen warehouse. The membership list of the strangely named
fraternity bore a remarkable similarity to that of the suppressed
Belfast Society of United Irishmen.

While in the North, Tone joined Neilson, Thomas Russell,
Henry Sheares, Robert Simms, and Henry Joy MacCracken for a
famous two-day meeting at MacArt's Fort on the Cave Hill overlooking Belfast. In this ruined redoubt, once the Gaelic stronghold of the great Hugh O'Neill's nephew, the six Unitedmen
made a solemn pact to never "desist from their efforts until they
had subverted the authority of England over their country, and
asserted their independence." Re-inspired, Sam Neilson's furtive
Belfast United group quickly hosted a clandestine convention to
reorganise the Society secretly on an islandwide basis. From this
point, the United Irishmen would talk little of politics, much of
measuring swords with the Crown.

THE PROTESTANT MEN

This brilliant modern song by Brian Warfield recalls the
efforts of the Society of United Irishmen to bring the disparate
religious and cultural groups of Ireland together to face the
Stranger. The point the songwriter makes is a valid one: with
some few exceptions, the founders of Irish republicanism were
all Protestants. When Wolfe Tone, for example, had written his
famous *Argument on Behalf of the Catholics of Ireland* in 1791,
he claimed to have not a single Roman Catholic acquaintance.
Later, when the twenty prize United Irish prisoners were interned in Scotland after the '98 risings, there were four Catholics,
six Dissenters, and ten Church of Ireland Protestants in the
group.

Clearly, the songwriter is subtly suggesting to the modern
Irish Catholic and Protestant listener alike that traditional Irish
nationalism was based on much more than religion. From the
time of Limerick in 1691 to the Easter Rising of 1916, the most
militant of Irish nationalists were Protestant. A 1914 letter published in the *Irish Worker* (written by James MacGowan in reply
to Sean O'Casey's assertion that the "revolution" should be that
of the *Catholic* working class) puts the case well:

If [*O'Casey's*] dictum had been the guiding principle of all classes in Ireland her history would, indeed, have been an inglorious one. We would have no Lord Edward or Tone or Napper Tandy to look back to for inspiration in '98, no Emmet or Russell in 1803, no Mitchel or O'Brien or Fintan Lalor in '48, no Kickham or O'Leary or Luby in '67, no George Henry Moore, no Parnell. All these men, it seems, lived and laboured under a delusion: they thought they had other interests to serve besides their own, and acted accordingly. And in our own days we have the Casements, the George Russels, and the Captain Whites making fools of themselves the same way.

The roster of Protestant leaders preaching violent Irish nationalism is long; it is a curious fact that the only major Catholic leader between 1691 and 1916 was the non-violent Daniel O'Connell.

The opening line of the ballad's fifth verse is worthy of special note. A subtle paraphrase of Hussey Burgh's famous comment during the 1779 "free trade debate" (*see p.* 248), the songwriter uses it to bridge the gap between the Volunteers and the United Irishmen.

It was back in history's page, the story's told
Of Napper Tandy, brave and bold,
With the scarlet and the green, he then was seen
With his big long gun and his fighting men.

And they beat the drum, they fired their gun,
And they shocked the English establishment;
The lords and peers, they then took their fears,
And Grattan got his Parliament.

Refrain:
So here's to those brave Protestant Men
Who gave their lives to free our land;
All the people sang their praises then,
For the brave United Irishmen.

In Belfast Town there lived a man
And his name was Samuel Neilson—
A minister's son, Presbyterian—
Had a paper called the *Northern Star*.

There was Henry Joy, the Green Volunteers,
And Thomas Russell, and MacCabe and MacTier;
And to them was known a man, Wolfe Tone,
And they formed the first United Irishmen.

Refrain

Sow your laws with dragon's teeth, and then you'll see
That you sowed the seeds of bigotry;
Then be England's fool, divide and they'll rule:
So they set to break the Unitedmen.

They killed them in the field and some in jail,
And some upon the gallows high;
When Willie Orr did die, his very last cry
Was "Unite and fight, brave Irishmen!"

Refrain

Cast dissensions to the wind, let all men lend
To the common name of an Irishman;
For across history's page, to rant and rage
Men crossed the Pales of biogtry.

There was the men of Ninety-Eight, those had their fate:
Lord Edward, Tone, and the brothers Sheares;
It was Emmet's plea in Eighteen-Three,
When he tried to set our country free.

As the Unitedmen were plotting, the Defenders were acting. Less than two weeks after the Belfast United Irish convention in May 1795, upward of two hundred Defenders were reported killed in an engagement with the militia in County Cavan. to the dismay of the authorities, a primitive infrastructure had begun to evolve among the previously parochial agrarian societies. Even more alarming was the evolution of some of the Defender bands into rude "patriotic" fraternities, particularly in the South.

The Defenders of Ulster, however, had little time to develop nationalist tendencies—they were altogether too busy trying to live up to their name. On 21 September the recurring struggle between the Peep o' Day Boys and the Catholics near Armagh culminated in the "Battle of the Diamond" where the Defenders were routed, leaving thirty dead behind. In celebration of their victory, the Protestant Boys founded a new organisation, the Orange Order, under the leadership of an obscure Loughgall innkeeper named James Sloan (one Thomas Verner was soon after installed as the first Grand Master of what was then called the Orange *Society*). This new fraternity was to provide the Ascendancy leaders with an instrument, easily manipulated, that could be used for those extra-legal activities that even the official forces were hesitant to attempt.

During 1795-96 recruiters for both the Defenders and the United Irishmen roamed the country organising for what was beginning to appear as inevitable—rebellion. In some few cases in Ulster, where tenuous contact had been made by the leaders of the two groups, these "committeemen" actually worked together. It was an alarming portent.

THE MAN FROM GOD KNOWS WHERE

Captain Thomas Russell was instrumental in the high councils of the United Irishmen from the very beginning. The Corkman was given the responsibility for organising County Down by the Society's May 1795 convention and, in the next year, was among the first of the United leaders to be arrested in the Crown crackdown. Jailed again before the 1798 rebellion, Russell would remain a guest of the authorities until 1802.

After his release, Captain Russell would immediately join the Unitedmen in France who were planning to rise again. Slipping furtively into Ireland the next year with the task of leading Ulster in rebellion, he was to be left without support after Robert Emmet botched the Dublin rising.

This famous ballad by Florence Wilson tells of Russell stopping for a night at Buck's Head Inn in east Down during the winter of 1795-96 when he was attempting to co-ordinate the county for the Unitedmen. The inn, called "Andy Lemon's" by the townsmen of Killyleagh, was filled with Defenders when Russell walked in out of the night. It is perhaps indicative of the nebulous connection between the two organisations that the patrons did not know who he was; neither was the Unitedman aware of their sentiments.

Eight years after that night, Russell would read the proclamation of the 1803 rising aloud from the capstone of the dolmen which stands by the roadside at the inn. Not long afterwards, the steadfast United Irishman was to be executed at the Old County Gaol in Downpatrick. Mary Ann MacCracken would raise his gravestone in the local Protestant cemetary, bearing the simple inscription, "The Grave of Russell."

The impact of this ballad has been significant; Thomas Russell is still often referred to by the song's title. The long folk-poem originally had thirteen verses. Seven are included here.

Into our townland on a night of snow
Rode a man from God knows where;
None of us bade him stay or go,
Nor deemed him friend, nor damned him foe,
But we stabled his big roan mare;
For in our townland we're a decent folk,
And if he didn't speak, why none of us spoke,
And we sat till the fire burned low.

It was closing time, and late forbye
When us ones braved the air—
I never saw worse (may I live or die)
Than the sleet that night and I says, says I,
"You'll find he's for stopping there."
But at the screek o' day, through the gable pane,
I watched him spur through the pelting rain,
And I juked from his roving eye.

Two winters more, the Trouble Year,
When the best that man could feel
Was the pike he kept in hiding near,
Till the blood of hate and the blood of fear
Would be redder, nor rust on the steel;
Us ones quit from minding the farms,
Let them take what we gave with the weight of our arms,
From Saintfield to Kilkeel.

All over Ulster the women cried
For the standing crops on the land—
Many's the sweetheart and many's the bride

Would liefer have gone to where he died,
And mourned alone by her man;
But us ones weathered the thick of it,
And we used to dander along, and sit
In Andy's side-by-side.

For a wheen o' days we sat waiting the word
To rise and go at it like men,
But no French ships sailed into Cloughey Bay
And we heard the black news on a harvest day
That the Cause was lost again;
And Joey and me and Willy Boy Scott,
We agreed to ourselves we'd lief as not
Have been found in the slick of the slain.

By Downpatrick Gaol I was bound to fare
On a day I'll remember, faith;
For when I came to the prison square,
The people were waiting in hundreds there,
And you wouldn't hear stir nor breath.
For the soldiers were standing, grim and tall,
Round a scaffold built there against the wall,
And a man stepped out for death.

I was brave and near to the edge of the throng,
Yet I knowed the face again,
And I knowed the set and I knowed the walk
And the sound of his strange up-country talk,
For he spoke out right and plain.
Then he bowed his head to the swinging rope
While I said, "Please God" to his dying hope
And "Amen" to his dying prayer;

That the Wrong would cease and the Right prevail.
For the man that they hanged at Downpatrick Gaol
Was the Man from God-Knows-Where!

Wolfe Tone had been making apparently unproductive representations to the French Minister in Philadelphia during autumn 1795 when he received a letter from Russell and John Keogh,[10] urging him to increase the pressure on the French.

Tone sailed forthwith for the continent, arriving at Le Harve in February 1796. His persuasiveness was evidently more effective in Paris; by that summer, the French began serious preparations for a large military expedition to Ireland, meanwhile making Tone a *chef-de-brigade* in the French service. The new French colonel seems to have been somewhat bemused by his good fortune. "Here I am," Tone wrote, "with exactly two louis in my exchequer, negotiating with the French government and planning revolutions." Reflecting later on the Unitedman's persuasive talents, even the Duke of Wellington would allow a bit of grudging admiration for Tone's audacity to creep in:

> Wolfe Tone was a most extraordinary man and his history is the most curious history of those times. With a hundred guineas in his pocket, unknown and unrecommended, he went to Paris in order to overturn the British government in Ireland. He asked for a large force; Lord Edward Fitzgerald for a small one. They listened to Tone. . . .

It is in fact doubtful if the future Hero of Waterloo ever understood just how vital Wolfe Tone's persuasive talents were to his *own* career. As Lieutenant Colonel Arthur Wellesley proceeded to the Cape to join the 33rd Regiment in the autumn of 1796 *en route* to India, the young British officer could not have known that Tone's glowing revolutionary description of the United Irishmen had caused the French to scrap a grandiose expedition to aid Tippoo Sahib against the English on the subcontinent. Tone's glib effrontery had convinced the French General Lazare Hoche to strike his blow against the British in Ireland. During the summer of 1796, Hoche had decided to land his sixteen thousand French regulars in Connacht rather than India; meanwhile he would dispatch a diversionary force to the coasts of Cornwall and Wales under Colonel Tate, an American adventurer, with the task of making sufficient noise to freeze potential Crown reinforcement to the Irish West. The future Lord Wellington was to be free to make his military reputation against Tippoo Sahib without French interference. Wolfe Tone, meanwhile, had his own date with destiny in Ireland.

Even before Tone had landed in France in early 1796, Dublin Castle had become alarmed at the growing militancy of both the Defenders and the United Irishmen. By the time Tone's mission began bearing fruit—a fact reported to the Castle by Thomas Collins and Leonard McNally who were privy to the United leaders in Dublin—the authorities were also concerned at a new development: it appeared that large numbers of Defenders were beginning to take the United Irish oath. In reaction to these alarming developments, the Crown brought in an Insurrection Act during March 1796 to "disarm" the populace. A yeomanry was created to enforce the new law. Augmenting the eighteen thousand militia and fifteen thousand regulars who were supposed to protect Ireland from the French, the "yeos" were a combination military/police force expressly designed to protect Ireland from the Irish.[11] Though quite effective in terrorising the peasant population, the yeomen were to prove no substitute for regular troops in battle against the French and rebels two years later.

In June 1796 the Dublin Directory of the United Irishmen—which now included John Sweetman, Dr. William MacNeven, and Thomas Addis Emmet—sent two of its most distinguished new recruits to France hoping to hasten aid. Lord Edward Fitzgerald (the aristocrat brother of the Duke of Leinster, Ireland's greatest peer) and Arthur O'Connor (an Irish M.P., former High Sheriff of Cork, and heir to a large estate in the Southwest) arrived in France seemingly unaware that Belfast was already being represented by Wolfe Tone. Napper Tandy was also in Paris demanding French assistance, further muddying the negotiations.

Dublin Castle was stirred to action. Based on information it was getting from inside the Society, the authorities determined to break the back of the United Irishmen. Sam Neilson, Thomas Russell, Henry Joy MacCracken, Charles Hamilton Teeling, and William MacCracken were all interned in September.[12] The arrests were not confined to the leaders. For example, James Porter, the Presbyterian curate of little Greyabbey on the Ards Peninsula, was jailed for publishing *Billy Bluff and Squire Firebrand*, a slim volume humourously lacerating the dignitaries of his parish. It was to cost him his life. When insurrection broke out two years later, the hapless minister would be hanged for treason in front of his own church.

During the second half of 1796 the authorities enforced the Insurrection Act with enthusiasm, the task of the yeomanry and militia being eased considerably by the suspension of the *Habeas Corpus* Act in October. In Ulster, the job was still easier; the Ascendancy leaders were stirring up the new Orange Society to offset the ecumenical nationalist efforts of the United Irishmen.

There was good reason for the Castle to be concerned. The Unitedmen, heretofore plagued by parochial organisation, had finally set up an executive—the National Directory—to coordinate the various provincial groups by the end of 1796. This Dublin-based council included Lord Edward Fitzgerald, Arthur O'Connor, Thomas Emmet, Oliver Bond, and Dr. William MacNeven. The Dubliners even sent Edward Lewins as a permanent "accredited" ambassador to France. Events threatened to overtake the Dubliners, however; perhaps unknown to them, the United prospectors already in Paris had hit a military motherlode.

On 16 December 1796 forty-three ships under Vice Admiral Morard de Galle hoisted sail from Brest. Aboard were fourteen thousand French troops under General Hoche. Wolfe Tone was returning to Ireland.

SHAN VAN VOCHT
(*Seanbhean Bhocht*)

After the English troops had been driven out of the Netherlands in 1794, the British share in the continental war against the French had been confined to a naval blockade. In the interim, the internal convulsions of the French Republic did not seem to be in any way constraining the French army in Europe. *Le Petit Caporal* Buonaparte was rampaging through Italy giving the world an indication of what was ahead. It was no secret that the United Irish and Defenders were expecting a French landing (the people, of course, had no way to know that the Dublin rebel leaders were as much in the dark as anyone as to when or where it might come). There was high excitement in Ireland in anticipation.

By the 1790s, the balladeers often represented the island in metaphor as a long-suffering and poor old woman, or *seanbhean bhocht*. Even in the modern era, Tommy Makem can sing of that "proud old woman" knowing that his audience understands immediately that he is referring to Ireland.

Oh, the French are on the sea, says the shan van vocht,
The French are on the sea, says the shan van vocht;
Oh, the French are in the bay, they'll be here without delay,
And the Orange will decay, says the shan van vocht.

Refrain: (last two lines of each verse)

And their camp it shall be where, says the shan van vocht,
Their camp it shall be where, says the shan van vocht;
On the Curragh of Kildare, the boys they will be there
With their pikes in good repair, says the shan van vocht.

Refrain

Then what will the yeomen do, says the shan van vocht,
What will the yeomen do, says the shan van vocht;
What should the yeomen do but throw off the Red-and-Blue,
And swear that they'll be true to the shan van vocht.

Refrain

And what colour will they wear, says the shan van vocht,
What colour will they wear, says the shan van vocht;
What colour should been seen where our father's homes have been
But our own immortal Green, says the shan van vocht.

Refrain

And will Ireland then be free, says the shan van vocht,
Will Ireland then be free, says the shan van vocht;
Yes, Ireland shall be free—from the centre to the sea!
Then hurrah, for Liberty! says the shan van vocht.

On New Year's Day 1797 Wolfe Tone was back in France—
the long awaited French expedition had proved an unqualified
bust. Admiral de Galle had sailed from Brest under cover of fog
to avoid Sir Edward Pellew's prowling British squadron, a fog
that cost the French admiral two ships which had run aground
in the limited visibility. Seven more vessels, including the flagship itself with de Galle and General Hoche aboard, had been
soon afterwards separated from the main fleet in the northeaster-
ly blizzard that replaced the fog. Although the spindrifting gale
continued to blow, the remaining thirty-four sail—now under
Rear Admiral Bouvet—had beat cautiously into Bantry Bay and
let go anchor on 22 December. Most of the vessels had dragged
their hooks through that first night; by the next morning, only
sixteen were left in the bay. When the fouling wind slackened a
bit on Christmas Eve, Brigadier Emmanuel de Grouchy had pre-

pared the remaining 6,500 French troops for landing on the holiday. That night, however, the yawing fleet had been hit with a new Atlantic storm and, when the fresh gale showed no signs of easing, the remaining French ships cut their cables one-by-one and slipped out to sea. The last did not quit Bantry Bay until 2 January 1797. The distinguished Sir Edward Creasy was to comment a half-century later that "Grouchy twice had in his hands the power of changing the destinies of Europe, and twice wanted nerve to act: first when he flinched from landing the French army at Bantry Bay in 1796 . . . [*Sir Edward's second example was, of course, Waterloo*]." Though the criticism was to be levied by an historian with little knowledge of the difficulty of manuevering sail-of-the-line close inshore for disembarkation amidst the howling gales of the North Atlantic winter, it *is* true that the most dangerous threat to six centuries of British hegemony in Ireland had sailed into the running sea with the departing French.

Dublin Castle was by now thoroughly alarmed, and understandably so. A wandering Clare poet called "Cormac," Patrick O'Kelly, perhaps afforded the most accurate picture of the Castle's relief at the dispersal of the Bantry Bay fleet:

While Admiral Bridport lay at rest,
And Colpoys everywhere was peeping,
Admiral de Galle stole from Best,
And thought to catch the Irish sleeping.

But a rare Admiral, General *Gale*,
Oh, may the gods give him a blessing!
Appeared in time with crowded sail,
And gave to frog-eaters a dressing.

The issue had indeed been decided by the arrival of O'Kelly's "volunteer general." Had Grouchy been able to land his troops there would have been nothing at all to stop him from taking most of Munster and Connacht. In truth, the woeful show of the yeomanry and militia twenty months later when faced by French regulars suggests there would have been little to stop the French commander even after the British *were* able to muster a defense. Two hundred years after the Spanish Armada had been blown onto the coast of Ireland, the Protestant Wind had arisen once more for the English, this time to blow the French away.

The news of the French fleet signalled increased United and Defender agitation—particularly in Ulster. When Lieutenant

General Gerard Lake, British commander in the province, heard that Colonel Tate's tardy French diversionary force had landed on the Pembroke coast of Wales in late February—and been immediately surrounded—it was enough to convince the English officer that the French threat had only been sidestepped. In March 1797 Lake placed the North under Martial Law. The Ulster authorities felt that the yeomanry and militia were not sufficient for the emergency. Brigadier Knox, commanding at Dungannon, wrote Chief Secretary Thomas Pelham suggesting the use of the Orange Society to "help disarm the United Irishmen" in his district.[13]   Soon there were volunteer mobs of Orangemen swarming over the province. The torching of houses and shooting of the occupants became commonplace. Lord Camden approved. Sympathising with the difficulty of Lake's task in Ulster, the Viceroy ordered the general to prevent the magistracy from interfering with the military's work merely because the law was being broken.

The authorities were not ignoring the United Irish leadership. Though most members of the highest councils were not yet bothered—the Castle's informers were providing a steady flow of information and the authorities did not want to jeopardise their sources until they had learned the date of the next French landing—the British suppressed the *Northern Star* and began to round up the lieutenants.[14]

BLARIS MOOR

As 1797 wore on, the Crown found that it had a particularly sensitive concern: Unitedmen within the ranks of its own forces. No less than seventy of the Monaghan Militia were made to confess that they had taken the United oath. One entire regiment had to be transferred away from Dublin because of its "Jacobin contamination." At one juncture, courts-martial were sitting on seduced soldiers in Cork, Belfast, and Limerick at the same time. It looked to some like a losing battle. One magistrate complained that "It answers no end to station small parties of the military in different cantonments, for they are regularly corrupted."

In the Belfast courts-martial in May, four militiamen from Monaghan were sentenced to death for being United Irishmen. Repeatedly refusing to inform on their comrades in exchange for pardons, the four troopers were carried to the village of Blaris just south of Lisburn; on 16 May 1797 William and Owen McKenna, Daniel McGillain, and Peter McCarren were shot dead by firing party.

The following year, this ballad by the Lurgan poet James Garland appeared on the streets of Belfast.

Ye muse grant me direction,
To sing that foul transaction,
Which causes sad reflection,
Late done at Blaris Moor
By wicked Colonel Barber;
Should I proceed much further
And call his conduct murder,
Twere treason, I am sure.

They were of good behaviour,
No heroes e'er braver,
But a perjured base deceiver
Betrayed their lives away.
For the sake of golden store,
This villain falsely swore,
And the crime we now deplore
In sorrow and dismay.

Then their foes held consultation
To find out combination,
And thus in exhortation
Cursed Barber did propose:
"Arise from your devotion,
Take pardon and promotion
Or death will be your portion
Unless you now disclose."

Some moments then they mused,
For their senses were confused,
Then smiling they refused
And made him this reply:
"We own we are United,
Of death we're not affrighted,
And hope to be requited
By Him who rules on high."

The guns were then presented,
The balls their bosom entered
While multitudes lamented
The shocking sight to see;
Those youthful martyrs four
Lying weltering in their gore,
And the plains besprinkled o'er
With the blood of cruelty.

In coffins they were hurried,
From Blaris Moor were carried
And hastily were buried
While thousands sank with grief,
Crying. *"Grania*, we must wonder
You rise not from your slumber
With voice as loud as thunder,
To grant us some relief!"

Only five years after Wolfe Tone and Sam Neilson had founded the Society of United Irishmen, Tone had sailed into Bantry Bay aboard the largest invasion fleet Ireland had seen since the Vikings almost a millennium before. In that short time, the Unitedmen had ignited an insolent flame of resistance whose intensity had caught the Crown by surprise. Though the embers would never quite be extinguished, the initiative was now to move to the side of the authorities. The execution of the militiamen at Blaris was merely the opening salvo in a Crown campaign that would make the coming rebellion hopeless before it had even begun.

CHAPTER NOTES (12)

1 — As has been seen, there were a small number of Catholic professionals and merchants also part of the emerging middle class. The prosperous papists were like the *noveau riche* anywhere, afraid to rock the boat. Their nervous support of the *status*

quo was to gain them the cant name "Castle Catholics."

2 — Captain Russell (the Corkman resigned his British Army commission in late 1791) had been in 1788 the first librarian of the Belfast Society for Promoting Knowledge, later to evolve into the Linenhall Library in Donegall Square North. When he returned to Belfast two years afterwards, he had jumped into the "Gaelic Renaissance" movement with both feet.

3 — The Irish Whig Club was better known at the time as the "Round Robin." Like its equivalent in Britain which included Charles James Fox and Edmund Burke, it had as members the brightest and most reputable political lights of late eighteenth century Ireland. Besides Grattan, Charlemont, and Tone, the membership included Lord William Fitzgerald, Duke of Leinster; John Philpot Curran, the island's finest barrister and orator; Dr. Archibald Hamilton Rowan, one of the great landowners of County Down; young George Ponsonby, who was later to lead the Ascendancy fight against the Act of Union; and James Napper Tandy, who was at home with any crowd having an anti-London bias.

4 — William and Henry Joy MacCracken were rich, young industrialists who were among the first customers of Belfast's newest business: shipbuilding. William and Hugh Ritchie founded the first shipyard on the River Lagan in 1791. The MacCrackens contracted for a ship the following year.

5 — The *Northern Star*, sometimes published as the *Morning Star*, was also known at the time as the "Union *Star*" . . . which raises a curious, if slightly confusing, point. The United Irishmen were familiarly called "Unionists" by their contemporaries. It must be remembered that the Act of Union did not come until later. Even in 1800 a disdainful Orange ballad sang of the United Irish "union," albeit with irony:

> As their union, union, republican union,
> Now would take place on the Shannon's green banks,
> And the liberty tree should there firm planted be,
> And from turf a gold cup made to give France their thanks.

Presumably the "union" that Tone *et al.* were trying to effect was an ecumenical one.

In late 1792 the first-ever Gaelic language magazine *Bolg an tSolair* was published by the *Northern Star*. The magazine was a 120-page amalgam of poetry (collected and translated by Charlotte Brooke), prayers, grammar, and vocabulary. Thomas Russell was apparently instrumental in the magazine's creation.

6 — John Keogh and Richard MacCormack who, along with Tone, were leading the Committee's fight for full papist emacipation, were finally persuaded that they could not win the battle. Tone was exasperated with his colleagues' acceptance of less, noting in his diary that merchants make bad revolutionaries.

7 — Robert Hobart, British Chief Secretary at the time, viewed the militia as:

> "the most useful measure to both England and Ireland that has ever been adopted . . . it will operate effectually to the suppression of volunteering, to the civilisation of the people, and to the extinction of the means which the agitators . . . have repeatedly availed themselves of to disturb the peace."

8 — The murders and robberies of the Defenders are well documented, rapes are not. On the contrary, contemporary accounts are remarkable for their silence about this very common mob crime. Considering the influence of the Catholic Church at the time, we should not be surprised.

The croppy priest was not above condoning a "little murther" in a good cause, but woe be the unwary papist who would violate the sanctity of an Irish woman. The Catholic Defender might stand staunchly before British bullets, but rare indeed was the peasant who would stand up to his parish priest.

9 — Hamilton Rowan managed to escape from prison in May 1794 and make his way first to France, thence to America. He seems to have avoided further entanglement with the United Irishmen.

10 — Keogh, Sweetman, and MacCormack, though maintaining their official posts with the Catholic Committee, had all joined the Unitedmen by this time.

11 — Parliament was presented with the proposal to raise 20,000 yeomen. The individual units functioned as sort of a Home Guard captained by local squires. By the time rebellion erupted in 1798, the yeomanry had mushroomed to 50,000 men. Perhaps half were Catholic.

12 — Most of the arrests were in Ulster. As the birthplace of the United Irish Society, the province was considered the "breeding-ground of rebellion" by the Castle. The impoundment of over 6,000 arms in the first series of government raids did nothing to dispel the notion.

13 — Knox had been urging this policy for some time. The previous year he had written to General Lake:

> "As for the Orangemen, we have rather a difficult card to play; they must not be entirely discountenanced—on the contrary, we must in a certain degree uphold them, for with all their licentiousness, on them we must rely for the preservation of our lives and properties, should critical times occur."

A century before Lord Randolph Churchill was to deal himself a hand in Ulster, the "Orange Card" was already being played.

14 — Sam Neilson and Thomas Emmet were already in gaol at this time. After their re-

lease in the summer of 1797, they helped Arthur O'Connor publish the Irish *Press* in Dublin that autumn to replace the suppressed Belfast journal.

13

The Eve of Rebellion

General Lake's measures to "subdue" Ulster began to have effect by mid-1797. It was no wonder. Lord Gosford, Crown Deputy for County Armagh, complained to his magistrates that "of no night passes that houses are not destroyed and scarce a week that dreadful murders are not committed." He was pleading to an unsympathetic audience. An Act of Indemnity had been passed giving a blanket pardon to those magistrates who had "in the previous half-year, exceeded their legal powers in the preservation of the public peace."

For some reason, Lord Camden and General Lake were not yet convinced of the Ulster yeomanry's loyalty. Consequently, the Ancient Britons, a notorious Welsh unit commanded by Sir Watkin Williams-Wynn, was brought into the province to help with the dragooning. The insulted local units thereupon redoubled their efforts to prove their fidelity to the Crown. The result was a sort of grisly competition in savagery. One English officer who happened upon the brutal rivalry in County Down reported that both the Welsh and Orange yeomanry were killing "old men, women and children." History does not record who won this bloody game of body-counts; the loser, of course, was the terrified peasantry.

As the Crown cowed the peasantry, the Ulster Directory of the United Irishmen became understandably anxious about the delay in the return of the French. Still active in Belfast were the brothers Simms and MacCracken, Reverend Dickson, Jamie Hope, and an attorney named MacGuckin (who was yet another Dublin Castle informer). As the downtrodden peasants turned in their weapons and took the oath of allegiance to the Crown in ever growing numbers, the northern group apprehensively urged the Dublin United leaders to precipitate rebellion whether or not the French were ready.

The Leinster Directory split over the issue: Lord Edward Fitzgerald and Arthur O'Connor spearheaded the support for the early rising demanded by the Belfast men, while John Sheares and Dr. William Lawless apparently led the faction wanting to wait for the French.[1]   Finally, the Dublin council narrowly defeated the Ulster proposal—agreeing, however, to send Dr. MacNeven to the continent to hurry the French along.

When the physician arrived in France in the summer of 1797, he found that the Batavian Republic (Holland's "republican" name) was mounting the new Irish expedition.   By the second week of July, fifty-two sail under Admiral de Winter were prepared to embark General Daendels' troops—and Wolfe Tone—at Texel.   Unfavourable winds, however, delayed boarding orders through August.   At that juncture the French General Hoche, co-ordinating the enterprise, fell ill unexpectedly, dying in mid-September as the fleet stood down in confusion.   Tone, despairing of the Dutch commitment, returned to Paris.   By the time de Winter finally sailed in October, the British were ready: Admiral Duncan's English fleet dispersed the Batavian fleet at the Battle of Camperdown, ending Irish rebel hopes for the year and Dutch pretensions to sea power forever.

The Crown intelligence operatives within the United Irish high command were proving particularly talkative throughout 1797.   The English were not concerned merely with French intentions toward Ireland; Napoleon was knocking off his continental opponents one-by-one and the British were apprehnsive that his next move might be against England itself.   One of the Crown's most important contacts was Samuel Turner, a former member of the Ulster Directory who had fled to Hamburg earlier when a warrant was issued for his arrest.   Joining several former comrades there, he had found himself at the nexus of the communications systems between Lord Edward Fitzgerald and the French Directorate.   Turner, feeling the cause lost, had contacted the British and agreed to work covertly for them in return for pardon of his earlier United activities.

Turner's information was now that the Irish were prepared to rise without regard to the French.   The intelligence was dubious—the Hamburg connection was Lord Edward's *private* pipeline to the continent—but it reassured the British who believed it implicitly.   Reasoning that, if the French were coming in force, Paris would be strongly urging the Unitedmen to keep their minions in check, Dublin Castle now changed its strategy.

The authorities started turning the screws in earnest. Not content any longer with dragooning the peasantry, the English began going after the United captains. The British now wanted to precipitate rebellion before any French aid could arrive.

One of the Ulstermen who had been arrested with Sam Neilson and Thomas Russell in 1796 was William Orr of Farranshane. After over a year of incarceration without indictment, Orr was suddenly charged with administering an illegal oath, an action proscribed under the Insurrection Act.

Orr was supposed to have given the United Irish oath to a militiaman, one Wheatley. In point of fact, it was not Orr but William McKeever of Londonderry who was the guilty party in the case.[2] The authorities had Orr in custody, however, and intended to make an example of him. They succeeded instead in making him a martyr.

The government badly mishandled the October 1797 trial. The "seduced" Wheatley retracted his evidence against Orr . . . and then retracted his retraction. Several jurymen who held out for acquittal were apparently swayed by a combination of blandishment, whiskey, and threat. In the end, the authorities got their verdict. William Orr was hanged just outside Carrickfergus on 14 October 1797. The execution of the Antrim farmer stunned a nation grown used to barbarity.

THE WAKE OF WILLIAM ORR

The Irish *Press*—founded this October by Arthur O'Connor in Dublin to replace the suppressed *Northern Star*—immediately protested the proceedings leading to Orr's death. Dublin Castle responded with a charge of libel against the printer, one Finnerty. The stage was set for a remarkable speech by John Philpot Curran, who had represented Orr and was now representing Finnerty. Rather than defend the printer, the extraordinary barrister attacked the government:

> It is not upon Finnerty you are sitting in judgement; but . . . upon the lives and liberties of the inhabitants . . . of Ireland. You are to say that it is a foul proceeding to condemn the Government of Ireland . . . that all is mildness and tranquillity; that there are no burnings, no transportations. . . .
>
> Gentlemen of the jury . . . you are called upon, on your oaths, to say that the Government is wise and merciful; the people

prosperous and happy; that military law ought to be continued . . . and that the statements of a contrary import . . . are libellous and false.

Let me ask you how you could reconcile with such a verdict the jails, the tenders, the gibbets, the conflagrations, the murders, the proclamations we hear of every day in the streets and see every day in the country? . . . What is the state of Ireland? And where shall you find the wretched inhabitant of this land?

You may find him perhaps in a gaol, the only place of security— I had almost said of ordinary habitation! If you do not find him there you may find him flying with his family from the flames of his own dwelling . . . or you may find his bones bleaching on the green fields of his country; or you may find him tossing on the surface of the ocean, mingling his groans with those tempests, less savage than his persecutors, that drift him a returnless distance from his family and his home—without charge, or trial, or sentence!

William Orr had given the United Irishmen a martyr whose death came to represent everything that they were struggling against, a feeling made clear in Curran's speech and by the following ballad by Dr. Drennan that appeared in the *Press* soon afterwards. Eight months after the Farranshane farmer's wake at Ballynure, Ulster insurrectionists would shout "Remember Orr!" as they strode into battle.

There our murdered brother lies;
Wake him not with woman's cries,
Mourn the way that manhood ought—
Sit in silent trance of thought.

Write his merits on your mind;
Morals pure and manners kind;
In his head, as on a hill,
Virtue placed her citadel.

Why cut off in palmy youth?
Truth he spoke, and acted Truth.
"Countrymen, *unite*! he cried,
And Died for what our Saviour died.

God of peace and God of love!
Let it not Thy vengeance move,

Let it not Thy lightnings draw—
A nation *guillotined* by law.

Hapless Nation, rent and torn,
Thou wert early taught to mourn;
Warfare for six hundred years
Epoch marked with blood and tears!

Hunted through thy native grounds,
Or flung reward to human hounds,
Each one pulled and tore his share,
Heedless of thy deep despair.

Hapless Nation! hapless Land!
Heap of uncementing sand!
Crumbled by a foreign weight:
And by worse, domestic hate.

Monstrous and unhappy sight!
Brothers' blood will not unite;
Holy oil and holy water
Mix, and fill the world with slaughter.

Angel of this sacred place,
Calm her soul and whisper peace:
Cord or axe, or *guillotine*,
Make the sentence—not the sin.

Here we watch our brother's sleep;
Watch with us but do not weep;
Watch with us through dead of night—
But expect the Morning Light.

Though the Crown had some success in intimidating the peasantry of Ulster, the country people in Leinster were so far uncowed. Seditious literature was read to villagers who met to hear it in much the same manner as their forefathers had assembled to listen to the *seanchaithe*. Ash trees—source of the legendary Irish pike—disappeared from gentlemen's estates with omnious frequency.[3] Peasants gathered to work the fields and cut the hay of their gaoled neighbors. Unitedmen were discovered with alarming regularity among the ranks of the militia and yeomanry. The Defenders ruled the countryside by moonlight. One well-heeled Member of Parliament felt compelled to rise and warn his honourable colleagues that they were "facing a war of the poor against the rich."

If the rebel leaders were not yet ready to rise, the people certainly were.

THE RISING OF THE MOON

The Crown's indiscriminate use of the Insurrection Act insured a great deal of grass-roots emotional support for the Defenders and Unitedmen. Many peasants went further, feeling they were "guilty" in the eyes of the authorities anyway. Blacksmiths and carpenters forged pikes which were swiftly hidden in the thatch of cottages all round. Extra arms were stockpiled and watchwords were exchanged. An electric expectancy hummed among the common people of Ireland.

John Keegan Casey, a young Fenian poet writing three-score years later under the name "Leo," imagined that time vividly in this ballad. Destined to die in prison at age twenty-three, the precocious Westmeathman wrote the song when he was only fourteen. The title of the ballad has since become synonomous with Irish Rebellion. For over sixty years it was the most widely sung of all rebel songs and is rivalled, even today, only by *Kevin Barry*.

"Oh then, tell me Shaun O'Farrell, why do you hurry so?"
"Hush, *a bhuachaill,* hush and listen," and his cheeks were all aglow.
"I bear orders from the captain, make your ready quick and soon,
For the pikes must be together by the rising of the moon."

Refrain:
By the rising of the moon,
By the rising of the moon;
For the pikes must be together
By the rising of the moon.

"Now then, tell me Shaun O'Farrell where the gathering is to be?"
"In the old spot by the river, right well known to you and me.
One word more—for signal token—whistle up a marching tune,
With your pike upon your shoulder by the rising of the moon."

Refrain

Out from many a mud-wall cabin, eyes were watching through the night,
Many a manly heart was throbbing for the blessed warning light;
Murmers ran along the valley like the banshee's lonely croon,
And a thousand blades were flashing by the rising of the moon.

Refrain

There beside the singing river that dark mass of men was seen;
Far above their shining weapons, hung their own beloved Green.
"Death to every foe and traitor! Forward! Strike the marching tune!
And, hurrah me boys, for Freedom! Tis the rising of the moon!"

Refrain

Well they fought for poor old Ireland and full bitter was their fate—
(Oh, what glorious pride and sorrow fills the name of Ninety-Eight)—
Yet thank God, e'en still are beating hearts, in mankind's burning noon,
Who would follow in their footsteps at the rising of the moon!

Refrain

Distressed by the bungling of the Orr incident, the Crown was now determined to move against the top councils of the Unitedmen. The authorities felt certain that pressure on the leadership would produce a premature rising. The strategy was ultimately to succeed beyond the Castle's wildest expectations.

Acting on a tip from Samuel Turner, the British arrested Arthur O'Connor at Margate in February 1798.[4] The Irish *Press* was closed down on 6 March. When Dublin Castle learned from Francis Magan—a government informer who, along with Thomas Reynolds, was on the Leinster Directory—that the Unitedmen had set "Old May Day" as the provisional date for the rebellion, the administration moved immediately to seize the rest of the southern leaders. Reynolds, County Kildare delegate and Treasurer for the Dublin Unitedmen, betrayed the Leinster Directory itself. The authorities struck on 12 March. Major Justice Swann of the Revenue Corps led a raid on Oliver Bond's house in the capital, netting about a dozen of the Leinster rebel leaders. Since many of the captured men also served on the

National Directory, the highest United councils were thrown into confusion. The raid was a blow from which the United Irishmen would never recover. In a very real sense, all hopes for rebel success died that day in Dublin.[5]

There were some few important Unitedmen who avoided the round-up. Two who had narrowly escaped, William Sampson and Richard MacCormack, fled the country. Others did not run. One provincial delegate, William Byrne of Wicklow, was to prove an able rebel captain when the fighting broke out. Another, Hans Dennistoun of Longford, would lead a rising after the French finally landed in late summer. Lord Edward Fitzgerald, already on the run, merely went further to earth.[6]

A new executive was hastily formed just before St. Patrick's Day at the now-famous Brazen Head in Dublin. Under the chairmanship of John Sheares, the new National Directory included his brother Henry; Robert Simms and Reverend Dickson from Ulster; and four men who had been involved with the former Leinster Directory, Sam Neilson, Dr. Lawless, Fitzgerald, and the informer Magan (though Reynold's treachery had been found out, Magan's had not . . . even though he had, of course, also escaped the trap at Bond's house). The fledgling Directory was to sorely miss the counsel of its captured leaders. Many of the provincial commanders had been picked up in the raid; setting up communications afresh with the men in the countryside proved to be beyond the capabilities of the new leadership.

The reconstituted Executive did set up a provisional chain-of-command. John Sheares was to be commander-in-chief, Fitzgerald his principal for Leinster; Simms and Dickson were apparrently appointed the leaders for Ulster. Henry Joy MacCracken, though nobody bothered to inform him, was chosen nominal commander for the North until the delegates returned from Dublin. The new council does not appear to have concerned itself with reorganising Munster.[7] Connacht, the remaining province, had never been a serious factor in the thinking of the United Irish high councils.

The authorities meanwhile expanded their campaign of terror in the countryside. Sir Ralph Abercrombie, appointed senior British military officer in January 1798, found that his regular forces could not control the excesses of the militia and yeomanry. When the Lieutenant General appealed to Dublin Castle for assistance, he found that Lord Castlereagh, acting Chief Secretary to Camden, was less than sympathetic. Abercrombie resigned in protest, leaving Ireland in early April.[8] His successor was Gerard Lake, an officer wholly in tune with the Camden/Castlereagh plan to provoke premature rebellion. Lake was happy to extend the policies he had been using in Ulster to the rest of the island.

The peasants to the south soon found out what kind of treatment their compatriots in the North had been getting. North Leinster was immediately proclaimed by the Crown. Tipperary was at the same time being "pacified" by a particularly brutal high sheriff, Thomas Judkin-Fitzgerald. His method of pacification was as simple as it was ruthless. The High Sheriff commonly collected the entire population of a town on the village diamond and then commenced "to flog each citizen until he told the truth," as the official told one horrified British general officer, the truth presumably being the names of the local Unitedmen and Defenders. Even "loyal" Wexford began to receive this kind of treatment as insurrection grew closer.

The last significant meeting of the National Directory of the Society of United Irishmen took place in Dublin on Friday, 18 May 1798. The policies of Camden and Castlereagh were bearing fruit. Lord Edward Fitzgerald, citing the deteriorating situation, demanded an immediate rising. It is perhaps indicative of the Unitedmen's desperation that John Sheares did not oppose his Leinster lieutenant's impatience; the chairman no longer wanted to wait for the French, either. Rather, Sheares had a strange new plan, suggesting that he could engineer a military coup by United sympathisers serving in the Kings County Militia.

It seems that Captain John W. Armstrong of that unit had been buying volumes cordial to the French Revolution at the shop of a trusted Unitedman. Naïvely judging the officer's political leanings solely on his "revolutionary" reading habits, the bookseller had, within the previous week, introduced the young captain to the brothers Sheares as a fellow radical. He was anything but. Armstrong reported the bizarre contact to his superiors and received orders to string his new friends along. To gain credibility with the Unitedmen, the militiaman suggested that he had disaffected friends in the officer corps of the units stationed around Dublin, hinting that they would be only too happy to rise in concert with the rebels. The credulous brothers swallowed the story whole.

A bitter debate broke out at the National Directory meeting. John and Henry Sheares were supported by Dr. Lawless.

The Rising of 1798

	Sunday	Monday	Tuesday	Wednesday	Thursday	Friday	Saturday
May	13	14	15	16	17	18 Last meeting of United Irish Directory	19 Fitzgerald captured; Napoleon sails from Toulon
	20	21 Sheares' captured	22	23 Mail coaches intercepted; Neilson jailed	24 Prosperous; Clane; Dunlavin	25 Naas; Carlow; Ball Alley Massacre	26 The Harrow; Tara; Rathangan
	27 Oulart Hill; Knockallen surrender	28 Enniscorthy; Ferns; Camolin	29 Gibbet Rath Massacre	30 Wexford taken by rebels	31	1 Newtown-barry	2
June	3	4 Tubber-neering; Gorey	5 New Ross; Scullabogue Massacre	6 Larne; Randals-town; Ballymena	7 Antrim	8	9 Arklow; Napoleon takes Malta
	10 Pike Sunday	11	12 Ballina-hinch	13	14	15	16
	17	18	19 Carrick-byrne	20 Bandon, Clonakilty; Cornwallis arrives	21 Vinegar Hill; Wexford falls; Bandon	22	23
	24 Castle-comer	25	26 Kilcomney Hill	27	28	29	30 Ballyellis
July	1 Wexford leaders hanged	2 Ballyrahee	3	4 Coolgreany	5	6	7
	8	9	10 Perry et al reach Timahoe	11	12	13	14
	15	16	17 Cornwallis offers amnesty	18	19	20 Amnesty Act by Irish Parliament	21 Napoleon wins battle of the Pyramids
	22	23 Aylmer surrenders	24	25	26	27	28 Billy Byrne hanged
August	29	30	31	1	2 Nelson wins Battle of Nile	3	4
	5	6 Humbert sails for Ireland	7	8	9	10	11
	12	13	14	15	16	17	18

The Rising of 1798

	Sunday	Monday	Tuesday	Wednesday	Thursday	Friday	Saturday
August	19	20	21	22 Humbert lands at Killala	23	24	25
	26	27 Races of Castlebar	28	29	30	1	2
September	3	4 Tandy sails for Ireland	5	6 Granard	7	8 Ballinamuck	9
	10	11	12 2nd Castlebar	13	14 Tone sails for Ireland	15	16 Tandy lands in Donegal
	17	18	19	20	21	22 Killala	23
	24	25	26	27	28	29	30
October	1	2	3	4	5	6	7
	8	9	10	11	12 *Hoche* yields off Tory Island; Tone taken	13	14
	15	16	17	18	19	20	21
	22	23	24	25	26	27	28
	29	30	31	1	2 Prisoners landed from *Hoche*	3	4
November	5	6	7	8	9	10 Tone condemned	11
	12 Tone cuts own throat	13 Date set for Tone's execution	14	15	16	17	18
	19 Tone dies	20	21	22	23	24	25

Fitzgerald, outraged by the wild new suggestion at such a late date, was supported by Sam Neilson and Reverend Dickson in calling for immediate and outright rebellion. Ironically, the deciding vote may have been cast by Francis Magan (apparently unaware of the "Armstrong ploy," the government spy was still following orders to do all he could to precipitate premature rebellion). The result splintered the United leadership irreparably: the Sheares brothers resigned and an overwrought Lawless fled the country.

With John Sheares gone, Lord Edward assumed the former chairman's position as United commanding general. In that capacity, Fitzgerald issued orders for the rising: on 23 May Unitedmen from south Meath and north Kildare were to muster and take Kilcock; at the same time, the north Meath rebel units were to join Dublin insurgents at Dunboyne. These two groups were then to converge on the Dublin suburb of Finglas and invest the capital city. The signal for the rising was to be the halting of the mail-coaches leaving Dublin on that day. They were the last orders Fitzgerald ever issued.[9] Alerted by Magan, the authorities took the United leader the following day.

LORD EDWARD

On 19 May 1798 Lord Edward Fitzgerald was holed up in a house in Thomas Street, Dublin. Bothered by a minor ailment, he was in sickbed on the second floor when Henry Sirr, Town Major of Dublin Police, raided the house with ten men. Major Swann of the Revenue Corps (the same who had led the raid at Oliver Bond's) and Captain Ryan of the Sepulchre's quickly rushed the stairs and burst into Fitzgerald's room.

Swann fired errantly as the United Irishman leapt at him with a stiletto. The major stumbled down the stairs for help, mortally wounded by Lord Edward's frantic defense. Before Sirr could react, Ryan and Fitzgerald also came tumbling down the stairs locked in combat. Ryan, armed with an unwieldy sword-stick, was getting much the worst of it until Major Sirr disarmed the rebel with a single shot to the Unitedmen's right shoulder.

The injured Fitzgerald was lodged in Newgate Prison. His wound grew unexpectedly worse and he died of complications on 4 June. This ballad seems to have been written soon after Lord Edward's demise.

What plaintive sounds strike on my ear!
They're Erin's deep-toned piteous groans,
Her harp, attuned to sorrow drear,
In broken numbers joins her moans.
In doleful groups around her stand
Her manly sons (her greatest pride),
In mourning deep, for by the hand
Of ruthless villians Edward died.

The assassin horde had him beset,
As slumbering on a bed he lay,
"Arise, milord," Swann cries, "Up get,
My prisoner you I make this day!"
Unawed our gallant chief up steps,
And in his vengeful hand he takes
His dagger keen—quite hard it grips,
Then to the savage crew he speaks.

"Come on who dare—your courage show,
Gainst Erin's steady children's chief;
Your burdened soul at single blow,
I'll from your body soon relieve!"
Fear-stricken at his manly form,
The bloodstained tribe, save Swann, back drew,
Who from our chieftain's potent arm
Received a stroke that made him rue.

Aloud he shrieked, then Ryan came
Unto his aid with trembling steps;
Mean caitiff Ryan, lost to shame,
With deeds most foul was full your cup.
Like vivid lightning at him flew
With well-aimed point, our hero sweet
The dastard's blood he forthwith drew,
And left his bowels at his feet.

So wide the gash, so great the gore,
That tumbling out his entrails came;
Poor groveling wretch, you'll no more
Attempt to blast unsullied fame;
A baser death should you await,
The hangman's rope—not Edward's hand,

The gallows tree should be your fate,
Your life deserved a shameful end.

Next came on Sirr, half dead with fear,
Deep stained with crimes his guilty mind,
He shook all through, by Lord Edward scared
Like aspen leaf before the wind;
With coward feet he advanced slow,
Dreading to feel our Edward's might,
Though eager for to strike a blow,
Yet fearful to appear in sight.

Assassin-like he took his stand
Behind the door—and there he stood
With pistol charged in either hand
So great his thirst for Edward's blood;
Upon his brow stood imp of hell,
Within his heart a devil foul,
Dire murder, dire, and slaughter fell,
Had full possession of his soul.

His bosom friend suggested then
A bloody deed—a devil's act—
A hell-framed thought! . . . ARISE YE MEN!
Revenge, revenge the horrid fact!
Sound, sound aloud the trumpet of war,
Proclaim that Edward's blood is spilled!
By traitor's hand, by coward Sirr;
Revenge! Revenge! For Edward's killed!

Upon hearing of Lord Edward's capture, John and Henry Sheares decided to reassert their authority. Perhaps not aware that Fitzgerald had already issued marching orders to the provincial leaders, the brothers Sheares were stubbornly still persuaded that a military coup was the most promising strategy for success. It is uncertain how many rebel leaders they contacted about their reborn scheme. What is certain, however, is that they did contact the duplicitous Captain Armstrong.

John and Henry Sheares were arrested on 21 May. It was but two days before the risings were due to begin, and the United Irish high council had effectively ceased to exist.

THE BROTHERS

After Francis Magan had betrayed Fitzgerald, Sam Neilson and the brothers Sheares were the only members of the United high command still at large. When the brothers had foolishly contacted Armstrong to pursue their own fanciful strategy, it demonstrated that they had lost all touch with the rebels in the field. When the Sheares' were taken, the incipient insurgency was left without a "national" organisation.

The trial and execution of the two attorneys was particularly distressing to the Establishment; as highly regarded professionals from a distinguished family, the brothers lent the Unitedmen an aura of respectability. As such, too, they were to become distinctly attractive martyrs within the rebel pantheon. One of the Confederacy Clubs of the Young Ireland movement a half-century later, for instance, was named in their honour.[10]

Captain Armstrong, of course, has been assigned a far different niche in the rebel tradition. The nationalist usage has pegged the militiaman as that most notorious of Irish traitors, the informer. The officer in fact considered himself a loyal and patriotic Irishman who owed his allegiance to the popularly elected Irish Parliament. It was a position not unusual at the time. Some of the men who were used to spy on the Unitedmen were bribed or intimidated, certainly, but most, like Armstrong, judged their activities in much the same way that a modern agent might when going undercover to infiltrate a terrorist organisation.

Jane Francesca Elgee wrote this ballad during the Young Ireland era. The poetess was a frequent contributor to *The Nation* under the *nom de plume* "Speranza." Later Lady Wilde, and mother of the famous poet, she was in 1848 a young firebrand (in a year of European firebrands) who could rise from the gallery of a courtroom and publicly declare herself the writer of a seditious article.

Tis midnight; falls the lamplight dull and sickly
On a pale but anxious crowd,
Through the court and round the judges thronging thickly,
With prayers they dare not speak aloud.
Two youths, two noble youths, stand prisoner at the bar—
You can see them through the gloom—
In the pride of life and manhood's beauty there they are
Awaiting their death-doom.

Before them shrinking, cowering, scarcely human,
The base informer bends,
Who, Judas-like, could sell the blood of true men
While he clasped their hands as friends.
Ay, could fondle the young children of his victim,
Break bread with his young wife
At the moment that, for gold, his perjured dictum
Sold the husband's and the father's life.

There is silence in the midnight—eyes are keeping
Troubled watch, till forth the jury come;
There is silence in the midnight—eyes are weeping—
"Guilty!" is the fatal doom.
For a moment o'er the brothers' noble faces
Came a shadow sad to see,
Then silently they rose up in their places
And embraced each other fervently.

A hymn of joy is rising from creation;
Bright the azure of the glorious summer sky;
But human hearts weep sore in lamentation
For the brothers are led forth to die.
Ay, guard them with your cannon and your lances—
So of old come martyrs to the stake;
Ay, guard them—see the people's flashing glances
For those noble two are dying for their sake.

Yet none spring forth their bonds to sever—
Ah! Methinks, had I been there,
I'd have dared a thousand deaths ere ever
The sword should touch their hair.
It falls!—there is a shriek of lamentation
From the weeping crowd around;
They are stilled—the noblest hearts within the nation—
The noblest heads lie bleeding on the ground.

Years have passed since that fatal scene of dying,
Yet life-like to this day
In their coffins still those severed heads are lying,
Kept by angels free from decay.
O! They preach to us, those still and pallid features,
Those pale lips yet implore us from their graves,

To strive for our birthright as God's creatures
Or die, if we can but live as slaves.

The arrest of the United Irish high command was not enough to stop the rebellion; the orders Lord Edward Fitzgerald had posted to the provincial leaders before his capture insured that Leinster, at least, would be ready to muster. All that was needed now was the order to halt the mail-coaches.

PAT O'DONOGHUE

Many men were waiting for the signal to rise. A number, smarting from General Lake's repressive measures, had fled to the hills and bogs, hiding from the troopers until word came down from Dublin.

One such rebel was the hero of this song. As a blacksmith, the Meathman was an obvious target of Crown suspicion (the steel pikeheads atop the ash pikes being confiscated from the peasantry were obviously not of King's-issue). Apparently Pat O'Donoghue's surreptitious smithing had been noticed by an informer. When Lord Roden's yeomen arrived to confront the blacksmith, O'Donoghue narrowly escaped into the forest. Without a rising, men like O'Donoghue must have felt they had no future at all.

Young Pat, he was as brave a boy
As ever hammer swung,
And the finest hurler that you'd find
The lads of Meath among;
And when the wrestling match was o'er
No man could boast he'd threw
The young dark smith of Currogha,
Pádraig O'Donoghue.

But Ninety-Eight's dark season came
And Irish hearts were sore,
The pitch-cap, shears and triangle,
The patient folks outwore.
The blacksmith thought of Ireland
And found he'd work to do,

"I'll forge some steel for freedom,"
Said Pat O'Donoghue.

The yeos are in Dunshaughlin,
The Hessians in Dunreagh;
And spread through fair Moynalty
Were the Fencibles of Reagh.
While Roden's godless troopers
Ranged from Screen to Mullachoo,
When hammered were the pikeheads first
By Pat O'Donoghue.

And so in Currogha each night
Was heard the anvil's ring,
While scouting on the highway
Were Hugh and Phelim King.
With Gilly's Matt and Duffy's Pat
And Mickey Gilsenan too,
While in the forge for Ireland,
Worked young Pat O'Donoghue.

But a traitor crept among them
And the secret soon was sold
To the captain of the yeomen
For the ready Saxon gold;
And a troop burst out one evening
From the woods of dark Kilbue,
And soon a rebel prisoner bound
Was Pat O'Donoghue.

"Down on your knees, you rebel dog!"
The yeoman captain roared,
As high above his helmet's crest
He waved his gleaming sword.
"Down on your knees to meet your doom,
Such is the rebel's due!"
But straight as pike-shaft 'fore him
Stood bold O'Donoghue.

The captain gazed in wonder,
Then lowered his keen-edge blade,
"A rebel bold is this," he said,

"'Tis fitting to degrade.
Here, man!" he cried, "Unbind him,
My charger needs a shoe;
The King shall have a workman
In this Pat O'Donoghue!"

A leap! A roar! A smothered groan!
The captain drops the rein,
And sinks to earth with hammer-head
Sunk deeply in his brain;
And lightly in the saddle
Fast racing towards Kilbrue
Upon the captain's charger sits
Bold Pat O'Donoghue.

A volley from the pistols,
A rush of horses feet—
He's gone and none can capture
The captain's charger fleet;
And on the night wind backwards
Comes a mocking loud "Halloo!"
That tells the yeomen they have lost
Young Pat O'Donoghue.

By 22 May 1798 Sam Neilson was the only member of the United Irish National Directory not in the hands of the Castle. Though he had been the founder of the Society seven years earlier, he was no longer deemed a threat: the authorities now considered Neilson a harmless alcoholic. They were half right.

Screwing himself up for a day of unaccustomed sobriety, Neilson spent the daylight hours of 23 May in furious activity, insuring that the mustering rebel units got the word to stop the mail-coaches. Only then did he enter a familiar public house and drink himself into incoherence. The last member of the United Irish Executive was arrested outside Newgate Prison that night as he hurled imprecations at the warders inside.

CHAPTER NOTES (13)

1 — Although it is impossible to be certain, it is likely that Henry Sheares and MacCormack supported John Sheares' inclination to await the French landing. The votes of Sweetman, Bond, McCann, and William Murphy are unclear. Francis Magan, acting secretly for Dublin Castle, probably voted against the request (the Crown policy to incite premature rebellion had not yet become official).

2 — Jamie Hope, the Templepatrick weaver, among others of the northern Unitedmen, knew the truth of the matter: he had helped smuggle McKeever out of the country. The Derryman spent the rest of his life in America.

3 — Myles Byrne remembered that:

> "the cutting down of young ash trees for that purpose awoke great attention and caused great suspicion of the object in view."

4 — After O'Connor managed to win acquittal on 22 May by parading a stream of famous and respected character witnesses into the English courtroom, he was rearrested as he tried to enter Ireland and was charged all over again under "Irish Law." By that time, of course, the rebellion was underway.

5 — In this one raid, the Crown netted almost the entire Leinster Directory. Taken were Thomas Emmet (who had been released from prison just the previous summer); John McCann, Secretary to the National Directory; Henry Jackson, ironmonger and businessman; Hugh Jackson, brother to Henry; John Sweetman, brewer; John Chambers, Secretary to the Irish Whig Club; Dr. William MacNeven; and the host, Oliver Bond. The Unitedmen also lost three important provincial representatives: George Cumming of Kildare, Michael Ivor of Carlow, and Robert Graham of Wexford.

Thomas Reynolds' position as undercover operative for the Crown was to become dicey at times. On the eve of rebellion, he was arrested as a Unitedman in Athy near his Kildare home at Kilkea Castle. The local yeomanry were not impressed with his story—many Unitedmen claimed to be working secretly for the authorities when they were captured. Reynolds' escape from the hanging tree was a narrow one. Presumably the £500 he had received for the Bond raid made his discomfiture easier to bear.

6 — There is some sketchy evidence that Fitzgerald had been tipped off about the raid in time for him to avoid the trap but not early enough for Lord Edward to warn the others.

7 — In any case, the arrest of Arthur O'Connor seems to have put an end to the United Irish liason with the Defenders in Munster (O'Connor's brother Roger was a Defender leader near Cork).

8 — Abercrombie's predecessor, the Earl of Carhampton, had resigned in January because he disagreed with Camden's policy of dragooning to foment premature rebellion.

The conditions must have been indeed outrageous for Abercrombie to object. The Scot was after all no liberal himself: he was the officer who had instituted the "free quarters" of British troops upon the civilian population of Ireland, a policy much like the *coyne* and *livery* of the Irish that Elizabeth Tudor's ministers had found so babarous some two centuries earlier.

Abercrombie was later to die a hero, gallantly fighting the French in Egypt.

9 — There remains a question as to what Ulster heard from Fitzgerald. Lord Edward's authority to issue military orders for Unitedmen outside his own command of Leinster may have been questioned at the time by the northern rebel leaders.

10 — Another indication of the Sheares' "rebel sainthood" occurred twenty years after their death when it was discovered that their bodies had not mouldered in their crypt under St. Michan's Church, Dublin. Though the incident was not unique—the Church Street vaults are extremely dry-aired—it is of such stuff that rebel legends are made. See the last verse of Lady Wilde's ballad.

___

14

Explosion in Leinster

The Risings of '98 began in the counties surrounding Dublin. Before Lord Edward Fitzgerald had been taken by the authorities, he had issued orders for rebellion. As has been seen, the signal was to be the interception of the mail-coaches leaving Dublin on Wednesday, 23 May. By this ingenious strategem, suggested by Sam Neilson, the provinces would learn within the day that insurrection had begun. Since the military mail journeyed on the same coaches with the civilian post, the stopping of the mail would have the added benefit of denying last-minute communication from Dublin Castle to the provincial garrisons.

The key to all the United Irish plans was County Kildare. The United commander in the county was a landowner from Johnstown, Michael Reynolds.[1] He was seconded by four United colonels: William Alymer of Kilcock, Hugh Ware and George Luby of Maynooth, and Dr. John Esmonde, who also served as a lieutenant in the Sallins yeomanry. Reynolds began mustering his forces according to schedule on the afternoon of 23 May, stopping the Munster mail-coach that same evening. The Year of Rebellion had begun.

Rebel bands began springing up like mushrooms. A thousand men from south Meath and north County Dublin halted the Belfast coach at Santry, just north of Dublin City. Other groups gathered at Tallaght and Rathcook along the road to the South, at Rathangan on the Kildare/Kings County frontier, and at several points in County Meath. One assemblage of about one thousand converged at Rathfarnum and Dalkey to stop the southbound coach at dusk. Another insurgent band reported halting the Athlone mail at Lucan; the Limerick coach, meanwhile, had been stopped by still one more rebel group on the Curragh of Kildare.

Lord Camden's strategy had worked—the Unitedmen were

in premature rebellion. There was no master plan for insurrection, no leaders left to establish one, and no French troops with which the Crown had to contend. Edward Cooke, Under Secretary to the Viceroy, wrote as the risings broke out:

> I consider this insurrection . . . the salvation of the country. If you look at the accounts that 200,000 are sworn in a conspiracy, how could that conspiracy be cleared without a burst? Besides, it will prove many things necessary for the future settlement of the country when peace arises.

The United Irish leaders would later explain the rebellion in different terms altogether. Not aware that Camden was fully in favour of the insurrection, they gave their reasons for rising in terms of Crown perfidy. The gaoled Thomas Addis Emmet blamed:

> The free quarters, the house burnings, the tortures, and the military executions in the counties of Kildare, Carlow, and Wicklow.

Myles Byrne of Wicklow, eighteen years old at the time of rising, agreed:

> Self-preservation was the motive which drove me into rebellion. . . . As to effecting a change of government, it gave me little trouble or thought. . . . It was private wrongs and individual oppression . . . which gave the bloody and inveterate character to the rebellion in the county of Wicklow. . . . The poor people engaged . . . had very little idea of political government.

Whatever the reason, the peasants had pulled their pikes from the thatch and taken to the fields. The next day insurrection began in earnest.

At dawn on Thursday 24 May, Lieutenant John Esmonde literally turned his yeoman coat inside-out and, as Colonel Esmonde of the Unitedmen, attacked the cotton-producing centre of Prosperous with a force of about five hundred. Thirty-eight of the fifty-seven defending City of Cork Militia were killed brutally, including their commander, Lieutenant Swayne, infamous in the district for his torture of the peasantry. Simultaneously, a smaller rebel force attacked a garrison of seventy at the nearby town of Clane. Richard Griffith's Crown troops easily repulsed the first onslaught on the village, but when the rebels were joined by reinforcements from Prosperous, the second assault was barely beaten off. Griffith decided to retreat upon Naas. When he did, the astonishing Dr. Esmonde was back in his accustomed position on the right flank as Lieutenant John Esmonde of the Sallins Yeomanry. Philip Mite—a yeo who

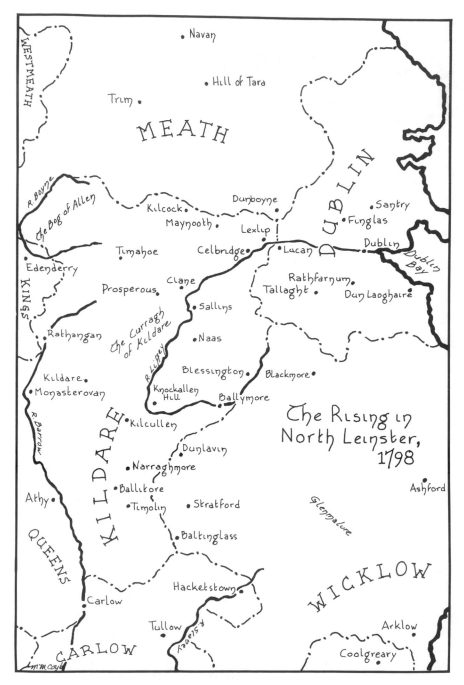

had deserted with the good doctor and helped him plan the attack on Prosperous—had also returned. Unfortunately for the coat-turning physician, Mite's bravado was not as complete as Esmonde's. The doctor-turned-rebel commander-turned-yeoman was later hanged at Prosperous.

When Griffith reached Naas, he found that he was not the only one who had been swamped by the rebels. Major General Lord Gosford and the Kildare garrison had also been forced to retreat to Naas, leaving the town to an army of two thousand insurgents under Roger McGarry. After securing the county town, McGarry's rabble-in-arms ambled west towards Monasterevin. Lieutenant General Ralph Dundas, commander of the military district, was himself in trouble at Kilcullen. His sixty men under Captain Erskine found themselves invested by a force of three hundred under a rebel leader named Perkins. Rallying at Kilcullen Bridge with reinforcements that brought his force up to 140, Dundas sent Erskine with a detachment of forty horse to charge the rebel band—which had doubled in the interim. The captain and twenty-two of his horsemen fell in the gallant charge, but the insurgents fled. The general hurriedly retreated north to join his lieutenants in Naas.

Further south in County Kildare, Ballitore and Narraghmore had fallen to the Unitedmen, while at Rathangan to the west, the militia hurriedly left defense of the town to the local yeomanry. In County Wicklow, however, the Crown backbone remained firm. Captain Beevor's Ballymore garrison gallantly withstood a rebel thrust of uncommon intensity; similarly, insurgent attacks were repulsed at Dunlavin, Stratford, and Baltinglass.

Naas had become the tenuous British eye in the swirling United Irish storm. The cut-off Crown forces desperately tried to gather intelligence from "croppy" prisoners, who were usually as ignorant of the military situation as their captors. The loyalist troops felt themselves stranded in the middle of what seemed to be general rebellion. It is not surprising that they treated their unfortunate prisoners to summary justice.

THE WEARING OF THE GREEN

Green has become, of course, the traditional colour of Ireland. Americans and others who are careful to wear it on 17 March as a badge of their heritage—real or imagined—are often surprised to learn that the wearing of the green was a capital offense in 1798. That the lyrics of the following ballad are not exaggerated may be verified by the number of men killed in that Irish year of rebellion for the mere act of wearing the Green Cockade. A 24 May dispatch to General Lake from Naas, for instance, reported that "more were brought in . . . together with three men with green cockades, all of whom were hanged in the public street."

The United Irishmen had adopted the colour from the French Tree of Liberty. By this time a sprig of green in the old battered hat of a cottier demonstrated defiance of the Crown. "Peasant girls had often thrown themselves enthusiastically into the United Irish movement," Lecky reports, "and attested their sentiments by their green ribbons." Outrages on the green-beribboned lasses by the rampaging soldiery had become legion. The bitterness resulting from such conduct can only be imagined.

The eloquent irony of this ballad masks the fact that it was born on the streets; that it survived is mute testimony to an unknown Belfast musician whose stinging lyrics caught the public imagination. "This little song," Frank O'Connor has commented, "written in pseudo-Irish dialect, probably by an Ulster Presbyterian and set to what seems to be an adaptation of a Scottish *pibroch* is our real national anthem."

The version of that pipe-song given here was rewritten for Dion Boucicault's play *Arrah na Pogue.* It is the one most often heard today.

Oh Paddy dear, and did you hear the news that going round?
The shamrock is forbid by law to grow on Irish ground;
St. Patrick's Day no more we'll keep, his colour can't be seen,
For there's a cruel law agin the wearin o the Green.

I met with Napper Tandy and he took me by the hand,
And said he, "How's poor Ireland, and how does she stand?"
"She's the most distressful country that ever yet was seen;
They're hanging men and women there for wearin o the Green!"

And if the colour we must wear is England's cruel Red,
Twill serve but to remind us of the blood that she has shed;
Then pull the shamrock from your hat and cast it in the sod,
But never fear, twill take root there, tho underfoot tis trod.

When laws can stop the blades o grass from growing as they grow,
And when the leaves in summertime their colours dare not show,
Then I will change the colour I wear in my *caubeen;*
But till that day, please God, I'll stick to wearin o the Green.

The major fighting in the midlands took place on 25 May. At dawn, an insurgent force over a thousand strong crept into the sleeping town of Carlow. Led by Michael Heydon—chief United organiser for the county since Michael Ivor's arrest in the March raid at Oliver Bond's—this rebel throng walked right into a trap. Colonel Mahon's concealed Ninth Dragoons ambushed the rebels in the centre of the town. The carnage among the insurgents was so great that the authorities were forced to dig a huge common grave. The "Croppy's Hole" was the end of rebellion for 649 Unitedmen. Heydon himself was hanged in the town diamond on the following day. The resiliance of the beaten rebels was, however, remarkable; later on the 25th, the remnants of the Carlow force joined a Wicklow band to attack Hacketstown fifteen miles to the cast.

Two other major rebel attacks marked that Friday. Roger McGarry's army from Kildare was repulsed after a bloody encounter at Monasterevin. General Michael Reynolds, meanwhile, led his Unitedmen in an attack on Naas itself. After desperate fighting, the superior firepower of the Crown prevailed. The rebels were thrown back, leaving three hundred dead at a cost to the British of twenty-two. The discouraged Reynolds fled to the Wicklow Mountains, leaving William Aylmer as the senior surviving rebel officer.

In addition to the three major attacks, there were three smaller actions on 25 May. Remnants of the insurgent band that had intercepted the southbound mail at Rathfarnum—and been dispersed near Clondalkin the next morning—had joined the group that had stopped the Belfast coach. This combined force made a desultory attack on Kilcock at dawn. Repulsed, the rebels followed with raids on Leixlip and Lucan later in the day, neither of which was driven home. After these abortive offensive efforts, most of this rabble drifted into the insurgent camp at Dunboyne, joining the rebels there in a march to the main Meath United camp at Tara.

PROSPEROUS

The Battle of Prosperous is fondly remembered by the rebel tradition as the one ringing 1798 victory-at-arms by the mid-Leinster Unitedmen. It was actually an attack on a sleeping and unprepared soldiery who were outnumbered by more than five-to-one.

A chronological ballad, *Prosperous* tells the story of the 24 May attack and that of the battle at Naas the following day. Too, it relates the curious tale of the extraordinary John Esmonde (the "colonel" of the song). John Devoy, the famous Fenian, claimed that this was still the favourite '98 ballad in County Kildare some fifty years after the rebellion.

On the twenty-fourth of May, at the dawning of the day,
Our lads went under arms, Prosperous to invade;
With heart in hand we marched under Captain Farrell's orders,
Twas in the town we halted and set it in a blaze.

There were red-hot balls a-flying, the groans of soldiers dying,
Flames in the air were frying, and Swayne expiring there;[2]
To retreat our colonel gave orders, but we never faltered,
Until wounded, killed and slaughtered, we won the battle there.

Next morning Naas was tattered and all our brethren slaughtered,
Many our valiant hero lay bleeding on the green;
Our colonel he forsook us and cursed Griffith took him,
He immediately was detected and hurled into Naas jail.

Phil Mite, the cruel informer, he robbed us of our "jewel,"
May heaven's high vengeance upon him pour down,
God and his holy angels, forever may they hate him,
May he be afflicted with the heavenly frown.

The boys we have forsaken, Kilcock Town have taken,
Leixlip, Lucan and Maynooth, with all its cavalry;
And home we then returned, Sparke's house then we burned,
To pay him back for Kennedy that died on the gallows tree.

Yet Colonel Aylmer bold had a valiant heart of gold,
He never was controlled, but fought on manfully;
He was general-in-chief and brought many foes to grief,
Maintaining Erin's rights and Her sweet liberty.

The bloody adulterous crew, they thought us to subdue,
But well we made them rue the day they did begin
Whipping and destroying; but Hibernia's brave boys
Soon they let them know we were brave Unitedmen.

If the West had took the dare like Wexford and Kildare,
The Green would fly on high through town and counterie;
To conclude and make an end, drink the health of Unitedmen,
May they live forever free and reign over bloody tyranny.

On the morning of 26 May part of Roger McGarry's band linked up with a marauding United Irish group from Kings County. This combined force swarmed into Rathangan, easily overrunning the yeomanry and nabbing their commander, a local land-agent named Thomas Spencer. The rebels promptly strung up the unfortunate yeo officer. The Saturday hanging proved to be the high water mark of the midland insurgency.

At the time Spencer was lynched,[3] the Unitedmen controlled County Kildare from just outside Kilcock in the North to Ballitore in the South, from Ballymore in the East to Spencer's scaffold in the West. Naas was beseiged, and even the Wicklow garrisons were outflanked by a rebel camp at Blackmore on the Dublin/Wicklow frontier. General Dundas, by now understandably convinced that the rebellion was countrywide, had no thought of offense—he was primarily concerned with strengthening his defenses and attempting to reopen his communications with Dublin.[4] Further north, most of County Meath had been overrun by the insurgents without serious quarrel from the Crown. The small garrison towns on the Dublin-Athlone road appeared to be hanging on between a potential pincers. There were fully thirty thousand armed Unitedmen roaming freely through the midlands. Presumably, this was not quite what Lord Camden had in mind when he had decided to foment premature rebellion.

The scenario began to change quickly—on the afternoon of 26 May the rebels were to get their first taste of British artillery. The United Irishmen of Meath had established their major camp on the Hill of Tara. Less active than their comrades-in-arms in Kildare, the Meathmen had few guns and little ammunition; there were, however, over eight thousand pikemen gathered around the *Lia Fáil* of the ancient Irish kings. A detachment of the Reay Fencibles commanded by Captains McLean and

Blanche, joined by a small yeoman unit under Lord Fingall (a former member of the General Committee of the Catholic Association), advanced on the Tara insurgent camp at midday Saturday. The Crown mission, numbering only four hundred men, seemed hopelessly quixotic at first blush. It was anything but . . . the Fencibles had a six-pound cannon. Unlimbering the gun as soon as it was in range, the British forces found quickly that the disorganised rebel leadership had no idea how to defend against it. It apparently never occurred to the terrified rebel captains to charge the gun. As the cannon took its toll, the insurgents began to melt away. When Blanche and McLean finally assailed the hill, the remaining rebels fled in bewilderment. The Unitedmen had lost three hundred killed, the yeomen and Fencibles, nine. The rebellion in County Meath was effectively over.

MICHAEL BOYLAN

After the rout at Tara, the beaten Meathmen scattered. During the next several months, Crown detachments roamed the countryside rounding up suspected Unitedmen. The authorities promised pardon to the underlings in return for information about the leaders. As might be expected under such circumstances, many of the frightened internees named anyone available to save their own necks.

This contemporary street ballad tells the story of one such "lieutenant" executed by the Crown.

Come all ye worthy members, your attention now I pray,
It's well you may remember these words I'm going to say;
I'm here in close confinement, no hopes of liberty,
Condemned to die for treason against His Majesty.

In Gullen I was taken, being on the third of June,
To Drogheda they conveyed me, where I received my doom;
I was in expectation that the bench would set me free
Till I received my sentence by Dan Kelly's perjury.

The day my trial came on my verdict first came clear,
Those Saxon prosecutors to me they proved severe;
Tom Harvey acted as a friend, he favoured me that day,
Till in came bought Dan Kelly and swore my life away.

He swore I had ten thousand men all at my own command,
To assist the French invaders as soon as they would land;
He swore I was a Committeeman for Lord Edward's lovely cause,
And the jury cried, "Mick Boylan, you must die by Saxon laws.

I owned I was United bold, and that I'll always be,
And many's the time I roved in spite of the yeomanry;
If I would a Fingall prove, I'd gaine my liberty,
But before I'd an informer prove I'll die on the gallows tree.

The rebel leaders in the field were perplexed. By 27 May they had been at arms for four days and there had been no word from either the Leinster Directory or the Dublin high command. The glib assurances that the yeomanry and militia would desert *en masse* in support of the Unitedmen had not come true. Finally, and perhaps most telling to rebel morale, there was no word about the overdue French.[5]

The individual leaders of the isolated rebel "armies" in Kildare had no way to know how successful the rebellion actually was; there was not only no co-ordination of movement among the various insurgent units, there was no real communication at all (nor, apparently, any provision for it). In truth, the insurrection had really been a series of isolated risings in which the individual rebel groups acted on the whims of their local captains. As far as one of the rebel leaders—Perkins—was concerned, he had been collecting volunteers for four days to no purpose. After the initial actions around Kilcullen, Perkins had set up camp on the nearby Knockallen Hill; since then, his force had grown from six hundred to over three thousand. The rebel captain had no idea what to do with them. For all the United commander knew, he was quite alone and surrounded by hostile loyalist forces. The puzzled Perkins decided finally to open negotiations with General Dundas, offering to surrender his men and their arms for free parole. The Englishman, cut off from his Dunlavin and Ballymore garrisons by the Knockallen camp (and outnumbered by Perkins three-to-one), understandably jumped at the offer. The Knockallen rebels were the last allowed to surrender peaceably under such terms.

When six thousand insurgents at Gibbet Rath on the Curragh agreed to disperse for similar terms, they were set upon by a militia force under Major General Sir James Duff. Between 200-

300 were massacred (according to Duff's dispatch to Dublin Castle) after they had stacked their arms. Duff had force-marched his six hundred men the seventy miles from Limerick to the relief of Kildare in forty-eight hours. After ousting the rebels from the county town, Duff had hurried his tired militia further eastward. Unknowingly, the militiamen had stormed right into the middle of the trucc procedures. The site is still known as the "Place of Slaughter."

Duff's was not the only counterattack from the west. A militia force from Tullamore had marched eastward through the Bog of Allen and attacked the insurgents at Rathangan. Thrown back initially, the Kings County soldiers were reinforced by Cork militia with artillery and forced the rebels from the town.

CAPTAIN DOORLEY AND THE BOYNE

Captain Doorley was the local commander of the United Irishmen for Rathangan. He seems to have mustered his men on 23 May, marching them to the Naas area to take part in the bloody interception of the mail-coach there. Were this ballad to be taken literally, Doorley would have had to have been present at every subsequent important encounter between the Crown and the Unitedmen in Kildare, Wicklow, and Wexford. More likely, of course, is that an anonymous street balladeer used Doorley's name as a vehicle to sing of all the battles.

We do know that the United captain was with Aylmer's insurgent army for some time. Since Doorley was finally hanged at Mullingar, it is likely that he left Aylmer's Timahoe camp some time before the United general's troops were given parole on 23 July.

Included here are nine verses dealing with Doorley's part in the Kildare campaign and his flight from vengeful Crown forces after the rebellion was broken. Variations of the ballad—including Doorley's alleged adventures in the southern counties—run to well over twenty verses.

Come all you true born Irishmen that love your liberty,
I hope you'll pay attention and listen unto me;
I was young and innocent when I dwelt in Lallymore,
Till I became the captain in the bold United corps.

My father is a farmer, a man of wealth and fame,
He reared me up quite tender till the captain I became;
I headed the Defenders from every neighboring town,
We're famous from here to Dublin and all the country round.

It's off to Naas we trampled on May the Twenty-Two,
To take the Dublin mail-coach all from an Orange crew;
We boldly strode up to the door and broke it with a sledge,
In Hamilton I lodged a ball, Packenham got my edge.

Prosperous Town we then did take, and Kilcock and holy Maynooth,
Our horse and foot came dashing on with our bold, undaunted youth;
We put the barn all to the torch, and to rout we put them all,
We searched for Colonel Saunders but he wasn't there at all.

Next to the town we did encamp and some time waited there,
Sparke's house we did break down so my men could get their share;
We slashed them down like reapers, their bodies could be seen,
Where Erskine and his troopers lay on Kilcullen green.

To Timahoe we then did go with five hundred men or more,
We battered all their cavalry, upwards of five score;
Sparing neither front nor rear, we left their forces weak,
We shot ten rounds from every man, the very earth did shake.

Then on to home we did return in honour and great fame,
To my surprise, when I came there, the yeos upon me came;
With horse and foot came thundering down, the battle-shout did sound,
"We're in search of Captain Doorley of sweet Rathangan Town!"

The yeos they did pursue me, they chased me to the Boyne,
To my chin up in the water (for that was my design);
For hours I lay bleeding with old Ireland on my mind,
For I'd made them well remember Captain Doorley at the Boyne.

I was born and bred in Kildare in a place that's dear to me,
I'm sure to be remembered in Irish history;
If those men had stood round me to the last degree,
They never would have taken me till I set old Ireland free.

By the beginning of June 1798 the rebellion in the midlands

had begun to assume a bizarre plural personality. Aylmer, Luby, and Ware controlled the entire Bog of Allen north of Prosperous and, from a camp at Blessington, held sway over a swath across the middle of County Kildare. Marauding Crown forces ran amok over the rest of the area, running down defenceless peasants for real or fancied United Irish activity. There was only sporadic skirmishing between the rebels and the government troops for the next month. The British were forced to be content with Aylmer's occasional forays: unexpected events forty miles to the south were to make it impossible to reinforce the Kildare garrisons for some time.

CHAPTER NOTES (14)

1 — Reynolds had held the position only a short time. The designated leader for County Kildare, George Cumming, had been one of the provincial leaders captured with the Leinster Directory at Bond's in March. The other projected Kildare commander had been Reynolds' namesake, Thomas of Kilkea Castle, by now well known as a Crown informer.

2 — Lieutenant Swayne perished, along with a score of his men, when the rebels set fire to the building in which his detachment was sleeping. As the terrified troops fled the building to escape the flames, the Unitedmen cut them down one-by-one.

3 — The word "lynch" dates back to the late fifteenth century in Ireland. Set in the wall of the Old Gaol in Galway is a black marble inscription dated 1624. Accompanied by a skull and cross-bones, the story tells itself:

> "This memorial of the stern and unbending justice of the chief magistrate of this City, James Lynch FitzStephan, elected mayor A.D. 1493, who condemned and executed his own guilty son, Walter, on this spot."

4 — Even the Viceroy had no idea how widespread the rebellion was in its early days. On 25 May Lord Camden reported that all communication with the South had been cut off.

5 — The Unitedmen who "were out" were largely under the impression that rising

orders would not have been issued unless the "French were on the sea." The orders had been issued, after all, *after* the arrest of Fitzgerald and the Sheareses. It is not surprising that the average United Irishman in the countryside assumed that a National Directory was still functioning.

In truth, had the United leadership been determined on unilateral action, it would have made little sense to wait until May when the peasants were in the fields. In February, before free quarters or martial law had been extended to the midlands, and before the Leinster leadership had been disrupted by the raid at Oliver Bond's, Lord Fitzgerald had calculated the number of armed Irishmen at 279,896. The estimate, though perhaps fanciful, demonstrates by the very exactitude of the number that there was reasonable organisation during the winter of 1797-98.

The Boys of Wexford

The major surprise of 1798 was rebellion in Wexford. Never considered a hotbed of United Irish activity, the county had been essentially written off by the United Directory and, therefore, by the authorities. The only regular troops in the area were at the fort of Duncannon, guarding the east side of Waterford Harbour, and at New Ross, twelve miles north at the junction of the Rivers Nore and Barrow. On the eve of the Wexford rising, the Crown had small militia garrisons in Enniscorthy, Gorey, Newtownbarry (modern Bunclody), the town of Wexford, and just across the Wicklow border at Arklow. The major Crown presence in County Wexford was the yeomanry.

Shortly before the Appointed Day, Dublin Castle discovered papers signed by Lord Edward Fitzgerald indicating that the town of Wexford could be used as a contingency landing site by the French. The authorities reacted with dispatch. The local yeoman companies were quickly supplemented by the North Cork Militia, and a savage search for weapons and Unitedmen was initiated. Half-hanging, the flogging triangle, and the "pitched-cap torture" were used indiscriminately on the bewildered peasantry.[1]

The peasants of Wexford, unlike the intellectual United Irish leaders, had no real knowledge of the goals of the French Revolution. They were perhaps insufficiently sophisticated to be stirred by such ideals as *Liberté, Égalité, Fraternité*, but they had no trouble choosing a side. Some began to cut their hair short in the style of the French *citizen* who had so effectively destroyed the *ancien régime*. This vague sign of sympathy with the French Revolution was considered more than a small sign of defiance by the yeomanry and militia; it was a sure sign of treason. The Protestants took to using the term "croppy" as a general denigrating description of the Catholic peasant.[2]

CROPPIES LIE DOWN

This song was a favourite of the yeomanry and militia at the time of the '98 risings. Still sung today with much gusto by the Orangemen of the North, it apparently was written by a Captain Ryan of the notorious North Cork Militia. The militia officer was stationed in County Wexford just before rebellion broke out; the lyrics of the ballad give us more than a hint of how Ryan must have treated the croppies.

There are scores of verses to the song; new ones show up regularly in Ulster to commemorate Orange successes over Catholics. Included here are five of over twenty sung in 1798.

We soldiers of Erin, so proud of the name,
Will raise upon rebels and Frenchmen our fame;
We'll fight to the last in the honest old cause
And guard our religion, our freedom and laws;
We'll fight for our country, our king and his crown,
And make all the traitors and croppies lie down.
Down, down, croppies lie down. . .

The rebels so bold—when they've none to oppose—
To houses and hay-stacks are terrible foes;
They murder poor parsons and also their wives,
But soldiers at once make them run for their lives;
And wherever we march, through country or town,
In ditches or cellars the croppies lie down.
And it's down, down, croppies lie down. . .

In Dublin the traitors were ready to rise,
And murder was seen in their lowering eyes,
With poison, the cowards, they aimed to succeed,
And thousands were doomed by the assasins to bleed;
But the Yeomen advanced, of rebels the dread,
And each croppy soon hid his dastardly head.
Down, down, croppies lie down. . .

Oh, croppies ye'd better be quiet and still,
Ye shan't have your liberty, do what ye will;
As long as salt water is formed in the deep,
Our foot on the neck of the croppy we'll keep.
Remember the steel of Sir Phelim O'Neill

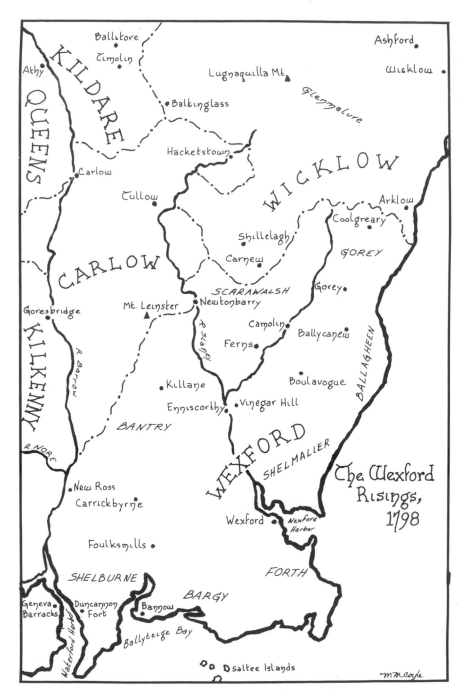

The Wexford Risings, 1798

Who slaughtered our fathers in Catholic zeal,
And down, down, croppies lie down. . .

When war and when dangers again shall be o'er
And peace with her blessings revisit our shore,
When arms we relinquish, no longer to roam,
With pride will our families welcome us home;
And drink, as in bumpers past troubles we drown,
A health to the lads that made croppies lie down.
Down, down, croppies lie down.

On the evening of 25 May, stories began to circulate through Wexford of twenty-eight prisoners executed in the Ball Alley at Carnew that morning, and of the shooting of others at Dunlavin. In the manner of the countryside, the tales were magnified in the retelling. The terrified peasants, reeling from the sudden campaign of depredation, were easily persuaded that murder had become official Crown policy; they had already taken to sleeping in the fields to avoid the night raids of the soldiers. The popular accounts of the incidents at Carnew and Dunlavin may have been exaggerated, but the reality was terrible enough.

DUNLAVIN GREEN

On Tuesday 22 May, Captain Saunders, commander of the Saunders-Grove corps of Wicklow yeomanry, had been advised of United Irish sentiment among his troops. Assembling his command in parade, he had announced his knowledge. After telling the men of the Monday capture of the brothers Sheares, and reminding his yeos that Lord Fitzgerald had been taken the previous Saturday, he had ordered the "misguided" nationalists to step forward.

Believing that their captain had been given their names, and presumably persuaded that the United cause was hopeless without its leadership anyway, about a score had decided to accept Saunder's promised parole. The men had been immediately slapped in irons and conveyed to the garrison at Dunlavin. After the insurgent attack on that town had been beaten off on the Thursday morning, the prisoners were summarily executed in reprisal.[3]

In the year of One Thousand Seven Hundred and Ninety-Eight,
A sorrowful tale the truth to you I'll relate,
Of thirty-six heroes to the world were left to be seen,
By false information were shot down on Dunlavin Green.

Bad luck to you Saunders, for you did their lives betray;
You said a parade would be held on that very day,
Our drums they did rattle—our fifes they did sweetly play;
Surrounded we were, and privately marched away.

Quite easy they led us as prisoners through the town,
To be slaughtered on the plain, we were then forced to kneel down;
Such grief and such sorrow were never before there seen,
When the blood ran in streams down the dykes of Dunlavin Green.

There is young Matty Farrell has plenty of cause to complain,
Also the two Duffys who were shot down on the plain;
And young Andy Ryan, his mother distracted will run
For her own brave boy, her beloved eldest son.

Bad luck to you Saunders, bad luck may you never shun,
That the widow's curse may melt you like the snow in the sun,
The cries of the orphans whose murmers you cannot screen,
For the murder of their dear fathers on Dunlavin Green.

Some of our boys to the hills they were going away,
Some of them are shot and some of them going to sea;
Micky Dwyer in the mountains, to Saunders he owes a spleen
For his loyal brothers who were shot on Dunlavin Green.

  The peasantry of County Wexford was becoming desperate. The yeomanry and militia were now in the business of teaching object lessons; guilt and innocence had long ceased to be criteria for Crown savagery. The shootings at Carnew and Dunlavin had convinced the people that the authorities were giving no quarter. The continued excesses of the troops were pushing the frightened peasants—increasingly of the opinion they had nothing left to lose—right into the laps of the insurrectionists. On the evening of 26 May, hard news of the Kildare risings reached the Wexford barony of Gorey. It was the spark needed to ignite resistance.
  Father John Murphy, curate of the parish of Kilcormuck

(serving the tiny villages of Monageer and Boulavogue), had been among the voices urging the peasants to turn in their weapons to avoid reprisal.[4] Apparently recognising the futility of the policy by this Saturday night, he had joined a number of his parishoners in the fields to avoid the midnight raids of the yeos. The frightened farmers were near The Harrow, a small country town, when they were accosted by a detachment of the Camolin Yeoman Cavalry under Lieutenants Thomas Bookey and John Donovan. The Goreymen piked Bookey and scattered the horsemen.[5] The rebellion in Wexford was on.

In reprisal for the lieutenant's death, the yeomanry sacked the entire district that night. Before Sunday dawn, they had burned down Murphy's chapel, 170 farmhouses, and had slaughtered a number of families taking shelter on the nearby Killthomas Hill. The butchery backfired; the homeless peasants flocked to the croppy priest's camp at Oulart Hill. Two deserters from the yeomanry, Sergeant Edward Roche and Morgan Byrne, were made officers and began to organise the stream of volunteers.

THE WIND THAT SHAKES THE BARLEY

A song that falls very definitely into the category of *caoine,* this ballad serves as both a love song and, more subtly, as a rebel song. The singer's quandry is the timeless one of Irish resistance: how to leave all he holds dear to march out and sacrifice his life for what probably is a hopeless Cause. In this case, the singer's problem is solved by a British bullet, and another young man sets off to join the Boys of Wexford at Oulart Hill.

The lyrics to this beautiful lament were written by Robert Dwyer Joyce, professor of English Literature at Dublin's Catholic University in the nineteenth century. Himself a rebel, Dr. Joyce was forced to flee to America due to his Fenian activities. After a successful career publishing Irish songs and ballads in the United States, he returned to Dublin to die in 1883.

I sat within the valley green,
I sat with my true love,
My sad heart strove to choose between
The old love and the new.

The old for her, the new that made me
Think of Ireland dearly;
While soft the wind blew down the glen,
And shook the golden barley.

How hard the bitter words to frame
To break the ties that bound us,
But harder still to bear the shame
Of foreign chains around us.

And so I said, the mountain glen
I'll seek at morning early;
And join the brave Unitedmen,
While soft winds shake the barley.

How sad I kissed away her tears,
Her soft arms round me clinging;
When suddenly the foemen shot
From out the wild woods ringing.

The bullet pierced my true love's side,
In life's young spring so early,
And on my breast in blood she died,
While soft winds shock the barley.

But blood for blood without remorse
I'll take at Oulart Hollow;
And I have lain her grey cold corse
Where I full soon must follow.

As round her grave I wandered drear,
Noon, night and morning early;
With breaking heart whene'er I hear
The winds that shake the barley.

Upon hearing news of the mid-Wexford rising, Colonel Foote and Major Lombard marched north from the town of Wexford with 110 men of the North Cork Militia, hoping to put down the insurgency before it got unmanageable. Foote was overoptimistic. When he reached Oulart Hill, he was too late. Murphy, Roche, and Byrne had already mustered about a thousand men on the prominence. The colonel wisely decided to settle in and wait for reinforcement. Unbeknownst to Foote, the ambitious Lombard—convinced that mere croppies would not stand against fully armed troops—gathered the militiamen and led them in a brash charge on the rebel position. It was an unqualified disaster. Colonel Foote stumbled back to Wexford with only three men for company.

The effect of the battle on the countryside was electric. The news of the 27 May battle spread swiftly all over the South of Ireland. Murphy had given the Wexford Irish what every successful rebellion needs—an early victory. Volunteers swarmed to join the rebel priest's insurgency. Father Murphy moved his burgeoning force five miles north to the Carrigrew Hill near Camolin, establishing a permanent camp that same Sunday night.

IRISH SOLDIER LADDIE

Some songwriters have the ability to create songs that can be applied to almost any "rebel era" with equal ease. Paddy McGuigan is such a writer. Having "paid his rebel dues" with a sojourn of internment on *HMS Maidstone,* he has fired off a barrage of rebel songs that are widely sung. This rousing, though perhaps not historically accurate, modern example is representative of the heady feeling in the South after the Oulart Hill fight in 1798. A few word changes, however, and we could place this Irish Soldier Laddie at the side of Patrick Sarsfield or Pádraig Pearse . . . or Seán MacStiofáin.

Twas morning in July, I was walking in Tipperary
When I heard a battle-cry from the mountains overhead;
I looked up to the sky and saw an Irish soldier laddie,
He looked at me quite fearlessly and said:

First Refrain:
"Will you stand by the band like a true Irishman
And go and fight the forces of the Crown?
Will you march with O'Neill to an Irish battlefield?
Oh, tonight we're going to free old Wexford Town!"

Said I to that soldier boy, "Would you take me to your captain?
It would be my pride and joy for to march with you today;

My young brother fell at Cork, and my son at Enniscorthy!"
And to the noble captain I did say:

Second Refrain:
"I will stand in the band like a true Irishman
And go and fight the forces of the Crown;
I will march with O'Neill to an Irish battlefield
Oh, tonight we're going to free old Wexford Town!"

As we marched back from the field in the shadow of the evening,
With our banners flying low to the memory of the dead,
We returned onto our homes, but without my soldier laddie,
Yet I never will forget those words he said:

First Refrain

On 28 May, the day after Oulart Hill, Father Murphy's growing army marched on nearby Camolin, finding about seven hundred muskets left behind in the wake of the yeomanry's hurried withdrawal. The rebels stayed on the heels of the yeoman cavalry as the horsemen retreated first to Ferns, and then to Enniscorthy. When the rag-tag insurgent army appeared before Enniscorthy early that Monday afternoon, it had grown to nine thousand men. The defenders under Captain Snowe numbered barely four hundred, including one hundred loyalist civilians. Recalling tactics used by their forebears six centuries earlier—probably storied in song—the rebels drove a herd of cattle before them as they attacked the town, creating great confusion. The Crown forces fled to Wexford over ten miles away after a gallant but brief defense. Murphy's rabble, after overrunning the town, set up a major camp on the nearby prominence of Vinegar Hill.[6] From this base by the River Slaney, the martial priest marched south towards the town of Wexford itself.

The insurgency continued to grow rapidly. Even though Murphy had left several thousand men behind at Vinegar Hill, by the time the rebel army set up a new camp at Three Rocks on the high ground west of Wexford on the night of 29 May, he had a force of about fifteen thousand. The loyal forces defending the town numbered about one thousand under the command of Colonel Maxwell, just arrived that morning from Duncannon Fort with two hundred Donegal militiamen to relieve Lieutenant

Colonel Watson.

General Fawcett, commanding at Duncannon, had meanwhile dispatched a major column for the relief of Wexford. Its spearhead, eighty-eight Meath militiamen under Captain Adams, marched their eighteen badly needed field guns unawares right by Three Rocks. The detachment was quickly annihilated. Watson, unaware of the action, sallied forth from Wexford to escort the relieving column, and was killed as his command was scattered. The main Duncannon force, now becoming painfully aware of the size of the insurrection, turned back.

Colonel Maxwell's military position at Wexford was untenable; outnumbered fifteen-to-one amidst a hostile population, he decided to abandon the town. Under the screen of negotiation with Murphy's forces, Maxwell managed to get his entire garrison safely away on the Duncannon road. The insurgents promptly entered the city.

Three prominent United Irishmen had been guests of the Crown gaoler in Wexford: Beauchamp Bagenal Harvey of Bargy Castle, Edward Fitzgerald of New Park, and Dr. John Henry Colclough of Ballyteigue. The bewildered Harvey, a Protestant squire who had been important in the United Irish Society earlier in the decade when it had been a legal debating society, was made Commander-in-Chief of the rebellion by the triumphant rebels. Fitzgerald and Colclough were made colonels. Captain Matthew Keough, a Protestant "half-pay" officer in the British Army, was made military governor of the town.

The rebel capture of Wexford on 30 May gave the insurgency control of the entire county of Wexford south of Gorey. With the Protestant United Irishmen in nominal command, the rebellion now had the appearance of organisation; it at least looked to be more than a simple rising of the Catholic peasantry.

BOULAVOGUE

The words of this late nineteenth century ballad by Patrick Joseph McCall are based on an earlier song dating from the '98 rising itself. Typical of the "chronological ballad" that tells the tale of an entire campaign, it sings the legend of Father John Murphy from the first skirmish near The Harrow to the priest's death at Tullow.

Of all the rebel songs, *Boulavogue* is perhaps the most

vocally demanding. This, rather than the ubiquitous *Danny Boy,*
is the ultimate in "Irish tenor ballads."

At Boulavogue, as the sun was setting
O'er soft May meadows of Shelmalier,
A rebel hand set the heather blazing
And brought the neighbors from far and near.
Then Father Murphy from old Kilcormuck
Spurred up the rocks with a warning cry:
"Arm, arm!" he cried, "For I come to lead you,
For Ireland's freedom we fight or die!"

He led us on against the coming soldiers,
The cowardly yeomen we put to flight—
Twas at The Harrow the Boys of Wexford
Showed Bookey's regiment how men could fight.
Look out for hirelings, King George of England,
Search every kingdom that breeds a slave,
For Father Murphy of the County Wexford
Sweeps o'er the land like a mighty wave.

We took Camolin and Enniscorthy
And Wexford storming, drove out the foes;
Twas at Slieve Coilte our pikes were reeking
With the crimson stream of the beaten yeos.
At Tubberneering and Ballyellis
Full many a Hessian lay in his gore:
Ah, Father Murphy, had aid come over,
The Green Flag floated from shore to shore.

At Vinegar Hill o'er the pleasant Slaney,
Our heroes vainly stood back-to-back;
And the yeos at Tullow took Father Murphy
And burned his body upon the rack.
God grant you glory, brave Father Murphy,
And open heaven to all your men;
For the Cause that called you may call tomorrow
In another fight for the Green again.

The insurgency continued to mushroom after the fall of
Wexford. Perhaps more important, for the first time a rude mili-

tary strategy began to emerge from the rebel leadership. Three distinct armies were created. The largest, under the command of Bagenal Harvey and seconded by Father Philip Roche and Dr. Colclough, marched off from Three Rocfks toward the British garrison at New Ross. A second column under Father Moses Kearns left Vinegar Hill to attack Newtownbarry. The third force rambled toward Gorey with a confused leadership. Ostensibly under the command of United General Edward Roche, the four rebel colonels with this last army (Father Michael Murphy of Ballycanew, Arthur Perry of Inch, William Byrne of Ballymanus, and the former prisoner Edward Fitzgerald of New Park) apparently feuded regularly with each other and with Roche.

The rebel column under Father Kearns attacked Newtownbarry on Friday, 1 June. The shock of the insurgent assault, three thousand strong, ousted Colonel L'Estrange's overmatched Kings County Militia in short order. The way to Carlow was open and the flank of the Gorey-bound force was secure . . . but only momentarily. The croppy priest not only failed to exploit his tactical advantage, he lost control of his men. The rebels went on a drunken rampage, pillaging the town. The Crown troops, though numbering no more than 350, took advantage of the rebels' poor discipline, counterattacking to great effect. The bewildered insurgent army was obliterated.

Harvey's force had meanwhile left Three Rocks on the Thursday night. The move toward New Ross was designed to secure the vital junction of the Rivers Barrow and Nore. If successful, it would strand the Crown fort at Duncannon, and open the way to Kilkenny and the western counties where there were large numbers of still quiescent, but presumably sympathetic, Defenders. The fall of New Ross would deny the authorities the opportunity to contain the Wexford *jacquerie* and, indeed, would threaten to transform the peasant rising into full-scale revolution.

Bagenal Harvey's army reached Carrickbyrne—a hill seven miles from New Ross—on Saturday, 2 June. Inexplicably, Harvey dawdled there for two days before pressing on to Corbet Hill overlooking the English garrison.[7] The delay turned out to be crucial. Colonel Luke Gardiner, Lord Mountjoy, arrived in New Ross on the Monday with two thousand men of the Dublin Milita and six badly needed pieces of artillery. In the meantime, the insurgents lost about an equal number of Bargymen when Colclough left in disgust at the rebel procrastination. When the battle was finally joined on the next day, it is likely that Harvey commanded slightly in excess of ten thousand. Major General Henry Johnson defended the garrison with about six thousand.

The 5 June Battle of New Ross was perhaps the most bitterly contested of the entire 1798 insurrection. Though enjoying numerical superiority, the rebels had no trained men to fire their captured cannon, no experienced infantry leaders, nor even expertise in the use of individual firearms—with the exception of some few men from the southeast coast who had their own long-barrelled fowling pieces. Most telling of all, the insurgents had little ammunition for the guns they did possess. The fight for New Ross was to be remembered as a story of hay-forks and pikes against artillery, of desperate courage and impetuous enthusiasm against overwhelming firepower.[8]

KELLY, THE BOY FROM KILLANE

The struggle at New Ross began when a group of about six hundred rebel Bantrymen under Lieutenant John Kelly of Kilann stormed the Bewley Gate. The carnage at the site earned the location the sobriquet of the *bearna bhaoil,* the "gap of danger." Repelling a countercharge by cavalry of the Fifth Dragoons, Kelly's pikemen managed to breach the gate. The rebels spilled into the town in their thousands.

Kelly, a massive figure of a man, became the central figure in the house-to-house fighting that raged murderously throughout the day. When he fell wounded as the Crown forces were in full retreat, the rebel attack slackened, giving the British officers the needed respite to rally their fleeing troops. The fury of the battle continued into the evening when the courageous but badly led insurgents finally broke off the action after almost fifteen hours of continuous fighting.

The butchery, however, did not halt. Angry Crown troops ran down rebel stragglers without mercy. Major Vesey, in command of the Dubliners in place of the fallen Lord Mountjoy, wrote that "no quarter was given. The soldiers were too much exasperated and could not be stopped." Dr. Jordan Roche, General Johnson's medical officer, filed this report describing the Tuesday night activities:

> The remaining part of the evening was spent searching for and shooting at the insurgents whose loss in killed was estimated at 2,806 men.[9]

This rousing nineteenth century ballad by Patrick Joseph McCall is still among the most popular of rebel songs.

What's the news, what's the news, oh me bold Shelmalier,
With your long-barrelled gun from the sea?
Well, what wind from the South brings a messenger here
With a song of the dawn for the free?
Goodly news, goodly news: do I bring ye youth of Forth!
Goodly news shall ye hear: Bargy men!
And the boys march at morn from the South to the North
Led by Kelly, the boy from Killane.

Tell me, who is the giant with the gold curling hair
That rides at the head of your band?
Seven feet is his height with some inches to spare,
And he rides like a king in command!
Well, me boys, that's the pride of the bold Shelmaliers,
The greatest of heroes, a man!
So fling your beavers aloft and give three ringing cheers
For John Kelly, the boy from Killane!

Enniscorthy's in flames and old Wexford is won,
And tomorrow the Barrow we cross;
On Corbet Hill o'er the town we have planted a gun
That will batter the gateway to Ross.
All the Forthmen and Bargymen will march o'er the heath
With brave Harvey to lead in the van,
But the foremost of all to that Grim Gap of Death
Will be Kelly, the boy from Killane.

But the bright sun of Freedom grew dark at New Ross,
And it set by the Slaney's red waves;
And poor Wexford, stripped naked, hung high on a cross,
With her heart pierced by traitors and slaves.
Glory O! Glory O! to her brave sons who died
For the cause of long-downtrodden man!
Glory O! to Mount Leinster's own, darling and pride,
Dauntless Kelly, the boy from Killane.

It is unlikely that there had been more than a few thousand sworn United Irishmen in County Wexford when the 1798 insurrection broke out. Since anywhere between thirty to fifty thousand men were to take up arms at one time or another during the Wexford rebellion, many members of the peasant army must have come from the ranks of the Defenders. As has been seen, there were large groups of Defenders openly challenging the militia as early as 1793. Though perhaps not as active as their namesakes throughout the rest of Ireland after that time, it is not illogical to presume that many of these Wexford men had been anxiously awaiting the opportunity to take to the field. In any event, both the authorities and the rebels used the terms "Unitedman" and "Defender" interchangeably in the county.

THE BANISHED DEFENDER

This broadside ballad by the northern poet James Garland appeared soon after the '98 risings were over. It is ostensibly the tale of a young lieutenant in Bagenal Harvey's rebel army who was captured the day after the Battle of New Ross. The sentence pronounced in his case, transportation "down under," was among the more merciful issued. The reference to "Van Dieman's Land" is, by the way, a generic allusion to *any* expulsion order to New South Wales or Tasmania—the penal colony in Tasmania was not actually in operation until 1803.

Religious bitterness is clearly apparent in the lyrics of the ballad. The key to the United Irish rebellion was supposed to be non-sectarianism. As both the song and the pre-eminence of croppy priests in the peasant army clearly demonstrate, however, the Wexford rising and Defenderism itself were characterised by their Roman Catholic nature. One result was the appalling massacre of some two hundred Protestant prisoners near Carrick-byrne.[10]

Poor Catholics of Erin give ear unto these lines I write,
I've fled to the mountains, forever I am banished quite,
For the sake of my religion I was forced to leave my native home,
I've been a bold Defender, and a member of the Church of Rome.

Then woe attend those traitors who forced me from my native soil,
Those perjured prosecutors that banished me in exile;
They swore I was a traitor and a leader of the Papist band,
For which I'm in cold irons, a convict in Van Dieman's Land.

Right well do I remember when I was taken in New Ross
The day after the battle as the Green Mountain Ferry I did cross;
The guards they did surround me, and bundle searched on the spot,
And there they found my green coat, my pike, two pistols and some shot.

The reason that they banished me, the truth I mean to tell you here,
Because I was a head leader of Father Murphy's Shelmaliers,
And for being a Roman Catholic I was trampled on by Harry's breed,
For fighting in defence of my God, my country and my creed.

Don't they know there's but one God and one true faith, the scripture says,
Don't they know there's but one church and out of that none can be saved?
She is a ship that can't be wrecked while Peter guides her with his oar;
The passengers that leave her deck are sunk and lost for evermore.

By the night of 5 June, two of the three insurgent columns had failed in their object. Father Moses Kearns' rebel band had ceased to exist as an effective unit. Bagenal Harvey's repulsed army was in disarray around Carrickbyrne (indeed Harvey was soon after supplanted as official leader of that force by Father Philip Roche). Everything now depended on the eastern column that was charged with taking Gorey, Arklow, and Wicklow, on the way to Dublin.

This army had in fact started its campaign promisingly. On 4 June the column had still been in camp at Carrigrew Hill when government forces had attempted to surround the rebel base. As Colonel Walpole was maneuvering his force of British Fencibles through the narrow pass at Tubberneering, he was ambushed by a large rebel band waiting in the foliage alongside the trail. The Crown troops were thoroughly routed.[11] In consequence, the worried authorities abandoned Gorey to the insurgents. Major General Loftus, nominal commander of the Gorey redcoats, retreated first to Carnew and then all the way to Tullow. The insurrection would still have a slim chance of success if the rebels followed up their advantage by marching rapidly on lightly defended Arklow. Instead, the rebel leadership made another fatal mistake.

The insurgents split their forces, sending a foray across the County Wicklow line after Loftus to avenge the Ball Alley executions. As they marched on Carnew, the rest of the army awaited the column's return to Gorey in what was becoming a charac-

teristic rebel manner: drinking and plundering. By the time the
rebel army was finally reorganised to march on Arklow, it was
Friday, 8 June. In the interim, General Francis Needham's garrison had been heavily reinforced. The insurgents had thrown
away their last chance to keep the rebellion alive.

IN DEEPEST SORROW I THINK OF HOME

This long ballad may be the single best example of rebel
music as history. It takes a chronological journey through the
campaign in Wexford from the piking of Lieutenant Bookey to
the eve of the Battle of Vinegar Hill. Each historical detail
that can be checked independently dovetails accurately. The
presumption is, of course, that other details included in such
songs not otherwise available to historians may also be considered accurate.

The ballad seems to have been sung almost immediately
after the rising; it is, quite simply, history from a rebel point of
view.

Come all you renowned warriors and honoured nobles,
Give ear unto my warlike theme;
And I will sing you how Father Murphy
Lately aroused from his sleepy dream.
Sure, Julius Caesar and Alexander
Nor brave King Arthur ever equalled him,
For armies formidable he did conquer,
Though with two gunmen he did begin.

Camolin Cavalry, he did unhorse them,
Their First Lieutenant he cut them down;
With shattered ranks and with broken columns
They soon returned to Camolin Town.
On the hill of Oulart he displayed his valour
Where a hundred Corkmen lay on the plain;
At Enniscorthy his sword he wielded,
And I hope to see him once more again.

When Enniscorthy became subject to him,
Twas then to Wexford we marched our men,
And on the Three Rocks took up our quarters

Waiting for daylight, the town to win;
The loyal townsmen gave their assistance,
"We'll die or conquer," they all did say;
The yeoman cavalry made no resistance,
For on the pavement their corpses lay.

With drums a-beating, the town did echo,
And acclamations came from door to door;
On the Windmill Hill we pitched our tents
And we drunk like heroes but paid no score.
On Carraigrua for some time we waited
And next to Gorey we did repair,
At Tubberneering we thought no harm,
The bloody army was waiting there.

The issue was a close engagement,
While on the soldiers we played warlike pranks—
Through sheepwalks, hedgerows and shady thickets,
There were mangled bodies and broken ranks.
The shuddering cavalry, I can't forget them,
We raised the brushes on their helmets straight—
They turned about and they bid for Dublin
As if they ran for a ten-pound plate.

Some crossed Donnybrook and more through Blackrock,
And some up Shankill without wound or flaw,
And if Barry Lawless be not a liar,
There's more went groaning up Luggelaw.
To the Windmill Hill of Enniscorthy,
The British Fencibles they fled like deers;
But our ranks were tattered and sorely scattered
By the loss of Kyan[12] and the Shelmaliers.

The streets of England were left quite naked
Of all its army both foot and horse,
The Highlands of Scotland were left unguarded,
Likewise the Hessians, the seas they crossed.
But if the Frenchmen had reinforced us,
And landed transports in Baginbun,
Father John Murphy would be their seconder
And sixteen thousand with him would come.

Success attend the sweet County Wexford,
Throw off its yoke and to battle run;
Let them not think we gave up our arms,
For every man has a pike and gun.

The rebel army—estimated at nineteen thousand by General Needham—appeared on the sandhills outside Arklow at 1600 on 9 June. Dublin Castle had been given two full weeks to strengthen Needham's defenses; though the government had been slow to recognise the strategic importance of the coastal town, reinforcements were now pouring in. The Durham Fencibles, destined to bear the brunt of the rebel attack, arrived scant minutes before the battle was joined.

Even though the sixteen hundred British were supported by artillery, the shock of the rebel attack stunned Needham's troops. Wave after wave stormed the Crown line in the face of grapeshot and concentrated firepower. Insurgents in their thousands surged against the redcoat redoubts. Needham was later to report to General Lake that:

> their perseverance was surprising, and their efforts to possess themselves of the guns on my right were most daring, advancing even to the muzzles, where they fell in great numbers.

At several different times during the bloody evening, General Needham felt in danger of being overrun; he went so far at one point to prepare a breakout to Wicklow. The assaults, however, began to slow with the gloaming—the insurgents had run out of ammunition. The 9 June sun set on the last real chance of rebel success in 1798.[13]

THE BOYS OF WEXFORD

The sheer valour of the Wexford rabble-in-arms surprised the Crown in nearly every engagement. Faced by troops led by professional British officers, however, Irish courage was not enough. The lack of comparable trained and disciplined leadership within the insurgency proved disastrous.

All three rebel columns in County Wexford squandered tactical victories when they failed to exploit them: in New Ross, the battle-weary insurgents had rested at the instant that pursuit of the fleeing British would have gained the field; in both Newtownbarry and Gorey, leaderless mobs had engaged in wild drinking and barbaric pillaging, giving their beaten foes time to regroup. There was little the Wexford pikemen had not done when asked by their officers; the misfortune arose from the lack of asking.

The ballad is credited to Robert Dwyer Joyce.

In comes the captain's daughter, the captain of the yeos,
Saying, "Brave United Irishmen, we'll ne'er again be foes;
A thousand pounds I'll give you and fly from home with thee,
I'll dress myself in man's attire and fight for Liberty!"

Refrain:
We are the boys of Wexford
Who fought with heart and hand,
To burst in twain the galling chain
And free our native land.

And when we left our cabins, boys, we left with right good will,
To see our friends and neighbors that were at Oulart Hill;
A young man from our ranks, a cannon he let go;
He slapt it into Lord Mountjoy, a tyrant he laid low![14]

Refrain

We bravely fought and conquered at Ross and Wexford Town,
And if we failed to keep them, twas drink that brought us down;
We had no drink beside us on Tubberneering day,
Depending on the long bright pike, and well it worked its way.

Refrain

They came into the country our blood to waste and spill,
But let them weep for Wexford and think of Oulart Hill!
Twas drink that still betrayed us—of *them* we had no fear,
For every man could do his part, like Forth and Shelmalier.

Refrain

My curse upon all drinking, it made our hearts full score,
For bravery won each battle but drink lost evermore;
And if, for want of leaders, we lost at Vinegar Hill,
We're ready for another fight and love our country still.

Refrain

During the next ten days, the Crown gradually squeezed the life from the remaining resistance in Wexford. Lake's forces slowly beat the rebels back to Vinegar Hill from the north and east. Meanwhile, General Johnson's garrison from New Ross joined Brigadier Sir John Moore's from Duncannon in a 19 June surprise attack on Father Roche's rebel camp at Carrickbyrne. The insurgent retreat was twofold: one group fled towards Enniscorthy hotly pursued by Johnson; the larger portion under Roche retreated in surprisingly good order towards Three Rocks, doggedly engaged by Moore.

By the next afternoon, the rebels remaining in the town of Wexford were frantic; Matthew Keough and Father Roche were desperately suing General Moore for terms before their army disappeared entirely into the surrounding countryside. Amidst the confusion, a rebel lieutenant named Thomas Dixon presided at a particularly bloody last-minute massacre of loyalist prisoners. Perhaps as many as a hundred were murdered on the Old-bridge and thrown into the mouth of the River Slaney.[15] On the next day, 21 June, Moore occupied the town.

Upriver, General Lake was drawing the net closed on the same afternoon. Father John Murphy had mustered about ten thousand rebels at Vinegar Hill. The Crown forces had almost completed surrounding the last insurgent stronghold in County Wexford; all that was needed was for Needham—still a day's march away—to close up on the southern gap in the ring.

Apparently foreseeing the incipient encirclement, Murphy seems to have initiated the battle. Lake was willing. After levelling a devastating cannonade on the summit of the 390-foot hill, the government troops charged. The rebels resisted stubbornly for almost two hours before they were overrun. At that juncture, one large band broke through the Crown lines at a point known to history as "Needham's Gap."

THE BATTLE OF VINEGAR HILL

If the fight for Arklow had sealed the fate of the Wexford insurrection, the battle by the River Slaney gave some indication how the British intended to deal with the rebel "veterans." The victors took few prisoners at Vinegar Hill, and the slain were buried hurriedly where they lay.[16] The dead had carried no K-rations into rebellion; their provisions consisted of raw wheat stuffed into their pockets. The following year, legend claims the wheat grew out of the shallow graves. The authorities, horrified, burned it. The next summer it renewed itself into an entire wheatfield—perhaps the most memorable gravestone in Irish rebel history.

This ballad by Father Patrick F. Kavanagh, as so many rebel songs, celebrates defiant courage in the face of certain defeat.

Proud marched the British army in scarlet and in gold,
Their trumpets loudly sounding, their banners all unrolled.
To meet the Wexford pikemen, those gallant men and true,
Who fought to raise our darling Green above the English Blue.

To Vinegar Hill their way they took, these English soldiers all,
Their lightfoot and their cavalry, their grenadiers so tall.
Resoved to make those pikeman bold their rashness sorely rue,
To dare to raise their darling Green against the English Blue.

For they thought of Tubberneering, New Ross and Wexford Town,
And in silence vowed they'd perish or rip that Green flag down.
Then a young ensign boldly spoke this, his scornful jest:
"I'll laugh to see the rebels run—their priest before the rest!"

Then said to him a captain, a grey-haired veteran he,
"I've met these men in fight before—no braver men there be.
We came upon them suddenly when we were two-to-one,
And fought them all the summer day till night was coming on."

Right soon that English army, twenty thousand strong,
Were marshalled round that hill, renowned in story and in song.
Whereon ten thousand pikemen, the flower of Ireland,
Had from homes and altars marched to make their final stand.

And then the battle's thunder broke o'er the echoing plain,
The cannon balls fell thickly and musket balls like rain;
Upon the hillside where there stood those peasant-patriots true,
Who fought to raise their Irish Green above the English Blue.

Soon many a dauntless Shelmalier lay weltering in his gore,
And many a valiant patriot bold had fallen to rise no more;
For thickly flew the cannon balls and musket balls like hail,
Till at the slaughter on the hill the stoutest heart might quail.

Then to their feet the pikemen sprang with fierce loud battle-cry,
Each firmly raised his trusty pike and raised his voice on high;
And suddenly on that hillside, a steel-tipped forest grew,
While borne aloft before their ranks, their gallant Green flag flew.

And rushing down the hill they came, a swift resistless tide,
Nor dared King George's veteran troops their onset fierce to bide,
But left a passage open wide before the gallant foe,
As with their Green flag flying, towards Wexford Town they go.

After the breakout from Vinegar Hill, most of the surviving rebels fled in small bands to avoid the fury of the government troops. Two coherent columns, however, did manage to offer organised resistance. One unit of two thousand men regrouped under Father John Murphy at Foulksmills and slipped through the Blackstairs Mountains into Kilkenny. The other, under William Byrne, wandered north into the forests along the Wexford/Wicklow frontier.

Murphy's renegades fought a successful rearguard action at Goresbridge and forged on, trying to raise the Defenders of northern Kilkenny. The call was answered only by a handful of disaffected colliers after the rebels had scattered a small yeoman force at Castlecomer. Pressed hard by Sir Charles Asgill's government troops, Murphy was forced to withdraw to Kilcomney Hill on the Queen's County border where his forces were dispersed after a last stand on 26 June. The croppy priest was captured, taken to Tullow, and hanged. In the custom of the time, his body was burned and his head festooned atop a spike at the market house in the town.[17] A Hessian troop under General Count Ferdinand Hompech meanwhile spread terror amongst the peasantry while chasing remnants of Murphy's band through the midlands.

While Murphy had been retreating westward, Billy Byrne's outfit had joined with a roving rebel band from the Wicklows under Edward Fitzgerald and become nettlesome to the Crown once again. An Ancient Briton detachment from Gorey attacked this combined unit on 30 June. Retreating about two miles to Ballyellis, Fitzgerald and Byrne drew the government forces into carefully prepared ambush and annihilation. A British relieving column under the infamous Captain Gowan was itself sent packing for Gorey, the triumphant rebels hot on its heels. Byrne set up camp on the Ballyrahee Hill the next day; Fitzgerald meanwhile took his men back into the Wicklows.

A large force of yeomanry under Captains Chamnay and Nickson assaulted the Ballyrahee position on 2 July. Both British officers were killed in the early fighting and, once again, the government troops retreated in confusion. It was by now, however, only a matter of time. Byrne's rebels were finally surrounded and overwhelmed at Coolgreany two days later. The insurgents were dispersed and William Byrne taken immediately to the Wicklow Gaol where he was imprisoned with two of his former comrades on the United Irish Leinster Directory, Oliver Bond and Sam Neilson. Rebellion was over in the South.

SWEET COUNTY WEXFORD

This chronological ballad dates to just after the Wexford rising and is one upon which Robert Dwyer Joyce based his later songs. It refers to Billy Byrne's short campaign of late June and early July in northern Wexford.

Down through the years this song has undergone some changes. Such metamorphosis is of course, not unusual to folksong. In the case of this ballad, though, it was not the words that were changed; rather, it was the order of singing them. Since Byrne's last-gasp campaign has never been really well known—most historians consider anything after Vinegar Hill a footnote—the general unfamiliarity with its chronology makes understandable the frequent juxtaposition of verses. The following version seems to be the way the ballad was sung at the time.

There is one apparent mistake of history in the ballad: *Colonel* Walpole was slain at Tubberneering more than three weeks prior to these events.

At Monaseed of a summer's morning,
Our brave boys halted, a rest to take;
The Ancient Britons in uniform
Upon Sliebh Beag a great show did make.
They thought we'd run when we saw them coming
But they were play for our heroes brave:
We marched before them to Ballyellis,
There is the place we made their grave.

As they from Gorey set out that morning,
You'd pity the groans and the women's tears;
But in that day we made them pay
When they came in view of our Shelmaliers.
We marched past the watch-house at Ballyellis,
To Pavey's Heights going towards Carnew;
That is the place we did engage them,
Such other pikemen you never knew.

The Gorey Cavalry that day did join them,
They were on bloody murder bent;
But soon our boys they did engage them,
They little thought that their glass was spent.
Cowardly Gowan when he saw us coming,
He called his men and away did run
Like a hunted fox; he crossed the rocks
When he saw the flash of a croppy's gun.

We left the town when the fight was over
(Our boys indeed had no more to do),
We crossed Brideswell, marched through Camolin,
And camped that night upon Carraigrua.
Twas early, early on the next morning,
Through Shillelagh we marched straight,
And that next evening at Ballyrahee
Gave Major Chamney a great defeat.

We did shoot Chamney and Captain Nixon
And General Walpole got no time to run,
And Long Smyth the slater—that bloody traitor—
He fell that day by a croppy gun.
Success attend the sweet County Wexford,
They are the boys that were ne'er afraid
Of Ancient Britons nor bragging yeomen,
But on such cowards great slaughter made.

In the wake of the suppression of the Wexford rebellion, the authorities took swift retribution against the rebel military leaders. John Colclough, Bagenal Harvey, and Matthew Keough were caught hiding in a cave on the Saltee Islands off the south coast of the county. Together with Father Philip Roche, they were hanged upon the Oldbridge at Wexford on 1 July. Their heads were piked over the courthouse and left on display for some weeks afterward. Such grisly exhibitions were not uncommon in Ireland over the next several months.

Many other famous rebels met the same fate. The legendary John Kelly of Kilann, for example, was also hanged at Wexford. Public execution was certain for any prisoner who could be shown to have had tactical authority among the insurgents.

BURKE'S DREAM

This broadside ballad is representative of the Celtic verse form of the *aisling*, the symbolic dream. In this case, the dreamer was presumably a minor officer in the Wexford peasant army awaiting his date with the hanging tree. The November reference suggests that young Burke had been able to elude the hemp-rope longer than most of his comrades.

Slowly and sadly one night in November
I laid down my weary head to repose
On a pillow of straw, which I long shall remember;
O'erpowered by sleep I fell into a doze,
Tired from working hard down in the felon's yard;
Night brought relief to my well-tortured frame,
Locked in my prison cell, surely an earthly hell:
I fell asleep and began for to dream.

Methought that I sat on the green hills of Erin,
Premeditating her victory won;
Surrounded by comrades, no enemy fearing.
"Stand!" was the cry, "Every man to his gun!"
Then on came the *Samagh* facing our Irishmen,
But they soon rallied back from our pike volunteers,
Whose cry it was shrill, "Hurrah boys! Father Murphy
And his brave Shelmaliers!"

Then methought that I seen our brave, noble commanders
All mounted on charges and in gorgeous array,
In green trimmed with gold, with their bright-shining sabres
On which danced the sunbeams of freedom that day.
"Oh!" was the battle-cry, "Conquer this day or die!

Sons of Hibernia, fight for liberty!
Show neither fear nor dread, vanquish the foe ahead!
Cut down their horse, foot, and artillery!"

Then on the cannon balls flew, men from both sides drew,
Our men were bound by oath to die and hold their ground;
So from our vengeance the *Samagh* fled,
Leaving the fields covered with dead.
While each man cried out gloriously:
"Come from your prison, Burke!
Irishmen have done their work,
God he was with us, old Erin is free!"

Then, methought, as the clouds were repeatedly flowing,
I saw a lion stretched on the crimson-gold places,
Beneath the pale moonbeams in death's sleep reposing,
The comrades I knew I would never see again.
Then over the mountain-path homewards I hastened back,
There saw my mother who fainted, gave a loud scream,
At the shock of which I awoke just at daybreak—
And found myself a prisoner and all but a dream.

The fate of the Wexford peasant—rebellious *or* loyal—was in some ways harsher than that of many of the insurgent captains. A few of the rebel leaders had been priests with no family; many others had been middle-class merchants and small landholders whose families had at least something to fall back on; yet others had been financially secure squires whose families' deprivations would be "merely" emotional. The lot of the humble croppy, on the other hand, bore cruel consequence for the economic future of his kindred.

The 1797 savagery in the North performed in the name of the Insurrection Act would now pale in contrast to the vindictiveness to be visited upon the peasantry of the Southeast in the name of vengeance. Even those peasants fortunate enough to escape the marauding bands of Crown avengers found no succour in the assizes. The luckiest of the prisoners were dispatched to Botany Bay at hard labour. Others were impressed into the Royal Navy—a "privilege" heretofore denied papists under the Penal Laws. Some three hundred were even given as slaves to Frederick Wilhelm III of Prussia to work in the mines. As far as their families were concerned, these woebegone Wexfordmen might as well have been slain in rebellion.

THE CROPPY BOY

A small settlement near the town of Passage on the western shore of Waterford Harbour was transformed into the major "croppy prison" after the Wexford insurrection. Named for a colony of Swiss gold and silversmiths who had settled there thirteen years earlier, it became the infamous Geneva Barracks after the '98 rebellion. Through its gates entered thousands of forlorn peasants suspected of some part in the risings. Few were to see their townlands again.

It has been said that there are as many versions of this ballad as there are counties in Ireland. This is one sung just after the fighting.

Twas early, early in the spring,
The pretty small birds began to sin;
They sang so sweet and so gloriously,
And the tune they played was Sweet Liberty.

Twas early, early last Thursday night,
The yeoman cavalry gave me a fright,
The fright they gave me was to my downfall—
I was prisoner taken by Lord Cornwall.

Twas in his guardhouse I was confined,
And in his parlour I was closely tried;
My sentence passed and my spirits low,
And to Duncannon I was forced to go.

My sister Mary is in deep distress,
She ran downstairs in her mourning dress;
Five hundred pounds she would lay down
To see me walking through Wexford Town.

As I was walking the hills so high,
Who could blame me if I did cry?
With a guard behind me and another before,
And my tender mother crying more and more?

So farewell father, and mother too,
And sister Mary, I have but you;
And if e'er I chance to return home,
I'll whet my pike on those yeomens' bones.

The United Irishmen of mid-Leinster had risen by design on 23 May. The peasants of Wexford had joined them out of "necessity" three days later. But in Rebel Ulster, the birthplace of the United Irish movement, there was an unaccountable silence. Eastern Ireland was to be roaring in revolt for two weeks before the republicans of the North joined the fight.

CHAPTER NOTES (15)

1 — *Half-hanging* involved tightening a noose around the victim's neck until he passed out, then repeating the procedure until the desired information was literally "wrung" out of the terrified peasant. The *flogging triangle* was a wooden structure upon which the victim was spreadeagled as the cat-o-nine-tails was liberally applied to the sufferer's back. It apparently made its debut at Athy as a Colonel Campbell rounded up black-smiths in a search for pikes. The *pitched-cap* was a paper crown filled with molten tar that was set alight. The victim was forced to rip his hair from his scalp to rid himself of the agony.

2 — There are several explanations for the origin of the term "croppy." One was that felons had their ears cropped in Ireland, another that the rich wore their hair *en queue* so that anyone who did not was by definition a "peasant." Still another involves the ancient Gaelic hairstyle of the Irish warrior. Yet one more suggests that the name emerged to describe the victims of the pitched-cap torture. It would not be surprising if in fact the name arose from an incorporation of all these to one degree or another.

  The infamous Hunter Gowan was the most notorious yeoman captain in Wexford before the rising. In response to the atrocities of his "Black Mob," some Catholics took to cropping the hair of Protestants so that they too might be targets of Gowan's outrages (Gowan considered anyone with short hair to be fair game for his men).

3 — The number arrested by Saunders and shot later at Dunlavin is still in dispute.

The ballad's contention that thirty-six were executed is supported by several contemporary accounts (John Mitchel, who had talked with many of the men who were out in '98, put the number at thirty-four). Sir Richard Musgrave, writing within two years of the rebellion, suggests that nineteen of Saunders' men were shot along with nine other treasonous militiamen from Narraghmore. In any case, the number would seem to be larger than the "twenty" given by most modern historians.

4 — Myles Byrne, in the thick of things in both 1798 and 1803, later escaped to join the French service, rising to *Chef-de-Batallion*. In his memoirs, he characterised Murphy as:

> "one of those Roman Catholic priests who used the greatest exertions and exhortations to oblige the people to surrender their pikes and fire-arms."

No republican, the croppy priest apparently was happy enough to serve the Crown until the yeomanry burned down his chapel. In those flames was born one of the brightest of Irish rebel legends.

5 — One of the most constant errors made by both the academicians and folk-historians of the Wexford rising is the canard that Father John Murphy and his original Wexford rebels were from the barony of Shelmalier. Murphy's chapel was in fact on the southern edge of the barony of Gorey.

The following entry, as dictated to his orderly, was the first in John Murphy's "military journal":

> "Began the republic of Ireland in Boulavogue in the county of Wexford, barony of Gorey and parish of Kilcormuck...."

There were actually portions of two coastal baronies—North and South Ballaghkeen—separating Gorey from Shelmalier. Shelmalier itself was just north of Wexford town, stretching from the St. George's Channel all the way to Foulksmills in the west. South of Wexford, covering the entire peninsula to Bannow Bay, were the baronies of Forth and Bargy.

6 — Vinegar Hill was often called "Windmill Hill" for the ruined mill on its summit. It should not be confused with the two heights *named* Windmill Hill upon which 1798 rebels also pitched camps: one overlooking the town of Ballinahich in County Down, the other near the Three Rocks outside of the town of Wexford.

7 — There is some evidence that the Crown garrison at Duncannon had established skirmishers at Foulksmills. If so, such a threat to his left flank would have sufficed to unnerve more experienced commanders than Bagenal Harvey.

8 — Charles Dickson cites an anonymous military analyst's report that it took twenty-three successive discharges of grapeshot to finally turn the rebel tide at New Ross, and that some of the British regulars fired 120 rounds during the battle. Interestingly, the

writer goes on to suggest that, had the English been supplied with twelve-foot lances
to counter the ten-foot pikes of the insurgents, such firepower may not have been
needed.

9 — Dr. Roche's "estimate" seems precise enough to be taken as accurate. The number
that fell in combat is something else again. Reverend James Gordon, a Protestant
minister on the scene, stated:

> "I have reason to think more men than fell in combat were slain in cold
> blood. No quarter was given to persons taken prisoner as rebels, with or with-
> out arms."

10 — The Scullabogue Massacre was a particularly vicious result of lack of effective
leadership among the rebels. About 175 Protestant civilians were confined in a barn
when it was set afire. As they tried to escape the horrible death inside, they faced a
forest of pikes thrusting them back into the flames. As can be seen by a later verse
written to *Croppies, Lie Down,* the Protestants did not forget the incident:

> Hundreds they've burned of each sex, young and old,
> From heaven the order, by priests they were told;
> No longer we'll trust them, no more to betray,
> But chase from our bosoms these vipers away...
> Derry down, down, croppies lie down!

11 — Among the wounded at Tubberneering was a captain of Kings County Militia,
John W. Armstrong, the same young officer who had successfully duped John and
Henry Sheares barely two weeks earlier. It may be indicative of the confusion in
Dublin at the time that the Crown would let its star witness take the field, thus jea-
pordising its case against the United Irish leaders.

12 — Captain Esmonde Kyan, the only rebel officer with any knowledge of artillery.
When his artificial arm was shot off by English cannon in the Battle of Arklow, he was
supposed to have remarked, "My loose timbers are flying—God bless the mark!—and
now for the right arm of the British line!" He was later hanged for his part in the
rebellion.

13 — This would probably have been later than the "eight-thirty" repeated by many
modern historians. Needham's dispatch to Dublin Castle suggests the battle was not
joined until 6 p.m., two hours after the rebels had appeared before Arklow. The combination of latitude and proximity to the summer solstice indicates a lingering twilight
on 9 June 1798, a clear, sunny day by all accounts. Since the contemporary reports
agree that the battle tapered off with the dark, the fighting before the town would
seem to have lasted at least three hours.

14 — Dr. Joyce is perhaps unfair to Lord Mountjoy. Indeed, it had been young Luke Gardiner who had been largely responsible for the Catholic Relief Acts of 1788 and 1783. As an unusually liberal politician during the heyday of the Patriot Party, Gardiner had introduced the legislation that had given Irish papists more freedom than they had enjoyed since the time of Charles II. It is yet another of the tragic ironies of Irish rebel history that he fell to a Catholic pike at New Ross.

15 — This massacre and the one at the Scullabogue barn are often offered as causal factors explaining the Crown's savage reprisals after the Wexford rising. Dixon, a merchant ship captain, disappeared from history after perpetrating the infamous butchery at Oldbridge.

16 — The estimates of casualties at Vinegar Hill are as numerous and dissimilar as the contemporary writers who made them. Most chroniclers, however, concurred that the majority of the dead did not fall in battle.

17 — After the sanguinary terrors experienced by the peasants by this juncture, it is unlikely that the growing number of ghastly trophies decorating the town diamonds served to further intimidate the rebels. In the case of Father John Murphy, however, the bloody gargoyle may have served its purpose: the superstitious insurgents had watched the martial priest survive unscathed through the thickest of the fighting. The peasants were convinced that Murphy had a Spartacus-like imperviousness to enemy weaponry. As in the case of the Roman slave-general, what government armament could not accomplish, the scaffold did.

16

Ulster Also Rises

The Crown had always considered Ulster the central hotbed of Irish republicanism. The Insurrection Act of 1796 had been brought in specifically to give General Lake, then in command in the North, the means to crush the Unitedmen in the province. As has been seen, Lake had become convinced by mid-1797 that Ulster was in worse shape than ever, and counselled even more coercion.[1] Lord Camden had been receptive to Lake's plea. The Viceroy, intent on precipitating premature revolt among the rebel Irish, had not blinked when Lake began to turn the northern screws in earnest. Camden's strategy in Ulster had ultimately backfired: the dragooning of the North had so thoroughly shattered the United Irish organisation in the province that when Leinster rose in May 1798, Ulster stood silent . . . to Dublin Castle's relief.

Robert Simms, the designated northern United leader, apparently had received Lord Edward Fitzgerald's orders for the rising, and seems to have made some effort to disseminate the word.[2] Curiously however, when the Belfast mail-coach had been intercepted at Santry on 23 May—the signal that the rising had begun—no marching orders had been issued in Ulster. Simms' failure to raise the North has never been satisfactorily explained. It does seem logical to assume that the northern leader was one of the few Unitedmen aware that the arrest of Fitzgerald and the brothers Sheares had left the Society without national leadership. Since Fitzgerald had been captured soon after issuing the rising orders, Simms may also have believed that the plans themselves had been blown. Also quite well aware that the French were *not* upon the sea, the northern commander may have opted for inactivity due to a realistic pessimism about the chances for success.[3] Whatever the reason, Ulster did not join the May rebellion.

About the beginning of June, a disgusted group of United Irish activists in the North decided to take matters into their own hands. Under the urging of a young firebrand, Thomas Bashford, these impatient radicals voted the old Ulster Executive out of office, deciding to rise in support of their comrades in the South. The new Northern Directory included Bashford, John Hughes of Belfast, Henry Joy MacCracken, and James Dickey, a Crumlin attorney. Another member of the council was Nicholas Magin, in reality an operative in the pay of Major General George Nugent, now the senior Crown officer in Ulster.

The fiery new Directory appointed Reverend William Dickson—earlier Simms' second and northern liason to the Dublin Executive—to command the United Irish troops in County Down. MacCracken was to be Commander-in-Chief and personally head the Unitedmen in County Antrim.

MacCracken began mustering his forces at the Donegore Hill, two miles east of Antrim on the night of 5 June—ironically, about the time Harvey's Wexford rebels were disengaging at New Ross, 160 miles to the south. The next day, the United general sent Samuel Orr to the west to take Randalstown and Toomebridge. Orr's mission was to secure the rebel flank against counterattack from Londonderry.[4] Another force was sent through Kells to Ballymena with the aim of cutting off Crown reinforcement from Coleraine. Still a third column was dispatched to take Larne on the east coast. This last unit was to act as a flanking threat to potential attack on the main rebel army from Carrickfergus. MacCracken's plan was to take the town of Antrim, wheel, and march on Belfast. Dickson's County Down rebels were expected to apply simultaneous pressure on the provincial capital from the south and east.

In theory, the United commander's strategy was sound. In practice, it was doomed from the beginning: Nicholas Magin had disclosed the entire plan to General Nugent. Even as MacCracken was gathering his forces on the Donegore Hill, the authorities were arresting Dickson and his adjutant. Concurrently, Nugent was working furiously to reinforce the precarious Crown garrison at Antrim.

Another serious problem confronted MacCracken: the five thousand Defenders that were to have joined the County Antrim rising did not appear on Donegore Hill. Although there has never been a definitive explanation for their absence, there are two conspicuous possibilities. First, there was a decided lack

of coherent communication within the new northern leadership—
it is quite possible that the Defenders were never informed.
Second, the sectarian nature of life in Ulster made the Roman
Catholics instinctively suspicious—it is certainly conceivable
that the missing papists just did not trust this new group of
Protestant leaders.[5]

Whatever the reason, MacCracken had mustered only three
thousand men when Sam Orr began the Antrim rising on 6 June
with his attack on Randalstown. Pressing the outmanned Crown
troops west into County Londonderry, Orr's band spent the rest
of that Wednesday day and night painstakingly dismantling the
bridge at Toome to prevent a counterattack. MacCracken's western flank was secure. Similarly, the northern rebel column secured MacCracken's rear, occupying both Kells and Ballymena.
The insurgents attacking Larne were also successful, forcing the
British there to retreat upon Carrickfergus. As MacCracken prepared his own "Defender-less" forces for the main assault on
Antrim the next morning, everything seemed to be proceeding
according to schedule. The plan began to unravel swiftly as the
sun rose on the Thursday.

The very success of the rising's first day began to cause unexpected problems. As word of the rebellion spread, unsolicited
volunteers poured into MacCracken's camp. The United general,
presumably still worried by the non-appearance of the Defenders,
decided to delay his attack as his lieutenants hurriedly attempted
to organise the new recruits. When the Unitedmen finally attacked the county town with a force grown to six thousand, it
was two hours past noon. The delay was to prove crucial.

The Antrim garrison had been there for the taking. Lieutenant Colonel Sir William Lumley's dragoons and Colonel Lord
John Skeffington's yeomen totaled only 150 men. MacCracken
had outnumbered the garrison by twenty-to-one at dawn. Now
he had doubled his forces. He had also given the English time to
get reinforcements on the road to Antrim.

When the rebel horde burst upon the town, even the grape-
shot-spewing artillery did not protect the Crown troops for long.
The garrison was beginning to break when the first elements of
the British relief column appeared just before 3 p.m.[6] This unit,
a detachment of Twenty-Second Light Dragoons under Lord
John O'Neill, fought gallantly but were also forced back by the
swarming rebel host. When their captain fell mortally wounded,
the dragoons broke . . . just as Sam Orr's Unitedmen appeared on

the scene from the west. As the redcoats fled, they ran right at the new arrivals. Orr's insurgents, mistaking the Twenty-Second's wild retreat for a desperate charge, themselves fled in confusion. The encouraged dragoons turned to make a stand. Within a half-hour, the rest of the English relieving column, under the tactical command of Colonels Durham and Clavering, charged boldly into the melee, narrowly succeeding in throwing the rebels back after fierce fighting. This battle in the North of Ireland marked one of the few times in military history that a flank attack on a beaten and unsupported foe "snatched defeat from the jaws of victory." As in the South, lack of tactical communication had torpedoed rebel hopes.

Although the rebels on the eastern coast did later succeed in taking Glenarm, the back of the Antrim rising was broken. Most of the Crown forces were freed to march south to deal with the Down insurgents. The rest, under Colonel Clavering, remained to mop up. The colonel first demanded the surrender of Randalstown; when the rebels refused, Clavering torched the town. The lesson was not lost on the Unitedmen in Ballymena, who quickly capitulated. By Monday morning 11 June, the remnants of the Antrim insurgency were trapped on Donegore Hill. When Clavering offered free pardon to all—except the leaders—who would lay down their arms and swear allegiance to the King, Henry Joy MacCracken's army disappeared. The United general was afterwards taken prisoner and executed at the Belfast Corn Market, less than one hundred yards from his home in Rosemary Lane.

HENRY JOY

Henry Joy MacCracken's place in the rebel tradition is secure. His hallowed position as a martyr of 1798 is rivalled perhaps only by Wolfe Tone and Lord Edward Fitzgerald. A young industrialist from Belfast, MacCracken had been one of the idealistic republican Dissenters stirred by the intellectual fervour of the French Revolution. Having the most to lose—he was probably the wealthiest of the Ulster Unitedmen—Henry Joy had nonetheless been active in the movement from the beginning, and had been among the select group of United Irishmen who had accompanied Tone and Sam Neilson to Cave Hill in 1795. MacCracken was the only founding member of the Society who actually took the field in 1798.

This quiet lament is still widely sung, particularly among the Republicans of modern Belfast.

An Ulsterman I'm proud to be,
From the Antrim glens I come;
And though I labour by the sea,
I have followed flag and drum.

I have heard the martial tramp of men,
I've seen men fight and die;
And, as to Eire, I remember when
I followed Henry Joy.

I pulled my boat in from the sea
And hid my sails away;
I put my nets under a tree
And I scanned the moonlit bay.

The boys were out—the redcoats, too—
I kissed my wife goodbye,
And there beneath that greenwood shade,
I followed Henry Joy.

Well we fought for Ireland's glory then,
For home and shire we bled;
Though our numbers few our hearts beat true
And five-to-one lay dead.

Aye, and many a mother mourned her lad,
And many a man his boy,
For youth was strong in that gallant throng
That followed Henry Joy.

In Belfast Town they built a tree
And the redcoats mustered there;
I heard him come with the beating drum
Sounding o'er the barracks square.

He kissed his sister, went aloft,
And said a sad goodbye;
And as he died, I turned and cried,
"You have murdered Henry Joy!"

HENRY JOY MacCRACKEN

Of all the slain heroes of 1798, MacCracken was perhaps the most dashing. Young, rich, and handsome, he sacrificed a much envied life for the cause of a republican Ireland. Not surprisingly, he has presented the nationalist balladeers with a perfect martyr.[7]

Most historians have tended to dismiss MacCracken's military leadership, correctly noting that better communication with Sam Orr's column and/or an earlier attack on Antrim may have won the day. If the United Irish general's tactical talents were limited, a case can be made that his rude strategic skill was not inconsiderable. It is at least debatable if the British would have been able to crush the Antrim rising so quickly had not General Nugent, privy to MacCracken's plan, been able to denude his County Down forces for the effort. Rare indeed is the successful general whose enemy knows in advance what he is going to do. Even without the five thousand "missing" Defenders, even with the decided lack of tactical communication, even without artillery, even with Crown pre-knowledge of rebel strategy, the United Irish defeat at Antrim was a close thing, turning on a case of mistaken intention at the critical moment of the battle.

Since British reinforcements were not sent to Wexford until after the Down rising was scuttled at Ballinahinch, it is interesting to speculate on possible Crown strategy had MacCracken still been in the field tying up the troops General Nugent would use against the Down rebels. In the event it is a credit to the professional skill of the English general officer that Dublin Castle never had to face the question.

This old ballad is representative of the many keens sung for the northern United Irish commandant. It is attributed to Dr. Drennan of the Dublin Unitedmen.

Twas on the Belfast mountains I heard a maid complain,
She vexed the sweet June evening with her heart-broken strain,
Saying, "Woe is me! Life's anguish is more than I can dree
Since Henry Joy MacCracken died on the gallows tree!"

"At Donegore he proudly rode and wore a suit of green,
And brave though vain at Antrim, his sword flashed lightning keen;
And when by spies surrounded, his band to Slemish fled,
He came into the Cave Hill for to rest his weary head."

"I watched for him each night as in our cot he slept;
At daybreak in the heather to MacArt's Fort we crept.
When news came from Greencastle of a good ship anchored nigh,
And down by yon green fountain we met to say goodbye."

"He says, 'My love, be cheerful, for tears and fears are vain.'
He says, 'My love, be hopeful, our land shall rise again!'
He kissed me very fondly, he kissed me three times o'er,
Saying, 'Death shall never part us, my love for evermore.' "

"That night I climbed the Cave Hill and watched till morning blazed,
And when its fires had kindled across the lough, I gazed—
I saw an English schooner at anchor off Garmoyle;
But alas! No good ship sailing away to France's soil."

"Twice that night a trampling came from the old shore road,
Twas Ellis and his yeomen (false Niblock with them strode);
My father home returning, the doleful story told—
'Alas!' he said, 'Young Harry Joy for fifty pounds is sold!' "

Now on the Belfast mountains this fair maiden's voice is still,
For in a grave they laid her on high Carmoney Hill;
The sad waves beneath her chant the Requiem for the Dead,
The rebel winds shrieks "Freedom!" above her weary head.

On 5 June, the day before the rescheduled risings were to begin in Ulster, the two senior United Irish officers for Down were arrested. Consequently, the Unitedmen who rose in that county took to the field group-by-group without co-ordination. Though some of the insurgents did gather on schedule, it was not until four days later that they were to have a commanding general. Henry Munro, a Scottish linen-draper with a shop in Lisburn, eventually emerged as leader of the United forces for Down—three full days after MacCracken's defeat at Antrim.

When Munro finally took command at the Windmill Hill just outside Ballinahinch, there were marauding bands of rebels already operating around Saintfield and Newtownards. General Nugent's plan was working admirably. His arrest of the Down military leadership had prevented the insurgents from working together, gaining the British general the time he needed to crush MacCracken. Now Nugent would be able to give the Down insurrectionists his undivided attention.

General Nugent moved before Munro had a chance to begin creating a cohesive military force out of the disorganised insurgency. Lieutenant Colonel Stewart's Argyleshire Fencibles were ordered to march on Ballinahinch from their Downpatrick base. Nugent meanwhile took personal command of the fifteen hundred troops *en route* from Belfast and Blaris.

On 9 June a rebel unit under a Dr. Jackson routed Colonel Stapleton's York Fencibles at Saintfield. The next day another independent rebel band attacked the redcoat garrison at Newtownards. Led by a schoolmaster named Fox, this second United group succeeded in ousting the defenders with great slaughter—earning the action the appellation "Pike Sunday." Unsure of what to do with his victory, Fox trooped his men to Jackson's camp at Saintfield. When he arrived, he found that their trek was not over; the men at Saintfield had been ordered by Munro to join the main body at Windmill Hill. The tired rebels straggled into the main rebel camp during the evening of 11 June. Munro's army was now seven thousand strong.

As Fox and Jackson arrived in the insurgent camp, General Nugent was sending Colonel Leslie's Monaghan Militia into the town of Ballinahinch itself. The militiamen quickly sunk to the same sort of wild drunkeness and pillaging that had plagued the Wexford rebels less than a week earlier. Whereas the professional British officers in the South had exploited such vulnerability to great advantage, the untrained United Irish captains in the North did not even recognise their opponents' weakness. After a fierce debate among the rebel officers, Munro decided to hold off his assault until daylight on the 12th. The delay cost dearly.

When the rested insurgents finally charged the town in the morning, the hungover Monaghan Militia found the pikemen impossible to check. General Nugent was compelled to send in his reserves as the bold rebel assaults—aided immeasurably by an unexpected fifth column of townspeople—forced the redcoats back.[8] In the meantime, however, Colonel Stewart's unnoticed Scottish Fencibles had flanked the main insurgent forces. Promptly unlimbering his artillery, Stewart stopped the rebel advance cold. After desperate fighting, the insurgent attack ebbed from the market square of the town; the superior tactical leadership and expertly trained artillery of the British had once again proved decisive. As was to be expected of untrained rebel forces, the retreat quickly turned into a rout.

The Down rising was over. Some of the fleeing rebels put up a halting defense at Saintfield but were soon dispersed. The Battle of Ballinahinch had marked the death knell of Rebel Ulster. After centuries of dominating Irish resistance to the English Crown, the northern province would henceforth look elsewhere for leadership.

GENERAL MUNRO

In addition to the four hundred dead the rebels left on the field at Ballinahinch, many others were soon run down by the pursuing Crown forces. One of those captued was the insurgent commander, Henry Munro. He was quickly tried and condemned. A scafford was erected directly across the street from his linen-drapery in Lisburn, and the unfortunate Scotsman was hanged with his family looking on from their living quarters above the shop.

The object lesson backfired on the English. The callous "subtlety" in the siting of the hanging tree transformed the inept military leader into yet another Irish rebel martyr. This lament, sung in the streets of the North soon after the Unitedman's death, is still heard today.

My name is George Campbell, at the age of eighteen
I joined the Unitedmen to strive for the Green,
And many's the battle I did undergo
With our hero commander, brave General Munro.

Have you heard of the Battle of Ballinahinch,
Where the people, oppressed, rose up in defense?
When Munro left the mountains his men took the field
And they fought for twelve hours and never did yield.

Munro being tired and in want of his sleep,
Gave a woman twelve guineas his secret to keep;
But when she had the money, the devil tempted her so
That she sent for the soldiers and surrendered Munro.

The Army they came and surrounded the place,
And they took him to Lisburn and they lodged him in jail;
His father and mother in passing that way,
Heard the very last words that their dear son did say.

"Oh, I die for my country as I fought for her cause,
And I don't fear your soldiers nor yet heed your laws;
And let every true man who hates Ireland's foe
Fight bravely for Freedom like Henry Munro!"

Twas early one morning when the sun was still low,
That they murdered our hero brave General Munro;
And high o'er the court house stuck his head on a spear
For to make the Unitedmen tremble with fear.

Then up stepped his sister and all dressed in green,
And with a sword by her side that was well-sharped and keen;
Giving three hearty cheers and away she did go,
Saying, "I'll have revengee for my brother, General Munro."

All ye good men who listen, just think of the fate
Of the brave men who died in the year Ninety-Eight;
For poor old Ireland would be free long ago
If her songs were all rebel, like *General Munro*.

There was some other scattered rebel activity in the North during 1798. Some peasants, bridling under the two-year dragooning of Ulster, used the risings as an excuse to settle scores with their local oppressors. Though not really associated with the United Irish hierarchy, they happily took to the field under the United "banner."

THE WILD HAZEL GLEN

Watty Graham of Crewe Hill led a localised rising in the Maghera area of County Londonderry. Rather than rising to Orr at Toome to join MacCracken's attack on Antrim, Graham's rebels concentrated on disposing of old accounts. When Billy Cuddy, one of the Maghera captains, was hanged after the rising was crushed, his neighbors managed to cut him down before he was dead. To cover his escape, the local people held a mock funeral complete with a procession to St. Lurach's Chapel. The lamented Billy's coffin was buried with great solemnity. There is still a stone in the old graveyard marking the "Buryingplace of William Cuddy." The corpse lived to a ripe old age in the United States.

This song is representative of such rebels. These were not men who rose for some theoretical political philosophy; these were poor peasants who revolted against the "red ruin" that the yeomanry left in their wake. As the song emphasizes, the blood of these bitter peasants "reddened the altars down many a wild hazel glen."

The yeoman trooped down on the village,
Red ruin they left in their trail,
And the flames licked the rooftops at midnight,
Like banners they streamed on the gale.
The groans and the shrieks of the dying
Woke the echoes again and again,
And the *caoines* were the wail of the banshee,
That night in the Wild Hazel Glen.

Young Diarmuid was bold as an eagle,
He was chief of the patriot band
Who were watching far off from the hillside
Awaiting the clash on the land.
And when morning's full glories were beaming
O'er the moor at long Carraig Fen,
They marched with their pike-blades a-gleaming
A-down through the Wild Hazel Glen.

They swept like the rain-swollen torrent,
Death poised on each keen-pointed blade,
And their bosoms were panting for vengeance
For their sisters and sweethearts betrayed.
And the wives and the fathers and mothers
That lay shroudless and coffinless then,
And the homes that were blackened and roofless
That morn in the Wild Hazel Glen.

But sad are the hearts that loved Diarmuid,
For he fell in the vanguard that day,
But whenever his rifle was levelled,
A yeoman went down in the fray.
Old Ireland, you never had martyrs
More true than the frieze-coated men
Whose life-blood has reddened the altars
Down many a Wild Hazel Glen.

Ulster had been no more successful in rebellion than had been the rest of Ireland. The northern Unitedmen had, in fact, risen haltingly, confusedly, and ultimately, ineptly. What the Irish National Tradition was to remember, however, was the intellectual and emotional legacy of the province: the United Irish movement had been born in Ulster, a movement that, for the first time in Irish history, had championed the rights of the common people of Ireland. The northern Unitedmen were not merely rebels, they were revolutionaries. The Ulstermen had introduced a concept into the national consciousness that has dominated the thinking of Irish nationalists ever since: The Republic.

CHAPTER NOTES (16)

1 — In a report to Dublin Castle from his post at Belfast in late spring of 1797, General Lake stated his opinion in the clearest possible terms:

"The lower order of the people and most of the middle class are determined Republicans . . . and will not be contented with anything short of revolution. . . . Nothing but coercive measures in the strongest degree can have any weight in this country."

2 — Reverend Dickson later reminisced about the events of May 1798:

"In that month several communications from the Executive *relative to the Insurrection* had been communicated. Special orders with respect to the Counties had been given. . . ." (*italics mine*)

3 — Simms' failure to act became, in at least one case, self-fulfilling insurance that his pessimism was well founded: a half-dozen cannon, secreted by the Unitedmen since the time of the Volunteers, were unearthed by the Crown (well after the day appointed for the rising). The rebels were badly in need of artillery after the Ulster fighting finally did begin.

4 — Sam Orr had good reason to be a stanch Unitedman. He was brother to Willie Orr, the "martyr" of 1797.

5 — It may have been that the Defenders' mistrust was well-founded. Robert Kee quotes a ballad sung soon after the fight at Antrim:

> Treachery, treachery, damnable treachery!
> Put the poor Catholics all in the front,
> The Protestants next was the way they were fixed
> And the black-mouthed Dissenters they skulked at the rump.

6 — The major reason that Lumley and Skeffington were able to hold on for almost an hour was their effective use of their cannon. The insurgents had only one piece of artillery at the outbreak of the battle. The gun blew up on its second discharge. MacCracken could dearly have used the six cannon the Crown had discovered at the end of May.

7 — Another reason that MacCracken is beloved by many Irish nationalists lies in his devotion to the retrieval of the lost Gaelic tradition of Ulster. Edward Bunting, the first collector of ancient Irish music, had an office in the MacCracken household in Rosemary Lane. Next door lived a good friend, the "Gaelic Preacher" of the Belfast Synod of the Presbyterian Community (whose duty it was to "preach in any place where he may have an Irish congregation and audience"). MacCracken was also a founding member in 1791 of the Belfast Harp Society which held the great harper's assembly of the next year (the music of which so impressed the impatient Wolfe Tone that he was caused to comment that "all the good Irish airs are already written").

Mary MacNeill has pointed out correctly that it was:

> "in the bosom of rationalist presbyterian Belfast the Renaissance of Irish music took place, the precursor by a century of the Irish Gaelic revival."

In the home of Henry Joy MacCracken, the Irish revival went far beyond the music.

8 — One of the townwomen who fought on the side of the rebels, the youthful Betsy Grey, emerged from this battle with a special place in the tragic folk tradition of Irish nationalism. Wounded during the fighting, Miss Grey and two companions who were attempting to help her escape after the battle were overtaken by the yeomanry and put to death.

17

Reprisal

In his speech from the dock in November 1798, Wolfe Tone would sum up the United Irish rebellion succinctly:

> In a cause like this, success is everything. Success in the eyes of the vulgar fixes its merits. Washington succeeded, and Kosciusko failed.

Tone was to suffer a harsher fate at the hands of the "vulgar" than his Polish contemporary; five months earlier, however, it was the poor peasants of Ireland who were paying the price for lack of success. A Protestant minister wrote of what was happening around him:

> From the commencement of the rebellion soldiers, yeomen, and supplementaries, frequently executed without any trial such as they judged worthy of death, even persons found unarmed in their own houses.

In order to understand why the authorities condoned savagery in dealing with the rebellious (and the innocent) peasants of '98, it is helpful to imagine once again how the insurrection must have appeared from the vantage of Dublin Castle. Consider, for example, the situation on 6 June, exactly two weeks after the interception of the mail-coaches.

On that day the news of the furious battle for New Ross reached the Castle. Even more disturbing, though, was another dispatch that arrived almost simultaneously from London: Bonaparte had sailed from Toulon on 19 May . . . destination unknown. The rebels had risen within four days of the French sailing. To the nervous Camden and Castlereagh, the timing must have seemed ominous.

If the lords of Dublin Castle were alarmed, it was understandable. The Irish insurgency had just fought a professionally led British garrison-in-force to a standstill at New Ross before retiring with army intact; another host of rebels had drawn the measure of the English column at Tubberneering and was known to be advancing on an outmatched Crown force at Arklow; marauding insurrectionists controlled the trackless mountains of County Wicklow; Aylmer's insurgent bands were roaming freely through County Kildare; General Nugent was warning that the North was about to explode; and now—Bonaparte!

Lord Camden had earlier cordially encouraged barbarism in the attempt to get the risings started prematurely. To the troubled Viceroy, it must now have looked as if his strategy might backfire—if Napoleon was headed for Ireland, he would land smack in the middle of an island already aflame. Under the circumstances, it would have been strange if the apprehensive Lord Lieutenant *had* tried to curb the ongoing excesses of his troops. Terror now had a new purpose: to discourage the still peaceful peasants from joining their treasonous fellows in the field. After the risings had been beaten down, the government was able to find yet another justification for the continuation of the savagery; terror could also be used to cow the peasantry so that the cottiers would not rise to the French banner if a landing finally did come.

RODY McCORLEY

As was happening already in Leinter—and was to occur in northern Connacht later in the year—the crushing of rebellion in Ulster was the signal for great brutality and slaughter by the authorities. Guilt or innocence of the victims was not normally of primary concern to the soldiery. Indeed, the Reverend James Gordon reported that the redcoats "often plundered without distinction of loyalist or croppy." Lecky's analysis of the carnage transported him to "distant and darker ages, in which the first conditions of civilised society . . . are unapplicable."

The National Tradition is dotted with the defiant deaths of obscure young insurgents whose names have been lost to recorded history. If lost to the scholars, their names have not been forgotten by the people. The songwriters have immortalised even minor rebel martyrs.

Ethna Carbery, a minor poet of the late nineteenth century, rewrote a 1798 ballad about just such a young rebel. Rody McCorley was a County Antrim Defender executed on the shore of Lough Neagh in the wake of the Ulster rising. His public hanging was not an atypical scene in the months, and years, after the United Irish failure.

　　The quatrain given immediately below is from the original ballad.　The song that follows it is the famous version written by Miss Carbery.　Such rewriting of old ballads is a common genesis of rebel balladry.

Traditional:

　　Come tender-hearted Christians, all attention to me pay
　　Till I relate these verses great, these verses two or three,
　　Concerning of a noble youth who was cut off in his bloom,
　　And died upon the gallows tree near to the bridge of Toome.

Ethna Carbery:

　　Ho!　See the hosts of fleetfoot men
　　Who speed with faces wan,
　　From farmstead and from fisher's cot
　　Upon the banks of Bann.
　　They come with vengeance in their eyes;
　　Too late, too late are they—
　　For young Rody McCorley goes to die
　　On the bridge of Toome today.

　　Oh!　Ireland, Mother Ireland,
　　You love them still: the best,
　　The fearless brave, who fighting fell
　　Upon your hapless breast;
　　But never a one of all your dead
　　More bravely fell in fray
　　Than he who marches to his fate
　　On the bridge of Toome today.

　　Up the narrow street he stepped
　　Smiling proud and young;
　　About the hemp-rope round his neck,
　　The golden ringlets clung,
　　There's never a tear in his blue eyes,
　　Both glad and bright are they,
　　As Rody McCorley goes to die
　　On the bridge of Toome today.

Because he loved the Motherland,
Because he loved the Green,
He goes to meet the martyr's fate
With proud and joyous mein;
True to the last, oh, true to the last,
He treads the upward way;
Young Rody McCorley goes to die
On the bridge of Toome today.

Lord Camden had repeatedly petitioned London for help from the day that insurrection broke out. Pitt, exasperated, decided that firmer hands were needed on the reins in Dublin. On 20 June, Lord Charles Cornwallis arrived in the Irish capital to take over the viceroyalty. The new Lord Lieutenant resignedly described the situation dumped into his lap:

> The violence of our friends and their folly in endeavouring to make it a religious war, added to the ferocity of our troops, who delight in murder. . . . The minds of the people are now in such a state that nothing but blood will satisfy them . . . their conversation and conduct point to no other mode of concluding this unhappy business, than that of extirpation.

Cornwallis was not the only English soldier who found his duties distasteful. General John Moore, overwrought at the conduct of some yeomanry units under his command, was moved to declare that "if I were an Irishman I would be a rebel."[1]

As early as 10 June there had been voices within the Castle counselling amnesty for rebels who wished to desert the United men.[2] The difficulty, of course, was that by this time there was no place for them to go. One Dublin official complained that Crown reprisals were actually prolonging the rebellion:

> Unfortunately, their houses are destroyed, their absence marked, and until it is wise to grant a general amnesty, no individual, irritated as the soldiery are, can safely leave their main body.

The first pardons were not to be issued by the authorities until the middle of July.

GREEN UPON THE CAPE

In the evolving tradition of Irish folk-song, different sets of

lyrics are often set to the same air. The collector Seán Ó Boyle
quotes an Armagh weaver-poet who spun lyrics along with her
yarn: "I always make my poems to the lie of a good tune."
In the North, some of these tunes were old pipe airs from across
the North Channel. In this Ulster variant of *The Wearing of the
Green,* the fleeing Defender is lucky indeed to chance upon a
ship with a Jacobin crew. There were few humble rebels who
made it to Paris.

     Most of those who "were out" with MacCracken and Munro
did not get the opportunity to flee. Those that did usually naïvely attempted to cross to the Lowlands. They were routinely
rounded up in Glasgow and shipped back for trial. Many of
those who survived the assizes found themselves embarked on
somewhat longer voyages than they had envisioned: the Irish
brogue was heard with increasing frequency in New South Wales
and on the lower decks of British sail-of-the-line. Some very
few, such as the rebel poet James Orr, were able to escape to
America.

I'm a lad that's forced an exile
From my own native land;
For an oath that's passed against me
In this country I can't stand;
But while I'm at my liberty
I will make my escape;
I'm a poor distressed croppy
For the Green on my cape!

Refrain:
For the Green on my cape!
For the Green upon my cape!
I'm distressed but not disheartened,
For the Green on my cape!

But I'll go down to Belfast
To see that seaport gay,
And tell my aged parents
In this country I can't stay.
Oh, tis dark will be their sorrow,
But no truer hearts I've seen,
And they'd rather see me dying
Than a traitor to the Green!

Refrain:
Oh, the wearing of the Green!
Oh, the wearing of the Green!
May the Curse of Cromwell darken
Each traitor to the Green!

When I went down to Belfast
And saw that seaport grand,
My aged parents blessed me,
And blessed poor Ireland.
Then I went onto a captain
And bargained with him cheap,
He told me that his whole ship's crew
Wore Green upon the cape!

Refrain:
Oh, the Green upon the cape!
Oh, the Green upon the cape!
God's blessing guard the noble boys
With Green upon their cape!

Twas early the next morning
Our gallant ship did sail;
Kind heaven did protect her
With a pleasant Irish gale;
We landed safe in Paris
Where victualling was cheap—
They knew we were Unitedmen
From the Geen upon our cape!

Refrain:
We wore Green upon the cape!
We wore Green upon the cape!
And they treated us like brothers
For the Green upon our cape!

Take courage now, my brave boys,
For here you have good friends,
And we'll send a convoy with you
Down by their Orange dens.
And if they should oppose us
With their weapons sharp and keen,

We'll make them rue and curse the day
That they e'er saw the Green!

Refrain:
That they e'er saw the Green!
That they e'er saw the Green!
We'll show them our authority
With wearing of the Green!

Oh, may the winds of Freedom
Soon send young Boney o'er,
And we'll plant the Tree of Liberty
Upon our shamrock shore.
Oh, we'll plant it with our weapons,
While the English tyrants gape
To see their bloody flag torn down
And Green upon the cape!

Refrain:
Oh, the wearing of the Green!
Oh, the wearing of the Green!
God grant us soon to see that day,
And in freedom wear the Green!

After the northern Unitedmen had been crushed, the Crown was able to move against the remaining rebel forces with very little constraint. British reinforcements poured across the Irish Sea.[3] As has been seen, General Lake had moved south toward the Wexford insurgent camp on Vinegar Hill. At the same time, the government had finally began to neutralise the Kildare insurrection. Shortly after the 12 June Battle of Ballinahinch in the North, William Aylmer had been forced from his Whelp Rock camp near Blessington. The rebel general retreated grudgingly across the county to Prosperous, on the edge of the great Bog of Allen. Constant government harassment convinced Aylmer that his position was still vulnerable; the Unitedmen consequently withdrew his forces into the bogland where the redcoats were loath to follow. By the end of June, his three thousand rebels were safely, if hungrily, encamped at easily defended Timahoe.

As the new month began, the United Irish rebellion had ceased to exist; Dublin Castle was by now treating its campaign as a mopping-up operation. By 8 July Cornwallis was able to report to London that there were only three isolated remnants of the revolt still causing problems. The Lord Lieutenant was referring to Aylmer in Kildare; to County Wicklow, where Joseph Holt and Michael Dwyer were leading guerrilla bands through the mountains; and to northern Wexford, where gadding groups of deserters from the militia and yeomanry were supposed to be roaming the forests. As regards the last, Lord Cornwallis' information was somewhat dated.

After William Byrne's surrender at Coolgreany on 4 July, the remnants of the Wexford insurgency had fled northward into the Wicklow Mountains. Several hundred refugees from Byrne's rebel force joined the last intact Wexford unit. This small army hiding in the forested hills was under the combined leadership of Edward Fitzgerald and Anthony Perry, the former Crown prisoners who had led the assault on Arklow, and Father Moses Kearns, who had commanded the rebel attack on Newtownbarry. The insurgent captains finally gathered about two thousand men and set off to the northwest. This rag-tag troupe somehow struggled through County Kildare undetected and, by 10 July, had linked up with Aylmer, Ware, and Luby at Timahoe.

The rebel officers argued bitterly about the future. The Kildare men and Fitzgerald were discouraged, arguing for negotiation with the Crown. Kearns and Perry were not convinced that the government was interested in talking. Indeed, they were of a mind with Lord Cornwallis who was having trouble calling off the hounds . . . even in College Green. When the Viceroy's acting Chief Secretary attempted to mute a parliamentary blood-hunt for Henry Grattan and John Philpot Curran, John Beresford accused Castlereagh, of all people, of being soft on traitors (Grattan and Curran—no friends of the rebels—had been protesting the malevolent reprisals of the Crown troops). It is little wonder that the Wexford men were not willing to take a chance on the government's mercy.

As Aylmer began tentative dealings with the Castle, Father Kearns and Anthony Perry struck off northwards across Meath trying to raise the countryside. It was far too late. The cowed peasants shunned the rebels and, as the insurgents moved into Louth—once a hotbed of Defenderism—their own forces began to desert. By the time the Wexfordmen decided to face reality, their time had run out. They straggled back to Timahoe to join the negotiations only to find that Alymer had already surrendered his army on 23 July. Aylmer's staff had been allowed self-exile and the United general himself was sent to Botany Bay; the rebels returning from Louth were not so fortunate. Perry and Kearns were caught and executed at Edenderry as they tried to escape to the West.

Lord Cornwallis was to find the men in the hills of Wicklow somewhat more elusive. The rebel bands under Joseph Holt and Mickey Dwyer knew the mountains intimately. The government, on the other hand, found the land impenetrable. Holt's Protestant guerrillas often took refuge in a beautiful but militarily forbidding chasm just northwest of Ashford called Devil's Glen. Dwyer's Catholics, like the men of Fiach MacHugh O'Bryne some two centuries earlier, operated out of the wild valley of Glenmalure. Though Holt was finally to come down from the hills in late autumn, Mickey Dwyer was able to keep his band intact for five years, and was to figure prominently in Robert Emmet's plans for rising in 1803.

MICHAEL DWYER (I)

Mickey Dwyer's continued defiance became a rallying point for the United Irish survivors of 1798. The importance of his guerrilla fight to the rebel tradition is underscored by this early twentieth-century ballad by Peader Kearney. The song recalls for the listener that at the gloomiest moment in rebel history, when the risings of 1798 had been crushed, Dwyer never quit. It is not surprising that the song was extremely popular among the men on the run during the dark days of the Black and Tan War.

Kearney is probably the most famous, and certainly was one of the most prolific, of rebel songwriters. His 1907 *The Soldier's Song* was later to become the national anthem of the Irish Republic.

Have you heard of Michael Dwyer and his mountain men,
Runs your blood like molten fire when you hear it again?
How he dashed like mountain torrent on his country's bitter foes,
Like a thundering, tearing torrent on the craven yeos?

Refrain:
Here's the chorus, chant it loudly on the still night air,
As the war-shout rises proudly o'er the trumpets blare;

Chant it! Peal it! till it echoes over every hill and glen,
Here's to gallant Michael Dwyer and his mountain men!

When the star of freedom vanished and our flag went down,
And the nation's hope was banished from each vale and town.
Borne intact through blood and fire, Ireland's banner waved again,
Held aloft by Michael Dwyer and his mountain men.

Refrain

Still the nation's hopes are burning as they burned of yore,
And the young and strong are yearning for the battle's roar;
But the blessed star of liberty shall never blaze again,
Till we strike like Michael Dwyer and his mountain men.

Refrain

One of the most curious features of the rebellion of 1798 was a non-event: the comparative quiet outside Leinster and Ulster. With the exception of Samuel MacTier's small group in Sligo, there was no really viable United organisation in all of Connacht. In truth, the United Irishmen had never done much proselytising in the western province and did not really expect much from the West. The real disappointment was the silence in Munster.

It is likely that the February arrest of Arthur O'Connor had much to do with the absence of rebellion in the Southwest. O'Connor's brother Roger, an influential Defender leader in County Cork, had been arrested when the risings first broke out. Since co-ordination between the United Irishmen and the Defenders was problematical in any case, the arrest of the brothers probably broke whatever fragile link that may have been forged between the two groups in Munster—particularly since there was no United Irish National Executive left by the time the insurrection exploded over the East and North of Ireland.

There *is* another plausible explanation for the quiet in the Southwest, one usually ignored by rebel historians. It is likely that the people of Munster were not as disaffected as the United-men believed. Certainly there had been no sign of incipient rebellion when the French fleet was in Bantry Bay back in December 1796. The *London Gazette* of 7 January 1797 had stated the situation clearly:

> . . . the greatest loyalty has manifested itself throughout the king-
> dom [*of Ireland*]; and in the south and west, where the troops
> have been in motion, they have been met by the country people
> of all descriptions with provisions and all sorts of accommodations
> to facilitate their march; and every demonstration has been given
> of the zeal and ardour of the nation to oppose the enemy. . . .

All available evidence does tend to indicate, as Lecky says:

> that the great body of Catholics did not at this time show the
> slightest wish to throw off the English rule, and that their spon-
> taneous and unforced sympathies were with the British flag.

There was, to be sure, one other reason for the Munstermen to stay quiet in 1798. The authorities in the province were extraordinarily ruthless in their attempt to root out suspected Defenders and Unitedmen. The High Sherrif of Tipperary, as has been seen, pacified that county by the brutal use of the flogging-triangle. His methods were the rule rather than the exception in Munster. It is not unlikely that many southwestern peasants were secretly rooting for their rebel countrymen but were fearful of taking to the fields themselves without leadership.

THE VOW OF TIPPERARY

There *was* one brief flare-up in Munster. On 20 June a small band of Defenders attacked a Westmeath Militia unit under Lieutenant Colonel Sir Hugh O'Reilly. The raid near Ballynascarthy, on the Bandon-Clonakilty road, was ostensibly a bid by the Defenders to free some comrades held by O'Reilly. The lack of any other action in Munster suggests that the swiftly suppressed "Cork Incident" was in no way connected with the United Irishmen.

This Thomas Davis song first appeared in *The Spirit of the Nation*. While it does not relate specifically to the events of 1798, it does give a vivid idea of the bitterness caused by the debilitating policies of the authorities in one Munster county.

From Carrick streets to Shannon shore,
From Slievenamon to Ballindeary,
From Longford Pass to Galtrymore,
Come hear The Vow of Tipperary.

Too long we fought for Britain's cause,
And of our blood were never chary;
She paid us back with tyrant laws,
And thinned The Homes of Tipperary.

Too long, with rash and single arm,
The peasant strove to guard his eyrie,
Till Irish blood bedewed each farm,
And Ireland wept for Tipperary.

But never more we'll lend a hand—
Hear us heaven and Virgin Mary!
Except in war for Native Land,
And *that's* The Vow of Tipperary!

To coax William Alymer's Kildare rebels into capitulating, Lord Cornwallis had offered an anmesty for all but the leaders on 17 July. The Irish Parliament had followed with an Amnesty Act three days later. After some negotiation that insured his officers' lives, Alymer had surrendered on 23 July. The submission of the Timahoe insurgents marked the end of the United Irish rebellion. If resistance was over, however, bloodletting was not. The yeomanry and militia showed marked enthusiasm in the sanguinary business of mopping up. The peasants soon found that the "Cornys," as the pardons were popularly known, were singularly ineffectual in defending them from the marauding redcoats in the countryside.

The ongoing savagery probably did not surprise the Lord Lieutenant. Cornwallis at this time had little respect for either the militia or the yeomanry. It was not merely the disdain of the professional military man for the amateur. In an 8 July letter to the Duke of Portland, he had written:

> The Irish militia are totally without discipline, contemptible before the enemy when any serious resistance is before them, but ferocious and cruel in the extreme when any poor wretches, either with or without arms, come within their power—in short, murder seems to be their favorite pastime.

Sixteen days later, the Viceroy had presumably decided that the yeomanry had outdone even the militia. In a dispatch to Major General Ross, Cornwallis complained of:

> numberless murders that are hourly committed by [*the yeomanry*]

without any process or examination whatever. These men have
saved the country, but now take the lead in rapine and murder.

The Lord Lieutenant's petulance did not translate into con-
straints upon the redcoats.

THE PATRIOT MOTHER

The years of 1797-98 had been disturbing ones for William
Pitt and the British Crown. The English had been reduced to the
role of spectators behind their so-far ineffective blockade while
most of Europe had been lost to the French. If the Crown
troops in Ireland were nettled by the Irish risings, they were
more concerned by the very real threat of a landing by French
regulars on the island. The true state of British morale was
perhaps best demonstrated in the early autumn when an hysteria
of relief greeted the dispatches announcing Nelson's victory at
Aboukir Bay. It is not unreasonable to deduce that some of
the British savagery in Ireland during 1798 may have been rooted
in the troops' feeling of helplessness as the French Army roamed
freely through Europe . . . if they could not get at the French,
they could make the "Frog-loving" natives suffer in the meantime.

The months following the suppression of rebellion in
Ireland passed with the tatoo of rolling drums providing somber
background about the scaffold. This mid-nineteenth century
ballad by "Eva of the *Nation*" tells the story of an unlucky
Kildare rebel for whom those drums beat. Mary Eva Kelly was a
famous rebel poet who was to wait patiently for a decade to
marry her fiancé, Kevin O'Doherty, a Young Irelander who was
in prison for his part in the 1848 outbreak.

"Come tell us the name of the rebelly crew
Who lifted the pike on the Curragh with you;
Come tell us the treason and then you'll be free,
Or right quickly you'll swing from the high gallows tree!"

"*Alanna*! *Alanna*! The shadow of shame
Has never yet fallen on one of your name,
And O may the food from my bosom you drew,
In your veins turn to poison, if *you* turn untrue."

"The foul words—O let them not blacken your tongue
That would prove to your friends and your country a wrong,
Or the curse of a mother, so bitter and dread,
With the wrath of the Lord—may they fall on your head!"

"I have no one but you in the whole world wide.
Yet false to your pledge, you'd ne'er stand at my side:
If a traitor you lived, you'd be father away
From my heart than, if true, you were wrapped in the clay!"

"O deeper and darker the mourning would be
For your falsehood so base, than your death proud and free;
Dearer, far dearer than ever to me,
My darling, you'll be on the brave gallows tree."

"'Tis holy, *agra,* from the bravest and best—
Go! Go! from my heart, and be joined with the rest,
Alanna machree! O *alanna machree*!
Sure a 'stag' and a traitor you never would be."

There's no look of a traitor upon the young brow
That's raised to the tempters so haughtily now;
No traitor e'er held up the firm head so high—
No traitor e'er showed such a proud flashing eye.

On the high gallows tree! On the brave gallows tree!
Where smiled leaves and blossoms, his sad doom met he!
But it never bore blossoms so pure or so fair
As the heart of the martyr that hangs from it there!

When the risings had begun on 23 May, most of the United Irish high command were already behind bars. As the rebellion continued through June and dragged into July, Dublin Castle began to prosecute the internees. The trials proceeded according to law, a courtesy not normally extended to the rebels in the field. The results, nonetheless, proved similar to those of the drum-head courts in the countryside.

The execution of Henry and John Sheares was soon followed by the hanging of John McCann. When Sam Neilson, Oliver Bond, and Billy Byrne were condemned, the United leaders began to get the message. They decided to trade information for their lives.

Dr. McNeven, Thomas Emmet, and Arthur O'Connor, with the acquiescence of the other United Irish prisoners, struck a deal with the government. The three agreed to tell all they knew of the Society's activities so long as they did not have to divulge names. In return, the Crown was to halt the executions and the prisoners were to be allowed to emigrate to the country of their choice. The Unitedmen were not aware that the government so far had tried only those prisoners whom they "had cold." The Castle was loath to use informers in open trial, the life expectancy of informers being notoriously short in Ireland. Without their testimony, on the other hand, the government had no real case against many of the prisoners. Castlereagh's Under Secretary complained that the most important Unitedmen "could not be disposed of without doing such a violence to the principles of law and evidence as could not well be justified."

In the event the prisoners were able to tell the Crown little that it did not know already from its operatives within the United Irish organisation. The United leadership spent the next four years as guest of His Majesty's Government at Fort George near Inverness in Scotland; they were not to be released until England and France signed the Peace of Amiens in 1802.

BILLY BYRNE OF BALLYMANUS

Three of the prize United Irish prisoners were held at Wicklow Gaol: Oliver Bond, Sam Neilson, and William Byrne. All three had already been sentenced to death when the United prisoners in Dublin entered into negotiations with the authorities. Indeed, there is considerable evidence that it was concern for the fate of the men at Wicklow that induced their comrades to negotiate in the first place. Emmet, O'Connor, and MacNeven, representing the Dublin prisoners, apparently believed that there was to be a hiatus in the executions until agreement could be reached.[4] Dublin Castle presumably was under no such impression.

Byrne was led to the scaffold on 28 July, some few hours before the agreement was accomplished in Dublin. Bond died shortly thereafter in what some claimed to be "mysterious" circumstances. The deaths were to have two major repercussions. First, Emmet and some others considered the Castle to have violated the agreement and, therefore, did not feel constrained to abide by it (a position solidified by four years of internment in Scotland rather than the self-exile promised). Second, young Myles Byrne, understandably outraged, became a lieutenant to Mickey Dwyer and, later, an important aide to Robert Emmet in 1803.

Come all you brave Unitedmen, I pray you lend an ear,
And listen to these verses I now will let you hear
Concerning noble Billy Byrne, a man of great renown,
Who was tried and hanged at Wicklow as a traitor to the Crown.

It was in the year of Ninety-Eight we got reason to complain,
We lost our brave commander, bold Billy Byrne his name;
He was lost at old Coolgreany and took to Wicklow Gaol,
And though we wished to free him, for him they'd take no bail.

When as prisoner he was taken the traitors forward came
To swear our hero's life away, and well they're known by name;
They had but little scruple his precious blood to spill,
And Wicklow lost, through perjury, the pride of Pleasant Hill.

Now of these false informers who in perjury agreed,
Were men that in his father's house so frequently did feed,
And at his brother's table where some of them you'd see;
Base informing paid the Byrnes for their generosity.

When they came forward for the Crown, they all against him swore
That he, among the rebels, a captain's title bore;
They swore he trained the cannon and the rebels did review,
And with that bloody cannon, he marched to Carraigrua.

Then here's to Billy Byrne, may his fame forever shine,
I will not forget his noble death when I am facing mine;
May the Lord send many more like him for it twas such men as he
Who stood upright for Ireland's Right and died for Liberty.

THE SUIT OF GREEN

If the United Irish political prisoners felt betrayed by

Dublin Castle's "abrogation" of the pact that saved their lives, the Unitedmen would find little sympathy among the peasantry. The humble folk, themselves confronted with summary execution on the whim of the rural magistracy—indeed on the caprice of many a private soldier—understandably resented the special treatment being afforded to the men who had started the whole business.

It had been dangerous to wear the colour green before the risings. Now, as has been seen, it had become a capital offense . . . or, at least, it was for the peasantry. That were options open to the upper-class Unitedmen is made evident in this scathingly satiric ballad. Such songs gave the common Irish an opportunity to voice their resentment of both "German George" and their own inept leaders.

Come all you pretty fair maids and listen to my melody,
When you hear my lamentation, I am sure that you will pity me;
Once I loved a young man, as neat a lad as could be seen,
He was torn from my arms for wearing of the suit of green.

It was on a summer's evening, as my love and I chanced to roam,
Folded in each other's arms as we strayed through yon shady grove;
He laid his head against my breast and most feelingly unto me did say,
"My life it lies in danger for wearing the suit of green."

"If this be true dear Willy, if this you tell to me be true,
I pray throw by your clothes, I'll buy for you a suit of blue!"
"No, no, my charming fair one, no cowardice shall e'er be seen,
For I am son to *Grania*, and I will always adore the Green!"

"I am a son to Erin, it was oft in my life was tore—
Our national colour and the shamrock that St. Patrick bore."
It was on a summer's evening as my love and I sat in a room,
Folded in each other's arms, immediately the guards they came.

It's with their guns the doors they broke, the moment that my love was seen;
He was torn from my arms for wearing of the suit of green.
My love he was then taken and under court-martial he was tried,
The colonel gave orders that at ten o'clock he should die.

I was sent for by my brother, a man that I wished to see,
He brought me to Dublin, the rights of law to give me;

He brought me to a merchant's shop, the neatest cloth that could be seen,
Embroidered with gold laces, he bought for me a suit of green.

I went unto His Majesty, my lamentations to make known,
Craving for his mercy, down on my bended knees did fall;
He says, "Rise up my blooming girl, your true love I shall set free,
I'll retore him to your arms and give him leave to wear the Green."

The Irish risings had been beaten down in as short a time as such an operation could effectively be performed. Ireland was more firmly under English control than it had ever been. The final chapter, however, had yet to be written. The Unitedmen in France had finally convinced their continental allies to move. If the Year of Rebellion was over, the Year of the French was just begun.

CHAPTER NOTES (17)

1 — This Scottish soldier was later knighted and, in 1808, was named Commander-in-Chief of His Majesty's forces in Portugal during the Peninsular War. In one of military history's most astonishing campaigns, Sir John led his apparently "trapped" army 250 miles across the midwinter mountains of Spain to the Galician port of Coruna. Attacked upon arrival by Marshal Soult's French, an army triple the size of Moore's, the British general led his troops brilliantly, falling—as had James Wolfe and Horatio Nelson—at the moment of victory.

An anonymous poem celebrating the soldier's gallantry, *The Burial of Sir John Moore*, was greeted with popular acclaim when it appeared in 1817:

> Slowly and sadly we laid him down,
> From the field of his fame, fresh and gory;
> We carved not a line, we raised not a stone—
> But we left him alone in his glory!

Attributed to Byron among others, the famous poem was later discovered to have been written by Dublin-born Charles Wolfe, a quiet country minister of County Armagh.

2 — Castlereagh, for one, urged the policy, pointing out correctly that the rebels were

already having trouble with desertions. Without such a policy, he argued, there was no reason for the peasants not to remain in the field and fight to the death. For his trouble, the Chief Secretary was accused of showing "criminal sympathy with traitors" by John Beresford and others of the Ascendancy.

3 — London by this time had intelligence that Napoleon was headed for other shores.

4 — MacNeven, writing after his release from Fort George, makes this point clearly:

> "An agreement was in consequence concluded and signed, which among other things stipulated for the lives of Byrne and Bond; but Government thought fit to annul this by the execution of Byrne. . . ."

Thomas Addis Emmet, on the other hand, indicates that the agreement was not presented in its final form until 4 August.

There appears to have been two agreements. The first, signed by the prisoners on 20 July may never have been presented to Dublin Castle after the prisoners heard of the execution of Byrne.

18

The Year of the French

By 1798 the French Directorate had already dispatched the armies of two nations to sea in aid of the United Irishmen. The first, French, had been defeated by heavy weather in December 1796; the second, Dutch, had been shattered by an English fleet in October 1797. The continental republicans had already lost tens of ships and thousands of men in the cause of Irish rebellion. As the risings broke out in Ireland in 1798, a small group of Unitedmen in France were almost beside themselves with frustration as they waited for still another promised invasion fleet to materialise.

Matthew Tone, Bartholomew Teeling, and Napper Tandy were forced to sit helplessly by as Matthew's brother Wolfe and Edward Lewins made repeated emotional representations to the French leaders. The United Irish ambassadors received responses that were correct, polite, non-committal, and extremely discomfiting to the anxious Irishmen. The Irish expedition was very decidedly on the back burner of a very crowded French stove.

The frowning British fleet in the English Channel had convinced Napoleon as early as February that an invasion of England itself was out of the question. Never one for half-measures, the astonishing young general had decided instead to found an empire in the Levant. With characteristic dispatch, he had created the Army of the Orient within the month, and had sailed for Malta on 19 May.[1]

The French had not forgotten their promise to the Unitedmen—indeed a diversion on England's back doorstep could only help Napoleon's Oriental adventure—but the Mediterranean enterprise had left the habitually bankrupt French Treasury once more bereft of funds. In addition, the British blockade made Gallic logistics a time-consuming overland business. As Lord

Cornwallis began his July mopping-up operations back in Ireland, orders were finally cut for the French expedition to the island. It was to be in four parts.

The initial three units were to be under the overall command of General Hardy and Commodore Bompard. First, a three-frigate flotilla under Captain Savary at La Rochelle was to land General Joseph Amable Humbert's one thousand troops and arms for five thousand insurgents on the "northwest coast" of Ireland. Humbert's task was to establish a secure beachhead, preferably in the Sligo area, meanwhile inciting the local peasants to rise to him while Savary returned to France for another three shiploads of French regulars. Second, Captain Rey, a French-American, was to sail from Normandy with an additional shipload of supplies for the supposedly "now-burgeoning" insurgency. Third, a larger fleet of ten sail was to land three thousand French troops in support of Humbert. This squadron, under the personal command of Hardy and Bompard, was to make up at Brest. A fourth unit, seven thousand men under the independent command of General Kilmaine, was to await encouraging news from Ireland before sailing to support the expected insurgency.

The French strategy was based on some rather staggering assumptions. Among other things, the French imagined that they could somehow choreograph the various sailings, voyages, and landings so that the different elements would dovetail precisely. They apparently assumed their piecemeal fleets would be able to elude the alert English naval patrols around Ireland. The weather, too, would have to co-operate so that the various units could synchronise precise landfalls. Perhaps the most remarkable presumption of all was that the peasants of the West were ready and waiting to rise. Every one of these suppositions proved wrong.

Much of the blame can be placed squarely on the fanciful planning of the French high command concerning the imagined capabilities of their vessels and their captains. The United Irish delegates to France, however, must be held culpable for misleading the French by repeated assurances that *all* Ireland would rise if only the "French were on the sea." The truth was that for whatever reason—remoteness, lack of local leadership, or even disinterest—no attempt had been made by the Unitedmen to organise the peasants of Connacht. To be sure, passive resistance and hatred of the Crown was a way of life in the West, but there

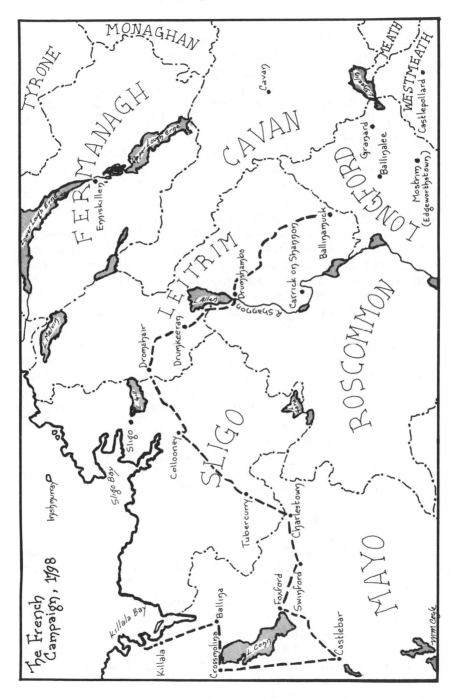

The French
Campaign, 1798

was no indication at all that Connacht was prepared to rise for the sake of some sort of intellectual egalitarian nationalism . . . there was not even a word for "republic" in Gaelic.[2]

Humbert sailed from La Rochelle on 6 August, accompanied by Bartly Teeling and Matthew Tone, both commissioned officers in the French Army. The three frigates gave a hovering British squadron the slip and set a roundabout course to Donegal Bay. When Captain Savary found difficulty beating upwind to his planned landfall near Sligo at the head of the inlet, General Humbert made the command decision to anchor in Killala Bay on 22 August. He had achieved complete surprise, dumbfounding the English . . . and the Connacht Irish as well.

The French landed on the same day, taking the town of Killala that evening after a brief skirmish with Captain William Kirkwood's local yeomanry. Leaving two hundred men behind to establish a base, Humbert marched on to Ballina, easily dispersing Colonel Sir Thomas Chapman's garrison of Leicestershire Fencibles on 24 August. The French general then swung his force around the northern end of Lough Conn, desparately trying to incite rebellion among the peasants. The day before Humbert had landed, Lord Castlereagh had submitted a secret report to the Irish Commons to which the Chief Secretary had appended the words of a treasonous Leinster ballad purporting to demonstrate how the peasantry would react to a French landing:

> They come, they come, see myriads come,
> Of Frenchmen to relieve us:
> Seize, seize the pike; beat, beat the drum;
> They come my friends to save us.
> Whilst trembling despots fly this land,
> To shun impending danger,
> We stretch forth our fraternal hand,
> To hail each welcome stranger.

Humbert would have dearly loved to grasp a Connacht equivalent of that Leinster fraternal hand in Mayo. In fact he was forced to be content with creating an "auxillary" force of about five hundred peasants under Neill Kerrigan, a Killala man, as the French moved southward from Crossmolina along the western shore of Lough Conn.

As Humbert attempted to raise the peasantry, General Gerard Lake arrived in Castlebar on 26 August to take personal command of the Crown forces in the county town. General Lord John Hutchinson had been able to muster over four thousand yeomanry and militia to meet the unexpected French threat. The fight for Castlebar was to be the first time that these troops would meet regular soldiers. It proved to be an inauspicious debut.

The competently officered French veterans were another story altogether from the badly led insurgents that Lake had routed at Vinegar Hill. Stealing a night march on the English, Humbert's eight hundred French regulars—and Kerrigan's five hundred auxillaries—roared into the county town before dawn on 27 August. Though outnumbered over three-to-one, Humbert set Lake's redcoats to running the storied "Races of Castlebar." The Irish cant name for the battle is not mere hyperbole. Terrified yeomen and militiamen from Castlebar fled as far as the city of Galway, some arriving in the distant town—forty miles away—within twenty-four hours after the fighting.

The French general seized upon the victory to proclaim the "Republic of Connacht" under the nominal leadership of John Moore, an ambitious young Mayo squire. It was apparently intended to be the first of four such provincial governments which would eventually come under the aegis of the "Irish Republic." In any event, it was the first "officially" proclaimed republic in Irish history. An Orange song that appeared the next year viewed Humbert's motives much as many suspicious Mayo peasants must have in August 1798:

> From Castlebar, the French declare it is their sole intention,
> On Connacht forthwith to confer freedom of *their* invention;
> What freedom this, you soon may guess by Humbert's proclamation;
> "You dogs," said he, "You shall with me go plunder your own nation!"

If the loyalist balladeers were not impressed with the "Republic" from the safety of elapsed time, no more was Lord Cornwallis ruffled at the instant. Britain's most celebrated military commander of the era, he had reason for confidence: there were nearly 100,000 men at arms in Ireland in the service of George III. The Viceroy took personal command of the redcoat response to Humbert after the debacle at Castlebar, swiftly organising a massive net in which to ensnare the French.[3]

General Humbert had established his bridgehead; unfortunately, he had neither time nor reinforcement available to make it secure. Indeed he had dispatched Savary's flotilla back to France for more men and munitions, cutting off his only

means of escape. He was committed . . . and already beginning
to despair of any large spontaneous uprising of the peasantry
in the West. Well aware of his precarious foothold, Humbert
set off rapidly along the southern side of the Ox Mountains
towards the town of Sligo, over forty miles to the northeast.
Briefed that there was still a United Irish group in that area, the
French general wanted to secure the port town as a base for the
future landings of Hardy and Kilmaine; it was, after all, where
he had originally planned to begin his campaign. Lake, presumably smarting from his Castlebar embarrassment, shadowed
the French leader from a safe distance, trusting to the growing
army of Cornwallis to run the fox to ground.

   Humbert easily brushed aside a yeoman force at Tubbercarry before his vanguard under Bartly Teeling met more serious
resistance near Collooney. Though Teeling drove the redcoats
off after a sharp fight at Carrignagat that cost the British sixty
lives against a handful of Franco-Irish casualties, Humbert was
apparently beginning to appreciate that not only were his forces
insufficient to hold Sligo for any extended period, but that it
might cost him dearly to take it in the first place. Cornwallis,
fresh from his triumphs in India, was no Gerard Lake and the
French commander knew it. Humbert's only hope for success
was to augment his force with more Irishmen. Reduced now to
grasping at straws, Humbert became inordinately encouraged by
a reported peasant rising near Granard in north County Longford
that was rumoured to be highly successful. When his van made
contact with a British unit of unknown strength at Dromahair,
Humbert took a deep breath, and turned inland hoping to link
up with the Granard rebels.[4]

   The melancholy truth was that Lord Cornwallis had put
down the Longford rising swiftly; a tentative companion rising
in neighboring Westmeath had died stillborn. The fox was in
fact marching straight for the hound. Even General Lake was
getting bolder. After Humbert crossed the River Shannon at
Drumshanbo, Lake's cavalry under Colonel Crawford set upon
the French rearguard before the bridge could be destroyed. It
cost Humbert sixty irreplaceable French regulars.

   On 8 September Cornwallis ran Humbert to ground at
Ballinamuck, four miles north of Drumlish on the Leitrim/
Longford frontier. The French, still nearly seven hundred
strong, put up a token defense against the Viceroy's ten thousand, and then surrendered *en masse*. The English graciously

accepted the French commander's sword. The thousand Irish that still marched with Humbert were not shown the same courtesy. Now outnumbered ten-to-one, they fought on bitterly—to little effect, as is demonstrated by this gloating Orange verse:

> When the open foe were prisoners made, twas then began the slaughter;
> Brave Roden's horse about them laid, amongst rebels from the altar.
> *Now* croppies speak, what think you of Lake, an't he a horrid *Delzo?*
> Of earth the scum, before him run, they can't digest his pills O![5]

Fewer than four hundred rebels escaped into the bogs.

THE MEN OF THE WEST

This ballad by the Gaelic League pioneer William Rooney, honours the rebel peasants of Mayo, men who fought with a courage that often amazed their French allies. As the Irish were being overrun in the closing minutes at Ballinamuck, one "Gunner" Magee loaded the last uncaptured French cannon with pots and pans as his ammunition ran out. When one of the gun wheels broke, two of Magee's cousins scampered under the axle to support the field piece with their backs. When the Gunner fired the last burst, their backs were broken by the recoil.

History does not disclose whether or not the shot struck home.

While we honour in song and in story
The names of the Patriot Men.
Whose valour has covered with glory
Full many a mountain and glen,
Forget not the boys of the heather
Who marshalled their bravest and best,
When Eire was broken in Wexford
And looked for revenge to the West.

Refrain:
I give you the "Gallant Old West," boys,
Where rallied our bravest and best,
When Ireland lay broken and bleeding;
Hurrah for the Men of the West!

The hilltops with glory were glowing,
Twas the eve of a bright harvest day,
When the ships we'd been wearily waiting
Sailed into Killala's broad bay.
And over the hills went the slogan
To waken in every bold breast,
The fire that has never been quenched, boys,
Among the true hearts of the West.

Refrain

Killala was ours ere the midnight
And high over Ballina town,
Our banners in triumph were waving
Before the next sun had gone down.
We gathered to speed the good work, boys,
The true men anear and afar,
And history can tell how we routed
The redcoats through old Castlebar.

Refrain

And pledge me "The Stout Sons of France," boys,
Bold Humbert and all his brave men,
Whose tramp, like the trumpet of battle,
Brought hope to the drooping again.
Since Eire has caught to her bosom
On many a mountain and hill,
The gallants who fell, so they're here, boys,
To cheer us to victory still.

Refrain

Though all the bright dreamings we cherished
Went down in disaster and woe,
The spirit of old is still with us
That never would bend to the foe.
And Connacht is ready whenever
The loud rolling tuck of the drum
Rings out to awaken the echoes
And tell us—the morning has come!

Refrain

THE FRENCHMAN

The long history of Irish resistance is replete with tales of foreign military aid coming (1) too early, (2) too late, or (3) without sufficient clout to prosper. Joseph Humbert's landing had been unique in that it had accomplished all three. The French general had left La Rochelle six weeks too early to work in concert with Hardy, for whom he was supposed to be establishing a beachhead. On the other hand, Humbert had sailed fifteen weeks too late to stoke the domestic fire of an island that had been already half aflame. Finally, his force was so small that even a victory of the magnitude of Castlebar had failed to encourage Kilmaine to sail with the main invasion army.

After Ballinamuck, the French prisoners of war were treated with the correct courtesy demanded by the conventions of the day. The French officers, in fact, became a sort of *cause célèbre;* the senior Englishmen, intensely curious about these soldiers from an army that had made such short work of the combined forces of Europe, entertained the captured officers lavishly while their exchange was being arranged. The Irish were not unaware that the British did not extend the same cordiality to the Irish officers with commissions in the French Army. Matthew Tone and Bartly Teeling were court-martialled, convicted of treason against the Crown, and hanged.[6]

This brilliant modern song by Pete St. John captures the spirit of the age-old Irish nationalist question: What if the French/Spanish/Germans/Americans had. . .?

On an angry August morning,
Sailing down Kilalla Bay,
Came the Frenchmen and their general,
Too late to save the day;
But my Nora waved them welcome
While I still licked my wounds,
Cruel marks from Tubberneering,
And all my dreams in ruins.

Refrain:
Ye Frenchmen, ah ye Frenchmen,
You've come too late again,
To save the flower of freedom,
Crushed in every glen;

And your fancy General Humbert,
Well intended though he be,
Will never reap the harvest
Promised to the free.

At Castlebar he chased them
Like foxes fore the hounds;
Lord Roden's vaunted cavalry,
They fled across the ground;
Seven hundred fiery Frenchmen,
Some peasants, two cannon guns,
And I thought of John at Tullow,
Lying dead with Wexford's sons.

Refrain

Then early in September
I saw it all again,
Cornwallis and his thousands
Drove Humbert down the glen;
And the Frenchmen just went back to France,
While the rebels they were slain,
With Tone and Teeling martyred,
And the banshee cried again.

Refrain

If the United Irish officers sporting the French Tricolour could at least count on courts-martial before their execution, very few of the peasant volunteers who marched with Humbert even made it to a courtroom. Lord Cornwallis remained in the village of Ballinalee, west of Granard, for two days after the Battle of Ballinamuck. During the Lord Lieutenant's visit, over 125 croppy prisoners were executed and buried in the old "Bully's Acre" graveyard outside the town. The number killed is curious: General Lake's dispatch to Dublin after the battle agrees precisely with an old Orange ballad reporting "The traitor Blake submits to Lake with ninety-three poor peasants. . . ." The Viceroy's earlier disgust with the yeomanry for murder without process or examination seems to have undergone a complete metamorphosis. After the yeos had slain the captured from

Ballinamuck—and an extra thirty peasants for good measure—Cornwallis issued a general commendation praising the corps of yeomanry. Presumably he was now able to identify with them.

PATRICK BRADY

This street ballad, apparently sung soon after the 1798 risings, recounts the unlikely adventures of a young Wexford farmer during the *bliain na bhFrancach*, the Year of the French. If the singer is to be believed, Patrick Brady's story went something like this:

The Brady brothers join Father Murphy's insurgency soon after Oulart Hill, are with Harvey at New Ross, speed back cross-country to join the sack of Carnew, and break out of the Vinegar Hill encirclement through "Needham's Gap."

Pat and his brothers then follow Murphy west into Kilkenny, somehow managing to escape the slaughter at Kilcomney Hill. Further stretching credibility, the Bradys next turn up in County Mayo at precisely the right moment to join the French for the Castlebar Races where Pat's brothers are slain. Pat Brady then marches with Humbert to Ballinamuck.

After the British rout the Franco-Irish force, Brady somehow manages again to escape—presumably through the bogs—and attempts to make his way home to County Wexford. The peripatetic Patrick Brady is finally captured on the Kildare/Kings border and hanged at Naas.
Whew!

Though it is, of course, extremely unlikely that one man could actually have experienced all these adventures, the chronological circumstances of the ballad are accurate, even to the coal miners who joined Murphy's band in northern Kilkenny. The anonymous street balladeer who wrote the song was almost certainly using some poetic license with his hero, but it is in itself notable that a street musician would have had such an accurate grasp of the events of the countryside.

Ye true born heroes, I hope you will now lend an ear
To a few simple verses, the truth unto you I'll declare.
My name is Pat Brady, the same I will never deny,
In Ross I was born and in Naas condemned to die.

I once had a home and a shelter from want and woe,

But I'm now among strangers where no person does me know;
Condemned for high treason to die on a gallows tree
For seeking the rights of poor Erin, my dear country.

My father, God rest him, was taken without any crime
And marched off a prisoner, and hanged in one hour's time;
Myself and two brothers to the wood were forced to fly—
We vowed for revenge or else by the sword we'd die.

It was early next morning to Gorey we all marched away,
Where the drums they did rattle and our fifes so sweetly did play;
Full twelve thousand heroes, nine hundred and forty-three,
We took all the cannon that day from their artillery.

It was early next morning to Wicklow we all marched away,
Our hearts most glorious with Liberty shining that day.
But entering of Ferns we were attacked by the yeomanry,
We fought them for four hours till we gained a complete victory.

We fought in New Ross and we fought upon Vinegar Hill,
And in sweet Castlecomer when the colliers joined us with a free will;
Out of fourteen engagements, we received not a wound or scar
Till I lost my two brothers at the battle of sweet Castlebar.

To march with the Frenchmen, it left me much troubled in mind,
To think I should go and leave my two brothers behind;
Through the sweet County Leitrim to Granard our way we took,
And were attacked by Cornwallis at the village of Ballinamuck.

We fought with good courage but defeated we were on that day;
We were forced to retreat, no longer our heroes could stay,
But the brave Longford heroes to fly with us they never could,
They never could yield till they'd lost the last drop of their blood.

When forced to retreat, for refuge we thought for to fly,
For all that were taken were certain and sure for to die;
To the sweet County Wexford for refuge, we thought for to face,
But were taken in Rathangan and twelve were hanged in Naas.

Come all you brave heroes, the truth unto you I'll relate,
From powder or ball, poor Brady has ne'er met his fate;
So all you good Christians who hear of my sorrowful fate,
You'll pray for Pat Brady, the hero of Ninety-Eight.

The French decision to make their landing in the northwest of Ireland is curious in retrospect. Why, it may properly be asked, would the French land in an area that had never been seriously organised by the United Irishmen?

The answer seems to lie in a combination of French strategic stupidity and persuasive United Irish duplicity. The French military leaders apparently valued surprise above other considerations. The diminutive size of their committment made it essential that the landing slip into Ireland almost unnoticed; for this purpose, the West was best. The original plan supposed that the British would have their hands full of rebellion on the opposite side of the island. Well aware that the Leinster and Ulster risings had been thoroughly crushed by the time of their sailing, the French commanders evidently did not alter their strategy to reflect reality.

Whatever the French thinking, they were certainly misled as to what they would find in Connacht. The frantic Unitedmen on the continent were ready to tell the French almost anything if only they would sail. Wolfe Tone was an English-speaking Protestant professional from Dublin with little, if any, knowledge of the Gaelic-Catholic farmers of the West;[7] neither had the other middle-class Irishmen who were acting as liason to the French. There was, for instance, only one known Irish-speaker with Humbert at Killala, and *he* spoke with a "Leinster *patois*" according to a loyalist eye-witness. Translation was accomplished through the few English-speakers among the peasantry (who of the Mayo cottiers had a command of French?). Although the United Irishmen were well aware of the hopeless poverty of the Catholic westerners, they blithely ignored the fact that the Connacht peasants had accepted their wretched lot for a century without a murmur, that even the Whiteboys and Defenders had never been in much evidence in the West. With the intellectual arrogance of a drawing-room Dubliner who had never been compelled to till the rocky topsoil of Mayo, Wolfe Tone had earlier described why he had thought it unnecessary to organise the western peasants:

> As no change could make their situation worse, I reckoned on their support to a certainty. . . . I well knew, however, it might be disguised or suppressed, there existed in the breast of every Irish Catholic, an inextirpable abhorrence of the English name and power.

"Abhorrence" of the English there may have been; whether it

would translate into "certain support" for the French was another question altogether. The Unitedmen were nonetheless able to persuade their continental allies that the peasants would rise against their oppressors . . . if only the French would hurry! General Humbert can be excused if he naïvely expected the peasantry to flock to the Tricolour when he landed.[8]

The men of Mayo turned out to be quite different from what the French officer had been led to expect, of course. Revolutionaries who are fond of quoting de Tocqueville's famous conclusion that a "grievance comes to appear intolerable once the possibility of removing it crosses men's minds," often forget the corollary that precedes it: "[*grievance is*] patiently endured so long as it seem[*s*] beyond redress." The Men of the West had spent a century and more stoically enduring under conditions that offered no redress at all. Taught by generations of scratching out subsistence on the poorest land in Ireland, these were men expert in patient survival and suspicious of promises. Happy to accept the proffered French guns, many promptly took the arms home for safekeeping before returning to Humbert with pike in hand . . . if they came back at all. In the time-honoured tradition of the Irish peasant, they would cheerfully tell the French—through interpretors—whatever they imagined the officers wanted to hear, and then march off and do exactly as they pleased.

As soldiers, the peasant "auxillaries" of Connacht baffled the French. Unlettered and ignorant, the Mayo men considered themselves to be fighting for the Roman Catholic Church—this with a French ally representing an anti-clerical revolution that had happily run the Pope out of the Vatican. One of the French officers was driven to comment upon the strange alliance to his prisoner, the Protestant Bishop of Killala:

> God help these simpletons; if they knew how little we care about the Pope or his religion, they would not be so hot in expecting help from us.

And yet these artless peasant soldiers exhibited sublime, if erratic, bravery in the field. In the face of impossible odds, they would stand dauntlessly pike-in-hand against riflemen, and then flee in helpless confusion at the sound of a single distant cannon.

THE BOYS FROM THE COUNTY MAYO

That this old ballad can fairly be sung about almost any rebel period is a singularly damning indictment of the ageless and unchanging lot of the hapless Connacht peasantry. The exiled singers could as easily be fugitive peasants who managed to escape the Curse of Cromwell as Mayo expatriates from the Great Hunger, the Fenian years, or the boycott time of the Land League. It is certainly not difficult to imagine the balladeers as peasant volunteers in the Year of the French who had become renegade after the Battle of Ballinamuck.

Far away from the land of the shamrock and heather
In search of a living, as exiles we roam;
But whenever we chance to assemble together,
We think of the land we once had a home.
But those homes are destroyed and our soil confiscated,
The hand of the tyrant brought plunder and woe;
The fires are now quenched and our hearts desolated,
In our once happy homes in the County Mayo.

Long years have now passed since with hearts full of sorrow,
The land of the shamrock we left far behind;
But how we would like to go back there tomorrow,
To the scenes of our youth which we still bear in mind.
The days of our childhood, it's now we recall them,
They cling to our vision wherever we go;
And the friends of our youth, we will never forget them,
They too are exiled from the County Mayo.

Then on with the Cause till our aim is accomplished,
Those who would fault us are cowardly and mean,
So stay in the fight till the Tyrant is vanquished
And expelled from our dear little island of Green.
With the foes of our land we have fought a long battle,
Soon they will get their last death-dealing blow,
When Old Nick has received them, their brains he will rattle,
For the wrongs they have done to the County Mayo.

After Ballinamuck, Lord Cornwallis leisurely conducted his pacification operations unaware that the French were again "on the sea." Had he been advised of the extent of the new French "threat," it is doubtful that he would have altered his schedule.

On 4 September, Captain Rey's corvette *Anacreon* sailed from Dunkirk with the now French General Napper Tandy aboard. This single vessel anchored off Rutland Island twelve days later with its hold full of munitions for the insurgency that Tandy expected to find. What he found instead was that the news of the disaster at Ballinamuck was common knowledge even in that lonely outpost off the rugged coast of Donegal. Since the ship carried primarily supplies for the now-nonexistant rebellion (there were a mere 180 men aboard), the newest French general officer, presumably seeing no other viable option, proceeded to drink himself into oblivion. Tandy awoke to find that he had been carried back aboard by the French marines, and that Rey had hoisted sail for the continent. The old war-horse's hangover, however, was just beginning. *Anacreon*, hotly pursued by English patrols on the return journey, was forced to slip into Hamburg. Tandy then suffered the final ignominy of extradition back to a British prison.

Six days after the issue had been settled at Ballinamuck, Commodore Bompard finally sailed from Brest with General Hardy's three thousand troops. Aboard the flagship *Hoche,* Wolfe Tone fretted over Humbert's fate: at the 14 September sailing, the last word Hardy had of the first landing force told of victories at Ballina and Castlebar, and indicated Humbert was planning to move towards Sligo. The dispatch had been eighteen days old.

What Tone could not know was that two days before the Brest fleet sailed, the last rebel assault of 1798 had already occurred when an unruly insurgent force was beaten off by the new Crown garrison in Castlebar. Tone presumably was still pacing the deck impatiently on 22 September, when a large detachment of Highlanders and militia under General Sir John Trench attacked the French-officered rebels Humbert had left behind to protect Killala. The nine hundred defenders under Colonel Truc were quickly overrun; six hundred had been butchered by the time the militiamen left off blood-letting and began pilfering. The liberated townspeople found the arrival of the redcoats a mixed blessing. As Bishop Stock caustically observed, "his Majesty's soldiers were incomparably superior to the Irish traitors, in dexterity at stealing." The last vestige of General Humbert's "Republic of Connacht" was erased amidst an orgy of British looting.

Wolfe Tone was to tread the deck-planking for almost three more weeks before his own melancholy confrontation with English firepower. On 12 October Commodore Bompard's fleet was intercepted ten miles off the Falcarragh coast of Donegal near Tory Island by Sir John Borlase Warren's squadron. Recognising immediately that his fleet was outgunned—the British had three ships-of-the-line, the only fully gunned French one was *Hoche*—Bompard ordered his smaller vessels away, joining battle with Warren to cover their flight. After a gallant defense that lasted a minute short of two hours (according to Admiral Warren's log), the French flagship was forced to strike.[9]

The English squadron finally landed the prisoners from *Hoche* in Lough Swilly three weeks later. Wolfe Tone was taken to Dublin for court-martial. The celebrated Unitedman was condemned on 10 November; he was to be hanged the following Monday, the 13th. Tone's request to be executed by firing party, as he claimed befitted his commission as *Chef-de-Brigade* "Smith" in the French Army, was refused on the Sunday. That same night, the prize prisoner cut his own throat with a hidden knife. A week later he was dead.[10]

There have been countless martyrs in the rebel history of Ireland, but none so firmly fixed in the public consciousness as Theobald Wolfe Tone. In reflecting on the eighteenth century, Seán Ó Faoláin says of the Unitedman, "Without him, indeed, it is hard to know what that century would have lent to the Irish National tradition."

Instrumental in the formation of the Society of United Irishmen, Tone was also a highly visible figure in the Catholic Committee, being largely responsible for the legislation that enfranchised the Catholic voter. Tone's avowal of French republicanism lifted a new spectre that continues even today to frighten the "haves" and inspire the "have-nots" in Irish (and British) society:

> If the men of property will not help us they must fall; we will free ourselves by the aid of that large and respectable class of the community—the men of no property.

Even in exile, Tone's constancy to the cause of the Irish Republic persuaded the French Directorate to dispatch three fleets to Ireland in as many years, a feat sufficient to make him legendary in his own time . . . even to his enemies. Indeed even before Tone had been landed at Lough Swilly, Castlereagh had written an

ebullient "thank-you note" to the Royal Navy. The Chief
Secretary delightedly congratulated London "no less on the cap-
ture of the *Hoche,* than I do Ireland on the value of her cargo.
The arch-traitor Tone is himself a very capital prize." After the
Unitedman's capture, even an Orangeman wrote an "auto-
biographical" song about him:

> From France to Lough Swilly I came,
> And that, by my soul, was a blunder;
> But I thought that my high-sounding name
> Would in Ireland perform some wonder;
> I stared and my friends all looked blue,
> When Sir John and his fleet did perceive us,
> For I knew, once he got us in view,
> The devil himself could not save us.

If Wolfe Tone's treason could be dismissed in ridicule by contemporary loyalists, it would be remembered with something
approaching reverence by those who followed in his footsteps.

BODENSTOWN CHURCHYARD

Fittingly, Tone was buried in Bodenstown Churchyard at
Clane, the village where the insurgents of Kildare had ignited the
rebellious flame of 1798. His grave is now honoured as an Irish
national shrine. Politicians troop dutifully to the revered site to
pay annual homage to the "patron saint of Irish Freedom."
When the public figures depart, they are replaced in front of the
grave by shadowy masked men—men, in the words of J. Bowyer
Bell, "red-necked and rumpled, men of no property, under the
distant wind of history, listening to the old litany." These men
consider themselves the true heirs to the legacy of Wolfe Tone.

Thomas Davis is commonly considered the finest of the
Irish rebel poets. In the old tradition, almost all of his poems are
sung. This may be the most hauntingly beautiful of them all.

In Bodenstown Churchyard there lies a green grave,
And wildly around it the winter winds rave;
Small shelter I ween are the ruined walls there,
When the storm clouds blow down on the plains of Kildare.

Once I lay on the sod that lies over Wolfe Tone,
And thought how he perished in prison alone,

His friends unavenged and his country unfreed;
"Oh, bitter," I cried, "is the patriot's meed!"

For in him the heart of a woman, combined
With a heroic life and a governing mind;
A martyr for Ireland—his grave has no stone—
His name seldom mentioned, his virtues unknown.

I was woke from my dream by the voices and tread
Of a band, who marched into the home of the dead;
They carried no corpse and they carried no stone,
And they stopped when they came to the grave of Wolfe Tone.

There were students and peasants, the wise and the brave,
And an old man who knew him from cradle to grave,
And children who thought me hard-hearted; for they,
On the sanctified sod were forbidden to play.

Then the old man who saw I was mourning there, said:
"We come, sir, to weep where bold Wolfe Tone is laid;
And we're going to raise him a monument, too—
A plain one, yet fit for the simple and true."

My heart overflowed and I clasped his old hand,
And I blessed him and blessed every one of his band;
"Sweet tis to find that such faith can remain
To the Cause and the Man so long vanquished and slain."

In Bodenstown Churchyard there lies a green grave,
And wildly around it the winter winds rave:
Far better they suit him, the ruins and the gloom,
Till Ireland, a nation, can build him a tomb.

WOLFE TONE

The importance of Wolfe Tone to the Irish rebel tradition is impossible to overemphasise. It was Tone who first clearly articulated centuries of Irish resentment to British rule. Perhaps even more important, he gave Irish nationalists hope that there was an answer:

> To subvert the tyranny of our execrable government, to break the connection with England, the never failing source of all our political evils, and to assert the independence of my country, these were my objects. To unite the whole people of Ireland, to abolish the memory of all past dissensions, and to substitute the common name of Irishmen in the place of the denominations of Protestant, Catholic, and Dissenter—these were my means.

Wolfe Tone's creed has been adopted by all succeeding Irish nationalists down to the modern era. The methods of his political heirs may have differed, but all—O'Connell's Repealers, Young Ireland, the Fenian Brotherhood, the Home Rulers, the Irish Republican Army, even today's Provisional Sinn Féin—have claimed Tone's philosophy as the basis of their own. It is the tragedy of Ireland that more attention has been paid to his "objects" than to his stated "means."

Pádraig Widger, in this lament for the United hero, captured the emotional tie that the Nationalist Irish still feel to Wolfe Tone.

In childhood days I loved to sit upon my father's knee
And hear the hates of *Granuaile* and the days that used to be;
I loved to dwell on what he'd tell, a story of his own
About a hero brave and true, his gallant name—Wolfe Tone.

His many deeds of bravery, the battles that he fought,
And how he died in prison cell, I saddened at the thought;
It left a spell, how can I tell of tears when all alone,
With childish grief, in true belief I prayed for poor Wolfe Tone.

In that sad uneven struggle of the weak against the strong,
When the anguished cry rose to the sky, "How long, oh God, how long?"
An empire's fate decreed a fate that made our people moan;
You did your best, with God you rest, Indomitable Tone.

A little grave at Bodenstown close by an ivied wall,
Where the dust of one of Ireland's best awaits the angels' call;
And with God's Will, he'll guide us still, till all our land we'll own,
Then swords of flame shall trace the name of our own unconquered Tone.

The death of Wolfe Tone marked the symbolic end of a rebellion that had been effectively crushed much earlier. The

United Irish risings in the midlands and Ulster had been brutally suppressed. The croppy rising in Wexford, the most nearly successful, had not lasted a month. The French landing in Connacht had come too late with too little. The sudden Longford rising had been smashed in infancy. The final French try had been thwarted before reaching Irish soil. Munster had remained quiet throughout. The only coherent rebel organisations still operating were small autonomous guerrilla bands holed up in the mountains of Wicklow.

Many of the insurgent political leaders were dead. The Unitedmen had lost Lord Fitzgerald, McCann, Bond, and the brothers Sheares in addition to Wolfe Tone. Not a few of the United Irish military leaders were dead as well, including Byrne, Munro, Teeling, and MacCracken among others. The surviving senior members of the Society were either in the hands of the Crown or in exile.

The rebel leaders who had emerged from the peasantry were gone, too. Kelly had been executed, as had been Fathers Kearns, Roche, and John Murphy. Father Michael Murphy had fallen in battle. Under the pressure of severe Crown reprisal, the *jacquerie* of the countryside had itself disappeared, becoming once again merely the cowed peasantry of rural Ireland. According to Dublin Castle, there had been less than twenty thousand Crown casualties, including the wounded; there had been over fifty thousand Irish *killed.*[11]

Shortly after Wolfe Tone's capture, three French corvettes appeared in Sligo Bay. Captain Savary had returned with three thousand French regulars to reinforce Humbert. Although the vessels hoisted sail as soon as they discovered the fate of the earlier expeditions, the lesson was not lost on the British: unless something "permanent" was done, Ireland was going to continue to be a problem.

CHAPTER NOTES (18)

1 — There is still some question as to how accurately the United Irish emissaries to France reported French intentions to their co-conspirators back in Ireland. Dublin Castle, whose secret operatives within the United high command were providing all available intelligence, had no idea that Napoleon had decided against an invasion of the British Isles as early as February. The Corsican had created an Army of the Orient by the next month—hardly an event that could have gone unnoticed by the United-men. Napoleon did not sail from the Riveria until 19 May, the same day that Lord Edward Fitzgerald was taken by the Crown. There was certainly sufficient time for Tone and Lewins to send the discouraging word to Dublin . . . and for the Crown to consequently learn of it.

It is barely possible that the French represented to the Unitedmen that the Toulan fleet's goal was Ireland (although, if so, why was Tone not in Provence with it as it made up?). Much more likely is that Tone and Lewins sent encouraging word back to Dublin to "keep their hopes up."

2 — *Poblacht na hÉireann*—the Republic of Ireland—entered the Irish language for the first time during 1798.

3 — Most of the Crown reinforcements to Ireland arrived on the island long after the risings in Leinster and Ulster had been put down. The militia and yeomanry, with a sprinkling of British regulars, had been more than sufficient to subdue the United-men and their croppy allies.

In the face of such a small French landing, Cornwallis did not muster all his forces, nor should he have from a military point-of-view. Most Crown forces were stationed as occupation forces to deal with potential "brush-fires" while Cornwallis, who had experience with this sort of thing in India, used only what force he thought might be necessary to deal with the French. Of the newly landed troops, only the Highlanders would get into the campaign against Humbert.

4 — Had Humbert opted to continue to the North, he would have found resistance minimal. The only opposition between the French and the easily defendable terrain of Donegal was untested yeomanry. In any case, it would have only prolonged his freedom by weeks against an opponent such as Cornwallis.

5 — The slang word *Delzo* is a contraction of "devil's own." It was a denigratory nickname used by the peasants for Orangemen and other loyalists, perhaps the rebel answer to "croppy."

According to Croker, the phrase "Lake's pills for a breaking out" was a common usage by the Orangemen, meaning simply "musket balls."

6 — Two other Irishmen with French commissions were also court-martialled, Blake and O'Keen. Blake was also executed but O'Keen convinced the military court that he had become a naturalised French citizen before taking up arms against the English. O'Keen was subsequently treated as a prisoner-of-war and exchanged with the other French officers. Humbert's formal protest of the proceedings was ignored.

7 — It is not recorded that Tone had even been in Connacht since 1792. On that occasion he had gone on Catholic Committee business during the Ballinasloe fair in east Galway. It is unlikely he talked to many poor farmers on that occasion. Indeed, he was the guest of Thomas Braughill, Tone tells us, whose purpose was to speak to the *gentry* of Connacht.

8 — The Dublin Executive had in fact sent one dispatch to Paris suggesting the French landing at one of three locations: *Oyster Haven,* if the initial objective was Cork City; *Lough Swilly,* if the bridgehead was to be Londonderry; or *Killybegs* (with a diversion in Sligo), if Ballyshannon was to serve as the invasion port. The eventual French strategy was remarkably similar to the third suggestion. It is likely that the 1797 missive went to France with MacNeven. The original, with the physician's signature, was in the hands of Dublin Castle shortly after the rebellion. Under questioning, MacNeven admitted its authorship.

9 — Commodore Bompard's tactics, though noble, were only marginally successful. Four of the fleeing French vessels were overhauled by Warren's squadron; two others were sailed down crossing the Channel.

Actually, the French had little chance of landing at all. As early as 17 September, Bompard had been sighted by scout sloops of the British Admiral Lord Bridport. On 4 October Bridport had dispatched Warren with three sail-of-the-line and five frigates to join three frigates that were already stalking the French invasion fleet. Warren found Bompard on the 11th and, still unsighted by the French, spent that night maneuvering his fleet upwind. When Warren attacked at dawn, Bompard's vessels were pinned against the coast.

10 — On 13 November, the day of Tone's scheduled execution, John Philpot Curran obtained a writ of *habeas corpus* for the prisoner (the Act had been reinstated by Cornwallis after the rebellion had been crushed). Arguing before the King's Bench that the prerogatives of the court were threatened by Tone's "illegal" court-martial, Curran apparently touched a nerve. When the Chief Justice, Lord Kilwarden, issued the writ, neither he nor Curran were aware that Tone had attempted his own life and the point was moot.

11 — It must be remembered that the "Crown casualties" during the 1798 rebellion were mostly among the yeomanry and militia, organisations that were themselves com-

prised of peasants, probably half of them Catholic. Almost all of the "Irish casualties" were among the peasantry.

Lest we leap to the conclusion that this was a civil war, however, we must also recall that the officers and political leaders determined the "reasons" for warfare in this era . . . even more so than they do today.

19

Bold Robert Emmet

The 1798 rebellion holds an honoured position in the tradition of Irish nationalism. Outside of Ireland, however, only those directly involved found it of any particular importance at the time. William Pitt, preoccupied with the grave events in Europe and the Levant, considered the Irish risings but a sideshow to the main event that was taking place in the Mediterranean, as did the French Directorate. On the other hand, the Prime Minister, perhaps somewhat surprised by the intensity of the rebellion, correctly surmised that it was a sideshow that might recur if not handled correctly.

After the news of Lord Nelson's August 1798 victory over the French fleet at the Nile reached London, Pitt was able to turn his attention to Ireland. The Prime Minister had long been an advocate of the parliamentary union of Ireland and Great Britain; now he was determined to press for an Act of Union to settle, in the by-now-commonplace phrase, "the Irish question once and for all." After six centuries of colonial status, the Irish were still behaving as if they were newly conquered; Pitt was genuinely, if naïvely, convinced that the civilising influence of Irish responsibility *within* the kingdom would engender "English patriotism" among the unruly natives of Ireland. It was, in any case, about all that had not been attempted. The Prime Minister's design included eventual Catholic Emancipation, a concept he defined as the abolition of peasant tithes and the admission of Catholic gentlemen into the British Commons. Those concessions, however, would be in the vague future; Pitt's first task would be to incorporate Ireland into a United Kingdom.

Union was not a new concept, nor was its unpopularity in Ireland. As has been seen, the mere rumour that the measure was to be introduced had produced riots in Dublin some four

decades earlier. Then, when a peer had dared suggest it to the
Viceroy in 1780 (as an alternative to the independent Irish Parliament urged by Charlemont and Grattan), Lord Buckingham had
responded:

> Let me earnestly recommend to you not to utter the word
> Union in a whisper, or to drop it from your pen. The present
> temper will not hear it.

With the Irish Volunteers a thing of the past and the United Irishmen in shambles, London was no longer so concerned with the
"temper" of the Irish.

As early as July 1798 the Baron of Auckland had begun
sounding Ascendancy opinion on the issue for the Prime Minister.   One letter that Auckland received in reply—from John
Fitzgibbon, the Lord Chancellor—is significant in that it expresses the genuine feeling among some of the great landowners
that there was no viable alternative:

> As to the subject of an Union with the British Parliament, I
> have long been of the opinion that nothing short of it can save
> this country. I stated the opinion very strongly to Mr. Pitt in
> 1793, immediately after that fatal mistake . . . in receiving an
> appeal from the Irish Parliament by a Popish democracy.

The Ascendancy was truly between a "rock and a hard place."
The country had to be protected from democracy to maintain
the prerogatives of the upper class, but the protection ironically
would involve shifting the landowners' political clout to the
middle-class burghers of the British Commons.

The Irish split over the issue, most choosing a side based on
what the Act of Union could do for them personally. The few
upper-class Catholics were largely disposed to accept Pitt's proposal.   Precluded from holding office in the Irish Parliament,
the papist gentry was hopeful of more sympathy from Westminster than had been shown them by the Protestants in College
Green.   Besides, Pitt was holding out the possibility of their
entering the British Commons. It was the Ascendancy itself
which stood to lose the most by the Union: the landowners,
who had complete control of the 300-seat Irish Parliament,
would comprise an ineffectual 100-seat minority in the proposed
new British assembly. Yet, the Protestant élite did not resist
the Union upon principle; rather, they fought the Prime Minister
tooth-and-nail for adequate compensation. They merely wanted
the government to pay them handsomely for giving up their
heretofore privileged position.

CHRONOLOGY (Bold Robert Emmet)

1799 . . . . . .Austria declares war on France, with Russians, capture Italy; Britain joins Turko-Russian alliance; Napoleon's *coup d' etat* dissolves Directory, establishes Consulate; Talleyrand named French Foreign Minister; political agitation for Union begins in Ireland, issue defeated in close vote in Irish Parliament.

1800 . . . . . .Malta falls to British; Napoleon buys Louisiana Territory from Spain to forestall English; First Consul also defeats Austrians at Marengo, recaptures Italy; Northern Armed Neutrality Pact against British blockade; Act of Union passes at College Green.

1801 . . . . . .Union takes effect, Union Jack becomes flag of England, Scotland, Wales, and Ireland; Nelson defeats Danish fleet off Copenhagen, Armed Neutrality Pact breaks up; Peace of Lunéville (Austria, France) marks end of Holy Roman Empire; French leave Egypt.

1802 . . . . . .Portugese independence recognised; Treaty of Amiens, United Irish prisoners from '98 freed; Napoleon named First Consul for life, suppresses Haitian revolt; Robert Emmet back in Ireland.

1803 . . . . . .Federal Republic established in Switzerland, leads to repudiation of Amiens; Louisiana Purchase by USA; Emmet leads abortive rising in Dublin, is captured and executed; Wellesley wins 2nd Mahratta War.

THE GALLANT MEN OF NINETY-EIGHT

The Protestant Ascendancy was in a dilemma: as deleterious as Union might be to its vested interests, the alternative could produce even more unwelcome results. The rebellion had shown just how precarious the status quo could be. The French, moreover, had demonstrated by arms that they considered Ireland to be the weak link in Britain's defenses. Union could damage the Ascendancy, to be sure, but without Union— and the British troops that would come with it—it was possible to lose all. The Lord Chancellor was quite persuasive when he rose in College Green to declare that, if the Union was adopted:

> The army of the Empire will be employed where it is most wanted . . . and so long as it is found necessary to garrison every district in Ireland, for the internal safety of the country, force may be stationed here.

The dreadful spectre of another bloody Wexford-like

jacquerie—"a Jacobin conspiracy with popish instruments," as Castlereagh had dubbed it—haunted Ascendancy dreams. To the landed Protestants, the nightmare was not far-fetched. The peasantry who by rights should have been respectfully licking their wounds were instead defiantly glorifying the traitors who had fought in the risings.

Republican songs were being sung in city street and peasant field. Nationalism was no longer an intellectual preserve of the middle-class Irish debating society and salon.

The spirit of our fathers bright
Inspires our hearts to firm unite,
And strike again for God and Right
As did the men for Ninety-Eight.
When Wexford and New Ross could tell,
And Tubberneering and Carnew,
Where many a Saxon foeman fell,
And many an Irish soldier, too!

Refrain:
Hurrah, brave boys, we vow to stand
Together for our fatherland
As did the bold devoted band,
The gallent men of Ninety-Eight.

Their altars and their homes, they rose
To guard from ruthless tyrant foes,
Who reeled beneath the vengeful blows
For Freedom dealt in Ninety-Eight.
The patriot's blood that reddened deep,
The soil where fell they in their gore,
Their memory green and fresh shall keep
Within our bosoms' inmost core.

Refrain

The political fight for Union was directed in Ireland by Cornwallis and Castlereagh, with Under Secretary Edward Cooke acting as point man for the Lords. The government leaders used the full power of Dublin Castle to seduce the leading Protestant politicians to the side of Downing Street. It soon became clearly apparent that the "independent" Irish Parliament achieved by Grattan and Flood in 1782 had a formidable rival in the "discretionary largesse" of the bureaucracy. When the first test came in 1799, the Irish Parliament rejected the Act of Union by a mere five votes.

Pitt, encouraged by the result of the balloting, urged his men in Dublin to pull out all stops to get the act passed the following year. Subtlety was no longer important. The Lord Lieutenant and the Irish Secretary freely and openly used their control of patronage to entice recalcitrant voters into the Prime Minister's camp. Some of the inducements offered were indeed conspicuous: sixteen new English and twenty-eight new Irish peers were created, titles clearly useless without corresponding seats in the Imperial House of Lords (which would, of course, exist only upon acceptance of the Union).

As the Crown steam-roller seemed certain to crush all before it, one Ascendancy voice thundered with the old passion on the other side of the aisle. Henry Grattan was strongly opposed to the dissolution of the Parliament that popularly bore his name; he was even more disdainful of the manner in which the administration was buying votes. With dripping irony, Grattan suggested that Ireland would have her vengeance: the bribery campaign would insure that Westminster would be sent "a hundred of the greatest scoundrels in the kingdom."

Even Lord Cornwallis seems to have shown some hesitation at the wholesale bribery which had as its object the political suicide of the Irish Parliament. He wrote during the 1800 legislative campaign that:

> The demands of our friends rise in proportion to the appearance of strength on the other side; and you . . . will be sensible of the difficulties which I must often have to keep my temper. . . . I shall, therefore, as much as possible overcome my destestation of the work in which I am engaged.

The Viceroy was presumably amazed at the extortionate price that the Ascendancy had put on the purchase of the Irish legislature. Most Irishmen were not at all surprised. As Jackson wryly observes, it was not the value of the Parliament that was being demonstrated, but rather the ability of the Irish gentry to "grab a guinea so tight that King George squealed for mercy."

Ireland became part of the United Kingdom on 1 January 1801. The English had used the 1798 rebellion to appropriate the cross of St. Patrick for the new Union Jack, much as they had used the Scottish '45 to grasp the cross of St. Andrew. Now, with Wales and England itself, both nations were part of one kingdom. Ironically, the United Irish attempt to eject the British from Ireland had ultimately resulted in the absolute domination of the island by London.

THE UNION

While Pitt was of the opinion that Catholic Emancipation should have been joined to the Act of Union, he was not prepared to quarrel with a reluctant George III on the subject. Pitt's notions became moot in any event when Addington replaced him over the scandal of the "purchase of the Irish Parliament." In any case as Ó Tuathaigh has pointed out, after the dragooning of the Irish peasantry in the wake of the '98 rebellion, "one may be permitted to doubt whether in fact even the concession of full political rights could have ensured the allegiance of the Catholic masses to the Union." Whatever *might* have occurred if Emancipation had been granted is perhaps irrelevant; concession of those rights was not forthcoming to the papists. What *was* to be of lasting significance was that the Presbyterians of Ulster were gradually to become the stalwart champions of Union, a process hastened as they began to realise the tangible economic benefits of the Act had put them in a separate category from the Catholics. In the long run, the Act of Union did not join Ireland and Britain inexorably together; rather, it divided the Irish.

This ballad by SLIABH CUILINN of the *Nation* reflects the Irish nationalist view of the Union at the time of Young Ireland. The *nom de plume* caused much inquiry into the identity of the author. It is likely that the poet was John O'Hagan, later a judge of the Supreme Court of Judicature and Judicial Commissioner of the Irish Land Commission. An accomplished linguist and skilled poetic translator, O'Hagan never acknowledged nor denied that the pen-name was his.

How did they pass the Union?
By perjury and fraud;
By slaves who sold their land for gold,
As Judas sold his God;
By all the savage acts that yet
Have followed England's track—

The pitchcap and the bayonet,
The gibbet and the rack.
And thus was passed the Union,
By Pitt and Castlereagh;
Could Satan send for such an end
More worthy tools than they?

How thrive we by the Union?
Look round our native land:
It ruined trade and wealth decayed
See slavery's surest brand;
Our glory as a nation gone;
Our substance drained away;
A wretched province trampled on,
Is all we've left today.
Then curse with me the Union,
That juggle foul and base—
The baneful root that bore such fruit
Of ruin and disgrace.

And shall it last, this Union,
To grind and waste us so?
O'er hill and lea, from sea to sea,
All Ireland thunders, No!
Eight million necks are still to bow—
We know our might as men;
We conquered once before, and now
We'll conquer once again,
And rend the cursed Union,
And fling it to the wind—
And Ireland's laws in Ireland's cause
Alone our hearts shall bind.

While the Ascendancy had squabbled over the spoils of Union, some of the defeated rebels had begun to reorganise for another try. The Defenders too had reappeared, particularly in the North where the Orange Order was becoming more visible. The few United Irishmen left in France had meanwhile established tentative contact with a shadowy new Dublin Directory of the Society. The machinery of resistance had been damaged seriously but, in the eyes of a few starry-eyed radicals, not irreparably.

Early in 1801 a young United representative arrived in France. Younger brother to the imprisoned Thomas Addis, Robert Emmet had been a republican student leader at Trinity College, Dublin, before the 1798 risings, and had been expelled for his refusal to take an oath of allegiance to "German George."[1] When young Emmet arrived in Paris shortly after the United Kingdom came into being, he found the French decidedly unenthusiastic about dispatching yet another expedition to Ireland. The strategic situation in Europe was vastly changed. Nelson's victory at the Nile had established British sea power in the eastern Mediterranean; after some ineffectual thrashing about, the French Army of the Orient had been stranded in Egypt. By 1800 the English had ousted the French from Malta, making the Mediterranean truly a British Sea.

As Emmet cooled his hot young heels in Paris, the likelihood of French military aid to Ireland grew even more remote— in April 1801 Admiral Nelson destroyed the Danish fleet at Copenhagen. Although the English were still unable to do much about Napoleon's stampeding armies on the continent, the genius of the French First Consul was being increasingly frustrated by the British mastery of the seas. Napoleon swiftly recognised the contretemps: he could not neutralise the English fleet in battle, any more than Addington dared dispatch troops to challenge the Corsican ashore. Accordingly, the Peace of Amiens was signed in March 1802.[2]

The naïve English optimism over the pact had one major result for the Irish separatists imprisoned in Scotland; no longer worried about a French invasion, the British authorities freed the remaining United Irish prisoners. Of the men released from Fort George, Arthur O'Connor, Sam Neilson, Dr. MacNeven, Thomas Russell, and Thomas Emmet made their way to France, apparently in mind to start up where they had left off. They were joined by Napper Tandy, released himself from an English cell. Neilson and Tandy were ailing, however, and both soon died. O'Connor and Emmet, always bitter opponents, quickly resumed their old ways, this time over who was to speak for the Unitedmen.[3] They shortly had one fewer to argue over when MacNeven, irked at the wrangling, sailed for America.

Robert Emmet left his exiled brother to the quarrel with O'Connor, returning himself to Ireland in October 1802. Within a couple months the younger Emmet was again actively involved with the members of the Dublin United Irish underground. These conspiratorial leaders had been successful in the interim in keeping their existence hidden from the authorities, an unusual feat indeed for Irish rebels.[4] Their obscuration, while effectively protecting their identities, had also the undesirable side-effect of making it extremely difficult for them to organise the men needed for a rising. The dashing young Emmet must have appeared to the secret council as the obvious choice to serve as their recruiter.

NO RISING COLUMN

There is some question as to whether Robert Emmet returned to Ireland with any idea of rejoining the United Irish conspiracy. If he did not, his nationalist spirit did not long remain dormant. The man who was to become the exemplar of Irish rebel martyrdom was himself to find his muse in the insurgents who had died in 1798. An abler poet then revolutionary, Emmet penned the following ballad in their honour during late 1802 or early 1803.

Many of the peasant prisoners from the '98 risings around Dublin had been interned in the infamous "riding school" of John Beresford in Marlborough Street, in the Prevot Prison of the Royal Barracks (presided over by Brigade-Major Sandys, brother-in-law to Under Secretary Cooke, and perhaps the most infamous of all the officials in the capital), and in Dublin Castle itself. Although there was much torture in the attempt to get confessions from the croppies, the trials themselves had been reasonably fair in Dublin, many of the accused even being allowed to give evidence of their innocence. In contrast to the summary justice of the countryside, some had even been acquitted. Enough had been condemned, however, to necessitate the digging of quicklime graves on Arbour Hill. The anonymous peasants buried there, to whom Emmet wrote these lines, were to be joined in the unconsecrated graves by another more famous group of Irish rebels after Easter 1916.

No rising column marks this spot
Where many a victim lies;
But oh! The blood which here has streamed,
To heaven for justice cries.

It claims it on the oppressor's head
Who joys in human woe,
Who drinks the tears by misery shed,
And mocks them as they flow.

It claims it on the callous judge
Whose hands in blood are dyed,
Who arms injustice with the sword,
The balance throws aside.

It claims it for his ruined isle,
Her wretched children's grave;
Where withered Freedom droops her head,
And man exists—a slave.

O Sacred Justice! Free this land
From tyranny abhorred;
Resume thy balance and thy seat—
Resume—but sheath thy sword.

No retribution should we seek—
Too long has horror reigned;
By mercy marked may freedom rise,
By cruelty unstained.

Nor shall a tyrant's ashes mix
With those our martyred dead;
This is the place where Erin's sons,
In Erin's cause, have bled.

And those who here are laid at rest,
Oh! Hallowed be each name;
Their memories are forever blest—
Consigned to endless fame.

Unconsecrated is this ground,
Unblest by holy hands;
No bell here tolls its solemn sound,
No Monument here stands.

But here the patriot's tears are shed,
The poor man's blessing given;
These consecrate the virtuous dead,
Just waft their fame to heaven.

MICHAEL DWYER (II)

When Robert Emmet began his task for the Dublin United-men, there was at least one enterprising insurgent captain still at large. Michael Dwyer and his Wicklowmen were the obvious ones about whom to base an insurrection. The rebel balladeers, remembering the rapparee tradition, sang of Dwyer's narrow escapes from a brutal but blundering soldiery, and of his brazen bravado in the face of almost overwhelming odds. Though many of his fabled escapades were certainly nearer legend than fact, the legend of the dauntless rebel leader was itself enough to cause constant irritation to Dublin Castle. The Crown began construction of the "Military Road" through the Wicklow Mountains specifically to render Dwyer's retreats accessible to the authorities.

This nineteenth century ballad by Timothy Daniel Sullivan, better known as "TD," tells of one of Mickey Dwyer's most remarkable adventures, this particular one authentic. On a February night in 1799, the rebel captain and four companions had been tracked by a hundred redcoats to the hamlet of Derryamuck on the south side of the Glen of Imaal. Sam MacAllister, one of Dwyer's band, had drawn the fire of the soldiers so that the guerrilla leader could escape. The Dwyer-MacAllister Cottage, the site of the incident, is now a national monument.

At length brave Michael Dwyer and his undaunted men
Were scented o'er the mountains and tracked into the glen;
The stealthy soldiers followed, with ready blade and ball,
And swore to trap the outlaw that night in wild Emall.

They prowled around the valley and towards the dawn of day
Discovered where the faithful and fearless heroes lay;
Around the little cottage they formed in a ring,
And called out, "Michael Dwyer, surrender to the King!"

Then burst the war's red lightning, then poured the leaden rain,
The hills around re-echoed the thunder-peals again;
The soldiers falling round him brave Dwyer sees with pride,
But, oh! One gallant comrade is wounded by his side.

Yet there are three remaining, good battle still to do;
Their hands are strong and steady, their aim is quick and true—

But hark! That furious shouting the savage soldiers raise!
The house is fired around them! The roof is all ablaze!

And brighter every moment the lurid flame arose,
And louder swelled the laughter and cheering of their foes;
Then spoke the brave MacAllister, the weak and wounded man—
"You can escape, my comrades, and this shall be your plan. . ."

He stood before the foeman, revealed amidst the flame;
From out the levelled pieces the wished-for volley came.
Up sprang the three survivors for whom the hero died,
But only Michael Dwyer burst through the ranks outside.

He baffled his pursuers who followed like the wind;
He swam the River Slaney and left them far behind.
But many a scarlet soldier he promised soon would fall
For those, his gallant comrades, who died in wild Emall.

The Peace of Amiens proved to be only a short interlude in Anglo-French warfare. Bonaparte—living up to his famous dictum, "The truth is not so important as what people think to be true"—had freely interpreted the treaty as merely a cease-fire giving him a free hand on the continent. The British and French were again at war by May 1803. Cheered by the resumption of hostilities, the Dublin Unitedmen corresponded with Thomas Emmet, urging him to petition Napoleon and Talleyrand for aid. They had mailed their missive to the wrong man. Arthur O'Connor, rather than his rival, led the faction of exiled United-men who had found favour with the First Consul and his remarkable Foreign Minister.[5]

It is doubtful that the French would have been receptive to yet another entreaty by the Unitedmen under any circumstances, even had it been presented by the influential O'Connor. Napoleon would dearly have loved to attack Britain itself, to be sure, but had never considered Ireland worth a concentrated assault while the English commanded the sea. He did keep an "Army of England" poised at Boulogne but wisely never launched it. The First Consul was never to consider the French Navy strong enough to protect a large invasion force. Napoleon's judgement on the relative worth of the fleets was to be proved unerringly accurate two years later at Trafalgar. In any event, the United Irishmen in Dublin were on their own.

By the spring of 1803 Robert Emmet had become the designated military leader for the Unitedmen. The clandestine Directory had provisionally scheduled the rising for July of that year, leaving to Emmet the actual planning. Taking residence in Butterfield Lane near Rathfarnum with his adjutant Myles Byrne, late of Dwyer's Wicklow band, Emmet busily set about putting together a plan in which he could use the scattered organisational rebel remnants from 1798. Apparently reasoning that, if the government could be overthrown the provinces would rise in sympathy, Emmet and Byrne made their target Dublin itself. The scheme had a few melancholy similarities to the one proposed by John Sheares five years earlier, the most glaring perhaps its *naïveté*.

The design was to use veterans from the 1798 rising as "strike groups." Men from Wexford, Wicklow, and Kildare were to make their way individually into Dublin on 23 July. Myles Byrne outlines to what use they were to be put:

> Now the final plan . . . consisted principally in taking the Castle, whilst the Pigeon House, Island Bridge, the Royal Barracks, and the old Custom House Barracks were to be attacked. . . . Obstacles of every kind to be created through the streets. . . . The Castle once taken, undaunted men, materials, implements of every description, would be easily found in all the streets . . . to impede the cavalry [*and*] infantry from passing through them.

The bands were to muster separately. The Wexford men were to join under Byrne at the Coal Quay (with a smaller detachment in Ship Street) to threaten both the main and west gates of Dublin Castle. The Kildare men were to put themselves under the command of Emmet himself at the main headquarters in a depot in Marshallea Lane off Thomas Street. Part of this muster, under the firebrand woollen-draper John Allen, was to take station in Crow Street and College Green. Meanwhile Arthur Devlin, one of Dwyer's lieutenants, was to lead a group of Wicklow men to a jumping-off point in the hills overlooking Rathfarnum. Emmet believed he could get two thousand men into the city without the knowledge of the authorities and take Dublin Castle before the Crown could react.

For once the Castle was not aware of the conspiracy's existence. Perhaps its own policy of using informers was to blame: the government was by this time so inundated by information from informers that "incipient rising" was like Peter's wolf; the

administration had accurate evidence of the plot, but just did
not believe it. Even an accidental explosion at a secret United
armoury in Patrick Street on 16 July did not seem to alarm the
authorities unduly. Emmet decided to go ahead with the rising
as planned.

With the bumbling inefficiency seemingly endemic to Irish
rebel leadership, Emmet was able to assemble only four score
men at his Marshallea Lane headquarters at the assigned hour.
The Coal Quay and Ship Street bands—about two hundred men
in all—were armed and ready to go but never got orders to rise
from Emmet.[6] Devlin was poised above Rathfarnum with the
Wicklow men, but the sky-rocket that Emmet was to set off
ordering them to move never lit the sky. Robert Emmet and
John Allen were busy arguing with the Kildare men.

When the grizzled peasant veterans had begun filtering into
town, they were met with a rumour that the rising had been
called off. Many went home. The ones that nonetheless continued on to Marshallea Lane were faced with an Emmet be-
decked in fantastic array. With a poet's idea of what a United
Irish general should look like, Emmet had had a uniform tailor-
made: a bright green blouse edged in gold lace, white breeches,
black knee-boots, gold shoulder epaulettes, gleaming sword,
and a cocked hat with a white plumed feather. The Kildare men
can perhaps be excused for having doubts about this Dublin
popinjay who swaggered about giving orders while looking for
all the world like a teenager. After carefully planning his insurrection for six months, Emmet found himself defending his
strategy on the day it was to begin. Among the other points
brought up by the peasants, it seems some of the Kildare men
were struck by the fruitlessness of capturing government buildings on a Saturday night when there was nobody of importance
in them. The thought seems never to have occurred to Robert
Emmet. The dubious Unitedmen became understandably curious about the rest of his plan. The discussions ended abruptly
when a messenger arrived with a false rumour of approaching
soldiers.

In a bravado born out of frustration, Emmet drew his
glittering sword and marched out into the Dublin Saturday
night. A ragged "army" of less than a hundred trailed out behind him. Rather than leading a revolution, the young United
Irish leader ended up spectator to a street fight. About thirty
lives were lost that night in Dublin, including that of the Lord

Chief Justice, Lord Kilwarden.[7]

FOR GOD AND IRELAND

The Rising of '03 was the epilogue to the activity of the Society of United Irishmen. It is fitting irony that a rising so badly fumbled would offer the Irish rebel tradition its most celebrated martyr.

This rallying-cry has often been criticised as an example of naïve nationalistic jingoism. If so, it is one we could easily imagine Robert Emmet singing on that swashbuckling July night before he stepped into the streets of Dublin.

For thee we stand, O Native Land,
To thee we pledge devotion;
Our love for thee will ever be
As boundless as the ocean.
For ages past, with voices massed,
Have poets hymned thy story;
But soldiers now, upon thy brow
Shall poise a crown of glory.

Refrain:
Then forward! For the hour is come
To free our fettered sireland;
To cannon boom and roll of drum
We'll strike for God and Ireland!

What matter if the foe be strong,
Our country we'll defend, boys;
What matter if the road be long,
We'll tread it to the end, boys;
From Rathlin Isle to Bantry Bay
Our fathers trod before us;
God send the sun of Freedom's Day
To flame in splendour o'er us.

Refrain

Lo! Yonder leap the beacon fires
That guide us from the valley;

Around us throng our martyred sires
To hearten and to rally.
Draw blade! For God and Ireland now!
Strike home for all we treasure!
And if the foemen drink, we vow
To give him brimming measure.

Refrain

Just before the explosion in Patrick Street, Thomas Russell
had slipped back into Ireland. In the week before the rising itself, Emmet had dispatched Russell to the North to contact
Jamie Hope and others among the former United leaders in
Ulster. Russell's charge was to incite a sympathetic rising. The
attempt was reflective of the slipshod planning. When Russell
issued a proclamation claiming the Unitedmen had arisen again,
attracting "vast multitudes in all parts of the country," few
bought the patently untrue story. He was easily run down by
the authorities and afterwards hanged at the Old County Gaol
at Downpatrick. Robert Emmet, meanwhile, was still on the
run.

TWENTY MEN FROM DUBLIN TOWN

Two centuries earlier when Red Hugh O'Donnell had
escaped from Dublin, it was to Glenmalure that he fled. Now,
with Myles Byrne and Arthur Devlin to guide him, Robert
Emmet also made his way into the trackless Wicklows to avoid
the forces of the Crown.
It has been often said that "if you scratch an Irish politician, you'll find a rebel." What is not as well understood is that
if you scratch the same Irish politician a second time, you will
likely also find a poet. Arthur Griffith, founder of Sinn Féin,
wrote this rousing battle-song honouring the men in the Wicklow
Hills after the failure of Emmet's rising.

Twenty men from Dublin Town
Riding on the mountainside,
Fearless of the Saxon frown,
Twenty brothers true and tried.

Blood flows in the city streets—
There the Green is lying low—
Here the Emerald Standard greets
Eyes alike of friend and foe.

Refrain:
Fly the city, brothers tried,
Join us on the mountainside,
Where we've England's power defied,
Twenty men from Dublin Town.

Twenty men from Dublin Town,
Full of love and full of hate;
Ah! Our chief, our Tone, is down,
Hand of God, avenge his fate.
Joy it is whene'er we meet
Redcoats on the mountain track;
Oh! As deer they must be fleet
If to Dublin they'd get back.

Refrain

Twenty men from Dublin Town
Every night around the fire,
Brimming methers toss we down
To our captain, Michael Dwyer.
Sláinte, Michael, brave and true,
Then there rings the wild hurrah,
As we drink, dear land, to you,
Eire Sláinte, Geal Go Brath.

About a week after the rising was crushed, arrangements began to be made for the escape of Robert Emmet and Myles Byrne to France. They had only, it appears, to wait safely in the hills until a suitable vessel could be secured to spirit them away. Demonstrating characteristic daring—and a usual lack of common sense—Emmet demurred. Instead, to be closer to his dying mother and his sweetheart, he took lodging in Harold's Cross under an alias in the house of a Mrs. Palmer. It proved to be a fatal, if romantic, gamble . . . Major Henry Sirr of the Dublin Town Police was closing in.

ANNE DEVLIN

Major Sirr, who had taken Lord Edward Fitzgerald five years earlier, appears to have been a dedicated and talented police officer. His methods, however, though not uncommon for the time, would scarce have endeared the officer to modern civil rights advocates.

Anne Devlin, youthful sister to the Wicklow rebel Arthur, had served as Emmet's housekeeper and confidant at the Butterfield Lane house in what was then rural Rathfarnum. A United Irish sympathiser, she had often been employed as messenger for her master. After the failure of the rising, it had been Anne who had found lodging for Emmet at the Palmer house. When Sirr "questioned" her soon after, she was bayonetted twice and then half-hanged. When she still refused to disclose any information, the steadfast servant was thrown into Kilmainham Gaol. Surviving the treatment, she lived on to the middle of the nineteenth century. Poetic justice, it is supposed, might have made her the "grand old dame of Irish Resistance" to the separatists of that era. Justice—poetic or otherwise—was however notably absent in Ireland during the Starvation Time. The tragic reality is that Anne Devlin died penniless and almost unnoticed in a famine hospital.

This haunting modern ballad by Pete St. John reaffirms her special place in the rebel tradition. The author is today perhaps Ireland's premier balladwriter, having been voted "Irish Songwriter of the Year" in both 1981 and 1982.

In Dublin town they sing
Of a brave Wicklow woman,
Of her troubles and her times
In cruel Kilmainham Gaol.
All the way from Butterfield Lane,
Anne Devlin was her name,
Friend to Robert Emmet,
She served his cause in vain.

Refrain:
And it's low, lie low,
Liffey keep on flowing;
Low, lie low,
Anne, your legend's growing.

Not torture nor the bribe
Could sway Anne Devlin's purpose,
Three years of living hell
In solitary's shame.
How proud Emmet met his fate
On the scaffold of the tyrant,
She saw her family passing
Like poor lilies in the storm.

Refrain

In Eighteen Fifty-One,
Anne Devlin met her maker;
But her story's with us still
As a lesson to the wise.
Not poverty nor fear
Can kill the heart of freedom;
Anne Devlin was the servant
To the spirit of our land.

Refrain

It took the ubiquitous Major Sirr less than a month to track down Robert Emmet. As Myles Byrne was safely asea for France, Emmet awaited his doom in an English prison.

EMMET'S FAREWELL

The myth of Robert Emmet gained a certain flair by the romantic circumstances surrounding the young Unitedman's capture. It was difficult to convince the strongly familial Irish that a loyal son, one who would risk his life and freedom to be close to his dying mother, could be the murderous criminal the Crown made him out to be. Too, the fact that Emmet was carrying love-letters from Miss Sarah Curran in the folds of his white neck-cloth when he was taken seemed to stir sympathy among the people.

The unfortunate young lady was the daughter of the great orator John Philpot Curran. For the first time, the famous attorney declined to defend a United Irish leader.[8] Outraged by his daughter's behaviour, Curran also refused to have any more to do with the unhappy Sarah. Miss Curran apparently shrugged off disownment by her father, refusing to repudiate her handsome young rebel.[9]

Farewell love, farewell love, I now must leave you,
The pale moon is shining her last beam on me;
In truth, I do declare I never deceived you,
For it's next to my heart is dear Erin to me.

Draw near to my bosom, my first and fond true love,
And cherish the heart that beats only for thee;
And let my cold grave with green laurels be strewn, love,
For I'll die for my country, dear Erin, and thee.

Oh, never again in the moonlight we'll roam, love,
When the birds are at rest and the stars they do shine;
Oh, never again shall I kiss thy sweet lips, love,
Or wander by streamlets with thy hands pressed in mine.

My hour is approaching, let me take one fond look, love,
And watch the pure beauty till my soul does depart;
Let the wrinkles fall on my face and brow, love,
Draw near till I press thee to my fond and true heart.

Farewell, love, farewell, the words are now spoken,
The pale moon is shining her last beams on me;
Farewell love, farewell love, I hear the death token,
Never more in this world your Emmet you'll see.

BOLD ROBERT EMMET

There could only be one result to Robert Emmet's trial. Fully aware of his predicament, the Unitedman decided to make the most of his short day in the sun.

Emmet's secure place in rebel history is founded upon his conduct *after* his unsuccessful rising. Inept as a revolutionary, he clearly has made a formidable martyr. The young rebel's ringing speech from the dock has been at the centre of republican sentiment since the day of his execution:

I have but one request to ask at my departure from this world; it is the charity of silence. Let no man write my epitath; for as no man knows my motives dare now vindicate them, let not prejudice or ignorance asperse them. Let them rest in obscurity and peace, my memory left in oblivion, and my tomb remain uninscribed until other men can do justice to my character. When my country takes her place among the nations of the earth, then, and not till then, let my epitath be written.

Poets may often make indifferent generals but, at least in Ireland, they make wonderfully articulate rebels.

On 20 September 1803 word was brought to Robert Emmet that his dying mother had finally succumbed. Some hours later, the young rebel was taken to Thomas Street and hanged. In accordance with the pronounced sentence, his body was afterward drawn and quartered.

This ballad, oftentimes attributed to Tom Maguire, commander of the old Irish Republican Army in Fermanagh, was popular before the Easter Rebellion and has been sung by every generation of nationalists since. As did the old IRA, today's Provisionals maintain that the epitath for Robert Emmet has yet to be written.

The struggle is over, the boys are defeated,
Old Ireland is surrounded with sadness and gloom;
We were defeated and shamefully treated
And I, Robert Emmet, awaiting my doom.

Refrain:
Bold Robert Emmet, the Darling of Erin,
Bold Robert Emmet will die with a smile;
Farewell companions, both loyal and daring,
I'll lay down my life for the Emerald Isle.

Hung, drawn and quartered, sure that was my sentence,
But soon I will show them no coward am I;
My crime was the love of the land I was born in—
A hero I've lived and a hero I'll die.

Refrain

The barque lay at anchor awaiting to bring me
Over the billows to the land of the free;

But I must see my sweetheart for I know she will cheer me,
And with her I will sail far over the sea.

Refrain

I was arrested and cast into prison,
Tried as a traitor, a rebel, a spy;
But no one can call me a knave or a coward—
A hero I've lived and a hero I'll die.

Refrain

Hark the bells tolling, I well know the meaning,
My poor heart tells me it is my death knell;
In come the clergy, the warder is leading,
I have no friends here to bid me farewell.

Refrain

MY EMMET'S NO MORE

Never again would an Irish rebel accept a sentence from an English magistrate without attempting a stirring speech from the dock. As Robert Kee has wryly noted, metaphorical handkerchiefs have been dipped in Robert Emmet's blood ever since.

One man who sported perhaps the most sanguinary linen came closest to defining the legacy of Robert Emmet. Pádraig Pearse, in a 1915 memorial ceremony at the grave of Wolfe Tone, would suggest that:

> No failure . . . was ever more complete, more pathetic than Emmet's. And yet he has left us a prouder memory than the men of Brian victorious at Clontarf or of Owen Roe victorious at Benburb. It is a sacrifice Christ-like in its perfection.

The baton of rebel martyrdom had been passed along for over a century by the time Pearse would insist that "the old heart of the earth needed to be warmed with the red wine of the battlefields." Obviously spurred by Emmet's example, Pearse would lead the Irish Republican Brotherhood out on Easter 1916 to make his own blood sacrifice.

Despair in her wild eye, a daughter of Erin
Appeared on the cliff of a bleak rocky shore,
Loose in the winds flowed her dark streaming ringlets
And heedless she gazed on the dread surge's roar.
Loud rang her harp in wild tones of despairing,
The time past away, with the present comparing,
And in soul-thrilling strains deeper sorrow declaring,
She sang Erin's woes and her Emmet's no more.

Oh Erin, my country! Your glory's departed,
For tyrants and traitors have stabbed thy heart's core.
Thy daughters have laid in the streams of affliction,
Thy patriots have fled or lie stretched in their gore!
Ruthless ruffians now prowl through thy hamlets forsaken—
From pale hungry orphans their last morsel have taken—
The screams of thy females no pity awaken,
Alas! My poor country, your Emmet's no more!

Brave was his spirit, yet mild as the Brahmin,
His heart bled in anguish at the wrongs of the poor;
To relieve their hard suffering he braved every danger,
The vengeance of tyrants undauntedly bore.
Even before him the proud villains in power
Were seen, though in ermine, in terror to cower;
But alas! He is gone, he has fallen, a young flower,
They have murdered my Emmet—my Emmet's no more.

NELL FLAHERTY'S DRAKE

During the 1803 Irish adventure, Robert Emmet had used various aliases as he travelled Leinster organising the rising. He most often went under the name of *Ellis.* While in hiding at Mrs. Palmer's house in Harold's Cross, he had used *Hewitt.* Another of the Unitedman's supposed code names, *Drake,* was to be adopted by the peasantry after Emmet's execution.

Using *Nell Flaherty* as a soubriquet for Ireland, this song gave the people a way to curse the agents of Emmet's death without the targets being the wiser. Unlike the rollicking rebel songs of more hopeful times, this one has a withering edge of bitterness. On the other hand, the inventiveness of the wryly stinging

lyrics suggest that military defeat did not mean defeat of the
spirit.   There are literally scores of variations; six of the most
popular verses are included here.

My name it is Nell, quite candid I tell,
And I live near Cootehill, I will never deny;
I had a large drake, the truth for to spake,
That my grandmother left me and she going to die.
He was wholesome and sound and he weighed twenty pound,
And the universe round I would roam for his sake;
But bad scram to the robber, be he drunken or sober,
That murdered Nell Flaherty's beautiful drake.

May his pig never grunt, may his cat never hunt,
That a ghost may him haunt in the dead of the night;
May his hen never lay, may his ass never bray,
May his goat fly away like an old paper kite.
That the flies and the fleas may the wretch ever tease,
And a bitter north breeze make him tremble and shake;
May an African bug build a nest in the lug
Of the monster that murdered Nell Flaherty's drake.

May his pipe never smoke, may his teapot be broke,
And to add to the joke, may his kettle ne'er boil;
May he ne'er rest in bed till the hour he is dead,
May he always be fed on goose grease and fish oil.
May he swell with the gout till his grinders fall out,
May he roar, bawl and shout with a horrid toothache;
May his temple wear horns and all his toes corns,
The scoundrel that murdered Nell Flaherty's drake.

May his spade never dig, may his sow never pig,
May each nit in his wig be as large as a snail;
May his door have no latch, may his house have no thatch,
May his turkey not hatch, may the rats eat his kale.
May every old faery from Cork to Dun Laoghaire
Dip him snug and hairy in some pond or lake,
Where the eel and the trout may dine on the snout
Of the hangman that murdered Nell Flaherty's drake.

May his dog yelp and growl with hunger and cold,
May his wife always scold till his brain goes astray;

May the curse of each hag who e'er carried a bag
Light on the wag till his beard it turns grey.
May monkeys still bite him and mad apes still fight him
And everyone slight him, asleep or awake;
May weasels still gnaw him and jackdwas still claw him,
The robber that murdered Nell Flaherty's drake.

The only good news that I have to diffuse
Is that long Peter Hughes and blind piper MacPeak,
That big-nosed Bob Manson and buck-toothed Bob Hanson,
Each man has a grandson of my darling drake.
My bird he has dozens of nephews and cousins
And one I must get or my poor heart will break;
To keep my mind easy or else I'll go crazy—
There ends the whole tale of Nell Flaherty's drake.

Robert Emmet's inchoate rising marked a watershed in Irish nationalist history. The Protestant intellectuals of the Dublin and Belfast salons had taken their best shot at a free and independent Ireland and had missed the mark badly. When next a viable national movement was to appear on the Irish stage, the leading player would be the son of a papist smuggler from the wilds of Kerry. The songs of the people, however, were to insure that the aims of the United Irishmen would never be forgotten.

CHAPTER NOTES (19)

1 — The Trinity College Historical Society, of which Robert Emmet was the radical leader before his expulsion from university in 1798, is the oldest collegiate debating society on the British Isles. Originally founded as simply "The Club" by Edmund Burke in 1747, it took its present name in 1770. Wolfe Tone became its auditor in 1785. Emmet joined in 1797 with his friend Thomas Moore.

2 — This treaty, lasting until a British ultimatum of April 1803, was the only time in Napoleon's career that he was not at war with the English . . . a period of thirteen

months.

3 — The feud apparently began during the 1797-98 United Irish debates over rising without French aid and continued at Ft. George where O'Connor and Emmet vied for precedence among the prisoners.

4 — Their success in camouflaging their identities apparently extended beyond their own time. As far as the author has been able to discover, history has had no better luck in determining the members of this indistinct Directory than did the contemporary British authorities. John Mitchel does list seventeen names—quoting a source that these were the "principal persons concerned" with Emmet—but they seem to be only those suspected by Dublin Castle.

5 — O'Connor, like Talleyrand-Périgord, seems to have enjoyed the favour of Napoleon at this time. Unlike the Foreign Minister, however, he maintained it, rising to the rank of general in the *Grand Armée*. Like Talleyrand, though, O'Connor managed to outlast the Corsican.

6 — In his memoirs, Myles Byrne claimed that at 2045 he had gotten impatient and actually taken a stroll through the Dublin Castle yard from Parliament Street. His recollection was that there was no alert and no extra guards visible.

7 — This was the same man who had issued the writ of *habeas corpus*, declaring the court-martial of Wolfe Tone illegal. The Chief Justice, no enemy to the people of Ireland, was pulled from his coach and piked. His horrified daughter was also witness to the murder of her husband in the middle of the street.

8 — Emmet secured Leonard McNally to conduct his defense, the same McNally who had been in the pay of the Crown since the arrest of the French spy Jackson a decade earlier. In the event it made little difference. Emmet was little disposed to make a defence; his route, rather, was defiance. He had little option. Besides the defendant's incriminating letters to Miss Curran, the Crown was able to parade eighteen witnesses through the court.

9 — Sarah Curran's conduct toward her doomed lover became celebrated in famous poem and prose by Thomas Moore and Washington Irving. Her mourning, however, did not last long. Sarah shortly thereafter married a British officer. She died in 1808 unreconciled with her father.

20

Conclusion

The period 1760-1803 had seen constant agitation in Ireland. The peasantry had emerged from seventy years of lethargy —first as Whiteboys, then as Defenders, and finally as uneasy allies of the United Irishmen. The Dissenters had meanwhile supported the landowners' successful struggle for an Irish Parliament and then, disappointed by the result, had led the island into unsuccessful armed rebellion with the help of the new French Republic. The Protestant Ascendancy had itself been out-maneuvered: the cynical landlords had ceded their power in return for riches only to find that the Crown had added the "cost" of the Act of Union to the Irish National Debt. From London, the British victory must have seemed complete.

England, however, was still learning the business of Empire and had not yet realised that she had already lost the battle most important to a colonial power—the battle for the minds and hearts of the subject people. Each British outrage, each Irish national effort against hopeless odds, came to have its effect on the consciousness of the Irish people. The imagination of the balladeers would ensure that the deeds of the lowliest rebel martyr would live on far out of proportion to their political significance. The street musicians celebrated the courage of the croppy and Unitedman in the face of overwhelming Saxon perfidy and firepower. Nationalist morale, rather than being shattered by the obvious failure of resistance, may actually have been strengthened.

THE DEAD WHO DIED FOR IRELAND

The rebel tradition had one inestimable advantage now. After 633 years of fighting the Stranger for individual reasons, there was now one single purpose with which every irredentist Irishman could identify, whatever his political stripe—vengeance. The United Irishmen came to be remembered as martyrs who had lived and died for *all* of Ireland, for—in a phrase that was to become increasingly popular—"Ireland for the Irish." Hereafter, there would always be those who would remember the sacrifice.

One such was Ellen O'Leary, the Tipperary poetess. Associated throughout her life with the Fenian activities of her brother John, she was not to let the Irish forget for whom those men had died.

The dead who died for Ireland,
Let not their memory die,
But solemn and bright, like stars at night,
Be they throned for aye on high.

The dead who died for Ireland,
In the lonely prison cell,
Far, far apart from each kindred heart,
Of their death pangs none can tell.

The dead who died for Ireland,
In exile, poor, in pain,
Dreaming sweet dreams of the hills and the streams
They never should see again.

The dead who died for Ireland,
Let not their memory die,
But solemn and bright, like the stars at night,
Be they throned for aye on high.

BREATHE NOT HIS NAME

While the street musicians and later rebel poets such as Ellen O'Leary would keep the glory of the fallen before the humble folk of Ireland, one aristocratic voice was able to prick the conscience of the upper class. Thomas Moore had been at Trinity with Robert Emmet and seems to have developed a fondness for the young rebel at that time. A regular in the drawing rooms and salons of the best society, Moore was stunned in 1803 when the extent of his former classmate's commitment to a republican Ireland was fully disclosed. From that time Moore's moral, if not political, identification with Emmet's sort of emotional nationalism would find expression in the poet's work.

This ballad to Robert Emmet's memory is among Moore's finest work. With his increasing reputation—Byron, among others, admired his work and considered him a close friend—Moore was assured of an audience among the most influential English circles. Ballads such as this made certain that intellectual England would hear another view of Irish nationalism than that emitting from Dublin Castle.

Oh! Breathe not his name,
Let it sleep in the shade,
Where cold and unhonoured
His relics are laid;
Sad, silent, and dark
Be the tears that we shed,
As the night-dew that falls
On the grass o'er his head.

But the night-dew that falls,
Though in silence it weeps,
Shall brighten with verdure
The grave where he sleeps;
And the tear that we shed,
Though in secret it rolls,
Shall long keep his memory
Green in our souls.

FORGET NOT THE FIELD

In 1807 Thomas Moore formed an association with Sir John Stevenson, a great collector of traditional Irish airs. For the next twenty-seven years Moore's original English-language poetry was set to a Gaelic musical background. Seán Ó Boyle describes the resulting songs as:

> nostalgic, pseudo-historical, whimsical, sentimental productions suited to the drawing rooms of the nineteenth century, and were in striking contrast to the living Gaelic love-songs, lullabies, aislingí

(vision poems), laments, drinking songs, hymns and work-songs of the Irish-speaking people.

As the modern folk-music critic would put it, they were not "ethnic."

Many of today's purists have a tendency to disparage Moore's work because it was not "Irish." The poet's audience, however, was never supposed to be the cottier of the Irish West; rather, he was singing to the very people who had never before bothered listening to the complaints of the Irish—the English.

Forget not the field where they perished,
The truest, the last of the brave,
All gone and the bright hope we cherished,
Gone with them quenched in the grave.

Oh! Could we from death but recover
Those hearts as they bounded before,
In the face of high heaven to fight over
That combat for freedom once more.

Could the chain for an instant be riven,
Which tyranny flung round us then,
Oh! Tis not in Man or in Heaven,
To let tyranny bind us again!

But tis past—and though blazoned in story
The name of our victor may be,
Accurst is the march of that glory,
Which treads o'er the hearts of the free.

Far dearer the grave or the prison,
Illumined by one patriot name,
Than the trophies of all who have risen
On Liberty's ruins to fame!

THE HARP THAT ONCE THROUGH TARA'S HALLS

The book jacket of *The Irish*—a volume by the American Richard O'Connor—describes a developing culture "in the halls of Tara while the peoples of western Europe were learning to paint on the walls of their caves." Though the statement is certainly more publisher's hyperbole than an accurate assessment of relative cultural levels, it does give an idea of the fondness with which the Irish still view their storied past. To the Irish of the early nineteenth century, six hundred years of English presence was but an irritating interlude in the 3,000-year march of *real* Irish history.

Thomas Moore captured that feeling for his English-speaking audience in this famous ballad.

The harp that once through Tara's halls
The soul of music shed,
Now hangs as mute on Tara's walls
As if that soul were fled.

So sleeps the pride of former days,
So glory's thrill is o'er,
And hearts that once beat high for praise
Now feel that praise no more.

No more to chiefs and ladies bright
The harp of Tara swells;
The chord, alone, that breaks the night,
Its tale of ruin tells.

Thus Freedom now so seldom wakes,
The only throb she gives
Is when some heart indignant breaks
To show that she still lives.

THE MINSTREL BOY

Most of Thomas Moore's nationalist songs are not chronologically specific. Rather than recounting or lamenting individual events in history, they supplied a metaphorical martial spirit that told the English-speaking Irishman, in effect, that it is all right to be an Irish rebel.

This memorable ballad is a case in point. Playing on the Irish love of poetic song, Moore created an entirely sympathetic minstrel-warrior. The universal compassion with martyrdom of the young made it immediately popular among an Irish people who remembered '98 and '03 first-hand. Of all the poet's songs, it is the one most often sung even today.

The minstrel boy to the war is gone,
In the ranks of death you'll find him;
His father's sword he has girded on,
And his wild harp slung behind him.—
"Land of song!" sang the warrior-bard,
"Though all the world betrays thee,
One sword, at least, thy rights shall guard,
One faithful harp shall praise thee."

The minstrel fell!—but the foeman's chain
Could not bring his proud soul under;
The harp he loved ne'er spoke again,
For he tore its chords asunder;
And sang, "No chains shall sully thee,
Thou soul of love and bravery!
Thy songs were made for the pure and free,
They shall never sound in slavery."

    The disappearance of Gaelic as the common tongue in Ireland was increasingly obvious in the early nineteenth century as the English-speaking towns became participant in the Industrial Revolution. The ascendancy of the English language was reflected in the music—joining the poor Irish labourers who flocked to Belfast and Dublin to earn English money in the new factories, many of the balladeers wrote music they could sell to an English-speaking market. The bogus picture of Ireland presented by these "false bards" so distressed Irish rebels that, as late as 1913, Sir Roger Casement would write to the *Ulster Guardian* that:

> When Irish history ceases to be written by buffoons and English music-hall artistes we shall begin to see that the simple title "an Irishman" is the common and glorious heritage of every son of this soil.

There were other bards, however, who would never forget the legacy of the men who had died "on the scaffold high, or on the battlefield."

BY MEMORY INSPIRED

This ballad is from the middle of the nineteenth century, as can be seen by the out-of-sequence references to Dan O'Connell and John Mitchel. The title is particularly significant: the "memory" involved here is the betrayal of the United Irish leaders, the "inspiration" presumably is to beware of informers.

One of the few ballads covering the events from October 1797 to September 1803 that makes no mention of the risings themselves, this one concentrates on the way the Crown dealt with the United political chiefs. The singer suggests Willie Orr was falsely convicted by a drunken jury; that Thomas Reynolds delivered John McCann, Oliver Bond, and Billy Byrne; that Captain Armstrong exposed Henry and John Sheares; and so on.

The ballad argues that the rebel leaders were merely unfortunate, that they might well have succeeded had they not been beguiled by deceivers. The corollary is, of course, that the task is not impossible; if the singers are careful not to make the same mistakes, they will be more successful.

By memory inspired
And love of country fired,
The deeds of Men I love to dwell upon;
And the patriotic glow
Of my spirit must bestow
A tribute to O'Connell that is gone, boys, gone!
Here's a memory to the friends that are gone.

In October Ninety-Seven,
May his soul find rest in heaven!
William Orr to execution was led on;
The jury, drunk, agreed
That Irish was his creed,
For perjury and threats drove them on, boys, on!
Here's to the memory of John Mitchel that is gone.

In Ninety-Eight, the month July,
The informer's pay was high,
When Reynolds gave the gallows brave McCann;
But McCann was Reynolds' first,
One could not allay his thirst,
So he brought up Bond and Byrne that are gone, boys, gone!
Here's to the memory of the friends that are gone.

We saw a nation's tears
Shed for John and Henry Shears,
Betrayed by Judas Captain Armstrong;
We may forgive, but yet
We never can forget
The poisoning of Maguire that is gone, boys, gone!
Our high star and true apostle that is gone.

How did Lord Edward die?
Like a man, without a sigh,
But he left his handiwork on Major Swann!
But Sirr, with steel-clad breast
And coward heart at best,
Left us cause to mourn Lord Edward that is gone, boys, gone!
Here's the memory of our friends that are gone.

September Eighteen-Three
Closed this cruel history,
When Emmet's blood the scaffold flowed upon;
O, had their spirits been wise
They might then realise
Their freedom—but we drink to Mitchel that is gone, boys, gone!
Here's to the memory of the friends that are gone.

THE THREE FLOWERS

The melodious weeping of the lament is a familiar sound in the lexicon of Irish rebel music. It is this memory-of-the-slain-in-song that has been largely responsible for creating the Pantheon of Martyrs that dominates the mythology of Irish resistance.

Success or failure has mattered little to the rebel balladeer; what has mattered is daring to strike the blow. The English have never fully understood the impact of the martyr on the Irish people and, so, have busily supplied the poets with a constant supply of graves over which to sing. Pádraig Pearse's bitterly shrewd keen over one of them, that of O'Donovan Rossa in 1915, should have given the Crown a clue:

> . . . the fools, the fools, the fools—they have left us our Fenian
> dead. And while Ireland holds these graves, Ireland unfree shall

never be at peace.

Had the British bothered to listen to the songs, they may have been able to prevent Pearse and his fellow poets from marching out the next Easter to offer their own blood sacrifice.

This ballad by Kenneth Reddin is typical of the *caoine*. Recalling Wolfe Tone and Robert Emmet with sorrow, the song equates their sacrifice with that of Mickey Dwyer who fought on alone against impossible odds when all seemed lost. It is a fine example of the regard in which those rebel heroes were—and are—held.

One time when walking down a lane
When night was drawing nigh,
I met a *cailín* with three flowers,
And she more young than I;
"St. Patrick bless you, dear," said I,
"If you will be quick and tell
The place where you did find those flowers
I seem to know so well."

She took a flower and kissed it once
And softly said to me,
"This flower I found in the Antrim hills
Outside Belfast," said she.
"The name I call it is Wolfe Tone,
The bravest flower of all;
But I'll keep it fresh close to my breast
Though all the world should fall."

She took a flower and kissed it twice
And sweetly said to me,
"This flower I found in Thomas Street
In Dublin City," said she.
"It's name is Robert Emmet,
The youngest flower of all;
But I'll keep it fresh close to my breast
Though all the world should fall."

She took a flower and kissed it thrice
And softly said to me,
"This flower I found in the Wicklow Hills,
Dew wet and pure," said she.

"It's name is Michael Dwyer,
The strongest flower of all;
But I'll keep it fresh close to my breast
Though all the world should fall."

"Then Emmet, Dwyer and Tone I'll keep,
For I do love them all;
And I'll keep them fresh close to my breast
Though all the world should fall."

THE MEMORY OF THE DEAD
(*Who Fears to Speak of Ninety-Eight?*)

This song may best personify the importance of rebel music in Irish history. John Kells Ingram, later to become a professor of Trinity College and president of the Royal Irish Academy, wrote the ballad when he was but a lad of twenty. First published anonymously in the April 1843 *Nation*—whose poetry section has been called by John McDonnell a "ballad history of Ireland"—the lay was reprinted two years later in *The Spirit of the Nation* with the melody to which it was already being sung in the streets and fields.

The ballad unabashedly makes martyrs of the men who fell in 1798. In the true tradition of the rebel song, it does more: it uses the memory of those martyrs to urge the listeners to follow in the footsteps of the men who fell at Vinegar Hill and Ballinahinch. Those who sing the song today also remember the men who fell at the Dublin G.P.O. and Brookeborough Barracks.

Who fears to speak of Ninety-Eight?
Who blushes at the name?
When cowards mock the patriot's fate,
Who hangs his head for shame?
He's all a knave, or half a slave,
Who slights his country thus;
But true men, like you men,
Will fill your glass with us.

We drink the memory of the brave,
The faithful and the few;

Some lie far off beyond the wave,
Some sleep in Ireland, too;
All, all are gone, but still lives on
The fame of those who died;
And true men, like you men,
Remember them with pride.

Some on the shores of distant lands
Their weary hearts have laid,
And by the stranger's heedless hand
Their lonely graves were made;
But though their graves be far away
Beyond the Atlantic foam,
They're true men, like you men,
Their spirit's still at home.

The dust of some is Irish earth,
Among their own they rest;
And the same land that gave them birth
Has caught them to her breast;
And we will pray that from their clay
Full many a race may start
Of true men, like you men,
To act as brave a part.

They rose in dark and evil days
To right their native land;
They kindled here a living blaze
That nothing can withstand.
Alas! That might can vanquish right!
They fell and passed away,
But true men, like you men,
Are plenty here today.

Then here's their memory! May it be
For us a guiding light,
To cheer our strife for liberty,
And teach us to unite!
Through good and ill, be Ireland's still,
Though sad as theirs your fate;
And true men be you, men,
Like those of Ninety-Eight.

In 1770 the great Samuel Johnson had roared forth from Fleet Street that the Empire was being served badly by British policy in Ireland. It would be more effective, he had argued:

> to restrain the turbulence of the natives by the authority of the sword, and to make them amenable to law and justice by an effectual and vigorous police, than to grind them to powder by all sorts of disabilities and incapacities.

Within the next half-century, the British government had decided to do both.

Strongbow had landed in Ireland with unsheathed sword six hundred years before Dr. Johnson's trenchant remarks. Rarely during the intervening years were the war-lord's colonialist heirs to use their scabbards. The Irish culture, two millennia a-building, was slowly but inexorably pushed to a precarious perch on the fringe of the evolving Anglo-Irish society. Native law, language, custom, and literature fell grudging victim to six centuries of increasing English hegemony. Along the way, however, the Irish had begun to pick up many Western European intellectual values. Concepts such as individual freedom, nationalism, ecumenism, and republicanism had been adopted in blood by the insurgent United Irishmen. These notions, once alien to the Irish tradition, had nonetheless become grafted into the one historical weapon that the Stranger had been unable to take away from the Gaelic Irish—the rebel song.

Now they would sing it in English.

IRISH GLOSSARY

Although the rebel song itself is an Anglo-Hibernian folk form of relatively recent vintage, its roots are very much in the ancient Irish poetic tradition of *rosg catha*. Its lyrics are a reflection of the reluctant metamorphosis of Irish society during the eight centuries of British presence in Ireland. The very existence of the song of resistance is in fact a mirror of the unwillingness of the Gaelic culture to slip silently into history: indeed, we find that many of the rebel ballads are to some degree macaronic. The Irish we discover sprinkled liberally throughout the English lyrics is sometimes phonetic or corrupted (*machree* for *mo chroí;* sometimes *passé* in usage (*file* now means simply "poet"); and sometimes representative of lyrical license even in the old language (*Mononia* for "Munster" is perhaps akin to the present-day English use of "Erse" for "Irish").

I hope the following glossary will be of some use to those readers even less familiar with the ancient tongue than the author. A special thanks is offered here to Caoimhín Ó Duhbhánaigh for setting aside his French, Persian, and Spanish studies long enough to patiently explain subtle shades of meaning in the old—and, sorrowfully, the modern—Irish to a fascinated but shame-faced student. If mistakes remain, they are in spite of the bemused best efforts of this young Gaelic scholar.

The meanings given below are those which best explain their use *in the context of this work*, not necessarily their primary (or modern) usage.

Aboo; abu; a bua — To Victory! (as a war-shout). "O'Donnell Aboo", for example, was the battle-shout of the lords of TyrConnell, "Butler Aboo!" the rallying-cry of the chiefs of Ormonde. "Crom Aboo!" was the war-cry of the Fitzgeralds of both Kildare and Desmond. During the time of Henry VII, these wild whoops of war had become so disconcerting to the English that an Act of Parliament was passed against their use. Curiously entitled "An Act abolishing the words Cromabo and Butlerabo," this flatulent legislation provided that "for the time being" the Irish warrior should "call only on St. George, or on the name of his Sovereign Lord the King of England." This surely stands as one of the most peculiar—and ineffective—pieces of legislation ever to emerge from Westminster.

Achadh Airt — Field of Art (metaphor for Ireland).

A chara — my friend, my dear.

A chroí — my friend, my darling, my heart.

A chuisle gheal mo chroidhe — bright pulse of my heart, shining vein of my heart.

Agra; a ghrá — my dear, my love.

Aisling — verse form; traditional mystical vision-poem. The usual scenario has the narrator come across a woman representing Ireland. Often the narrator awakes to find he has been dreaming.

Alanna machree; a leanna mo chroí — my dear child.

Annála Ríoghachta Eireann — Annals of the Kingdom of Ireland. Better known as *The Annals of the Four Masters* or, sometimes, *The Irish Chronicles.*

Ard Rí — High King.

Aroon, a rúin — my [dear] secret. Used as a term of endearment: my darling.

Astoreen; a stóirín — my little treasure.

Bacach — lame.

Banba, Fódhla, and *Érie* — names of three royal sisters of the ancient *DéDanann.* Each extracted a promise from *Amairgen,* High Druid of the conquering *Melesians,* that the island would be named after her (all three names, therefore, are now used as poetic metaphors for Ireland).

Bean dubh an ghleanna — dark lady of the glen. Name of famous Gaelic song that has since become yet another sobriquet for Ireland.

Bearna bhaoghail; or *bearna bhaoil* — the gap of danger; often translated incorrectly, if poetically, as the "grim gap of death." It refers to the point of bitterest fighting in a battle.

Bliain na bhFrancach — the Year of the French. Cant name for 1798.

Bodhrán — hand-held Irish war drum used from antiquity. Now an integral part of most "traditional" Irish folk bands.

Bonnacht; buanacht — Irish mercenary. Originally meant "soldiers' quarters" (see *coyne* and *livery*), it came to mean the soldier so quartered. After the Desmond Wars some entire displaced clans hired themselves out to Hugh O'Neill.

Bóirmhe; bóruma — of the tributes. Because cattle were the basis of wealth in ancient Ireland, "of the *cattle* tributes" is correct in idiom.

Bothóg — shelter. Temporary "portable" shelters for the Catholic Mass were common throughout the 17th and 18th centuries.

Bouchal; buachaill — boy, lad.

Brehon; breitheamh — judge, poet, lawyer; heir to Druidic tradition.

Buachaillí Bána — Whiteboys.

Cailleach ghranna — the ugly hag. Used in Connacht to describe Elizabeth Tudor.

Cailín; colleen — young girl, lass.

Cáitilín ní Uallacháin — Kathleen, daughter of Houlihan (metaphor for Ireland).

Cáitilín ní Triall — Kathleen, daughter of Tyrell (metaphor for Ireland).

Cáit ní Dhuibhir — Kate, daughter of Dwyer (metaphor for Ireland).

Caoine; keen — death song, lament.

Carraig; carrick — large rock. Often used in combination with another word to designate a particular outcropping or large hill (i.e. *Carraigrua* in Wexford).

Clár Chormaic — Plain of Cormac (ancient metaphor for Ireland).

Clár na bhFionn — Plain of the Fair Ones (ancient metaphor for Ireland).

Clárseach — the Irish harp.

Cnota Bán — white knot. Used as synonym for the "White Cockade" of the French Bourbon kings.

Combarba — heir apparent, successor, tanist. Properly, it is an ecclesiastical term.

Coyne and *livery* — ancient custom which required henchmen of a Celtic king to quarter the king's troops and provide them with supplies. In later times, it could be paid in either money or kind. Also called *bonnacht*.

Creach — plunder, loot.

Cró Chuinn — the Fold of Conn (ancient metaphor for Ireland).

Crom — pagan god of antiquity still invoked in Irish curse. "*Crom Aboo!*" was the war-shout of the Fitzgeralds and is now their motto.

Décies — shortened and slightly corrupted form of *Deasmbumban* ("South Munster"). The area referred to roughly coincides with modern Waterford.

Dhoun; donn — brown-haired, brunette.

Drimindubh deelish; or *dhroimeann dubb dílis* — my dear white and black-backed cow (metaphor for Ireland).

Dubb — dark, black, raven-haired.

Dun; dúin — stronghold, fort, aerie.

Éraic; éiric — blood debt. Under Celtic law, a formalised debt was incurred for taking a life. In terms of Anglo law, it would be a civil rather than criminal offense. The system of "repayment" was complicated but usually involved a payment of cattle (and, later, money . . . from which sprung the perjorative English description of the custom as "blood money").

Erin go bragh; Eireann go brách — Ireland forever!

Fiadh Fuinidh — Land of the West (ancient metaphor for Ireland).

Fionn — fair one, white, beautiful.

File, filí — poet, poets (*pl.*). In early times, "poet" falls far short of really defining the Gaelic word. In pre-Christian Ireland, the *filí* were official court genealogists, seers, and judges in addition to their saga-making.

Fitz — Norman patronymic signifying "son of." Gradually, it also became "of the family of." The Fitzgeralds, for example, took their family name from Gerald FitzMaurcie (Gerald, son of Maurice), 1st Baron of Offaly in the late twelfth century. Hence they were called the Geraldines.

Foras Feasa ar Éirinn — Basic Knowledge on Ireland. This work by Seathrún Céitinn (Geoffrey Keating) is normally called *Keating's History* or, more simply, *The History of Ireland.*

Gallóglaigh; gallowglass — foreign youth, foreign mercenaries. The Irish first got these fierce adventurers from the savage tribes of Wales and Britain. In later times, they were to be recruited from Scotland and the Hebrides.

Geal — bright, silvery, white.

Go de thu, mavourneen slaun; or *Ga dté tú, a mhuirní slán* — may you go [safely], farewell my darling.

Grá — love.

Granuaille; Gráinne Mhaol — corruption of Gráinne ní Máille (Grace O'Malley), 16th century Queen of Clare Island and Clew Bay (metaphor for Ireland).

Iomarbhaigh na bhFilí — counterboasting of the poets, the "Bardic Contention."

Inis; inish; innis — isle, island.

Inis Fáil — Isle of Destiny (metaphor for Ireland).

Kern; ceithearn — band of soldiery. Properly a plural word, it is sometimes improperly used to signify a single soldier. In later years, the meaning has expanded in slang to mean the "common folk."

Laighean — Leinster.

Lia Fáil — the coronation stone of the ancient kings of Tara. Legend tells us that if the "true" High King were being crowned, the stone would groan.

Lillibulero Bullenala — a corruption from the Irish, perhaps of "*An Lile ba léir dhó, ba linn an lá.*" Considering the era, that would roughly translate as "The Lily [of France] appeared certain to him [Tyrconnell], but the day was ours." Sparling repeats another, somewhat more fanciful possibility: "*Lí! li Beur! lear-a! Buille na la!*" This suggestion, supposed to be "part of a solar hymn, astronomical and druidical . . .", would translate as "Light! light on the sea! beyond the promontory! Tis the stroke of morning!"

Lough; loch — lake, arm of the sea.

Mac — Celtic patronymic denoting "son of." Systemised patronymics became prevalent in Ireland at the time of Brian Boru (whose father's name was Cinnéide, making Boru's proper name Brian McKennedy).

Machree; mo chroí — my love, my darling, my heart.

Mavrone; mo ghrón — my grief; sometimes rendered "alas."

Mononia — poetic name for ancient Munster.

Mór; More — big, large, the great (as in Malachy *Mór*).

Na géanna fiáine; or *na geana fiadhaine* — "The Wild Geese."

Na nGall — of the foreigners.

Ní — Celtic patronymic denoting "daughter of." Female equivalent of *Mac*. In Gaelic Ireland a married woman maintained her "maiden" name (it would, of course, have been absurd for her to take her husband's name since it meant "son of" or "descended from").

Nóra Críonna — Sage Old Nora (ancient metaphor for Ireland).

Ó; O' — Celtic patronymic signifying "descended from." Usually, the family name was taken from the most notable of ancestors (the O'Neills, for example, claim descent from Niall of the Nine Hostages).

Ochon — alas.

Óg; Oge — young, the younger, "Junior" (as in Garret *Oge* Fitzgerald).

Ogham — primitive form of early Irish cipher.

Ollamh, ollúna — High Druid, High Druids (*pl.*). Chief of the pre-Christian bardic order, the *ollamh* was at once classical poet, arbiter of genealogical dispute, seer, and judge of last resort.

Paidrín — rosary beads.

Poblacht na hÉireann — the Republic of Ireland.

Port — redoubt, fortress, harbour.

Príosún — gaol, prison.

Reacaire — professional "reciter" of poetry in ancient Ireland.

Roe; rua; ruadh — red-headed, ginger-haired, the red (as in Owen *Roe* O'Neill), foxy.

Róisín dubh — the little black rose, dark Rosaleen (metaphor for Ireland).

Rosg catha; Rosg-Cata — an address for [of] battle. The term was used to denote the "war song of the *file*," the rabble-rousing lay used to incite the kern on the eve of battle.

Sassenach; Sasanach — Saxon. The term later evolved into a perjorative nickname for any stranger (usually in the sense of "English-lover").

Scáthlán — shelter. Popularly used to describe the areas used for the Mass in rural areas.

Seanchaí, seanchaithe — storyteller, storytellers (*pl.*). In ancient Ireland, this class of apprentice poets occupied the lowest rung of the Druidic ladder.

Seán Ó Duibhir an gleanna; or *Sheáin Uí Dhuibhir an ghleanna* — Sean O'Dwyer of the glen.

Senchus Mór — the ancient code of Brehon Law. Though this name was not used until the old laws were committed to paper by scholars, the phrase has come to be synonomous with "Brehon Law" itself.

Shan van vocht; or *seanbhean bhocht* — poor old woman (metaphor for Ireland).

Sinn Féin — we ourselves. If the popular translation of "ourselves alone" is specifically incorrect, the double positive in emphasis makes it close enough for all but purists.

Sláinte — health. As in a toast, "to your health."

Slieve; sliabh — mountain.

Spailpín fánach; spalpeens — occasional migratory labourers. Collective term for casual day-workers. Through some strange metamorphosis, on the streets of New York City, "spalpeen" (or "spaldeen") refers to the ubiquitous hard rubber spheroid used in stickball.

Stor machree; or *stór mo chroí* — treasure of my heart.

Súgán — Rope made of straw. Idiomatic way of saying "illusory."

Tanist, tánaist — the heir apparent to an ancient Irish chieftain (from the Gaelic for "the expected one"). Under the system of *tánaisteacht,* the tanist was elected from among the royal families of the clan. The theory was that by electing a successor while the king was still alive, a bloody fight for the Crown could be avoided when the chieftain died. In reality, such divisive squabbles were the rule anyway. A parallel in Anglo history might be the 1707 Act of Union that not only created Great Britain, but provided that Princess Sophia of Hanover was heir presumptive to William III. The Stuarts no more gracefully acceded to that agreement than the pretenders to Gaelic titles did to those of tanistry.

Thomond; Tuaidhmhumham — northern Munster. The specific realm of Thomonod came to be County Clare and part of north County Limerick.

Tory; toraidhe — pursuer, outlaw, bandit, highwayman, rapparee.

Tuath — tribe, clan sept (in anthropologic terms). To a lesser degree (in political terms) the concept also encompassed the domain over which the clan held sway.

Ulaidh; Ulladh, Ulidia — Ulster. In antiquity, only the eastern portion of the modern province was named.

Umhalach — henchman, faithful follower, liegeman.

BIBLIOGRAPHY

To some degree all histories are presumptuous. When we are tempted to pontificate on the "whys" of centuries past, it is well that we remember Golo Mann's caution as he traced the career of the remarkable Wallenstein:

> It has always been no more than a historian's postulate, credulously accepted, that mankind's bloody imbecilities require causes commensurate with their horror, or even causes at all.

The interpretation of events *is* perhaps better left to philosophers than historians. If I have occasionally forgotten Mr. Mann's warning, it is not because of the volumes listed below. The years of collective research that must have gone into their writing is staggering, and I have little hesitation in admitting that my text is unabashedly dependent on their authors' Herculean efforts. In one way or another each of these books have been of use to me. I hope that some comments upon them may encourage others to make use of them, too.

C. ANDERSON, *Historical Sketch of the Native Irish and Their Descendants*, Edinburgh, 2nd Edition, 1830. Gives a fascinating view of the Crown's attempts to eradicate Gaelic "literature, education, and oral instruction."

H. ARBMAN, *The Vikings*, London, 1961. Useful to gain perspective of the full extent of Norse expansionism.

O. ARMSTRONG, *Edward Bruce's Invasion of Ireland*, London, 1923.

R. BAGWELL, *Ireland Under the Tudors*, London, 1890. Still the touchstone work on the era.

J. C. BECKETT, *The Making of Modern Ireland 1603-1903*, London, 1966. Should be near the historian's desk from the Plantation times forward.

J. B. BELL, *The Secret Army: The IRA, 1916-1979*, Cambridge, Massachusetts, 1970;

4th Edition, 1980. An emotionally sympathetic yet intellectually objective historian has made a spectacular start in filling in the blanks.

R. BERLETH, *The Twilight Lords,* New York, 1978. History that reads like a saga. Here is an author who does not skip swiftly over the dramatic complexities of the Desmond Wars.

J. A. BLACK, *Your Irish Ancestors,* Seacaucus, New Jersey, 1978. Fine narrative history from an unexpected source.

B. L. BLAKELEY and J. COLLINS (Eds.), *Documents in English History Early Times to the Present,* New York, London, Sydney, Toronto, 1975. From Tacitus to Bernadette Devlin.

D. BRENNAN, "Paintings in a Military Academy," CARA, Vol. 14, No. 4, 1981. An interesting treatment of the Wild Geese who "made good" in the Austrian service.

R. B. BROWN, "A Nation Without a King," BRITISH HISTORY ILLUSTRATED, Vol. V, No. 4, 1978. Fascinating look at the events precipitated by the death of the Maid of Norway.

H. CALKIN, "For and Against the Union," ÉIRE-IRELAND, Winter 1978. Fine account of the "public-relations fight" for votes and minds.

J. CARSWELL, *From Revolution to Revolution: 1688-1776,* New York, 1973. Valuable treatment of an England entering the Industrial Revolution. The author's research into population, and his resulting table, are themselves sufficient reason to pick up the book.

N. CHADWICK, *The Celts,* Harmondsworth, Middlesex, 1970, 1978. Covers the rise and spread of the Celts in less than 300 pages. A good read by a noted scholar.

G. CHRISTIANSON, "Landlords and Land Tenure, 1790-1830," ÉIRE-IRELAND, Spring 1974.

W. L. S. CHURCHILL, *A History of the English-Speaking Peoples,* London and New York, 1956-1958.

J. I. C. CLARKE, "The Fighting Race" in Dunn and Lennox, *The Glories of Ireland,* Washington, 1914.

A. COSGROVE, "The Gaelic Resurgence and the Geraldine Supremacy" in Moody and Martin, *The Course of Irish History,* Cork, 1967, 1978.

E. CREASY, *The Fifteen Decisive Battles of the World,* London, 1851, 38th Ed., 1894. A sweeping view of world military history by the British Chief Justice of Ceylon. The work provides an insight into the colonial mind of a man whose contemporaries fought Napoleon.

T. C. CROKER, *Popular Songs, Illustrative of the French Invasions of Ireland,* London, 1845-1847. The title is deceptive. This slim volume is a treasure-house of balladry and history alike. Croker had access to much primary source material no longer available . . . including personal correspondence with some of the principals involved.

M. CULLIGAN-HOGAN, *The Search for Galloping Hogan,* New York, 1979. A sort of historical detective story (the author is in search of an ancestor) that should be at least faintly familiar to any scholar who has traipsed off searching errant information.

E. CURTIS, *A History of Medieval Ireland,* London, 1923. Sheehy, who should know, calls this still the "best general account of the Norman invasion."

G. DANGERFIELD, *The Damnable Question,* Boston and Toronto, 1976. A valuable treatment of the Anglo-Irish Troubles of the early twentieth century.

C. DICKSON, "The Battle of New Ross," in Hayes-McCoy, *The Irish at War,* Cork, 1964, 1969.

−, *The Wexford Rising in 1798,* Tralee, 1955. Essential.

J. DUNN and P. J. LENNOX (Eds.), *The Glories of Ireland,* Washington, 1914. Un-abashedly nationalist with essays by such as Roger Casement, Douglas Hyde, and Alfred Percival Graves. And yet. . . .

P. DWYER, *The Siege of Londonderry,* London, 1893. Reverend Dwyer has presented the "essential" *A True Account of the Siege* by George Walker in this volume.

R. D. EDWARDS, *An Atlas of Irish History,* London, 1973, 1981. If ever a book "filled a gap in the literature," this is it. Should be on the shelf of anyone at-tempting to read, or write, intelligently about Irish history.

E. E. EVANS, *Prehistoric and Early Christian Ireland,* London, 1966. Useful introduction into the nebulous mists of Irish prehistory.

C. FALLS, "The Battle of the Yellow Ford" in Hayes-McCoy, *The Irish at War*, Cork, 1964, 1969.

—, *Elizabeth's Irish Wars*, London, 1950. Falls demonstrates far more knowledge of Elizabethan Ireland than either the Tudor court or the Irish war-lords of the age.

J. P. FRAYNE and C. JOHNSON (Eds.), *Uncollected Prose by W. B. Years, Vol. 2: Reviews, Articles and Other Miscellaneous Prose, 1887-1939*, New York, 1976. For those of us who cannot put him down.

P. GALVIN, *Songs of Irish Resistance*, London, 1955. This little book blazed a trail for those of us who stumble along in its wake.

S. R. GARDINER, *Cromwell's Place in History*, London, 1897. A remarkable work, one of the few that does not "take a side" on Cromwell's legacy. Perhaps *the* historian of seventeenth century England, Gardiner's portrayal here of the Lord Protector as the precursor of nineteenth century liberalism is essential to an understanding of a man who has slipped unfocused into history.

J. B. GORDON, *History of the Rebellion in Ireland, 1798*, London, 1803. Lecky uses the cleric's eyewitness account as a valued primary source. We could do worse.

T. GRAY, *The Irish Answer*, Boston and Toronto, 1966. A journalist's view of Ireland on the eve of the present troubles.

C. D. GREAVES, *The Easter Rising in Song and Ballad*, London, 1980. A fine "ballad treatment" of the 1916 watershed in Irish history.

E. HAHN, *Fractured Emerald: Ireland*, Garden City, New York, 1971. One of the best quick-read histories of Ireland. An ideal volume for those with little time for intense study who still wish an overview of the Irish past.

H. C. HAMILTON and R. P. MAHAFFY (Eds.), *Calendar of State Papers, Ireland*, 11 vols., London, 1860-1912.

G. A. HAYES-McCOY (Ed.), *The Irish at War*, Cork, 1964, 1969. Seven of the major battles in Irish history as presented in the Thomas Davis Lectures on Radio Éireann during 1955-1956. The editor's own contributions, "The Battle of Benburb" and "Militant Ireland," are particularly valuable.

G. A. HAYES-McCOY, "The Tudor Conquest" in Moody & Martin, *The Course of Irish History*, Cork, 1967, 1978.

G. HILL, *An Historical Account of the Plantation in Ulster at the Commencement of the Seventeenth Century 1608-1620*, Belfast, 1877. The author's prejudices do not diminish the fascination.

K. HOAGLAND, *1000 Years of Irish Poetry*, Old Greenwich, Connecticut, 1947. One reviewer called this volume "a major contribution to world literature." The comment is not hyperbole.

R. HOGAN (Ed.-in-Chief), *Dictionary of Irish Literature*, Westport, Connecticut, 1979. Writing about Ireland without this work close at hand would be like trying to read history without an encyclopedia in the room.

R. HOLINSHED, *Chronicles*, London, 1807-1808. Updated by unknown hands.

R. HOLTMAN, *The Napoleonic Revolution*, New York, 1967. A fine survey of the Corsican's career. Without some such perspective of Napoleon's goals, it is impossible to reach an understanding of French motives *vis-à-vis* those of the United Irishmen.

K. HUGHES, "The Golden Age of Early Christian Ireland" in Moody & Martin, *The Course of Irish History*, Cork, 1967, 1978.

T. A. JACKSON (Ed. by C. D. GREAVES), *Ireland Her Own*, London, 1947, 1976. An admitted partisan, the author articulates the "Socialist view" of Irish history better than some others. His facts, if sometimes selective, are accurate. As an "outline history of the Irish struggle," it is useful.

E. M. JOHNSTON, *Ireland in the Eighteenth Century*, Dublin, 1974, 1980. Dispassionate if somewhat dry treatment of the political realities. Solid treatment of the Ascendancy infighting, a subject heretofore needing precisely this sort of examination. Less useful in its handling of the submerged Irish nation.

J. JONES, *An Impartial Narrative of Each Engagement Which Took Place Between His Majesty's Force and the Rebels, During the Irish Rebellion, 1798*, New York (Amer. Ed.), 1833. Not so "impartial," but fascinating.

R. KEE, *The Most Distressful Country*, London, 1976 (Volume I of what was originally published as *The Green Flag*, London, 1972). The author, who has been attacked so violently for the recent BBC series on Ireland, deserves more than a little respect for *this* admirable work. If the "true" video story of Ireland remains on the cutting-room floor, Mr. Kee's prose work suggests that it is not his fault.

J. KENYON, "The English Civil Wars," BRITISH HISTORY ILLUSTRATED, Vol. V, Nos. 2, 3, & 4 (series), 1978. Professor Kenyon has made a noble attempt to untangle the snarled military and political tumult of those confusing years. I would wistfully urge him to make the same attempt at concurrent events in Ireland.

B. KIELY, "A Terrible Beauty" in Podhoretz (Ed.), *The Irish Uprising 1916-1922,* New York, 1966.

A. F. KINNEY, *Elizabethan Backgrounds: Historical Documents of the Age of Elizabeth I,* Hamden, Connecticut, 1975.

E. KNOTT, *Irish Classical Poetry,* Cork, 1957, 1978. This little paperback contains a wealth of information on both the poetry and poets of early Ireland.

D. KRAUSE, *The Letters of Sean O'Casey, Volume I,* New York, 1975. The early letters demonstrate the impact of the Irish rebel tradition on a poor Dublin Protestant of the early twentieth century.

B. KRIMM, *W. B. Yeats and the Emergence of the Irish Free State,* Troy, New York, 1981. Spendid coverage of the Senator-poet's later production when, as the author points out, Yeats was "living in the explosion." Especially rewarding is Mr. Krimm's treatment of the poet's preoccupation with the Dermott-Dervogilla theme.

R. LACEY, *Sir Walter Raleigh,* New York, 1974. Freebooting in Ireland on the way to the top.

W. E. H. LECKY, *A History of Ireland in the Eighteenth Century,* London, 1892. As has been said by many others, Lecky is still indispensible for an understanding of the era. His rambling introductory is also informative and worth more attention than it usually gets.

J. F. LYDON, *Ireland in the later Middle Ages,* Dublin, 1973. A fine treatment of an extremely neglected period of Irish history.

M. MacCURTAIN, *Tudor and Stuart Ireland,* Dublin, 1972, 1979. Excellent narrative history that will satisfy both the scholar and the dilettante.

L. MacMANUS, "The Rising of 1641" in S. MacManus, *The Story of the Irish Race,* New York, 1921, 1973.

S. MacMANUS (Ed.), *The Story of the Irish Race,* New York, 1921; 23rd printing, 1973. This thinly-disguised nationalist work has obviously touched the same nerve in several generations of readers. I would not be surprised to learn that Seumas MacManus' name appears on more private bookshelves than any other Irish author. A modicum of scholarship and an excess of passion have made this volume a publishing phenomenom.

M. MacNEILL, *The Life and Times of Mary Ann McCracken,* Dublin, 1960. An insightful view of life in Rosemary Lane.

G. MacNIOCAIL, *Ireland Before the Vikings,* Dublin, 1972. Perhaps the best treatment of the "unsullied" Gaelic society.

H. O. MACKEY (Ed.), *The Crime Against Europe by Roger Casement,* Dublin, 1966.

F. X. MARTIN, "The Anglo-Norman" in Moody and Martin, *The Course of Irish History,* Cork, 1967, 1978.

R. MASON, *The Song Lore of Ireland,* New York, 1911; Ann Arbor, Michigan, 1971. The "march" of Irish balladry.

R. K. MASSIE, *Peter the Great, His Life and World,* New York, 1980. The Pulitzer Prize-winning historian of Russia includes a valuable treatment of William III and a fascinating glimpse of the London visited by the young Tsar in 1698.

W. A. MAXWELL, *History of the Irish Rebellion in 1798,* London, 1845, 1887. Includes some valuable eyewitness accounts, not least of which are entries from the diaries of Dr. Joseph Stock.

J. McDONNELL, *Songs of Struggle and Protest,* Dublin, 1979. A Socialist view of history through the medium of song.

R. B. McDOWELL, "The Protestant Nation" in Moody and Martin, *The Course of Irish History,* Cork, 1967, 1978.

J. MITCHEL, *The History of Ireland from the Treaty of Limerick to the Present Time/ being a continuation of the History of the Abbé MacGeoghegan,* New York, Montreal, and Boston, 1868. A marvelous companion volume to the history of Irish resistance. Mitchel had access to a great deal of primary source material and, fortunately for the reader, included much of it *in toto*. Various clues suggest that Lecky kept this volume close by while writing his great history of eighteenth century Ireland. Indeed between the history by the Ascendancy landowner and this one by the celebrated Young Irelander, a reasonably accurate picture of the time emerges.

—, *The Life of Hugh O'Neill, Prince of Ulster,* Dublin, 1845. A younger Mitchel here, one with more fire and perhaps less scholarship.

T. W. MOODY and F. X. MARTIN (Eds.), *The Course of Irish History,* Cork, 1967, 1978. A fine introduction to Irish history by twenty-one distinguished modern scholars. Chapter authors whose work I have used are acknowledged individually in this bibliography.

J. MORRIN (Ed.), *Calendar of the Patent and Close Rolls of Chancery in Ireland of the reigns of Henry VIII, Edward VI, Mary, and Elizabeth,* 2 vols., Dublin 1861. Amidst the grants to royal favourites and pardons to presumably penitant rebels can be found Elizabeth's correspondence to an ever-changing group of official servants. The Queen's commands—following the invariable "Right trustie and welbeloved, wee greete youe well"—are specific, warmly imperious, and consistantly uniformed as to the true state of the realm.

D. MURTAGH, "The Battle of Aughrim" in Hayes-McCoy, *The Irish at War,* Cork, 1964, 1969.

NATION, The Writers of THE, *The Spirit of the Nation, Ballads and Songs,* Dublin, 1845, 2nd Ed., 1882. The poetic "Bible" of the Irish rebel tradition.

K. NICHOLLS, *Gaelic and Gaelicised Ireland in the Middle Ages,* Dublin, 1972; 3rd Edition, 1981. Reading between the lines of the *Four Masters* and the *State Papers.*

S. Ó BOYLE, *The Irish Song Tradition,* Dublin, 1976. A minor classic well worth the read. In many ways, the author's career resembles that of the American folk collector Alan Lomax.

C. C. O'BRIEN, "Holy War," NEW YORK REVIEW OF BOOKS, 6 November 1969.

L. Ó BROIN, *The Unfortunate Mr. Robert Emmet,* Dublin and London, 1958. Useful treatment of the '03 leader.

M. R. O'CONNELL, *Irish Politics and Social Conflict in the Age of the American*

Revolution, Philadelphia, 1965.

D. Ó CORRÁIN, *Ireland Before the Normans,* Dublin, 1972, 1980.   Gaelic Ireland *sans* romance.

B. Ó CUÍV, "Ireland in the Eleventh and Twelfth Centuries" in Moody and Martin, *The Course of Irish History,* Cork, 1967, 1978.

J. O'DONOVAN (Trans., Ed.), *Annals of the Kingdom of Ireland by the Four Masters, From the Earliest Period to the Year 1616,* 5 vols., Dublin, 1854; 7 vols., New York, 1966. A staggering work of history and literature, both by O'Cleary and his brother Franciscans, and by the nineteenth century translator. Hoagland calls it simply "one of the largest collections of national, civil, military, and family history ever brought together." The Donegal clerics used every available source in the writing; their purpose was to save Irish history before the records were lost. O'Donovan similarly used every chronicle still extant to check his translation (as well as the services of the last few Irish scholars who could still understand the vernacular involved); his purpose was to get an accurate translation into English before it was no longer possible. The result is that O'Donovan's notes are almost as important as the text.

S. Ó FAOLÁIN (Ed.), *The Autobiography of Theobald Wolfe Tone,* New York, London, *et al.,* 1937. The United Irishman's original "autobiography" was published by his son in Washington during 1826. This edition includes material omitted from the original (William had edited his father's diary indiscretions) and reduces the unwieldy two volumes to a single one, easily read. The result of Ó Faoláin's editing is that, for all the legend, Wolfe Tone appears as a man.

—, *The Great O'Neill,* London, 1942; Cork, 1981. The best biography of the renaissance Gael. Although the author is firmly grounded in the Irish nationalist tradition—he fought on the Republican side during the Civil War—he shows a scholar's disdain for romantic nonsense. Here may be found the realistic story of a tenth-century culture fighting hopelessly against the advent of the seventeenth century . . . and of the one great Irish chieftain who saw it coming.

T. Ó FIAICH, "The Beginnings of Christianity" in Moody and Martin, *The Course of Irish History,* Cork, 1967, 1978.

J. O'MEARA (Trans., Ed.), *The First Version of the Topography of Ireland by Geraldus Cambrensis,* Dundalk, 1951. A journey into another world.

G. Ó TUATHAIGH, *Ireland Before the Famine 1798-1848,* Dublin, 1972. An excel-

lent introduction to nineteenth-century Ireland. The author had the toughest
of all tasks in the Gill Series: to describe O'Connell, Young Ireland, and the
Great Hunger with only a brief lead-in on the times of the United Irishmen. The
result is admirable.

F. PAKENHAM, *The Year of Liberty: the Great Irish Rebellion of 1798*, London,
1969. In little over a decade this volume has moved onto centre stage in every
study of the Year of the French. Absolutely essential.

R. R. PALMER, *Twelve Who Ruled*, Princeton, 1941. A flavour of the tumult in
France during the Year of Terror.

L. DE PAOR, "The Age of the Viking Wars" in Moody and Martin, *The Course of Irish
History*, Cork, 1967, 1978.

—, *Divided Ulster*, Harmondsworth, Middlesex, 1970. The early pages give a good cap-
sule history of the roots of the modern problem in the North. Short but extremely valuable account on the birth of the Orange Order.

J. H. PARRY, *The Establishment of the European Hegemony: 1415-1715*, New York,
1959, 1966 (originally published as *Europe and a Wider World*, London, 1949).
Includes a fine account of the impact of colonialism on the colonial powers
themselves, including the English. Professor Parry also explains why Barbados
and the American colonies needed cheap labour, providing along the way a
lucid picture of the conditions faced by both willing and unwilling new arrivals
across the Atlantic.

W. PETTY, *Political Survey of Ireland, with the Establishment of that Kingdom, when
the late Duke of Ormonde was Lord Lieutenant*, London, 1672; 2nd Edition,
1719. Who was who in Ireland after the Restoration.

J. H. PLUMB, *The First Four Georges*, London, 1952, 9th printing, 1972. The flavour
of life at the top by the great modern biographer of Walpole.

—, *The Growth of Political Stability in England 1675-1725*, New York, 1967; Baltimore, 1969. An edition of the Ford Lectures as delivered at Oxford by one of
the most distinguished historians of our time. Professor Plumb's throwaway
lines themselves speak volumes.

M. PODHORETZ (Ed.), *The Irish Uprising 1916-1922*, New York, 1965. Stands head
and shoulders above most volumes published to commemorate the 50th anniversary of the Easter Rebellion.

J. P. PRENDERGAST, *The Cromwellian Settlement of Ireland*, London, 1870. The author's prose is occasionally purple, but it is worth the read for all that.

A. and B. REES, *Celtic Heritage: Ancient Tradition in Ireland and Wales*, New York, 1961, 1978. The subtitle of this volume gives a hint as to its real value. Not merely a study of the *Irish* Celtic tradition, this admirable work affords a perspective not always found in more narrow studies.

D. RYAN, *The Sword of Light*, London, 1939. Intellect and emotion from the man who was secretary to Pearse and fought beside his captain at the Dublin G.P.O.

M. SHEEHY, *When the Normans Came to Ireland*, Cork and Dublin, 1975. Perhaps now *the* expert on the *Laudibilitier*, Professor Sheehy gives a complete translation of it here. In this little paperback, he affords a succinct view of Ireland on the eve of the Norman landing, the situation that piqued Strongbow's interest in the first place, the invasion itself, and the immediate effects on the island resulting from it.

C. SHRODES, C. JOSEPHSON, J. R. WILSON (Eds.), *Reading for Rhetoric*, New York, 1962, 1967.

J. G. SIMMS, *Jacobite Ireland 1685-1691*, London, 1969. James II and the War of the Two Kings.

—, "The Restoration and the Jacobite War" in Moody and Martin, *The Course of Irish History*, Cork, 1967, 1978.

H. H. SPARLING (Ed.), *Irish Minstrelry*, London, 1887. This tiny old volume by Charles Gavan Duffy's friend is a delight.

J. R. TANNER, *English Constitutional Conflicts of the Seventeenth Century 1603-1689*, Cambridge, 1928; 10th printing, 1966. Professor Tanner accomplishes the impossible: in simple, clear prose, he makes explicable the bewildering events of that tumultuous century.

G. M. TREVELYAN, *British History in the Nineteenth Century (1782-1901)*, London, 1922. To understand British policy in Ireland, it is necessary to understand the English preoccupation with events elsewhere. The number of pages devoted to Ireland should alone give us that perspective.

—, *A Shortened History of England*, New York, 1960 (abridged edition of his *History of England*). There should be at least one reputable British historian of the old school at the elbow of every Irish historian. Trevelyan is mine.

M. WALL, "The Age of the Penal Laws" in Moody and Martin, *The Course of Irish History*, Cork, 1967, 1978.

—, *The Penal Laws 1691-1760*, Dundalk, 1967. For those of us that tend to examine the Penal Times with the intellectual arrogance of the academic, this should be required reading. Maureen Wall reminds us brilliantly that the humble folk most affected were real people, not footnotes on the pages of history.

A. WARD, G. PROTHRO, and S. LEATHES (Eds.), *The Cambridge Modern History, Volume VIII, The French Revolution*, Cambridge, 1904. More than "merely" a reference book, this monumental work is sufficiently comprehensive to include information about the French expeditions to Ireland not usually reported in Irish histories.

C. V. WEDGEWOOD, *Thomas Wentworth, First Earl of Strafford 1593-1641*, London, 1964. A remarkable book about a more remarkable man.

C. WOODHAM-SMITH, *The Reason Why*, New York, 1953, 1960. An admirable treatment of the events leading to the notorious Charge of the Light Brigade. Along the way, the author makes some insightful observations about Irish rural life as she traces the bumbling career of the absentee third Earl of Lucan.

W. B. YEATS, *Plays and Controversies*, London, 1923; New York, 1924.

A. YOUNG, *A Tour in Ireland: With General Observations on the Present State of that Kingdom, 1776, 1777, 1778*, 2 vols., Dublin and London, 1780. An English agricultural expert's view of the unruly Irish. Stendahl once said that a novel is a "mirror carried along a highway." Young's journey is valuable because he was not concerned with his own reflection.

G-D. ZIMMERMAN, *Songs of Irish Rebellion*, Hatboro, Pennsylvania, 1967 (published the same year in Dublin under the name *Irish Political Street Ballads and Rebel Songs 1780-1900*).

DIRECT QUOTATIONS

For those who may be disappointed by the absence of individual references to justify each of my "assertions" within the text, I offer this simple explanation: my purpose has not been to write a "monographic history" for academicians. I have cluttered the text quite enough with footnote numbers; to interject several hundred more merely for ease of reference would tend to sink the volume in the swamp of scholarship. My aim has been the average reader, not the academician. If this be treason. . . .

In defense, I offer the recent testimony in THE NEW YORK REVIEW OF BOOKS by Gordon S. Wood of Brown University concerning the present trend among historians to write "technical, specialized analyses of particular events or problems in the past":

> The results of all this for history have been little short of chaotic. The technical monographs pour from the presses in overwhelming numbers. . . . Historians are more and more specialized, experts on single decades or single subjects. . . . Most now make no pretense of writing for the educated public. They write for each other. . . .

If my approach has enabled me to put a bit of living flesh upon one or two of the ghostly skeletons that drift with unnecessary anonymity through the lyrics of Irish balladry, then I have accomplished my purpose.

That now off my perhaps paranoid chest, I shall now attempt to make amends to those I may have indicted. Each direct quotation that I have used in the text, and its source, is listed below in its chronological order of appearance in *Blood on the Harp*. For more information on the sources, please refer to the **Bibliography** of the antecedent pages.

1. Introduction

HAVE A TENDENCY . . . NEIGHBORS: George Dangerfield, *The Damnable Question.*

SOME LORDS USED . . . EFFECT: Emily Hahn, *Fractured Emerald: Ireland.*

A BLESSING ON . . . ON IT: Alwyn and Brinley Rees, *Celtic Heritage.*

ADVENTURES OF . . . NEWSPAPERS: Rees', *ibid.*

NO LARGER NATION . . . CENTURIES: John F. Kennedy, 1963 speech to Dáil Éireann.

HAD A WIDESPREAD . . . LEARNING: Ruth Dudley Edwards, *An Atlas of Irish History.*

FROM THE BEGINNING . . . IRELAND: R. Hogan (Ed.), *Dictionary of Irish Literature.*

FREQUENTLY SENTIMENTAL . . . FORGOTTEN: C. Desmond Greaves, *The Easter Rising in Song & Ballad.*

VERSE WAS . . . MUSIC: Eleanor Knott, *Irish Classical Poetry.*

THE TRADITION OF . . . WORLD: Patrick Galvin, *Songs of Irish Resistance.*

IRISHMEN WILL NEVER . . . VAIN: Hamilton and Mahaffy (Eds.), *Calendar of State Papers, Ireland* (hereafter called simply "*State Papers*").

PROVISIONAL IRA . . . FUTURE: Published in extract by several of the "Provo newspapers," among them AN PHOBLACHT. Entitled "Northern Ireland: Future Terrorist Trends," the report was dated 4 January 1979 and authored by the man who was later to become commanding general officer in Northern Ireland, General Glover.

Chapter Notes (1)

VARYING IN NUMBER . . . IN LENGTH: Tomás Ó Fiaich, "The Beginnings of Christianity."

ONE OF THE . . . EDUCATION: Kathleen Hughes, "The Golden Age of Early Christian Ireland."

2. The Coming of the Stranger

THE WIND . . . SCANDINAVIANS: Graciously translated—with English alliteration that captures the spirit of the Gaelic—by Caoimhín Ó Duhbhánaigh. The quatrain is literally an aside, found in the margin of "St. Gall Priscian" (cited in Stokes and Strachan, *Thesaurus Palaebibernicus*, 1903).

A SORT OF . . . RACKET: Tony Gray, *The Irish Answer.*

FROM HIS BARSTOOL . . . CHARING CROSS: Benedict Kiely, "A Terrible Beauty."

MARCH INTO . . . PRESERVED: Maurice Sheehy, *When the Normans Came to Ire-land*.

NEVER, NEVER . . . PLACE: William Butler Yeats, "The Dreaming of the Bones," *Plays and Controversies*.

WAS SOUND ENOUGH . . . WOMAN: Edmund Curtis, *A History of Medieval Ireland*.

USED THE WOODS . . . ENTRENCHMENTS: J. O'Meara (Trans., Ed.), *The First Version of the Topography of Ireland by Giraldus Cambrensis*.

ALTHOUGH THE IRISH . . . CULTURE: O'Meara, *ibid*.

THEY WEAR MANTLES . . . COUNTRYSIDE: O'Meara, *ibid*.

IT IS ONLY IN . . . EVER SEEN: O'Meara, *ibid*.

ARE SO REMOVED . . . ALTOGETHER: O'Meara, *ibid*.

Chapter Notes (2)

THE FLEET OF . . . OF MAIL: John O'Donovan (Trans., Ed.), *Annals of the Kingdom of Ireland by the Four Masters* (hereafter called simply "*Four Masters*").

3. Assimilation of the *Sassenach*

AN EASH PASTORAL . . . INVADERS: Seán Ó Faoláin, *The Great O'Neill*.

NO GREATER DEFEAT . . . TIME: *Four Masters, op. cit.*

GREAT AND GENERAL . . . GAEL: *Four Masters, ibid.*

DESTROYER OF ALL IRELAND . . . HIS TIME: *Four Masters, ibid.* O'Donovan is here citing Mageoghegan's translation. The Four Masters' account, while not as complete, agrees generally . . . including upon the apparent cannibalism.

THE DISTINCTION . . . EXTENDED: George Macaulay Trevelyan, *A Shortened History of England*.

MANY MEN OF . . . IRISHMEN: *State Papers, op. cit.*

MAN ENGLISH . . . DECAYED: Hahn, *op. cit.*

THE WHOLE LAND . . . REBELS: James Lydon, *Ireland in the Later Middle Ages*.

HOW THAT HIS . . . COMMANDMENTS: Hahn, *op. cit.*

THE PRINCIPLE OF . . . FIGHT: Lydon, *op. cit.*

Chapter Notes (3)

I SAW MACMURROUGH . . . MAN: Lydon, *ibid*.

THAT WHEREAS . . . MADE: Lydon, *ibid*.

4. The Twilight of the Gael

THE MOST ILLUSTRIOUS . . . TIME: *Four Masters, op. cit.*
410 OF THE . . . PREY: *Four Masters, ibid.*
HE WAS KILLED . . . EARL: *Four Masters, ibid.*
YOUR HIGHNESS . . . ENCREASETH: *State Papers, op. cit.*
CRAMPERNED AND . . . COUNTRY: *State Papers, ibid.*
THE COUNTRY . . . COUNCIL: *State Papers, ibid.*
IRISHMEN WILL NEVER . . . WAR: *State Papers, ibid.*
THE CHIEF WAS . . . ASSASINATION: Thomas Alfred Jackson, *Ireland Her Own.*
THE SAID KING'S . . . OFFALY: Acts of Parliament, 3rd and 4th Philip and Mary.
THAT OLD BLIND . . . A FIG: Ó Faoláin, *op. cit.*
MIGHT HAVE BEEN . . . ENGLISH: *Four Masters, op. cit.*
POWERFULLY NOSTALGIC . . . OF LIFE: Ó Faoláin, *op. cit.*
TO WRITE SHANE . . . ACHIEVEMENT: Margaret MacCurtain, *Tudor and Stuart Ireland.*

Chapter Notes (4)

TEIGE O'COFFEY . . . POETRY: *Four Masters, op. cit.*

5. The Desmond Wars

DURING THE REIGN . . . COMPUNCTION: Richard Berleth, *The Twilight Lords.*
FOR ENGLISH CONTEMPORARIES . . . KHAN: Ó Faoláin, *op. cit.*
JAMES, THE SON . . . PARLIAMENT: *Four Masters, op. cit.*
OUTLAWED BARDS . . . BLOOD: Berleth, *op. cit.*
THE LURKING REBELS . . . ARMY: Berleth, *ibid.*
IT IS FANTASTICALLY . . . HER NEEDS: Ó Faoláin, *op. cit.*
SHEWED MERCY . . . PEOPLE: *Four Masters, op. cit.*
WERE LAID . . . COVERT: Cyril Falls, *Elizabeth's Irish Wars.*
WERE A MAN . . . ALL: Falls, *ibid.*
THE RECRUITS . . . LOST: Falls, *ibid.*
THEY TOLD THEIR . . . WAR: Hughes, *op. cit.*
DRIVEN TO EAT . . . EXAMPLES: Raphael Holinshed, *Chronicles.*
SO BARREN . . . ELSEWHERE: Holinshed, *ibid.*
PICTURES OF . . . HISTORY: William Edward Hartpole Lecky, *A History of Ireland in the Eighteenth Century.*
ROBERT GARDINER . . . PLOT: James Morrin, *Calendar of the Patent and Close Rolls of Chancery in Ireland*, Volume II (hereafter called "*Calendar of Chancery*").

CALL BACK THE . . . GALLOWGLASS: Berleth, *op. cit.*, is citing Michael Drayton.
A LOVING . . . PEOPLE: Kathleen Hoagland, *1000 Years of Irish Poetry.*

Chapter Notes (5)

DIVERS HOUSES . . . LAWS: *Calendar of Chancery, op. cit.*
PROSECUTE, INVADE . . . AUTHORITIE: *Calendar of Chancery, ibid.*
GOOD SUBJECTS . . . 'CLANCAIR': *Calendar of Chancery, ibid.*

6. The Nine Years War

REPRESENTED GAELIC . . . THE SAGAS: Ó Faoláin, *op. cit.*
WE ARE INFORMED . . . REALM: *Calendar of Chancery, op. cit.*
BROKEN CAUSEY . . . WOOD: MacCurtain, *op. cit.*
THE IRISH WARS . . . FOREST: Ó Faoláin, *op. cit.*
THERE WERE MORE . . . TO DECLARE: Ó Faoláin, *ibid.*
WAS NEVER TO . . . ENVIED: Berleth, *op. cit.*
THE STATE OF . . . FIELD: Berleth, *ibid.*
HUGH, EARL OF . . . TYRONE: *Calendar of Chancery, op. cit.*
LIEUTENANT-GENERAL . . . FORCES: *Calendar of Chancery, ibid.*
THE GREATEST VICTORY . . . ENGLISH: Cyril Falls, "The Battle of the Yellow Ford."
OUR GRACIOUS INTENTION . . . THEM: Arthur F. Kinney, *Elizabethan Backgrounds: Historical Documents of the Age of Elizabeth I.*
MOUNTJOY WAS . . . OBSTINATE: Ó Faoláin, *op. cit.*
LORD MOUNTJOY . . . HEAD: Lecky, *op. cit.*
THERE BE SOME FEW . . . THEMSELVES: Ó Faoláin, *op. cit.*
THE GREATEST MARCH . . . HEARD OF: Ó Faoláin, *ibid.*
WHILE MANY OF HIS . . . IRISH: Hoagland, *op. cit.*

Chapter Notes (6)

THE CROWN HAD NEVER . . . PROTECTION: Berleth, *op. cit.*
PARDON OF RORY . . . O'DONELL: *Calendar of Chancery, op. cit.*

7. Plantation

IN SUCH CIRCUMSTANCES . . . ENGLAND: Trevelyan, *op. cit.*
FROM SCOTLAND . . . JUSTICE: George Hill, *An Historical Account of the Plantation.*

PRIESTS LAND HERE . . . SYNAGOGUE: *State Papers, op. cit.*

THE NATIVES WERE . . . DEFIANCE: Conor Cruise O'Brien, "Holy War."

THEY WERE FUNDAMENTALLY . . . CRITICISM: J. H. Plumb, *The Growth of Political Stability in England.*

LAUD AND THE BISHOPS . . . GOVERNMENT: Trevelyan, *op. cit.*

IT WAS TO HIM . . . PROTESTANTS: C. Veronica Wedgeworth, *Thomas Wentworth, First Earl of Strafford.*

TO ROUSE AND KEEP . . . COUNTRY: Knott, *op. cit.,* is quoting that giant of Gaelic scholarship, Eugene O'Curry.

COLOSSAL PIECE OF . . . TO END: Ó Faoláin, *op. cit.*

NO SUCH CONSIDERATIONS . . . THOROUGH: Wedgeworth, *op. cit.*

THE COUNTRY HAD NOT . . . BRUCE: Trevelyan, *op. cit.*

Chapter Notes (7)

BECAUSE THE IRISH . . . INDIANS: D. B. Quinn, *The Elizabethans and the Irish.*

THE IRISH ANALOGUE . . . RIGHTS: Lecky, *op. cit.*

8. The Great Rebellion

POPISH MASSACRE . . . GOSPEL: John Mitchel, *The History of Ireland.*

THE FAVOURITE ENJOYMENT . . . SO ON: Mitchel, *ibid.*

IF ONE PRESUMED . . . *REVENGE:* Mitchel, *ibid.*

THIS ILL NEWS . . . ENGLAND: J. R. Tanner, *English Constitutional Conflicts of the Seventeenth Century.*

TO WOUND, KILL . . . ARMS: Lecky, *op. cit.,* who does his usual job of paraphrasing, suggests this order was issued in 1644. L. MacManus, in "The Rising of 1641," cites "Carte's 'Ormonde' " as dating the decree to 25 February 1642. Since James Butler was trying to establish the Ormonde Peace by the later date, it is likely that the earlier is in fact accurate.

IF WE BEAT . . . SLAVES: John Kenyon, "The English Civil Wars."

SOMETHING OF PARNELL . . . JACKSON: G. A. Hayes-McCoy, "The Battle of Benburb."

IT HAS PLEASED GOD . . . BELONGS: *State Papers, op. cit.*

UPON TUESDAY THE 10TH . . . GLORY: Brian Blakeley and Jacquelin Collins (Eds.), *Documents in English History.*

CROMWELL IN IRELAND . . . CROMWELL: Winston Chruchill, *A History of the English-Speaking Peoples.*

HE STANDS FORTH . . . JUDGED: Samuel R. Gardiner, *Cromwell's Place in History.*

9. The War of the Two Kings

A MAN MIGHT TRAVEL . . . BIRD: J. P. Prendergast, *The Cromwellian Settlement of Ireland.*

THE IRISH CATHOLIC LANDLORD . . . STAYED: Jackson, *op. cit.*

THE FOUNDATION OF . . . IRELAND: Lecky, *op. cit.*

THERE MUST BE NEW . . . ENGAGEMENTS: MacCurtain, *op. cit.,* and others.

THE CATHOLICS OF IRELAND . . . LOYALTY: J. G. Simms, "The Restoration and the Jacobite War."

THERE WAS A TRADITION . . . BIRTHRIGHT: Plumb, *op. cit.*

THAT WHISTLED A . . . KINGDOMS: MacCurtain, *op. cit.*

IT BOLDLY ANNOUNCED . . . NATION: MacCurtain, *ibid.*

ALL HIS OTHER SUBJECTS . . . THEM: MacCurtain, *ibid.*

WAS A CALVINIST . . . LOUIS: Robert K. Massie, *Peter the Great.*

IN THE YEAR 1690 . . . IRELAND: Trevelyan, *op. cit.*

SARSFIELD, THE HERO . . . NATION: Trevelyan, *ibid.*

NOT WITH DREAMS . . . IRON: Algernon C. Swinburne, "A Word for the Country."

AUGHRIM WAS MORE FATAL . . . HANDS: Diarmuid Murtagh, "The Battle of Aughrim."

THE ROMAN CATHOLICS . . . SAID RELIGION: Lecky, *op. cit.,* and Mitchel, *op. cit.*

THE ARTICLES WERE NOT . . . EXCEPTIONS: MacCurtain, *op. cit.*

NO IRISH WAR . . . IRISH: MacCurtain, *ibid.*

Chapter Notes (9)

IN 1654, ALL HARPERS . . . DESTROYED: Seán Ó Boyle, *The Irish Song Tradition.*

TRANSPORTATION MEANT . . . SUPPOSED: J. H. Parry, *The Establishment of the European Hegemony.*

10. Ascendancy and Wild Geese

I AM SURE THAT . . . FOR IT: Massie, *op. cit.,* cites Peter Geyl's *History of the Low Countries* for this quotation.

HE ACQUIESCED IN . . . LOUIS: Massie, *ibid.*

CONQUERED AND HOSTILE . . . STRENGTH: Lecky, *op. cit.*

PRESUME ANY SUCH PERSON . . . CATHOLIC: Quoted by both Mitchel, *op. cit.,* and Lecky, *ibid.* Lecky's use of many of the same excerpted quotations as Mitchel—such as this one—point to the presumption that the Protestant landowner wrote his brilliant history with a copy of the Young Irelander's effort at his elbow.

THESE DISTRICTS . . . THE LAW: Lecky, *ibid.*

WHETHER THERE BE . . . IRISH: Mitchel, *op. cit.,* and Lecky, *ibid.*

THERE ARE TOO MANY . . . SUBJECTS: Mitchel, *ibid.,* and Lecky, *ibid.*

TO FIGHT FOR . . . BARBADOES: Caroline Shrodes, Clifford Josephson, and James R. Wilson (Eds.), *Reading for Rhetoric,* reprints the famous essay in its entirety.

DEVELOPED THE VICES . . . WHEREVER POSSIBLE: Jackson, *op. cit.,* cites "Hayden and Moonan: *Short History of the Irish People*" for this quotation.

THESE PEOPLE OF . . . NATIONALITY: Jackson, *ibid.*

THERE WERE IRISH CATHOLICS . . . CORPORATIONS: Joseph I. C. Clarke, "The Fighting Race."

11. Peasants and Patriots

IF YOU ASK A MAN . . . I DO: Cecil Woodham-Smith, *The Reason Why.*

THE LOWER ORDERS . . . SUFFERING: Lecky, *op. cit.*

OF FIRE AND POWER . . . SURVIVES: Donal Brennan, "Paintings in a Military Academy."

THE COTTAGES OF . . . STRAW: Arthur Young, *A Tour in Ireland.*

SLAVES EVEN IN THE . . . LIBERTY: Young, *ibid.*

NEVER BEFORE IN IRELAND . . . POLICY: Lecky, *op. cit.*

BY FREE TRADE . . . RUIN: Mitchel, *op. cit.*

THE IRISH PROTESTANT . . . SLAVE: Lecky, *op. cit.,* and Mitchel, *ibid.*

SOWED THEIR LAWS . . . ARMED MEN: Mitchel, *ibid.*

NO PARLIAMENT HAD . . . IRELAND: Mitchel, *ibid.*

A CITIZEN BY LEARNING . . . FELLOW-SUBJECTS: Mitchel, *ibid.,* includes the complete text of the fourteen major resolutions of the Dungannon convention.

IRELAND, NEWLY ESCAPED FROM . . . OTHER: Mitchel, *Ibid.*

Chapter Notes (11)

WERE USED WORSE THAN . . . MASTERS: Lecky, *ibid.*

THE LANDLORD OF . . . HIS WILL: Young, *op. cit.*

A DEGREE OF DOMESTIC . . . IMAGINE: Cited by Gale E. Christianson, "Landlords and Land Tenure in Ireland, 1790-1830."

A REWARD OF . . . EXISTENCE: Lecky, *op. cit.*

THE POLITICAL POETRY . . . ENDEARMENT: In John P. Frayne (Ed.), *Uncollected Prose of W. B. Yeats.*

12. The United Irishmen

NEARLY EVERY POST OF . . . MOST ABLE: Lecky, *op. cit.*

EVERYWHERE THE DEFENDERS . . . LONGFORD: Lecky, *ibid.*

THE GOVERNMENT OF . . . PEOPLE: Quoted by numerous sources, among them Jackson, *op. cit.*

BUT FROM THE DAY . . . EMPIRE: Lecky, *op. cit.*

DESIST FROM THEIR . . . THEIR INDEPENDENCE: Ó Faoláin, *The Autobiography of Theobald Wolfe Tone.*

IF [*O'CASEY'S*] DICTUM . . . SAME WAY: The complete text of the letter is given in David Krause, *The Letters of Sean O'Casey.*

HERE I AM . . . PLANNING REVOLUTIONS: Ó Faoláin, *The Autobiography of Theobald Wolfe Tone.*

WOLFE TONE WAS . . . TO TONE: Quoted by Ó Faoláin in his introduction, *ibid.*

GROUCHY TWICE HAD . . . IN 1796: Edward Creasy, *The Fifteen Decisive Battles of The World.*

IT ANSWERS NO END . . . CORRUPTED: Lecky, *op. cit.*

Chapter Notes (12)

MERCHANTS MAKE BAD REVOLUTIONARIES: Ó Faoláin, *The Autobiography of Theobald Wolfe Tone.*

THE MOST USEFUL MEASURE . . . PEACE: Lecky, *op. cit.*

AS FOR THE ORANGEMEN . . . OCCUR: Liam de Paor, *Divided Ulster*, cites P.R.O.I. Rebellion papers 620/24/106.

13. The Eve of Rebellion

OF LATE NO NIGHT . . . COMMITTED: Robert Kee, *The Most Distressful Country*, citing B. M. Add. MSS. 33104/331. Also by Jackson, *op. cit.*

IN THE PREVIOUS . . . PEACE: The wording of the Irish Parliament's legislation is given in Jackson, *ibid.*

IT IS NOT UPON FINNERTY . . . SENTENCE: Mitchel, *op. cit.*, includes almost the entire speech. Jackson, *ibid.*, quotes extracts from the remarkable oration.

TO FLOG EACH CITIZEN . . . TRUTH: Mitchel, *ibid.*, identifies the officer as Brigadier Sir John Moore.

Chapter Notes (13)

THE CUTTING DOWN OF . . . IN VIEW: Mitchel, *ibid.*, makes much use of Byrne's eyewitness testimony. It is at least possible that the Young Irelander had personally met the venerable old Unitedman.

14. Explosion in Leinster

I CONSIDER THIS INSURRECTION . . . ARISES: Lecky, *op. cit.*

THE FREE QUARTERS . . . WICKLOW: Mitchel, *op. cit.*

SELF-PRESERVATION WAS . . . GOVERNMENT: Mitchel, *ibid.*

MORE WERE BROUGHT IN . . . STREET: John Jones, *An Impartial Narrative of Each Engagement . . . During the Irish Rebellion, 1798.*

PEASANT GIRLS HAD . . . RIBBONS: Lecky, *op. cit.*

THIS LITTLE SONG . . . ANTHEM: To my acute embarrassment, I have not been able to track down my source for this quotation. I scribbled it down well before I had any idea of writing a book . . . and did not register the source. My apologies, it was just too apt to leave out.

15. The Boys of Wexford

NO QUARTER WAS . . . STOPPED: Jones, *op. cit.*

THE REMAINING PART . . . 2,806 MEN: Charles Dickson, "The Battle of New Ross."

THEIR PERSEVERENCE . . . NUMBERS: Lecky, *op. cit.*

Chapter Notes (15)

ONE OF THOSE ROMAN . . . FIRE-ARMS: Mitchel, *op. cit.*

BEGAN THE REPUBLIC . . . KILCORMUCK: Desmond Ryan, *The Sword of Light.*

I HAVE REASON TO . . . WITHOUT ARMS: James B. Gordon, *History of the Rebellion in Ireland, 1798.*

16. Ulster Also Rises

Chapter Notes (16)

THE LOWER ORDER OF . . . COUNTRY: Lecky, *op. cit.*

IN THAT MONTH . . . GIVEN: Kee, *op. cit.*

TREACHERY, TREACHERY . . . THE RUMP: Kee, *ibid.*

IN THE BOSOM OF . . . REVIVAL: Mary MacNeill, *The Life and Times of Mary Ann McCracken.*

17. Reprisal

IN A CAUSE LIKE THIS . . . FAILED: Ó Faoláin, *The Autobiography of Theobald Wolfe Tone.*

FROM THE COMMENCEMENT . . . HOUSES: Gordon, *op. cit.*

OFTEN PLUNDERED WITHOUT . . . CROPPY: Gordon, *ibid.*

DISTANT AND DARKER . . . UNAPPLICABLE: Lecky, *op. cit.*

THE VIOLENCE OF . . . EXTIRPATION: Lecky, *ibid.*

IF I WERE . . . REBEL: Jackson, *op. cit.*

UNFORTUNATELY, THEIR HOUSES . . . MAIN BODY: Lecky, *op. cit.*

I ALWAYS MAKE . . . GOOD TUNE: Ó Boyle, *op. cit.*

THE GREATEST LOYALTY . . . THE ENEMY: T. Crofton Croker, *Popular Songs, Illustrative of the French Invasions of Ireland.* Croker cites other issues of the LONDON GAZETTE between 3-17 January 1797 in which specific instances of peasant help to the militia (clearing snowbound roads, etc.) can be found.

THAT THE GREAT BODY . . . FLAG: Lecky, *op. cit.*

THE IRISH MILITIA . . . PASTIME: Mitchel, *op. cit.*

NUMBERLESS MURDERS . . . MURDER: Mitchel, *ibid.*, includes the entire letter.

COULD NOT BE DISPOSED OF . . . JUSTIFIED: Lecky, *op. cit.*, is quoting Edward Cooke.

Chapter Notes (17)

AN AGREEMENT WAS . . . BYRNE: Mitchel, *op. cit.*, gives the complete text of the MacNeven, Emmet, and Sweetman affadavits as well as the entire agreement itself (dated 29 July and supposedly signed by over seventy United Irish prisoners).

18. The Year of the French

AS NO CHANGE COULD . . . POWER: Ó Faoláin, *The Autobiography of Theobald Wolfe Tone.*

GOD HELP THESE . . . FROM US: Dr. Joseph Stock's diary is liberally extracted in both W. H. Maxwell, *History of the Irish Rebellion in 1798*, and Mitchel, *op. cit.*

HIS MAJESTY'S SOLDIERS . . . STEALING: Maxwell, *ibid.*, and Mitchel, *ibid.*

WITHINOUT HIM, INDEED . . . TRADITION: Ó Faoláin, *The Autobiography of Theobald Wolfe Tone.*

IF THE MEN OF . . . PROPERTY: Ó Faoláin, *ibid.*

NO LESS ON . . . CAPITAL PRIZE: Croker, *op. cit.*, claims to have seen this letter personally.

RED-NECKED AND . . . OLD LITANY: J. Bowyer Bell, *The Secret Army: The IRA, 1916-1979.*

TO SUBVERT THE TYRANNY . . . MY MEANS: Ó Faoláin, *The Autobiography of Theobald Wolfe Tone.*

19. Bold Robert Emmet

LET ME EARNESTLY . . . BEAR IT: Lecky, *op. cit.*

AS TO THE SUBJECT . . . DEMOCRACY: Lecky, *ibid.*

THE ARMY OF THE . . . STATIONED HERE: Lecky, *ibid.*

THE DEMANDS OF OUR . . . ENGAGED: Lecky, *ibid.*

GRAB A GUINEA . . . MERCY: Jackson, *op. cit.*

ONE MAY BE PERMITTED . . . THE UNION: Gearóid Ó Tuathaigh, *Ireland Before the Famine 1798-1848.*

NOW THE FINAL PLAN . . . THROUGH THEM: Mitchel, *op. cit.*

I HAVE BUT ONE REQUEST . . . WRITTEN: Emmet's speech from the dock is the most famous of all Irish orations. Unfortunately, it is famous in a number of different versions. Though the rhetoric was said to transfix the courtroom, each listener seems to have come out with a different version of what young Emmet actually said. Robert Kee, *op. cit.*, has profoundly observed that since "it was as legend that this speech took wings it seems unimportant that the exact text is probably not wholly accurate."

NO FAILURE . . . PERFECTION: Quoted by numerous sources, among them Kee, *ibid.*

THE OLD HEART OF . . . BATTLEFIELDS: Quoted by numerous sources, among them Midge Podhoretz (Ed.), *The Irish Uprising 1916-22.*

20. Conclusion

NOSTALGIC, PSEUDO-HISTORICAL . . . PEOPLE: Ó Boyle, *op. cit.*

IN THE HALLS OF . . . CAVES: Richard O'Connor, *The Irish.*

WHEN IRISH HISTORY . . . THIS SOIL: H. O. Mackay (Ed.), *The Crime Against Europe.*

THE FOOLS, THE FOOLS . . . PEACE: Numerous sources but my favourite is Dangerfield, *op. cit.*, who follows Pearse's famous keen at the Rossa funeral with a comment made by the pragmatic James Connolly that same day. The ICA commander was heard to sarcastically say that "he wished people would stop blethering about dead Fenians 'and get us a few live ones for a change'."

A BALLAD HISTORY OF IRELAND: John McDonnell, *Songs of Struggle and Protest.*

INDEX OF BALLADS

After Aughrim's Disaster 185

Anne Devlin 428

Avenging and Bright 27

Ballad of Galloping Hogan, The 176

Banished Defender, The 336

Bard of Armagh, The 241

Battle of the Boyne, The 172

Battle of Callann, The 34

Battle of Vinegar Hill, The 342

Billy Byrne of Ballymanus 382

Black-Backed Cow, The 161

Blackbird, The 206

Blacksmith of Limerick, The 180

Blaris Moor 281

Bodenstown Churchyard 404

Bold Captain Freney 222

Bold McDermott Roe 266

Bold Robert Emmet 430

Boulavogue 331

Boyne Water, The 171

Boys from the County Mayo, The 401

Boys of Mullaghbawn, The 265

Boys of Wexford, The 340

Breathe Not His Name 438

Brennan on the Moor 254

Brian Boy Magee 132

Brian the Brave 20

Bridge of Athlone, The 183

Brigade at Fontenoy, The 218

Brothers, The 301

Burke's Dream 347

By Memory Inspired 443

Cailín, Dhoun, The 213

Captain Doorley and the Boyne 318

Carraigdhoun 212

Cean-Salla 105

Clare's Dragoons 201

Croppies Lie Down 323

Croppy Boy, The 349

Dead at Clonmacnois, The 40

Dead Who Died for Ireland, The 437

Death of Owen Roe, The 147

Dirge of O'Sullivan Bear, The 208

Downfall of the Gael, The 58

Dunlavin Green 325

Emmet's Farewell 419

Erin go Bragh 211

Flower of Finae, The 204

Follow Me Up to Carlow 78

Fontenoy 216

For God and Ireland 425

For the Green 198

Forget Not the Field 439

Frenchman, The 395

Gallant Men of '98, The 413

Galloping O'Hogan 178

Gaol of Clonmel, The 234

Garryowen 239

General Munro 363
Geraldines, The 68
Glenswilly 108
Granuaille 228
Green Upon the Cape 371

Harp that Once Through Tara's Halls,
    The 440
Hedge Schoolmasters, The 119
Henry Joy 358
Henry Joy MacCracken 360
Honest Owen 237

In Deepest Sorrow I Think of Home
    338
Irish Brigade, The 215
Irish Soldier Laddie 329
Irish Volunteer, The 245

John O'Dwyer of the Glen 113

Kathleen ni Houlihan 251
Kelly, the Boy from Killane 334
Kincora 18

Lament for Art O'Leary, The 231
Lament for Patrick Sarsfield 188
Lillibulero 163
Lisnagade 256
Lord Edward 298

Maiden City, The 167
Man From God Knows Where, The 273
Memory of the Dead, The 446
Men of the West, The 393
Michael Boylan 316

Michael Dwyer (I) 376
Michael Dwyer (II) 421
Minstrel Boy, The 441
My Emmet's No More 432

Native Swords 263
Natives of this Nation, Ye 184
Ned of the Hill 194
Nell Flaherty's Drake 433
No Rising Column 419
No Surrender 166

O'Donnell Aboo 97
O'Driscoll War Song, The 76
O'Neill's War Song 92
Our Heritage 9
Owen Roe's Address 136

Pat O'Donoghue 303
Patrick Brady 397
Patriot Mother, The 380
Prosperous 314
Protestant Men, The 270

Redmond O'Hanlon 156
Rising of the Moon, The 292
Rocks of Bawn, The 153
Rody McCorley 369
Róisín Dubh 252
Rory O'More 128

Shady Woods of Truagh, The 139
Shan Van Vocht 278
Shane O'Neill 63
Shule Agra 199
Siege of Maynooth, The 54
Song of O'Rourke, The 24

Suit of Green, The 383
Sweet County Wexford 345

Taxes 243
Three Flowers, The 444
To the Battle, Men of Erin 223
True Irish King, The 31
Twenty Men from Dublin Town 426

Union, The 416
unnamed ballads 16, 247

Volunteers of '82, The 249
Vow of Tipperary, The 378

Wake of William Orr, The 289
Wearing of the Green, The 311
Wexford Massacre, The 146
When Shall the Day Break in Erin 46
White Cockade, The 220
Wild Hazel Glen, The 364
Wind that Shakes the Barley, The 327
Wolfe Tone 405

INDEX OF SUBJECTS

A

Abercrombie, British Lt. Gen. Sir Ralph, 294-295, 307

Aboukir Bay (Nile), 1798 naval battle of, 380, 418

Acheson, Maj. Gen. Arthur, 2nd Viscount and 1st Earl of Gosford, 287, 311

Act of Indemnity (1797), 287

Act of Oblivion (1604), 126

Act to Prevent Further Growth of Popery (1703), 196

Act of Settlement (1701), 225

Act of Renunciation (1783), 252-253

Act of Union (1801), 252, 412-417, see also Union, of Britain and Ireland

Adams, Captain of Meath Militia, 331

Addington, Prime Minister Henry (afterwards Viscount Sidmouth), 416, 418

Adrian IV, Pope (Nicholas Breakspeare), 23, 65

Adventurer's Act (1642), 134

Affane, 1565 skirmish at, 67

Agincourt, 1415 battle of, 29, 186

Agrarian crime/societies, see Defenders; Oakboys; Peep o' Day Boys; and Whiteboys

Aguila, Don Juan del, 1601 Spanish commander at Kinsale, 104, 107

Aix-la-Chapelle, 1748 Treaty of, 225

Alen Archbishop John, Dublin Master of the Rolls, 54

Alexander III, King of Scots, 36

Alexander III, Pope, 23

Allen, Bog of, in 1798 insurrection, 318, 320, 374

Allen, John, 1803 rebel, 423-424

American(s), 122, 200, 311, 327, 395; Civil War, 176, 239; Colonies, 153, 201, 242-243; Declaration of Independence, 209; War of Independence, 242-248, 257-258; privateers, 245

Amiens, 1802 Peace of, 382, 418, 422, 435-436

Amnesty Act (1798), 318, 379; movement towards, 371, 385-386

Amsterdam, 201

Anabaptists, see Dissenters

Anacreon, French corvette, 402

Ancient Britons, Welsh yeoman unit, 287, 344-346

Anglicans, see England, Church of; Ireland, Church of; and Protestant Ascendancy

Annals of Clonmacnoise, 39

Anne, Stuart, Queen of England, 163, 191-192

Anne Boleyn, Queen of England, 54, 65

Answer to Burke's Reflections (Wollstonecraft), 262

Antrim, County, 1798 insurrection in, 355-361, 364, 367

Antrim town, 1798 battle of, 355, 357-358, 360, 364, 367

Antrim, Jacobite General Lord, see

MacDonnell, Alexander

Antrim of Dunluce, Lord, *see* MacDonnell, Randall

Apprentice Boys of Derry, in 1688 siege, 166-168, 190

Arbour Hill, 1798 croppy graveyard, 419

Ardee, in 1599 campaign, 101-102; 1641 action at, 129

Ardscull, 1316 battle of, 38

Argument on Behalf of the Catholics (Tone), 261, 270

Argyle, 8th Earl of, *see* Campbell, Archibald

Argyle, 10th Earl of, *see* Campbell, Archibald

Argyle and Greenwich, Duke of, *see* Campbell, John

Argyleshire Fencibles, in 1798 battle of Ballinahinch, 362

Aristophanes, Greek playwright, 7

Arklow; 1641 rebel attack on, 131; in 1798 insurrection, 322, 337-338; 1798 battle of, 340, 342, 352, 369, 375

Armada, Spanish, *see* Navy/fleets, Spain

Armstrong, John Warneford, Kings Co. Militia captain; and Sheareses' 1798 coup plans, 295, 298, 300-302; in Wexford campaign, 352; folk-legacy of, 443-444

Army/armies, *Anglo-Dutch Williamite;* Marlborough's in Ireland, 163, 175; Schomberg's, 170; William III's, 170-182; Doublas', 175; de Ginckel's, 180, 182, 185-187; Mackay's in Ireland, 182-184; Mackay's in Scotland, 193

—, *Austrian Imperial,* 214; Eugene's, 204; Irish in, 218-219, 231

—, *Dutch, Batavian,* Daendal's, 288

—, *Dutch, Orange,* 163, 192, 202;

Alliance, 216

—, *English, Cavalier,* 142; Rupert's, 135; royalist insurrectionist, 143; Ormonde's, 129, 133-134, 142-144, 147-148; Hamilton's, 134; Coote's, 134-135; Inchiquinn's, 134, 136, 139, 143-144; Broghill's, 144; Ashton's, 144-145; O. R. O'Neill's, 147-148; MacMahon's, 149

—, *English, Parliamentary;* Coote's, 134, 147, 149; Cromwell's, 135-136, 144-148; New Model, 135-136, 141-143; Inchiquinn's, 136, 142; Jones', 142-144, 147; Broghill's, 149; Ireton's, 149

—, *English/British, Royal,* 6, 11, 38, 113, 131, 194, 197, 278, 322, 374; Richard II's, 44; Poynings', 53; Skeffington's, 54-56; St. Leger's, 57; Sidney/Perrot, 71-73; Pelham/Butler/ Maltby, 75, 77; Grey's, 78-82; Zouche's, 82; Duke's, 90-91; Bagenal's, 91, 97-99; Russell's, 94; Burgh's, 96; Clifford's, 96, 101; Essex's, 100-102, 110; Docwra's, 102, 104; Mountjoy's, 103-107; Carew's, 104-105; Wentworth/ Charles I, 122, 124-125; Charles II/ James II, 162, 176; Marlborough's continental, 201-202; Cumberland's continental, 216-219; Cumberland's in Scotland, 220; Burgoyne's, 245; Cornwallis' in America, 248; Dundas', 311, 317; Johnson's, 334-336, 342; Loftus', 337; Needham's, 338, 340, 342, 397; Moore's, 342, 385; Lake's, 342, 374; Asgill's, 344; Nugent's, 357-358, 360-363; Hutchinson/Lake, 390-393; Cornwallis' in Ireland, 391-392, 401-402, 408

—, *French Imperial;* of England, 422; *Grand Armée,* 436

—, *French Revolutionary,* 263, 265, 307, 309, 391; Napoleon's, 278, 288; Hoche's, 278-279; Grouchy's, 279-280, 283, 377; Tate's, 276, 281; of the Orient, 387, 408, 418; Humbert's, 277, 388-402, 408-409; Hardy's, 388, 392, 395, 402; Kilmaine's, 388, 392, 395

—, *French Royal;* Irish Brigade in, 199, 202-206, 208, 212, 214-219, 225; Villeroi's, 202, 204; de Saxe's, 216-219; Thurot's, 259

—, *Irish;* Yorkist, 49; Lancastrian, 49; Garret More's, 53; Fitzmaurice's Papal, 74; Sir John of Desmond's, 75; O'Byrne's rebel, 79-80, 82; T. O'Neill's, 81-82; Pale Earl's, 77-82-83; O'Donnell/Maguire, 90-91, 101; Tyrell/*Súgán* Earl, 100; Tyrone's, 96-102, 110; 1641-1642 Ulster rebel, 128-129; O. R. O'Neill's Confederate Catholic, 134, 136-141, 143, 147-148; Preston's Confederate Catholic, 134, 139, 141-142; Taafe's Confederate Catholic, 142; Inchiquinn's Confederate Catholic, 143

—, *Irish, Jacobite;* Tyrconnell's, 161, 163, 167-168, 179-192; Antrim's, 166; Grace/Sarsfield, 175; Berwick's, 170, 175-182; St. Ruth/Tyrconnell, 182-188; Sarsfield, 188

—, *Irish, 1798 rebel,* 336; Reynolds', 309, 311, 313; Alymer's, 313, 318, 320, 369, 374-376, 379; Heydon's, 313; McGarry's, 311, 313, 315; Perkins', 311, 317; at Gibbet Rath, 317-318; Murphy's, 329-338, 342, 344, 397; Harvey's, 333-337, 340, 351-352, 368; Kearns', 333, 337, 340-341; E. Roche's, 333, 337-338, 340-341, 369; P. Roche's, 337, 342; Byrne's, 344-345, 375; McCracken's,

355-358, 360, 372; Munro's, 361-372; Perry/Kearns, 375-376; Fitzgerald's, 344-345

—, *Papal/Spanish;* di San Joseppi's, 81-82

—, *Portugese,* 178, 218

—, *Scottish;* Wallace's, 36-37; Bruce's, 37-39; Leslie's Covenanter, 124-125, 134-135; Monroe's Covenanter, 132-137, 139, 141; Hamilton's Engager, 143, 148-149; Dundee's Jacobite, 193; Mar's Jacobite, 205; New Pretender's, 220

—, *Spanish,* 178; d'Aguila's, 104-107

Arnold, American rebel General Benedict, 245

Artillery, at 1535 siege of Maynooth, 54; at 1798 battle of Tara, 315-316; at 1798 battle of New Ross, 334, 341; at 1798 battle of Arklow, 352; in 1798 Ulster insurrection, 357, 360, 366-367

Arrah na Pogue (Boucicault), 312

Asgill, British Major General Sir Charles, in 1798 Kilkenny campaign, 344

Ashton, Sir Arthur, Cavalier commander at 1649 defense of Drogheda, 144-145

Askeaton, Desmond Fitzgerald stronghold, 75, 77, 100

Athankip, 1270 battle of, 35

Athenry, 1316 battle of, 39

Athlone, 1691 battle of, 183-185

Auckland, Baron of, *see* Eden, William

Aughnanure, 1572 fall of, 73

Aughrim, 1691 battle of, 185-187, 189-190

Austrians, Austria, 12, 201, 214, 218, *see also* Army/armies, Austrian Imperial

Austrian Succession, War of, *see* War,

Non-Irish

B

Bagenal, Sir Henry 'of the Battle-Axes', Marshal of Newry, 91, 105; at Yellow Ford, 98-99, 139

Baginbun, 339

Bagenal, Nicholas, British Lord of Monaghan, 87

Baker, Maj. Henry, in 1688-1689 Londonderry siege, 168

Balfours, Fermanagh planters, 131

Ball Alley executions, *see* Carnew

Ballaghkeen, North and South, Wexford baronies, 351

Ballina, 1798 French occupation of ('1st Ballina'), 390, 394, 402

Ballinacor Mountain, O'Byrne stronghold, 79, 85, 89

Ballinafanad (Curlew Hills), 1599 battle of, 101

Ballinahinch, 1798 battle of, 360-363, 367, 374, 446

Ballinalee, 1798 executions at, 396

Ballinamuck, 1798 battle of, 392-398, 401-402

Ballinasloe, in 1691 campaign, 185

Balliol, John de, Lord of Galloway, King of Scots, 36

Ballitore, in 1798 insurrection, 311, 315

Ballyellis, 1798 battle of, 332, 344-346

Ballymena, 1798 action at, 355, 357-358

Ballymore, 1648 battle of, 143; 1798 battle of, 311; in 1798 insurrection, 315, 317

Ballymore, 1594 campaign around, 90

Ballynascarthy, *see* Bandon, 1798

incident near

Ballyneety, 1690 Jacobite raid on ('Sarsfield's Raid'), 176-180, 184

Ballyrahee, 1798 action at, 345-346

Ballyshannon, in Nine Years War, 90, 96

Baltimore, 1631 Algerian pirate sack of, 76, 122

Baltinglass, 1798 action at, 311

Baltinglass of Ballymore, Lord, *see* Eustace, James FitzRoland

Bandon, 1798 incident near, 378

Bannockburn, 1314 battle of, 37-38

Bantry, town of, founded, 13

Bantry, Wexford barony, 334, 336

Bantry Bay expedition, *see* French, 1796 Irish expedition

Baptists, *see* Dissenters

Barbados Colony, Drogheda survivors sent to, 145; Irish orphans sent to, 153, 191; Swift on, 210

Bardic Contention ('Counterboasting of the Poets'), 123

Bargy, Wexford barony, 335, 351

Baronies, establishment of, 36; Wexford, 36, 351; Mayo, 258

Barrett, Richard, Mayo poet, 237

Barry, Gerald de, ('Gerald of Wales', 'Geraldus Cambrensis'), 27-28

Barry, Kevin, 1920 IRA man, 292

Barry, Michael Joseph, Young Ireland songwriter, 146

Barry, Robert de, Norman knight (brother to Gerlad of Wales), 24

Barrys of Limerick, 68

Bashford, Thomas, Ulster Unitedman, 355

Bastille, 1789 Fall of the, 257, 263

Bavaria, 201; Elector of, 202

Beachy Head, 1690 naval battle of, 180

BealBoru ('Brian's Castle'), 18, 176

Becket, Thomas à, Archbishop of Canterbury, 23

Beevor, 1798 militia Captain, 311

Behan, Bredan, writer, 225

Belfast, 281, 284, 358-359, 366-367, 435; and Irish Volunteers, 245, 261; Directory of United Irishmen, 261-262, 265, 269-272, 287, 355; and France, 277; in 1798 rising, 354-355, 362

Bellaclynthe (Ford of Aclint), 1599 parley at, 101-102

Benburb, 1646 battle of, 136-141, 148, 432

Bentinck, William Henry Cavendish, 3rd Duke of Portland, 379

Beresford, John Claudius, Chief Commissioner of Revenue, 269, 375, 386, 419

Berkeley, George, Bishop of Cloyne, 209

Bermingham, Edwardian General John de, 38

Berwick, Duke of, *see* Stuart, General James 'FitzJames'

Billy Bluff and Squire Firebrand (Porter), 277

Bingham, Charles, Lord Lucan, 237

Bingham of Sligo, Sir George, Elizabethan freebooter, 90, 94

Bingham, Sir Richard, Elizabethan Lord President of Connacht, 96, 100, 110, 230, 237

Binghams of Connacht, 88-90, 94, 96, 100, 110, 230, 237

Bishops, 1688 Trial of the Seven, 162-163

Black and Tan War ('War for Irish Independence', 'Anglo-Irish War'), *see* Irish rebellion, Black and Tan War

Black Death, *see* Plague in Ireland

Blacker, Lieutenant Colonel William, Orange songwriter, 171

'Black Mob', in 1798 dragooning of Wexford, 350

Blackmore, 1798 rebel camp at, 315

'Black Oath' (Oath of Supremacy), Ulster Presbyterians made to take, 124

Blake, Galway Unitedman in 1798 French expeditionary force, 396, 409

Blake, James, 1602 English assassin, 107

Blanche, Captain of Irish Militia, at 1798 battle of Tara, 316

Blaris, 1797 executions at, 281-283

Blenheim, 1704 battle of, 201

Blessington (Whelp Rock), 1798 rebel camp at, 320, 374

Blockade, British, on French continental republics, 278, 300, 387

'Bloody Assizes', reprisals following Monmouth rising, 162

Bodenstown churchyard, Tone's grave at, 404-406

Bog of Allen, *see* Allen, Bog of

Blount, Sir Charles, 8th Baron Mountjoy (afterwards Earl of Devonshire), 126, 133; Viceroy, 103; 1601 campaign, 104; at battle of Kinsale, 105-106; O'Neill submits to, 107, 111

Bodhrán, Irish war-drum, 2, 79

Boisseleaux, Jacobite Governor of Limerick, 175

Bolg an tSolair, Gaelic magazine, 284

Bompard, J. B. B., French Commodore of 1798 naval expedition to Ireland, 388, 402-403, 409

Bonaparte, *see* Napoleon Bonaparte

Bond, Oliver, Dublin Unitedman; early United Irish activities, 263, 278; Crown raid on Leinster Directory at house of, 293, 298, 306,

313, 320-321, 443; in Wicklow Gaol, 345, 381-382, 386; death of, 382, 407

Bonnacht, see Mercenaries, Irish

Bookey, Camolin Yeoman Lieutenant Thomas, 327, 332, 338

Book of Leinster, 6

Boru, Brian MacKennedy, King of Dál Cais, King of Munster, High King of Ireland ('Emperor of the Irish'), 9, 99, 102, 176, 203, 230; Munster campaigns, 16, 29; 1002 'Grand Tour', 16, 29; 1004 coronation as Emperor, 16; 1013-1014 Clontarf campaign, 8, 17-18, 432

Bosworth Field, 1485 battle of, 52

Botany Bay, New South Wales prison colony, 266, 336, 348, 372, 376

Boucicault, Dionysius Lardner, playwright, 76, 312

Boulavogue, in 1798 insurrection, 327, 331-332

Bouvet, French Rear Admiral; tactical commander in 1796 Bantry Bay expedition, 279

Bowes, John, Baron Bowes of Clonlyon, Lord Chancellor (afterwards Lord Justice) of Ireland, 198

Boycott, Captain; target of Land League agitation, 225, 401

Boyle, Parliamentary Lieutenant General Sir Roger, Baron Broghill (afterwards 1st Earl of Orrery), 144, 149

Boyne, 1690 battle of the, 170-175, 184, 189-190, 205, 256, 260

Brady, Field Marshal Thomas, Austrian Privy Councillor, Governor of Dalmatia, 218

Braughill, Thomas, Catholic Committeeman, 409

Breakespeare, Nicholas, *see* Adrian IV, Pope

Brehon(s), 7, 21, 33

Brehon/Druidic Law, 3-7, 12, 21, 26, 36, 43, 48, 74-75, 92, 110, 448; and Gaelic succession, 58, 61, 103, 110, 113, 215

Brian Boru, *see* Boru, Brian MacKennedy

Bridport of Somerset, Baron, *see* Hood, Admiral Alexander

Britain, conquered by Vikings, 17; Henry II's knowledge of, 23; politics, 47, 49; *see also* English/Imperial Government and influence *and* Parliament, English/Imperial

British Government in Ireland, *see* Dublin Castle (English Government in Ireland)

Broghill, Lord, *see* Boyle, Roger

Brooke, Charlotte, Gaelic scholar and translator, 284

Brookeborough Barracks, 1956 IRA raid on, 446

Brown, Sir Valentine, Elizabethan adventurer, 83

Bruce, Edward the ('Edward I' of Ireland), 37-39, 48

Bruce, Robert de, Lord of Annandale; claimant to Scottish Crown, 36

Bruce, Robert the, *see* Robert I, King of the Scots

Bruce Invasion of Ireland, 37-39

Buckingham, Lord, *see* Grenville, Lord George Nugent-Temple-

Buckingham, Earl (afterwards Duke) of, *see* Villiers, George

Bully's Acre, croppy grave at Ballinalee, 396

Bunting, Edward, Irish music collector, 206, 224, 367

Burial of Sir John More (Wolfe), *The,* 385

Burgh, Thomas, 5th Lord, Lord Deputy of Ireland, 96-97

Burgh, Walter Hussey, Prime Serjeant of Irish Bar, Patriot Party leader, 247-248, 271

Burgo, Richard de, 2nd Earl of Ulster, 4th Earl of Connacht (the 'Red Earl'), 38

Burgo, Walter de, 1st Earl of Ulster, 35

Burgoyne, British General Sir John; in American Saratoga campaign, 245

Burke, Edmund, British statesman and political writer, 262, 284, 435

(MacWilliam) Burke, John MacOliver, Lord of Mid-Connacht, 71

Burke, Richard, Sligo clan chief, 94

(MacWilliam) Burke, Theobald, Connacht rebel, 96-97

Burke, Ulick, Sligo rebel, 94

Burke, Ulick Finn, Lord of Clan-Ricarde, 53

Burke Regiment (of the French Irish Brigade), 204

(MacWilliam) Burkes of Connacht; change name from de Burgo, 40, 45, 52; accept earldom of ClanRicarde, 57, 65, 68, 71, 73, 82, 85, 91, 100, 110

Butler, Sir Edmund of Cladh (son of Black Earl), 68

Butler, Sir Edward (son of Black Earl), 68

Butler, James, 5th Earl of Ormonde, Earl of Wiltshire, 49

Butler, James, 13th Earl (afterwards 1st Marquis) of Ormonde, 133-134, 142-148; after Restoration, 156, 159, 191

Butler, Sir John of Ormonde (brother to 5th Earl), 49

Butler, Pierce, 9th Earl of Ormonde, Earl of Ossory, 52, 57

Butler, Thomas Boleyn, Viscount Rochford, 8th Earl of Ormonde, Earl of Wiltshire, 53-54

Butler, Elizabethan Lieutenant General Thomas FitzJames, 11th Earl of Ormonde (the 'Black Earl'); feud with Desmond, 67, 71; in Desmond Wars, 77, 81-84; in Nine Years War, 99-100, 102

Butlers of Ormonde, 38, 45, 49, 52-54, 57, 65, 67-68, 71, 77, 81-84, 97, 100, 102, 133-134, 142-144, 147-148, 156, 159, 191

Byrne, Edward, Catholic Committee-man, 261

Byrne, Captain Morgan, yeoman deserter, Wexford Unitedman, 327-328

Byrne, United Captain Myles (afterwards French Colonel), 306, 309, 351; in Emmet Rising of 1803, 383, 423, 426, 436; escapes to France, 427, 429

Byrne, United Colonel William ('Billy'); escapes net at Bond's, 294; in Wexford insurrection, 333; after Vinegar Hill, 344-345; Coolgreany surrender of, 375; trial and execution of, 381-383, 386, 407, 443

Byron, Lord George Gordon, 6th Baron, British poet, 385

C

Callanan, James Joseph 'Jeremiah', poet and Gaelic translator, 208, 220, 225

Callann, 1261 battle of, 48

Cambrensis, Geraldus, *see* Gerald of Wales

Camden, Earl of, *see* Pratt, John Jeffreys

Camolin, 1798 action at, 330, 332

Camolin Yeoman Cavalry, 327, 330, 338

Campbell, Colonel of Irish Militia, 350

Campbell, Archibald, 8th Earl and 1st Duke of Argyle ('Lord Lorne'), 124

Campbell, Archibald, 10th Earl and 1st Duke of Argyle, 162, 193

Campbell, John, Earl of Breadalbane, Duke of Greenwich, 2nd Duke of Argyle, 205

Campbell, Thomas, Scottish poet, 241

Campbells, Argyle, 125, 193, 220

Camperdown, 1797 naval battle of, 288, 387

Carbery, Ethna, *see* MacManus, Anna Johnston

Carew, George, Lord President of Munster, Baron (afterwards Earl) of Totnes, 104-106

Carew, Sir Peter, Elizabethan soldier and freebooter, 68, 78

Carhampton, Earl of, *see* Luttrell, Henry Lawes

Carlisle, 1745 fall of, 220

Carlow town; 1798 battle of, 313; goal of Kearns' Wexford rebels, 333

Carmelites, Discalced, 118

Carnew; 1798 Ball Alley executions at, 325-326, 337; 1798 rebel attack on, 337, 397, 414

Carrickbyrne Hill, in 1798 insurrection, 333, 336-337, 342; *see also* Scullabogue, 1798 massacre at

Carrickfergus (earlier 'Knockfergus'); 1640s base of Covenanter army, 132-133, 141; in 1689-1690 Williamite campaign, 170; in 1798 rising, 355, 357

Carrignagat, 1798 action at, 392

Casement, Sir Roger, Irish republican, 271, 442

Case of Ireland's being bound (Molyneux), *The*, 209

Casey, John Keegan ('Leo'), Fenian poet, 292

Cashel, ancient Munster throne, 14

Cassano d'Adda, 1705 battle of, 204-205

Castlebar, 1st 1798 battle of ('Castlebar Races'), 391-392, 394-398, 402; 2nd 1798 rebel attack on ('2nd Castlebar'), 402

Castlecomer, in 1798 resurrection, 344, 397-398

Castleisland, in Desmond Wars, 77

Castleknock, 1171 battle of, 26

Castlemaine, in Desmond Wars, 77

Castlereagh, Viscount, *see* Stewart, Robert

Catherine of Braganza, Queen of England, 160

Catholic Association ('Catholic Committee'), 316; 1759 founding of, 242; and 1st Catholic Relief Act, 248; radicalisation of, 261; Tone joins, 262, 403, 409; and 3rd Catholic Relief Act, 262-263

Catholic Confederation, *see* Confederate Catholics of Ireland

Catholic Emancipation, 411, 416

Catholic Relief Acts; of 1778 (1st), 248, 256; of 1782 (2nd), 249, 256; of 1793 (3rd), 262-263, 403

Catholics and the Church, 118-120, 126, 191, 256, 259, 262, 265-266, 723; under the Tudors, 54, 70-71, 74-75, 78, 82, 84-85, 94, 112; and the Papacy, 65-66, 74-75, 82, 118, 120, 160, 173, 205, 225, 400; rallying-point for Irish rebellion, 70-71, 74-75, 78, 82, 211, 213 (*see also* Confederate Catholics of Ireland); confiscation of monasteries, 84, 94,

118, 127; and early Stuarts, 112,
118-127; outlawed by Long Parliament, 129, 146; and Cromwellian
Settlement, 152-153; and Restoration Stuarts, 155-156, 158, 160-162,
191; Popish Plot, 160, 191; and Tyrconnell, 161, 163-165; and William
III, 173; as 'enemies' of Government,
190, 213, 223-224; in Penal Times,
196-199, 207-209, 212-213, 221,
223-225, 227-228, 231, 240, 257,
263, 348; and Scottish Jacobite rebellion, 205, 223; and middle class,
223, 227, 242, 260, 263, 283-284,
348; and Patriot Party, 248, 254;
and Irish Volunteers, 249; and Relief
Acts, 248-249, 254, 262-263, 284;
and French republicans, 260, 400;
and United Irish leadership, 270,
399, 409; and Orangemen, 323 (*see
also* Defenders *and* Peep o' Day
Boys); Emancipation and the Union,
411-412, 416; *see also* Priests/clergy,
Irish Catholic

Cattle, ancient Irish measure of wealth,
14, 161

Cattle-raids, 4-7, 27, 30, 68, 76, 153

Caulfield, James, 4th Viscount and 1st
Earl of Charlemont; and 1760 Thurot
raid, 259; and Whig Club, 261, 284;
leader of Patriot Party, 244-246, 252,
254, 412; Irish Volunteer commander, 248-250, 253

Cavaliers, 125, 135, 141-145; *see also*
Army/armies, English Cavalier;
Charles I; *and* Charles II

Cavan, 1595 rebel raids into, 94

Cave Hill (MacArt's Fort), United
Irish meeting at, 270, 358

Cecil, Robert, 1st Viscount Cranborne,
1st Earl of Salisbury, 91, 95, 104

Cecil, William, 1st Baron Burghley,

Elizabethan Secretary of State, 85

Cellachán, 10th Century Munster King,
14

Chambers, John, Dublin Unitedman,
306

Chamnay, Yeoman captain in 1798 insurrection, 345

Chapman, Fencible Colonel Sir
Thomas; in 1798 French campaign,
390

Charlemagne (Charles the Great), King
of the Franks, 7

Charlemont, Earl of, *see* Caulfield,
James

Charles I, Stuart King of Great Britain,
17; and Parliament, 121-127; and
Irish rebellion, 131-132; and Civil
Wars, 134-136, 141-143; execution
of and its impact, 144, 151, 156, 159

Charles II, Stuart King of Great Britain, 151, 156, 159-161, 188, 353

Charles V, Holy Roman Emperor, 65

Charles Edward Louis . . . Stuart, *see*
Stuart, 'Bonnie Prince' Charles

Chesterfield, Lord, *see* Stanhope,
Philip Dormer

Chichester, Elizabethan Major General
Sir Arthur (afterwards Lord Chichester of Belfast), Jacobean Lord
Deputy of Ireland, 104, 107, 116

Chichester, Sir John, Elizabethan
soldier, 96

Christianity, arrival of in Ireland, 6-8

Church of England, *see* England,
Church of

Church of Ireland, *see* Ireland, Church
of

Churchill, Major General John, Earl
(afterwards Duke) of Marlborough,
163; in 1690 Limerick campaign,
175, 180; European campaigns, 201-
202

Churchill, Lord Randolph, 19th Century Unionist, 285

Churchill, Sir Winston, 146

'Citizen Soldier' Address, 263, 268

City of Cork Militia, in 1798 insurrection, 309, 314, 320

Civil War, American, 136, 176

Civil Wars; 1st English, 121, 134-136, 150, 191; 2nd English, 143-149, 191; *see also* Confederate Catholic Wars

Clady, 1689 battle of, 167

Clan Connell (ClannConnaill), *see* O'Donnells of Tyrconnell

Clane, 1798 rebel attack on, 309, 404

ClanRicarde, Earls of, *see* (MacWilliam) Burkes of Connacht

'Claragh', *see* MacDonnell, Shane

Clare, Earl of, *see* Fitzgibbon, John

Clare, Lords, *see* O'Brien, Charles, 5th and 6th Viscounts of

Clare, Richard de, 6th Earl of Hertford, 8th Earl of Clare, Lord of Thomond, 39

Clare, Richard FitzGilbert de, 2nd Earl of Pembroke, Earl of Striguil ('Strongbow'), 20, 23, 26, 30, 69, 468

Clarence, Prince Lionel, Duke of, *see* Lionel of Antwerp

Clarendon, Earl of, *see* Hyde, Edward

Clavering, British Colonel; at 1798 battle of Antrim, 358

Clement VIII, Pope, 102

Clifford, Sir Conyers, Elizabethan Commissioner of Connacht, 96, 99, 100, 105

Clondalkin, in 1798 resurrection, 313

Clonmacnois, monastic university at, 7-8, 40-41

Clonmel, 1650 battle of, 148

Clontarf, 1014 battle of, 18-20, 23, 230, 432

Clontibret, 1595 battle of, 91, 94

Cloughoughter, 1641 action at, 131; Owen Roe's death at, 147-148

Cockades, as battlefield identification, 173, 192; white, as Bourbon symbol, 173, 220-221, 256; green, as United symbol, 256, 312; *see also* Green, colour; *and* Orange, colour

Cockayne, John, English attorney, Crown spy, 268

Colclough, United Colonel Dr. John Henry, 331, 333, 346-347

Coles, Fermanagh planters, 131

Colleen Bawn (Boucicault), *The,* 76

Collegians (Griffin), *The,* 76

Collins, Thomas, Dublin Unitedman, Crown informer, 261, 276

Collooney, 1798 action near, 392

Colonialism, British, 64, 113, 116, 201

Colpoys, Vice Admiral Sir John, 280

Columbanus, 7

Columbus, 68

Columcille (Columba of Iona), 7, 63

Commonwealth, establishment of British, 144, 159, 162

Congreve, William, English dramatist, 210

Conn of the Hundred Battles ('the Hundred-Fighter'), early High King, 11, 31, 41

Connacht, division into counties, 83, 110; 1798 'Republic' of declared, 391, 402; and United Irishmen, 294

Confederate Catholics of Ireland ('Kilkenny Confederation'), founding of, 134; negotiations with Charles I, 135-136; internal disputes, 136, 139, 141-144; defeated, 149

Confederate Catholic Wars (1542-53), *see* Irish rebellion

Connell, Johnny, 239-240

Connor, 1315 battle of, 38

Connor, Flaherty O'Malley, Gaelic poet, 118

Conway, Owen, Mayo land agent, 237-238

Cooke, Edward, Undersecretary for Military Affairs, 269, 382, 414, 419

Cooley, Cattle-Raid of (Táin Bó Cuailnge), 6

Coote, Sir Charles (the younger), Lord President of Connacht (afterwards Earl of Mountrath), 134, 136, 147, 149

Coolgreany, 1798 rebel surrender at, 345, 383

Copenhagen, 1801 naval battle of, 418

Corbet Hill, rebel position at New Ross, 333, 335

'Cork Incident', *see* Bandon, 1798 incident near

Cork City; founding of, 13; 1690 capture of by Marlborough, 175, 180

Cormac MacArt, 3rd Century High King, 9

'Cormac', *see* O'Kelly, Patrick

Cornwall, 1648 rising in, 143

Cornwallis, General Marquis Charles, Viceroy, 248, 349, 371; mops up 1798 insurrection, 375-376, 379-380, 387-388; and French landing, 391-392, 396, 408; on yeomanry and militia, 371, 379-380, 396-397; after Ballinamuck, 401; re-instates *Habeas Corpus* Act, 409; and Union, 414-415

Corũna, 1808 battle of, 385

Cosby, Sir Francis, Governor of Kings and Queens counties, 74

Council of State, Commonwealth, 144

Courcy, John de, Norman knight, 27

Covenant with God ('National Covenant of 1638'), 124, 128

Coyne and *Livery* ('Free Quarters'),

43, 307; *see also* **Irish Glossary**, 452

Cranmer, Archbishop Thomas, Primate of England, 54

Crawford, Colonel, in 1798 action at Drumshanbo, 392

Crécy, 1346 battle of, 29

Credan, 1258 battle of, 47

Cremona, 1702 battle of, 204, 205

Croft, James, Duke of Monmouth, 162

Cromwell, Lieutenant General Oliver (afterwards Lord Protector of the Commonwealth); in English Civil Wars, 135-136, 143; in Ireland, 144-149; and Charles II, 151; as Lord Protector, 152; legacy of in Ireland (the 'Curse of Cromwell'), 146, 149, 373, 401

Cromwellian Settlement, 146, 152-153, 182

Cross Keys, 1862 American battle of, 136

'Croppy's Hole' at Carlow, 313

CúChulainn (Setanta MacSualtim, 'Cullan's Hound'), legendary Gaelic warrior, 6, 31, 63, 73, 90, 109

Cuddy, 1798 Derry rebel Captain William, 364

Culloden Moor, 1746 battle of, 220, 225

Culmore; 1600 British landing at, 102; in 1688-1689 siege of Londonderry, 168

Cumberland, Prince William Augustus, 'Bloody' Duke of; at Fontenoy, 216-217; in Scottish Forty-Five, 220

Cumming, George, Kildare Unitedman, 306, 320

Curlew Hills, *see* Ballinafanad, 1599 battle of

Curragh of Kildare, in 1798 insurrection, 308, 317-318

Curran, John Philpot, advocate and

political orator; defends Rowan, 268; defends Orr and Finnerty, 289-290; and Whig Club, 284; protests 1798 reprisals, 375; obtains *habeas corpus* for Tone, 409; refuses to defend Emmet, 429-430

Curran, Sarah, 429-430, 432, 436

Curry, Dr. John, Catholic Committeeman, 242

Custer, American General George Armstrong, 239

Custom House Barracks, target of 1803 rising, 423

Custume, Jacobite Sergeant, at Athlone, 183

C

Daendels, 1797 Dutch General, 288

Dálcassians, 14, 16, 19, 29

Dalkey, 1798 mail-coach halted at, 308

Danes, *see* Vikings

Danny Boy, ballad, 332

Dark Lady of the Glen, ballad, 194

Darnley, Lord, *see* Stewart, Henry

Davis, Thomas, Young Ireland poet, 31, 69, 147, 169, 202, 215-216, 249, 264, 378, 404

Declaration of Independence, 1782 Irish, 252

Declaration of Right (1780), 248

Declarations of Indulgence (1687, 1688), 162

Declaratory Act of 1719, 252

Defenders, Catholic agrarian societies, 265-267, 272-273, 285, 292, 336, 367, 375, 417; and Connacht, 399; and the Diamond, 273; emergence of, 256, 437; and 1796 French expedition, 278, 280; and 1798 insurrection, 333, 336, 344, 355, 357, 360;

and Militia conscription, 265; and Munster, 295, 378; and Peep o' Day Boys, 256-257, 265-266; and Ulster, 272-273; and the United Irishmen, 268, 273, 277, 336, 355, 357, 377-378

Del Oro, Fort, 1580 massacre of 'Spanish' at, 81-82

Denmark, 201

Dennistoun, Hans, Longford United leader, 294

Derby, 1745 Scot Jacobite advance to, 220

Derry, *see* Londonderry

Derryamuck, 1799 action at, 421-422

Dervogilla, wife to Tiernan O'Rourke, 24-25

Desmond Fitzgeralds (Fitzgeralds of Munster)

Desmond, Captain of, *see* Fitzgerald, Sir James FitzMaurice

—, 1st Earl of, *see* Fitzgerald, Maurice FitzThomas

—, 7th Earl of (the 'Greal Earl'), *see* Fitzgerald, Thomas FitzJames

—, 8th Earl of, *see* Fitzgerald, James FitzThomas

—, 11th Earl of, *see* Fitzgerald, Thomas Oge

—, 14th Earl of (the 'Pale Earl'), *see* Fitzgerald, Gerald FitzJames

—, 15th Earl of, *see* Fitzgerald, James FitzGerald

—, Sir John of, *see* Fitzgerald, John FitzJames

—, *Súgán* Earl of, *see* Fitzgerald, James FitzThomas

Desmond Wars, *see* Irish rebellions

Devereux, Robert, 2nd Earl of Essex, 100-102, 110

Devereux, Walter, 1st Earl of Essex, 74, 100

Devlin, Anne, confidant to Emmet, 428-429

Devlin, Arthur, 1803 United captain, 423-424, 426, 428

Devon, 1688 landing of Willem and Mary at, 163

Devon Commission of 1844, 227

Devoy, John, American Irish Fenian, 314

Diamond, 1795 'battle' of the, 273

Dickey, James, Crumlin Unitedman, 355

Dickson, Reverend William, Ulster Unitedman, 287, 294, 298, 355, 366

Dicuil, Irish missionary, 7

Digges, American Unitedman, 261

Dillon, Sir Luke, Elizabethan adventurer, 83

Dillon, Sir Robert, Elizabethan adventurer, 83

Dillon, Regiment (of French Irish Brigade), 204

Dissenters, 12-22, 125, 160, 191, 223-225, 260, 265, 416, 437; and Ulster, 120-122, 127, 416; and Cromwell, 143; and Restoration Stuarts, 151, 162, 191; and Penal Laws, 191, 223-225, 228; and emerging middle class, 223-224, 260-261; control Catholic Committee, 261-262; and nationalism, 261-270, 367; and French Revolution, 260-261; and Union, 416; *see also* Oakboys, Peep o' Day Boys; *and* United Irishmen

Dixon, United Lieutenant Thomas; perpetrates 1798 Wexford massacre, 342, 353

Docwra, Sir Henry, Elizabethan soldier, 102, 104

Dodington, Captain, Ulster planter, 127

Donald, Scot Prince of Mar; at Clontarf, 18

Donegal Militia, in 1798 insurrection, 330

Donegal town, in Nine Years War, 104

Donegore Hill, 1798 rebel camp at, 355, 358, 360

Donnelly, Patrick, Archbishop of Armagh, 241

Donagh MacBrian, son of Boru, 19

Donore, in 1690 Boyne campaign, 170

Donovan, Lieutenant John, of Camolin Yeoman Cavalry, 327

Doon, Rock of, O'Donnell coronation stone, 89, 107, 110

Doorley, Kildare United captain, 318-319

Dorrington, Irish Jacobite Brigadier, 175

Douglas, Williamite Brigadier, 175

Douglas, Sir James, Lord of Douglas (the 'Black Douglas'), 37

Down, 1798 insurrection in, 355, 358, 360-364, 367

Downing, D. J., poet, 46

Downpatrick; 1260 battle of, 31, 35; in 1798 rising, 362; 1803 execution of Russell at, 274, 426

Drapier's Letters (Swift), 210

Drennan, Dr. William, Unitedman, pamphleteer, songwriter, 129, 261, 263, 290

Drogheda; 1460 parliament at, 45-46; 1495-1495 parliament at, 53; 1641 siege of, 129, 145; 1649 sack of, 144-146, 149; in 1690 campaign, 172

Dromahair, 1798 action at, 392

Druids, *see* Ireland, Gaelic/Celtic; *and* Poets/poetry, Irish

Drumshanbo, 1798 action at, 392

Drury, Sir William, Elizabethan Lord President of Munster, 75

Dublin; in Viking times, 13, 16-18;

claimed by Henry II, 26; Saxon plantation in, 26, 57; in Silken Thomas rebellion, 54; 1601 O'Neill feint towards, 104; 1647 Cavalier surrender of, 142; 1648 Cavalier investment of, 143-144; in 1690 Williamite campaign, 171-172; as target of 1798 risings, 295, 298, 300, 337; 1798 trials in, 419

Dublin Castle (building); target of Silken Thomas rebellion, 54; target of 1641 conspiracy, 128, 150; 1798 reprisals in, 419; target of Emmet rising, 423, 436

Dublic Castle (English/British Government in Ireland); Norman, 26-27, 34-36, 38, 41, 43-46; Yorkist, 49-50, 52; Tudor, 52-54, 56, 66-67, 71, 74-75, 78, 83, 86-87, 90-91, 94-97, 107, 126; early Stuart, 113, 116, 118, 133-134; Civil War/Protectorate, 141-145; Restoration Stuart, 160-161, 191; Jacobite, 163-164; Williamite, 193-194; Georgian, 201, 210, 242-246, 248-249, 252, 412; 1782-1798 era, 252, 263, 265, 269, 276-277, 280-283, 288-290, 292-295, 298, 306, 354; during 1798, 308-309, 315, 319, 320, 340, 352, 366, 368-369, 371, 374-375, 381-384, 385-386, 390, 403-404, 408; post-1798, 412-416, 423-424, 444-445, 448

Dublin Militia, at 1798 battle of New Ross, 333

Duff, Major General Sir James, 1798 Limerick District O/C, 317-318

Duffy, Charles Gavan, Young Irelander, 139

Duke, Sir Henry, Elizabethan soldier, 90-91

Duleek, 1690 action at, 171-172

Dunbar, 1650 battle of, 149, 151

Dunboyne, in 1798 insurrection, 298, 313

Duncan, British Vice Admiral Adam (afterwards Viscount Camperdown), 288

Duncannon Fort; 1649-1650 parliamentary siege of, 148; in 1798 Wexford campaign, 322, 330-331, 333, 342, 349, 351

Dundalk, in 1689 Williamite campaign, 170

Dundas, General Sir Ralph, 1798 British O/C in Kildare, 311, 315, 317

Dundee, 'Bonny', *see* Graham, John

Dungannon; 1602 English capture of, 107; 1646 action at, 137; 1782 Volunteer convention at, *see* Volunteers, Irish

Dungannon, Barons of, *see* O'Neill, Conallagh; O'Neill, Hugh; *and* O'Neill, Matthew

Dungan's Hill, 1647 battle of, 142

Dunkeld, 1689 battle of, 193

Dunlavin; in 1798 insurrection, 311, 317, 325; 1798 executions at, 325-326, 350-351

Durban, 1640 Scot Covenanter invasion of, 124

Durham, British Colonel; at 1798 battle of Antrim, 358

Durham Fencibles, at 1798 battle of Arklow, 340

Dutch/Holland/the Netherlands, 201; 1664 war with English, 160; sea power, 121, 180; in War of Two Kings, 170; at Fontenoy, 214, 216-217; 1793-1794 war with France, 263, 278; 1797 Irish expedition, 288, 387

Dwyer, Michael, United Irish guerrilla captain, 326, 375-377, 383, 423, 445-446; at Derrynamuck, 421-422;

after 1803 rising, 427

Dysert O'Dea, 1318 battle of, 39

E

East India Company of London, 125, 201

Easter Rebellion of 1916, *see* Irish rebellion, Easter (1916)

Eden, William, Baron of Auckland, 412

Edict of Nantes, *see* Huguenots

Edinburgh, 1648 seizure by Cromwell, 143

Edward I ('Edward Longshanks'), Plantagenet King of England, 36-37

'Edward I of Ireland', *see* Bruce, Edward the

Edward II, Plantagenet King of England, 37-38

Edward III, Plantagenet King of England, 40-41

Edward IV, Yorkist King of England, 49-50, 52

Egypt, Napoleonic campaign in, *see* Levant, Napoleonic campaign in the

Elgee, Jane Francesca (afterwards Lady Jane Wilde), 'Speranza', poet, 301, 307

Elizabeth, Charlotte, Orange songwriter, 168

Elizabeth I, Tudor Queen of England, 58, 62, 67, 87, 112, 118, 120, 230, 307; and Shane O'Neill, 61-63; and Desmond Wars, 70-71, 73, 80, 83-84; and Nine Years War, 86, 89-92, 95-97, 100-101, 103, 107, 110-111

Emigration; of the Irish after 1607, 108; of the 'Scotch-Irish', 258

Emmet, Robert; at TCD, 418, 438; in France, 418; contacts Dublin United Directory, 419; made O/C of 1803

rising, 423; sends Russell north, 426; Rising of '03, 424-425; flees to Wicklows, 426-427; and Anne Devlin, 428-429; aliases, 433; capture, death and myth of, 271-272, 430-436, 444

Emmet Rising of 1803, *see* Irish rebellion, Emmet (1803)

Emmet, Thomas Addis, Dublin Unitedman, 278, 309; on National Directroy, 278; and Irish *Press,* 285-286; 1798 arrest of, 306; negotiates with Government, 382, 386; after 1802 release, 418, 422; feud with O'Connor, 436

'Engagement', between Scots and Charles I, 142

England, Church of, 121-122, 124-125, 127-128, 142, 156, 160, 162, 188, 228; *see also* Cavaliers; Church of Ireland; *and* Protestant Ascendancy

English/Imperial Government and influence; Norman, 11, 26, 31, 35-36, 46-47, 53, 56; Tudor, 56-58, 64, 67-68, 71, 73, 82, 86-87, 91, 95-96, 100, 102-103, 112; early Stuart, 112-113, 120, 129, 131-132, 134; Civil War/Protectorate, 144-145, 152-153; Restoration Stuart, 155-156, 160; Williamite, 163, 182, 193; Georgian, 196-199, 201, 205, 210, 245, 246, 248-249, 251-252, 269, 288; during 1798, 368, 371, 375, 380, 411; post-1798, 412-416, 418, 457

Enniscorthy; in 1798 Wexford campaign, 322, 342; 1798 battle of, 330, 332, 335, 338

Enniskillen, 175; 1594 campaign for, 90-91; 1688-1689 campaign for, 163, 167, 224

Eóghanacht kings of Munster, 14

Erskine, British Captain; at 1798 battle of Kilcullen Bridge, 311, 319

Erskine, John, Duke of Mar; at 1715 'battle' of Sherrifmuir, 205

Esmonde, United Colonel Dr. John (and lieutenant in Sallins Yeomanry), 308-310, 314

Essex, 1st Earl of, *see* Devereux, Walter

Essex, 2nd Earl of, *see* Devereux, Robert

Eugene of Savoy, Prince, expatriate general in Imperial service, 204

Eustace, James FitzRoland, Viscount Baltinglass of Ballymore, 78, 81-82

Eva, Princess of Leinster, *see* MacMurrough, Eva

Eva of the *Nation*, *see* Kelly, Mary Eva

F

Fairfax, Sir Thomas, 3rd Baron of Cameron, 135, 143-144

Falkirk, 1298 battle of, 37

Famine; of 1581, 82; of 1582, 83; of 1651-1654, 152; of 1845-1849 ('The Great Hunger', 'The Great Starvation'), 257, 401, 428

Farsetmore, 1567 battle of, 63

Faughart, 1318 battle of, 38

Fawcett, 1798 British General, 331

Féini, pre-Celtic Irish, 5

Fenian Brotherhood (Irish Republican Brotherhood), 314, 327, 401, 406, 432, 438, 444

Ferguson, Sir Samuel, poet and antiquarian, 59, 161

Ferns; MacMurrough demense, 21; in 1798 insurrection, 330

Ferriter, Confederate Catholic General Pierce, poet, 131, 149-150

5th Dragoons, at 1798 battle of New Ross, 334

Filí, *see* Poets/poetry, Irish

Finae, 1646 action at Bridge of, 150

Fingall, Lord, *see* Plunkett, Arthur James

Fingals, in 1798 rising plans, 298

Finn MacCool, 9

Finnerty, printer of Irish *Press*, 289-290

Firearms, introduction to Irish battlefield, 53

Fitzgerald of New Park, United Colonel Edward, 331, 333, 344-345, 375

Fitzgerald, Lord Edward, Leinster Unitedman, 322; and French, 276-277, 288; on National Directory, 278; urges insurrection, 288, 295, 298; issues 1798 rising orders, 298, 303, 307-308, 354; capture of, 298-300, 321, 408, 428, 444; death of, 272, 407; legacy of, 271, 358

Fitzgerald, Garret 'Mór' FitzThomas, 8th Earl of Kildare, Lord Lieutenant, 50, 52-53

Fitzgerald, Garret Oge, 9th Earl of Kildare, Lord Lieutenant, 53-54, 56, 65

Fitzgerald, Gerald FitzJames, 14th Earl of Desmond (the 'Pale Earl'), 85, 89, 95, 103; confined at Southwark, 67-68; freed, 74; in 2nd Desmond War, 75-78, 81-83

Fitzgerald, Gerald FitzMaurice, 3rd Earl of Desmond ('Gerald the Rimer'), Justiciar of Ireland, 40, 43

Fitzgerald, James FitzGerald, 15th Earl of Desmond (the 'Tower' or 'Queen's Earl'), 103

Fitzgerald, Sir James FitzMaurice, Captain of Desmond (the 'Arch Traitor'), 67-68; in 1st Desmond War, 70-71,

73; in 2nd Desmond War, 74-75, 81

Fitzgerald, James FitzThomas, 8th Earl of Desmond, 50

Fitzgerald, James FitzThomas, *Súgán* (or 'Hayrope') Earl of Desmond (nephew to Pale Earl), 95-97, 99-100, 103, 107

Fitzgerald, Jame Oge (nephew to Pale Earl), 78

Fitzgerald, Sir John FitzJames (brother to the Pale Earl), 67-68, 74-75, 81-82

Fitzgerald, John FitzThomas, Lord of the Décies, 34, 48

Fitzgerald, Maurice FitzJohn, Prince of the Décies, 48

Fitzgerald, Maurice FitzThomas, 1st Earl of Desmond, 39, 48

Fitzgerald, Sir Robert, 17th Knight of Kerry, 228

Fitzgerald, Thomas, 7th Earl of Kildare, Lord Lieutenant, 50

Fitzgerald, Thomas FitzGarret, Lord Offaly, afterwards unconfirmed 10th Earl of Kildare ('Silken Thomas'), 54-56

Fitzgerald, Thomas FitzJames, 7th Earl of Desmond, Lord Lieutenant (the 'Great Earl'), 49-50, 52

Fitzgerald, Thomas Judkin-, *see* Judkin-Fitzgerald, Sir Thomas

Fitzgerald of Kildare, Sir Thomas Oge, 52

Fitzgerald, Lord William Robert, Duke of Leinster, 277, 284

Fitzgerald of New Park, United Colonel Edward, 331, 333, 375, 344-345

Fitzgeralds of Desmond, 34, 45, 47-50, 65, 68-70, 77-78, 109

Fitzgeralds of Kildare, 38, 45, 48, 50, 52-56, 68-70

Fitzgibbon, John, Earl of Clare (after-

wards Lord Fitzgibbon of Sidbury), Lord Chancellor, 412

FitzHenry, Myler, Welsh knight, 24

FitzMaurice, Sir James, *see* Fitzgerald, James FitzMaurice

FitzStephan, Robert, Welsh knight, 24

Flight of the Earls, 9, 31, 108, 112, 116, 128, 188

Flight of the Wild Geese, *see* Wild Geese

Fitzwilliam, Lord William, Elizabethan Lord Lieutenant, 80, 86-87, 90

Fitzwilliam, Earl of, *see* Wentworth, William

Flodden, 1512 battle of, 186

Flogging triangle, 322, 350, 378

Flood, Henry; Patriot Party leader, 169, 242-243; Vice Treasurer of Ireland, 244, 248; rejoins Patriots, 249-250, 252-254, 415

Fontenoy, 1745 battle of, 214-220, 264

Foote, North Cork Militia Colonel, 328-329

Foras Feasa ar Éireann (Keating), 123

Fort George, Scottish prison, 270, 382, 386, 418

Fort of the Shields, 29

Forth, Wexford barony, 36, 335, 351

Fosterage, 66

Foster's Corn Law (1784), 258

Foulksmills, in 1798 insurrection, 344, 351

Four Masters, Annals of the, 123

Fox, 1798 United Captain, 362

Fox, Charles James, Whig parliamentary leader, 284

Franciscans, Capuchin, 118

Frederick II ('the Great'), Hohenzollern King of Prussia, 214, 219

Frederick Wilhelm III, King of Prussia, 349

Free Quarters, *see Coyne* and *Livery*

Free Trade movement, *see* Non-importation movement

French, Percy, songwriter, 178

French/France, 31, 35, 121, 163, 199, 224, 284, 295, 317, 321-322, 339, 380, 395, 413, 437; early centre of learning, 7; St. Bartholomew's Eve massacre in, 71; Huguenots, 121, 162; Edict of Nantes, 170; and Irish War of Two Kings, 169-170, 172-176, 180, 182, 184-188, 192; subsequent Bourbon war with English, 193-194, 198, 201-202, 204, 214, 216, 219-220; and Stuart pretenders, 163, 205, 225; Thurot Raid, 259; and American War of Independence, 245-246; emergence of Republic, 257, 260, 263; National Guards, 264; Committee of Public Safety, 268; Paris Jacobin Society, 262; agent Jackson sent to Ireland, 268-269; and United Irishmen (*see* United Irishmen, and French); 1796 Irish expedition, 276, 278-281, 283, 294, 377-378, 387; Directorate, 288, 387, 403, 411; 1798 Irish expeditions, 387-410; *see also* Army/Armies, French; Napoleon Bonaparte; *and* Navy/fleets, French

French Revolution/French Republic; influence on Irish, 46, 220, 257, 260-261, 263, 268-269, 284, 295, 312, 322, 358, 400, 403; and English Levellers, 150-151; and Catholic Church, 260, 400

Freney, Captain, highwayman, 222-223

Furlong, Thomas, songwriter and translator, 114

G

Gaelic cultural tradition, *see* Ireland, Gaelic/Celtic

Gaelic language, *see* Irish language

Gaelic League, 393

Gaelic Revival, *see* Irish Renaissance

Gaelicisation, 69; of the Vikings, 8, 14; of the Normans, 30, 40-41, 43-45; of the English, 50-51, 56, 73

Galle, Admiral Morard de, naval commander of 1796 French expedition, 278-280

Gallowglass, *see* Mercenaries, English, Hebridian, and Scottish

Galway City, Gaelic threat to, 65, 74

'Gap of the North', *see* Moyry Pass

Gardiner, Dublin Militia Colonel Luke, Viscount and 1st Baron Mountjoy, 333-334, 341, 353

Gardiner, Robert, Elizabethan freebooter, 83

Garland, James ('The Lurgan Poet'), 282, 336

Gates, American rebel General Horatio, 245

Geneva Barracks, 1798 croppy prison, 349

Geohegan, Arthur Gerald, Dublin poet, 198

George II, King of Great Britain, Elector of Hanover, 215

George III ('German George', 'Mad George'), Hanoverian King of Great Britain, 332, 344, 384-385, 415-416, 418

Gerald, 1st Baron of Offaly, 48

Gerald of Wales ('Geraldus Cambrensis'), *see* Barry, Gerald de

Geraldine Confederacy, 68, 71, 74-78, 81, 83, *see also* Irish rebellions, 1st Desmond *and* Irish rebellions, 2nd

Desmond

Geraldines, *see* Fitzgeralds, Desmond, *and* Fitzgeralds, Kildare

Gibbet Rath, 1798 massacre at, 317-318

Gibralter, 201

Gilbert, Captain (later Sir) Humphrey, Elizabethan, 68, 71

Ginckel, Williamite General Godert de (afterwards Earl of Athlone), 180, 182, 184-186, 188

Giolla MacLiag, poet to Brian Boru, 18-19

Glarmorgan, Lord, *see* Somerset, Edward

Glenarm, in 1798 insurrection, 358

Glencoe, 1692 massacre of MacDonalds at, 193

Glendower, Owen, Welsh rebel leader, 44

Glenflesk, 1565 battle of, 62

Glenmalure; 1580 battle of, 78-82; Red Hugh escapes to, 89, 426; refuge of O'Dwyer after 1798, 376; Emmet flies to after 1803, 426

GlenMáma, 998 battle of, 16

Glorious Revolution, *see* Irish rebellions, of the Two Kings

Godwin, Mary Wollstonecraft, English writer and feminist, 262

Gordon, Reverend James B., eyewitness chronicler of 1798 insurrection, 352, 368-369

Goresbridge, 1798 action at, 344

Gore (Wexford barony), in 1798 insurrection, 326, 351

Gorey town, in 1798 insurrection, 322, 331, 333, 337, 339, 341, 344, 346, 398

Gorey, Yeoman Cavalry, in 1798 insurrection, 346

Gormanston, Lord, Confederate Catholic leader, 122, 134

Gosford, Lord, *see* Acheson, Major General Arthur

Government, British Instrument of, *see* Instrument of Government, English

Government, English in Ireland, *see* Dublic Castle

Gowan, yeoman Captain Hunter, in 1798 dragooning and insurrection, 344, 346, 350

Gowran, Castle, 1650 massacre at, 148

Grace, Colonel Richard, Jacobite Governor of Athlone, 175, 184

Graces, The, 121, 123-125, 127

Graham, John, Viscount Dundee of Claverhouse ('Bonny Dundee'), 193

Graham, Robert, Wexford Unitedman, 306

Graham, Derry rebel Captain Watty, 364

Granard, 1798 rising near, 294, 392, 398

Grand Alliance of 1701, 201

Grattan, Henry, Patriot Party leader, 169, 244-245, 247-248, 252, 254, 271, 412, 415; Whig Club, 260, 284; and Irish Volunteers, 246, 250, 253; protests 1798 reprisals, 375; opposes Union, 415

'Grattan's Parliament', *see* Parliament, Irish

'Grazier Tribe', *see* Landlords, Connacht

Great Rebellion of 1641-2 (the 'Great Popish Massacre'), *see* Irish rebellions

Great Seal of England, 163, 188

Green, colour, as nationalist symbol, 173, 198, 256, 311-313, 372-374, 384

Gregory XIII, Pope. 74

Grenville, Sir Richard, Elizabethan

freebooter, 68

Grenville, Lord George Nugent-Temple-, 1st Marquis of Buckingham, Viceroy, 412

Grey, General Arthur, Baron de Wilton, Viceroy, 78-82, 92

Grey, Betsy, 1798 Down rebel, 367

Griffin, Gerald, novelist, 76

Griffith, Arthur, founder of *Sinn Féin*, 1st President, Provisional Government of the Irish Free State, 426

Griffith, Captain Richard, in 1798 insurrection, 309, 311, 314

Groomsport, 1689 Schomberg landing at, 170

Grouchy, French Brigadier (afterwards Marshal) Emmanuel de; in 1796 Bantry Bay expedition, 279-280

Guilds of London, in Ulster Plantation, 113, 127

Gunpowder Plot ('Guy Fawke's Affair'), 112, 126

H

Haakon IV, King of Norway, 35

Habeas Corpus Act of 1781, 249; 1796 suspension of, 277; 1798 reinstalment of, 409

Hacketstown, 1798 rebel attack on, 313

Half-hanging, 322, 350, 428

Hamburg, United Irish intelligence operations in, 288

Hamilton, Cavalier General Sir Frederick, 134

Hamilton, Engager General Lord James, 3rd Marquis and 1st Duke of, 143

Hamilton, Sir James (afterwards Viscount Claneboye), Lord Deputy of
Ireland, 116

Hamiltons, Fermanagh planters, 131

Hampden, John, Puritan parliamentary leader, 132

Hardy, French General, French expeditionary commander, 388, 392, 395, 402

Harps/harpers, 3, 12, 28, 119, 191, 206, 440-402; assembly of 1792, 206

Harrington, Sir Henry, Elizabeth soldier, 85

Harrow, The; in 1798 insurrection, 327, 332

Harvey, United Irish General Beauchamp Bagenal, 261; O/C Wexford rebels, 331, 351; New Ross campaign, 333, 336, 355, 397; replaced 337; executed, 346-347

Hastings, 1066 battle of, 29

Hay, Lieutenant Colonel Lord Charles, 3rd Marquis of Tweeddale; with British 1st Foot Guards at 1745 battle of Fontenoy, 216-217

Heart of Oak Boys, *see* Oakboys

Hearth Tax, *see* Taxation

Hedge Schools/hedge schoolmasters, *see* Schools, hedge

Heffernon, Blind William, poet, 251

Helen of Troy, 24

Henrietta Maria, Queen of England, 121-122

Henry II, Plantagenet King of England, 23, 26, 230

Henry IV, Lancastrian King of England ('Henry Bolingbroke', 'Henry of Lancaster'), 44

Henry VI, Lancastrian King of England, 45, 50

Henry VII, Tudor King of England ('Henry of Richmond'), 52-53

Henry VIII, Tudor King of England,

54, 56, 65, 337; 'Surrender and Re-grant' policy, 57-58, 61, 67, 71; King of Ireland, 57

Herbert, Lord Thomas, 8th Earl of Pembroke, Viceroy, 223-224

Hessians, in 1798 insurrection, 304, 332, 339, 344

Heydon, Captain Michael, Carlow Unitedman, 313

High Commission, abolition of, 125

Highland(s, -ers), Scottish, 220; feuds, 124, 142; Jacobite, 169, 175, 193, 220; in 1798 Irish insurrection, 339 408

History of Ireland (Keating), 123

Hobart, Sir Robert (afterwards 4th Earl of Buckinghamshire), Chief Secretary, 285

Hoche, French man-of-war; in 1798 Irish expedition, 402-404

Hoche, French General Lazare, com-mander of 1796 expeditionary force, 276, 278-287, 288

Hogan, Michael ('Bard of Thomond'), 92

Hogan, Michael ('Galloping Hogan')' rapparee, 176-180, 194, 254

Hogan, Portugese Major General Andre Miguel, 178, 218

Holt, United Colonel Joseph; Wicklow guerrilla leader, 375-376

Home Rule, Irish, 45-46, 53, 94-95, 210, 406

Hompech, Hessian General Count Ferdinand; in 1798 insurrection, 344

Hood, Admiral Alexander, Baron Brid-port of Somerset (afterwards Vis-count Bridport), 280, 409

Hope, James, Antrim Unitedman, 286, 306, 426

Hughes, John, Belfast Unitedman, 355

Huguenots; Villiers' belated aid to,

121; and French Dragonnades, 162, in Williamite army,173; Edict of Nantes, 170

Humbert, French General Joseph Amable, commander of 1798 French landing, 388, 390, 399; Races of Castlebar, 391, 402; battle of Ballina-muck, 392, 397; surrender of, 393, 395

Hundred Years War, *see* War, non-Irish

Hutchinson, General Francis; at 1798 battle of Castlebar, 390-391

Hyde, Ann (mother to Queens Mary and Anne), 163, 191-192

Hyde, Lord Edward, 1st Earl of Clarendon, chief Minister to Charles II, 191

I

Inchicronan, 1651 battle at Pass of, 149

Inchiquinn, Earl of, *see* O'Brien, Mur-rough

India, 276, 408

Indulgence, 1st (1687) and 2nd (1688), *see* Declarations of Indulgence

Industrial Revolution; English, 228, 247; Irish, 442

Informers, *see* Irish informers

Ingram, John Kells, poet and academic, 446

Innocent X, Pope, 139

Instrument of Government, English, 152

Insurrection Act (1796), 277, 289, 292, 348, 354; *see also* Yeomanry, Irish

Ireland, Anglicisation of, 56-59, 63-64, 109, 113-116, 120, 448

Ireland, Church of; 'plantation', 70,

128, 188; tithes to, 228, 411; declares Dissenters 'enemies', 191; *see also* Protestant Ascendancy *and* Protestants, Irish

Ireland, Gaelic/Celtic, 4-7, 10-12, 28, 30, 46, 74, 95, 440-441; demise of, 108-109, 448, *see also* Ireland, Anglicisation of

Ireland, metaphors for, 17, 85, 198, 230, 241, 251-252, 259, 278, 433; *see also* **Irish Glossary,** 449

Ireton, Parliamentary Brigadier, Henry, 143, 148-149

Irish (O'Connor), *The,* 440

Irish armies, *see* Army/Armies, Irish; Army/Armies, Irish Jacobite; Army/Armies, 1798 rebel; *and* Irish Republican Army

Irish Brigade (-s), 212, 225; American, 239; French, 199, 201-204, 206, 208, 214-219; recruiting sergeants for, 199; *see also* Wild Geese

Irish informers, 24-25, 208, 303, 380-382, 408, 423-424; Armstrong, 295, 298, 300-302, 443-444; Collins, 261, 276; Magan, 293-294, 298, 306; Magin, 355; MacGuckin, 287; McNally, 268, 276, 436; Mite, 309, 311, 314; Puxley, 208; Reynolds, 293-294, 306, 443

Irish independence, first declared, 45-46

Irish Jacobites, *see* Jacobites/Jacobitism

Irish/Gaelic language, 4, 7, 14, 26-27, 30, 43, 109, 158, 192, 231, 234-235, 250-251, 253, 259, 284, 316-317, 390, 399, 408, 442, 448

Irish middle class, *see* Middle class, Irish

Irish mititia, *see* Militia, Irish

Irish Monthly, 198

Irish National Land League, *see* Landowners/land/land tenure

Irish nationalist folk-memory/heritage, 4, 39, 92, 104, 111, 118, 127, 146, 149, 173, 175-176, 190, 206, 211, 220, 251, 258-259, 301, 307, 358, 366, 395, 404-406, 408, 428-429; Gaelic tradition, 8-11, 27, 59, 64, 89, 102, 116, 123, 213, 228, 367, 440-441; 'martyrdom', 258, 289, 301, 360, 363, 403, 419, 425, 430-432, 437-438, 441-442, 444, 446; tradition of violence, 2-3, 9, 16, 46, 129, 180-181, 183, 292, 334, 421, 437, 444-446; *see also* United Ireland

Irish Parliament, *see* Parliament, Irish

Irish population, 191, 223, 226

Irish *Press,* United Irish journal, 286, 289-290, 293

Irish public opinion, 224, 245

Irish rebellions, insurrections, risings, and wars, 9, 16-17; military solutions to, 10-11, 56; religion first used as basis for, 71; and foreign military aid, 395; *Dálcassian (954, 982, 988, 994),* 14-15, 29; *Limerick Norse (967),* 16; *Dublin Norse (998-999),* 16; *Dublin/ Leinster coalition (1013-1014),* 8, 17-20; *MacLochlainn/MacMurrough (1156-1171),* 21-24; *TyrOwen (1258-1260),* 31, 33-35; *MacCarthy (1261),* 34-35, 48; *O'Connor Sligo (1270),* 35; *Bruce Invasion (1315-1318),* 37-39; *O'Donnell/O'Connor (1316),* 39; *O'Brien (1318),* 39; *Art MacMurrough (1356-1362),* 41; *Art Oge MacMurrough (1390-1394),* 44, 48; *Art Oge MacMurrough (1395-1400),* 44; *Lancastrian (1453-1462),* 49; *Simnel (1487),* 52; *Thomond/Clan-Ricarde (1502-1504),* 53; *Silken Thomas (1534-1535),* 54-56; *Laois/ Offaly (1540-1546),* 57; *Shane O'Neill (1599-1567),* 61-63, 72-73;

Antrim Scots (1560-1593), 62, 86;
  1st Desmond (1569-1673), 68-73;
  2nd Desmond (1579-1583), 74-85;
  Nine Years (1594-1603), 90-107;
  O'Dougherty (1608), 109; *Great Rebellion (1641-1642)*, 126, 128-129,
  131-134, 150, 156, 160, 164; *Confederate Catholic (1642-1653)*, 134-
  149, 158; *of the Two Kings (1688-
  1691)*, 160-161, 163, 166-170, 174-
  175, 190, 230; *Thurot Raid (1760)*,
  see French, Thurot Raid; *Bantry Bay
  (1796)*, *see* French, 1796 Irish expedition; *Midlands (1798)*, 298-299,
  303, 308-321, 374-376, 379, 397-
  399, 407; *Wexford (1798)*, 114, 261,
  320-353, 393, 397-399, 407-408,
  413-414; *Ulster (1798)*, 274, 277,
  290, 355-364, 366, 374, 397-399,
  407; *Connacht (1798)*, and *Longford
  (1798)*, *see also* French, 1798 Irish
  expedition *and* Risings, 1798 Irish;
  Emmet (1803), 273-275, 376, 383,
  423-426, 442-443; *Young Ireland
  (1848)*, 380; *Easter (1916)*, 10, 253,
  260, 270, 419, 431-432, 445-446;
  Black and Tan (1919-1921), 376
Irish Renaissance ('Gaelic Revival'),
  284, 367
Irish Republic/republicanism, 10, 64,
  351, 366, 376, 408, 448; French
  heritage of, 260-261, 263, 268-269,
  295, 322, 358, 403; Protestant
  championship of, 209-212, 224, 270-
  272; 1st declared, 351 or 391
Irish Republican Army (IRA), 406,
  431; Provisional, 11, 431
Irish Republican Brotherhood (IRB),
  see Fenian Brotherhood
Irish tribal nobility, decline of, 63, 83-
  84, 108-109, 112-115, 152-153, 181
Irish Volunteers, *see* Volunteers, Irish

Irish Worker, 270
Irving, Washington, American writer,
  436
IslandBridge Barracks, target of 1803
  rising, 423
IslandMagee Peninsula, 1642 massacre
  at, 132
Isle of Man, 1760 naval battle of, 259
Italians/Italy; Napoleon in, 278; in
  Desmond Wars, 81-82
Iveagh, Lord, Jacobite soldier, 170
Ivor, Michael, Carlow Unitedman, 306,
  313

J

Jackson, Dr., 1798 Antrim rebel, 362
Jackson, Henry, Dublin Unitedman,
  263, 306
Jackson, Hugh, Dublin Unitedman,
  306
Jackson, Richard, Squire of Forkhill,
  265-266
Jackson, CSA General Thomas Jonathan ('Stonewall'), 136-137
Jackson, Reverend William, French
  spy, 268-269, 436
Jacobin Society, Parisian, 262, 268
James I, Stuart King of Great Britain
  (James VI of Scots), 100, 102, 109,
  112, 121, 126
James II, Stuart King of Great Britain
  (James VII of Scots), 173, 187, 189-
  190, 198, 200, 205, 215, 241; as
  Duke of York and Albany, 160-161;
  early sympathy to Catholics, 161-
  162, 191; becomes king, 176; deposed in England, 163-164; Kinsale
  landing, 167, 192; at Londonderry
  siege, 168-169; and Patriot Parliament, 169-170; and the Boyne, 170-

171, 174; death of, 225

James Francis Edward Stuart (the 'Old Pretender'), *see* Stuart, James Francis Edward

Jesuits/Society of Jesus, 118, 160

Jocelyn, yeoman cavalry Colonel Robert, 2nd Earl of Roden, 303-304, 393, 396

John, King of Scots, *see* Balliol, John de

John XXII, Pope, 48

John *Sans Terre*, Count of Mortain (afterwards John 'Lackland', Plantagenet King of England), Lord of Ireland, 26-27, 57

John Scotus Eriugena, Irish missionary, 7

Johnson, Major General; in 1798 insurrection, 334, 342

Johnson, Lionel, British poet, 17

Johnson, Dr. Samuel, Englishman of letters, 448

Johnston, Anna, *see* MacManus, Anna Johnston

Jones, parliamentary General Michael, 142-144

Joyce, Dr. Robert Dwyer, balladwriter and folklorist, 181, 327, 341, 345, 353

Judkin-Fitzgerald, Sir Thomas (afterwards Baronet of United Kingdom), High Sheriff of Tipperary, 295, 378

Julianstown Bridge, 1641 battle of, 129

K

Kavanagh, Donal, *see* MacMurrough (Kavanagh), Donal

Kavanagh, Fr. Patrick F., balladwriter, 343

Kavanaghs of south Leinster, *see* MacMurrough (Kavanaghs)

Kearney, Peadar, poet, playwright, rebel, songwriter, 376

Kearns, Fr. Moses, United Irish colonel, 333, 337, 375-376, 407

Keating, Fr. Geoffrey (Seathrún Céitinn), Gaelic historian, 123

Kellistown, 1398 action at, 44

Kells (Antrim); 1315 battle near, 38; in 1798 insurection, 355, 357

Kells (Meath), 1315 battle of, 38

Kelly, United Lt. John; at 1798 battle of New Ross, 334-335; execution of, 347, 407

Kelly, Mary Eva ('Eva of the *Nation*'), 380

Keogh, John, Catholic Committeeman and Unitedman, 261-262, 284-285

Keough, Captain Matthew, 1798 rebel governor of Wexford town, 331, 342, 346-347

Kerrigan, 1798 rebel Captain Neill, 390-391

Kerry during Penal Times, 207-209, 225

Kevin Barry, rebel ballad, 292

Kickham, Charles Joseph, Young Ireland, Fenian, novelist, poet, 271

Kieran, St., 7, 40

Kilcock, in 1798 insurrection, 298, 313-315, 319

Kilcommedon Hill, Jacobite position in 1691 battle of Aughrim, 185

Kilcomney Hill, 1798 rebel surrender at, 344, 397

Kilcullen, in 1798 insurrection, 311, 317, 319

Kildare, County, 1798 insurrection in, *see* Irish rebellion, Midlands (1798)

Kildare Geraldines (Fitzgeralds of Kildare)

Kildare, 7th Earl of, *see* Fitzgerald, Thomas

Kildare, 8th Earl of, *see* Fitzgerald, Garret FitzThomas

Kildare, 9th Earl of, *see* Fitzgerald, Garret Oge

Kildare, 10th Earl of, *see* Fitzgerald, Thomas Fitzgarret

Kildare, Sir Thomas of, *see* Fitzgerald, Thomas Oge

Kildare town, 1798 action at, 311, 318

Kilkenny, County, 1798 insurrection in, 344, 397

Kilkenny, Statutes of, 41, 43-44, 53

Kilkenny Confederation, *see* Confederate Catholics of Ireland

Killala; 1798 French landing/occupation of, 390, 394-395; 1798 British attack on ('2nd Killala'), 402; Bishop of, *see* Stock, Joseph

Killiecrankie, 1689 battle of, 193

Killthomas Hill, 1798 massacre at, 327

Kilmaine, French General Charles Edward, supreme commander, 1798 Irish expeditionary forces, 388, 392, 395

Kilmallock, in Desmond Wars, 71, 75

Kilwarden, Lord, *see* Wolfe, Arthur

Kincora, Brian's castle at, 18-20

King's Council, *see* Privy Council, English

Kings County, institution of, 57-58

Kings County Militia in 1798 coup plans, 295; in 2798 insurrection, 333, 352

Kings/kingship in Ireland, 4-7, 13-14, 16-21, 23-27, 29, 31, 35, 39; British, 57, 65-66; Gaelic (and Gaelic succession), 58, 61, 89-90, 110, 116; Scottish, 38, 48; *see also* Irish tribal nobility

Kinsale, Spanish expedition to, *see* Spanish, Spain, *and* Nine Years War

Kinsale; O'Neill/O'Donnell 1601 march to, 104-105; 1601 battle for, 104-107; 1689 landing by James II at, 192; 1690 Marlborough campaign for, 175, 180

Kinsalla, Thomas, poet, 231

Kirk, Scot Presbyterian, *see* Scotland, Presbyterians and Church in

Kirkwood, 1798 yeoman Captain William; at 1798 1st Killala, 390

Knockallen Hill (Knockaulin), 1798 rebel camp at, 317

Knockdoe ('Hill of the Axes'), 1504 battle of, 53

Knox, Brigadier, 1797 British O/C Tyrone, 281, 285

Kosciusko, General Thaddeus, Polish patriot, 368

Kyan, Captain Esmonde; 1798 rebel at battle of Arklow, 339, 352

L

Lacy, Hugh de, Lord of Meath, 26

Lacy, Major General Count Peter, Tsarist campaigner, 218

Lake, British Lieutenant General Gerard, 285, 312, 340; in dragooning of Ulster, 281, 287, 354, 366; as O/C Ireland, 295, 303; in 1798 Wexford campaign, 340, 342, 374; in 1798 Ballinamuck campaign, 390-393, 396

Lalor, James Fintan, Young Irelander and Fenian, 271

Lambeg drums, used in Orange celebrations, 171

Landen, 1693 battle of the River, *see* Neerwinden, battle of

Landowners/land/land tenure, 4, 14, 120, 235, 437; difference in Gaelic and English ownership laws, 57-58,

113, 116, 228; and Tudors, *see* Surrender and Re-grant Policy *and* Plantation, Irish land; Undertakers, 116; and 1642 Adventurer's Act, 134; Cromwellian Settlement, 146, 152-153, 155-156, 175, 182; Restoration Claims Court, 156; speculation, 153, 227; in Penal Times, 193, 196-197, 228; land agents, 234, 236-238; subdivision and sub-letting, 227; absentee ownership, 227-228, 243, 258; the 'Grazier Tribe' of Connacht, 236, 243, 257-258; 'Ulster Custom', 258; 1778 Catholic Relief Act, 248, 256; 1782 Catholic Relief Act, 244, 254, 256; and agrarian violence, 234-235, 256, 265; Irish National Land League, 225, 401

Lane, Denny, Young Ireland songwriter, 212

Laois (Leix) Plantation, *see* Plantation, Queens

Larne; 1315 Bruce landing at, 37; 1798 action at, 355, 357

Laud, Archbishop William, Primate of England, 122-124, 127

Laudabilitier, papal bull, 23, 26, 65-66

Lauzun, French Duke of, Jacobite officer, 175

Law, English/British, 3, 26, 36, 41-42, 48, 58, 74, 113, 119, 199, 212, 248, 281, 289-290, 306, 382; protectionist, 209, 258; *see also* Dublin Castle; *Habeas Corpus* Act; Parliament, English/Imperial; Navigation Laws; *and* Penal Laws

Law, Irish, *see* Brehon/Druidic Law

Lawless, Dr. William, Dublin Unitedman, 288, 294-295, 298

Leicestershire Fencibles, at 1798 action at Ballina, 390

Leinster, on eve of 1798 insurrection, 291-292, 295, 350

Leixlip, 1798 rebel attack on, 313-314

Leslie, Monaghan Militia Colonel; at 1798 battle of Ballinahinch, 362

Leslie, Scot General Alexander, Earl of Leven, 124-125, 135

L'Estrange, Kings County Militia Colonel; at 1798 battle of Newtownbarry, 333

Levant, Napoleonic campaign in the, 387, 411, 418

Leveller Movement (Puritan egalitarians), 141-142, 150-151

Levellers (Irish agrarian society), *see* Whiteboys, Whiteboyism

Leven, Earl of, *see* Leslie, Scot General Alexander

Lewins, Edward John, United Irish legate to France, 278, 387, 408

Lía Fail, ancient Irish coronation stone, 315

Lifford; in Nine Years War, 104; in War of Two Kings, 167

Lilburne, John, Puritan Leveller leader, 150

Limerick; founding of, 13; in Viking wars, 14, 16; in Desmond Wars, 71; 1651 siege of, 149; 1690 siege and battle for, 175-178, 180, 184, 189; 1691 campaign for, 183

Limerick, 1691 Treaty of (Capitulation of Limerick), 188, 190, 193-194, 196, 206, 209, 211, 217-218, 221, 226, 254, 270

Lincoln, Earl of, *see* Pole, John de la

Lionel of Antwerp, Earl of Ulster, Duke of Clarence, 41, 43

Lisnagade, 1791 incident at ring fort of, 256-257

Literacy in Ireland, 4-5, 7-9, 12, 116, 118-120; *see also* Penal Laws *and* Schools, Irish

Loftus, British Major General; in 1798 Wexford insurrection, 337

Lombard, North Cork Militia Major; at 1798 battle of Oulart Hill, 328-329

London, City of, 125, 201; in Ulster Plantation, 113; and Covenanters, 135; occupied by Fairfax, 142

Londonderry, town of ('Derry' until 1613); 1600 Crown capture of, 102; City of London plantation of, 113; 1688-1689 siege of, 163, 166-169, 192; legacy of siege, 175, 189, 224

Louis XIII, Bourbon King of France, 123

Louis XIV, *Roi Soleil* (the 'Sun King'), Bourbon King of France, 162-163, 169-170, 173, 176, 184, 187-189, 198, 204, 225

Louis XV, Bourbon King of France, 214-217, 219

Louis XVI, Bourbon King of France, 263

Luby, Colonel George, Kildare Unitedman, 308, 320, 375

Luby, Thomas Clarke, Fenian, 271

Lucan, in 1798 insurrection, 308, 313-314

Lucan, Baron, *see* Bingham, Charles

Lucan, Lord, *see* Sarsfield, Major General Patrick

Lucas, Charles, 18th-century Irish anti-government gadfly, 169, 250

Luck of Barry Lyndon (Thackeray), 222

Lumley, Lieutenant Colonel Sir William; at 1798 battle of Antrim, 357, 367

Lundy, Robert, 1688 Mayor of Londonderry, 166, 168

Luttrell, Colonel Henry (afterwards Dutch Major General), Jacobite cavalry commander secretly in Williamite service, 185

Luttrell, Lord Henry Lawes, 2nd Earl of Carhampton, 1797 O/C Ireland, 307

Luxembourg, Francis Henry of Montmorency-Bouteville, Duke of; Marshal of France, 176

Lynch, James FitzStephan, Mayor of Galway, 320

Mc/Mac

MacAllister, Samuel, Wicklow guerrilla, 421-422

MacArt, Cormac, 3rd century High King, 9

MacArtmoyle, 1601 rebel, 103

MacArt's Fort, *see* Cave Hill

MacBrody of Clare, Conor, 17th century Gaelic scholar, 127

MacCabe, Thomas, Ulster Unitedman, 261, 272

McCall, Patrick Joseph, balladwriter, 79, 158, 331, 335

McCann, John, Secretary to United Irish National Directory, 306, 381, 407

McCann, Michael Joseph, scholar, journalist, and balladwriter, 98

McCarren, Peter, Monaghan militiaman; executed, 282-283

MacCarthy, Cormac MacTiege, 1st Earl of Clancarty, 77-78

MacCarthy, Donnell, Earl of Clancar, 85

MacCarthy, Fineen MacDonnell, 34

MacCarthys of Kerry, 34-35, 45, 48, 68, 77-78, 85, 190

MacCool, Finn, 3rd-century commander of the Fenians, 9

MacCooleys of Tyrone, 91

McCorley, Rody, Antrim Defender, 369-371

MacCormack, Richard, Catholic Committeeman and Unitedman, 261, 284-285, 294, 306

MacCracken, Henry Joy, 109, 272, 372; joins United Irishmen, 261; at Cave Hill, 270; 1796 arrest of, 277; and shipbuilding, 284; on Ulster Directory, 287, 294; O/C Ulster Unitedmen, 355; at Donegore Hill, 355-356; and battle of Antrim, 357-358, 361, 364; execution of, 358-361, 407; military ability of, 360

MacCracken, Mary Ann, 274

MacCracken, William, Ulster Unitedman, 261, 277, 284

MacCuartha, Seamus Dall ('Blind Jamie' MacCarthy), Gaelic poet, 190

McDermott Roe, Roscommon Defender captain, 266-267

MacDonalds, Highland, 193, 220

MacDonnell, Jacobite General Alexander, 3rd Earl of Antrim; at 1688 Londonderry siege, 166, 168

MacDonnell, Angus 'the Haughty', Prince of the Route, 62

MacDonnell, Angus Oge, Prince of the Route, 87, 97

MacDonnell, James, Lord of the Isles, 62

MacDonnell, Lord Randall, 2nd Viscount Dunlace, 2nd Earl and 1st Marquis of Antrim, 132

MacDonnell, Shane ('Claragh'), Gaelic poet, 206

MacDonnell, Sorley Boye, Prince of the Route, 62-63, 86, 132

MacDonnells of the Route, 62-64, 74, 86-87, 96-97, 132, *see also* Mercenaries, Redshank

MacEgan, Bishop Beotius, Confederate Catholic, 149

MacEgan of Tipperary, Flann, 17th-century Gaelic scholar, 127

McGarry, Captain Roger, Kildare Unitedman, 311, 313, 315

McGillain, Daniel, Monaghan militiaman, 282-283

MacGowan, James; adversary correspondent of O'Casey, 270

MacGuckin, Ulster Unitedman, Crown informer, 287

McGuigan, Paddy, folksinger and songwriter, 329

McKeever, William, Derry Unitedman, 289

McKenna, Owen and William, Monaghan militiamen, 282-283

MacKennas of Monaghan, 87, 139-141

McLean, Fencible Captain; at 1798 battle of Tara, 315-316

MacLendon, Pádraig, harper and poet, 147

MacLiag, Giolla, *see* Giolla MacLiag

MacLochlainn, Murtough, Lord of Ulster, 21

MacMahon, Brian MacHugh, The MacMahon, 94, 103

MacMahon, Costelloe, The MacMahon, 139

MacMahon, Bishop Herber MacTurlough, Confederate Catholic, 149

MacMahon, Hugh Oge (grandson to Hugh O'Neill), 1641 conspirator, 150

MacMahons of Monaghan, 58, 87, 91, 94, 97, 103, 139, 150

MacManus, Anna Johnston ('Ethna Carbery'), poet, 132, 369-370

MacManus, Seumas, playwright, balladwriter, and short story writer, 64, 119

MacMurrough, Art, Lord of south
Leinster, 41

MacMurrough, Sir Art Oge, Lord of
south Leinster, 44, 48, 116

MacMurrough, Dermott (Diarmuid
'na nGall'), Lord of Leinster, 21, 23-
26, 264

MacMurrough (Kavanagh), Donal, Lord
of Leinster, 39

MacMurrough, Eva, daughter of Dermott, 23-24, 26

MacMurrough (Kavanaghs) of south
Leinster, 21, 23-26, 39, 41, 44-45,
48, 68, 78, 116, 264

McNally, United Irish attorney
Leonard, Crown informer, 268, 276,
436

MacNamee, Giolla Brighde, poet to
Shane O'Neill, 31

MacNeven, Dr. William James, Dublin
Unitedman; and Catholic Committee,
261; on United Irish Dublin Directory, 277; United legate to France,
288, 409; 1798 arrest, 306; deals
with government after rising, 382,
386; release of, 418

MacQuillans of Antrim, 62

McSheeys of Limerick, 68, 71, 95

MacStiofáin, Seán; former Chief-of-
Staff, Provisional IRA, 329

MacSweeneys of TyrConnell, 97

MacSwineys of Limerick, 68, 71, 95

MacTier, Samuel, Sligo Unitedman,
261, 272, 377

MacWard, Owen Roe, Gaelic poet, 252

MacWilliam Burkes of Connacht, see
Burkes

M

Mackay, Williamite Major General

Hugh, 182-185, 193

MaelMórdia, King of Leinster, 17-18

Maeve, pre-historic Queen of Connacht, 9

Magan, Francis, Dublin Unitedman and
Crown informer, 293-294, 298, 301,
306

Magee, 'Gunner', 1798 rebel, 393

Magennis, Sir Hugh, Elizabethan soldier, 81

Magennisses of Ulster, 58

Maghera, in 1798 insurrection, 364

Magin, Ulster Unitedman Nicholas,
Crown informer, 355

Magistracy, Irish, after Flight of the
Earls, 128; in Penal Times, 197, 199;
and Defenders, 265; and dragooning
of peasantry, 281, 287

Maguire, Conor MacBrian, 2nd Baron
of Enniskillen; 1641 Catholic conspirator, 126, 150

Maguire, Cuconnacht Oge (Conn Oge),
Lord of Fermanagh, 104-105, 111

Maguire, Hugh MacCuconnacht, Lord
of Fermanagh; and border war with
Bagenals, 88-89; and Nine Years War,
90-91, 94, 96-97, 111

Maguire, Thomas, Commander, 2nd
WesternDivision, IRA, 431

Maguires of Fermanagh, 58, 88-91,
94, 96-97, 104-105, 107, 131

Mahon MacKennedy, Dálcassian King
of Munster, 14, 16

Mahon, British Colonel at 1798 battle
of Carlow, 313

Maidstone, HMS, early 1970s prison
ship, 329

Mail-coaches, halting of as signal to
begin 1798 insurrection, 298, 305,
308, 318-319, 354, 368

Makem, Tommy, folksinger, innkeeper,
and songwriter, 278

Malachy MacDonnell (Malachy '*Mór*'),
King of the Southern O'Neill (Meath),
High King of Ireland, 16-20, 29, 99
Mallow, 1598 rebel siege of, 100
Malta, in Napoleonic Wars, 387, 418
Maltby, Nicholas, Elizabethan O/C
Munster (afterwards) Governor of
Connacht, 75, 77, 79, 82, 84
Manchester, Earl of, *see* Montagu,
General Edward
Mangan, James Clarence, poet, 18,
106, 189, 253
Mar, Duke of, *see* Erskine, John
Mar, Prince of, *see* Donald, Scot Prince
of Mar
Margaret ('Maid of Norway'), Princess
of Scotland (granddaughter to
Alexander III of Scotland and Henry
III of England), 36
Marlborough, Earl (afterwards Duke)
of, *see* Churchill, Major General John
Marshallea Lane, headquarters of 1803
rebels in, 423-424
Maria Theresa, Queen of Bohemia and
Hungary, Holy Roman Empress, 219
Marston Moor, 1644 battle of, 135
Martial law, in period previous to 1798
insurrection, 281, 295, *see also* Insur-
rection Act (1796)
Mary I ('Bloody' Mary), Tudor Queen
of England, 57-58, 160
Mary II, Stuart Queen of England, 163,
188, 191-192, 225; *see also*, William
III
Mary Beatrice of Modena, Queen of
England, 161-162
Mary Stewart (Stuart), Queen of Scots,
62, 70, 86, 112
Mass, Catholic, 6, 119, 197, 199
Massareene, Lord, *see* Skeffington,
Colonel John Clotworthy
Maxwell, militia Colonel in 1798

insurrection, 330-331
Maynooth; 1535 siege of, 54-56; 1798
action at, 314, 319
Meagher, American Brigadier Thomas
('Meagher of the Sword'), Young
Irelander, 239
Meath, 1798 insurrection in, *see* Irish
rebellion, Midlands (1798)
Meath Militia, in 1798 insurrection,
331
Mellifont Abbey, 1603 submission of
Tyrone at, 107, 111
Meloniere, 1691 Huguenot Williamite
officer, 185
Mercenaries; English, 13; Flemish, 24,
29-30; German (Hessian), 52, 304,
332, 339, 344; Hebredian, 31, 73;
Irish *bonnacht*, 92, 98; Irish Wild
Geese, *see* Wild Geese; Redshank
(Antrim Scot), 62-64; Scot *galló-
glaigh*, 13, 18, 31, 35, 54, 62, 76-77,
84, 90, 92, 98
Middle class, Irish, 223-224, 227, 257,
260, 263, 283
Middle Nation, *see* Old English of
Ireland
Militia, Irish, 281, 317; founding of,
265; in dragooning, 281, 326; infiltrated by Unitedmen, 281; complained of by Abercrombie, 294; in
Wexford 1798, 322-323, 408; in
Midlands, 408; deserters from, 375;
vs. French, 391, 402; conduct in
battle, 280, 379, 391; reprisals, 379;
Cornwallis' attitude towards, 371,
379-380, 396-397; 1798 casualties,
409-410
Minorca, British Crown Colony, 201
Missionaries, Irish, 7-8, 118
Mitchel, John, Young Irelander, journalist, historian, 131, 271, 351, 436,
443-444

Mite, Philip, Sallins Yeoman, Kildare Unitedman, 309, 311, 314

Modest Proposal (Swift), *A*, 210

Molyneux, William, Williamite Home Ruler, 169, 209, 243, 250

Monaghan, Fort, 1595 siege of, 91, 94

Monaghan Militia; Unitedmen within, 291; at battle of Ballinahinch, 362

Monaster (Monasteranenagh Abbey), 1579 battle of, 75, 79

Monasterevin, in 1798 insurrection, 311, 313

Monastic communities; early Irish, 7; Viking attacks on, 8, 13-14; Tudor destruction of, 84-85, 118; and Statutes of Kilkenny, 43; in Penal Times, 197

Monmouth, duke of, *see* Croft, James

Monroe, Scot Covenanter Major-General Robert, 134; 1642 Antrim landing, 132; IslandMagee massacre, 132-133; at 1646 battle of Benburb, 136-141

Montagu, parliamentary General Edward, 2nd Earl of Manchester, 135

Montgomery, Sir Hugh, Down planter, 116, 126

Moore, George Henry, 1850s Mayo M.P., Irish Tenants' League leader, parliamentary destructionist, 271

Moore, British General Sir John, 295, 342, 371

Moore, Thomas, poet and songwriter, 25, 441-442; at TCD, 435-436; and Emmet/Curran, 436, 438-439; audience, 440

Morning Star, *see Northern Star*

Mortimer, Roger de, 4th Earl of March, Viceroy, 44

Mortimer, Roger de, 8th Baron Wigmore, Lord of Meath (afterwards 1st Earl of March), Viceroy, 38

Mountjoy, 1689 Williamite relief ship, 168

Mountjoy, Baron, *see* Blount, Charles

Mountjoy, Colonel Lord, *see* Gardiner, Colonel Luke

Moyry Pass ('Gap of the North'); description of, 90; in 1318 campaign, 38; in 1597 campaign, 96; in 1599 campaign, 102

Muddler's Club, Belfast United Irish front group, 270

Mullaghamast, 1577 massacre at Rath of, 74

Munro, United General Henry, Down rebel commander, 361-364, 372

Munster; divided into counties, 83; and United Irishmen, 295, 377-378

Murphy, United General Fr. John, 109, 337-339, 347, 351; begins 1798 Wexford insurrection, 326-327, 331-332; leads Wexford rebels, 327-332, 342-343; after Vinegar Hill, 344; execution of, 331-332, 353, 396, 407

Murphy, United Colonel Fr. Michael, 333, 407

Murphy, William, Dublin Unitedman, 306

Murrough MacBrian, son of Boru, 18

Murtough of the Leathern Cloaks, King of the Northern O'Neill, 14

Music/musicians/musical instruments, 28, 43, 191, 206; and poetry, 9-11, 73, 190, 213; *see also* Harps/harpers *and* pipes/pipers

N

Naas; in 1798 insurrection, 309, 311-312, 315, 318-319; 1798 battle of, 313-314

Nantes, Edict of, *see* Huguenots

Napoleon Bonaparte, French soldier and First Consul, 374, 435-436; early successes, 278, 288; Army of Orient, 368-369, 387, 408; Peace of Amiens, 418, 422; resumption of hostilities, 422; and the United Irishmen, 368-369, 387, 422, 436

Narraghmore, in 1798 insurrection, 311

Naseby, 1645 battle of, 135

Nation, 1840s nationalist journal, 139, 146, 380, 446

National Guard, United Irish, 263

Navigation Laws, 244-248, 260

Navy/fleets, Dutch, 121, 180, 288, 387

Navy/fleets, French, 188, 259, 278-280, 283, 377, 387-389, 391, 402-403, 407, 409, 422

Navy/fleets, Royal, 121, 169, 180, 197, 220, 348, 372, 390, 402, 404, 411; under Commons, 135, 143; in blockade of European republics, 278-279, 387-389, 403, 409, 418, 422

Navy/fleets, Spanish, 86-87, 90, 95, 104, 280

Needham, 1798 British General Francis (afterwards Earl of Kilmorey), 338, 340, 342, 352, 397

Neerwinden (River Landen), 1693 battle of, 198

Neilson, Samuel, founder of United Irishmen, 260-261, 283; and *Northern Star*, 262, 271; effect of Fitzwilliam's recall on, 269; reorganisation of Ulster Unitedmen, 270; Cave Hill meeting, 270, 358; helps found Irish *Press*, 285-286; 1796 arrest of, 277, 289; supports Fitzgerald, 298; National Directory after Bond raid, 294; activity before rising, 305; suggests 'mail-coach strategy', 308;

condemned, 381; in Wicklow Gaol, 345, 381-382; 1802 release of 418

Nelson, Admiral Viscount Horatio, 380, 385, 411, 418

Nenagh; 994 sack of, 29; Whiteboys near, 234

New English of Ireland ('Pale English'), 30, 36-37, 39-40, 43, 45

Newgate Prison, 298, 305

New Ross; in 1798 insurrection, 322, 333, 342; 1798 battle of, 334-337, 340-341, 343, 351-353, 355, 368, 397-398, 414

Newcastle, 1640 seizure of by Leslie, 125

Newry; in 1595 campaign, 91; in 1689 campaign, 170

New South Wales, *see* Botany Bay

Newtonwards, 'Pike Sunday' at, in 1798 insurrection, 361-362

Newtownbarry (Bunclody); 1798 battle of, 333, 340-341; in 1798 insurrection, 322, 375

Newtownbutler, 1689 battle of, 167

New York (Niew Amsterdam), 160

Niall of the Nine Hostages, Irish High King, founder of the O'Neill line, 31, 63

Nickson, yeoman captain in 1798 insurrection, 345

Nile, battle of, *see* Aboukir Bay (Nile), battle of

Nine Years War, *see* Irish rebellion

Ninth Dragoons, at 1798 battle of Carlow, 313

Non-importation movement, Irish, 247, 250

Normans, coming of to Ireland, 4, 8, 22-23, 28-31, 34, 86, 228

Norris, Sir John, Elizabethan Lord President of Munster, 86, 99

Norris, Sir Thomas, Elizabethan Lord

President of Munster (afterwards Lord Justice of Ireland), 100

North Cork Militia; in Wexford dragooning, 322-323; at 1798 battle of Oulart Hill, 328-329

Northern Star ('Morning Star', 'Union Star'), United Irish journal, 261-262, 265, 281, 284, 286

Northumberland, 1639-1640 Covenanter invasion of, 124

Nugent, British Major General George, 1798 O/C Ulster, 355, 360-362, 369

O

Oakboys, Oakboyism, 234, 242, 256, 265

Oates, Titus, and the Popish Plot of 1678, 160-161, 191

Oath of Supremacy, *see* Black Oath

O'Breslans of Tyrconnell, 33

O'Brien, Turlough MacMurrough, grandson of Boru, 18

O'Brien, Charles, 5th Viscount Clare, *Maréchal-de-Camp* in French Army of Flanders, 201-205

O'Brien, Charles, 6th Viscount Clare, Comte de Thomond (afterwards Marshal of France), 215-218

O'Brien, Conor, Lord of Lemaneagh Castle, 149

O'Brien, Conor MacDonagh, 3rd Earl of Thomond (Conor 'the Longnailed'), 71

O'Brien, Darby, 239-240

O'Brien of Thomond, Margaret, 50

O'Brien, Murrough MacDermot ('Murrough of the Burnings'), 6th Baron (afterwards 1st Earl of) Inchiquinn, 134, 136, 139, 142-144

O'Brien, Turlough, Lord of Thomond, 53

O'Brien, William Smith, Young Irelander, 271

O'Briens of Clare (Thomond), 18-19, 31, 39, 45, 57, 71

O'Brudair, Daithi, poet, 190

O'Byrne, Fiach MacHugh, Wicklow rebel, 78-82, 85, 89, 376

O'Byrnes of Wicklow, 35, 39, 76, 78-81, 85, 95

O'Cahan, Donal Ballagh, Lord of Dungiven, 127

O'Cahans of Tyrconnell, 33, 37, 97, 127

O'Casey, Seán, poet, balladwriter, playwright, 270-271

O'Cleary, Michael, Gaelic historian, 123, 127

O'Cleary, Br. Peregrine, Gaelic historian, 127

O'Coffey, Teige, Gaelic poet and teacher, 66

O'Connell, Daniel ('The Liberator'), 114, 230-231, 225, 271, 406, 435, 443

O'Connell of Connacht, Hugh, 39

O'Connor, Arthur; United Irish legate to France, 277; on National Directory, 278; and Irish *Press*, 286, 289; supports rising, 288; arrest in England, 293; acquittal and re-arrest, 306; liason with Defenders, 306, 377; deals with Dublin Castle on behalf of prisoners, 382; Ft. George imprisonment, 436; release of, 418; feud with Emmet, 436; favourite of Napoleon, 422, 436

O'Connor, Charles, founder of Catholic Association, 242

O'Connor, Frank (Michael O'Donovan), novelist, translator, critic, short story writer, 231, 312

O'Connor of Roscommon, Hugh MacFelim, 35

O'Connor, Roger, Cork Defender leader, 306, 377

O'Connor, Rory, King of Connacht, High King of Ireland, 21, 26-27

O'Connor, Turlough, King of Connacht, High King of Ireland, 20-21

O'Connor Offaly, Brian, 57

O'Connor Sligo, Lord of Roscommon, 84

O'Connor Sligo, Felim, 39

O'Connors of Connacht, 20-21, 26-27, 31, 35, 39, 45, 68, 76, 81, 84-85

O'Connors of Kerry, 34

O'Connors of Offaly, 52, 57, 74, 78, 83, 95

Octennial Act of 1767, 242

O'Curry, Eugene, Gaelic antiquarian, 106

O'Daly, Doighre, poet to the O'Byrnes, 79

O'Doherty, Cahir, *see* O'Dougherty, Cahir

O'Doherty, Kevin Izod, Young Irelander, 380

O'Donnell, Calvagh MacManus, The O'Donnell, 62-63

O'Donnell, Donal Oge, The O'Donnell, 35, 47

O'Donnell, Godfrey MacDonal, The O'Donnell, 47

O'Donnell, Hugh MacCalvagh ('Black Hugh'), The O'Donnell, 63, 86-87, 89, 93, 110

O'Donnell, Hugh Oge, The O'Donnell ('Red Hugh'); kidnapped, 86; freed, 88-89, 110, 426; in Nine Years War, 90, 93-99, 101, 103, 105; flight to Spain and death, 106-107, 111, 138

O'Donnell, Joanna (daughter to Black

Hugh, wife to Hugh O'Neill), 87

O'Donnell, Sir Nial Garv, O'Donnell pretender, 103-104, 107, 110

O'Donnell, Rory McHugh, Earl of TyrConnell, The O'Donnell, 107-108, 111, 118, 126

O'Donnells of TyrConnell ('Clann-Connell'), 31, 35, 41, 45, 47, 62-63, 71, 81, 86-90, 93-99, 101, 103, 105-107, 109-111, 118, 126, 138, 426

O'Donnellys of Ulster, 61, 66

O'Donovan, Jeremiah ('O'Donovan Rossa'), Fenian, 444

O'Donovan, John, Gaelic antiquarian, 106

O'Donovan, Michael, *see* O'Connor, Frank

O'Dougherty, Cahir, Lord of Inishowen, 109

O'Dougherty, Kevin, *see* O'Doherty, Kevin Izod

O'Dougherty Rebellion of 1608, *see* Irish rebellions

O'Doughertys of TryConnell, 97, 103, 109

O'Driscolls of Kerry, 34, 76-77

O'Dowds of Connacht, 110

Ó Duhbhánaigh, Caoimhín, translator, 231-232

O'Duigenan, Peregrine, Gaelic historian, 127

O'Dwyers of Tipperary, 68

O'Faoláins of the Décies, 68

Offaly, Lord Gerald, *see* Gerlad, 1st Baron of Offaly

Offaly, Lord Thomas, *see* Fitzgerald, Thomas FitzGarret ('Silken Thomas')

Offaly Plantation, *see* Plantation, Kings

O'Flaherty, Donnell Crone, The O'Flaherty (Donnell 'of the Wars'), 73, 85, 110

O'Flaherty, Sir Murrough 'of the Battle-axes', O'Flaherty pretender, 73, 85, 110

O'Flahertys of Connemara, 71, 73-74, 76-77, 82, 85, 110

O'Gara, Ferghal, patron of Four Masters, 127

O'Gillain, Angus, Gaelic poet, 40

O'Gnive, Farley, poet to Shane O'Neill, 58-59

Ogham cypher, 12, 41

O'Hagan, Judge John ('SLIABH CUILINN'), Young Ireland ballad-writer, 416

O'Hagans of Tyrone, 33, 37, 88-90

O'Hanlon, Barnaby, poet, 184

O'Hanlon, Redmond, Armagh rapparee, 156, 158-159

O'Hanlons of Armagh and Monaghan, 33, 37, 58, 97, 131, 156, 158-159

O'Higgins, Spanish Captain General Ambrose, 218

O'Higgins, Bernardo, Chilean Liberator, 218

O'Higgins, Blind Teige, Gaelic poet, 102

O'Hussey, Eochy, poet to Hugh Maguire, 105

O'Keen, Irish officer in 1798 French expeditionary force, 409

O'Kelly, Patrick ('Cormac'), Gaelic poet, 280

Oldbridge at Wexford; 1798 massacre at, 342, 353; execution of rebels at, 346-347

Oldbridge Ford, at 1690 battle of Boyne, 171-172

Old English of Ireland (the 'Middle Nation', the 'marcher lords'), 8, 30-31, 34-37, 39-41, 43-45, 47, 49-50, 56, 69, 125; in Kilkenny Confederation, 134-136, 139, 141-143

Old Mill Glen (Ballycarry), 1597 action at, 96

Old Pretender, *see* Stuart, Prince James Francis Edward

O'Leary, Irish-Austrian Colonel Arthur, 231-233

O'Leary, Eileen, Gaelic poet, 231

O'Leary, Ellen, Fenian poet, 438

O'Leary, John, Fenian, 271, 438

Ollúna, see Poets/poetry, Irish

O'Luinighs of Strabane, 66

O'Mahonys of west Cork, 76

O'Malley, Grace, Lord of Clew Bay ('*Granuaile*'), 76, 85, 230

O'Malleys of Mayo, 76, 85, 110, 230

O'More, Eoiny MacRory, Queens Co. rebel, 66, 100-103

O'More Gillapatrick, Lord of Laois, 57

O'More, Confederate Catholic Colonel Rory MacCalvagh; instigator of 1641 Catholic conspiracy, 66, 126, 128-129, 150

O'More, Rory MacConnell, Captain of Laois, 66

O'More, Rory Oge, 1570s Queens Co. rebel, 66, 80, 100

O'Mores of Laois (Queens Co.), 39, 57, 66, 74, 78, 80, 100-103

O'Moriarty, Owen MacDonal, Kerry chieftain, 83

O'Mulcrony, Farfassa, Gaelic historian, 127

O'Neill, Art MacFerdoraghe (brother to Hugh), 61

O'Neill, Art MacSeán (son of Shane), 103

O'Neill, Art Oge (nephew to Hugh), 108

O'Neill, Brian of TyrOwen, The O'Neill, 31, 35

O'Neill, Brian MacArt (nephew to Hugh), 103, 270

O'Neill, Brian MacFerdoraghe (brother to Hugh), 61

O'Neill, Connallagh *Bacagh* (Conn 'the
Lame'), 1st Baron Dungannon, 1st
Earl of Tyrone, The O'Neill, 57-58,
61, 110, 126, 132

O'Neill, Cormac MacFerdoraghe
(brother to Hugh), 61, 66

O'Neill, Sir Felix (Feidlimidh *Ruadh*),
leader of 1641 rebellion, 126, 128-
129, 131, 133-134, 139, 149-150,
323

O'Neill, Hugh (Aodh Mac Ferdoraghe),
3rd Baron Dungannon, 2nd Earl of
Tyrone, The O'Neill (the 'Arch
Rebel'), 63, 66-67, 123, 126, 270;
'fostered' by Sidneys, 61, 65-66, 92;
installed in Dungannon, 65, 91; in
Desmond Wars, 71, 87; made Earl,
86; solidifies hold in Ulster, 87-92;
joins rebels, 91; in Nine Years War,
92-105, 107, 110-111; Flight of the
Earls, 108, 118, 138

O'Neill, Black Hugh MacArt Confederate Catholic, 148-149

O'Neill, Hugh *Gaveloch* ('Fettered'
Hugh; son of Shane), 87

O'Neill, Captain John, 1st Viscount; at
1798 battle of Antrim, 357

O'Neill, Matthew (Ferdoraghe MacSeán),
2nd Baron Dungannon, 61, 65

O'Neill, Confederate Catholic General
Owen MacArt (Owen Roe), 123, 158;
in Flight of the Earls, 108; return to
Ireland, 134, 188, 202; and battle of
Benburb, 135-141; after Benburb,
143-144, 432; death of, 147-148

O'Neill, Phil, songwriter, 137

O'Neill, Seán MacConallagh (Shane
'Donnelly'), The O'Neill (Shane 'the
Proud', the 'Grand Disturber', 'The
Great O'Neill'), 59-67, 71, 87, 103,
110; and the O'Neill succession, 58,
61; and the Crown, 61-62; battle of

Farsetmore, 63; death of, 63, 138;
sons of, 89

O'Neill, Turlough, 1641 rebel, 128

O'Neill, Turlogh MacConallagh (Turlough 'Luineach'), Captain of Tyrone,
Earl of Clanconnell, The O'Neill
('Dragon of Tara'), 61, 66, 71, 76,
78, 81-82, 87

O'Neill henchmen, *see* MacMahons;
Magennisses; Maguires; O'Breslans;
O'Cahans; O'Donnellys; O'Hagans;
O'Hanlons; *and* O'Shiels

O'Neills of Ulster, 31, 33, 35, 37, 45,
50, 52, 57-67, 71, 76, 78, 81-82, 86-
87, 89, 91-92, 94-105, 107-111, 118,
123, 126, 128-129, 131-134, 136-
141, 143-144, 147-150, 158, 188,
202, 270, 323, 357, 432

O'Rahilly, Egan, Kerry poet, 149

Orange, colour, as loyalist symbol,
173, 256

'Orange Card', 285

Orange folk-memory/tradition/heritage,
74, 131, 164, 167-168, 171-175,
180, 190, 192, 256-257, 323, 352,
391, 393, 396, 404, 416

Orange Order/Society, 408, 417;
emergence of, 256-257, 273; sash,
192; in dragooning, 277, 281, 285,
323-324; in yeomanry, 287

O'Reilly, Colonel Sir Hugh, in 1798
'Cork Incident', 378

O'Reilly, Colonel Myles 'Slasher',
Confederate Catholic, 131, 137,
150

Ormonde, 8th Earl of, *see* Butler,
Thomas Boleyn

Ormonde, 9th Earl of, *see* Butler,
Pierce

Ormonde, 11th 'Black' Earl of, *see*
Butler, Lieutenant General Thomas

Ormonde, 13th Earl of, *see* Butler, James

Ormonde, Sir John of, *see* Butler, Sir John

Ormonde Peace, 141-142

O'Rourke, Brian, Lord of Leitrim, 90, 102

O'Rourke, Brian Oge, Lord of Leitrim, 90, 96-97, 101

O'Rourke, Tiernan, Lord of Breffny, 21, 24-25

O'Rourkes of Leitrim, 21, 24-25, 77, 81-82, 90, 96-97, 102-102

Orr of Ballycarry, James, rebel poet, 262, 372

Orr, Captain Samuel, Farranshane Unitedman; in 1798 insurrection, 355, 357-358, 360, 364, 366

Orr, William, Farranshane Unitedman; 1796 arrest of, 289; 1797 trial of, 289, 293; 1797 execution of, 272, 289, 366, 443; legacy, 290-291

O'Ryan, Edmund ('Ned of the Hill'), rapparee and Gaelic poet, 194, 196

Osbourne, Sir William, Patriot Party leader, 242

O'Sheas of Kerry, 76

O'Shiels of TyrConnell, 33

Ossian, legendary Gaelic warrior-poet, 6

O'Sullivan, Murtogh Oge, Kerry smuggler, 208-209

O'Sullivans of Kerry, 34, 76

O'Toole, Luke, Confederate Catholic, 131

O'Tooles of Connacht, 39

O'Tooles of Wicklow, 35, 39, 78, 131

Oulart Hill; 1798 rebel camp at, 327-328; 1798 battle of, 329-330, 338, 341, 397

Oxford University, 210

P

Padilla, Spanish Admiral, commander of 1597 fleet to Ireland, 96

Paine, Thomas, American political theorist and writer, 261-262

Palmer, landlady to Emmet, 427-428, 433

Papacy, *see* Vatican

Parez (sometimes 'Parese'), commander of 1535 Maynooth garrison, 54-56

Parliament, English/Imperial, 53, 58, 411-412; vs. the Crown, 120-121, 124, 132, 159-163; Elizabethan, 120; of James I, 121; of Charles I, 121-122, 124, 131-132; Short, 124-125; Long, 125, 129, 131, 134-135, 141-142; Rump, 143-144; Protectorate, 145, 150, 152-153; of Charles II, 150, 156, 159-161; of James II, 161-163; of William III, 163, 193-194; of George III, 244-245, 247-248, 252-253; and Union with Ireland, *see* Union of Britain and Ireland

Parliament, Irish, 50, 194, 301, 247, 412; 1366 Kilkenny, 41, 43; 1460 Drogheda, 45-46; 1495-96 Drogheda, 53; 1689 Patriot, 167, 169-170; 1759 riots at, 224, 411-412; Patriot Party Opposition in, 242-245, 248; declared independent by Irish Volunteers, 249; Free Trade debate in, 247-248, 271; Grattan's (1782-1800), 210, 250, 252-254, 260, 269, 271, 292, 412-413, 415, 437; and 3rd Catholic Relief Act, 263; warned of peasant-French connection, 390; debate on 1798 reprisals, 374; and Amnesty Act of 1798, 379; Union with British, *see* Union of Britain and Ireland

Parnell, Charles Stewart, Irish parliamentary leader, 136, 271

Pass of the Plumes, 1599 battle at the, 101

Patrick, St., 17

Patriot Party, Irish, 253-254, 259, 261, 353; 1759 founding of, 242; and Octennial Bill, 242; American effect on, 243-245, 257; and Irish Volunteers, 245-250, 257; and Declaration of Independence, 252

Paul III, Pope, 65

Pearse, Pádraig, poet and 1916 rebel, 253, 329, 432, 444-445

Peasantry, Irish, 153, 240, 247-248, 254, 256, 260, 291-292, 303, 320, 350, 353, 437; in Great Rebellion, 128; and Penal Laws, 208-210, 212, 227-228, 236, 242-243, 254, 258 (*see also* Defenders; Peep o' Day Boys; Oakboys; *and* Whiteboys); Protestant, 228, 258, 369; of the West, 236-237, 388-389, 390-394, 396-397, 399-401, 409; as *jacquerie*, 291-292, 326, 350, 365, 407, 413-414; and Patriot Party, 243, 247-248, 257; and Catholic Committee, 248; dragooning of, 287, 289-292, 309, 312, 322-323, 325-326, 350-351, 354, 364-365, 378; and 1798 risings, 368, 379, 407, 409-410; and 1798 French landing, 388-389, 390-394, 396; 1798 reprisals against, 348-350, 369-371, 384, 386, 396-397, 416, 419; *see also* Catholics and the Church

Peep o' Day Boys ('Wreckers', 'Protestant Boys'), anti-Catholic agrarian society, 256-257, 265-266, 273

Pelham, Sir Thomas (afterwards 2nd Earl of Chichester), Chief Secretary, 281

Pelham, Sir William, Elizabethan Lord

President of Munster (afterwards Lord Justice of Ireland), 75, 77-78

Pellew, British Admiral Sir Edward; and 1796 French expedition, 279

Pembroke, Earl of ('Strongbow'), *see* Clare, Richard FitzGiblert de

Pembroke, 8th Earl of, *see* Herbert, Thomas

Penal Laws/Penal Times, 188, 192, 197-198, 212, 219, 221, 231; Ascendancy protections under, 196, 227-228; Catholic avoidance of, 199, 207-208, 212, (*see also* Whiteboys, Whiteboyism); estrangement of cottiers and landowners, 197-198, 212-213, 227-228, 236-237, 243; informers and priest hunters, 208-209, 241, 259; smuggling trade flourishes under, 207-209, 225; and Dissenters, 223-225, 234; easing of, 223, 242, 248-249, 254

Perkins, Kildare United commander, 311, 317

Perrot, Sir John, Elizabethan Lord President of Munster, 71, 73, 90

Perry, United Colonel Anthony, 333, 375-376

Peter 'the Great' Romanoff, Tsar of Russia, 218

Petty, Sir William, Cromwellian Physician General, 191

Philip II, King of Spain and Portugal, consort to Mary of England, 57-58, 74, 86-87, 95, 97

Philip III, King of Spain, 102, 104, 106

Phoenix, 1689 Williamite relief ship, 168

Píbroch, see pipes/pipers

Pigeon House, target of 1803 rising, 423

'Pike Sunday', *see* Newtownards, 'Pike Sunday' at

Pilltown, 1462 battle of, 49

Pitched-cap torture, 322, 350, 417

Pipes/pipers, 73, 79, 190-191, 206, 219-220, 312

Pitt (the Younger), William, British Prime Minister, 371, 380, 411-412, 414-417

Pius VI, Pope, 400

Plague in Ireland, 40, 48

Plantation, Irish land, 7, 100; Antrim, 116; Down, 116, 126; Connacht, 123, 127; Dublin/Pale, 26, 57; Kings/ Offaly, 57-58; Longford, 116; Mun-ster, 68, 71, 74, 83-84; Queens/Laois, 57-58; Ulster (Armagh, Cavan, Cole-raine&'Gaelic Countrie', Donegal, Fermanagh, Tyrone), 9, 113-116, 126-128, 158; Westmeath, 116; Wex-ford, 116; Wicklow, 116

Plunkett, Arthur James, 8th Earl of Fingall, yeoman officer in 1798 in-surrection, 316

Plunkett, Joseph Mary, poet, editor and 1916 rebel, 9

Plunkett, Oliver, Archbishop of Armagh, 191

Pole, John de la, Earl of Lincoln, champion of Simnel, 52

Poets/poetry, Irish, 10-11, 24, 39, 76, 95, 92, 119, 123, 190, 206, 251, 259, 291; *fili*, 5-8, 11-12, 30-31, 40, 43, 58-59, 84, 118, 137, 150; *rosg catha*, 3-4, 9, 73, 79, 137

Ponsonby, George, Irish parliamentary opposition leader, 284

Popish Plot of 1678, *see* Oates, Titus

Population, Irish, *see* Irish population

Port Republic, American battle of, 136

Portland, 3rd Duke of, *see* Bentinck, William Henry Cavendish

Portmore (Blackwater Fort), 1597-98 siege of, 96-98

Porter, Reverend James, cleric and pamphleteer, 277

Portugese/Portugal, 201, 218, 385

Poynings, Sir Edward, 1494-95 Crown military commander in Ireland, 53

Poynings Law of 1494, 53

Pratt, John Jeffreys, 2nd Earl of Cam-den (afterwards Marquis of Camden), 382, 386; named Tory Viceroy, 268; approves use of Orangemen in dra-gooning, 281, 287, 354; orders Lake to ignore magistracy, 281; attempts to foment premature rebellion, 294-295, 307-309, 315, 354, 369; reports Dublin cut off during 1798 insurrec-tion, 320; reaction to Napoleon's sailing/risings, 368-369; replaced by Cornwallis, 371

Prendegast, Maurice de, Welsh Norman knight, 24

Presbyterians in Ireland, *see* Dissenters, Irish

Presbyterians in Scotland, *see* Scot-land, Presbyterians and Church in

Press, see Irish *Press*

Preston, 1648 battle of, 143

Prestonpans, 1745 battle of, 220

Preston, Confederate Catholic General Thomas (afterwards 1st Viscount Tara), 122, 134, 139, 141, 148, 188

Pretenders, Jacobite, *see* Stuart, 'Bonnie Prince' Charles *and* Stuart, Prince James Francis Edward

Prevot Prison at Dublin's Royal Bar-racks; after 1798 insurrection, 419

Priests/Clergy, Irish Catholic, 43, 112, 138; as teachers, 118-119; and ban-ning of bishops, 259; hunted during Penal Times, 197, 217, 240-241; and Relief Act of 1782, 249; 'croppy', in 1798 insurrection, 348, 351 (*see also* Kearns, Moses; Murphy, John; *and*

Murphy, Michael, *and* Roche, Philip)

Privy Council, English, 56-57, 162

Privy Council, Irish, 118

Proposals for the Universal Use (Swift), 210

Prosperous, in 1798 insurrection, 309, 311, 314-315, 319-320, 374

Protestant Ascendancy, 131, 156, 188, 190, 193-194, 196-198, 201, 209-212, 220, 223-225, 227-228, 242-243, 252, 257, 263, 269; and French Revolution, 260; Irish Whig Club of, 260, 284; and United Irish leadership, 270; and Orangemen, 273, 277; and the Union, 412-415, 417, 437; *see also* Patriot Party *and* Landowners

Protestants, Irish; and Great Rebellion, 128, 131; and Restoration, 156; and Tyrconnell, 161, 163-165; and Londonderry siege, 166-169; and 1798 risings, 336; and nationalism, 209-210, 214, 224, 261, 270-272; *see also* Church of Ireland; Dissenters; *and* Protestant Ascendancy

Provisional Irish Republican Army, *see* Irish Republican Army (IRA), Provisional

Provisional *Sinn Féin, see Sinn Féin* Provisional

Prussia, 201, 348

Puritans, 121-122, 124-126, 135, 142, 153, 182; *see also* Army, Parliamentary; Civil Wars, English; Cromwell, Oliver; *and* Parliament, English

Pym, John Puritan leader of English Commons, 132

Q

Quakers, *see* Dissenters, Irish

Queens County (Laois, Leix); instituted, 57-58; 1599 Essex campaign in, 101

Queens plantation, *see* Plantation, Queens

R

Raftery, Anthony, poet, 186

Raleigh, Walter (afterwards Sir Walter), Elizabethan freebooter and soldier, 68

Ramillies, 1706 battle of, 201, 205

Randalstown, in 1798 insurrection, 355, 357-358

Rapparees, Irish highwaymen and rebels, 158, 176-180, 186, 194, 199, 221-222, 225, 254-255

Ratcliffe, Lord Thomas, 3rd Earl of Sussex, Lord Deputy of Ireland, 61-63, 71

Rathangan, 1798 events in, 308, 311, 315, 318-319

Rathcook, 1798 rebel muster at, 308

Rathfarnum; in 1798 insurrection, 308, 313; in 1803 rising, 423-424, 428

Rathlin Island, 1575 massacre at, 74, 86, 100

Rathmines, 1649 battle of, 144

Rathmullen, 1607 Flight of the Earls from, 108

Recaire, professional reciter of poetry, 12

Reay Fencibles, at 1798 battle of Tara, 315-316

Rebel balladry, evolution of, 2-4, 9-10, 173, 175, 180, 184, 190, 206-207, 211, 213, 224, 237, 251-253, 256, 259, 292, 376, 390, 425-426, 433-435, 437, 441-442, 444-448

Reddin, Kenneth, poet, 445

Redshanks, Lord Antrim's Jacobite, 166

Redshanks, Scottish, *see* Mercenaries, Redshank

Renault, 1691 French Admiral, 188

Repealers, Irish, 406

Reprisals, 1798 against peasantry, 371, 375, 379-380, 384, 417, 419; Midlands, 317-319, 369, 375-376, 379-381; Ulster, 363, 367, 369; West, 369, 396; Wexford, 369, 396

Republic of Ireland, *see* Irish Republic, republicanism

Republic of Connacht, *see* Connacht, 1798 'Republic' declared

Restoration, 1660 Stuart, 155-156, 160, 191

Rey, French-American Captain; in 1798 Rutland Island expedition, 388, 402

Reynolds, Kildare United Irish General Michael, 308, 320, 313

Reynolds of Kilkea Castle, Thomas, Treasurer to the Dublin Directory of United Irishmen, Crown informer, 293-294, 306, 320, 443

Richard I, *Couer de Lion*, Plantagenet King of England, 28

Richard II, Plantagenet King of England, 44, 116

Richard III, Yorkist King of England, 52

Richard Plantagenet, Duke of York, Viceroy (afterwards 'Lord of Ireland'), 45-46, 49

Richelieu, Cardinal Armand Jean du Plessis de, French Minister, 121, 123

Riding School, Beresford's, 1798 prison, 419

Rightboys, *see* Whiteboys, whiteboyism

Rights of Man (Paine), *The* 266

Rinuccini, Bishop Giovanni Battista, papal legate to Confederate Catholics, 136, 139, 141-144

Riot, 1759 Dublin, 224, 411-412

Ripon, 1640 'Treaty' of, 125, 132, 141

Rising of 1803, *see* Irish rebellions, Emmet (1803)

Risings, 1648 English royalist, 143

Risings, 1685 English and Scottish, 162

Risings/Rebellion, 1798 Irish, 211, 224-225, 270, 273, 283, 308-386, 415-416; planning of, 295, 298, 300-301, 303, 305, 307-308; casualties in, 407, 409, 410; legacy of, 410, 416; *see also* French, 1798 Irish expedition; Irish rebellions, Midlands (1798), Wexford (1798), Ulster (1798); *and* United Irishmen

Ritchie, Hugh and William, Belfast shipbuilders, 284

Robert I ('Robert the Bruce'), King of Scots (earlier Earl of Carrick, Lord of Annandale, 37-38, 124

Robinson, Lord Chief Justice of Ireland, 198

Roche, United General Edward (yeoman sergeant), 327-328, 333

Roche, Fr. Philip, 1798 Wexford rebel general, 333, 337, 342, 346-347, 407

Roches of Fermoy, 68

Roden, Lord, *see* Jocelyn, Robert

Rolleston, Thomas William Hazen, essayist, scholar, and translator, 40

Romans, 4, 9, 31

Rooney, William, Gaelic Leaguer, 393

Roscommon town, Defender activities around, 267

de Rosen, French Jacobite General; in Boyne campaign, 170

Ross, British Major General, correspondent of Cornwallis, 379

Rosg catha, see Poets/poetry, Irish, rabble-rousing

'Rossa', Jeremiah O'Donovan, *see* O'Donovan, Jeremiah

Rothe, David, Bishop of Ossery, titular Senior Bishop of Ireland; 'elder statesman' of Catholic Confederation, 134, 142-143

Rowan, Archibald Hamilton, Secretary to Dublin Unitedmen, 263, 268, 284-285

Royal Barracks, Dublin; as 1798 prison, 419; as target of 1803 rising, 423

Rupert, Prince, Count Palantine of the Rhine and Duke of Bavaria, Cavalier general, 135

Russell, Captain Thomas (the 'Man From God Knows Where'), 260, 284; and founding of United Irishmen, 261, 272; at Cave Hill meeting, 270; organiser for Down, 273-274; 1796 arrest of, 273, 289; 1798 arrest of, 273, 277; 1802 release of, 273, 418; in 1803 rising, 273-274, 426; legacy of, 271, 275

Russell, Sir William, Elizabethan Lord Deputy of Ireland, 90, 94

Russians, 218

Rutland Island, 1798 French landing at, 402

Ryan, Sepulchre Captain, in capture of Fitzgerald, 298-299

Ryan, Captain, of North Cork Militia, 323

S

St. Bartholomew's Eve, 1572 massacre of, 71

Saintfield, in 1798 insurrection, 274, 361-363

St. John, Captain Oliver, Elizabethan soldier, 158

St. John, Pete, songwriter, 395, 428

St. Leger, Sir Anthony, Tudor Lord Deputy of Ireland, 57

St. Patrick's Day, 311-312

St. Ruth, French Captain-General; in 1691 Jacobite campaign, 182-185, 192

Saladin, 28

Sallins Yeomanry, in 1798 insurrection, 308-309

Sampson, William, United Irish attorney, 294

Sandys, Brigade-Major, in 1798 insurrection, 419

San Joseppi, Bolognese Colonel Sebastiano di; in 1580 Smerwick landing, 81-82

Santry, in 1798 insurrection, 308, 354

Saratoga, 1777 battle of, 245

Sarsfield, Jacobite Major General Patrick, titular Earl of Lucan, 109; 1690 Limerick campaign, 175-182; 1691 Aughrim campaign, 184-185, 187; leads Flight of the Wild Geese, 188-190; death and legend of, 181, 198, 329

Sarsfield's Raid, *see* Ballyneety, 1690 Jacobite raid on

Saunders, Captain of Saunders-Grove Yeomanry, 319, 325-326, 350-351

Saunders, Fr. Nicholas, papal legate to Geraldine Confederacy, 74, 78, 82

Saunders-Grove Yeomanry, executions among, 325

Savary, French Captain; in 1798 expeditionary force, 388, 390-391, 407

Savoy, 201

Saxe, Hermann Maurice de, Marshal of

France, at 1745 battle of Fontenoy, 216-217

Scarriffhollis, 1651 battle of, 149

Schiltron, 36-37, 48

Schomberg, General Frederick Hermann, Baron of Teyes, Earl of Brentford, Marquis of Harwich, and Duke of (formerly Marshal of France), 170-174

Schools, Irish, 12, 197; bardic, 8, 118; monastic, 7-8; hedge, 119-120; *see also* Literacy in Ireland

Scotland, 128, 132, 186; Wallace revolt, 36-37; Bannockburn campaign, 37; and Garret More Fitzgerald, 53; in Elizabethan era, 62, 70, 100; Solemn League and Covenant, 135, 141; *see also* Armies, Scottish; Civil Wars, English; Irish rebellions, Bruce Invasion; War, Scottish Fifteen; *and* War, Scottish Forty-Five

Scotland, Presbyterians and Church in, 121, 127, 142, 151, 220; Kirk and 1638 National Covenant, 124, 143; *see also* Army/armies, Scottish

Scots of the Route (Antrim Scots), *see* MacDonnells of the Route

Scottish Jacobites, 161, 169, 175, 193, 201, 205-206, 220, 223, 242

Scottish war-pipes, *see* Pipes/pipers

Scullabogue, 1798 massacre at, 336, 352-353

Seanchaithe, see Poets/poetry, Irish

Sedulius Scotus, Irish missionary, 7

Senchus Mór (*Seanchus agus Félineachus na hEireann*), ancient Celtic law, 5-6; *see also* Brehon/Druidic Law

Sheares, Henry; joins United Irishmen, 261; at Cave Hill meeting, 270; and National Directory, 294-296, 298, 306; capture, trial and execution of,

272, 300-303, 321, 325, 354, 381, 407, 443-444; legend of, 307

Sheares, John, United Irishman, 261, 272, 288; as United Commander-in-Chief, 294-296, 300; capture, trial and execution of, 272, 300-303, 321, 325, 354, 381, 407, 443-444; legacy of, 307

Sheehy, Fr. Nicholas, rebel martyr, 258

Shelmalier, Wexford barony, 332, 335, 337, 339, 343, 346-347, 351

Sherrifmuir, 1715 'battle' of, 205

Sidney, Sir Henry ('Big Henry of the Beer'), Lord Chancellor of Ireland, 61, 71, 77, 85

'Silken Thomas', *see* Fitzgerald, Thomas FitzGarret

Silken Thomas Rebellion of 1534-5, 54-56

Simmons, Fr. Richard, and Simnel, 52

Simms, Robert, Ulster Unitedman, 261, 287; and *Northern Star*, 262; at Cave Hill meeting, 270; after Bond raid, 294; O/C Ulster, 355; fails to issue rising orders, 354, 366

Simms, William, Ulster Unitedman, 261-262, 287

Simnel, Lambert ('Edward VI'), pretender to English Crown, 52

Sinclair, William, Ulster Unitedman, 261

Sinn Féin, Provisional, 404, 406, 431

Sirr, Henry Charles, Town Major of Dublin; captures Fitzgerald, 298, 300, 444; captures Emmet, 427-429

Sitric, Ostman King of Dublin, 17

Skeffington, Colonel Lord John Clotworthy, 2nd Earl of Massareene; yeomanry commander at 1798 battle of Antrim, 357, 367

Skeffington, Sir William; Tudor soldier,

54, 56

Slaughterford Bridge, in IslandMagee massacre, 132-133

SLIABH CUILINN, *see* O'Hagan, John

Sligo; 1269 seizure of by de Burgo, 35; in Nine Years War, 90-91, 96; in 1798 French campaign, 388, 390, 392, 402

Sloan, James, founder of Orange Society, 273

Smerwick, in Desmond Wars, 81-82

Smith, Josua, Elizabethan freebooter, 83

Smuggling, during Penal Times, 207-209, 225

Snowe, 1798 Captain of militia, 330

Solemn League and Covenant of 1643, 135

Soldier's Song (Kearney), *The*, 376

Somerset, Edward, 6th Earl and 2nd Marquis of Worcester, titular Earl of Glarmorgan, Cavalier Lieutenant General; Stuart emissary to Confedeate Catholics, 135-136

Soult, Nicolas Jean de Dieu, Marshal of France, in Peninsular War, 385

Spalpeens, 238-239

Spanish/Spain, 31, 33, 61, 111, 121, 218, 395; and Desmond Wars, 81; 1588 Armada, 86-87, 90, 95, 280; and Nine Years War, 95-97, 104-107, 111; 1779 war with England, 245-246

Spanish Netherlands, British campaigns in 198, 201-202, 204

Spencer, Yeoman Captain Thomas; at 1798 battle of Rathangan, 315

Spenser, Edmund, English poet, 92

'Speranza', *see* Elgee, Francesca

Spirit of the Nation, Young Ireland ballad book, 378, 446

Springfield (*Gort na Tobrad*), 1579

battle of, 75

Stanhope, Philip Dormer, 4th Earl of Chesterfield, Viceroy, 223, 235, 258

Stanley, Sir William, Elizabethan soldier, 79

Stapleton, York Fencible Colonel; in 1798 insurrection, 362

Star Chamber, abolition of, 125

Steelboys, *see* Oakboys

Stevenson, Sir John, Irish music collector, 439

Stewart, Lieutenant Colonel of Argyleshire Fencibles; in 1798 insurrection, 362

Stewart, Henry, Lord Darnley, 62

Stewart, Mary, *see* Mary Stewart (Stuart), Queen of Scots

Stewart, Robert, Viscount Castlereagh, Earl (afterwards Marquis) of Londonderry, Acting (afterwards official) Chief Secretary for Ireland, 368, 390, 403-404, 414; forces Abercrombie's resignation, 294; attempts to foment premature rebellion, 295; accused of being soft on rebels, 375, 385-386; and Union, 414-415, 417

Stirling Bridge, 1297 battle of, 36

Stock, Joseph, Bishop of Killala, 400, 402

Stoke, 1487 battle of, 52

Story of the Irish Race (MacManus), *The*, 64

Strafford, 2nd Earl of, *see* Wentworth, Thomas

Stratford, 1798 action at, 311

'Strongbow', *see* Clare, Richard Fitz-Gilbert de

Stuart, 'Bonnie Prince' Charles Edward Louis Philip Casimir (the 'Young Pretender', 'The Blackbird'), 173, 205-207, 220-221, 225

Stuart, CSA General J.E.B., 176

Stuart, Jacobite General James 'Fitz-James', Duke of Berwick, 170, 175-176, 190

Stuart, Prince James Francis Edward, Jacobite James III of Great Britain, James VIII of Scots (the 'Old Pretender', 'James Edward'), 162, 173, 205-207, 220-221

Sullivan, Timothy Daniel ('TD'), Lord Mayor of Dublin, essayist, poet, and editor, 421

Surrender and Re-grant Policy of Henry VIII, 57-58, 61, 67, 71

Sussex, 3rd Earl of, *see* Ratcliffe, Sir Thomas

Svein, King of Denmark and Britain, 17

Swann, Revenue Major Justice; leads raid on Leinster Directory, 293-294; in capture of Fitzgerald, 298-299, 444

Swayne, Lieutenant of City of Cork Militia, 309, 314, 320

Sweetman, John, Dublin Unitedman, Catholic Committeeman, 266, 277, 285, 306

Swift, Jonathan, Dean of St. Patrick's, essayist, novelist, pamphleteer, 156, 169, 210-211, 214, 223, 225, 247, 250

Swinburne, Algernon, English poet, 186

Synge, Edward, Archbishop of Tuam, 210

T

Taafe, Theobald, Earl of Carlingford, Confederate Catholic general, 142

Tadg MacBrian, son of Boru, 19

Taín Bó Cuailnge, see Cooley, Cattle-Raid of

Talbot, Archbishop Peter, 191

Talbot, Richard, Earl (afterwards Duke) of Tyrconnell, Lord Lieutenant, Jacobite general, 175, 190-192; and Irish standing army, 161; campaigns of 1688-90, 163-165; campaign of 1691, 187; sudden death of, 188

Tallaght, 1798 rebel muster at, 308

Talleyrand-Périgord, Charles Maurice de, French Minister, 422, 436

Tanderagee, 1641 seizure by rebels, 131, 158

Tandy, James Napper, Dublin Volunteer and Unitedman ('Tribune of the Plebs'), 312; on Dublin Corporation, 259; Whig Club, 284; Irish Volunteer officer, 248, 253; Dublin Unitedman, 259, 261; and Irish National Guard, 263; flees Ireland, 268; in France, 259, 268, 277, 387; in Rutland Island expedition, 259, 402; 1802 release and death of, 259, 418; legacy of, 271

Tanists/tanistry, succession in Brehon Law, 61, 74, 110

Tara; seat of ancient Irish kings, 4-5, 17, 41, 440-441; 1798 battle of, 313, 315-316

Tasmania, *see* Van Dieman's Land

Tate, French Colonel, William, American adventurer; in French 1796-7 expeditionary force, 276, 281

Taxation, in Ireland, 197, 228, 243-244

Teeling, Bartholomew, Unitedman in French Army, 387, 390, 392, 395-396, 407

Teeling, Charles Hamilton, United Irishman, 277

Terence, Roman playwright, 7

Thackeray, William Makepeace, English

novelist, 222

Thomond, Earl of, *see* O'Brien, Conor MacDonagh

Three Rocks, 1798 rebel camp at, 330-331, 333, 338, 342, 351

Thurot, French naval commander in 1760 Antrim raid, 259

Timahoe, 1798 rebel camp at, 318, 375, 379

Tippoo Sahib of Mysore, Indian rebel, 276

Tiptoft (sometimes 'Tibetot'), Sir John 'the Butcher', Earl of Worcester, 50

Tithes, 228, 411

Tocqueville, Alexis de, French political writer, 400

Tone, Matthew, United Irishman in French service, 387, 390, 395-396

Tone, Theobald Wolfe, Dublin United-man, 202, 260, 284, 435-436, 445-446; pamphleteer, 261, 270; effect of French republicanism on, 403; and founding of United Irishmen, 262-263, 403; and Catholic Committee, 262-263, 403; allowed self-exile, 268-269; at Cave Hill meeting, 270; effect of Fitzwilliam recall on, 269; in America, 275; contacts with French, 268, 275-277, 387, 399, 408; and 1796 Bantry Bay expedition, 278-279, 283; and 1797 Dutch expedition, 288; view of 1798 insurrection, 368; knowledge of peasantry, 399, 409; 1798 French expedition, 402-404, 407; death of, 403, 406-407, 409; Wellington's appraisal of, 276; legacy of, 271, 358, 403-406, 432

Toomebridge, in 1798 insurrection and aftermath, 355, 357, 364, 370-371

Tory, origin of word, 158, 191-192

Toulon, Napoleon's 1798 departure from 368, 387, 408

Tower of London, 50, 53-54, 57, 107, 125

Towns, early Irish, 8, 13-14

Towton Field, 1461 battle of, 49

Trafalgar, 1805 naval battle of, 422

Tralee, 1641 rebel capture of, 131

Tree of Liberty, as republican symbol, 284, 312, 374

Trench, 1798 British General William, 402

Trim, 1647 siege of, 142

Trimleston, Lord Barnewell, 5th Baron of; Elizabethan soldier, 96

Trinity College, Dublin ('TCD'), 210, 418, 435, 446

Trinity College Historical Society ('The Club'), 435

Truc, French Colonel; at 2nd battle of Killala, 402

Tubbercarry, 1798 action at, 392

Tubberneering, 1798 battle of, 332, 337, 339, 341, 343, 345, 369, 395, 414

Tullow, in 1798 insurrection, 331-332, 337, 344, 396

Tullyallen, in 1690 battle of the Boyne, 171

Turner, Samuel, Ulster Unitdman, Crown informer, 288, 293

Turpin, Ben, English highwayman, 222

22nd Light Dragoons, at 1798 battle of Antrim, 357-358

Two Kings, Irish War of the ('Glorious Revolution'), *see* Irish rebellion

Tyrconnell, 1st Duke, of, *see* Talbot, Richard

TyrConnell, 2nd Earl of, *see* O'Donnell, Calvagh MacManus

TyrConnell, 3rd Earl of, *see* O'Donnell, Black Hugh

TyrConnell, 4th Earl of, *see* O'Donnell, Rory MacHugh

Tyrone (TirOwen), 1st Earl of, *see* O'Neill, Connallagh *Bacagh*

Tyrone, 2nd Earl of, *see* O'Neill, Hugh

Tyrell, Captain Richard, lieutenant to Hugh O'Neill, 96, 100

Tyrellspass, 1597 action at, 96

U

Ufford, Ralph de, Norman adventurer; in 1270 Sligo campaign, 35

Ufford, Robert de, Lord Justice of Ireland, 34

Uisneach, ancient Druidic centre, 5, 7

Ulster; kinship with Scots, 37; forests of, 86, 113-115; *sine qua non* in conquest of Ireland, 86; inaccessibility to Elizabethan English, 86, 89-90; 1797 dragooning of, 277, 281, 285, 287, 291, 354, 364; modern, 171-172; *see also* Defenders; Irish rebellion, Nine Years; Irish rebellion, Great Rebellion; Irish rebellion, Ulster; Oakboys; *and* Peep o' Day Boys

Ulster, Scots of ('Scotch-Irish'), 113, 116, 120, 125, 127, 164, 256, 258; harassed by Wentworth, 122, 124; 1641 massacre of, *see* Irish rebellions, Great Rebellion

Ulster Guardian, 442

'Ulster Custom', *see* Landowners, 'Ulster Crustom'

Undertakers, *see* Landowners, Undertakers

Union, of England and Ireland, 269, 411, 416; 1759 Dublin riots over, 224, 411-412; Irish parliamentary fight over, 284, 412-415; 1801 Act of, 252, 437

United Ireland, as nationalist goal/folk-memory, 8-9, 16, 45, 60, 95, 103, 132

United Irishmen, Society of, 129, 259-261, 264, 272, 283, 285, 358, 360-362, 366, 374, 403, 412, 429, 433; agitation after Bantry Bay, 280; 1795 Belfast convention of, 270, 272; debating clubs, 262, 331; Committeemen, 273; and Connacht, 377, 388, 390; and Defenders, 268, 276, 336; and Emmet Rising, *see* Emmet Rising of 1803; executions of, 381-383; and French, 278, 387, 399-400, 408-409, 417-418, 422; informers, 301, 443; and Insurrection Act, 292; and Irish Volunteers, 271, 273; and Kildare, 308; leaders of, 293, 384, 407, 418, 436; legacy of, 435, 438, 448; Leinster (Dublin) Directory of, 261, 277, 288, 293-294, 306, 317, 345; and militia and yeomanry, 281, 291-292; and Meath, 313, 315; and Munster, 295, 377-378; National Directory (Executive) of, 278, 281, 294-295, 300, 321, 377, 409, 417, 419, 422-423; National Guard, 263; and *Northern Star*, 265; number in arms (1798), 309, 321; prisoners, 270, 311, 381-384, 386, 395-396, 418; and Orr, 289-291, 366; and peasants, 384, 388, 390, 399, 409, 437; risings of 1798, *see* Irish rebellion; sectarianism within, 336; and Sligo, 377, 392; suppression of, 268, 293, 298, 303, 305; and Ulster, 354; Ulster (Belfast) Directory of, 261-262, 269-270, 287, 307, 355, 366; called 'Unionists', 284; and Wexford, 322, 328, 331, 335

United Kingdom, 411, 415, 418

United States of America, *see* America

d'Usson, French Jacobite Major General; at 1691 battle of Athlone, 182-184

Utrecht, 1713 Treaty of, 201

V

Van Dieman's Land (Tasmania), prison colony, 336

Vatican, 120, 225, 400; and the Stuarts, 160, 173, 205; *see also Laudabilitier*

Vendôme, French Duke of, 204

Vere, Robert de, Marquis of Dublin, 44

Verner, Thomas, 1st Grand Master of the Orange Society, 273

Vesey, Major of Dublin Militia; at 1798 battle of New Ross, 334

Victoria, Queen of United Kingdom, 62

Vikings ('Danes', 'Norse', 'Northmen', 'Ostmen', 'Foreigners of the West of Europe'), 20, 23, 76-77, 106, 230; onslaught on Ireland, 8, 13-14, 283; establish Irish towns, 13; merge with Gaelic culture, 14, 59; conquer Britain, 17; last attempts at Irish control, 16-19

Villeroi, Marshal of France; at 1706 battle of Ramillies, 202

Villiers, George, Earl (afterwards 1st Duke) of Buckingham, 121

Vindication of the Rights of Women (Wollstonecraft), 262

Vinegar Hill; 1798 rebel camp at, 330, 333, 351; 1798 battle of, 332, 338-339, 341-345, 353, 374, 391, 397-398; casualties at, 342, 446

Volunteers, Irish, 260, 366, 412; origins and growth, 245-248; 1781-2 conventions of, 249-250, 263; and religion, 249; and legislative independence, 251-253, 257; distrusted by authorities, 263; Crown raids on, 265; and United Irishmen, 271-272; and Irish Militia, 285

W

Wakefield, 1460 battle of, 45

Walker, Reverend George; in 1688-89 siege of Londonderry, 168, 173-174

Wales, 416; longbowmen of, 37, 44, 48; 1400 Glendower Rising in, 44; 1648 rising in, 143; 1797 French landing in, 276, 281

Wall, Don Ricardo, Spanish Prime Minister, 218

Wallace, William, 1297 Scottish rebel, 36, 124

Wallop, Sir Henry, Lord Justice (afterwards Lord Treasurer) of Ireland, 83-84, 95-96

Walpole, British Colonel, at 1798 battle of Tubberneering, 337, 345-346

Walpole, Sir Robert (afterwards 1st Earl of Orford), 'Prime' Minister of Great Britain, 210

War, non-Irish; *Hundred Years* (1337-1453), 40; *of the Roses* (1455-84), 45, 47, 49-50, 67; *Anglo-Spanish* (1588), 86-87, 95, 280; *Thirty Years* (1618-48), 212; *Anglo-Dutch* (1664-67), 160; *of the League of Augsburg/ Grand Alliance* (1686-97), 169-170, 173-174, 193, 198; *of the Spanish Succession* (1701-14), 201-202, 204-205; *Scottish Fifteen* (1715), 205-206, 220; *of the Austrian Succession*

(1740-48), 214-219, 225; *Scottish Forty-Five* (1745-46), 214, 220, 223, 242, 416; *Seven Years* (1756-63), 245; *for American Independence* (1775-83), 209, 242-248, 257-258; *Anglo-Franco* (1793-98), 263, 278, 380, 387, 411, 418; *Napoleonic* (1799-1802, 1803-14, 1815), 280, 382, 385, 418, 422, 435-436; *American Civil* (1861-65), 136-137, 176, 239; *Zulu* (1878-79), 99; *see also* Civil Wars, English; Scotland, Bannockburn campaign; *and* Scotland, Wallace revolt

Warbeck, Perkin ('Prince Richard'), pretender to English Crown, 52

Ware, Colonel Hugh, Kildare Unitedman, 308, 320, 375

Warfield, Admiral Sir John, 1798 Royal Navy squadron commander, 403-404, 409

War-shouts, Irish, 55, 68, 70, 79, 93

Washington, American rebel General George (afterwards President), 368

Waterford town, 13, 26; 1649-50 siege of, 148

Waterloo, 1815 battle of, 276, 280

Watson, Lieutenant Colonel Jonas; at 1798 battle for Wexford, 330-331

Wellesley (formerly *Wesley*), Arthur, 1st Duke of Wellington, 276

Wentworth, Sir Thomas (afterwards Earl of Strafford), Viceroy, 122-125

Wentworth, William, 2nd Earl of Fitzwilliam, 1794 Whig Viceroy, 269

Westmeath Militia, in 1798 'Cork Incident', 378

Wexford, County, 1798 insurrection in, 326-348, 351-353, 360, 368-369, 374-375, 407

Wexford town; founding of, 13; claimed by Henry II, 26; 1649 mas-

sacre at, 145-147, 149; 1793 Defender action at, 265, 336; as possible 1798 French landing site, 322; 1798 campaign for, 322, 330-332, 335, 338-339, 341-344, 414

Wharton, Thomas, 1st Marquis, Ascendancy politician and songwriter, 164, 192

Whig Club ('Round Robin'), Irish, 260, 284

Whigs, 162, 210, 269, 306; origin of, 191-192; ministry after Yorktown, 248-249

White, Captain Jack, O/C Irish Citizen Army, 271

'White, Sergeant', Jacobite rapparee, 176

Whiteboys/whiteboyism, agrarian societies, 235, 238-240, 242, 254, 265-266; emergence of, 234, 437; executions of, 234-236, 258

Wicklow, County, 1798 insurrection in, 309, 311, 325, 337-338, 340, 352, 369, 375-376

Wicklow town; 1641 attack on Black Castle, 131; in 1798 insurrection, 337, 398; Wicklow Gaol, 345, 382-383

Widger, Pádraig, songwriter, 406

Wigmore, Baron of, *see* Mortimer, Roger de

Wild Geese, 178, 264; Flight of the, 188-189, 199-200, 248; in battle, 201-208, 212-220, 224

Wilde, Lady Jane, *see* Elgee, Jane Francesca

William III (Willem, Stadtholder of Orange-Nassau), King of England ('Dutch William', 'King Billy'), 187; marriage to Mary Stuart, 163; Devon landing, 163; coronation of, 163, 167, 169; 1690 Carrickfergus landing,

170; at the Boyne, 170-174; at
1690 siege of Limerick, 176-182;
and Treaty of Limerick, 188; and the
Scots, 169, 193; and the French, 175;
and Parliament, 193-194

Williams-Wynn, Sir Watkin, commander of Ancient Britons, 287

Wilson, Florence, balladeer, 273

Windmill Hill at Ballinahinch, 1798
rebel camp at, 351, 361-362

Windmill Hill at Wexford, 1798
rebel camp at, 339, 351

Windsor, 1175 Treaty of, 26-27

Winter, Dutch Admiral Jan Willem de,
O/C 1797 expedition, 288

Winter, Sir William, Elizabethan
soldier, 78

Wogan, John de, Lord Deputy of Ireland, 35-36

Wolfe, Lord Chief Justice Arthur,
Baron Kilwarden of Newlands (afterwards 1st Viscount Kilwarden);
issues *habeas corpus* for Tone, 409,
436; death of, 424-425

Wolfe, Rev. Charles, Armagh cleric
and poet, 385

Wolfe, British Major General James,
Hero of Quebec, 385

Wollstonecraft, Mary, *see* Godwin,
Mary Wollstonecraft

Wolsey, Cardinal Thomas, Primate of
England, 54

Wool-carding, 234, 258

Worcester, 1651 battle of, 149, 151

Wreckers, *see* Peep o' Day Boys

Wyse, Thomas, Catholic Committeeman, 242

Y

Yeats, William Butler, poet, playwright,
folklorist, Nobel laureate, 24, 259

Yellow Ford, 1598 battle of the, 93,
98-100

Yeomanry ('yeos'), Irish, 281, 304,
306, 317, 339; 1796 creation of,
277, 285; composition of, 285; in
dragooning, 281; conduct in battle,
277, 280, 316, 391; Abercrombie on,
294; Cornwallis on, 379-380, 396-
397; deserters from, 375; in 1798 insurrection, 319, 322-323, 326-327,
332, 367, 391, 408; casualties, 409-
410; 1798 reprisals by, 379-380, 396-
397

York Fencibles, in 1798 insurrection,
362

Yorkshire, 1648 rising in, 143

Yorkists, 45, 49-50, 53

Yorktown, 1781 British surrender at,
248

Youghal, 1570 sack of, 77

Young, Arthur, English agriculturist,
236-237, 258

Young Ireland, 131, 139, 380; Confederacy Clubs of, 301

Young Ireland rising, *see* Irish rebellion, Young Ireland (1848)

Young Pretender, *see* Stuart, 'Bonnie
Prince' Charles

Ypres, Irish Dames of, 202, 204, 205

Z

Zouche, Captain John Elizabeth,
Elizabethan soldier, 82-83

Zulu Wars, 99

Ireland